Clinical Practice
and
the Law

Second Edition

For Grace – with all my love

Clinical Practice
and
the Law

Second Edition

SIMON MILLS

MB, BCh, BAO, BA (Dubl), BCL (NUI), MICGP,
Barrister-at-law (of King's Inns), MSc (Lond), MFF&LM

Published by
Tottel Publishing Ltd
Maxwelton House
41–43 Boltro Road
Haywards Heath
West Sussex
RH16 1BJ

Tottel Publishing Ltd
Fitzwilliam Business Centre
26 Upper Pembroke Street
Dublin 2

ISBN 978-1-84592-786-8
© Tottel Publishing Ltd 2007
First published 2002
Second edition 2007

British Library Cataloguing-in-Publication Data
A catalogue record for this book is available from the British Library

Typeset by Marlex Editorial Services Ltd., Dublin, Ireland
Printed and bound in Germany by Bercker GmbH & Co., Kevelær

Foreword to the First Edition

The relationship between medicine and the law is like a long-standing yet stormy marriage. It is at one and the same time a partnership and a battlefield. Each party regards the other with a mixture of respect, admiration, impatience and contempt.

Yet as Simon Mills, himself a barrister and a doctor, demonstrates in this lucid and compassionate book, it is impossible to practise law or medicine effectively and efficiently without an informed understanding of the issues and challenges of the extensive terrain wherein both meet.

He deals with issues such as the definition of death, the decision not to resuscitate, consent to treatment, medical evidence, confidentiality, the insanity defence, issues that are legal as well as medical minefields and does so with an impressive grasp of and respect for the facts.

The result is a book that is mandatory reading for all doctors and lawyers, trained and in training.

Professor Anthony Clare

3 October 2002

Preface to the First Edition

Surgeons must be very careful
When they take the knife!
Underneath their fine incisions
Stirs the culprit, - Life!

   Emily Dickinson

The evolution and provision of health services are among the hallmarks of a modern civilised society. Similarly any civilised society will find it nearly impossible to function without laws or other similar rules of conduct. It is true that laws – being engines of an essentially human desire to regulate social living – will be human and imperfect, but their necessity is doubted by few. One of the accusations levied with mutual recrimination – although perhaps with diminishing frequency – by the professions at which this book is directed, namely clinical practitioners and lawyers, is that to each the other's profession and professional standards are somewhat opaque.

I hope that this text will give the clinical practitioner an insight into the mind of the law and help her to see that she is not being forced to conduct her practice on shifting sands, but rather on a largely certain footing, where few enough areas of legal uncertainty exist. The idea of the law as a threat to the practitioner is in part a product of fear and misunderstanding. The converse hope is that that those approaching law and clinical practice from a legal perspective will gain something of an insight into the way that medicine and the allied clinical arts are practised within a legal framework.

But while this book is in some measure about the relationship between health care practitioner and lawyer, it is more particularly about the relationship between practitioner and patient. The bulk of the ways in which law affects clinical practice do not involve lawyers at all: instead the law simply lays out ground rules for contact between practitioner and patient in the common scenarios in which they find themselves. It is true that some situations, such as the question of 'informed consent', may be complex, but others, such as prescribing or the notification of deaths to the coroner, are largely straightforward and essentially administrative and all are in some measure legally regulated. In his wonderful book, *The Doctor, Father Figure or Plumber*,[1] written at a time when "litigation [was] still uncommon", James McCormick presciently drew on a quotation that identifies a source of litigation not in the clash between clinician and lawyer, but in the shortcomings of the therapeutic relationship:

> "Let's start with…your relationship (or lack of one) with your patient. Isn't it strange that the person who first comes to you in complete confidence, fully prepared to refer to you fondly as "my doctor" is the very same person who sues the heck out of you? Quite obviously, somewhere along the line, something went wrong to cause such a wonderful start in a mutually beneficial relationship to end up fraught with suspicion, frustration and anger…

---

[1] London, 1979

"You can blame anyone or anything you want – the law, lawyers, courts, juries, insurance companies or the changing times, But if you don't examine yourself, your patient and how the two of you are doing in your human relationship, you will be putting the blame in the wrong place."[2]

This may be overstating the matter somewhat (the quote above is, after all, that of a lawyer) but there is a kernel of truth to it. A successful practitioner-patient relationship is all about communication and a misapprehension of the law can be another stumbling block to good communication. This book then should be regarded as a handbook for good practice – in a legal rather than clinical sense – of the relationship between practitioner and patient. It will not teach the clinical student or practitioner how to be a lawyer, nor will it coach the law student in the intricacies of medico-legal courtroom work but it is hoped that clinician, lawyer and perhaps more importantly, patients will benefit in some measure from the information contained herein.

How to use this book

If you want to, you can simply ignore the footnotes. This book is not of necessity an academic work, although it can – and hopefully will – be read as one, but is intended to be something of 'user's handbook', albeit a detailed one. I have attempted as far as possible to consign to the footnotes everything that is not essential for a non-legal, non-academic understanding of the subject matter or that would otherwise distract from the explanation of broad principles. For similar reasons, the footnotes can be found at the end of each chapter, rather than at the bottom of each page It is there that the legal reader, or the person with an interest in reading more widely, will find case names, details of statutes and references for articles. The clinically minded reader should hopefully find in the main body of the text alone a thorough review of law as it affects clinical practice written in neither medical nor legal jargon. Hopefully, the legal reader will find the absence of esoteric language – in either medical or legal dialects – an advantage as well.

The non-legal reader who wishes to know more about the law should consider reading Appendix I. References to legal reports are deciphered in the list of common abbreviations found at the back of the book. Each legal case generally comprises the year of the case in brackets, together with the law report text in which the case is found, followed by the page of the report on which the account of the case begins. So [1997] 3 IR 456 refers to a case in volume three of the 1997 Irish Reports, page 456. All the important law reports are to be found on the shelves of the law section in the University libraries. Many other recent or significant judgments are recorded on the excellent UCC-based website http://www.irlii.org (The Irish Legal Information Initiative).

The reader who is more pressed for time can consult the quick reference guides that pepper each chapter. At the end of many sections of the text, important material is summarised in a digestible form. The interested – or confused – reader may then refer back to the text for clarification or elucidation of any topic that whets the appetite or requires greater detail for a more thorough understanding. Whether there is enough

---

2   E Blake Moore, 'Anaesthesia and Analgesia – Current researches', *Lancet,* (1976), no 5, 756. Cited at p 37 of *The Doctor, Father Figure or Plumber.*

material in the quick reference tables alone to get the undergraduate through his or her exams, only time – and students brave enough to rely on the tables alone – will tell. The Tables have their own specific and separate list of their whereabouts at the beginning of the book.

A note on gender

The he *vs* she dilemma foxed the author for quite some time. I was not happy to simply rely on the old shibboleth that "where used in the text, the word 'he' also connotes the female." Instead, I have opted to recognise the reality of 21st century clinical practice in Ireland, namely that the majority of the student and practising body in most fields of clinical endeavour is – or, if present trends continue soon will be – female. Accordingly I have opted to use the female pronoun in the text to denote the clinical practitioner and the male pronoun to denote the patient. It is hoped that no one will be offended or perhaps – more pessimistically – that all will be offended equally. This convention is only departed from where it would make a nonsense of the text to adhere to it slavishly, for example by referring to a pregnant patient as 'he'.

I have attempted to ensure that the law and facts contained in this book are up to date as of the 16th September 2002, although it has been possible to involve a few developments occurring after this date.

Simon Mills

Christchurch

16 September 2002

Preface to the Second Edition

A great deal has changed, both in my life and in the world of law, since the first edition of this text. From a professional point of view, I have pursued a career at the Bar and as a consequence spend less time in the practise of medicine. In addition, I passed a very enjoyable and challenging year studying Medical Ethics at Imperial College London. Each of these experiences has, no doubt, had its effect on the content of this second edition. There is more law to it than there was to the earlier edition and for this there is no apology made: it is hoped that the non-legal reader will still find the text palatable and the legal reader will find everything she needs to know in the footnotes (the change from endnotes, used in the first edition, to footnotes is born both of my own experience of using legal texts in courts and the kind suggestions of colleagues).

There is also, as a result of my experiences of the last few years, a slightly greater emphasis on medical ethics alongside law. I have not, I hope, strayed too far into medical ethics (having read many texts on 'medical ethics and law', I am increasingly convinced that – with the honourable exceptions of Emily Jackson's *Medical Law* and Deirdre Madden's *Medicine, Ethics and the Law* – it is almost impossible to write a text that covers both topics well), but I also hope that the interested reader will find enough to whet her appetite and the resources she needs to explore the ethical aspects of some of the more contentious areas of this book.

The changes in the law, however, are those that have had the greatest impact on this text. There is hardly a sentence that has not been re-written and many chapters have needed to be fundamentally re-cast in response to changes in the law on mental health and regulation of the professions, as well as many proposed changes to areas such as coroners' law.

A number of people have been of great help in the genesis and growth of this text. The foreword to the first edition was written by the late Prof Anthony Clare and, then as now, a contribution that I hugely value from a man whom I enormously admired. For me, as for many of my medical colleagues, he was a role model and an example. His cruel and untimely death in 2007 robbed Irish medicine of one of its finest practitioners and Ireland of one of her – to use his own words – most lucid and compassionate citizens. Professor Roy Spence, who acted as Consultant Editor to the first edition, is responsible for the first edition ever being published and, in turn (albeit at second hand), for this second edition. The seeds for this book were first sown while I spent a year in UCD and I reiterate too the thanks uttered in the first edition to Prof Denis Cusack, Asim Sheikh and Cliodhna McGovern. As far as those who have helped birth this second edition are concerned, I am extremely grateful for the forbearance, guidance and encouragement shown by Sandra Mulvey at Tottel, especially in the face of delays and the spectre of further delays occasioned by my other commitments. In addition, Marian Sullivan, who typeset the book, Orla Fee, who edited it, and Andrew Turner, who indexed it, have my deepest gratitude. Mark Tottenham BL helped enormously, both thanks to his compendious back catalogue of medico-legal case reports and his calm and calming presence in the office we share. Dr Mary Gray read proofs of this book and made some extremely useful and perceptive comments, for which I am also thankful.

I have been greatly enlightened by the students I have taught over the last five years and, in particular, those at Blackhall Place and the Royal College of Surgeons in Ireland, from whom I have learned far more (I fear) than they have learned from me. I thank, too, my medical colleagues who have been kind enough to ask me to lecture them on occasion over the last few years and on the basis of whose store of practical wisdom I hope I have been able to apply this book to practical matters facing doctors and other clinicians.

My greatest thanks (and my love), however, go to my wife, Grace, and to my three daughters Sorcha, Anna and Emily; they are my greatest inspiration.

The law stated in this text is correct as it stood in November 2007.

Simon Mills
Arran Quay
14 November, 2007

Contents

Chapter 4   Consent

Chapter 5   Clinical Records and Prescribing

Chapter 6   Clinical Negligence

Chapter 7   The Practitioner and the Family

Chapter 8   Health in the Workplace

Chapter 9   The Practitioner and the Lawyer

Quick Reference Guides

Table of Cases

L

M

Q

R

S

Table of Statutes

Bunreacht na hÉireann

Other Jurisdictions

European Legislation

Statutory Instruments

Chapter 1

Introduction and History

INTRODUCTION – SOME DEFINITIONS

[1.01] This book is predominantly concerned with the subject of 'legal medicine' although, somewhat counter-intuitively, the phrase 'legal medicine' itself is rarely used in the text. The reasons for this apparent paradox are twofold. The first is simple: the book is not intended solely for practitioners of medicine, but for those, from whatever clinical or non-clinical discipline, who are interested in how the law interacts with clinical practice. The second reason is that the term is not always understood to mean the same thing by all those who hear or use it. Some believe the term to be unnecessarily restrictive or prefer to call the discipline 'forensic medicine', 'medical jurisprudence' or 'medical law'.

[1.02] A definition of 'legal medicine' might be the professional and academic discipline concerning itself with legal aspects of medical science, medical practice and other healthcare delivery problems. 'Forensic medicine' is a narrower construct, concerned predominantly with using clinical, medical or other scientific measures to achieve the ends of a legal process, such as a successful criminal prosecution or the resolution of a paternity dispute. 'Medical jurisprudence' is, in its technical sense, an examination of the legal principles (as distinct from practice) that underpin medicine, its professional ethics and the practitioner–patient relationship. 'Medical law', finally, is often used to describe the study by lawyers of the way that law applies to medicine.

[1.03] One reason why the term 'legal medicine', rather than a vaguer and more generic term such as 'legal clinical practice', does remain relevant to the aims of this book is that it is in the specifically medical arena that the great majority of the legal principles set out in this book have been expounded and tested. The Irish Medical Council's *Guide to Ethical Conduct and Behaviour*[1] is the most thorough and considered Irish expression of clinical ethical and legal practice. Similarly, it is the doctor–patient relationship that has tended to give rise to the bulk of the case law forming the backdrop to the legal principles discussed in this text. Finally, the author comes from a medical background, which may lend a certain unavoidable slant to affairs. For all the foregoing reasons, this text will necessarily appear, in places, to have something of a medical bias; any apparent bias simply reflects the fact that much of healthcare and clinical litigation itself has a certain medical bias. The fact is, however, that the lessons learned from medicine's encounters with the law are generally applicable to all clinical professions.

[1.04] This book contains elements of forensics, jurisprudence, legal medicine, medical law and medical ethics, but its ultimate aim is to give a comprehensive view of the interaction of law and legal frameworks with the everyday practice of the various clinical disciplines. Hence, in order to convey accurately the extent of the area reviewed, it is

---

[1]   Medical Council, *Guide to Ethical Conduct and Behaviour* (6th edn, 2004).

necessary to give the book a title that reflects that broad canvas: *Clinical Practice and the Law.*

A NEED FOR CLINICAL LEGAL TRAINING?

[1.05] Most (if not all) Irish law courses offer modules, usually optional, in medical law, while all of the medical schools teach a compulsory course in forensic/legal medicine. Most non-medical clinical curricula also include modules on legal matters relevant to the practice of the particular discipline. However, the value placed on such courses in the curriculum is of crucial importance to how the lessons taught will be valued and absorbed by students. Many have bemoaned the lack of emphasis given to medico-legal training in the modern university, especially in the case of medical students. Some have suggested that legal medicine is losing out in an 'overcrowded curriculum'[2] and, insofar as this is true, it is regrettable.

[1.06] Legal aspects of clinical practice confront clinicians in almost every aspect of their working lives. It may be a matter of apparently routine conduct, such as completing a driver's licence application for a patient,[3] or it may be a knottier question, such as whether to respect a patient's decision to refuse treatment even where that refusal means the patient will die.[4] In either of these scenarios (and in many other situations), a grasp of the law can help to ease the doubts that may arise in the mind of the conscientious practitioner who is aware of the legal ramifications of her practice. Other clinical processes that have more than a whiff of law about them include examining assault and accident victims, the certification of death, reporting deaths to a coroner, writing medico-legal reports and giving evidence in court. There have been suggestions from a number of sources that standards in areas of practice such as recording the cause of death[5] or describing wounds[6] fall short of the ideal. Yet, the solution is by no means set in stone: what constitutes adequate training in the legal aspect of medical training? Opinions vary; however, one list of topics considered mandatory by some sources is set out at Figure 1.1.[7]

---

2   Mant, 'The decline in the teaching of legal medicine' (1986) BMJ; 293:1390; see also Mant, 'A survey of forensic pathology in England since 1945' (1973) J Forensic Sci Soc 13, 17.
3   See Ch 16 'The Practitioner and the Driver', para **[16.05]***ff.*
4   See Ch 12 'The Extremes of Life II: Death', para **[12.05]***ff.*
5   James and Bull 'Information on death certificates: a cause for concern?' (1996) Journal of Clinical Pathology 49(3), 213–216; Doyle, Harrison and O'Malley, 'A study of selected death certificates from three Dublin teaching hospitals' (1990) Journal of Public Health Medicine 12(2), 118–123. Both studies showed fundamental problems with the information contained on death certificates; the latter study in particular demonstrated frequent and egregious discrepancies between the cause of death recorded on certificates and the cause of death established at autopsy.
6   Milroy and Rutty, 'If a wound is "neatly incised" it is not a laceration' (1997) BMJ; 315:1312 (letters).
7   Mant, 'The decline in the teaching of legal medicine' (1986) BMJ; 293:1390; Simpson, 'Postgraduate training in forensic pathology.' (1971) Proc Royal Soc Med 64, 146–147.

Figure 1.1 Important medico-legal and forensic skills

- What to do (and what not to do) with a dead body where there are suspicions of an unnatural death
- Certification and disposal of the dead
- The preparation of medico-legal reports and the giving of evidence
- Litigation and compensation
- The interpretation of injuries
- Sexual assault victim examination
- Principles of medical ethics

[1.07] The list set out in Figure 1.1 may be criticised for its apparent bias towards the forensic aspects of legal medicine and that bias is unsurprising, for its origins were mooted by academic forensic pathologists. A more exhaustive list might include issues of medical negligence and consent and topics dealing with mental illness, children and questions of confidentiality, all of which areas, together with forensic matters, are dealt with in this text. In the United Kingdom, attempts have been made, led by the General Medical Council,[8] to shore up the teaching of medico-legal topics with an agreed 'core curriculum' in medical law and ethics (Figure 1.2).[9] The 12 themes identified in the core curriculum form the 'core academic content necessary to produce "doctors who will engage in good ethically and legally informed practice".'[10] In counterpoint to the criticism made of the forensic medicine bias in the skill sets referred to in Figure 1.1, the 'core curriculum' in Figure 1.2 seems to regard forensic matters as lying wholly outside its remit.

Figure 1.2 The UK 'Core Curriculum' on Medical Ethics and Law

1. Informed consent and refusal of treatment
2. The clinical relationship: truthfulness, trust and good communication
3. Confidentiality
4. Medical research
5. Human reproduction
6. The 'new genetics'
7. Children—age of consent; parent/child conflicts; child abuse
8. Mental disorders and disabilities
9. Life, death, dying and killing
10. The duties of doctors (and medical students); the General Medical Council and professional regulation; responding to clinical mistakes
11. Resource allocation
12. Rights—what rights are; their links with moral and professional duties; the importance of rights (including human rights) for good medical practice

---

[8] General Medical Council, *Tomorrow's Doctors* (GMC, 1993).

[9] See Consensus Group of Teachers of Medical Ethics and Law in UK Medical Schools, 'Teaching medical ethics and law within medical education: a model for the UK core curriculum' (1998) J Med Ethics 24, 188–192.

[10] Doyal, Gillon, 'Medical ethics and law as a core subject in medical education' (1998); BMJ 316:1623–1624 (Editorial).

[1.08] As will be seen, the aim of this text is to cover, in some measure, all of the areas mentioned in both Figures 1.1 and 1.2. The more informed a practitioner is about the legal framework within which she practises, the better she can be expected to avoid the ever-present legal pitfalls of her everyday work. Knowledge and comprehension of even the barest rudiments of legal aspects of patient care can provide certainty and reassurance for practitioner and patient, together with guidelines for best clinical–legal practice and greater confidence in clinicians' communications with patients on legal matters. Ignorance of the law is one of the clinical practitioner's worst enemies; ignorance may beget fear, errors and taciturnity in the face of any questions about the legal propriety of any course of action.

A (VERY) BRIEF HISTORY OF LEGAL MEDICINE AND MEDICAL ETHICS

[1.09] There are few countries in possession of ancient historical records that cannot lay at least a tentative claim to having played host to the genesis of legal or forensic medicine. The truth, however, is that legal medicine as an independent and discrete subject within the medical corpus is a comparative latecomer, dating back to no earlier than the late seventeenth century, although, as we note below, some doctors were discharging forensic or coroners' duties long before then. Academia's historical quest has been for something akin to what playwright Arthur Miller termed 'echoes down the corridor':[11] the process of teasing out elements of ancient medicine that bear the primitive hallmarks of what we now call 'legal medicine', even though the ancient world called it no such thing. Such a historical tour can, however, be a relatively enlightening one, insofar as it demonstrates the side-by-side evolution of clinical skills and law and an early recognition that the relationship between the two could and should be a symbiotic rather than an antagonistic one.

The dawn of legal medicine

Egypt

[1.10] Imhotep (c.2686–c.2613 BC) was at various times the Grand Vizier and Chief Justice of Egypt and physician to Pharaoh Djoser and he is considered by some to have been one of the first 'medico-legal' experts. In truth though, there was little at which he was not adept—he excelled as an administrator, architect, sage and physician and had the decided advantage, rare at that time, of living a long life. He was later deified,[12] becoming one of the few Egyptian commoners (and probably the only doctor ever) to achieve that distinction; the Ancient Greeks and Romans came to identify him with Aesculapius, the god of healing. Until the nineteenth century, he was thought to have been a mythological figure, until archaeological evidence transplanted him from legend into history. Imhotep is associated with the Edwin Smith Papyrus, in which more than 90 anatomical terms and 48 injuries are described.[13] He may also have founded a school of

---

[11] Miller, *The Crucible* (Penguin, 2000).

[12] Much later: his deification occurred sometime in the period 664 BC–525 BC, following hundreds of years of worship; it has been suggested that early Christians may also have venerated him.

[13] See Nunn, *Ancient Egyptian Medicine* (British Museum Press, 1996), Ch 2.

medicine at Memphis, some two millennia before the 'father of medicine', Hippocrates, was even born.

China

[1.11] As long ago as the fifth century BC,[14] there was an official in China with responsibility for investigating suspicious deaths. A text from that time, *The Lu's Spring and Autumn Annals*, describes how the body decomposes and provides information on the diagnosis of wounds such as bruises and fractures. Around 221 BC, the Qin Dynasty[15] emerged dominant from a period of turmoil and established the first centralised Imperial administration in China, including within its bureaucracy one of the first coroner-type[16] roles, the 'lingshi', who was required to examine corpses and to produce reports on certain categories of death. A prevailing attitude in the administration of Chinese justice at that time was that punishment should be proportional to the injuries inflicted on the corpse of the victim, so evidence disclosed by examination was potentially vital in the ultimate determination of the sanction to be imposed on a wrongdoer.

[1.12] In one recorded case,[17] an official by the name of Zhang Ju performed an experiment to try to prove a homicide had taken place; the wife of a dead man was suspected of his murder and of burning the body, but she claimed her husband had been burned to death in a fire. To determine the matter, Zhang Ju burned two pigs, one living and one dead. Subsequent examination of the pigs showed that the pig that was dead before the fire started had no ashes in its mouth, while the pig that had been immolated alive had inhaled evidence of the fire. No ashes had been found in the mouth of the dead man, permitting the inference that he had died before the fire started; confronted with this evidence, the wife admitted her guilt.

[1.13] By the seventh century AD, the Chinese had recognised that fingerprints could be of use in identification (although the formal process of fingerprint classification and their use in crime detection lay many years in the future).[18] By the time of the Song Dynasty (c.1000 AD), the law required the appointment of an officer who was obliged, in cases of murder, to visit the scene as soon as possible and was subject to statutory penalties for failing to do so. The officer, who was not necessarily a doctor, was required to examine the body, certify the death and furnish a post-mortem report, including a

---

14 During the period known as 'The Warring Kingdoms'; see Jia, Cameron and Wang, 'A Brief History of Forensic Medicine in China' (1988) 12 The Criminologist 67.

15 From which China gets its name.

16 For a discussion of the history and role of coroners, see Ch 13 'Coroners and the Aftermath of Death', para **[13.12]***ff*.

17 Described in *Yi Yu Ji* ('A Collection of Criminal Cases'), dating from the Wu Dynasty in the Three Kingdoms' 264–277. See also Lu and Needham, 'A history of forensic Medicine in China' (1988) Med Hist 32 357–400, 363. Medical evidence similar to this has been used in modern cases.

18 Thomas Bewick, a nineteenth-century English naturalist, used engravings of his own fingerprints to identify books he had published. The last years of the nineteenth century ushered in the use of fingerprints as a means of identification and crime detection: see Figure 1.3.

front and rear sketch of the body (although oriental modesty meant that the genitalia were not included in the sketch).

[1.14] Another significant early medico-legal text dates from the second century of Song rule (c. 1247 AD); although heavily amended in subsequent editions, *Hsi Yuan Chi Lu* (most commonly translated as *The Washing Away of Wrongs*) remained the authoritative text on forensic and legal medicine in China until 1911, when the last emperor was deposed. Among the guidance contained in the text was how to distinguish between victims of drowning and strangulation and the classification of wounds caused by different weapons. The text also contains an early example of forensic entomology.[19] The author tells of a murder in a Chinese village in which the victim was repeatedly slashed; the local magistrate thought the wounds might have been inflicted by a sickle, but investigations had been fruitless. Finally, the magistrate ordered all the village men to assemble, each with his own sickle. In the hot summer sun, flies were attracted to one sickle because of the residue of blood and small tissue fragments still adhering to the blade and handle; the owner of the sickle confessed to the crime.

[1.15] Many other texts demonstrated the evolution of knowledge in China concerning the legal ramifications of medical knowledge—a text from 1694 described subcutaneous haemorrhages for the first time; another, from 1777, described the fracturing of the hyoid bone as a sign of hanging or strangulation. However, progress at the interface of law and medicine slowed in China as years went by and as the empire waned and atrophied. Several elements contributed to this. The first was the institutional reluctance of the Imperial rulers to open their doors to outside influences. Secondly, the process of post-mortem examination in China tended to be confined to external examination, limiting the degree to which advances in physiological and anatomical understanding could be made. Finally, the humanist revolution that swept Europe during the Renaissance meant that huge strides were being taken in the European knowledge of the sciences (including anatomy and physiology) and humanities in which the isolated Chinese could not share and by which they were, in terms of knowledge, left behind.

The 'western' world

[1.16] The Middle East, Greece and Rome were the cradles of our own civilisation: our alphabet, numerical systems and many of our modern administrative and legal structures are recognisable in the history that flows from those eras. The origins of modern medical ethics also have their roots in the Ancient World that bordered the Mediterranean.

The Ancients

[1.17] One of the earliest formalised legal codes, dating from approximately 1750 BC, is the *Code of Hammurabi* (a king of Babylonia), which was found engraved on a diorite column at Susa in Iran. The code consists of 282 provisions and the justice it meted out was rooted firmly in the 'eye-for-an-eye' school of thought. So, in dealing with the specific issue of medical or surgical accidents, the code states:

---

[19] Using insects—and particularly their larvae—as an adjunct to solving crime: see Ch 14 'Forensic Medicine, DNA Testing and Terminology of Injuries', para **[14.16]***ff.*

'If a physician makes a large incision with the operating knife and kills his patient, or opens a tumour with the operating knife and cuts out the eye, his hands shall be cut off.'[20]

[1.18] Hippocrates, Galen and Aristotle also flourished in the Mediterranean region. Hippocrates, who is closely associated with the Greek island of Kos, was not only a physician but is also often characterised as the father of medical ethics. The 'Hippocratic' Oath—written about 400 BC—may not have been authored by Hippocrates and may not even have been the prevailing ethical standard of the day,[21] but it continues to exercise an influence over the practice of medicine in the modern era. Many medical schools in the USA and UK have a 'swearing' ceremony in which graduating medical students swear an oath that is often (but by no means always) based on the Hippocratic Oath.[22] The Oath deals with many concerns that remain current in medical practice, such as confidentiality, acting for the good of the ill, euthanasia and abortion, while also dealing in less accepted coin, such as a gendering of medicine (men only). Although there is no definitive translation, one version is as follows:

'I swear by Apollo the Physician and by Asclepius and by the God [of Health] Hygeia and Panacea and by all the gods as well as goddesses, making them judges [witnesses], to bring the following oath and written covenant to fulfilment, in accordance with my power and judgement;

To regard him who has taught me this *techné* [art and science] as equal to my parents, and to share, in partnership, my livelihood with him and to give him a share when he is in need of necessities, and to judge [his] offspring equal to [my] brothers, and to teach them this *techné*, should they desire to learn it, without fee and written covenant,

And to give a share both of rules and of lectures, and of all the rest of learning to my sons and to the [sons] of him who has taught me and to the pupils who have made a written contract and sworn by a medical convention but by no other.

And I will use regimens for the benefit of the ill in accordance with my ability and my judgement, but from what is to their harm or injustice I will keep [them].

And I will not give a drug that is deadly to anyone if asked [for it], nor will I suggest the way to such a counsel.

And likewise I will not give a woman a destructive pessary.

And in a pure and holy way I will guard my life and my *techné*.

I will not cut and certainly not those suffering from the stone, but I will cede [this] to men [who are] practitioners of this activity.

Into as many houses as I may enter, I will go for the benefit of the ill while being far from all voluntary and destructive injustice, especially from sexual acts upon women's bodies and upon men's, both of the free and of slaves.

---

[20] Provision 218. Doctors fare comparatively well in the code: if a building collapsed and killed the inhabitants, the builder who erected it could be put to death together with his children (provisions 229—230). In all cases, the penalties for killing a slave were less onerous than those for killing a freeman; the doctor whose negligence killed a slave would not forfeit her hands, but could instead merely replace the slave.

[21] See Miles, *The Hippocratic Oath and the Ethics of Medicine* (Oxford, 2004).

[22] Mills 'Oaths and Courses' (2002) IMJ 95:10.

And about whatever I may see or hear in treatment, or even without treatment, in the life of human beings—things that should not ever be blurted out outside—I will remain silent, holding such things to be unutterable [sacred, not to be divulged].

If I render this oath fulfilled, and if I do not blur and confound it [making it to no effect] may it be granted to me to enjoy the benefits both of life and of *techné*, being held in good repute among all human beings for the eternal. If, however, I transgress and perjure myself, the opposite of these [shall be my fate].'[23]

[1.19] The Hippocratic Corpus (the name given to the wider body of medical documents dating from that era) also deals with medico-legal issues, including the relative fatality of wounds in different parts of the body, the possibility of super-foetation,[24] the average duration of pregnancy, the viability of embryos before full term, and malingering. The Graeco-Roman physician, Galen, also considered medico-legal problems and wrote on the need for research and empiricism in medicine,[25] while Aristotle estimated the time of the 'animation' of the foetus (the date on which its soul was conferred and it became a 'person') at 40 days.[26]

[1.20] The Romans passed laws with medico-legal relevance: the *Lex Aquila* of 572 BC dealt with the lethality and criminal gravity of certain wounds. In 44 BC, the murdered body of Julius Caesar was subjected to a post mortem examination by the physician Antistius, who concluded that of the 23 stab wounds inflicted by the conspirators, only one—a stab wound to the chest—was fatal.[27] The later *Code of Justinian*, dating from the sixth century AD, was a massive compendium of all Roman legislation and among many other things provided for regulation of the practice of medicine, surgery and midwifery and enumerated the recognised classes of physicians. It also drew a distinction between medical and other witnesses in legal proceedings, expounding the principle, valid then as now: *'Medici non sunt proprie testes, sed majus est judicium quam testimonius'*—a medical expert is most useful when assisting the court, rather than her own side, with testimony.[28]

The dark ages

[1.21] When Germanic peoples began, from the late fourth century AD onwards, to overrun, conquer and then re-conquer at will the increasingly disjointed Roman Empire, among the laws that were laid down under the new dispensation, the *Leges Barborum*,[29]

---

[23] Slightly adapted from a version cited in Miles, *The Hippocratic Oath and the Ethics of Medicine* (Oxford, 2004), Ch 1. See also von Staden, '"In a pure and holy way": Personal and professional conduct in the Hippocratic Oath' (1996) J Hist Med Allied Sci 51:406–408.

[24] Fertilisation of a second ovum after a pregnancy has begun; it results in two foetuses of different ages in the uterus at the same time.

[25] Van der Eijk, *Medicine and Philosophy in Classical Antiquity* (Cambridge, 2005), Ch 10.

[26] This question of the 'animation' of the foetus played an important role in the approach of early courts (which were frequently religious courts) to the question of abortion.

[27] Suetonius, *Lives of the Twelve Caesars* (Oxford Classics, 2000).

[28] See Ch 9 'The Practitioner and the Lawyer', para **[9.30]***ff.*

[29] 'The Barbarians' Laws', a generic term for the many sets of rules introduced by the successive waves of invaders, each set typically bearing the name of the invading tribe whose writ ruled Rome at the time (eg the fifth-century *Lex Visigothorum* or the seventh-century *Lex Langobardorum*).

were statutes compelling courts to rely on medical expertise when evaluating wounds. In turn, born out of these laws were exhaustive compilations of categories of injury and the compensation payable for any injury (the 'Wergeld')[30] by an assailant. Similar laws were still being passed 500 years later—the *Sachsenspiegel* ('Saxon mirror') of 1225 provided for medical experts, having sworn an oath, to assist the courts. Laws such as these helped to codify society's response to violent death and to avoid, or at least modify, the idiosyncrasies and excesses of personal vendettas and blood feuds.

[1.22] German legal thinking was a significant factor in the development of law and its relationship with medicine elsewhere in mainland Europe. The academic Irnerus was teaching Langobardic (a German tribe) law as well as Roman law during the last part of the eleventh century in the college that was later (in 1119) to become the University of Bologna. Germanic legal influence was also evident in an edict of the Norman King Roger II of Sicily of 1154 that provided for the appointment of physicians to help the courts.[31] These edicts in turn had a strong influence on the Italian town charters of the thirteenth to sixteenth centuries, which contributed much to the development of a systematically consolidated medico-legal discipline.

Mediaeval and Renaissance Europe

[1.23] Twelfth-century Norman England was the wellspring of the office that most clearly unites the role of the clinician and the lawyer in modern Ireland and Britain—the coroner's office dates from 1194, during the reign of King Richard the Lionheart (Richard I).[32] However, there was little else in the way of development at the interface between medicine and law in these islands and when evidence of the burgeoning relationship did emerge, it was in mainland Europe. The argument has been made that it was the difference in legal systems that led to the growth of the role of the medical expert in mainland Europe—while England and its dominions relied on a jury-based justice system, law in Europe was typically administered by an inquisitorial judge who acted as both investigator and judge.[33] Another factor may have been the greater organisation of legal medicine in continental Europe, allied to schemes for comparatively lucrative remuneration of experts in exchange for their time and expertise.[34] In the thirteenth century (1252), Bologna was the first city in Europe to demand an expert medical investigation in all cases of offences against the person.

---

[30] 'Blood-price': it was paid to the victim or his family (in the case of murder) by the suspect criminal. The amount depended on the type of injury and the status of the victim. If the wound exposed brain or bowel, the fee was higher than if only blood was shed and the greater status of the victim the higher the Wergeld.

[31] Roger II is also credited with being the first Western administrator to insist that doctors pass a qualifying examination. Examinations for Chinese doctors are thought to have been introduced in 493 AD and the Caliph of Baghdad introduced similar tests in about 931 AD. See also Lu and Needham, 'A history of Forensic Medicine in China' (1988) Med Hist; 32:357–400.

[32] See Ch 13 'Coroners and the Aftermath of Death', para **[13.12]***ff*.

[33] See Crawford, 'Legalizing medicine: early modern legal systems and the growth of medico-legal knowledge' in Clark and Crawford (eds), *Legal Medicine in History* (Cambridge University Press, 1994).

[34] Ibid.

Caroline code

[1.24] The *Constitutio Criminalis Carolina* was a landmark in the history of legal medicine. The law, which translates approximately as the *Criminal Code of Emperor Charles* or the *Caroline Code*, was introduced by the Holy Roman Emperor, Charles V, in 1532, but was based on an earlier law of 1507 drawn up for the governance of the town of Bamberg.

[1.25] The Caroline Code articulated the fact that many questions could not be answered by purely legal methods and obliged judges therefore to take the evidence, sworn in advance, of physicians in cases where death had resulted from criminal or accidental violence. The code explicitly laid down that expert medical testimony was necessary to guide judges in cases of murder, wounding, poisoning, hanging, drowning, infanticide, abortion, and in other circumstances relating to personal injuries. The code also introduced a practice of obligatory medico-legal autopsies. The Caroline Code is interesting in part because it coincided, chronologically and geographically, with the flourishing of the Renaissance and associated rapid advances in the medical sciences, led by practitioners such as Vesalius. This in turn meant that the autopsies ordered by law could feed off flourishing anatomical knowledge in Europe and vice versa. Contemporary records show that unlike in China, where examinations were almost solely external, wounds in Europe were opened to show their depth and direction, although complete autopsies were probably not performed in every case.

Other developments in the sixteenth and seventeenth centuries

[1.26] The French surgeon Ambroise Paré, published his *Traicte des rapports, et du moyen d'embaumer les corps morts* at Paris in 1575. It was reprinted many times thereafter and translated into English in 1634, with the title *How to make reports, and to embalm the dead*. The first book on poisons, Battista Codronchi's *De morbis veneficis*, was published in Venice in 1595. The first comprehensive European text on medico-legal matters was *De relationibus medicorum*, published by Fortunato Fedele at Palermo in 1602, although this work was soon supplanted by Paolo Zacchia's *Quaestiones medico-legales*, which was published in Rome in the 1630s. The latter text canvassed all questions likely to require medical explanation to non-medical judges. By the mid-seventeenth century, Michaelis and Bohn had begun to give forensic pathology lectures at Leipzig University.

The 18th century onwards

[1.27] The importance of expert medical knowledge was increasingly recognised in England from the eighteenth century; between 1730 and 1760 medical testimony was heard at more than half the homicide trials at the Old Bailey.[35] More generally, the medical profession gradually started to organise discussions based on the new knowledge base, forensic monographs became almost commonplace and the discipline of legal or forensic medicine began to emerge as a subject distinct from the general practice of medicine or law by the end of the seventeenth century. By the eighteenth century, chairs had been established in German universities for legal medicine, Leipzig

---

[35] Ibid.

being the first in about 1720. The French followed suit with chairs in forensic medicine in Paris, Strasbourg and Montpellier by the end of the eighteenth century and there was a professorship in legal medicine in Vienna by 1804. In Great Britain, Edinburgh became the first to establish a chair in forensic medicine in the opening decade of the nineteenth century, with Glasgow University following suit by 1839; London appointed its first professor of medical jurisprudence in 1834.

[1.28] In 1900, early laws dealing with clinical non-therapeutic research had been passed in Prussia,[36] prohibiting experimentation on non-consenting adults, minors and the mentally incompetent and demanding that participants be properly informed of possible adverse outcomes. These laws were later, in 1931, to become the basis for national laws (*Richtlinien*), which in turn were pointedly and savagely ignored once the Nazis came to power.

[1.29] In Britain and Ireland legislation began to be laid down, some of which is still applicable today. The Offences Against the Person Act 1861, which criminalised abortion, is still in force in Ireland. In parallel, courts began to reach judgments that helped to crystallise the way in which medicine and allied clinical disciplines are practised today. In the 1920s the American case of *Schloendorff v Society of New York Hospital*[37] crystallised the principles of consent to medical treatment that still govern thinking on the topic. The modern concept of the law of negligence dates from the 1930s' English case of *Donoghue v Stevenson*.[38] The second half of the twentieth century saw major re-evaluations of the law relating to medical negligence and to informed consent and we will return to these matters in their proper place in the text.

FORENSIC DEVELOPMENTS

[1.30] As medicine and law evolved side by side, so too the scientific basis for medicine developed. From rudimentary conceptions of the human body and its functioning,

---

[36] Sass, 'Reichsrundschreiben 1931: Pre-Nuremberg German regulations concerning new therapy and human experimentation.' (1983) J Med Philos 8:99–111; also Capron, 'Human experimentation' in Veatch (ed), *Medical Ethics* (Jones and Bartlett, 1997), 135–184. Also in 1900, as it happens, a bill was presented to the US Senate to provide rules for human experimentation. The bill required a scientific rationale demonstrating the need to conduct further research; independent approval of research; exclusion of vulnerable groups from research; and informed consent: the bill was thrown out by the Senate. See Lederer, *Subjected to Science: Human Experimentation in America before the Second World War* (Johns Hopkins Press, 1995).

[37] *Schloendorff v Society of New York Hospital* (1914) 211 NY 125 at 126. The law on consent to medical treatment can be traced back as far as *Slater v Baker & Stapleton* 95 Eng. 860, 2 Wils KB 359 (1767). In that case, a doctor initially set a patient's femoral fracture in accordance with practice at the time, but at a follow-up visit re-broke the healing fracture and placed the re-broken bone in a mechanical device. The judge concluded that obtaining a patient's consent was a custom of physicians and ruled that consent should have been obtained by the physician as part of the duties of his profession: see Mazur, 'Influence of the law on risk and informed consent' 2003 BMJ 327: 731–731. As Mazur observes, it was only much later that the notion of information became linked to consent.

[38] *Donoghue v Stevenson* [1932] AC 562.

science came to have a great comprehension of anatomy, physiology and ultimately genetics, lending medicine greater force when it came to undertaking legal obligations. Some significant events in the development of forensic medicine are set out in Figure 1.3.

Figure 1.3 Some modern milestones in the evolution of forensic medicine

Year/Era	*Event*
1813	Mathieu Orfila, a Spanish professor at the University of Paris, published his *Treatise on Toxicology*. Orfila is also credited as one of the first to attempt the use of a microscope in the assessment of blood and semen stains.
1823	Jan Evangelista Purkinje, Professor of Anatomy at the University of Breslau in Czechoslovakia (who also gave his name to the fibres in the heart's conduction system), published the first paper on the nature of fingerprints and suggested a classification system based on nine major types. He did not recognise their potential for identification or crime detection.
1836	James Marsh, Scottish chemist and inventor of the Marsh test for the presence of arsenic, was the first to present toxicological proof of poisoning (with arsenic) in a trial.[39]
1863	The use of hydrogen peroxide as a test for the presence of blood was discovered.
1880	Henry Faulds, a Scottish physician, published a paper suggesting that fingerprints at the scene of a crime could identify the offender. He used fingerprints to eliminate an innocent suspect and to identify the real perpetrator of a Tokyo burglary.
1880	Henry Faulds, a Scottish physician, published a paper suggesting that fingerprints at the scene of a crime could identify the offender. He used fingerprints to eliminate an innocent suspect and to identify the real perpetrator of a Tokyo burglary.

---

[39] Arsenic had cropped up in a murder trial before, although a test for its presence in the body's organs did not then exist. In 1752, a 31-year-old spinster, Mary Blandy, murdered her father with arsenic in a dispute over her proposed marriage. The witness, Dr Addington, did not possess the knowledge to prove absolutely that the powder Mary used was arsenic, but he convinced the court beyond reasonable doubt that the powder was arsenic. Blandy had mixed white arsenic in gruel and given it to her father, who fell ill and died. Some of the leftover gruel was eaten by a charwoman and a maid, who also became unwell. The pan used to prepare the gruel was examined and a white sediment was recovered from the bottom. The sediment had exactly the same physical characteristics as arsenic and behaved the same way in chemical reactions. Blandy was convicted and sentenced to death.

1880	Henry Faulds, a Scottish physician, published a paper suggesting that fingerprints at the scene of a crime could identify the offender. He used fingerprints to eliminate an innocent suspect and to identify the real perpetrator of a Tokyo burglary.
1896	Edward Richard Henry developed the modern fingerprint classification and identification system, based on nine points of identification on the fingerprint.
1900	Landsteiner discovered human blood groups (for which he received the Nobel Prize in 1930).
c.1910	Victor Balthazard used photographic enlargements of bullets and cartridge cases and recognised the possibility of connecting a fired bullet to a particular weapon. Balthazard, a professor at the Sorbonne, also studied the forensic uses of human hair.
1910s	Lattes, a professor at the Institute of Forensic Medicine in Turin, developed the first antibody test for ABO blood groups.
1930s	Holzer, working at Innsbruck University, developed the absorption-inhibition ABO typing technique that forms the basis of the test that continues to be used in present-day laboratories.
1940s	Lundquist, in the University of Copenhagen, developed the acid phosphatase test for semen.
1960s	Culliford, working in the Metropolitan Police laboratory in London, initiated gel-based methods to test for isoenzymes in dried bloodstains and was instrumental in the development and dissemination of methods for detecting proteins and isoenzymes in blood and other body fluids.
1985	Alec Jeffreys published his discovery of the DNA profiling test.
1988	The first use of DNA to solve a crime (involving the rape and murder of two girls)[40] and also—in the process—to exonerate an innocent suspect.

---

[40] *R v Pitchfork* (1988) The Guardian, 23 January. Using his DNA technique, Jeffreys compared semen samples from both murders against a blood sample from a suspect and conclusively proved that both girls were killed by the same man, but not by the suspect. The police consequently undertook the world's first DNA mass screening, covering all adult males in three villages—a total of 5000 men—who were asked to volunteer and provide blood or saliva samples. Blood grouping was performed and DNA-profiling then carried out on the 10 per cent of men who had the same blood type as the killer. Initially the testing proved fruitless, but it later came to light that Colin Pitchfork had asked a friend to submit a sample in place of him. A sample was taken from Pitchfork and he proved to be the killer. For more on DNA testing, see Ch 14 'Forensic Medicine, DNA Testing and Terminology of Injuries', para **[14.21]***ff.*

Chapter 2

Healthcare Professions and Regulation

INTRODUCTION

[2.01] This chapter commences by looking at what constitutes a profession, before examining the various clinical disciplines in Ireland, together with their organisation and regulation. We highlight in particular the disciplinary measures created by relevant legislation. Finally, we examine the question of the free movement of healthcare professionals within Europe.

WHAT IS A PROFESSION?

[2.02] It is hard to fasten on a definition of a 'profession' that is at once both precise and concise. Historically, the term tended to apply only to the pursuits of medicine, law and divinity, but the term has become less selective in its application over time: teaching, nursing and banking, for example, might well be regarded as professions in the modern world. Some criteria that can probably be used to define a profession include:

- the acquisition of learning as a necessary precursor to entry into the profession;
- the presumption of continued learning within the practice of the profession;
- a degree of self-direction and control over the pace and scheduling of work;
- a possibility of advancement to higher levels within the profession.[1]

[2.03] In general, as well as having the four characteristics listed above, a profession will also typically generate its own sense of separate identity, which separateness and significance outside observers have come to accept. Most professions will also have an ethical code of conduct. This code of conduct may simply be regarded as a benign guide, setting down rules of conduct through which the profession ensures that those depending upon the profession receive the best possible care or service. However, a more caustic view may also be taken of such profession-mediated rules of conduct, namely that they are not essential for the patient or client but rather for the continuance of the profession itself and its hegemony over the delivery of the service in which the profession specialises. A professional principle, for example, stating that the patient must always come first, has benefits not only for the patient, but also for the profession: it may well encourage practitioners to work longer hours and to undertake difficult tasks. A professional code may furthermore encourage junior practitioners within the profession to adopt a subservient role in the hierarchy 'in the interests of the patient', but also in the interests of the profession which enshrines its hierarchy and protects the traditional career structure. A proscription against (or restrictions placed upon) advertising, which is another common

---

[1] Scruton *A Dictionary of Political Thought* (Pan, 1984). See also the discussion in Ch 6 'Negligence' para **[6.32]**.

feature of professional ethical codes, can also help to protect professional hierarchies by maintaining the existing system: practitioners remain within the existing system, rather than branching out on their own (and advertising the fact that they have), in order to acquire the skills that are deemed necessary by the profession for the practitioner to reach the pinnacle of her discipline.

Statutory and non-statutory professions

[2.04] More recently and with the advent of legislation aimed at regulating professions, there arose a distinction between those clinical disciplines that were regulated by legislation (such laws generally created regulatory bodies with disciplinary powers over the profession in question) and those that were not. Traditionally, the former group comprised medicine, nursing, pharmacy and dentistry, while the latter included practitioners such as physiotherapists, radiographers and occupational therapists. However, the passage of the Health and Social Care Professionals Act 2005[2] has largely obliterated this distinction and has placed 12 designated professions (with the possibility of further additional professions being 'designated' as coming under the provisions of the legislation) under the auspices of a new regulatory body. This Act is dealt with in greater detail below (see para **[2.33]***ff).*

THE REGULATION OF HEALTHCARE PROFESSIONS

[2.05] The features of statutory regulation are relatively uniform across those professions that are regulated by legislation: generally speaking, the following features are common to all—

- a specific regulatory body for the profession(s) in question;
- a register of the members of that profession, created and maintained by the regulatory body (or some other organ created by the legislation, as in the cases of the Health and Social Care Professionals Act 2005 – see para **[2.33]***ff*);
- it is an offence to practise the relevant profession when one is not a registered member of the profession;
- certain acts and omissions are made grounds for complaints against practitioners;
- the regulatory body has the power to investigate and, where necessary, punish those who are found to have breached rules relating to conduct;
- the regulatory body has oversight of matters such as continuing education and training.

[2.06] The advantages of placing the regulation of a healthcare profession on a state-sponsored self-regulatory footing are obvious: it becomes possible for the profession's regulatory body to set nationwide standards for training, conduct and competence that are binding on all members of the relevant profession. The regulatory body is also empowered to take the necessary steps to maintain the standards of the profession by

---

[2] England had long had similar legislation for the regulation of allied health professions: see the Professions Supplementary to Medicine Act 1960; Osteopaths Act 1993; Chiropractors Act 1994.

dealing with those practitioners whose continued practice represents an unacceptable risk to the public or otherwise renders them unfit to be registered members of the relevant profession. The overriding aim of regulatory bodies therefore is to represent the public and the public interest and it is, in part, this imperative that has lent impetus to changes in the composition of regulatory bodies. However, the need to ensure that the public interest is not only protected, but also represented, by regulatory bodies has led to marked reform.

Post-2005 reform

[2.07] Important changes in the regulation of the professions have taken place since 2005, with the passage of the Health and Social Care Professionals Act 2005, followed by the Medical Practitioners Act 2007 and the Pharmacy Act 2007. Each of these Acts inaugurated sharp changes in the way in which professions are regulated. Traditionally, the clinical disciplines had been, in the simplest sense of the word, 'self-regulating'. The regulatory bodies and their disciplinary committees had been overwhelmingly comprised of members of the profession being regulated by the body in question. So, under the Medical Practitioners Act 1978, there could only be a maximum of four persons on the Medical Council who were not registered medical practitioners; now, under the 2007 Act, it is possible (although not mandatory) for the majority of the Medical Council to be comprised of 'lay' persons. Similarly, the post-2005 legislation has broadened the grounds on which complaints may be made against clinical practitioners as well as altering the mechanisms by which complaints must be investigated and disciplinary inquiries conducted.

[2.08] Regulation of the nursing and dental professions, both covered by 1985 legislation, has yet to be updated and the more 'old-fashioned' approach to regulation apparent in the cases of both these professions is highlighted in the text that follows. It should, however, be observed that the Government has undertaken to modernise the regulation of both of these professions in keeping with the new approach evidenced by the post-2005 clinical regulatory legislation.

[2.09] We turn now to examine the legislation regulating and policing each of the clinical disciplines in turn. On the grounds (as has been observed) that there are many common features shared by regulatory legislation, we will deal first, and in some detail, with regulation of the medical profession, before turning to the other professions in less detail save for the identification of those areas where regulation of other professions differs significantly from the regulation of medicine. Following a consideration of the features of each of the regulated professions, we examine the area of disciplinary proceedings where, again, many common features are apparent.[3]

---

[3] That is to say that there are many common features shared by the pre-2005 professions (particularly dentistry and nursing) and other common features shared by the post-2005 professions.

Medicine

[2.10] The medical profession in Ireland is regulated by the Medical Council according to the provisions of the Medical Practitioners Act 2007.[4] Historically, the Medical Council had a majority of medical members,[5] but the 2007 Act gives rises to a scenario under which there may be a medical majority, but which does not guarantee that majority.[6] The 2007 Act creates a 25-member Medical Council, drawn from three broad categories (broken down in Table 2.1):

- those who are registered medical practitioners,

- those who may be medical practitioners, and

- those who are not, and never have been, medical practitioners.

---

[4] The 2007 Act repealed the Medical Practitioners Act 1978. The pre-1978 ancestor of the Medical Council was the Medical Registration Council, established in 1927 and with strong ties to the UK General Medical Council (GMC); there was Irish representation on the GMC until 1979. At the time of writing (October 2007) the Act has not been commenced but it is presumed that it will come into force in late 2007 and is therefore treated as being the law in force. A description of the Medical Council and its procedures under the Medical Practitioners Act 1978 can be found in Mills, *Clinical Practice and the Law* (1st edn, Tottel Publishing, 2002), Ch 2. As this text was going to press, certain amendments were proposed to the Medical Practitioners Act 2007 by the Health (Miscellaneous Provisions) Bill 2007. None of the proposed changes materially affect the discussion set out in this chapter.

[5] Under the 1978 Act, the 25-member Council was composed of a minimum of 21 doctors (there were four ministerial appointees, of whom three could not be registered medical practitioners); the 21 doctors were 11 representatives of the medical schools and of the various medical specialties as well as 10 doctors elected by the medical profession.

[6] Recommendations in favour of a 'lay'/non-medical majority on the regulatory bodies of healthcare professions have been made in countries other than Ireland. The UK House of Commons Health Committee (in *Procedures Related to Adverse Clinical Outcomes in Medical Care*, HC 549-I, session 1999–2000) recommended that the lay membership of the UK Medical and Nursing Councils be increased to a majority. See also Department of Health, *Trust, Assurance and Safety – The Regulation of Health Professionals in the 21st Century* (London, 2007) which called for an end to the medical majority on the General Medical Council (see para 1.10): 'The [UK] Government is convinced that in order to establish and sustain confidence in the independence of the regulators, all councils should be constituted to ensure that professionals do not form a majority.'

Table 2.1 – Composition of the Medical Council[7]
Medical Council – Total Membership 25

Must be doctors – 10	Must not be doctors – 11	May be doctors – 4
1 medical practitioner nominated by each of:	1 nominee of each of the following:	2 nominees of approved bodies delivering undergraduate medical education
(a) Royal College of Physicians	(a) Royal Irish Academy	2 nominees of the Health Service Executive who are representative of the management of the public health sector
(b) Royal College of Surgeons	(b) Minister for Education and Science after consultation with the Higher Education Authority	
(c) Irish College of General Practitioners		
(d) Irish Psychiatric Training Committee or equivalent approved body	(c) An Bord Altranais (must be a registered nurse or midwife)	
6 medical practitioners elected (in accordance with s 18 of the Act) by the profession to include 1 representative of each of the following branches of the profession;	(d) Health and Social Care Professionals Council (must be a 'registrant' or a member of a designated profession within the meaning of the Act)[8]	
(a) Obstetrics and Gynaecology	(e) Health Information and Quality Authority	
(b) Public Health Medicine		
(c) Anaesthesia	(f) Independent Hospitals Association of Ireland	
(d) Pathology or Radiology	5 nominees of the Minister for Health who have such qualifications, expertise, interests or experience as, in the opinion of the Minister, would enable them to make a contribution to the performance of the Council's functions.	
(e) Non-consultant hospital doctors		
(f) A registered medical practitioner who does not fall within the foregoing categories.		

Functions of the medical council

[2.11] Members of the Medical Council hold office for a term of 5 years and no member may serve more than two consecutive 5-year terms.[9] The explicit statutory object of the Medical Council is to 'protect the public by promoting and better ensuring high standards of professional conduct and professional education, training and competence

---

[7] Medical Practitioners Act 2007, s 17. Note that s 18 of the Act—referred to in column 1 of Table 2.1—states the Minister for Health 'may' make regulations relating to the conduct of elections; although the Act does not explicitly say so, it is to be assumed that in the absence of the Minister making such regulations, it falls to the Medical Council to lay down the rules under which any elections will be conducted.

[8] HSCP Act 2005, s 3.

among registered medical practitioners'[10] and the Council is explicitly required to discharge its functions in the public interest. A wide range of other functions of the Medical Council are also set out in the Act[11] which may be summarised as follows:

- **Medical registration**: maintaining a medical register and setting the criteria for entering into and staying on the register.

- **International functions:** acting as the competent body for the purpose of the recognition (mutual or otherwise) of foreign medical qualifications.

- **Professional ethics:** giving guidance to the profession on matters of professional ethics and standards.[12]

- **Disciplinary functions:** creating committees for the receipt, investigation and hearing of disciplinary matters; powers to issue punishments.

- **Other functions:** include informing the public on matters of interest relating to the Council and any other function that is conferred upon it by the Medical Practitioners Act 2007 or any other Act.[13]

[2.12] The Minister of Health has the power to make certain orders relating to the training of doctors or the implementation of European Directives and Regulations,

---

[9]   Medical Practitioners Act, Sch 2. The Minister has certain powers to remove members (and indeed the entire Council) from office in limited circumstances; members will also cease to be members in certain stated cases of financial, ethical or criminal misdemeanours or where failing to attend meetings without reasonable excuse—Medical Practitioners Act 2007, s 23. Members are also required to make disclosure of any conflicts of interest that arise in the discharge of their duties: ss 30–31.

[10] Medical Practitioners Act 2007, s 6.

[11] Medical Practitioners Act 2007, s 7.

[12] Including a specific obligation to regulate practice relating to 'advertising by registered medical practitioners...and...the disclosure of appropriate information relating to the fees to be charged for [such services]' – Medical Practitioners Act 2007, s 7(3). Note that the remit of the Minister to dictate to the Medical Council does not extend to ethical guidance. For an example of an unsuccessful challenge to the ethical guidelines (on advertising) of the Medical Council, see *Hemat v The Medical Council* [2006] IEHC 187.

[13] In discharging its various functions under the 2007 Act the Council is expected to have regard to:

- functions performed by bodies that are similar or ancillary to the functions of the Medical Council
- the need to co-operate with other public bodies (in particular the HSE), where the functions of those bodies could affect the health of the public
- the need to promote efficiencies in specialist and intern training through the development of standard practices.
- the policies and objectives of the Government or any Minister of the Government to the extent that those policies may affect or relate to the functions of the Council.
- available resources and the need to secure the most beneficial, effective and efficient use of those resources (Medical Practitioners Act 2007, s 7(4)).

The Council also has the power to make the necessary rules for the successful operation of the Act, subject both to a consultation process with the profession and the public and to the approval of the Oireachtas – Medical Practitioners Act 2007, s 11.

subject to the approval of the Oireachtas. The Minister can also give general policy directions to the Medical Council, except for any matters relating to professional conduct and ethics or disciplinary matters (Parts 7,8 and 9 of the Act).[14] In a novel development, the Council is also obliged to publish a Statement of Strategy, Business Plan and Annual Report.[15] We turn now to consider the most important roles of the Medical Council, namely those relating to registration, education and disciplinary matters.

Registration

[2.13] A person cannot practise medicine unless she is registered with the Medical Council.[16] Similarly, such titles that might be used by a registered medical practitioner may, under the new legislation, be reserved solely for doctors or specific classes of doctor: so, it may be that the term 'consultant' or 'specialist' might in future be designated as being applicable only to certain categories of doctor. To practise medicine without being registered or for a particular medical practitioner to practise under a title that she is not entitled to use is an offence.[17] The Medical Council is therefore obliged to maintain a register[18] of medical practitioners, divided as follows:[19]

(a)　*The General Division*

　　Admission into this division is open to those who have completed medical training in Ireland, in the EU,[20] or elsewhere and/or who have completed any required examinations and/or who have satisfactory evidence of experience sufficient to permit registration.

---

[14]　Medical Practitioners Act 2007, ss 8–9. Note that the increased ministerial powers of direction and control contained in the act as well as the requirement to have regard to policy and resources (see previous fn) have led to concerns that the Medical Council's independence will be compromised.

[15]　Medical Practitioners Act, Pt 3 (ss 12 16).

[16]　Medical Practitioners Act 2007, s 37. This restriction is subject to the exception that dentists, nurses etc… may "practise medicine" in a fashion ancillary to their main profession. Such persons do not contravene s 37.

[17]　Medical Practitioners Act 2007, s 41. A person found guilty of an offence under s 41 on summary conviction can be fined up to €5,000 and/or be jailed for up to six months; following conviction on indictment the maximum sanctions are up to €130,000 and/or five years' imprisonment (for a first offence) or €320,000 (for a second or subsequent offence). It is also an offence to make representations on behalf of another person to the effect that the other person is a registered medical practitioner or is entitled to employ a title to which she is not, in fact, entitled.

[18]　Medical Practitioners Act 2007, s 43. The Act also allows for the inclusion in the register of such identifying particulars of the practitioner as the Council thinks appropriate. Where conditions have been attached to a practitioner's registration, the fact and particulars of those conditions shall be entered into the register (s 43(6)).

[19]　Medical Practitioners Act s 43–50.

[20]　The mutual recognition of qualifications under EU Directive 2005/36/EC is dealt with in para **[2.66]**.

(b)   *The Specialist Division*

Admission to this division is open to those who have completed specialist medical training in a medical specialty recognised by the Council and who possess evidence from an appropriate body that satisfies the Medical Council.

(c)   *The Trainee Specialist Division*

Admission to this division is open to qualified doctors who are practising medicine in 'an individually numbered, identifiable post which has been approved by the Council for the purpose of medical specialist training'.[21] Doctors employed in their one-year internship at a centre approved by the Council are also included in the trainee specialist division.

(d)   *The Visiting EEA Practitioners Division*

This division is for practitioners who are established in medical practice in a Member State and who wish to practise medicine in Ireland on a 'temporary and occasional' basis. The practitioner is required to notify the Medical Council of intended dates and scope of practice within this State and to make certain declarations as to good standing in her native country.

All practitioners who are registered (on payment of the appropriate fee, set by the Council) are given a certificate of registration, which is to be displayed for the duration of the practitioner's registration at the principal place where the practitioner practises medicine. The register itself is a public document that must be published by the Medical Council.[22]

[2.14] The practitioner's registration number is 'to be included on all medical prescriptions and all other documentation and records, whether in paper or electronic format, relating to that practitioner's practice as a registered medical practitioner.'[23] A practitioner may only be registered in one division of the register at any given time,[24] but can apply – for example, on the completion of specialist training – to be moved from one division of the register to another. Similarly, a practitioner can apply to have her name removed from the register, although the Council may refuse such a request where the practitioner is the subject of a complaint which has not yet been dealt with by the Council or has been convicted of a criminal act. In either case, the Council has the power

---

[21]   It is open to the Council to register not only Irish and EU Member State nationals (who have evidence of medical qualification and the completion of an intern year or equivalent and hold a numbered post) in this division, but also non-nationals (including EU non-nationals) or refugees who have passed examinations set for the purpose of testing competence (or who have —for reasons laid down in applicable rules—been exempted from such examinations).

[22]   Medical Practitioners Act 2007, s 56(1). 'The Council need not make available for inspection or publish the residential addresses, home telephone numbers or e-mail addresses of registered medical practitioners or other similar details that, in its opinion, should, in the interests of the security of the practitioners, be protected from disclosure.'—s 56(2), but note that this section does not forbid the Medical Council from publishing the home contact details of registered medical practitioners.

[23]   Medical Practitioners Act 2007, s 43(8).

[24]   Medical Practitioners Act 2007, s 45(3). However, there is nothing to prevent a practitioner being registered under two different specialities within the Register of Medical Specialists.

to determine, prior to the voluntary removal by the practitioner of her name, whether the practitioner should be sanctioned.[25]

[2.15] The Medical Council is not obliged to register a practitioner (or restore to the register the name of any practitioner whose name was previously removed from the register), but where it declines to do so, it must notify the practitioner with the date of its decision and the reasons for that decision; the practitioner in question has three months in which to appeal any decision to refuse registration to the High Court.

Education and training

[2.16] The Medical Council is the body responsible for certifying any institution that proposes delivering medical education and training as fit to do so[26] and prescribes the standards of medical education as well as ensuring that those standards continue to be met by educational organisations delivering undergraduate and post-graduate medical training (and in particular the numbers and standards of intern and specialist training posts).[27] To this latter end, the Medical Council is empowered to carry out inspections of relevant bodies and places delivering that training. The Medical Council also has the authority (in consultation with the Minister) to determine which medical specialities it recognises and to accord approval to training programmes and training bodies responsible for the training of such specialists.[28]

Maintenance of professional competence

[2.17] The Act also place an obligation on the Medical Council to satisfy itself 'as to the ongoing maintenance of the professional competence of registered medical practitioners' and is required to have established a competence assurance scheme by the date of the first anniversary of the commencement of the Act. The Council is entitled to appoint (and, where necessary, to cancel the appointment of) bodies that it has otherwise recognised for the delivery of education and training to assist it in the delivery of competence assurance.

[2.18] Medical practitioners are obliged to participate in applicable professional competence schemes and to abide by any rules made by the Medical Council with respect to competence assurance.[29] Where the Medical Council considers that a registered medical practitioner, who is not participating in professional competence programmes:

---

[25] Medical Practitioners Act 2007, s 52(1)–(3).

[26] Medical Practitioners Act 2007, s 88. Under s 87 it is also the competent body with regard to Directive 2005/36/EC (see para **[2.66]**).

[27] The setting of numbers of intern and specialist training posts is carried out in consultation with the Health Service Executive: see para **[2.19]**.

[28] Medical Practitioners Act 2007, s 89. Any decision to refuse or to withdraw accreditation may be appealed by the relevant undergraduate or specialist training body to the High Court with 21 days of the relevant organ receiving notice of the refusal or withdrawal: s 90.

[29] Medical Practitioners Act 2007, s 94. The Medical Council's power to make rules arises from s 11. S 94 also applies to those practitioners who are directed to undergo competence training or assessment pursuant to an undertaking or 'consent' given under s 67(1) – see para **[2.52]**.

- has refused, failed or ceased to co-operate with rules relating to professional competence made by the Medical Council;

- has contravened a direction of the Council to participate in professional competence arising out of an undertaking or 'consent' given to the Medical Council;

- may pose an immediate risk of harm to the public [presumably due to the risk caused by a lack of competence and a lack of willingness to remedy shortcomings]; or

- may have committed a serious breach of its guidance on ethical standards and behaviour,

then the Council is obliged to make a complaint in respect of that practitioner. Confidentiality applies to all information relating to professional competence schemes, except where disclosure is necessary to allow the functioning of the professional competence scheme or where it is necessary for a person to perform functions (including disciplinary functions) under the Medical Practitioners Act. The Freedom of Information Acts 1997 to 2003 do not operate to secure disclosure of information relating to professional competence matters, but the Act does not prohibit the making of court orders mandating disclosure of information.[30]

The role of the Health Service Executive

[2.19] The Medical Practitioners Act 2007 for the first time places an onus upon health administrators in relation to the practice of medicine and provides principally that the Health Service Executive (HSE):

- shall facilitate the basic medical education and training of students training to be registered medical practitioners.

- shall, with respect to specialist medical and dental education and training:

  (a) promote the development of specialist medical and dental education and training and co-ordinate such developments in co-operation with relevant councils and training bodies;

  (b) undertake appropriate medical and dental practitioner workforce planning for the purpose of meeting specialist medical and dental staffing and training needs of the health service on an ongoing basis;

  (c) assess on an annual basis the number of intern training posts and the number and type of specialist medical training posts required by the health service and, pursuant to that assessment, put proposals to the Council in relation to the Council's role in approving intern and specialist training posts;[31]

  (d) assess on an annual basis the need for and appropriateness of other non-consultant, non-specialist training medical posts;

---

[30] Medical Practitioners Act 2007, s 95. See Cusack and Mills, 'Legislating for competence assurance – cool water on a hot topic' (2001) 7 MLJI 2.

[31] Pursuant to Medical Practitioners Act 2007, s 88(3)(a) and (4)(a).

(e)   advise the Minister, after consultation with the medical and dental training bodies and with such other bodies as it may consider appropriate, on medical and dental education.[32]

Disciplinary and health matters

[2.20] The overall principles and practice of disciplinary proceedings in the statutory professions, including issues of fair procedure and definitions of misconduct, are dealt with below at para **[2.37]***ff.* Here, we focus particularly on certain issues peculiar to the Medical Council.

Committee structures

[2.21] As with the other statutory professions whose regulatory affairs have been overhauled post-2005, the Medical Practitioners Act 2007 envisages three committees:[33]

–   a Preliminary Proceedings Committee (PPC), to give initial consideration to complaints

–   a Fitness to Practise Committee (FTPC), to inquire into complaints

–   a Health Committee, to perform such functions as are specified by the Council in support of medical practitioners with relevant medical disabilities and those who have given 'consents' under the Act[34] (the issue of 'consents' in this context is dealt with at para **[2.52]** below).

Non-members of the Medical Council may be appointed as members of any these committees. Neither the PPC or FTPC may be chaired by the President or the Vice-President of the Council. There can be no overlap between the memberships of PPC and FTPC[35] but the membership of the various committees is subject to the following strictures:

–   at least one third of the membership of the FTPC shall consist of medical practitioners.

–   the majority of the membership of the FTPC shall consist of persons who are not medical practitioners.

–   the majority of the membership of a committee other than the FTPC shall consist of medical practitioners.[36]

---

[32] Medical Practitioners Act 2007, s 86(2). The HSE is also obliged to facilitate the maintenance of professional competence of registered medical practitioners (as are non-HSE employers): s 93.

[33] Medical Practitioners Act 2007, s 20. The PPC and FTPC are both mandatory under the Act (s 20(2)); the health committee is optional (s 20(4)). Note that under the Pharmacy Act 2007 (s 34) and the Health and Social Care Professionals Act 2005 (s 51) the establishment of a Health Committee is mandatory.

[34] Medical Practitioners Act 2007, s 67(1)(c).

[35] Any overlap in membership would clearly give rise to the possibility of a fitness to practise hearing being conducted by a person who had already reached a determination on the matter as part of the Preliminary Proceedings Committee which in turn could give rise to a reasonable apprehension of bias. See para **[2.58]** on fair procedures below.

[36] Medical Practitioners Act 2007, s 20(9)–(11).

Nursing

[2.22] The nursing profession, including midwives, is regulated by An Bord Altranais (The Nursing Board), which was created by the Nurses Act 1985.[37] The Board comprises 29 members, elected or appointed by for a term of five years; 17 are elected by their fellow nurses, while 12 are ministerial appointees. The composition of the board is as follows:

- five nurses engaged in the training of nurses;[38]
- five nurses who are engaged in nursing administration;
- seven nurses who are engaged in clinical nursing practice;[39]
- twelve persons appointed by the Minister for Health after consultation with relevant bodies but who must include the following:
    - a registered medical practitioner from each of three hospitals where (a) general nurses, (b) psychiatric nurses and (c) midwives respectively are trained;
    - a representative of HSE management;
    - a representative of hospitals other than those under HSE management,
    - two representatives of the Department of Health;
    - a person experienced in the field of education;
    - a representative of a third-level institution in which nurses are trained;
    - a registered nurse;
    - two representatives of the interests of the general public.

As with the Medical Council, An Bord Altranais has responsibility for compiling and maintaining the register of nurses and can refuse to register a person it deems unfit to be registered.[40] The nursing register takes account of the particular division of nursing (paediatric, psychiatric, general or midwifery) in which each nurse is trained to practise. The Board also oversees education and training of the profession, including setting curricula for any courses and examinations, appointing examiners and approving training institutions.[41] In addition, the Board publishes ethical guidelines for nurses.[42]

---

[37] Replacing the Nurses Act 1950. Reform of the Nurses Act 1985 (presumably along the lines of the Medical Practitioners Act 2007) has been promised by the Department of Health and Children. The UK House of Commons Health Committee (in *Procedures Related to Adverse Clinical Outcomes in Medical Care*, HC 549-I, session 1999–2000) recommended that the lay membership of the UK Medical and Nursing Councils be increased to a majority. See also Department of Health, *Trust, Assurance and Safety – The Regulation of Health Professionals in the 21st Century* (London, 2007) para 1.10.

[38] One each from general, paediatric, psychiatric and mental handicap nursing and one from midwifery (the same allocation applies to those nurses elected to represent nursing administration). Each elected nurse must be resident in the Republic of Ireland.

[39] Two each from general and psychiatric nursing; one from each of paediatric and mental handicap nursing and from midwifery.

[40] Nurses Act 1985, ss 27–30. See also, An Bord Altranais, *Nurses Rules* (2007): available for download from http://www.nursingboard.ie/en/publications_current.aspx (last accessed October 2007).

[41] Nurses Act 1985, ss 31–37.

[2.23] An Bord Altranais has a Fitness to Practise Committee to look into allegations of misconduct or unfitness to practise due to physical or mental disability. Its powers include recommendations of erasure or suspension from the register or the attachment of conditions to the continuation of practice (with any such decision, as with the Medical Council, subject to scrutiny and ratification by the High Court – see para **[2.37]** *ff* below). As with doctors, the Board may admonish or censure a nurse rather than opting for a sanction that impacts on her ability to continue in practice. A nurse's name may be erased or suspended from the register if she is convicted of a serious offence. Any decision concerning the erasure, suspension or restoration of a nurse's name with respect to the register must be notified to the Minister and, where known or appropriate, to the nurse's employer.[43]

As with the medical profession, it is an offence for anyone to hold herself out as being a nurse who is not on the register or for anyone to practise in a specialty of nursing in which she is not registered or to misuse or falsely obtain registration documents.[44]

[2.24] The Act makes a number of specific provisions for midwifery. A midwife who is not employed by the HSE or a hospital and who is practising midwifery in a specific area must notify the HSE section responsible for that area and the HSE in turn must exercise 'supervision and control' over the midwife.[45] No one may attend on a woman in childbirth, except in an emergency, unless she is:

- a midwife;
- a registered medical practitioner;
- a person who is undergoing training to become a midwife or registered medical practitioner or training in the area of obstetrics as part of a course of wider training.[46]

Dentistry

[2.25] The dental profession came under statutory control with the passage of the Dentists Act 1985. This legislation replaced the former Dental Board with the Dental Council,[47] which in turn comprises 19 members who serve on the Council for a five-year term. The composition[48] is as follows:

---

[42] An Bord Altranais, *The Code of Professional Conduct for each Nurse and Midwife* (2000). Although a shorter document than its medical or dental equivalents, it is based on the same ethical and legal principles. Also see An Bord Altranais, *Guidance to Nurses and Midwives Regarding Ethical Conduct of Nursing and Midwifery Research* (2007): both available for download from http://www.nursingboard.ie/en/publications_current.aspx (last accessed October 2007).

[43] Nurses Act 1985, ss 38–47.

[44] Nurses Act 1985, s 49.

[45] Nurses Act 1985, s 57.

[46] Nurses Act 1985, s 58.

[47] http://www.dentalcouncil.ie. Reform of the Dentists Act 1985 (presumably along the lines of the Medical Practitioners Act 2007) has been promised by the Department of Health and Children.

[48] Dentists Act 1985, s 9. The Minister can vary the composition of the Dental Council by ministerial order s 9(1). In practice, although the Act stipulates that only seven members shall be 'fully registered dentists', the Dental Council operates with a professional majority.

- two persons appointed by the University College Cork;
- two persons appointed by the University of Dublin;
- two persons appointed by the Medical Council;
- a person appointed by the Royal College of Surgeons in Ireland;
- a person appointed by the Minister for Education and Science;
- seven dentists appointed by election by registered dentists;
- four persons appointed by the Minister for Health and Children of whom at least two must not be registered dentists and who will represent the interest of the public as consumers of dental services.

The Dentists Act 1985 is cast from a near-identical mould to that of the Nurses Act 1985 and the powers and responsibilities of the Dental Council are closely analogous to those exercisable by An Bord Altranais. The Dental Council maintains a register of practitioners,[49] including a register of specialists. There is scope for temporary registration, but no equivalent of trainee or trainee specialist registration. The Dental Council has responsibility for overseeing training and education of dentists in the State, including both primary and postgraduate training[50] and responsibility for curbing the practice of those dentists who are unfit to practise due to misconduct or because of physical or mental disability.[51] The Council publishes ethical guidelines[52] and similar sanctions are available to the Council as those available to an Bord Altranais, namely censure, attachment of conditions to practice, suspension from the register and erasure from the register. It is an offence to claim to be or to imply that one is a registered dentist or to practise dentistry if one is not on the register.[53] The Dental Council also oversees the designation, training and roles of auxiliary dental workers (such as dental hygienists) including the determination of what work auxiliary staff may undertake, the registration of auxiliary dental workers and the titles such workers may claim.[54]

---

[49] Dentists Act 1985, ss 26–33.

[50] Dentists Act 1985, ss 34–37.

[51] Dentists Act 1985, ss 38–48.

[52] *Professional Behaviour and Dental Ethics*, Dental Council, Dublin 1998. This guide stresses the 'general principle' of ethical dental practice as 'the three-fold aim of safeguarding the health of patients, promoting the welfare of the community and maintaining the honour and integrity of the dental profession.' Available online at http://www.dentalcouncil.ie/g_dentalethics.php (last accessed October 2007).

[53] Dentists Act 1985, ss. 50–51.

[54] Dentists Act 1985, ss. 53–55. The Dental Council also publishes *Dental Nurses: Ethics and Conduct Code Of Practice* (September 2002), available online at http://www.dentalcouncil.ie/g_dentalnurses.php. See *Kenny t/a Denture Express v. Dental Council* [2004] IEHC 29 in which the plaintiff tried unsuccessfully to get an order directing the Dental Council to recognise his auxiliary discipline of 'denturist'.

Opticians

[2.26] Dispensing and ophthalmic opticians are regulated by Bord na Radharcmhastóirí – the Opticians Board – that was founded under the Opticians Act 1956.[55] It is an 11-member board:[56]

— four ministerial appointees who must be registered medical practitioners

— one other ministerial appointee, who may or may not be a registered medical practitioner

— six members elected by the body of registered opticians. One must be a registered dispensing optician and five must be registered ophthalmic opticians.

The Board maintains two separate registers, one for dispensing opticians and the other for optometrists[57] and the Board has the power to recognise qualifications based on acquired experience or on satisfactory qualifications obtained outside the State. The Opticians Board takes the decision whether to register any person and a decision not to register a person must be notified to the applicant, who has the right to appeal such a refusal to the High Court within three months of the date of such refusal.[58] One area in which the powers of the Opticians Board differ significantly from those of the Medical and Dental Councils and An Bord Altranais is where a person is removed from either register of opticians: there is no automatic High Court scrutiny of the decision, although the affected party does have a right of appeal to the High Court.

[2.27] The Opticians Board has responsibility for overseeing the training and examination of opticians and for approving the institutions that are suitable for training purposes. Only a person who is registered optician (or medical practitioner) may prescribe or dispense spectacles and a person who does so without being an optician or who claims to be an optician and is not registered is guilty of an offence.[59]

Pharmacists

[2.28] The regulation of the profession of pharmacy was fundamentally re-shaped by the Pharmacy Act 2007. The new Act provides for a modern framework for the operation of the Pharmaceutical Society of Ireland (PSI), together with a new system of regulation of

---

[55] As amended by the Opticians (Amendment) Act 2003.

[56] Opticians Act 1956, ss 7–10. The Minister for Health and Children also appoints the President of the Board. Note that there is no guaranteed lay (in the sense of non-clinical members of the public) representation on this board at all.

[57] Part III of the Act is concerned with the Register of Optometrists and Part IV with the Register of Dispensing Opticians, although the broad rules are the same for both. The register of optometrists was known as the register of ophthalmic opticians prior to the Opticians (Amendment) Act 2003.

[58] Opticians Act 1956 (as amended), s 24–25 (for optometrists) and 33–34 (for dispensing opticians)

[59] Opticians Act 1956 (as amended), ss 47–51. The Opticians (Amendment) Act 2003, significantly increased the financial penalties that may be imposed for an offence under the Act.

the pharmacy profession in Ireland, including the creation of an amplified fitness to practise regime.[60]

The essential elements of the Act are:

- a stronger statutory basis for the Pharmaceutical Society of Ireland, to include governance of the PSI, and wider non-pharmacist representation on its Council;

- updating regulations for the registration of pharmacists, including non-EU/ EEA graduates, and introducing registration for pharmacy businesses;

- matters concerning the delivery of community pharmaceutical services, such as linguistic and forensic competence and experience for supervisory pharmacists;

- the removal of the prohibition or 'derogation' on non-Irish graduates being supervising pharmacists in pharmacies less than three years old;

- fitness to practise provisions.

The Council of the Pharmaceutical Society of Ireland

[2.29] The Council of the PSI is in effect the regulatory body of the profession and its principal duties[61] are to—

- protect patients and the public interest;

- maintain registers of pharmacists and pharmacies;

- inspect pharmacy practices and enforce pharmacy legislation;

- draw up codes of conduct for pharmacists and pharmacy owners;

- promote and ensure high standards of education and training including continuing education in pharmacy;

- conduct inquiries where necessary to determine 'fitness to practise' and 'fitness to operate';[62]

- process complaints relating to pharmacy practice and operation;

- act as the registration authority for pharmacists outside of Ireland and the EU and as the competent authority for recognition of qualifications from other EU countries;[63]

- give relevant advice to the Minister and Oireachtas.

---

[60] The Pharmaceutical Society of Ireland is the professional regulatory body of Pharmacy in Ireland. It was originally founded by the Pharmacy Act (Ireland) 1875 but its statutory footing was more recently updated by the Pharmacy Act 1962.

[61] Pharmaceutical Society of Ireland, *Preliminary Overview – Pharmacy Act 2007, A New Beginning* (Dublin 2007). Available for download from: http://www.pharmaceuticalsociety.ie/ Pharmacy_Act_2007/Pharmacy_Act_2007/Navigation.html (last accessed October 2007). Parts 1 (other than s 4), 2 and 3 of the Act, together with ss 18 and 76 and Sch 1 were commenced in May 2007: Pharmacy Act 2007 (Commencement) Order 2007 (SI 243/2007).

[62] Neither of these terms formally appears in the Act, but they describe the conduct of individual pharmacists and the operation of retail pharmacies respectively.

[63] Pharmacy Act 2007, s 7. Other functions include appointing officers for the purposes of discharging functions under the Misuse of Drugs Act 1977 and the Irish Medicines Board Act 1995. Further functions may also be conferred on the Society by the Minister.

[2.30] The Council of the Pharmaceutical Society of Ireland is a 21-member body:

– 11 members shall be persons who are not and never have been registered as pharmacists, pharmaceutical chemists or dispensing chemists and druggists within the State and who are not registered outside the State or otherwise qualified there as pharmacists and those 11 are appointed as follows:[64]

　o three persons nominated (1 each) by the Irish Medicines Board (as representative of the management of the regulation of medicinal products), the Health Services Executive (as representative of public health sector management) and by the Minister (as a representative of the provision of continuing professional development);

　o three shall be persons with such qualifications, expertise, interests or experience as would, in the opinion of the Minister, enable them to make a substantial contribution to the performance of the Society's functions;

　o five others nominated by the Minister;

– nine shall be members of the Society who have been selected by its members[65]

– one shall be a member of the Society appointed as representing third level establishments engaged in the training of pharmacists.

[2.31] The PSI Council's duties to publish a register extend to both pharmacists and retail pharmacies and the Council is obliged to keep the register up to date[66] and each pharmacist and pharmacy is issued with relevant certificates of registration. The regulator will ensure that each pharmacist must be 'fit to practise' on an annual basis and all pharmacies must be 'fit to operate' on an annual basis. A new code of professional conduct for pharmacists and pharmacy owners will be put in place[67] and enforced. The Act contains specific provisions outlawing too close a business relationship between registered pharmacy owners and registered medical practitioners, in the sense of either a pharmacist having a share in a medical practice or pharmacies and medical practices being co-located on the same site.[68]

Complaints and disciplinary system

[2.32] Complaints or disciplinary matters arising will be dealt with by the Council in its capacity of pharmacy regulator[69] and the Act confirms powers upon the Council that are broadly analogous to those given to the Medical Council (disciplinary practice and

---

[64] In essence, six non-pharmacists must be appointed in accordance with the stipulations of the Act, but the Minister then has a free hand in respect of the appointment of the other five non-pharmacists. The President and Vice-President of the Council must be registered pharmacists, although the former is not permitted to be a member of any disciplinary committee.

[65] In accordance with rules made under s 11(2)(b) of the Act.

[66] Pharmacy Act 2007, Pt 4, ss 13–24. Note that at the time of writing (October 2007), only s 18 of this Part has been commenced, which permits the Minister to make regulations for the purposes of the health, safety and convenience of the public, relating to most aspects of the day-today running of pharmacy businesses.

[67] Pharmacy Act 2007, s 7(2)(iii). Any such Code of Conduct must be placed before the Oireachtas for approval (s 76).

[68] Pharmacy Act 2007, ss 63–64.

[69] Pharmacy Act 2007, Part 6, ss 33–65. Note that at the time of writing (October 2007), this Part has yet to be commenced.

procedure is discussed at greater length at para **[2.37]***ff* below). Complaints can be initiated by any relevant party, including the Registrar of the Pharmaceutical Society of Ireland relating to a pharmacist or pharmacy.

Other clinical professions

[2.33] Previously, the clinical professions other than those already discussed could loosely be grouped under the heading of the 'non-statutory' professions. However, the passage of the Health and Social Care Professionals (HSCP) Act 2005 has set in train the process by which other 'paramedical' professions will regulated in an analogous fashion to more traditional statutory professions. The Act[70] sets out certain designated professions to be regulated by the Health and Social Care Professionals Council. Each of the designated professions will have its own registration body and the membership of the Council reflects that fact:

-   a Chairperson, appointed by the Minister,[71] who may not be a person who is registered as a member of a designated profession;

-   a member of the registration body of each designated profession and nominated by that registration body;

-   nine other persons:

    o   one representative of the management of the public health sector, the public social care sector (or both);,

    o   one representative of the management of a voluntary or private sector organisation concerned with health or social care;

    o   one representative of third level educational establishments involved in the education and training of persons practising the designated professions;[72]

    o   six representatives of the interests of the general public;[73]

-   three persons who have such qualifications, interests and experience as, in the opinion of the Minister, would be of value to the Council in performing its functions.

Designated professions and registration bodies

[2.34] Unlike the Medical Council and other such bodies, the HSCP Act 2005 does not formally specify the size of membership of the Health and Social Care Professionals Council. The Council's membership is elastic, in part because the number of 'designated professions' (each of which has a nominee on the Council) is itself elastic: while the Act

---

[70] The Act has only been partially commenced: Pts 1 and 2, ss 92–96 and the Schedule were commenced in March 2007 by HSCP Act 2005 (commencement) Order 2007 (SI 126/2007). The Act has only been partially commenced: Pts 1 and 2, ss 92–96 and the Schedule were commenced in March 2007 by HSCP Act 2005 (commencement) Order 2007 (SI 126/2007). Parts 1 and 2 (together with Schedule 1) deal with preliminary matters and the establishment of the Health and Social Professionals Council. The provisions dealing with registration, education/training and disciplinary matters remain to be implemented at the time of writing.

[71] Under the Act, all members are appointed by the Minister for Health (HSCP Act 2005, s 9).

[72] Nominated by the Minister for Education and Science.

[73] Appointed with the consent of the Minister for Enterprise, Trade and Employment.

stipulates 12 'designated professions',[74] the Act also provides that the Minister may by regulation designate other professions for the purpose of the Act.[75]

Accordingly, with the passage of years, the Council may grow in size.[76]

[2.35] Within each designated profession, the Act creates a registration board[77] comprising 13 members, six of whom are registered members of the profession in question and seven of whom are appointed by the Minister.[78] Each registration board has the power to set rules for the appointment of registered members including necessary qualifications and language proficiency. The principal duties of each registration board are to:[79]

— establish and maintain a register of members of the designated profession;

— issue certificates of registration;[80]

— give guidance to registrants concerning ethical conduct and give guidance and support to them concerning the practice of the designated profession and continuing professional development;

— monitor[81] the continuing suitability of programmes approved by the board for the education and training of applicants for registration; and

---

74 HSCP Act 2005, s 4(1): (a) clinical biochemist; (b) dietitian; (c) medical scientist; (d) occupational therapist; (e) orthoptist; (f) physiotherapist; (g) podiatrist; (h) psychologist; (i) radiographer; (j) social care worker; (k) social worker; (l) speech and language therapist.

75 HSCP Act 2005, s 4(2). It is to be presumed that a profession will only be so designated where it meets the definition of a 'health and social care profession' set out at s 4(3), namely 'any profession in which a person exercises skill or judgment relating to any of the following health or social care activities: (a) the preservation or improvement of the health or wellbeing of others; (b) the diagnosis, treatment or care of those who are injured, sick, disabled or infirm; (c) the resolution, through guidance, counselling or otherwise, of personal, social or psychological problems; (d) the care of those in need of protection, guidance or support.'

76 Membership of the Council may, for example, come to include members of complementary healthcare professions; the UK has long had regulation for such clinical disciplines: see Osteopaths Act 1993 and Chiropractors Act 1994.

77 HSCP Act 2005, Pt 3: not in force at the time of writing (October 2007).

78 HSCP Act 2005, s 28(1). The six 'registrants' are to be split between 3 practitioners of the profession, two managers of the profession and one engaged in education and training. The seven ministerial appointees are (a) one each from (i) public health/social care, (ii) a voluntary or private sector organisation concerned with health or social care and (iii) a third level establishment educating or training members of that designated profession and (b) four representatives of the interests of the general public (appointed with consent of Minister for Enterprise, Trade and Employment).

79 HSCP Act 2005, s 27(3).

80 The obligation to issue certificates and to notify applicants of any decision to refuse to grant registration or to restore a person's name to the relevant register is set out at s 41. Any decision to refuse such an application may be appealed to the Council (s 43) and an appeal lies to the High Court from any decision of the Council (s 44).

81 In accordance with s 49, which states that such reviews of training should place no less frequently than every five years.

– make recommendations with respect to sanctions to be imposed on registrants of the designated profession.

Disciplinary matters

[2.36] The Health and Social Care Professionals Council has disciplinary powers[82] relating to any registered person that are broadly analogous to those of the Medical Council and will be dealt with under the broad heading of disciplinary proceedings in the statutory professions, to which we now turn.

Quick Reference Guide 2.1

Features common to statutory regulatory bodies

❖ Created by a specific law to take responsibility for the regulation of a particular profession

❖ Responsible for
  o laying down ethical guidelines for the profession
  o maintaining registers of members of the profession
  o disciplinary and other fitness to practise issues within the profession
  o education and training standards within the profession

❖ Have powers to punish those guilty of misconduct or unfitness to practise
❖ Reforms post-2005 affect the Medical Practitioners Act 2007, the Pharmacy Act 2007 and the Health and Social Care Professionals Act 2005
❖ Dentistry and Nursing both continue to be regulated by 1985 legislation, while the Opticians Act was somewhat reformed in 2003

❖ The post-2005 reforms include
  o diminished professional representation on the regulatory bodies
  o the creation of separate preliminary proceedings, professional practice and health committees

❖ The Medical Council is also afforded powers to monitor and compel ongoing professional competence under the Medical Practitioners Act 2007

DISCIPLINARY PROCEEDINGS IN THE STATUTORY PROFESSIONS[83]

[2.37] From the point of view of the practitioner, one of the most daunting powers of the statutory regulatory bodies is their wide-ranging entitlement to impose sanctions on a practitioner. These powers have, in the case of the more recent regulatory statutes, been both refined and increased. We examine here the way in which complaints, investigations, fitness to practise proceedings and fair procedures operate in the context of the disciplinary proceedings of the statutory profession. While the broad brushstrokes of principle applicable across the profession are the same,[84] the reader's attention is

---

[82] Contained in Pt 6 of the Act: not in force at the time of writing (October 2007).

[83] See de Prez, 'Self-Regulation and Paragons of Virtue: The Case of 'Fitness to Practise", (2002) 10 Med L Rev 28.

[84] With the exception that the Opticians Board's processes do not include the automatic High Court scrutiny that is an inherent part of the disciplinary procedures of the other statutory.

again drawn to the differences inherent in the post-2005 reforms of statutory professions and in particular the difference that now exists between the 'new dispensation' in medicine, pharmacy and the health and social care professionals and the 'traditional' professional regulation of dentistry and nursing. Older rules continue to apply in the case of the nursing and dental professions. In the sections that follow therefore we look (in less detail)[85] at disciplinary measures under the older dispensation and (in greater detail) at the approach born of post-2005 legislation in this area.

Complaints

[2.38] A practitioner's name may be suspended or erased from the register for something as simple as failing to pay her retention fee, but her name may also be erased or suspended, or conditions may be attached to her retention on the register, on foot of a complaint made to the relevant body. Anyone, including a Board or Council itself, may bring an allegation of misconduct or unfitness to practise against a practitioner.[86] The manner in which a complaint is dealt with reflects in part the nature of the complaint – one feature common to the modern form of statutory regulation of the professions is the creation of separate Health Committees and Professional Practice Committees. The former deals with cases where a practitioner is unfit to practise by reason of ill-health (which may include addiction or alcoholism), the latter deals with cases where the issue is one of misconduct or competence.

Traditional grounds for complaint

[2.39] Under the traditional dispensation, this dichotomy between differing reasons underlying a person's unfitness to practice was dealt with by a single committee (the Fitness to Practice Committee), but the complaint against the practitioner could be framed in one of two ways:

(a)   alleged professional misconduct; or

(b)   alleged unfitness to engage in such practice by reason of physical or mental disability.[87]

Complaints under the new dispensation

[2.40] In the post-2005 legislation regulating statutory professions, the grounds for complaint against a practitioner have been significantly re-categorised, although the two 'gold standard' grounds of 'professional misconduct' and 'unfitness to practise' are still represented. Under the Medical Practitioners Act 2007 a complaint may be made to the Medical Council on the grounds of:

(a)   professional misconduct;

(b)   poor professional performance;

(c)   a relevant medical disability;

---

[85]   The justification for giving less attention to these older approaches to disciplinary measures is the express intention of the Oireachtas to introduce new legislation for the Dental, Nursing and Midwifery professions along the lines of that already introduced in the post-2005 reforms.

[86]   Indeed, there may be circumstances where the Council is obliged to bring a complaint: see para **[2.18]** dealing with professional competence in the medical profession.

[87]   Dentists Act 1985, s 38(1); Nurses Act 1985, s 38(1).

(d)   a failure to comply with a relevant condition;

(e)   a failure to comply with an undertaking or to take any action specified in a consent;[88]

(f)   a contravention of a provision of the Act (including a provision of any regulations or rules made under the Act); or

(g)   a conviction for a serious offence.[89]

A complaint of professional misconduct or poor professional performance may be made to the Medical Council in relation to any doctor registered with the Council even if the matter to which the complaint relates occurred outside Ireland.[90]

Investigating a complaint

[2.41] Just like the grounds on which complaints may be made, so the position on investigating a complaint has been modified by the more recent legislation regulating the clinical professions and it is sensible to look at both the traditional approach to investigation and the more refined approach mandated by the post-2005 reforms of the medical, pharmaceutical and other professions.

'Traditional' approach to investigation

[2.42] Under the Dentists and Nurses Act of 1985, the entire process of dealing with an allegation of fitness to practise falls to the Fitness to Practise Committee (FTPC) of the relevant body, which conducts an initial investigation of the complaint and decides whether there is sufficient substance to that complaint. It also determines into which section of the legislation the complaint falls – misconduct or unfitness to practise on medical grounds (or possibly both). If the FTPC does not think the complaint warrants further investigation, then that decision is forwarded to the full Council or Board for approval and, with the approval of the Council or Board, the matter does not proceed any further.[91]

---

[88]   A 'consent' in this context is an undertaking, given in the face of disciplinary proceedings, to the relevant Council to refrain from the alleged objectionable conduct in future; to undertake such necessary training to improve competence; to undergo medical treatment or to accept admonishment or censure from the Council.

[89]   Medical Practitioners Act 2007, s 57(1). Similar grounds arise in the HSCP Act 2005 and the Pharmacy Act 2007. Convictions that may be grounds for a complaint are defined in the various Acts: conviction within the State for 'an offence triable on indictment or a conviction outside the State for an offence consisting of acts or omissions that, if done or made in the State, would constitute an offence triable on indictment.' The fact that a practitioner has been cleared of an offence at trial does not mean that a disciplinary hearing may not proceed in respect of the same matters that were alleged in the criminal proceedings: *A (A) v Medical Council* [2001] IEHC 211 (11 October 2001).

[90]   Medical Practitioners Act 20007, s 51(2). Similar provisions relating to misconduct outside the State apply in both the Pharmacy Act 2007 (s 35(1)(a)–(b)) and the HSCP Act 2005 (s 52(2)).

[91]   In the United Kingdom, the General Medical Council appoints a 'screener' to conduct the initial review. If she concludes there is no case to answer, then that decision is referred to a lay member of the Council to ensure that she agrees with the screener's decision. If the screener or lay reviewer feels matters should be investigated further, the case goes first to a Preliminary Proceedings Committee and the if necessary to the appropriate decision-making committee. This approach is reflected in post-2005 Irish legislation by the PPC.

If there is substance to the allegation,[92] then the second stage of the process is activated, which is an inquiry into the complaint. In the traditional setting, such inquiries are held in private, although they may be held in public in exceptional circumstances.

Investigations under the new regulatory dispensation[93]

[2.43] Under the new regulatory approach,[94] three separate committees (which may broadly be termed 'disciplinary committees') are called for:

– Preliminary Proceedings Committee (PPC);

– Fitness to Practise Committee (FTPC) or Professional Conduct Committee (PCC);[95]

– Health Committee.[96]

In the Medical Council the FTPC must have a non-medical (or 'lay') majority; there is no such restriction on the Health Committee or the PPC.[97] On the Council of the Pharmaceutical Society of Ireland, all three committees are required to have a 'lay' majority,[98] while under the HSCP Act 2005, the majority of the members of any disciplinary committee must be registered members of the designated professions.[99]

Preliminary Proceedings Committee

[2.44] The role of the PPC is to conduct initial investigations in an expeditious manner, while keeping the complainant informed of the progress of the complaint.[100] Other persons may be appointed by the Medical Council to assist it in its endeavours.[101] The

---

[92] Or where the relevant Board of Council disagrees with the FTPC's decision that there is no case to answer, in which case it may direct that an inquiry be held.

[93] In this section we focus on the regulatory regime established by the Medical Practitioners Act 2007, but the same principles apply (with the necessary modifications) to the other recently reformed regulatory processes under the Pharmacy Act 2007 and the HSCP Act 2005.

[94] See Medical Practitioners Act 2007, s 20(1)–(4); Pharmacy Act 2007, s 34(1); HSCP Act 2005, s 51(1).

[95] This is the term used in the Pharmacy Act 2007 and the HSCP Act 2005.

[96] Note that under the Medical Practitioners Act 2007, the creation of a Health Committee is optional; Health Committees are mandatory under the Pharmacy Act 2007 and the HSCP Act 2005.

[97] Medical Practitioners Act s 20(10)–(11). There is no requirement that the membership of the PPC or FTPC ('section 20(2) committees' in the Act) must be drawn from the Medical Council, but at least one-third must be Medical Council members; at least one-third of the FTPC must comprise medical practitioners.

[98] At least one third of the members of any committee must be registered pharmacists (at least two of whom must be registered pharmacists who are pharmacy owners): Pharmacy Act 2007, s 34(4)–(5). Where a complaint is against a pharmacy owner, then a meeting of a disciplinary committee will only be quorate when at least one of the pharmacy owners on the committee in question is present.

[99] Although at least one third of the membership of any committee must consist of persons other than registrants, at least one of whom shall be representative of the interest of the general public: HSCP Act 2005, s 51(4).

[100] Medical Practitioners Act 2007, s 57(3)–(4).

[101] Medical Practitioners Act 2007, s 58.

only exception to its investigatory function is where it receives a complaint relating to a criminal conviction for a serious offence, in which case the Act directs that the PPC refer that matter directly to the Medical Council.[102]

[2.45] At the end of its consideration of any complaint, the PPC will determine whether there is sufficient cause to warrant further action being taken. The PPC may request further evidence from a complainant and may, in the case of the Medical Council, refuse to proceed with its investigation where that information is not forthcoming. The PPC may also demand such information as it requires from the practitioner who is the subject matter of the complaint[103] and the practitioner is obliged to supply that information. Where the PPC is of the opinion that the complaint is not one that requires the attention of the Medical Council, it may inform the complainant that another forum is more appropriate.[104] If the complaint is withdrawn during the PPC's investigation, then the PPC may discontinue its investigation or, if appropriate, proceed to investigate the matter as if the complaint had never been withdrawn.[105]

[2.46] If at the end of the investigation process the PPC forms the opinion that there is no cause for further action, or that the complaint is one that is amenable to mediation, or (in the case of the Medical Council), that the complaint should be directed to another body for investigation, then it will inform the relevant Council of that view. In the case of the PSI Council and the Health and Social Care Professionals Council, the recommendation of the PPC that the matter should not proceed further is conclusive and neither Council has the power to direct the issue to another forum. However in the case of the Medical Council, it may accept and follow the view of the PPC, but also has the authority to

- refer the complaint to a professional competence scheme;
- refer the complaint for resolution by mediation or other informal means; or
- if it considers it necessary to do so, refer the matter to the FTPC.

Mediation[106]

[2.47] Mediation is a new element of the post-2005 reforms of statutory professions. It is open to the relevant bodies (but not mandatory) to develop guidelines for the mediation of certain complaints. While there is no compulsion attached to the introduction of

---

[102] Conviction for a serious offence means 'conviction in the State for an offence triable on indictment or a conviction outside the State for an offence consisting of acts or omissions that, if done or made in the State, would constitute an offence triable on indictment'. This obligation to immediately refer in the case of conviction of an indictable offence exists only under the Medical Practitioners Act 2007, s 57(5)–(6).
Where the offence in question is sufficiently serious such as to 'render the practitioner permanently unfit to continue to practise medicine, and...it is in the public interest that it take action immediately' it is open to the Medical Council to cancel the practitioner's registration. If the offence is not of sufficient seriousness to warrant immediate cancellation, then the investigation of the complaint will proceed in the normal fashion.

[103] Medical Practitioners Act 2007, s 59 (3)–(7); HSCP Act, s 53(5); Pharmacy Act, s 38(2)(c).

[104] For example, the complaints process established under Pt 9 of the Health Act 2004.

[105] Medical Practitioners Act 2007, s 59(10); HSCP Act 2005, s 62; Pharmacy Act 2007, s 44.

[106] Medical Practitioners Act 2007, s 62; HSCP Act 2005, s 55; Pharmacy Act 2007, s 37.

mediation or other alternative dispute resolution, the Acts indicate what such mediation might include and further lay down certain stipulations as to the limitations to be placed on mediation. Suggested ingredients of mediation include mechanisms for:

–   determinations to be made about whether a complaint can in fact be resolved by mediation or other informal means;

–   identifying the persons who may attempt to mediate or otherwise resolve the complaint;

–   recording of the manner in which the complaint was resolved and of the agreement of the complainant and the registered medical practitioner the subject of the complaint to the resolution;

–   the steps to be taken if the complaint cannot, in the opinion of the person attempting to do so, be resolved by mediation or other informal means;

[2.48] There is a prohibition against forcing mediation upon unwilling participants: both complainant and practitioner must consent to mediation taking place. Where as part of mediation a practitioner gives a 'consent', that consent or undertaking cannot be taken as an admission of any allegation. No answer or statement made by the practitioner in question in the course of attempting to resolve a complaint through mediation can be communicated to any person other than those involved in the mediation, nor can it be used in any disciplinary, civil or criminal proceedings. The resolution of a complaint through mediation facilitated by the Medical Council cannot include the payment of compensation.[107]

Conduct of inquiries

[2.49] Where the PPC is of the opinion that there is a *prima facie* case against a practitioner, then it may refer the case to the FTPC.[108] The medical practitioner who is the subject of the complaint must then be notified of the referral, of the nature of the complaint and the evidence supporting that complaint, of her right to be represented and to defend herself at the hearing and of the right to apply (or for witnesses to apply) for the hearing or certain portions of it to be heard in private.[109] The presumption under the post-2005 reforms of the statutory profession is in favour of public hearings although applications may be made by the subject of the nature of the complaint that the inquiry be heard wholly or partly in private.[110] In the case of the Medical Council, any witness

---

[107]   Medical Practitioners Act 2007, s 62(6).

[108]   As has already been observed above, in the case of the Medical Council, where the PPC initially holds that there is not complaint to answer and informs the Council of that fact, the council may direct nonetheless that the matter be referred to the FTPC: Medical Practitioners Act 2007, s 61(2)(e).

[109]   Medical Practitioners Act 2007, s 64. Under the Dentists Act 1985 and Nurses Act 1985 (and, indeed, under previous Medical Practitioners legislation) the presumption was in favour of hearings held in private.

[110]   Medical Practitioners Act, s 65(2). It is possible that Health Committee hearings of the Medical Council would be more likely to be heard in private: the HSCP Act 2005 explicitly states that Health Committee hearings should be in private unless it would be appropriate to do otherwise: HSCP Act 2005, s 58(3).

before the inquiry may also apply to have the hearing heard wholly or partly in private. The decision whether to hold an inquiry in public or in private (*in camera*) lies with the relevant Council,[111] and the Council in question may choose to have the hearing in private when they consider it 'appropriate' to do so. Even in a private hearing, the Supreme Court has held that the person who is the subject of the complaint has the right to be accompanied by her expert witnesses.[112]

[2.50] Fitness to practise inquiries are akin to a court hearings and the FTPC can call witnesses, examine them under oath and compel the production of relevant documents, including confidential clinical records. It is important to observe that the complaint, once made to and substantiated by the PPC becomes, in effect, the property of the Council, so that it is the FTPC that presents the case against the practitioner and not the person who made the initial complaint, although the complainant will almost certainly be required to give evidence. The evidence relied on by the FTPC must be evidence that is heard by the Committee (although it need not be given orally)[113] and which can be cross-examined and tested by the subject of the complaint or her legal representatives.[114] Witnesses may also be questioned not only by legal representatives for the Council and the clinician, but also by the members of the FTPC itself.

[2.51] The powers and privileges of the members of an FTPC are similar, but not identical,[115] to those of a High Court judge—the Committee can enforce the attendance of witnesses, examine witnesses on oath or otherwise, and compel the production

---

[111] *Barry v Medical Council and Fitness to Practise Committee of the Medical Council* [1997] IEHC 204, [1998] 3 IR 368. Courts have also previously directed that a hearing must be heard in private: *Eastern Health Board v Fitness to Practice Committee of the Medical Council* [1998] IEHC 210, [1998] 3 IR 399.

[112] *O'Ceallaigh v The Fitness To Practise Committee Of An Bord Altranais* [1998] IESC 60, [1999] 2 IR 552.

[113] Medical Practitioners Act 2007, s 66(3), it may also be given on affidavit (sworn statement); the Medical Council has the power (under s 11) to set its own rules of practice.

[114] *Borges v Fitness to Practice Committee of the Medical Council* [2004] IESC, [2004] 1 IR 103. In that case, the Medical Council relied upon, among other evidence, transcripts of evidence that had been given against Dr Borges in fitness to practise hearings before the UK General Medical Council and used those transcripts as the basis for a finding of misconduct against him. Evidence was not heard from his UK-based accusers because they were unwilling to travel to Ireland for the hearing. The Supreme Court observed (per Keane CJ, 119):

> 'It is sufficient to say that the applicant cannot be deprived of his right to fair procedures, which necessitate the giving of evidence by his accusers and their being cross-examined, by the extension of the exceptions to the rule against hearsay to a case in which they are unwilling to testify in person.'

The Court left open the question of whether the Medical Council might be able to rely upon transcript evidence in circumstances where a witness at an earlier hearing had subsequently died or become incompetent to give evidence.

[115] The Fitness to Practice Committee cannot, for example, directly punish someone for contempt (for example, in not appearing as a witness): it must go to the High Court to seek the appropriate orders. Note that under the Pharmacy Act 2007, the Council of the PSI also has the power to award legal costs to any party: s 43(1)(d).

(including discovery) of records. Traditionally, it has been the case that Medical Council (and similar) fitness to practise inquiries have been conducted according to the 'beyond reasonable doubt' standard of proof. It is not clear whether that standard, which is usually reserved exclusively for criminal trials, will continue to be applied following the re-constitution of FTPCs along new lines.[116] If a complaint is withdrawn while being considered by an FTPC, the hearing of the complaint may be discontinued or may proceed nevertheless.

Consents

[2.52] One new facet of the post-2005 regulatory legislation is that a practitioner may consent to disciplinary measures being imposed. Once a complaint has been referred to an FTPC, the Committee may call upon the practitioner who is the subject of the complaint to give one or more of the following undertakings or consents:

- if appropriate, undertake to not repeat the conduct that was the subject of the complaint;

- undertake to be referred to a professional competence scheme and to undertake any requirements relating to the improvement of the practitioner's competence and performance which may be imposed;

- consent to undergo medical treatment;

- consent to being censured by the Council.[117]

If the practitioner gives the requested consent, then that may dispose of the disciplinary matter and no further investigation need be conducted; if the request for an undertaking or consent is rejected, then the matter proceeds. If the undertaking or consent is given, but is not subsequently honoured, then that failure or refusal to honour the consent or undertaking is grounds for the Council to proceed again against the practitioner.

---

[116] See Department of Health, *Trust, Assurance and Safety – The Regulation of Health Professionals in the 21st Century* (London, 2007): 'The [UK] Government agrees…that the civil standard of proof, with its sliding scale, should be the common standard of proof for all the regulatory bodies in fitness to practise proceedings.' Whether this 'sliding scale' approach to the balance of probabilities (ie flexibly applied to take into account the circumstances and gravity of individual cases, with more serious matters requiring a greater degree of probability of the evidence being true) represents the law in Ireland was discussed in the judgment of O'Flaherty J in *O'Laoire v Medical Council* (27 July 1997, unreported) SC (at p 8):

> 'The essence of a disciplinary enquiry into alleged professional misconduct…is to find out by clear evidence the pith and substance of the misdeed being investigated and decide whether the case has been established against the person, always bearing in mind the grave consequences that such a finding will, in general, have for the person whose conduct is called into question but also remembering that the public has an interest in making sure the proper standards of professional misconduct are upheld. The graver the allegation the greater will be the care which the tribunal will take to make sure that the case has been brought home against the person whose conduct is impugned'

[117] Medical Practitioners Act 2007, s 67(1). Similar powers exists under the Pharmacy Act 2007 (s 46) and the HSCP Act 2005 (s 61).

Conclusion of the inquiry – sanctions

[2.53] At the end of any inquiry, the FTPC makes a decision in respect of the complaint made and reports on that decision to the Council. If the FTPC exonerates the practitioner, the matter will generally end there and the complaint will be dismissed. The appropriate sanction will depend on the nature of the complaint proven against the practitioner. The range of sanctions open to the Medical Council (any combination of which may be imposed) under the 2007 Act is as follows:

- an advice or admonishment, or a censure, in writing;
- a censure in writing and a fine not exceeding €5,000;
- the attachment of conditions to the practitioner's registration, including restrictions on the practice of medicine that may be engaged in by the practitioner;
- the transfer of the practitioner's registration to another division of the register;
- the suspension of the practitioner's registration for a specified period;
- the cancellation of the practitioner's registration;
- a prohibition from applying for a specified period for the restoration of the practitioner's registration.[118]

The practitioner is notified of the finding, the punishment and any details of the punishment (such as the size of a fine or the duration of any suspension), together with the date of the decision and the reasons for the imposition of the sanction. In certain situations, even where a clinician is found not to have met the criteria for professional misconduct, the Board or Council may still be permitted to attach conditions to her continued registration.[119]

Role of the High Court

[2.54] The potential consequences of a decision that a practitioner is guilty of professional misconduct or otherwise unfit to practise are immense. Because of the enormity of such a decision, the final say on any disciplinary decision taken by a statutory body that significantly affects the livelihood of a professional must be subject to review by the courts before it can be legally binding.[120] Accordingly, if the Medical Council imposes a sanction more punitive than an advice, admonishment or censure, it must apply to the High Court to make that decision final. When a practitioner, against

---

[118] Medical Practitioners Act 2007, s 71. The Council of the PSI and the Health and Social Care Professionals Council do not have the power to fine practitioners and nor does the power to transfer practitioners to another division of the register arise in the case of either of those bodies.

[119] *Casey v The Medical Council* [1999] IEHC 171, [1999] 2 IR 534, [1999] 2 ILRM 481. It is likely that a case such as this, where a doctor was not found guilty of misconduct, but was found to have professional competence issues, would now be dealt with under the Medical Council's professional competence powers: Medical Practitioners Act 2007, s 91 et seq.

[120] In *Re Solicitors Act 1954* [1960] IR 239. The process now followed by the Medical Council, Dental Council and An Bord Altranais whereby sanctions are imposed by a FTPC but must be confirmed by the courts was challenged, but upheld: *Re M* [1984] IR 479; *M v Medical Council* [1984] IR 485.

whom a finding of unfitness to practise has been made, is notified of the decision, she has 21 days to apply to the High Court to have that decision overturned.[121] If she does not do so, then the Council or Board must nonetheless apply to the court to have its decision made final.[122] Once the order of the Council is confirmed, the practitioner must be notified.

[2.55] On an appeal the High Court has the power to hear any evidence put before it, but the court will generally recognise a certain sphere of autonomy within which the Council in question is free to set its own rules of conduct, so long as fair procedure is not infringed.[123] The court is free to hear expert evidence as to whether any conduct complained of in the original allegation constitutes professional misconduct in the opinion of the expert.[124] The court may, on appeal by a practitioner, make any order that seems just, whether upholding the Council's sanction, cancelling the punishment or substituting a different punishment.[125] Where there is a power of temporary registration, there is no obligation on the court to review a decision not to renew temporary registration if the decision in relation to registration is not a direct result of the deliberations of a Fitness to Practise Committee.[126]

Dispensing with an inquiry in the public interest

[2.56] In general, where a complaint is found to have substance, then an inquiry will follow as a precursor to any sanction being imposed. However, where a complaint is of such gravity and the Medical Council is of the opinion that immediate suspension is necessary to protect the interests of the public, then it may apply *ex parte* to the High Court for an order to suspend the registration of the practitioner in question. Such an application will ordinarily be heard in private.[127]

---

[121] Under the Pharmacy Act 2007 and the HSCP Act 2005, practitioners have 30 days to appeal to the High Court.

[122] Medical Practitioners Act 2007, ss 74–76.

[123] *CK v An Bord Altranais* [1990] 2 IR 396.

[124] *Perez v An Bord Altranais* [2005] IEHC 400, [2005] 4 IR 298.

[125] Medical Practitioners Act 2007, s 75. See also *Cahill v Dental Council* [2002] IEHC, 15 June 2001. Following problems that arose during Dr Cahill's attempts to sedate a child patient prior to surgery and following a FTPC inquiry, the Dental Council imposed a number of conditions on his practice of dentistry, including that he be prohibited from performing dentistry involving the use of anaesthesia or sedation, that he should complete a course in paediatric dentistry approved by the Council and that he should display a notice in his premises drawing attention to the conditions attached to his practice. The court lifted the requirement to display a notice and limited the restriction on the use of anaesthesia or sedation to only those patients under the age of 16 years. The requirement to complete a course in paediatric dentistry was upheld.

[126] *Anachebe v The Medical Council* [2000] IEHC 193 (12 July 2000). The plaintiff had been found guilty of professional misconduct and was censured (which does not require the supervision of the court). When subsequently he applied for renewal of his temporary registration, the Medical Council declined to renew it, citing the previous finding of misconduct.

[127] Medical Practitioners Act 2007, s 60(1). The court has the power to make such order as it sees fit: see the summary of events contained in the *ex tempore* judgment of Kelly J in *An Bord Altranais v Ní Cheallaigh* [1997] IEHC 186 (17 December 1997). (contd/)

Quick Reference Guide 2.2

Outcomes of fitness to practise inquiries

❖ Any interested party, whether a member of the public or the regulatory Council or Board itself, may make an allegation against a practitioner. There are circumstances (such as where the Medical Council becomes aware that a practitioner is not maintaining professional competence) where a body must make a complaint against a practitioner.

❖ How a complaint is dealt with will depend on whether the profession in question is one that is policed by post-2005 reforms. The pre-2005 professions (nursing and dentistry) allow for the investigation and hearing of complaints by the Fitness to Practise Committee of the relevant body. Hearings are traditionally held in private.

❖ The post-2005 professions (medicine, pharmacy and the health and social care professions) require separate investigative and hearing roles, by the preliminary proceedings and professional practice committees respectively. Hearings are heard in public unless there is a reason to do otherwise.

❖ Among the post-2005 reforms are provisions for:

    o the use of mediation and other alternative dispute resolution as part of the complaint process;

    o the option for the practitioner, on request, to give to the disciplinary authority a consent to refrain from certain behaviour, to be referred for relevant competence assessment or training, to undergo medical treatment or to be censured by the relevant council.

❖ In the case of all Fitness to Practise Committees, there is a variety of available sanctions, ranging in severity from admonition or censure to suspension or striking off from the relevant register.

❖ Any sanction more stringent than censure or admonition may be appealed to the High Court by the practitioner within a stipulated timeframe. Where no appeal occurs, the regulatory body must nonetheless apply to the High Court for confirmation of the sanction.

What is 'professional misconduct'?

[2.57] The Medical Council has the following definition of professional misconduct:

'Professional misconduct is:

(a) Conduct which doctors of experience, competence and good repute consider disgraceful or dishonourable; and / or

---

[127] (\contd) In that case, an order prohibiting a midwife from continuing to practise was not applied in the case of five couples who wished to continue to avail of the midwife's services. The court ordered that they be given the opportunity of knowing of the allegations of the midwife and then choosing whether they still wished to retain her for delivering their babies. See also the facts in *Medical Council v O* [2004] IESC 22; [2004] 2 ILRM 161. In *Medical Council v PC* [2003] 3 IR 600, the Supreme Court stated that, in determining whether to exercise its discretion to suspend a practitioner pending a hearing of the FTPC, the High Court was required to be satisfied that the public interest required that such an order be made and that the public interest outweighed the constitutional right of the practitioner to practise and earn a livelihood.

(b)   Conduct connected with his or her profession in which the doctor concerned has seriously fallen short by omission or commission of the standards of conduct expected among doctors.'[128]

Professional misconduct must obviously relate to some aspect of the clinician's professional activity, although it need not relate to want of clinical skill or judgment and must have an element of moral failure (such as dishonesty) or persistent recklessness or negligence or to it. The courts, in *O'Laoire v Medical Council*, have defined professional misconduct more exhaustively:[129]

'(1)   Conduct which is "infamous" or "disgraceful" in a professional respect is "professional misconduct" ...;

(2)   Conduct which would not be "infamous" or "disgraceful" in any other person, if done by a medical practitioner in relation to his profession, that is, with regard either to his patients or to his colleagues, may be considered as "infamous" or "disgraceful" conduct in a professional respect;

(3)   "Infamous" or "disgraceful" conduct in turn is conduct involving some degree of moral turpitude, fraud or dishonesty;

(4)   Conduct which could not properly be characterised as "infamous" or "disgraceful" and which does not involve any degree of moral turpitude, fraud or dishonesty may still constitute "professional misconduct" if it is conduct connected with his profession in which the medical practitioner concerned has seriously fallen short, by omission or commission, of the standards of conduct expected among medical practitioners.

Usually negligence or recklessness will have to occur on more than a single occasion for it to be regarded as professional misconduct[130] and typically the misconduct should arise in the course of the practitioner's clinical duties, although that need not always be the case.[131]

Fair procedure and disciplinary matters

[2.58] We have observed already that legal fair procedure requires that it is a judge of the High Court who gives or withholds final approval to any sanction imposed by a statutory disciplinary body.[132] There are certain things the Courts will be especially concerned about when examining the decision made by a FTPC. It will want to know that the decision reached by the Board or Council was reasonable, although it will not generally examine the minutiae of the decision. It will be more interested in ascertaining whether fair procedures were followed in making the decision. Any decision made by a body

---

[128] *Guide to Ethical Conduct and Behaviour* (6th edn, 2004), para. 1.5. The guidelines also specify certain forms of conduct, such as deliberately causing the death of a patient.

[129] Per Keane J in *O'Laoire v Medical Council* (27 January 1995, unreported) HC, 109. See also *Re Richard Lynch and Malachy Daly* [1970] IR 1.

[130] *McCandless v General Medical Council* (1995) 30 BMLR 53.

[131] In *Roylance v General Medical Council* [1999] Lloyds Rep Med 139, a non-practising doctor who was the head of a National Health Service Hospital Trust which knowingly permitted substandard paediatric cardiac surgery to take place was found guilty of professional misconduct.

[132] *In Re Solicitors Act 1954* [1960] IR 239.

such as the Medical Council and indeed any decision made that affects a person's livelihood or career[133] must observe the rules of fundamental justice. There are many facets to the principle of fair procedures, and we look here at some of the most important.

Delay

[2.59] Any allegation against a practitioner must be made and investigated, where possible, without undue delay. Delay can adversely affect a person's ability to defend herself. Where there is an excessive delay between the occasion on which a practitioner was allegedly guilty of misconduct and the making of a complaint[134] (or the decision to act on that complaint by a disciplinary body), then that delay may operate to deprive the practitioner of a fair trial. The need for prompt action cuts both ways: a person who delays in challenging disciplinary proceeding may find that her right to challenge the proceedings evaporates due to her delay.[135] Similarly, a delay in raising an important legal point at the first available opportunity in disciplinary proceedings may preclude the practitioner from attempting to rely on that point later in the proceedings.[136]

Notice

[2.60] A person charged with wrongdoing must have notice of the charges against her, the evidence[137] and against her and of any hearing where matters are to be decided.[138] The Medical Practitioners Act 2007 directs that the PPC must notify the practitioner who is the subject of the complaint of the complaint, the nature of the complaint and the name of the complainant.[139] Without notice of what is going on, a person cannot defend herself against allegations. To ensure fair procedure, when an allegation of misconduct is

---

[133] *Gunn v National College of Art and Design* [1990] 2 IR 168.

[134] See *Michael Shine v Fitness to Practise Committee of the Medical Council* (19 December 2006, unreported) HC (O'Donovan J). The High Court permitted the Fitness to Practise committee of the Medical Council to inquire into allegations of professional misconduct concerning Mr Shine's treatment of nine of his former patients, but restrained the committee from proceeding with an inquiry into the conduct of Dr Michael Shine in respect of complaints by 12 other patients: in four of those cases, the issue of prejudice arose, due to a delay of many years in reporting alleged assaults. It is not enough that there is delay in the disciplinary process: the delay must result in some prejudice to the practitioner who is the subject of the complaint by preventing her from defending herself.

[135] *O'Flynn v Mid-Western Health Board* [1989] IR 429 (HC), [1991] 2 IR 223.

[136] *A(A) v Medical Council* [2003] IESC 70, [2003] 4 IR 302, [2004] 1 ILRM 372.

[137] A disciplinary body does not need to share *every* piece of information available to it with the person facing disciplinary proceedings, but only that material which has a bearing on ensuring the procedure is fair: *Georgopulous v Beaumont Hospital Board* (4 June 1997, unreported) SC. There may be no need to hand over all details to the person complained of if the investigating body is still at the stage of deciding whether a complaint should or should not be entertained: *O'Flynn v Mid-Western Health Board* [1991] 2 IR 223 (SC).

[138] *O'Laoire v Medical Council* (27 January 1995, unreported) HC: a person facing disciplinary proceedings must have 'adequate notice of the allegations made against him so as to enable him to conduct his defence and to meet [the allegations] with whatever legal assistance was appropriate and with the production of whatever evidence was necessary.'

[139] Medical Practitioners Act 2007, s 59(5). Similar provisions exist in the other regulatory statutes.

received against a practitioner, the practice is to notify the practitioner concerned and invite her to give her comments on the matter. The practitioner must then be given notice of any hearing and then notice of any decision taken on foot of the hearing.

Fair procedure at the hearing

[2.61] The more serious the consequences of any disciplinary action or the greater the uncertainty concerning the facts at the centre of the issue, the greater the need for an oral hearing of the matter and the greater need for formality and legal representation in that hearing.[140] In general at disciplinary hearing of the regulatory bodies the case against the practitioner is presented by barristers on behalf of the Council or Board, while the practitioner's legal team mounts her defence. A person who is not given the opportunity to present her side of the case in a disciplinary scenario will generally be able to ask a court to overturn the decision.[141]

[2.62] If a person has the opportunity to challenge evidence—for example, at a hearing—and passes up the opportunity to do so, it is difficult for her to subsequently challenge the evidence, so the opportunity presented by a hearing of the case should be taken very seriously.[142]

Reasons

[2.63] In the same way that a person must be given the evidence against her, she must also be given the reasons for any decision that is taken concerning her. Without reasons, it would be impossible for her to decide whether an appeal was possible or what part of the decision she should appeal against. The reasons need not be exhaustive, merely sufficient for a person to understand how and why the decision was made.

Prejudice and bias

[2.64] A disciplinary procedure or hearing is not fair if there is someone involved who has already made up his mind on the matter or who has already heard the evidence and reached an opinion upon it. So, the person who initially screens a complaint against a practitioner, decides that she has a case to answer and refers the matter to the Fitness to Practise Committee, cannot also sit on the Committee hearing the case as she has prejudged the matter and it would not be fair.[143]

---

[140] In *Flanagan v University College Dublin* [1988] IR 724 a student was subjected to a formal college hearing concerning alleged plagiarism without being offered the opportunity of legal representation (her only representation was from the Students' Union). The High Court held that the potential consequences were so great (being sent down from the university) that representation was necessary.

[141] *Aziz v Midland Health Board* (29 October 1999, unreported) SC. A doctor was dismissed for refusing to obey lawful instructions. The Court was satisfied that it was reasonable to dismiss him but criticised the fact that he was not allowed to present his side of the story.

[142] *State (Boyle) v General Medical Services Board* [1981] ILRM 14.

[143] In *O'Neill v Beaumont Hospital Board* [1990] ILRM 419, a court refused to allow three members of the hospital board to sit on a disciplinary panel considering a surgeon's conduct because they had already committed themselves to positions that suggested they had prejudged the matter. Similarly, in the Medical Practitioners Act 2007 (and in the analogous post-2005 Acts), the membership of the PPC and FTPC cannot be allowed to overlap.

Bias is a slightly different and subtler matter: there does not have to be actual prejudice, but merely the appearance that a person involved in the decision-making process could have been biased for some reason. Bias can come in many forms, such as a personal relationship, a financial interest in the matter, or a political or personal position that makes it likely that a decision-maker could be hostile or partial toward a person appearing before the decision-making committee.[144]

Proportionate punishment

[2.65] The punishment should fit the crime. Where a sanction imposed on a practitioner is disproportionate to the decision reached by the disciplinary committee, the court may refuse to uphold it or where it concerns attaching conditions to the clinician's practice, it may alter those conditions.[145]

Quick Reference Guide 2.3

Fair procedure

> ❖ **Where any practitioner is facing disciplinary inquiries she is entitled to fair procedure in the form of:**
>   - o **the avoidance of delay**
>   - o **notice of complaints and evidence against her**
>   - o **fair procedure at the hearing, including legal representation where desired and the opportunity to examine witnesses**
>   - o **reasons for any decisions taken by the disciplinary body**
>   - o **the avoidance of prejudice and bias**
>   - o **punishments proportionate to the offence committed**

MOVEMENT OF HEALTH CARE PROFESSIONALS THROUGHOUT EUROPE

[2.66] While application by a non-European Union (EU) clinician to practise in an EU country may be met with resistance, the case of EU citizens who wish to practise in other EU countries is very different. The EU system enshrines what are sometimes called the 'four freedoms'

- – free movement of goods;
- – free movement of capital;
- – free movement of workers;
- – freedom to establish oneself in business and to provide or obtain services.

What these 'freedoms' mean in essence is that the presence of national borders within the EU should not be an obstacle to the free market. A product that can be sold in Germany should be capable of being sold just as easily in Greece and Ireland. By extension into the clinical field, a practitioner qualified in an EU country should also be free to work in other EU countries. Health professionals, depending on whether they are

---

[144] See *O'Donoghue v Veterinary Council* [1975] IR 398, where the person in whose name the complaint was made was also sitting on the panel that decided the fate of the vet in question. The decision of the panel was therefore void.

[145] *Cahill v Dental Council* (15 June 2001, unreported) HC.

employees or self-employed have rights under the free movement of workers and the freedom of establishment respectively.

[2.67] There are some obvious stumbling blocks to free movement of health professionals, among them the facts that qualifications obtained in different countries may not be equivalent and that a person coming from outside the country may lack linguistic proficiency. There is an obvious allure in deciding to exclude from practice a clinician whose qualifications do not, on paper, match the host country's equivalent and who does not speak the language of the host country. In order to overcome the difficulties, the European Union introduced a series of Directives to regulate how the free movement of health and other professionals should work. Many Directives were formerly profession-specific,[146] together with broader guidelines[147] that brought the bulk of clinical disciplines within their remit, but the principles of the recognition of qualifications necessary to achieve the end of free movement and freedom of establishment have been consolidated in Directive 2005/36/EC.

[2.68] The rules for the mutual recognition of qualifications are comparatively straightforward and have not been significantly altered by the 2005 consolidation.[148] A person who wishes to take up a regulated (and regulated is defined loosely in the general directive, to include all those professions carried on under a professional body, whether statutory or not) profession in another EU country must satisfy minimum criteria laid out in the Directive and including, where applicable, evidence that she has pursued within the EU the equivalent the required basic higher education course in the profession in question[149] and that she has completed the necessary professional or specialist training in an EU Member State.

[2.69] Once these conditions are met, an EU country cannot refuse someone permission to practise on the basis of her lacking qualifications. However if the course or training is markedly different from that provided in the host State, then the host State can offer the

---

[146] The Directives formerly applying to the various professions and to professionals generally included: for the medical profession: Directive 75/362/EEC; Directive 75/363/EEC; Directive 86/457/EEC and Directive 93/16/EEC. For the dental profession: Directive No 78/686/EEC and Directive 78/687/EEC. For the nursing profession: Directive 77/452/EEC and Directive 77/453/EEC (general nursing) and Directive 80/154/EEC and Directive 80/155/EEC (midwifery). For pharmacy: Directive 5/432/EEC and Directive 90/658/EEC. All of these Directives passed into law by being made ministerial Regulations. See also European Communities (European Economic Area) (Recognition of Qualifications in Pharmacy) Regulations 1994, which give free movement rights to pharmacists from the European Economic Area as well as those from the EU.

[147] See Directive 89/48/EEC, which laid out the basis ground rules for mutual recognition of third-level professional qualifications. See also Directive 92/51/EEC, which allows for mutual recognition of shorter diploma courses and of other educational certificates.

[148] There are some differences, but they lie outside the remit of the present text.

[149] Article 24 of Directive 2005/36/EC sets out that 'basic medical training shall comprise a total of at least six years of study or 5 500 hours of theoretical and practical training provided by, or under the supervision of, a university.'

clinician the choice between an aptitude test[150] and a period of adaptation in the host country. An EU country that refuses to allow an EU citizen with an EU professional qualification to practise within its borders must give reasons for doing so and allow the applicant a legal right of appeal against the decision.

---

[150] Which can be in the language of the host country, thereby testing the applicant's linguistic competence.

Chapter 3

Confidentiality and the Practitioner–Patient Relationship

INTRODUCTION

[3.01] The relationship between patient and clinician is arguably founded on a trinity of essential components: confidentiality, consent and the duty to provide competent care. Of these three elements, it is trust that is often most pivotal to the therapeutic relationship, a confidence not merely in the skill of the clinician, but also in her professional ethics and her dispassionate professionalism. A healthcare practitioner is expected to remain silent on what takes place behind the veil of the therapeutic setting. However, there are also exceptions to the obligation of confidentiality (and indeed, there may even be circumstances, discussed below, where there is an obligation to breach confidentiality) and in this chapter we examine both confidentiality and the exceptions to it.

[3.02] The second part of the chapter examines the practical and legal basis of the practitioner–patient relationship, including the differences that arise between public (state-funded) and private healthcare. There are many other facets to the broad term 'practitioner-patient relationship', including elements of sociology, philosophy and the inter-personal skills of the parties involved, but in this chapter we will attempt only to tease out a working legal definition of the relationship.

CONFIDENTIALITY

[3.03] Confidentiality is one of the foundational principles of the therapeutic relationship and has an ancient lineage. The Hippocratic Oath (see para **[1.18]**) demanded that doctors preserve confidentiality and similar requirements are common to all modern declarations of medical ethics.[1] We will see below that the exhaustive Hippocratic rule of confidentiality (which meant that even knowledge gleaned outside of medical practice was to be guarded as a 'sacred' secret) is no longer the case in modern medical law, but nonetheless the requirement to maintain confidentiality remains an onerous one.

The need for confidentiality

[3.04] The importance of confidentiality is obvious; many aspects of the therapeutic relationship float on trust and confidence. A patient who is completely open with his doctor about his past or present issues can in turn expect the doctor to provide better and more rounded medical care. In turn, the assurance of confidentiality held out by the doctor permits that greater disclosure by the patient. The Medical Council *Guide to Ethical Conduct and Behaviour* states the following about confidentiality:

---

[1] For example, the original Declaration of Geneva (World Medical Association, 1948): 'I will respect the secrets which are confided in me, even after the patient has died'.

Confidentiality is a time-honoured principle of medical ethics. It extends after death and is fundamental to the doctor/patient relationship. While the concern of relatives and close friends is understandable, the doctor must not disclose information to any person without the consent of the patient, subject to exceptions [discussed below at para **[3.15]***ff*].[2]

Courts too have recognised the role that confidentiality plays in society both on an individual and general level:

[Confidentiality] is crucial not only to respect the sense of privacy of a patient but also to preserve his or her confidence in the medical profession and in the health services in general. Without such protection, those in need of medical assistance may be deterred from revealing such information of a personal and intimate nature as may be necessary in order to receive appropriate treatment and, even, from seeking such assistance, thereby endangering their own health and, in the case of transmissible diseases, that of the community.[3]

The legal basis for confidentiality

[3.05] Confidentiality is not only rooted in medical ethics; the courts have identified that there are circumstances where there is a legally binding requirement for confidentiality and respect for privacy and that the therapeutic setting is one such circumstance. The rule has been arrived at, in part, by the courts accepting that without confidentiality many aspects of commercial, professional and civic life, including the provision of medical care, would be impossible.[4] However, the requirement of confidentiality is not only based on the decisions of courts; it has other origins too, including both the Irish Constitution and European human rights law.

The Constitution

[3.06] Irish courts have recognised in a number of cases that a citizen has a right to privacy, which is derived from Article 40 of the Constitution,[5] although the right, as with all rights, is not absolute.[6] Flowing from the acknowledgment of a right of privacy is the implication that medical confidentiality is a practical expression of that right. In the *Kennedy* case (in which two journalists took an action against the State following the illegal tapping of their phones), the Supreme Court stated:

Though not specifically guaranteed by the Constitution, the right of privacy is one of the fundamental personal rights of the citizen… It is not an unqualified right. Its exercise may be restricted by the constitutional rights of others, or by the requirements of the common good, and it is subject to the requirements of public order and morality… [T]he nature of

---

2   Medical Council, *Guide to Ethical Conduct and Behaviour* (6th edn, 2004), para 16.1.
3   *Z v Finland* (1997) BMLR 107.
4   *W v Egdell* [1990] 1 All ER 835.
5   Article 40 of the Constitution refers to the 'personal rights' of the citizen without setting out explicitly what those rights are; referred to as 'unenumerated' rights, the courts have over the years recognised several such rights, including the right to privacy and the right to bodily integrity—see para **[4.03]**.
6   See *McGee v Attorney General* [1974] IR 284, which concerned the right of a married couple to use contraception. The Supreme Court was less inclined to recognise a right to privacy in the case of a homosexual relationship, at a time when homosexuality was illegal in the state—see *Norris v Attorney General* [1984] IR 36.

the right to privacy must be such as to ensure the dignity and freedom of an individual in the type of society envisaged by the Constitution.[7]

Human rights law

[3.07] The European Convention on Human Rights, of which Ireland is a signatory and which has been incorporated into Irish law by the European Convention on Human Rights Act 2003, guarantees a 'right to respect for…family and private life.'[8] The European Court of Human Rights has stated:

> [T]he protection of personal data, not least medical data, is of fundamental importance to a person's enjoyment of his or her right to respect for private and family life as guaranteed by Article 8 of the Convention. Respecting the confidentiality of health data is a vital principle in the legal systems of all the contracting parties to the Convention.[9]

This adds a human rights dimension to the obligation to maintain confidentiality, although as with the non-absolute nature of the constitutional right to privacy, there are analogous limitations to the rights derived from the Convention on Human Rights. It is open to a state to infringe the right to privacy where that infringement is 'in accordance with the law and necessary in a democratic society':[10] so, in the case of *TV v Finland*, the European Court of Human Rights regarded as justified the disclosure of a prisoner's HIV status to prison staff.[11]

[3.08] More generally, and as is discussed more fully in the section that follows, courts have also recognised a 'public interest' in trying to maximise confidentiality within the practitioner–patient relationship. As we will see, it is only where there is a countervailing 'public interest' outweighing the presumption of confidentiality that confidentiality can and will be set aside.

The courts and confidentiality

[3.09] We need first to examine how the courts define and regard the obligation of confidentiality in the clinical setting. In *Hunter v Mann*[12] an English court offered this summary of the duty of confidentiality:

> [I]n common with other professional men (*sic.*)…the doctor is under a duty not to disclose [voluntarily], without the consent of his patient, information which he, the doctor, has gained in his professional capacity.

In that case, police sought information from a doctor as part of an investigation into a road traffic accident. As well as outlining the general duty of confidence above, the court reasoned that in circumstances where disclosure could aid in the detection of a crime, a doctor could breach confidence.[13] The court also observed that where a patient

---

7   *Kennedy v Ireland* [1987] IR 587 at 592 per Hamilton P.
8   Article 8(1) of the European Convention on Human Rights.
9   *Z v Finland* (1997) 45 BMLR 107.
10 Article 8(2) of the European Convention on Human Rights.
11 *TV v Finland* No 21780/93 76 ADR 140.
12 *Hunter v Mann* [1974] QB 767.
13 In Northern Ireland there is a legal obligation on doctors to disclose information where they believe that a patient they have treated may have been involved in criminal (contd/)

consents to disclosure, the doctor's obligation of confidentiality is lifted. We will see below that consent and the prevention of crime are just two of a number of mechanisms that operate to permit clinicians to breach the obligation of confidentiality normally owed to patients.

When does a matter become confidential?

[3.10] The courts recognise that not every interaction between parties is confidential and, similarly, not every transaction between a doctor and patient may be deemed 'confidential'. While it might be prudent to err on the side of discretion, it may nonetheless be the case that a cross-table conversation in a crowded pub between a doctor and her friend on the subject of that friend's health would probably not necessitate the same regard for confidentiality as a situation where the same friend consulted the same physician in her surgery. Broadly speaking, the courts have recognised that there are three elements to deciding whether a matter is confidential.

(a) Nature of the information

[3.11] One judge offered the opinion (in the context of commercial secrets rather than medical confidentiality, although the principle is precisely the same) that in order to be confidential the subject-matter of any interaction must have 'the necessary quality of confidence about it, namely, it must not be something which is public property and public knowledge.'[14]

(b) Nature of the encounter

[3.12] According to another case concerning commercial secrets, the test of whether something is confidential is whether 'a reasonable man in the shoes of the recipient of the information would have realised that upon reasonable grounds the information was being given to him in confidence.'[15]

(c) Nature of any disclosure

[3.13] The last feature of a confidential encounter is that any disclosure of the confidential information, gleaned in a confidential setting, would be 'unconscionable' or unfair in some way. In the case of *AG v Guardian Newspapers*,[16] the court stated:

> [A] duty of confidence arises when confidential information comes to the knowledge of a person (the confidant) in circumstances where he has notice, or is held to have agreed, that the information is confidential, with the effect that it would be just *in all the circumstances* that he should be precluded from disclosing the information to others [*italics* added].

---

[13] (\contd) In Northern Ireland there is a legal obligation on doctors to disclose information where they believe that a patient they have treated may have been involved in criminal—and particularly terrorist—activity: Criminal Law Act (NI) 1967, s 5(1); Prevention of Terrorism (Temporary Provisions) Act 1976.

[14] *Saltman Engineering Co v Campbell Engineering Co* (1948) 65 RPC 203, 251.

[15] *Coco v AN Clark (Engineering) Ltd* [1969] RPC 41.

[16] *AG v Guardian Newspapers* [1988] 3 All ER 545, per Lord Goff.

A combination of these three elements yields a good working definition of when a matter is confidential:

- The information should be confidential in nature;

- The circumstances should imply confidentiality;

- There would be an element of unfairness or unconscionability about disclosure of the information.

The duty of confidentiality extends to information concerning the patient that the practitioner learns from sources other than the patient (for example, from a referral letter) while acting in her capacity of caring for the patient.[17]

Confidentiality and anonymous information

[3.14] Information that is not capable of identifying someone is not normally regarded as being confidential. Anonymous data incapable of identifying any patient or patients may be released, processed or even sold without being a breach of confidentiality, so long as all necessary steps have been taken to safeguard the privacy of the individuals to whom the information relates.[18] The legal test is not whether the information is said to be anonymous but whether in fact and in effect it really *is* anonymous. Information that is theoretically anonymous (in that nothing explicitly identifies the person to whom the information relates) may nonetheless have the practical effect of making it possible to identify a person and may therefore require protection or restriction in some way. For example, to disclose information that a medical condition affects a member of a small community (such as an inhabitant of a particular village or a dentist in a particular hospital), even without specifically naming the individual, could be tantamount to infringing that person's right to confidentiality because of the ease with which that individual might be identified within that community (see Case Study 3.1).

Case study 3.1 Anonymous or not?

One example of 'anonymous' information that was held to be confidential is a case in which the courts protected two HIV-infected doctors when their right to privacy was threatened by newspapers.[19] The papers planned to identify the doctors or, failing that, to identify hospitals in which they had worked as well as the dates of their employment in those hospitals. However, the courts refused to permit either course of action: to detail hospitals in which the doctors had worked together with the dates they worked there would effectively lead to their identification.

This broad principle that nominally anonymous information should be examined for its capacity to identify and therefore breach confidentiality, applies to any clinical information obtained in confidence. The obligation to maintain confidentiality over

---

[17] Gurry, *Breach of Confidence* (Clarendon Press, Oxford, 1984), 148–149.

[18] *R v Department of Health, ex parte Source Informatics Ltd* [2000] 1 All ER 786. This principle is also adopted in the Data Protection Acts 1988 to 2003, s 5(1)(h); see Ch 5 'Clinical Records and Prescribing' para **[5.32]**ff.

[19] *X v Y* [1988] 2 All ER 648.

clinical information only extends insofar as that information has the potential to identify the patient to whom it relates.

Who is bound by the duty of confidentiality?

[3.15] Confidentiality is the patient's prerogative. A patient may, after a consultation with a doctor, go straight out and discuss every detail of the consultation and nothing of consequence will flow from that disclosure. Conversely, a doctor who did the same thing would be guilty of a breach of confidence; the onus of preserving confidentiality is not bilateral.

A distinction between confidentiality and 'legal privilege'

[3.16] There is an apparent comparison to be made between confidentiality and legal or sacerdotal[20] privilege, but the comparison is apparent rather than real. 'Privilege' describes the fact that a consultation with a lawyer or confession with a priest is exempt (or 'privileged') from being used as evidence in a courtroom. It is true that privilege does not irrevocably bind the client or penitent, in the same way as the confidentiality of the therapeutic relationship does not bind the patient. The client or the parishioner cannot be compelled to testify about consulting with his lawyer or priest, but if he decides to do so there is nothing that the lawyer or priest can do to muzzle him. Similarly, the cloak of confidence that covers the doctor and patient in consultation is the patient's to set aside as he wishes, in spite of any protestations that the obligation of confidentiality should cover both parties to the consultation.[21]

[3.17] However, the comparisons stop at the unilateral quality shared by confidentiality and privilege, because the confidential clinical encounter is not exempt from being used in evidence in legal proceedings. The clinical encounter is not privileged; a court can, and will if it deems it necessary, order a doctor to disclose material relevant to legal proceedings that arose in the therapeutic context notwithstanding the fact that the information would otherwise be considered confidential.[22]

---

[20] Of or relating to the priesthood; confessional secrecy, for example.

[21] *Johnson v Church of Scientology* (30 April 1999, unreported), HC. Note that in this case, sacerdotal privilege was found not to apply to the Church of Scientology.

[22] The Eleventh Report of the UK Criminal Law Revision Committee (1972) considered recommending that the doctor–patient relationship should be made legally privileged; however, the idea was rejected and the Committee concluded that:

> For example, it would be a scandal if a criminal who had been injured when blowing a safe or committing a robbery could prevent the doctor who had attended him from revealing what the criminal told him about how he came by his injury.

The Committee did propose limiting the application of legal privilege to psychiatrists alone, but that idea too was shelved. In some jurisdictions the therapeutic relationship between psychoanalyst and client is privileged: see O'Leary, 'A Privilege for Psychotherapy' Bar Review 12(1) & 12(2).

Quick Reference Guide 3.1

The obligation of confidentiality

❖   Confidentiality is enshrined in the ethics of clinical practice but it is also a legal obligation.

❖   Confidentiality in Ireland is based on the decisions of the courts, the Irish Constitution and human rights law.

❖   A matter is confidential when:

      o   it concerns information that is – by its very nature – confidential

      o   is transmitted in circumstances that suggest a desire for confidentiality and

      o   it would be wrong or unconscionable for that information to be disclosed

❖   Confidentiality extends not only to what the patient tells the practitioner but also to information the practitioner receives from other sources when acting as the patient's health carer .

❖   Where information is incapable of identifying an individual then the release of that anonymous information does not breach the identity of the people to whom it relates.

❖   The obligation of confidentiality binds only the practitioner and not the patient.

Breaching confidentiality

[3.18] We observed above that legal authorities grounding the right of confidentiality concur that the right is not an absolute one. The court in *Hunter v Mann*[23] drew attention to the fact that a patient might consent to disclosure; both the Irish Constitution and the Convention on Human Rights have been explicitly interpreted as affording only a limited right to privacy that must give way where necessary for the operation of a just and democratic society. In this section we examine the lifting of the veil in confidentiality in two discrete contexts: first, where the patient gives his consent; and secondly, those scenarios in which confidentiality may be breached in the absence of patient consent.

Disclosing confidences with consent

[3.19] When consent is given to the disclosure of confidential information, then the obligation of confidentiality no longer applies; it is atomised. As we have already observed, consent binds the doctor, but not the patient, and if the patient wishes his doctor to disclose confidential medical information (for example, for the purposes of obtaining life insurance), then the clinician is free to do so. However, there are three important caveats that are as much to do with common sense as law:

(a)   It should be clearly understood between patient and practitioner precisely what information is to be released;

(b)   It should be clearly understood to whom that information is to be released;

(c)   The consent of the patient to disclosure should be recorded.

---

[23]   *Hunter v Mann* [1974] QB 767.

Oral consent by the patient to the release of otherwise confidential information is adequate and sufficient, but it is generally preferable (and a more permanent and reliable record than human memory) to secure written consent.[24]

[3.20] There is often a presumption that consent to disclosure of confidential information is automatically implied when a patient is under the care of several doctors or practitioners from a range of disciplines. However, the argument may be made that even within such a team care arrangement, the patient's consent should be sought in advance for disclosure within the members of the team. The question of inter-professional communication concerning a patient whose care is the shared responsibility of several healthcare professionals is not explicitly dealt with in current Irish ethical guidelines. It might be reasoned that such inter-professional communications are exempt from the normal rules on confidentiality because they are deemed (by the carers) to be in 'the interests of the patient'; however, it is interesting to note that the UK General Medical Council is more circumspect:

> **Sharing Information in the Health Care Team or with Others Providing Care**
> 10. Most people understand and accept that information must be shared within the health care team in order to provide their care. You should make sure that patients are aware that personal information about them will be shared within the health care team, unless they object, and of the reasons for this. It is particularly important to check that patients understand what will be disclosed if you need to share identifiable information with anyone employed by another organisation or agency who is contributing to their care. You must respect the wishes of any patient who objects to particular information being shared with others providing care, except where this would put others at risk of death or serious harm.
> 11. You must make sure that anyone to whom you disclose personal information understands that it is given to them in confidence, which they must respect...
> 12. Circumstances may arise where a patient cannot be informed about the sharing of information, for example because of a medical emergency. In these cases you must pass relevant information promptly to those providing the patient's care.[25]

Disclosing confidences without consent

[3.21] There are a number of different ways of classifying the grounds on which confidential information may be disclosed in situations where the patient will not (or cannot) consent to that disclosure, but we adopt here the categories set out in the Irish Medical Council's *Guide to Ethical Conduct and Behaviour*:

> There are four circumstances where exceptions may be justified in the absence of permission from the patient:
>
> (1)   When ordered by a Judge in a Court of Law, or by a Tribunal established by an Act of the Oireachtas.
>
> (2)   When necessary to protect the interests of the patient.

---

[24] See Ch 4 'Consent' (para **[4.11]**) where the issue of written *versus* oral consent is discussed in greater detail.

[25] General Medical Council, *Confidentiality: Protecting and Providing Information* (April 2004) http://www.gmc-uk.org/guidance/current/library/confidentiality.asp (last accessed October 2007).

(3)   When necessary to protect the welfare of society.

(4)   When necessary to safeguard the welfare of another individual or patient.[26]

Broadly speaking, it can be said that each of these exceptions exemplifies a matter of 'public interest' or in other words an aspect of democratic civic life that can operate to override the usual presumption in favour of confidentiality. So, while there may well be a public interest in ensuring that doctor–patient confidentiality be preserved, there is also a public interest in ensuring, for example, that dangerously psychotic individuals who pose a real threat to others are not permitted to cause harm. In such cases, will the public interest involved in detaining such a patient, including the requirement that the doctor discuss the patient's condition with a hospital in order to facilitate admission, win out over the public interest in confidentiality? The rule of law, the preservation of life and limb, or the integrity of the fabric of society may be of such great public interest as to require (or at least to permit) the disclosure of information that would otherwise be confidential. We discuss in the sections that follow this balancing act (and it is, in essence, a question of balancing competing interests), identifying some circumstances in which this public interest modification to the obligation of confidentiality may occur.

[3.22] The area is somewhat complicated by the absence of a precise definition of 'public interest'. By way of limited clarification, it has been said that 'there is a wide difference between what is interesting to the public and what it is in the public interest to make known.'[27] So it might be concluded that the mere fact that a person holds celebrity status might not be grounds for disclosing that person's medical records while conversely a person who, by reason of severe mental illness, poses a threat to the public, might meet the criteria for disclosure.

[3.23] We examine in the sections that follow each of the four categories of exception enumerated by the Medical Council. It should also be pointed out that even where a patient articulates an express prohibition against the disclosure of confidential information, the exceptions below, sensibly and logically applied, still operate to override such express prohibition. Because the starting point of both the law and medical ethics is that confidentiality is the default setting for the clinical relationship, express refusal to consent to disclosure of the confidential information really adds very little to the status quo.

Exception 1: The operation of law

The law can operate in a number of ways to militate against confidentiality.

Litigation

[3.24] Once a legal action is in progress, a doctor can be compelled to testify, notwithstanding that the subject-matter of the testimony would ordinarily be confidential.[28] Even prior to an action being taken, or where a particular doctor is not

---

[26]   *Guide to Ethical Conduct and Behaviour* (6th edn, 2004), para 16.3.

[27]   *British Steel Corporation v Granada Television Ltd* [1981] 1 All ER 417 at 455, per Lord Wilberforce.

[28]   In *JF v DPP* [2005] 2 IR 174, [2005] IESC 24, Hardiman J (at 179) stated '… a plaintiff who sued for damages for personal injuries must be taken to waive his right to the privacy and the confidentiality which he would otherwise enjoy in relation to his medical condition.'

likely to be required to be a witness, it may nonetheless be desirable or necessary for one party to legal proceedings to have access to the medical records of another party. Often, consent will dispense with the necessity to seek a court order compelling disclosure of clinical records, but a court will, where necessary, order the discovery, inspection or production of clinical records.

Investigation

[3.25] During the investigation of a crime, the need to identify perpetrators might also undermine any claim to confidentiality over clinical records. As we have noted, that was the opinion of the court in the case of *Hunter v Mann*[29] where police sought a doctor's records as an aid to the detection of the culprit in a road traffic offence. The conclusion of the court in that case was that the balance of public interest lay in favour of disclosure in order to achieve the ends of the legal system.

Legislation

[3.26] There may also be express statutory provisions that mandate the disclosure of otherwise confidential information. The Infectious Diseases Regulations[30] place an obligation on doctors to notify public health authorities upon the diagnosis of certain 'notifiable' diseases. Although the notification will necessarily include the identity of the patient in order to assist with tracing the source of the infection and any potential contacts of the affected patient, it will not amount to an unlawful breach of confidentiality because of the statutory obligation upon the doctor. Similar obligations exist in respect of the registration of births and deaths.

Exception 2: Protecting the interests of the patient

[3.27] Precisely where the 'interests of the patient' lie is not always clear, but adherence to the principle of respect for autonomy seems necessarily to imply that where a patient is competent to do so, then he, rather than his doctors, will determine how his interests are best served. So, if a patient does not want information about him to be disclosed, even in his own interest (and where there is no other reason for disclosure, such as a legal obligation or to protect another important public interest), then that refusal must generally be respected.

[3.28] Examples of where confidentiality might be breached in the interests of a competent person who does not consent to disclosure are comparatively few. One set of circumstances might be where a person is the victim of abuse and, although capable of consenting, is so far under a spell of fear or duress that he or she will not consent to disclosure of the abuse. In such cases, especially where minors are concerned,[31] the lifting of confidentiality could be justified. It would also be possible, of course, to justify such disclosure (especially where the abuser in question was a threat to others) on the basis of the welfare of society (see the following section).

---

[29] *Hunter v Mann* [1974] QB 767. See also fn 13 above.
[30] Made pursuant to the Health Act 1947, s 29.
[31] See for example *Re C (a minor)(Evidence: Confidential Information)* (1991) 7 BMLR 138.

Exception 3: When necessary to protect the interests of society

[3.29] The elements of the balancing act involved in weighing competing public interests is especially apparent when considering the question of disclosure in the interests of wider societal welfare. A classic example might be the doctor who, although not specifically an occupational health physician working for his patient's employer,[32] becomes aware that his patient, who is a pilot, is suffering from new-onset epilepsy. Clearly the risk to prospective passengers (not to mention those living under an airline's flight paths) will justify disclosure.

Case Study 3.2 Disclosure in the Interests of Society

A psychiatrist was asked to review a prisoner by the prisoner's solicitors, who were planning an application for early release. The psychiatrist ascertained that the patient (in gaol for murdering 5 people and wounding 2 others) could not prudently be recommended for release, not least because of his ongoing interest in firearms and explosives. The prisoner's solicitors did not proceed with the application for release at that time. However, they did renew the application some time later on the basis of a new and more favourable psychiatric report and the application for release made no mention of the earlier doctor's report. Concerned that his findings were of extreme importance and that the prisoner might be wrongly released, the original psychiatrist communicated his concerns first to the prison authorities and then passed his report on to the UK Home Secretary (with whom ultimate responsibility lies for early releases). The prisoner, on learning of this disclosure, brought an action against the doctor alleging that confidentiality had been wrongfully breached.

In this case[33] the court summed up the balancing act between individual interests and societal interests that must take place before confidential information may be disclosed:

Although the basis of the law's protection of confidence is that there is a public interest that confidences should be preserved and protected by the law, nevertheless that public interest may be outweighed by some other countervailing public interest which favours disclosure.

Accordingly, in *Egdell* the court held that the very real threat to society posed by the mooted release of this prisoner, together with the fact that this threat had not been communicated to the relevant authorities by the prisoner's solicitors, justified Dr Egdell's decision to release the information to the relevant responsible bodies.

'Need to know' disclosure

[3.30] There was one other aspect of the disclosure in *Egdell* that ensured that it met with the approval of the court, namely the nature and scope of the disclosure itself. It is clear from the law on breaching medical confidentiality that even where circumstances exist to justify the fact of the breach, careful attention must nonetheless be paid to the manner of the breach. So, in *Egdell*, the doctor did not go to the media, but rather took a circumspect and step-by-step approach, discussing the matter first with relevant prison authorities before being directed to the appropriate highest authority.

---

[32] The special situation of doctors in the occupational health setting is discussed in Ch 8 'Health in the Workplace'.

[33] *W v Egdell* [1990] 1 All ER 835.

[3.31] The proper approach to the disclosure of confidential information without a patient's consent is best described as 'need to know' disclosure—only those who need to know the information should be told it and, even then, they should only be told what they need to know to effect any necessary steps arising from the disclosure.

Case Study 3.3: 'Need to know' disclosure

A doctor in New Zealand became aware that one of his patients was suffering from a heart condition that could potentially make him unsafe to do his job, which was driving a bus. The patient did not wish to stop driving and did not consent to any disclosure of his medical condition. Dr Duncan contacted the police to see about having the driver's licence revoked, but also discussed the patient with other patients and spoke to some other patients about organising a petition. A complaint was made to the New Zealand Medical Practitioners Disciplinary Committee (MPDC), which censured Dr Duncan, who in turn responded to being censured, not by appealing the decision, but by giving interviews to the national media in which he again revealed details of his patient's medical condition. Another complaint was made to the MPDC and at this second time of asking, Dr Duncan's name was removed from the register.

[3.32] In the *Duncan* case[34] the GP appealed the decision to strike him off, but his erasure was upheld by the New Zealand courts:

> ...professional confidence can only be breached in most exceptional circumstances and then only if the public interest is paramount...A doctor who has decided to communicate [confidential information] should discriminate and ensure that the recipient is a responsible authority.

Exception 4: Safeguarding the welfare of another individual

[3.33] The Irish Medical Council addresses one specific scenario where a doctor may forego the obligation of confidentiality to his patient in order to protect the welfare of another individual:

> Where others may be at serious risk if not aware that a patient has a communicable infection, a doctor should do his/her best to obtain permission from the patient to tell them, so that appropriate safeguards can be put in place. If the patient refuses to consent to disclosure, those who might be at risk of infection should be informed of the risk to themselves.[35]

The classic example of a serious infectious disease is HIV or Hepatitis C infection. A patient who is positive for either of these conditions (which are sexually transmissible) and who has a partner known to or identifiable by the doctor, should be counselled to advise the partner of the risk of infection. Where the patient will neither tell the partner nor consent to the doctor doing so, then the doctor will, according to these guidelines, be ethically justified in breaching confidentiality.[36]

---

[34] *Duncan v Medical Practitioners Disciplinary Committee* [1986] 1 NZLR 513.

[35] Medical Council, *Guide to Ethical Conduct and Behaviour* (6th edn, 2004) para 16.8.

[36] A similar situation may arise where a doctor (or other practitioner) becomes aware, in a professional and therefore confidential setting, that a colleague is suffering from a condition or addiction that might impinge on her ability to practise medicine. (contd/)

[3.34] Statute law also recognises the imperative for disclosure that might arise where a person poses a serious risk to another individual; the Data Protection Act 1998 includes an exception to the effect that:

> Any restrictions in this Act on the disclosure of personal data do not apply if the disclosure is … required urgently to prevent injury or other damage to the health of a person or serious loss of or damage to property.[37]

There has been no Irish decision on the subject of the disclosure of confidential information where there is a threat to a third party, but the issue has been litigated in other jurisdictions. In *Tarasoff*,[38] a student confessed to a psychologist/counsellor that he harboured obsessive feelings towards another student (Tarasoff). The psychologist did not communicate the fact of this threat to the college authorities or to the woman in question and shortly afterwards the girl was killed by the obsessed student. When the deceased girl's family pursued a claim against the university, the court, speaking the language of balancing competing public interests, observed:

> In this risk-infected society we can hardly tolerate the further exposure to danger that would result from a concealed knowledge of the therapist that his patient was lethal. If the exercise of reasonable care to protect the threatened victim requires the therapist to warn the endangered party or those who can be reasonably expected to notify him, we see no sufficient societal interest that would protect and justify concealment. The containment of such risks lies in the public interest.[39]

[3.35] The *Tarasoff* decision held that once a psychologist (and by reasonable extension, any comparable physician) knows that a client/patient poses a danger of violence to another, the psychologist has a duty to exercise reasonable care to protect the foreseeable victim of that danger. Discharging the duty may mean warning the potential victim, but *Tarasoff* did not impose an absolute obligation on clinicians to warn third parties of the risks posed by a patient. Although a warning may be the only practicable way of protecting a patient, it is perhaps better to think of a 'duty to protect', rather than a 'duty to warn'.

Can there be an obligation to disclose confidential information?

[3.36] We have already observed that sometimes legislation or judicial orders can compel the disclosure of otherwise confidential information and we have noted that the courts, in cases such as *Tarasoff*, recognise that clinicians have duties to third parties. But are there other circumstances where a specific legal obligation to warn might arise? Consider the scenario in Case Study 3.4:

---

[36] (\contd) In such cases, the doctor who became aware of her colleague's debility would probably be justified in communicating the relevant information to the appropriate committee of the Medical Council (assuming that efforts to get the affected doctor to seek help of to modify her practice had failed). See also para 4.3 of the *Guide to Ethical Conduct and Behaviour* (6th edn, 2004).

[37] Data Protection Act 1988, s 8(d).

[38] *Tarasoff v Regents of the University of California* 17 Cal 3d 425, 551 P.2d 334 (1976).

[39] Ibid at 442.

Case Study 3.4

A couple present to a GP. They intend to become engaged and to commence sexual relations, but they wish to be screened for serious transmissible infections. Both patients undergo HIV testing. The man comes back for the result of his test, which is positive. He is counselled to tell his partner. He does not do so and instead presents to his partner a forged negative test result. The woman, whose HIV test was negative, attends the GP's practice looking for the contraceptive pill, which puts her doctor in the position of being aware that she is planning to engage in unprotected intercourse with her partner. The doctor does not advise her that her partner is HIV-positive and she contracts HIV.

Cases such as this[40] point to possible circumstances in which an obligation to warn might be created; the American case of *Reisner*[41]reached a comparable conclusion. A case on behalf of a third party against a clinician for the clinician's failure to warn that third party would appear to necessitate the following elements:

(1)   the presence of a potentially serious harm posed to a third party;

(2)   the presence of a serious likelihood of that harm occurring;

(3)   the identity of the third party at risk should be known to the clinician;

(4)   it should be possible for the clinician to notify the third party.

[3.37] Where the third party is not foreseeable and/or identifiable by the clinician, then it is unlikely that a claim by a third party injured by a patient will succeed.[42] It should further be observed that, generally speaking, there is no 'duty to rescue' in Irish (or UK law); it is not clear whether, even if the criteria set out above were met, an Irish court would impose such a duty on Irish doctors, but where the person to be warned was also the doctor's patient, that would seem to increase the likelihood that a duty to warn exists.[43]

Confidentiality after death

[3.38] As has been observed above, the Medical Council's *Guide to Ethical Conduct and Behaviour* (among other sources)[44] asserts that the obligation on the practitioner to

---

[40]   *PD v Dr Nicholas Harvey* [2003] NSWSC 487.

[41]   *Reisner v Regents of the University of California* (1995) 31 Cal App 4th 1110. A doctor discovered that blood he had given to a female patient was HIV-positive. He did not tell her of this fact. She began a sexual relationship with Daniel Reisner. Two years later, the doctor told his patient about the HIV-positive blood and Reisner discovered that he too was HIV-positive. He was successful in his action against the doctor for the doctor's failure to inform his patient of the risk to her, such that Reisner would have had due warning.

[42]   *Palmer v Tees Health Authority* [1999] Lloyds L Rep (Med) 351 (CA). In *Palmer*, a negligently discharged psychiatric patient attacked a woman. However, on the basis that the victim was not one who could reasonably have been identified or foreseen as the victim of the attack, it was held that the doctors treating the patient had not been negligent in failing to protect the woman from the attack.

[43]   See Mason and McLaurie, *Mason and McCall Smith's Law and Medical Ethics* (7th edn, Oxford, 2006) para 8.38. Contrast with McLean and Mason (the same Mason!), *Legal and Ethical Aspects of Healthcare* (Greenwich Medical Media, 2003) 42: 'The probability is that there would be no legal obligation to warn the person at risk ...'

[44]   *Guide to Ethical Conduct and Behaviour* (6th edn, 2004) para 18.1; a similar stipulation appears in the Declaration of Geneva. (contd/)

maintain confidentiality extends even after the death of the patient. This is probably correct insofar as it is a statement of ethical principle, but the argument has been made that, as a matter of law, there may be few if any legal consequences of a post-mortem breach of confidence. The right to confidentiality (the argument goes) is a personal one and peculiar to the individual relationship between the practitioner and the patient in question. Therefore, the imperative of confidentiality and more particularly the right to sue for any breach of that confidentiality, dies with the patient. In the same way that only a living person can sue for libel, it may be the case that only the specific individual affected by the disclosure of his secrets would have a right to bring legal proceedings. In effect, therefore, after the death of the patient there may be no-one who could sue the practitioner for failing to maintain confidentiality relating to the now deceased patient.[45]

Quick Reference Guide 3.2

Breaching confidentiality

❖ Patient consent to the release of information relieves the practitioner of her obligation to maintain confidentiality in respect of that information. However, she may only reveal the information that the patient permits to be disclosed and only to the entity to whom the patient wishes it released.

❖ Regarding consent to the release of otherwise confidential information, that consent should be recorded in writing.

❖ Best practice suggests that the consent of the patient should be obtained for the sharing of information between professionals who co-operate in the care of a patient.

❖ In general terns, where a patient does not consent to disclosure, there are four recognised situations where disclosure of confidential information may nonetheless occur:

  o Where a law or a court demands the disclosure

  o Where the disclosure protects the interests of a patient

  o Where a disclosure protects the welfare of society

  o Where necessary to safeguard the welfare of another individual or patient

❖ The test for disclosure is whether the public interest inherent in the integrity of the therapeutic relationship is outweighed by a public interest compelling disclosure. In general, a risk posed to society or an individual that provides grounds for disclosure should be a grave risk.

❖ If disclosure of confidential information is made without consent, then both the information and the recipients of the information should be kept to the minimum necessary.

❖ If a serious risk is posed to an individual by a patient, and the identity of the person at risk is known, the doctor may be under a duty to the person at risk to breach her duty of confidentiality. In any event, she will be justified in doing so on the basis of the risk posed to society and the individual.

❖ The requirement to maintain confidentiality towards the patient extends – in theory at least – even after the death of the patient.

---

[44] (\contd) The UK General Medical Council takes a similar approach: see *Good Medical Practice* (London: GMC, November 2006), (http://www.gmc-uk.org/guidance/good_medical_practice/index.asp); and *Confidentiality: Protecting and Providing Information* (London: GMC, April 2004), (http://www.gmc-uk.org/guidance/current/library/confidentiality.asp) (both last accessed October 2007).

[45] See Kennedy and Grubb, *Medical Law* (3rd edn, OUP) 1081–3.

[3.39] However, the reality may be a little subtler. As some commentators have observed, some legal obligation (quite aside from any ethical or moral mandate) does probably adhere to the practitioner and it seems likely that the practitioner probably does continue to labour under some obligation to preserve confidential information about patients after their deaths. Firstly, even if a patient is no longer alive to bring a legal action, the Medical Council (or the relevant regulatory body for the clinician in question) may nonetheless choose to initiate disciplinary proceedings, if the actions of the clinician are contrary to the applicable code of practice, in the interests of present and future patients of the practitioner in question. Secondly, even if the patient cannot bring an action, there may be limited circumstances in which the family might be able to do so.[46]

Legal remedies for breach of confidence

[3.40] It is not clear exactly how one sues for breach of confidence in the medical setting. In one New Zealand case[47] it was successfully argued that breach of confidentiality could be construed as negligence, but this is not a line of legal reasoning that has prospered over the years. Generally, actions arising out of breach of confidence are equitable[48] in nature and, as such, the reliefs are likely to be equitable in nature and will include injunctions;[49] so, in the *X v Y* case,[50] the court granted an injunction preventing newspapers from publishing information that would either identify or be capable of identifying two HIV-positive dentists. Of course, if the breach of confidence has already taken place the damage may already have been done and there may be little practical effect to any injunction save for preventing a repeat of the disclosure. If any disclosure is not imminent or has already taken place, then instead of an injunction, one might more appropriately seek a declaration from the court that any dissemination of confidential information would be, or was, unlawful. Such a declaration would, in effect, prevent repetition of any breach already made and may also lay the grounds for an action in damages should the breach of confidence subsequently occur or be repeated.

[3.41] Whether damages may be sought for the fact of a breach of confidence is not clear, but any compensation is likely to be limited to that measured against any distress or injured feelings caused by the disclosure. Financial loss, such as loss of business, might also be compensated. In Irish case law there is little guidance to be found as to

---

[46] See Berg, 'Grave Secrets: Legal and Ethical Analysis of Post mortem Confidentiality' (2001) Connecticut Law Review 81. She identifies three categories of arguments against post-mortem disclosure of confidential information: (a) interests of current patients in knowing that their own information will remain secret after death; (b) interests of the deceased, insofar as the information is the 'property' of the deceased; (c) interests of third parties (possible genetic issues; emotional distress).

[47] *Furniss v Fitchett* [1958] NZLR: a doctor's duty of care 'must extend also to the exercise of care in deciding whether [confidential information] should be put in circulation in such a way that is likely to cause harm to another'.

[48] A branch of law dealing with legal obligations that arise in the interests of 'equity' or fairness.

[49] A legal remedy that—if successful—prevents the wrongdoing party from continuing with a particular course of action, such as trespassing or (as in the present discussion) disclosing confidential information.

[50] *X v Y* [1988] 2 All ER 648; see Case Study 3.1.

whether, or to what extent, compensation might arise for distress occasioned by a breach of confidence. In England, the Law Commission Report on *Breach of Confidence*[51] recommended that damages for mental distress caused specifically by a betrayal of confidence should be available. There has been no statutory authority given to this recommendation, but there is English case law in which such damages for distress have been awarded.[52]

THE LEGAL BASIS OF THE PRACTITIONER–PATIENT RELATIONSHIP

[3.42] In Ch 2 we looked at the questions of 'Who is a clinician?' and 'How are the professions regulated?', but the question remains, 'Who is the patient?' One obstacle to answering this question is the concurrent existence of 'two tiers' of healthcare in Ireland—some patients receive entirely (or substantially) free healthcare funded from the public coffers, while others opt to pay for their healthcare, typically through health insurance.

The funding of healthcare

[3.43] Although the policy and politics of healthcare funding lie outside the scope of this text, the way in which any particular healthcare transaction is funded has certain implications for the legal relationship between practitioner and patient.[53] The principal division in funding, as indicated above, is between publicly- and privately-funded healthcare.

Public funding

[3.44] In terms of public care, approximately 30 per cent of the Irish population is entitled to coverage by some aspect of the General Medical Services (GMS) scheme.[54] The main manifestation of the GMS is the 'medical card', which allows the bearer to avail of free primary care (general practitioner) services and (in most cases) free prescription medications. Medical cards are issued on the basis of either age or financial need. The majority of patients with GMS eligibility are also entitled to free medical appliances, as well as dental, aural (for example, hearing tests and hearing aids) and optical services.

[3.45] Since July 2000 all Irish citizens over 70 years of age are entitled to a medical card, irrespective of the state of their finances. For those under 70 years of age, cards are issued predominantly on the basis of financial need, although in borderline cases the presence of chronic disease (necessitating frequent medical attendances) may also be a

---

[51] Law Commission, *Breach of Confidence* (Cmnd 8388; Report No 110, 1981).

[52] *Cornelius v De Taranto* (2001) 68 BMLR 62. Damages were awarded on foot of disclosure of a psychiatric report (containing several potentially damaging statements) circulated without the patient's consent and the compensation was—in part—for 'injury to feelings caused by breach of confidence'.

[53] For some interesting overviews of the past, present and future states of the Irish healthcare system, see Leahy and Wiley (eds), *The Irish Healthcare System in the 21st Century* (Oak Tree Press, 1998) and Wren, *An Unhealthy State: Sixty Years of a Sick Society* (New Island Books, 2003).

[54] Donnellan, 'Medical card holders on the rise' (2006) Irish Times, 10 January.

factor in the decision to issue a card. The factors taken into account in means-testing patients for GMS services include age, household size, marital status and financial expenditure on accommodation (mortgage or rent).

[3.46] Furthermore, since October 2005 two levels of GMS cover have existed. The majority of card-holders, as noted above, are entitled to free primary care and prescription medication; a smaller number of people—on the margins of means-tested assessment for medical cards—are entitled to 'doctor-only' (GP visit) cards, which permit the patient to attend his general practitioner, but which do not cover medications.

[3.47] Other state-funded services exist for certain categories of patients: pregnant women can avail of mother and infant services for the duration of their pregnancy and immediate post-partum period and primary childhood vaccinations are provided free by the State. Certain diseases also entitle the sufferer to free or subsidised medical care, eg patients who contracted Hepatitis C directly or indirectly from the use of Human Immunoglobulin-Anti-D or another blood product or a blood transfusion within Ireland are entitled to GP, nursing and home-help services as well as counselling services, regardless of income. Persons suffering from certain chronic medical conditions may obtain without charge the drugs, medicines and medical and surgical appliances necessary for the treatment of that condition under the Long Term Illness Scheme. As with the Hepatitis Scheme, this is not a means-tested scheme.

[3.48] There is other state funding that mitigates, but does not eliminate, the cost of healthcare for all citizens. Since 1991 the provision of hospital-based medical care has been extended to the entire population. All persons, irrespective of income, are entitled to free in-patient services in public hospitals, out-patient clinic care and maternity and infant services. Nominal charges are levied for non-GMS cardholders staying as in-patients in hospital, but there is a maximum charge of ten billable nights per annum. Similarly, a charge is levied on non-GMS cardholders attending Accident and Emergency Departments, but that fee is waived where a patient has attended his general practitioner before coming to the hospital.

[3.49] The final state-funded scheme which mitigates the cost of healthcare for non-GMS card-holders discussed here is the Drug Payment Scheme—under this programme, any individual or family (including dependent children) pays a monthly maximum of €85 for approved prescribed medicines and appliances. Medical card-holders are already entitled to approved prescribed drugs and medicines free of charge, so they are not eligible for this scheme.

Private funding

[3.50] As we have observed, approximately 30 per cent of the Irish population is entitled to GMS cover, whether 'doctor only' or full cover. The remaining 70 per cent of the population must make its own provision for healthcare payment (subject to the mitigating schemes discussed above). Approximately 52 per cent of the population has private health insurance, which provides varying degrees of cover for patients to see doctors as private patients and to avail of either private hospitals or private accommodation within public hospitals.

Who is the patient?

[3.51] Has the previous section answered the question, 'Who is the patient?' Probably not. We have certainly identified categories of patient, namely private and public, but no more than that. The question of whether a person is a patient is not answered simply by reference to whether or not someone is paying for healthcare.

[3.52] In the UK National Health Service (NHS), the majority of people are registered with a particular general practitioner. In such a case it is relatively easy to say that a person registered with a particular practice is a patient of the professionals working in that practice, who may include doctors, nurses, physiotherapists and so on. In Ireland, it is less simple. True, some people are—thanks to the GMS 'Choice of Doctor' scheme—registered with particular doctors, but many more people are not attached in this way to any particular practice and, even if apparently attached to a particular practice, may well attend any other medical practices depending on circumstances. So, a patient may have attended Doctor A for a minor ailment in 2002 and Doctor B for another (or even the same) problem in 2007. Is that person a patient of either doctor in the period between the two consultations? Once he has attended the second doctor, does he immediately become a patient of that second doctor, or does he remain a patient of both? In an emergency, would either doctor—or both—be under an obligation to attend the patient? These are potentially complex questions. One logical answer is that, as an element of patient autonomy and the right to consent to treatment, it is the patient who chooses the doctor and not the other way around. It might be a more accurate reflection of affairs, especially in the sphere of private medicine, to talk about the 'patient and his clinician', rather than the 'clinician and her patient'.

[3.53] A patient might then be described, from this autonomy-centred perspective, as a person who seeks healthcare, or is found to require it as a matter of emergency or necessity. Put another way, it is a question of patient-orientated circumstances, either by choice or by necessity, giving rise to the practitioner–patient relationship. Similarly, the patient may terminate the relationship, as in the example of the patient who chooses to attend a different doctor or to seek a second opinion. The patient in such circumstances owes little or nothing to the doctor other than, perhaps, what courtesy might dictate. The doctor, however, continues to labour under an obligation to preserve the notes of consultations with her erstwhile patient and might still be the subject of legal action concerning the care documented in those notes, or may receive a request to send those notes on to a new practitioner.

[3.54] Of course, such a patient-orientated definition of the patient is not always true; a patient will not invariably be free to choose his doctor. A person may choose a particular doctor or hospital, but other healthcare providers will come 'bundled' with that choice. A patient who chooses to attend a particular hospital will implicitly be compelled to accept that certain nurses, radiographers, occupational therapists and other staff, over whom the patient has little or no real choice, will come as part of the patient's initial choice. Some healthcare is also delivered in a way that militates against choice; for example, public psychiatric care in Ireland is administered according to strict geography—only in exceptional cases will a patient be treated by a doctor or hospital other than the one with responsibility for the catchment area in which he lives. It is difficult, therefore, to say that patient choice always informs the practitioner–patient relationship; any particular relationship may be formed as the result of circumstances beyond the patient's control. However, the idea of patient autonomy as the primary determinative factor in the practitioner–patient relationship is nonetheless a valid and important one.

The practitioner–patient relationship in legal terms

[3.55] The State, as we have seen, pays for all or some of the healthcare of many people, while others pay for their own medical care. This can have an impact on the precise legal relationship that arises between the clinician and the patient, although it will *not* affect the broad legal duty that the doctor owes to take care of the patient.

When a person avails himself of free medical care, there is no direct financial link—and therefore no contract—between the doctor and the patient; rather, any contract is between the doctor and the institution that pays her. Of course, the doctor's employment contract will necessarily mean that she is obliged to care for the patients whose treatment is part and parcel of her job, but there is no formal legal contract between patient and doctor.

[3.56] Conversely, where a patient pays a doctor, either directly out of his own pocket or through the medium of an insurance policy, that payment establishes a direct financial link between patient and clinician and creates a contractual element that is absent in the 'free' public healthcare setting.

[3.57] The legal basis of the therapeutic relationship is ultimately a 'quasi-contractual' one, but the distinction that needs to be stressed is that the only direct and legally enforceable contract is between the practitioner and whoever is paying her, whether that is a private patient, an employer or a third party such as an insurance company. What must also be stressed is that this somewhat variable legal arrangement makes no difference to the standard of care that must be provided by the clinician to the patient. Simply because one is paying for private healthcare does not mean that one is entitled to, or will necessarily receive, better quality of care.

Practical effects of the distinction

[3.58] The legal difference becomes most apparent when something goes wrong. Because the paying patient has a direct contractual link with a doctor, then typically the doctor herself will be sued by the patient (we discuss elsewhere the issue of who it is that is sued when something goes wrong—see para **[6.52]**). The doctor can be sued for breach of her duty to the patient but can also be sued for breach of contract.

[3.59] Where the patient is a public patient and the doctor an employee of a body such as the Health Services Executive, then while legal action can be taken against the practitioner culpable for a negligent act or omission it is more often the case that the 'real' defendant will be the institution employing the doctor.[55] With the advent of Enterprise Liability and the Clinical Indemnity Scheme, the ultimate liability for

---

[55] The legal scenario where an employer is legally liable for the actions of its employees is known as 'vicarious liability'—see para **[6.54]**.

negligent acts and omissions occurring in public hospitals (even in the case of private patients in public hospitals) lies with the 'enterprise' where the negligent act occurred (see para **[6.89]**). Because there is no contract between the patient and doctor, there can be no question of the patient suing for breach of contract (in contrast to the private patient).

[3.60] The formal legal relationship between the clinician and the patient depends therefore primarily on the nature of the transaction that brings them into contact. In the case of the private patient, the situation is one of a legal contract between doctor and patient *as well* as the duty the profession owes to the patient to take care of him competently.[56] The patient pays the practitioner for her professional skill and she, in turn, is obliged to provide that care diligently and competently as part of the contract that is formed by the fact that the patient is paying for care. One reason why a direct contract may be important is that any contract may have specific terms that the practitioner will be compelled to satisfy over and above the regular professional duty of care[57] (or—more rarely—terms that limit the patient's right to sue the doctor).

[3.61] In the case of the clinician in the public system, such as a hospital senior house officer or physiotherapist, there is no legal contract between patient and doctor. Instead, as we have noted, any contract is between the practitioner and her employing authority. The legal relationship between the patient and the healthcare professional is instead the clinician's general obligation to provide competent medical care and to do no harm to the patient through negligent acts or omissions: the 'duty of care'.

Other issues

[3.62] A therapeutic relationship may also arise in emergency situations and not due to the express wish of either party. Nonetheless, the duty of the doctor towards the patient to diligently discharge her duty remains once she undertakes the care of the patient.[58]

[3.63] Finally, the legal relationship between the doctor and patient is sometimes described as a 'fiduciary' one. This means that the doctor has a duty of trust to protect the patient's welfare in every respect; the patient entrusts her with confidential information and with his health and the doctor must zealously preserve that trust. Some

---

[56] The expected 'standard of care' is discussed in para **[6.23]***ff.*

[57] In general, the outcome of litigation based on negligence will be the same whether or not a contract is present. However, one potentially relevant distinction is that it may be easier to hold a doctor to 'warranties' as to outcome that are made in the context of a contract: see for example *La Fleur v Cornelis* (1979) 28 NBR (2d), where the doctor said, 'There will be no problem; you will be very happy'; see also *Guilmet v Campbell* (1971) 188 NW 2d 601 (Mich SC) in which the doctor said, 'Once you have an operation, it takes care of all your troubles.'

[58] Note the discussion of the 'Good Samaritan' scenario in para **[6.11]**. In general a 'Good Samaritan' scenario arises where (i) the doctor has no prior notice that treatment will be required; (ii) the only treatment given is emergency treatment; and (iii) no payment is sought for the doctor's services.

judges take this fiduciary approach in interpreting the duties owed by doctors to patients,[59] but it is by no means universally accepted.[60]

Quick Reference Guide 3.3

The practitioner-patient relationship in legal terms

> ❖ Whether a patient is paying for medical care or not makes absolutely no difference to the care he is due from the clinician.
>
> ❖ In principle, the relationship between clinician and patient is most like a contract. However, there is only a direct contract if the patient is paying the doctor.
>
> ❖ A doctor who breaches his duty to the patient may be guilty of negligence but, if there is a direct contractual link between him and the practitioner, he may sue the practitioner for negligence and breach of contract.
>
> ❖ The additional direct contractual right of the paying patient is in general of little practical significance. It may be of significance if there is some element of the contract that explicitly changes the usual terms of the practitioner-patient relationship. One area where the existence of a contract between practitioner and patient may be relevant is where there is a specific promise made by the practitioner about the outcome of treatment.

---

[59] Especially in Canada: see *McInerney v McDonald* (1992) 93 DLR (4th) 415.
[60] Bartlett, 'Doctors as Fiduciaries: equitable regulation of the doctor–patient relationship' Med Law Rev, Vol 5, Summer 1997, 193–224; Kennedy, 'The Fiduciary Relationship and its Application to Doctors and Patients', in Birks (ed), *Wrongs and Remedies in the Twenty-first Century* (Clarendon Press, 1996) 111.

Chapter 4

Consent

INTRODUCTION

[4.01] Consent, except in unusual circumstances, is an indispensable precursor to lawful medical treatment or research and is therefore one of the most important issues in clinical practice. If a clinician examines, treats or operates upon a person without that person's valid consent in a situation where consent could and should have been obtained, then the doctor is committing an unlawful act. The law starts from the fundamental premise that almost all touching of another person is unlawful and consent is required to make that touching, which may be anything from a surgical operation to a football tackle, lawful. Consent and its mirror image, the withholding of consent, form the kernel of this chapter.

We examine the manner of consent, together with its essential ingredients, in particular the questions of 'capacity' to consent and 'informed consent'. We look at those circumstances in which consent cannot be obtained. We also examine what happens when consent is withheld and the reasons for which it can be withheld. In addition, we deal with some of the alternative methods for dealing with medical treatment of the person who lacks mental capacity.

WHY IS CONSENT NECESSARY?

[4.02] Consent is rooted in the legal and philosophical notion of autonomy, which in turn is the idea that humans are free agents with the power to reason and to take decisions. While definitions of what constitutes autonomy vary,[1] the best-known modern expression of the legal imperative for autonomy remains:

> 'Every human being of adult years and sound mind has a right to determine what shall be done with his own body; and a surgeon who performs an operation without the patient's consent commits an assault.'[2]

---

[1] See, for example, the distinction between 'principled' autonomy and 'sheer, mere' autonomy that is drawn in O'Neill, *Autonomy and Trust in Bioethics* (Cambridge, 2002).

[2] *Schloendorff v Society of New York Hospital* (1914) 211 NY 125 at 126 per Cardozo J. This enlightened view contrasts markedly with one nineteenth century judicial view: 'Your patient has no more right to all the truth than he has to all the medicine in your saddle bags.', Holmes, *Currents and Counter Currents in Medicine* (Boston, 1861). The law on consent to medical treatment can be traced back as far as *Slater v Baker & Stapleton* 95 Eng 860, 2 Wils KB 359 (1767). In that case, a doctor initially set a patient's femoral fracture in accordance with practice at the time, but at a follow up visit re-broke the healing fracture and placed the re-broken bone in a mechanical device. The judge concluded that obtaining a patient's consent was a custom of physicians and ruled for that consent should have been obtained by the physician as part of the duties of his profession: see Mazur, 'Influence of the law on risk and informed consent' 2003 BMJ 327: 731–734. As Mazur observes, it was only much later that the notion of information became linked to consent.

It should be noted that autonomy is not an absolute guarantee held out as part of medical treatment—in order to exercise automony, a person must generally be an adult and of sound mind; we return below to each of these necessary elements for valid consent. Once we accept that a person has a right to autonomy then the opportunity for others, including clinicians acting in discharge of their clinical duties, to interfere with that right is curtailed. It is consent that makes it legal for a person to encroach upon another person's bodily integrity. It would be obviously unlawful for a person to walk down the road and, without permission, to jab a needle into everyone she encountered, even if she is a medical practitioner and the needle contains a beneficial vaccine. But when a patient attends his doctor seeking vaccinations and gives consent to the administration of the relevant injections, the act of sticking a needle in that person is no longer unlawful.

[4.03] The constitutional right of personal autonomy in the face of medical treatment has been recognised by the Irish courts,[3] but rights are not absolute and the right to autonomy is no exception. We have already noted that it may be curtailed in young people or those who lack mental capacity; in such cases, consent may involve a balancing act between the rights of the person seeking to assert his right to consent and the need of society and the medical profession to try to serve the best interests of individuals and to protect those who are not competent to make decisions from the consequences of that lack of competence. In resolving this tension, as we will see below, the courts may be required to step in.[4]

THE MANNER OF CONSENT

[4.04] Consent can come in different guises—it may be express, which is to say positively affirmed by the person giving consent, or it may be implied by the conduct or silence of the person whose consent is required. Similarly, consent may be given orally or in writing. In general, the best permanent record of a person's agreement to treatment is express consent in writing.

---

[3] *In Re A Ward of Court (withholding medical treatment) No 2* [1996] 2 IR 79. The court relied on Article 40.3.1° of the Constitution. Article 40.3.1° stipulates that 'the State guarantees in its laws to respect, and as far as practicable, by its laws to defend and vindicate the personal rights of the citizen'. Article 40.3.2° contains an obligation on the State to 'by its laws protect as best it may from unjust attack and, in the case of injustice done, vindicate the life, person, good name and property rights of every citizen'. Finally it should be observed that s 4 of the Health Act 1953 enshrines a statutory principle of autonomy and freedom of religion in the case of health care:

> 4.—(1) Nothing in this Act or any instrument thereunder shall be construed as imposing an obligation on any person to avail himself of any service provided under this Act or to submit himself or any person for whom he is responsible to health examination or treatment.
>
> (2) Any person who avails himself of any service provided under this Act shall not be under any obligation to submit himself or any person for whom he is responsible to a health examination or treatment which is contrary to the teaching of his religion.

[4] It is partly to streamline mechanisms for dealing with those who lack capacity, and in particular mental capacity, that the Law Reform Commission has proposed legislation to help to deal with those who lack capacity: *Vulnerable Adults and the Law* (LRC 83–2006).

Express versus implied consent

[4.05] Consent can be implied or express and there is no legal difference in value between the two (just as there is no difference in value between written consent and its oral counterpart). However, as with written consent, express consent has a greater quality of certainty.

Implied consent

[4.06] If a patient attends his doctor with an ailment and undergoes an examination, it would generally be implied that he was consenting to be examined and, if appropriate, to be treated or, in other words, 'actions speak louder than words'.

Case Study 4.1

Emigrants to the United States in the late 19th century underwent vaccination against smallpox before disembarkation and one woman who had been inoculated during a voyage subsequently sued for damages resulting from alleged battery. The court found that in queuing up to be vaccinated and holding out her arm to be examined and inoculated, she had given her implied consent and therefore could not claim to have suffered battery.[5]

[4.07] Consent may also be implied in situations where treatment is a matter of extreme urgency. If a person is unconscious and bleeding heavily, there may not be time to enquire whether for any reasons, such as religious conviction, he is implacably opposed to blood transfusions and in such cases consent to intervention can be said to be implied.[6] Similarly, during an operation, it may become clear that an unanticipated problem has arisen that necessitates immediate treatment.[7] In such circumstances, courts are prepared to accept that there was implied consent to the additional procedure. The Canadian case of *Mohr v Williams*[8] discussed in broad overview when consent may be implied:

'If a person should be injured to the extent of rendering him unconscious, and his injuries were of such a nature as to require prompt surgical attention, a physician called to attend him would be justified in applying such medical or surgical treatment as might be reasonably necessary for the preservation of his life or limb, and consent on the part of the injured person would be implied. And again, if in the course of an operation to which the patient consented, the physician should discover conditions not anticipated before the operation was commenced and which, if not removed, would endanger the life or health of the patient, he would, though no express consent was obtained or given, be justified in extending the operation to remove and overcome them.'

---

[5] *O'Brien v Cunard SS Co* (1891) 28 NE 266.

[6] Note that some writers (see Kennedy and Grubb, *Medical Law* (4th edn, 2000) 591) argue that examples of the patient who is anaesthetised or *in extremis* are not really illustrations of implied consent, but of the necessity of treatment in the individual circumstances. Consent, they argue, is not an issue at all in such cases.

[7] *Marshall v Curry* (1933) 3 DLR 260.

[8] *Mohr v Williams* (1905) 104 NW 12.

Limits to implied consent – necessity versus convenience

[4.08] In *Mohr v Williams*,[9] the court drew a distinction that is both important and of lasting validity—there is a critical difference between a necessary intervention and a merely convenient one. Compare these two cases: in one, a surgeon discovers and removes a gangrenous testicle during a routine operation, although she does not have consent to do so;[10] in the other, while a surgeon is removing fibroids[11] from a woman's womb, he performs a sterilisation without her consent.[12] In the former case, the intervention was necessary, so the surgeon could rely on implied consent, while in the latter scenario the surgeon could not rely on necessity; the sterilisation could easily have been performed at any later date with the patient's full consent. It was, in other words, merely convenient to carry it out.

Express consent

[4.09] Express consent is explicit agreement on the part of the patient with the course of action that is being proposed. It can be given orally, but the preferable method of securing express consent is through the medium of the consent form. Different consent forms have different wordings depending on the specific context in which they are used, but there are many common features.[13] Signing a consent form is not the end of the matter, however; getting a patient to sign a form which states that 'the effect and nature of the operation have been explained to me' is a worthless endeavour if the effect and nature of the procedure have not, in fact, been properly explained to the patient. Courts have properly warned against scenarios where the consent is 'expressed in form only and not in reality'.[14] The explanation given to the patient must be adequate and the patient must understand the explanation. The question of how thorough any explanation must be is dealt with in more detail when we consider 'informed consent' (see para **[4.45]***ff*).

Limits to express consent

[4.10] As with implied consent, express consent is a finite concept. So, when a patient signs a consent form including a clause to the effect that he agrees to 'such further or alternative measures as may be found necessary', there is a limit to the latitude that is

---

[9]   (1905) 104 NW 12; see fn 20 below.
[10] *Marshall v Curry* (1933) 3 DLR 260.
[11] Non-cancerous, sometimes painful, lumps in the wall of the womb.
[12] *Parmley v Parmely and Yule* [1945] 4 DLR 81.
[13] The features of consent forms typically include: (i) the name and other personal details of the patient; (ii) the nature of the intervention to be performed; (iii) confirmation that the nature of the intervention has been explained (and sometimes that any of the patient's questions concerning the procedure have been answered); (iv) in the case of operations performed in public (and occasionally in private) hospitals, a caveat that the operation may not be performed by any particular surgeon; (vi) a statement that the patient consents to such additional procedures as may be thought necessary during the main intervention; (vii) space for both the patient and doctor to sign.
[14] *Chatterton v Gerson* [1981] 1 All ER 257 at 265 per Bristow J. This was also an early case in which it was affirmed that failure to obtain consent should generally be considered to amount to negligence rather than battery (see para **[4.12]***ff* below).

conferred by such a disclaimer and whether an act exceeds the express consent given very much depends on the nature and degree of any collateral act carried out under the umbrella of the original consent. So, in one case where consent was given to a muscle biopsy and 'such further or alternative measures as may be found necessary', that agreement was found to have given the surgeon sufficient discretion also to take a small biopsy from a diseased area of bone adjacent to the area of the muscle biopsy.[15] In another case, the court found that consent to laparoscopy[16] also included consent to the snipping of adhesions.[17] However, where a problem that differs widely from the original procedure to which consent was given and not requiring urgent intervention is identified, then the surgeon would be required 'to consult further with the patient and obtain further consent to the major operation.'[18]

Oral versus written consent

[4.11] Consent can be given orally and is just as valid as written consent. The obvious problem with oral consent, however, is that it is much more difficult to prove in retrospect that the consent was ever given, so that if, for example, a patient subsequently denies having given consent or has died and is therefore not able to testify to having consented, difficulties may arise. The practical approach, therefore, should be to seek to obtain consent in writing wherever possible. If that is not possible, then there should be witnesses to the oral consent and those witnesses should attest in writing in the patient's clinical notes to the fact that oral consent was given.

The consequences of acting without consent

[4.12] If touching a person without his permission is unlawful, it follows that the doctor who treats a patient without consent is breaching the law. But what law is being breached? If proper, valid consent is not obtained from a patient, then the patient has one of two legal actions open to him—battery or negligence—although it is the latter that has come to predominate in the law courts of Ireland.

Battery

[4.13] Battery[19] occurs when there is an intentional harmful or offensive contact with the person of another individual without consent or other lawful justification. A crucial element in the definition is that the offensive contact is sufficient—no actual physical or psychological harm need result. If a surgeon operates on an individual with perfect skill

---

15 *Bruschett v Cowan* [1991] 2 Med LR 271. The plaintiff suffered bone damage as a result of the biopsy being taken.

16 Using a camera inserted through the abdominal wall to examine the abdominal and pelvic organs and to guide surgical tools also inserted through the abdominal wall.

17 *Pridham v Nash* (1986) 33 DLR (4th) 304. Adhesions are small stringing connections that sometimes arise between organs or between organs and the abdominal wall. The court concluded that snipping the adhesions permitted a more effective laparoscopy to be executed.

18 *Pridham v Nash* (1986) 33 DLR (4th) 304 per Holland J.

19 Battery is a tort and a tort is in turn a legal wrong or disagreement that typically arises between private individuals or between companies. Negligence, defamation, trespass and nuisance are also torts (tort is an old French word for 'wrong').

and a textbook outcome, her dexterity and success are to no avail if no valid consent was obtained prior to commencing the operation.[20]

Negligence

[4.14] The more common remedy in modern law is that the practitioner who proceeds without valid consent is sued for negligence. As with battery, the actual conduct of the operation or treatment need not be negligent in any way; simply failing to obtain the required consent is enough to amount to negligence, although it is a necessary corollary of the law on negligence (as distinct from the law of battery) that harm must result to the patient.[21]

Why negligence rather than battery?

[4.15] In theory then, any failure to obtain consent could result in a charge of battery, but in practice courts in Ireland[22] have taken a policy decision that failure to disclose facts to a patient that are material to consent is negligence rather than battery. The reasons for preferring a negligence-based approach to a battery-based approach are many, but they include the fact that finding a doctor guilty of battery may appear to criminalise her when in fact no truly criminal act has taken place.[23] Accusations of battery are reserved for situations where there has been an extreme failure to obtain consent from the patient, for example, where the doctor has deliberately and/or fundamentally misled the patient as to the nature[24] or purpose of the intervention in question or the identity of the person carrying out the intervention.[25]

---

[20] *Mohr v Williams* (1905) 104 NW 12. In *Mohr*, the patient had consented to an operation on his right ear. When the operation commenced, the surgeon observed that the right ear did not require surgery while the left ear was diseased; although he did not have consent to do so, he proceeded to carry out surgery on the correct ear with all due skill. The court nonetheless found that the doctor's actions constituted a battery.

[21] See Ch 6 'Negligence', para **[6.07]**. So, in order for a consent action in negligence to succeed, the failure to obtain consent must have led to some harm, such as causing the patient to undergo an operation that was not required (*Appleton v Garrett* 34 BMLR 23 (QBD)) or causing the patient to undergo an operation with a poor outcome in circumstances where, if the patient had been properly informed of the possibility of that poor outcome, he would not have undergone the operation (*Rogers v Whittaker* (1992) 67 AJLR 47).

[22] And in England: *Chatterton v Gerson* [1981] 1 All ER 257. This line of reasoning was approved in Ireland in *Walsh v Irish Family Planning Services Ltd* [1992] 1 IR 496.

[23] Although a doctor who has committed a battery may also be guilty of the crime of assault and face criminal charges (see fns 24 & 25).

[24] An example might be the case of *R v Williams* [1923] 1 KB 340 where a man convinced a woman that the act of sexual intercourse was a procedure necessary to improve her singing voice. In that case, the woman consented but the consent was meaningless because she was so intrinsically misled as to the nature and purpose of the encounter to which she was consenting.

[25] In *R v Tabassum* [2000] 2 Cr App Rep 328, it was held that where a person lied about being a doctor, that would be sufficient for examinations carried out by that person to amount to an assault. However, misleading patients about status (in the case of a dentist who continued to treat pre-existing patients after she had been suspended from the register) was not held to constitute an assault: *R v Richardson* 43 BMLR 21 (CA). See Somerville, 'Structuring the issues in informed consent' (1981) 25 McGill Law Journal 740.

THE ESSENTIAL INGREDIENTS OF CONSENT

[4.16] The three most significant elements of consent, each of which will be dealt with in turn in the sections that follow, are:

1. Consent must be given (or withheld) voluntarily;

2. Consent must be given (or withheld) by an individual who has the legal capacity, in terms of age and mental competence, to do so;

3. Any decision relating to the giving or withholding of consent should be based on sufficient relevant information.

This last ingredient, 'sufficient relevant information', is a vexed issue and one that is woven into the fabric of the concept of 'informed consent'. As we will see when we look at informed consent below, the question of precisely what is 'sufficient' and what is 'relevant' and who sets the standard for the quality of information to be imparted to a patient is not always easy to resolve.

Voluntary consent

[4.17] Where consent is not voluntary, then it is not valid and the same applies to the refusal of consent—it, too, must be voluntary. In the English case *Re T*,[26] a woman required a blood transfusion. She was a lapsed Jehovah's Witness and initially indicated that she would have the blood transfusion. However, following this assent, she was visited by her mother who was still a practising Witness. After her mother's visit, T indicated that she no longer wished to have the transfusion. An application was made to the courts and her refusal to give consent was declared invalid on the ground[27] that it had not been voluntary because she had been placed under duress and undue influence.

[4.18] In institutional settings, such as prisons or psychiatric hospitals (or indeed in general hospitals, where the institutional aura surrounding the clinician can be very great), a person's 'voluntary' consent may be more apparent than real.[28]

Capacity to consent

[4.19] We have noted already the legal declaration that 'every human being of adult years and sound mind has a right to determine what shall be done with his own body...'[29] and this provides us with a departure point for a discussion of capacity. A person has the capacity to consent when he:

(a) has sufficient capacity in terms of age; and

(b) has sufficient mental capacity.

We examine each of these aspects of capacity in turn.

---

26 *Re T (adult: refusal of treatment)* [1992] 4 All ER 649.

27 The court also had doubts about both her capacity to consent, given her blood loss, and whether she had been properly informed by the medical staff as to the consequences of refusal (and the availability of non-blood treatment options consistent with the beliefs of Jehovah's Witnesses).

28 See *Freeman v Home Office (No 2)* [1984] QB 524. This case related to inmates in a prison 'consenting' to medical interventions and the court noted that the institutional context in which consent is given is important. See also McLean, *Old Law, New Medicine—Medical ethics and human rights* (Pandora, 1999).

29 See fn 2 above.

Quick Reference Guide 4.1

The basics of consent

> ❖   Without consent, medical treatment is unlawful, save for exceptional cases. Consent must be voluntary, informed and be given by an adult with sufficient mental capacity.
>
> ❖   Where there is no proper consent a practitioner may be, in theory, guilty of assault or battery and, in practice, guilty of negligence.
>
> ❖   Consent can be 'express' (generally in writing) or 'implied' (generally by conduct or when a patient is unconscious and in danger). Both forms of consent are equally binding, but it is easier to prove whether a patient consented when the decision is recorded in writing.
>
> ❖   Merely signing a consent form does not necessarily amount to valid consent.
>
> ❖   Consent to a given procedure – for example an operation – can be exceeded when it is *necessary* to do so, but not where it is merely *convenient* to do so unless the additional procedure is relatively minor. So if a patient consents to an operation (whether consent is express or implied) and during the operation another critical condition or relevant finding is discovered, consent would extend to dealing with the new condition as well as conducting the procedure to which the patient consented.

Age and capacity

[4.20] Irish law recognises that one becomes an adult for the purposes of consent to medical treatment at the age of 16[30] and one is an adult with full autonomy at the age of 18. However, there are apparent limits to the consent that is conferred on individuals aged 16 and 17 that have not yet been teased out in Irish law (although they have been considered in other jurisdictions). Accordingly, we examine separately the distinct, but in some ways similar, situations of the over-16s and the under-16s.

Over-16s

[4.21] Section 23 of the Non-Fatal Offences Against the Person Act 1997 states:

> (1) The consent of a minor who has attained the age of 16 years to any surgical, medical or dental treatment which, in the absence of consent, would constitute a trespass to his or her person, shall be as effective as it would be if he or she were of full age; and where a minor has by virtue of this section given an effective consent to any treatment it shall not be necessary to obtain any consent for it from his or her parent or guardian.
>
> (2) In this section 'surgical, medical or dental treatment' includes any procedure undertaken for the purposes of diagnosis, and this section applies to any procedure (including, in particular, the administration of an anaesthetic) which is ancillary to any treatment as it applies to that treatment.

[4.22] Two things may be observed. The first is that this is a right to consent only; there is nothing in the legislation to say that 16- and 17-year olds have the right to refuse treatment. In England, where there is an identical legislative provision in force,[31] the

---

[30]   Non-Fatal Offences Against the Person Act 1997, s 23.
[31]   Family Law Reform Act 1969, s 8.

courts have considered whether the provision confers a right on over-16s to refuse treatment. The balance of the decisions is that where a 16- or 17-year old seeks to refuse treatment that would, if given, be in the minor's best interests, then the courts will intervene and direct that treatment be given.[32]

[4.23] The second issue that arises from s 23 is the fact that the 16- or 17-year old's power to consent to medical treatment extends to 'surgical, medical or dental treatment' only. So, for the purposes of psychiatric treatment a person is only considered an adult from the age of 18.[33] The use of the word 'treatment' also creates a certain tension—where a medical intervention is not a treatment or a procedure in the commonly understood sense of the word, such as the prescription of a contraceptive pill, then does the 16- or 17-year old have the power to consent to it? The law is not clear on this point, although it can be observed that the English courts, when considering the identical English statutory provision, have interpreted the word 'treatment' in its widest sense.[34]

Under-16s

[4.24] The preponderance of legal opinion is that under-16s in Ireland have no personal power to consent to medical treatment.[35] The seed of this reasoning is the special position of the family recognised in Article 41 of the Irish Constitution,[36] which vests authority for decisions relating to the family within the family and therefore in effect vests decision-making authority with the parents. In *North Western Health Board v W(H)*[37] the Supreme Court found that in most circumstances and in keeping with the family's rights under the Constitution, the welfare of a child is best served by deferring healthcare decisions to a child's parents. The court held that there would be circumstances where, in the face of a grave threat to the welfare, health or life of the

---

[32] See *Re W (a minor)(medical treatment)*. The rationale is that, unlike in adults, the consent of the 16- or 17-year old is only one of three possible sources of lawful consent for minors: parents and courts may also give their consent and can do so when the minor's proposed course of action is contrary to his best interests.

[33] Mental Health Act 2001, s 2.

[34] *Re W (a minor)(medical treatment)* [1993] Fam 64 CA; the definition of 'treatment' was discussed also in *Gillick v West Norfolk and Wisbech AHA* (1985) 2 BMLR 11.

[35] Law Society's Law Reform Committee, *Rights-based Child Law: The Case for Reform* (Dublin, 2006), Ch 8. See also *Irish Medical Law*, Tomkin & Hanafin (Dublin: Round Hall Press, 1995), 37–44. Madden appears to be less pessimistic: see *Medicine Ethics and the Law* (Tottel Publishing, 2002), 490–491.

[36] Article 41.1 of the Constitution:

> 'The State recognises the Family as the natural primary and fundamental unit group of Society, and as a moral institution possessing inalienable and imprescriptible rights, antecedent and superior to all positive law.'

The position of the family and further questions of dealing with it in a healthcare setting are considered in Ch 7 'The Practitioner and the Family'.

[37] *North Western Health Board v W(H)* [2001] 3 IR 622, [2001] IESC 70. This case did not concern the rights of an older child, but the rights of the child within the family were discussed as part of the judgment. See Mills, *'PKU:* Please Keep Unclear?' (2002) 23 DULJ 180. See also the judgment of Keane C.J. in which he recognised the existence of the particular individual and personal rights of the child.

child, a court would displace the decision-making authority of the parents, but that the facts in *W(H)* did not warrant such a step. The court did not stipulate the circumstances in which the child's rights would take precedence over the parents' rights as decision-makers, but an example might be where parents were proposing to refuse life-saving treatment directed at the minor.[38]

[4.25] The *W(H)* case concerned[39] a very young minor and was a case where, as in child care cases (the other forum in which the rights of the child within the family are most commonly discussed) the dispute was in effect between the State (in this case a health board) and the parents. Such cases need to be distinguished from cases in which the minor himself wishes to assert his own rights or wishes the court to vindicate his rights (which he is capable of holding and articulating) against his parents and where the right to medical treatment that the minor wishes to assert is one that is consistent with his best interests.[40] Such cases appear to the author to be different and one possible outcome of such application to the courts (although of course, by no means the only possible outcome) would be acknowledgment of *Gillick*-type competence in Ireland. Irish legislation also recognises explicitly the need to take account of the wishes of the child,[41] as well as judicial recognition of personal rights inhering in the child,[42] lending

---

[38] 'Gardaí called as parents refuse transfusion for boy' (2000) Irish Times, 3 March. The child was taken into HSE care and the transfusion was administered. Such a case would probably be an example of the 'exceptional circumstances' described in *W(H)*.

[39] The *W(H)* case arose from the attempts of the North Western Health Board to perform a PKU test (to detect a congenital metabolic condition) on a child. The parents refused. The court concluded that while there were of course circumstances where a court would intervene to safeguard a child, this was not such a case: the testing was not compulsory, the condition was rare and it was evident, in any event, that the child did not have the condition. In such circumstances, even though one of the judges said that he was 'impatient with the attitude' of the parents, the court was reluctant to interfere with the parental decision, an example of the strength of the family's position in Irish law.

[40] We discuss below the case of the under-16 minor who wishes to take a course of action that is contrary to his best interests: see para **[4.30]**.

[41] Child Care Act 1991, s 3(2)(b)(ii) refers to the fact that in questions of care of the child, the courts should 'in so far as is practicable, give due consideration, *having regard to his age and understanding*, to the wishes of the child' [italics added]. While this law refers only to care proceedings, the deference it gives to the decision-making possibilities of the minor is arguably significant. The Child Care Act 1991 is reviewed in Ch 7 'The Practitioner and the Family', para **[7.42]***ff*. Also in the Criminal Justice (Forensic Evidence) Act 1990, consent must be given to the Gardaí obtaining body samples from people suspected of crimes. In the case of those aged between 14 and 17, consent must come from parents/guardians *and* the minor himself, again suggestive of the law's recognition of limited autonomy of the minor. The Criminal Justice (Forensic Sampling and Evidence) Bill 2007 also allows 12- to 18-year-olds to consent to the taking of intimate forensic samples (although that consent can be countermanded by the parents). Note also the requirement in Sch 1, Pt 4 of the Clinical Trials on Medicinal Products for Human Use Regulations 2004 to inform minors in clinical trial and to take account of their wishes in accordance with their capacity to comprehend the issues involved.

[42] *G v An Bord Uchtála* 1980] IR 32; see also Donnelly, 'Capacity of Minors to consent to medical and contraceptive treatment' (1995) MLJI 18–25.

at least some credence to the argument that decision-making authority wielded by under-16s is consistent with Irish constitutional principles.

Where parents refuse treatment of children

[4.26] In general, the younger a child is, the more certain one can be that the parents will be the decision-makers. It will be observed, however, that the sphere of autonomy granted to parents does not extend to taking decisions that will endanger the child, even when the basis for their decision would be sufficient grounds for the parents to refuse treatment for themselves (such as religious convictions). The rationale for overriding the parents' decisions in such circumstances was phrased as follows:

'Parents may be free to become martyrs themselves, but it does not follow that they are free in identical circumstances to make martyrs of their children beforselves.'[43]

Where parents differ on treatment of minors

[4.27] The capacity of each parent to exert his or her will over treatment decisions relating to children may become relevant where parents disagree over a proposed course of treatment for a minor. Where parents are not married or do not otherwise shared joint guardianship of a minor, then it will generally be the parent who is the guardian of the minor whose wishes prevail, assuming that the decision does not fall foul of the caveats set out in *W(H) v North Western Health Board* (see para **[4.24]**). Where parents who do share guardianship differ in their wishes for treatment of their child, then it appears likely that it is the wishes of the parent whose approach to treatment is more consistent with the minor's best interest that will prevail.[44]

Gillick competence

[4.28] *Gillick* competence is the shorthand term for the capacity of the mature under-16 to consent to medical treatment and its origins were discernable in English law for some time before the decision in the *Gillick* case was decided.[45] *Gillick v West Norfolk and Wisbech AHA*[46] concerned a mother's attempts to seek a declaration that her children

---

[43] *Prince v Massachusetts* (1944) 321 US 158 at 170 per Rutledge J. Note, however, the decision of the European Court of Human Rights in *Glass v UK* [2004] 1 FLR 1019 in which the court found that it breached the rights of the mother for a hospital to decide not to resuscitate a (profoundly disabled) child against the wishes of the mother without having first obtained the authority of the court.

[44] See *B (a child)* [2003] EWCA Civ 1148, [2003] 73 BMLR 152. This English case concerned unmarried parents who differed about whether the MMR vaccine should be given. On the basis of expert evidence, the Court of Appeal upheld the decision of the High Court that the MMR vaccine should be given in the minors' best interests. Whether the same decision would be reached in this jurisdiction in the case of non-married parents is not clear: it might be that the decision of the guardian parent will always win out so long as it will not pose a serious harm to the health, life or welfare of the minor. Where the parents are married or otherwise share joint guardianship of a minor, it is submitted that *Re B* would be followed in Ireland.

[45] See *Hewer v Bryant* [1969] 3 All ER 578, 582 per Lord enning MR:

'[T]he legal right of a parent to the custody of a child ends at the eighteenth birthday [as was the case when he wrote these words; it is 16 now]; and even up till then, it is a dwindling right which the courts will hesitate to enforce against the wishes of the child, the older he is. It starts with a right of control and ends with little more than advice.'

[46] *Gillick v West Norfolk and Wisbech AHA* (1985) 2 BMLR 11.

(who were younger than 16) would not be prescribed the oral contraceptive pill without her knowledge or consent. The court decided that children had a right to consent to medical treatment and their conclusion was summarised as follows:

> '[T]he parental right to determine whether or not their minor child below the age of 16 will have medical treatment terminates if and when the child achieves a sufficient understanding and intelligence to enable him or her to understand fully what is proposed.'[47]

[4.29] In essence, the core of *Gillick* competence is the idea that a minor may give consent to his own treatment once he is mature enough to be capable of understanding what is involved. The *Gillick* principle has also been approved in Canada[48] and there is legislation in Scotland[49] giving effect to the principle. The full test established by the court in *Gillick*, to be applied before treating a minor for contraceptive purposes, is more complex than mere ascertaining of maturity and it is offered here for guidance:

(i) The doctor must form the opinion that the girl (although under 16 years of age) will understand his advice;

(ii) The doctor cannot persuade her to inform her parents or to allow him to inform her parents that she is seeking contraceptive advice;

(iii) The minor is very likely to begin or to continue having sexual intercourse with or without contraceptive treatment;

(iv) The doctor must form the opinion that, unless she receives contraceptive advice or treatment, the minor's physical or mental health or both are likely to suffer;

(v) The minor's best interests require the doctor to give her contraceptive advice, treatment or both without the parental consent;

(vi) Any advice on contraception that will lead to unprotected intercourse must be accompanied by advice on safe sex.

Limits to Gillick competence

[4.30] There are limits to *Gillick* competence analogous to the restrictions placed on the right of the 16- and 17-year old to refuse consent. So, while many jurisdictions acknowledge the *Gillick* competent minor's right to seek and to consent to treatment, they are markedly more reluctant to give full rein to that mature minor's decision to refuse treatment, especially where that refusal is of treatment that would be in the 'best interests' of the minor. In such circumstances, courts will more readily uphold the right of the parents or courts to give consent to treatment.[50] The overriding impression is that courts are happy to permit a minor to take decisions consistent with improving his health, but not decisions that would be injurious to health, welfare or life.

---

[47] Per Lord Scarman.

[48] *C v Wren* (1987) 35 DLR (4th) 419: in this case, a minor sought the right to undergo a termination of pregnancy against the wishes of her parents, who had refused to give consent.

[49] Age of Legal Capacity (Scotland) Act 1991, s 2(4) states that a child under the age of 16 has legal capacity to consent to any surgical, medical or dental treatment or procedure so long as that child is capable of understanding the nature and consequences of the proposed treatment or procedure. Note also the discussion at fn 41.

[50] *Re R (a minor) (wardship: medical treatment)* [1991] 4 All ER 177.

Consent and pregnancy

[4.31] The question of the pregnant woman who refuses treatment, where that refusal would place her life and/or the life of her unborn foetus at risk, is not one that can be categorically answered in the present state of Irish law. A woman who refuses treatment and whose refusal will inevitably result in the death of her foetus places a court in a difficult position—should they uphold the right of the foetus to life and therefore compel the woman to undergo treatment or respect the right of the mother to refuse treatment?[51] The courts in both England[52] and the United States[53] have reasoned that it is the mother's right to choose or to refuse treatment, even if such a decision is at the expense of the foetus she is carrying. In Ireland, the Attorney General has issued an opinion that it would be permissible to turn off the life support machine of a pregnant woman, but the matter has not formally come before the Irish courts.[54] Issues regarding the unborn child in Irish law are dealt with in greater detail in Ch 12.

Quick Reference Guide 4.2

Consent and minors

> ❖ For the purposes of medical, surgical and dental treatment, a person becomes an adult at the age of 16.
>
> ❖ It is not clear whether the 16- or 17- year old's right to consent also includes a right to refuse treatment and it is also not certain whether a 16- or 17- year old only has a right to consent to treatment, but not to consent to non-treatment inverventions (for example, perventative measures).
>
> ❖ In the case of under-16s, there is no Irish equivalent of *Gillick* competence, which is the right of the mature under-16 minor to consent to medical treatment. It is arguable that such a right exists in Irish law but the matter has not been determined by the Irish courts. The younger and more immature a minor is, the more likely it is that the parents will take healthcare decisions on behalf of the minor.
>
> ❖ In general, the right of minors (that is to say, all under-18s) to refuse treatment may be overridden where the treatment refused by the minor is one that would be in his best interests.
>
> ❖ Where parents refuse treatment of their children, the courts will intervene where that refusal by the parents puts the life, health or welfare of the minor at serious risk.

---

[51] Where a person consents to a clinical intervention (other than an abortion) that will result in intra-uterine death as a necessary, although undesired, corollary, the law will not interfere.

[52] Following a case which called into question the right of the competent pregnant woman in the UK to both assert her competence and to refuse a caesarean section (see *Re S (Adult: refusal of treatment)* [1992] 4 All ER 671), the right of the pregnant woman to refuse caesarean section was affirmed in *St George's NHS Trust v S* [1998] 3 All ER 673.

[53] *Re AC* (1990) 573 A 2d 1253.

[54] See (2001) Irish Times, 15 June, 'Brain-dead woman kept alive due to pregnancy'. Note also the case of a woman who was pregnant and HIV-positive and who refused to undergo treatment that would have had the effect of reducing the risk of transmitting the virus to her unborn child. Finnegan P advised her that if she refused to give birth in hospital he would have to make 'much more serious orders affecting her bodily integrity.' (2002) Irish Times, 20 July.

Mental capacity and consent[55]

Defining capacity

[4.32] Finding a workable and universally agreed definition of mental capacity to consent is not easy. The United States President's Commission[56] listed three elements they considered essential to decision-making capacity:

1.   possession of a set of values and goals;

2.   the ability to communicate and understand information;

3.   the ability to reason and to deliberate about one's choices.

[4.33] The English Mental Capacity Act 2005[57] states that a person *lacks* mental capacity 'if at the material time he is unable to make a decision for himself in relation to the matter because of an impairment of, or a disturbance in the functioning of, the mind or brain.'[58] The Act goes on to state that 'it does not matter whether the impairment or disturbance is permanent or temporary'[59] and that lack of mental capacity renders a person unable to make a decision when that person is unable to:

(a)   understand the information relevant to the decision;

(b)   retain that information;

(c)   use or weigh that information as part of the process of making the decision; or

(d)   communicate his decision (whether by talking, using sign language or any other means).[60]

[4.34] It has also been suggested that the required capacity is greater as the import and consequences of the decision in question grow:

---

55   It should be observed that patients may lack capacity to consent for physical reasons, eg extreme pain or for mental reasons that are not caused by a mental disorder, such as severe side-effects of medication: Raymont et al, 'Prevalence of mental incapacity in medical inpatients and associated risk factors: cross-sectional study' (2004) 364 The Lancet 1421–1427.

56   United States President's Commission for the Study of Ethical Problems in Medicine and Biomedical and Behavioural Research, *Making Health Care Decisions* (Washington, 1983).

57   The Act was based closely on English Law Commission Report, *Mental Capacity* (No 231, 1995). There is no equivalent legislation in Ireland although reform has been proposed and presented in draft form by the Law Reform Commission, *Vulnerable Adults and the Law* (LRC 83–2006). A Private Members Mental Capacity and Guardianship Bill 2007 was introduced to the Seanad in early 2007 but has not progressed at the time of writing (October 2007).

58   Mental Capacity Act 2005, s 2(1).

59   Mental Capacity Act 2005, s 2(2).

60   Mental Capacity Act 2005, s 3. This 'functional' definition of capacity was endorsed by the Law Reform Commission Report, *Vulnerable Adults and the Law: Capacity* (LRC 83–2006). The definition is derived from the English case *Re C* [1994] 1 All ER; [1994] 1 WLR 290, later approved in *Re MB* [1997] 1 FCR 274. In the former case, although the patient suffered from severe schizophrenia with florid delusions (that he was a celebrated doctor), there was no evidence to show that his condition imposed on his decision, in this case, to refuse the amputation of a gangrenous leg.

'When the consequences for well-being are substantial, there is a greater need to be certain that the patient possesses the necessary level of capacity. When little turns on the decision, the level of decision-making capacity required may be appropriately reduced (even though the constituent elements remain the same) and less scrutiny may be required about whether the patient possesses even the reduced level of capacity. Thus a particular patient may be capable of deciding about a relatively inconsequential medication, but not about the amputation of a gangrenous limb.' [61]

The preferred test of mental capacity is individualised and based on the personal capacity[62] of the patient who is facing the choice in question. What matters is not what the patient's diagnosis is, but what effect that diagnosis has on the particular patient's ability to make a particular decision. So a patient who suffers from a condition such as schizophrenia may have no difficulty in consenting to surgery in circumstances where the symptoms of his condition do not impinge on his ability to comprehend that choice, even if those symptoms do affect his thinking in other ways. It seems likely that this 'functional' or 'capacity' approach reflects the common law in Ireland.[63]

Practical effects of a capacity-based approach

[4.35] Examples of cases in which the presence of a mental disorder does not affect capacity to consent are legion. They arise in cases of ongoing and severe psychiatric disorder,[64] as well as in cases of fluctuating capacity. As an example of the latter, there was a US case[65] in which a woman who suffered from intermittent periods of confusion and forgetfulness was found to be competent to refuse to consent to an amputation because her senile symptoms (when she was at her most lucid) could not be shown to impinge at all upon her decision to withhold consent and she had, when lucid, refused the surgery.

The patient who is incapable of consenting

[4.36] Where an adult patient cannot consent to treatment because she is, for example, comatose, *in extremis* or suffering from a severe intellectual disability, then what is the mechanism for ensuring that treatment is lawful? In such cases a 'proxy' consent is required, a consent that stands in the place of the consent that would have been obtained

---

[61] President's Commission, fn 55 above, 60. A similar approach was adopted in *Re MB* [1997] 1 FCR 274, but the notion that capacity should be dependent on the outcome of the proposed decision has been criticised in some quarters (see Buller, 'Competence and risk-relativity' 15 *Bioethics* 93–109) and supported in others: see Buchanan and Brock, *Deciding for Others: the Ethics of Surrogate Decision-Making* (Cambridge, 1989), 62 et seq.

[62] This 'functional' or 'capacity'-based approach to competence to consent contrasts with the 'status' approach, whereby the patient's condition is determinative of whether or not he can consent. See Kennedy, *Treat Me Right* (OUP, 1988), 57–58; also Law Reform Commission, *Vulnerable Adults and the Law* (LRC 83–2006), 26:

'The status approach to capacity is evident in the Wards of Court system and in respect of enduring powers of attorney under the Powers of Attorney Act 1996, both of which involve a broad assessment of general legal capacity.'

[63] *In the Matter of a Ward of Court* [1996] 2 IR 73, [1995] 2 ILRM 401, although see fn 62 above.

[64] *Re C* [1994] 1 All ER; [1994] 1 WLR.

[65] *Lane v Candura* (1978) 376 NE 2d.

from the patient in the ordinary course of events to ensure that treatment is lawful. There is no automatic right of spouses or next of kin to consent to treatment on behalf of an incompetent adult (although such power may be purportedly conferred upon them by a mechanism such as an 'advance statement').[66] Where a patient cannot consent at all, then the decision may fall to the courts.[67] But the courts have, in reaching decisions, laid down rules that can guide clinicians in the delivery (or withdrawal)[68] of treatment in those situations where a patient is unable to consent to treatment. Broadly speaking, there are two approaches to the treatment of the patient who cannot consent:

(a)   a 'best interest' test (the test preferred in Ireland); or

(b)   a 'substituted judgment' test.

Best interests test

[4.37] Although the court in *Re A Ward of Court* was concerned with the withdrawal of treatment from an incompetent adult, it seems clear that it is authority for the proposition that a patient's 'best interests' would be the basis for the giving of treatment as well. Certainly English courts have adopted a best interests test to treatment as well as to the withdrawal of treatment.[69] We discuss in Ch 12 what is meant by the term 'best interests' when it comes to withdrawing treatment from the incompetent adult,[70] but we discuss here what the best interests approach means when it comes to providing treatment to the same category of persons.

[4.38] It seems clear from the discussion of withdrawing treatment in the Irish setting contained in the *Ward* case that in discharging the best interests of a patient, the decision is a predominantly clinical determination, but the wishes of the family should be taken into account and the decision should be taken (or will be taken, where the courts become involved) from the standpoint of a 'prudent, good and loving parent'. In England the courts have reasoned that previously expressed wishes of the incompetent patient, even if not of sufficient force to determine the matter, may also be factored into any decision.[71] However, in imposing treatment on an incompetent patient, further considerations come into play—the necessity or otherwise of the treatment may serve to

---

[66]   See Ch 12, 'The Extremes of Life II: the end', para **[12.32]**. Note also the recommendations of the Law Reform Commission relating to personal guardians as proxy decision-makers and extension of the role of the enduring power of attorney into the domain of healthcare decisions: *Vulnerable Adults and the Law* (LRC 83–2006).

[67]   *In the Matter of a Ward of Court* [1996] 2 IR 73, [1995] 2 ILRM 401: in this case there was a dispute over whether treatment could be withdrawn from a patient in a near-PVS (persistent vegetative state).

[68]   Ch 12 'The Extremes of Life II: the end', para **[12.09]**.

[69]   *Airedale NHS Trust v Bland* [1993] AC 789 at 868 per Lord Goff. English law has subsequently put the best interests test on a statutory footing: Mental Capacity Act 2005.

[70]   See para **[12.13]**.

[71]   See *Re T (Adult: Refusal of Treatment)* [1992] 3 WLR 782 at 787 per Lord Donaldson. Note also that the Supreme Court did not criticise the High Court for having taken into account evidence of what the incompetent ward herself would have wanted: *In Re a Ward of Court* [1996] 2 IR 79, [1995] 2 ILRM 401 at 415 per Hamilton CJ. Discussed in Ch 12 'The Extremes of Life II: the end' (para **[12.13]**).

indicate whether or not it should be given;[72] where it is not necessary (and where the treatment would be very invasive, as in the case of sterilisation of the incompetent patient),[73] there may be some hesitancy in the court assenting to the performance of the procedure. In general, too, best interests is taken to describe the patient's best medical interests although there have been exceptions. In one English case, a mentally incompetent woman was the only possible bone marrow match for her sister. Although becoming a bone marrow donor would confer no medical benefit on the mentally incompetent donor, the court held that the benefit the donation would confer on the sister (and the 'emotional, psychological and social benefit' conferred on the donor by her family's gratitude and her sister's anticipated survival) would suffice to justify the court authorising the operation.[74]

A competing view—substituted judgment

[4.39] The best interests test can be contrasted with the so-called 'substituted judgment' approach, which is the preferred mechanism for proxy treatment decisions (including treatment withdrawal) concerning the incompetent patient in the US. It arises when the court attempts to decide what decision would be made by the individual if he were competent. The court 'dons the mental mantle of the incompetent and substitutes itself as nearly as possible for the individual in the decision making process.'[75] The substituted judgment test is arguably 'less overtly paternalistic than the best interests test, since it attempts to extend the principle of self-determination to patients who are in fact incapable of making their own decisions',[76] but the difficulties of substituting one person's judgment for that of another, no longer competent, person are obvious.[77] Another issue is whether there is, in reality, as much difference between the best interests test and the substituted judgment test in circumstances where the former may frequently involve an inquiry (via the next of kin) into the values and circumstances of the incompetent patient.[78]

Where mental capacity is uncertain

[4.40] There may be circumstances where a patient's mental capacity is in doubt. Although conscious and capable of expressing himself, a patient may nonetheless, due to

---

[72] *Re F (Mental Patient: Sterilisation)* [1990] 2 AC 1 HL.

[73] In *Re A (Medical Treatment: Male Sterilisation)* [2000] 1 FLR, the court held that sterilisation of a mentally incompetent man was not necessary for a man in the same way that it might be for a similarly mentally incompetent woman (who would of course run the risk of becoming pregnant).

[74] *Re Y (Mental Incapacity: Bone Marrow Transplant)* [1996] 2 FLR 787, [1997] 2 WLR 556.

[75] *Superintendent of Belchertown State School v Saikewicz* 370 NE 2d 417 (1977).

[76] Jackson, *Medical Law* (Oxford, 2006), 205.

[77] See Elliott, 'Patients doubtfully capable or incapable of consent' in Kuhse and Singer (eds), *A Companion to Bioethics* (Blackwell, 1998), 452–462. See *Re Lucille Boyd* (1979) 403 A 2d 744 (DC Cir) for an example of the substituted judgment test in action. Substituted judgment is discussed again in Ch 12 'The Extremes of Life II: the end', para **[12.14]***ff*.

[78] See above fn 71.

the effects of a medical condition, the operation of a particular phobia,[79] or rapidly evolving clinical circumstances, be on the borderline of capacity to consent. In such cases, the presumption will generally be in favour of capacity, but there may be circumstances in which genuine concerns arise about the capacity of the patient to refuse. The Medical Council states that:

> 'A competent adult patient has the right to refuse treatment. While the decision must be respected, the assessment of competence and the discussion on consent should be carried out in conjunction with a senior colleague.'[80]

Where it is proposed that a patient will be treated in the face of a refusal and where there is uncertainty about the patient's capacity to refuse, a court may be asked to rule on the lawfulness of treatment in the circumstances. Although there is no considered Irish case law on the issue of applications to the court in respect of doubtfully competent individuals,[81] there is substantial guidance from the English courts that where it is proposed to seek a court order declaring a patient's refusal of treatment invalid, then that application should be made on notice to the patient and the patient should, where possible, be represented at the hearing of the action.[82]

Wards of court and other mechanisms for overcoming incompetence

[4.41] There are two types of wardship.[83] One, the bulk of such cases, relates to adults who may require the court's protection because they are mentally incapacitated and unable to manage their affairs. The second category comprises minors (under 18 years of age) who require the court's protection for particular reasons;[84] lack of mental capacity is not a necessary prerequisite for a minor to be made a ward. Any mental incapacity

---

[79] In *Re MB (Caesarean Section)* [1997] 2 FLR 426, 38 BMLR 175, the court determined that the existence of a phobia about needles sufficiently over-rode the patient's capacity to refuse a caesarean section.

[80] *Guide to Ethical Conduct and Behaviour* (6th edn, 2004), para 17.1.

[81] Although note the ex tempore decision of Abbott J in *Fitzpatrick & Ryan v K and Attorney General* [Record 2006 No 4427P] 21 October 2006 in which the judge directed that it would be lawful for a hospital to transfuse a Jehovah's Witness who had suffered a substantial haemorrhage following the delivery of a child; see also the ex tempore decision of Finnegan P in *JM v The Board of Management of Saint Vincent's Hospital and Justin Geoghegan and PM* (Notice Party) [2003] 1 IR 321, where the court directed treatment in circumstances where the patient had not clearly indicated whether she had consented to or refused the treatment.

[82] *Re MB (An adult: medical treatment)* [1997] 2 FLR 426, [1997] 38 BMLR 175; *St George's NHS Trust v S* [1998] 3 All ER 673. See also the discussion of refusing medical treatment at para **[4.65]***ff.*

[83] What follows is only a brief summary: for more information see O'Neill, *Wards of Court in Ireland* (Firstlaw, 2004); also Courts Service, *Office of Wards of Courts—an information booklet* (2003) available from www.courts.ie (publications section). Abolition of the Ward of Court scheme and the introduction of a new personal guardianship scheme has been proposed by the Law Reform Commission in *Vulnerable Adults and the Law* (LRC 83–2006). The report proposed a new Office of the Public Guardian. Similar recommendations were made in the Law Reform Commission *Consultation Paper on Law and the Elderly* (LRC CP 23–2003).

[84] The most common situation is where the minor has been awarded substantial damages by a court and has special housing or care needs.

giving rise to an adult becoming a ward may be either permanent[85] or temporary.[86] If a person recovers from the disability that caused him to be taken into wardship, he can then apply (on the basis of medical evidence that he can now manage his affairs) to be discharged from wardship.

[4.42] An application is made by a solicitor to the registrar of the Office of Wards of Court on behalf of (usually, but not always)[87] the family of the ward; the solicitor provides the registrar with all available details in relation to the medical condition, next of kin, assets and income of the person to be protected. Although it depends on the circumstances of the case, the formal application will usually be made by way of 'petition' in the High Court, accompanied by two sworn medical statements ('affidavits'). Only a single medical report or affidavit is required where the person who is to be taken into wardship is of limited means;[88] in rare cases (where there is no one to act as petitioner), the application may be made by letter to the Office of Wards of Court. Finally, where the proposed ward is a minor, the application is made by way of a 'summons'.

[4.43] Once the decision is made, a 'committee', which generally consists of only one person and is usually the family member who initiated the application (or a 'guardian' in the case of a minor) is appointed by the court to take routine decisions relating to the ward's finances, property and welfare. Contentious decisions can be referred to the courts and there are certain matters that specifically require the court's approval, such as a change of residence or consent to medical treatment (other than emergency treatment, which can be provided without the court's leave). Any disputes are settled by the court.

[4.44] In cases where a person who is now competent is expected to become mentally incompetent over time, as happens in dementia, the preferable approach may be to confer power of attorney on a person who will then take decisions on behalf of that person when he becomes incompetent. Advance statements are another mechanism of 'planning' for loss of mental capacity, and both power of attorney (which cannot currently be used as a basis for proxy healthcare decisions)[89] and advance statements are dealt with in Ch 12, 'The Extremes of Life II: the end', at para **[12.32]**.

---

[85]   This is what happened in *In the Matter of a Ward of Court* [1996] 2 IR 73. The question of whether the ward in question should have life-sustaining treatment withdrawn could not be decided by committee and was decided ultimately by the Supreme Court. This is dealt with in more detail in Ch 12, para **[12.09]**.

[86]   *JM v The Board of Management of St Vincent's Hospital* [2003] 1 IR 321. In this case, there was uncertainty about whether JM had validly refused a blood transfusion. She was admitted to wardship and the court directed that the transfusion should be given.

[87]   Other prospective applicants include the person's own solicitor, his doctor or the hospital authorities if he is a patient in a hospital.

[88]   In which case, the application may also be brought in the Circuit Court instead of the High Court.

[89]   The Law Reform Commission has recommended that an enduring power of attorney should be capable of permitting an attorney to make certain healthcare decisions on behalf of the donor where the donor lacks capacity to make the decision: (contd/)

Table 4.1 Consent and mental capacity

– The law has moved away from automatically classifying individuals according to their status and towards examining the individuals' capacity or functional ability to consent

– While definitions of mental capacity vary, the approximate test is whether or not a particular patient has sufficient capacity to take the particular decision facing him. It is frequently suggested that the greater the import of the decision facing a person, the greater the capacity required to take the decision

– Where a person lacks the mental capacity to consent to treatment, there are two approaches to making decisions on that person's behalf:

    o Best interests: where the court attempts to determine what would be in the person's 'best interests' (the approach taken in Ireland).

    o Substituted judgment: where the court attempts to establish what the now-incompetent person would have wanted.

– A person who is permanently or temporarily mentally incapacitated may be made a Ward of Court, allowing the court or a court-appointed person to take decisions on his behalf. A person who is likely to become mentally incompetent can confer a Power of Attorney on another person that is activated when the incompetence takes hold. The Law Reform Commission has advocated substantial reform of the law in this area, including the creation of an office of guardianship.

Information disclosure ('informed consent')[90]

Introduction

[4.45] The third element of valid consent (together with the requirements that it be voluntary and given or withheld by someone with the requisite capacity) is that the patient has sufficient relevant information on which to base his decision. This last ingredient is often referred to as 'informed consent'. It is not always clear what is meant by 'informed consent'—one judge has argued that the 'oft-used and somewhat

---

[89] (\contd) The Law Reform Commission has recommended that an enduring power of attorney should be capable of permitting an attorney to make certain healthcare decisions on behalf of the donor where the donor lacks capacity to make the decision: *Vulnerable Adults and the Law* (LRC 83–2006), para 4.32. However, the Commission also recommended that certain major healthcare decisions such as non-therapeutic sterilisation, the withdrawal of artificial life-sustaining treatment and organ donation should be specifically reserved for the High Court (para 6.72). The draft 'Mental Capacity and Guardianship Bill' annexed to the report advocates (instead of the wards of courts system) a system of personal guardians (to be overseen by a new Office of the Public Guardian) to operate as a more flexible proxy decision-maker in circumstances where a person may possess the capacity to taken certain decisions, but lack it in respect of others. Where an enduring power of attorney is activated and registered, any powers of an assisting decision-maker which conflict with those of an attorney will cease to have effect unless the Guardianship Board (which will have actual responsibility for the appointment of personal guardians) determines otherwise.

[90] A good summary of this area, up to and including the *Bolton* decision (below), is to be found in Gaughran, 'Informed Consent to Medical Treatment: A Case of Medical Negligence' (1997) DULJ 178.

amorphous phrase "informed consent"[91] should not be used at all. Many prefer to talk instead of the duty to disclose information. On this reading of matters, consent is 'informed' when a doctor has discharged her duty to sufficiently inform the patient concerning whatever intervention consent is being sought for. But this definition, although perhaps more helpful than relying on the content-free mantra of 'informed consent', is not without difficulties—what is the basis for a doctor's duty to disclose and how extensive does disclosure have to be? Put another way: how 'informed' does informed consent have to be?

[4.46] That the basic nature and purpose of a procedure should be conveyed to the patient is true beyond doubt.[92] But setting aside black-and-white questions such as the nature of the procedure, what about the greyer ancillary areas of information, such as outlining side effects, complications, alternative treatments or the possibility of pain? It is generally upon such matters that the question of informed consent turns. In the sections that follow we examine three areas:

- the standard of disclosure;
- informed consent in Ireland;
- the question of 'causation' in information disclosure cases.

How much information should be disclosed?

[4.47] If 'informed consent' is grounded in a requirement that a doctor disclose relevant information to a patient prior to treating him, then the next question that falls to be considered is the extent of the doctor's duty of disclosure. When has she given her patient sufficient information that he can be said to be properly informed? There are two competing tests for assessing whether a patient has been properly informed:

(a) the 'reasonable doctor' approach;

(b) the 'reasonable patient' approach.

The 'reasonable doctor'

[4.48] As we have observed already (see para **[4.12]**), the failure to obtain consent is generally regarded as giving rise to a negligence action. The essential question in professional negligence[93] is whether the doctor has been proved to be 'guilty of such failure as no medical practitioner of equal specialist or general status and skill would be guilty of if acting with ordinary care.' In other words, to establish negligence it is necessary to compare the conduct of the defendant doctor with that of reasonable comparable doctors. In a case of a lack of information giving rise to negligence, the issue would be whether the doctor disclosed less information than any reasonable comparable doctor would have done. This test, whereby the information provided by the doctor is compared with the level of information that doctors would ordinarily provide, can be termed the 'reasonable doctor' or 'doctor-centred' test.

---

[91] *Rogers v Whittaker* (1992) 67 AJLR 47 at 55.

[92] *R v Williams* [1923] 1 KB 340, see fn 24 above.

[93] Ch 6 'Negligence', para **[6.23]**.

[4.49] In the earliest 'informed consent' cases[94] the issue was always whether the doctor had provided such information as a reasonable, comparable doctor would have provided. If the doctor had given such advice or warnings as a reasonable doctor would give (and, just as importantly, if anything he withheld was consistent with reasonable comparable medical practice), then there was no negligence. This doctor-centred test is applied in England:

> '[A] doctor, bearing in mind the best interests of the patient and bearing in mind the patient's right [to] information which will enable the patient to make a balanced judgement must decide what information should be given to the patient and in what terms the information should be couched.'[95]

It should be observed that one corollary of applying negligence principles to information disclosure is that the important limitation imposed in the leading English[96] and Irish[97] cases on medical negligence apply. The mere fact that a doctor defends his actions by pointing to a reasonable body of medical opinion is not an automatic defence—courts can and will consider whether the professional standard relied on by the doctor is so obviously defective that it is insufficient to save the doctor from negligence.

The doctor-centred approach was for a long time (and probably still is—see the discussion at **[4.54]** below) the position in Ireland and we return to the Irish situation below.

The 'reasonable patient'?

[4.50] There are problems with a test that allows the medical profession, in effect, to set its own standard of information disclosure.[98] What of the patient who wants to know

---

94 *Salgo v Leland Stanford, Jr, University Board of Trustees* (1957) 154 Cal App 2d 560.
95 *Sidaway v Board of Governors of the Royal Bethlem Hospital* [1985] AC 871.
96 *Ibid.*
97 *Dunne v National Maternity Hospital* [1989] IR 91.
98 Whatever the standard for disclosure, there is always a positive obligation on doctors tell the truth. The Medical Council's *Guide to Ethical Conduct and Behaviour* (6th edn, 2004) stipulates (at para 3.3) that:

> 'A request for information from a patient always requires a positive response. In general, doctors should ensure that a patient...[is] as fully informed as possible about matters relating to an illness...They should be encouraged to ask questions. These should be answered carefully in non-technical terms...'

Cf also White, *Medical Negligence Actions*, 158:

> There is... no doubt that, when a medical practitioner is directly questioned by his patient concerning the risk associated with the proposed therapy, he must give a direct and full answer to the patient's questions unless he can rely upon a compelling therapeutic privilege; and the scope of the operation of such a privilege is necessarily strictly limited in the face of a direct request for information by the patient.

In effect, general questions may be answered generally while specific questions warrant more minute attention. It will only be in exceptional individual patient circumstances that the doctor's answers may be economical or circumspect with the truth. See also *Hopp v Lepp* (1980) 112 DLR (3d) 67: (contd/)

more[99] or who is, because of some special circumstances, in a position of needing more information before he can be said to be properly informed? In the case of *Canterbury v Spence*[100] a US court observed:

'Respect for the patient's right of self-determination…demands a standard set by law for physicians rather than one which physicians may or may not impose upon themselves.'

[4.51] A similar conclusion that it should not be up to the practitioner to set the standard for information disclosure emerged from the later Canadian case of *Riebl v Hughes*:[101]

'To allow expert medical evidence to determine what risks are material and, hence, [what risks] should be disclosed and, correlatively, what risks are not material is to hand over to the medical profession the entire question of the scope of the duty of disclosure, including the question whether there has been a breach of that duty.'

[4.52] The clearest exposition of the 'patient-centred' approach to information disclosure came in the Australian case of *Rogers v Whitaker*.[102] The court reasoned that it was 'illogical' that a patient should be expected to decide on a procedure based only on the information that the doctor was prepared to share and that the doctor could hide behind the opinion of her colleagues that the information provided connoted an acceptable level of disclosure. It phrased its decision in terms of a doctor's duty to disclose 'material' facts to the patient, subject to an exception called 'therapeutic privilege'. Of 'material' risks, the court said:

'[A] risk is material if, in the circumstances of the particular case, a reasonable person in the patient's position, [103] if warned of the risk, would be likely to attach significance to it or if the medical practitioner is or should reasonably be aware that the particular patient, if warned of the risk, would be likely to attach significance to it. This duty is subject to the therapeutic privilege.'[104]

---

[98] (contd/)

[Specific] questions must be answered, although they invite answers to merely possible risks. If no specific questions are put to possible risks, the surgeon is under no obligation (although he may do so) to tell the patient that there are possible risks since there are such risks in any operation. It becomes a question of fact how specific are any questions that are put.

[99] Indeed, what of the patient who wants to know nothing? Is there an obligation on doctors to inform the patient who wishes to nothing of the risks of treatment? See the discussion of 'authorisation' at para **[13.64]**.

[100] *Canterbury v Spence* (1972) 464F 2d 772.

[101] *Riebl v Hughes* (1980) 114 DLR (3d) 1.

[102] *Rogers v Whittaker* (1992) 67 AJLR 47.

[103] In the *Rogers* case, the patient only had sight in one eye. An operation was proposed that could restore the sight in her blind eye. There was an approximately one in 14,000 chance that the operation would not only fail to restore the sight in her affected eye but would also cause her to go blind in the good eye. This is what happened. The doctor, accused of negligence, brought forward evidence from reasonable comparable experts to the effect that they would never warn of the risk of 'reflex' blindness because it was so rare.

[104] In *Canterbury v Spence* (see fn 100) the court stated that '[a] risk is material when a reasonable person in… the patient's position would be likely to attach significance to the risk or cluster of risks in deciding whether or not to forego the proposed therapy.' (contd/)

So, in *Rogers*, the failure to tell the patient of the risk of losing the sight in her good eye, in circumstances where that would leave her totally blind, was held (notwithstanding that the surgeon followed the general accepted practice of reasonable comparable doctors), to be negligence.

[4.53] The therapeutic privilege, identified in *Rogers*, refers to the fact that a doctor may choose not to disclose material facts where there would be a serious risk of serious psychological harm to the patient if told of the risk in question. It is generally the case that therapeutic privilege will only apply in the most exceptional cases.[105] In recent years there have been moves in Ireland towards the 'patient-centred' test for disclosure and we turn in the next section to consider the Irish situation.

Informed consent in Ireland: shifting sands

[4.54] Withholding information from patients was not always anathema in Ireland. In one Irish case, a needle broke and a portion of it lodged in a woman's perineum during stitching after childbirth and the doctor elected not to tell the woman until she had recovered from childbirth. The court accepted that the doctor had the right not to tell the patient about the incident until she had made a recovery from the rigours of labour.[106]

The Bolton and Walsh cases

[4.55] The acceptance that there was in fact a duty to inform patients was confirmed by the Irish Supreme Court in two cases.[107] The logic of these two decisions (which adopted the 'reasonable doctor' test) can be summarised as follows:

 – failure to obtain valid consent is negligence;

 – the question of valid consent, including the question of whether consent is informed, should be judged by the standard test of negligence;

 – this means comparing the conduct of the clinician to a reasonable body of medical opinion held by practitioners of similar skill and specialisation to the doctor whose conduct is being questioned;

 – in general, if the practitioner's conduct in giving information to the patient is consistent with that of a reasonable body of opinion held by comparable medical professionals, then she will not be negligent;

---

[104] (\contd) In the *Reibl v Hughes* case (see fn 101), the patient was not told of the 10 per cent risk of a stroke that was attendant upon the procedure. This too was held to be a 'material risk' of which the patient should have been told.

[105] General Medical Council, *Seeking patients' consent: the ethical considerations* (1998), para 10:

> 'You should not withhold information necessary for decision making unless you judge that disclosure of some relevant information would cause the patient serious harm. In this context serious harm does not mean the patient would become upset, or decide to refuse treatment'.

[106] *Daniels v Heskins* [1954] IR 73, per Kingsmill-Moore J:

> I cannot admit any abstract duty to tell patients what is the matter with them…All depends on the circumstances—the character of the patient, her health, her social position, her intelligence, the nature of the tissue in which the needle is embedded…

[107] *Walsh v Irish Family Planning Ltd* [1992] 1 IR 496; *Bolton v Blackrock Clinic* (23 January 1997) SC.

    – however, if the court is not happy with the standard of disclosure adopted by the profession, it can set a higher standard.

While both of these cases confirmed that the duty to disclose information would be judged by the standards of the reasonable doctor,[108] they also brought two comparatively novel elements to the duty to disclose: the first related to the 'elective' nature of the procedure and the second to the obligation to warn of the risk of chronic pain. As far as the 'elective' nature of the procedure or treatment is concerned, it is clear that in Irish law the duty on the doctor to disclose information increases as the urgency and necessity of the therapeutic intervention lessens; in other words, a non-essential operation, such as a vasectomy or cosmetic surgery, demands a higher level of disclosure.[109] There is some uncertainty, however, as to what is meant by 'elective'. In *Walsh* (a case which concerned the duty to warn of the risk of chronic pain and impotence following a vasectomy) one of the judges stated that an operation was elective where it 'is not essential to health or bodily well-being.'[110] However, in the later *Bolton* decision[111] the judge stated that the plaintiff's surgery was 'undoubtedly elective surgery in the sense that it was a matter for [her] to decide whether or not she would undergo such an operation.'[112] This latter definition seems to muddy the waters for, according to one reading of those words, all operations are 'elective' and therefore attract a higher degree of disclosure. The apparent divergence can perhaps be resolved by the following logic: all operations where a patient is capable of exercising a choice are (even if urgent or necessary) elective to some degree and therefore mandate disclosure of relevant information as to benefits, risks and alternatives. However, this obligation grows as the operation becomes less of a medical necessity and more of an exercise of free will by the patient.[113]

---

[108] Although note that, in the *Walsh* case, O'Flaherty J seemed to base his judgment on decision in *Reibl v Hughes* (1980) 114 DLR (3d) 1 (although he referred to *Reibl* as being 'resolved on the established principles of negligence', which was not exactly the case). In the *Bolton* case, the single judgment of Hamilton CJ approved and applied the 'doctor-centred' negligence test of *Dunne v National Maternity Hospital* [1989] IR 91. The decision to apply *Dunne* principles has been criticised: White, *Medical Negligence Actions* (Oak Tree Press, 1996), 189–90. See the discussion of *Geoghegan v Harris* below (para **[4.58]**).

[109] *Walsh v Irish Family Planning Ltd*, 496 per Finlay CJ:

    '[T]he obligation to give warning of the possible harmful consequences of a surgical procedure which could be said to be at the other end of the scale to the extent to which it is elective, such as would undoubtedly be the operation of vasectomy, may be more stringent and more onerous'.

[110] *Walsh*, 509 per O'Flaherty J.

[111] The case concerned warnings prior to sleeve resection surgery of the bronchus. The issue was whether the surgeon warned of narrowing of the bronchus as a complication, which would require removal of the lung. This, in fact, occurred and the plaintiff required a second operation in which the recurrent laryngeal nerve was damaged.

[112] *Bolton*, 182 per Hamilton CJ.

[113] This assessment that some operations, even where a choice is open to a patient, are more elective than others seems to be borne out by the observation of Hamilton CJ in *Bolton* when, commenting on the failure by the defendant to warn the plaintiff of a risk (laryngeal nerve damage) that eventuated as a result of a second operation that was necessary to correct complications of an earlier operation, he stated (at 213): (contd/)

[4.56] The second issue to arise from the *Bolton* and *Walsh* decisions was the obligation, in the case of any elective procedure, wherever there is 'a risk—however exceptional or remote—of grave consequences involving severe pain stretching for an appreciable time into the future and involving the possibility of further operative procedures', to warn of that risk of pain 'in the clearest possible language'.[114] Although we have noted the difficulty with the definition of 'elective' above, it seems to follow from that discussion that the 'more elective' a procedure is, the greater is the obligation to warn of pain and, where a procedure is wholly elective, such as a vasectomy or a purely cosmetic procedure, the obligation borders on the absolute.

[4.57] Following these two cases, Irish law appeared clear: a doctor was obliged to disclose information on the basis of the 'reasonable doctor' or 'doctor-centred' test; the less urgent and necessary the operation, the greater the disclosure required and in elective procedures there was an obligation to warn of any risk of chronic pain extending into the future, however remote. However, the case of *Geoghegan v Harris*[115] changed the landscape somewhat.

Geoghegan v Harris and *Fitzpatrick v White*

[4.58] In *Geoghegan*, a man had presented to a specialist dentist and dental implant surgery was performed which necessitated the taking of a small bone graft from the jaw; this latter procedure left the patient in severe and long-lasting pain. At issue in the case, then, was whether he should have been warned of the risk of this pain. The plaintiff said he had been given no warning as to pain; the defendant argued that he had given the warning but that, even if he had not, the chance of chronic pain of this nature was so remote that he was not obliged to warn. The court concluded, applying the *Walsh* decision, that the defendant was obliged to warn of the risk of pain. However, in reaching this decision, the judge held that the rationale for warning the patient was that it was a 'material risk' of which the reasonable patient would wish to know. In other words, the court departed from the doctor-centred rule applied in *Bolton* and *Walsh*[116] and instead applied the patient-centred test of cases such as *Rogers* and *Reibl*. The judge stated that

---

[113] (contd/)

> The learned trial judge stated in his judgment that:-
>
> > "I am satisfied, however, on the evidence which I have heard that the second operation and its effect was adequately explained to the Plaintiff by Mr. Wood. It is true that he did not mention to her that there could be a risk of damage to her laryngeal nerve. Such nerve damage was in fact caused. But the risk of this happening was small and I do not think that every conceivable contingency has to be explained to a patient. It was absolutely essential that the Plaintiff should undergo a complete pneumonectomy and I think it inconceivable that any additional information would have had the effect that she would have refused to have the operation."
>
> Having regard to the fact that the operation was necessary, it was open to the learned trial judge to so find.

[114] *Walsh* 510 per O'Flaherty J.

[115] *Geoghegan v Harris* [2000] 3 IR 536 at 561–564.

[116] Kearns J was not persuaded that the entitlement of the court to set aside the standard of reasonable medical practice (when relied on as a defence) was sufficient safeguard to ensure that patients would be properly informed and drew a distinction between the obligation of doctors to treat and the obligation of doctors to disclose information (546, per Kearns J): (contd/)

'[e]ach case it seems to me should be considered in the light of its own particular facts, evidence and circumstances to see if the reasonable patient in the plaintiff's position would have required a warning of the particular risk.'[117]

[4.59] It should be observed that one aspect of the *Geoghegan* decision, namely the determination of how 'informed consent' legal cases are to be decided (see para **[4.63]**) found prompt approval in Irish law. However, for some time it remained unclear whether the significant broader restatement of the law contained in *Geoghegan* (the 'reasonable patient' test) would find approval from the Supreme Court.

[4.60] The matter appears to have been settled by the decision of the Supreme Court in *Fitzpatrick v White*,[118] a case which concerned a failure to give a warning to a patient prior to eye surgery. Giving the judgment of the Court, Kearns J stated that Australian authorities in particular supported:

> '...the argument that the giving of an adequate warning, far from being a source of nuisance for doctors, should be seen as an opportunity to ensure they are protected from subsequent litigation at the suit of disappointed patients. I am thus fortified to express in rather more vigorous terms than I did in *Geoghegan v Harris* my view that the patient centred test is preferable, and ultimately more satisfactory from the point of view of both doctor and patient alike, than any "doctor centred" approach favoured by part of this Court in *Walsh v Family Planning Services*'.

In *Fitzpatrick v White*, the court rejected the plaintiff's appeal on the basis that the warning given to him was adequate. However, many more 'failure to warn' cases stand or fall (and more frequently the latter) not on the quality of the warning but on the issue of causation and it is to this that we now turn.

CAUSATION – THE EFFECT OF NOT INFORMING

[4.61] We have observed above (see para **4.12**]) that to proceed without consent is negligence; we have also observed that one element of negligence (the standard of the reasonable doctor) may, if it is the preferred test of the court, inform how much information should be given. However, there is one other important element of

---

[116] (contd/)

> Finlay CJ (in *Walsh*) invoked the exception in the following manner at p 511:-
>> "...it may be, certainly in relation to very clearly elective surgery, that the court might more readily reach a conclusion that the extent of warning given or omitted contained inherent defects which ought to have been obvious to any person giving the matter due consideration than it could do in a case of complicated medical or surgical procedures,"
> With considerable diffidence, I venture to suggest that this statement really only highlights the unreality of relating or contrasting the duty of disclosure to or with complicated medical treatment which is a separate and quite different function.

[117] At 550, citing McCarthy J in *Walsh* (521):

> ...those concerned, if they knew of such a risk, however remote, had a duty to inform those so critically concerned with that risk. Remote percentages of risk lose their significance to those unfortunate enough to be 100% involved.

[118] *Fitzpatrick v White* [2007] IESC 51. In reaching its decision the court placed reliance on both *Rogers v Whitaker* (1992) 175 CLR 479 and the more recent decision of Kirby J (at paras 143–5) in *Rosenberg v Percival* [2001] HCA 18.

negligence that must be considered, no matter what test for disclosure is applied by the court, and that is 'causation'.[119] In order for a person to prove negligence, he must show that the negligent action caused his harm. Consider Example 4.1:

Example 4.1

Dr Dorian is a plastic surgeon. He is approached by a promising young actress, Ms Leigh, who wishes to undergo a 'nose job'. She says she needs it for her career because she has been told her nose is 'too big' for film or television. She is, she says, desperate for her big break and that is why she is opting for surgery. Dr Foster discusses the operation with her, but does not advise her of the rare (0.1 per cent) chance of her nose being left permanently deformed and swollen. In fact, this is what happens.

In a case such as this one, where the surgery is elective and the doctor knows that the patient needs a beautifying outcome, it is at least arguable that she should have been warned of the risk of swelling and deformity. Let us assume, then, that a court finds that she should have been warned; there is still a further element to be satisfied, namely that of causation. Ms Leigh has to prove that the failure to warn caused her harm; in other words, she has to show that but for the negligent warning she would not have undergone the operation. This is the test of causation in 'informed consent' cases: 'the patient obviously has no complaint if [she] would have submitted to the therapy notwithstanding awareness that the risk was one of its perils.'[120]

Subjective, objective or both?

[4.62] There are clearly at least two ways to approach the issue of whether the lack of information caused harm to the patient. The first is the 'objective' test: what would the reasonable person, if warned of the risk of an adverse outcome, have done? This is the approach formerly taken in Ireland.[121] The second is a 'subjective' test: what would the particular person have done if warned of the risk? This is the approach taken in England.[122] There are difficulties with the subjective test, for a person suing will always (and perhaps truthfully) claim that he would not have undergone treatment[123] had he been warned of the risk that eventuated. But there is a third way and this 'mixed

---

[119] See Jackson, Medical Law (Oxford, 2006) 290: for a person to win an 'informed consent' action:

'she must prove

(1) that she has suffered an injury that has made her worse off than she would have been if the procedure had not been performed; *and*

(2) that her injury is the materialization of the undisclosed risk or outcome; *and*

(3) that if she had been informed of this risk of outcome, she (or a reasonable patient) would not have consented to the procedure and [therefore] the injury would not have occurred.'

Causation is discussed at greater length in Ch 6 'Negligence', see para **[6.36]**.

[120] *Canterbury v Spence* (1972) 464 F 2d 772 at 790.

[121] See *Walsh v Irish Family Planning* [1992] 1 IR 496; also *Canterbury v Spence* (1972) 464 F 2d 772.

[122] *O'Keefe v Harvey-Kemble* 45 BMLR 74 (CA); see also the Australian case of *Ellis v Wallsend District Hospital* [1990] 2 Med LR 103.

[123] Or would have sought a second opinion or postponed the operation: see *Chester v Afshar* [2004] 3 WLR 927; *Chappel v Hart* (1998) 72 AJLR 1344.

approach' is the route taken in *Geoghegan v Harris* and is one that has subsequently been followed in a number of cases:

'It seems to this court that both approaches are valuable in different ways and that both should be considered. In the first instance it seems to me that the court should consider the problem from an objective point of view… However, it seems to me that any objective test must sometimes yield to a subjective test when, but only when, credible evidence, and not necessarily that of the plaintiff, in the particular case so demands… If this dual and combined approach smacks of pragmatism, so be it. It is in my view well justified if it achieves a better result in terms of deciding what probably would have occurred.'[124]

[4.63] This 'mixed' approach (objective first and then subjective if the evidence warrants it) to determining the issue of causation was subsequently approved by the Supreme Court in case of solicitors' professional negligence[125] and has been applied in the context of several medical information disclosure cases.[126] There is a practical corollary of the causation hurdle in informed consent cases, which is that it is very difficult for a plaintiff to prove that a lack of information (even if it is proved that the information should have been given) did, in fact, cause him to undergo the procedure and, as a result, successful 'failure to warn' cases are a rarity.[127]

Quick Reference Guide 4.3

Informed consent

> ❖ Informed consent is a somewhat vague concept. It depends on a determination of whether a person has been given enough information in order to be able to base his consent on all the relevant facts.
>
> ❖ Although there had been some uncertainty in Irish law for many years about the correct standard for the disclosure of risks of any treatment or intervention, recent jurisprudence indicates that in Irish law the 'patient-centred' test to disclosure is to be preferred.
>
> ❖ The patient-centred test involves disclosing all the information regarding risks that a reasonable patient in the position of the person undergoing the procedure in question would regard as 'material' or significant.
>
> ❖ A clinician has a 'therapeutic privilege' to withhold information where she feels that the information would be harmful to the patient. This therapeutic privilege does not amount to a license to lie in response to a direct question.
>
> ❖ Where a patient claims that his consent to treatment was not informed, he must prove that if he had been properly informed, he would not have undergone the treatment.

---

[124] *Geoghegan v Harris* [2000] 3 IR 536 at 557; a 'mixed' approach was also proposed in the English case, *Smith v Barking Health Authority* [1994] 5 Med LR 285 at 289 per Hutchison J: the court was very careful to warn of the risks of accepting a patient's retrospective claims of what he would have done if the information he received had been different.

[125] *O'Carroll v Diamond* [2005] 4 IR 41.

[126] *Callaghan v Gleeson and Lavelle* [2002] IEHC 32; *Farrell v Gleeson* [2003] IEHC 286; *Winston v O'Leary* [2006] IEHC 440.

[127] According to the sources available to the author, no case that has gone to court and been decided by a judge to date has resulted in a victory for the plaintiff (although some cases have settled just prior to or during hearing).

A GUIDELINE FOR INFORMING PATIENTS AND DISCLOSING MATERIAL FACTS

[4.64] A useful summary of the issues regarding disclosure (and therefore how 'informed' the patient is) to bear in mind when seeking a patient's informed consent was provided by the Australian Law Reform Commission.[128] The Commission suggested (see Table 4.1) that when it comes to disclosing 'material facts' in the context of obtaining consent from a patient, it was possible to compile a checklist that goes some way towards covering all bases:

Table 4.2 Australian Law Reform Commission checklist for obtaining informed consent

Matters to be considered when seeking the informed consent of a patient to clinical intervention include the following:
- the personality and temperament of the patient and the patient's attitude
- whether the patient wants information
- whether the patient asks questions
- the patient's level of understanding
- the nature of the proposed treatment
- the magnitude of any possible harm
- the likelihood of the risk of any possible harm occurring
- the general surrounding circumstances

It is suggested that a checklist of this nature applied to each situation where consent is being sought could help to provide the doctor with the best protection for ensuring that he or she has obtained a patient-centred consent.

WITHHOLDING CONSENT

[4.65] It should be clear from what has gone before that a patient does not have to consent if he does not want to. Flowing from the principles of autonomy and self-determination is the corollary that a patient 'of sound mind and adult years' capable of giving consent to a given treatment is similarly free to refuse his consent to the same treatment, even if the consequences of refusal will be worse than the consequences of giving consent: '*The patient has a right to be wrong.*'[129] Furthermore, the extent to which the patient is allowed to be wrong is also clear: 'Competent adults... are generally at liberty to refuse medical treatment even at the risk of death.'[130] The right to withhold consent also includes the right to change one's mind and even to withdraw consent

---

[128] Australian Law Reform Commission, *Informed Decisions about Medical Procedures* (1989). See also Manning, 'Informed Consent to Medical Treatment: The Common Law and New Zealand's Code of Pateints' Rights' (2004) 12 Med L Rev 2, 181–216.

[129] *Hopp v Lepp* (1979) 98 DLR (3d) 464 [italics in original].

[130] *Malette v Shulman (Ont CA)* [1990] 72 OR (2d) 417. See also *Re B (Adult: Refusal of Medical Treatment)* [2002] 2 All ER 449; [2002] FCR 1. In this case a competent, ventilator-dependent woman wished to have her ventilator turned off by doctors, allowing her to die. (contd/)

during a procedure:[131] 'consent should be considered as a process, not an event, and it is important that there is continuing discussion to reflect the evolving nature of treatment.'[132]

[4.66] This right of refusal that is granted to the adult of sound mind exists even if the decision appears not only to be wrong, but even irrational, to the onlooker. In the English case of *Re T* the court had to consider the decision of a woman who, for reasons ostensibly rooted in her childhood faith as a Jehovah's Witness, declined a blood transfusion. The court reasoned that the patient's

> '[r]ight of choice is not limited to decisions which others might regard as sensible. It exists notwithstanding that the reasons for making the choice are rational, irrational, unknown or even non-existent.'[133]

Withholding consent in Ireland

[4.67] In Ireland the right of autonomy, including the right to refuse medical treatment, is enshrined in the 'unenumerated' rights protected by the State under the Constitution,[134] which have been held to include a right to bodily integrity.[135] The Supreme Court has stated (explicitly approving the English decision in *Re T*):

> 'The consent which is given by an adult of full capacity is a matter of choice. It is not necessarily a decision based on medical considerations. Thus, medical treatment may be refused for other than medical reasons or reasons most citizens would not regard as rational, but the person of full age and capacity may make the decision for their own reasons.'[136]

---

[130] (\contd) This latter case appears to raise interesting legal points: conscientious objection was explicitly recognised and perhaps more importantly the court made a detailed inquiry into Ms B's reasons for refusing treatment, apparently as a precondition for finding her competent, which seems to contradict earlier case law where it has been asserted that competent patients can refuse treatment for no reason at all (see para **[4.70]** below).

[131] *Ciarlariello v Keller* [1993] 2 SCR 119.

[132] British Medical Association, *Consent Tool Kit* (BMA Books, 2001) 9.

[133] *Re T (adult: refusal of treatment)* [1992] 4 All ER 649, per Lord Donaldson. In *Re T* the court found that the woman had come under undue influence from her mother, which meant that her refusal was not voluntary and therefore not valid: see para **[4.17]** above.

[134] Article 40.3.1° of the Constitution. The rights are 'unenumerated' because they are not specifically listed in Article 40.3 of the Constitution; instead, judges have decided that they exist. See also fn 3.

[135] *Ryan v Attorney General* [1965] IR 294, per Kenny J.

[136] *In Re A Ward of Court (withholding medical treatment) No 2* [1996] 2 IR 79 at 156 per Denham J. This statement on withholding consent was upheld in *North Western Health Board v W(H)* [2001] 3 IR 622, [2001] IESC 70.

In essence then, voluntary refusal of medical treatment by an adult of sound mind and in possession of all the relevant information is generally final.[137]

Quick Reference Guide 4.4

The Irish approach to informed consent

> ❖   'Informed consent' is the name given to the courts' recognition that doctors have a duty to disclose information to patients.
>
> ❖   The extent of the duty to disclose information is generally measured according to one of two standards:
>
> > o   The 'doctor-centred' standard: the doctor is obliged to disclose what the reasonable doctor would disclose;
> >
> > o   The 'patient-centred' standard: the doctor is obliged to disclose what the reasonable patient would wish to know.
>
> > Irish law is at a crossroads in terms of the test to be adopted.
>
> ❖   Broadly speaking a doctor is obliged to disclose the significant risks of any treatment to the patient, but may have some limited discretion to withhold information in certain limited circumstances.
>
> ❖   The law in Ireland appears to mandate a greater degree of disclosure when:
>
> > o   A procedure is elective; it appears that the more elective (in the sense of non-essential) a procedure or treatment is, the greater the onus on the practitioner to disclose the risks of that procedure or treatment;
> >
> > o   Where an elective procedure involves a risk of long-lasting or severe pain, there is a substantial onus on the practitioner to disclose that risk of pain
>
> ❖   The Irish Supreme Court has adopted a doctor-centred approach to the duty to disclose, but there is some High Court jurisprudence to the effect that the patient centred test is to be preferred.
>
> ❖   If the patient asks questions, the clinician should answer them as truthfully as possible.
>
> ❖   Any person alleging negligence as a result of a failure to obtain proper consent must show that the failure caused harm by causing the person to undergo the procedure and suffer injury in circumstances where he would not have undergone the procedure had he been properly warned. The assessment in Irish law of whether the patient would have taken a different course if properly informed is based on a mixture of a subjective and objective tests.

Limits on withholding consent

[4.68] There are a number of situations in which the right to refuse treatment is curtailed.

---

[137] Although note the *ex tempore* decision of Abbott J in *Fitzpatrick & Ryan v K and Attorney-General* [Record 2006 No 4427P] October 21, 2006 in which the judge directed that it would be lawful for a hospital to transfuse a Jehovah's Witness who had suffered a substantial haemorrhage following the delivery of a child; see also the *ex tempore* decision of Finnegan P in *JM v The Board of Management of Saint Vincent's Hospital and Justin Geoghegan and PM (Notice Party)* [2003] 1 IR 321, where the court directed treatment in circumstances where the patient had not clearly indicated whether she had consented to or refused the treatment.

Minors

[4.69] As we have observed above (see sections **[4.22]**, **[4.27]**) the right of mature minors (assuming they have the right to consent) and those aged 16 and 17 years to refuse is frequently abridged by the courts in circumstances where the minor wishes to take a decision that would be against his best interests.

Irrational decisions as evidence of mental disorder

[4.70] It may also be noted that notwithstanding the fact that patients are said to be free to refuse treatment for 'irrational' reasons, there are occasions on which irrational decisions to refuse treatment will be scrutinised by the court, in part to ensure that the irrationality of the decision is not evidence of a mental disorder that might, in turn, mean that the patient lacks the capacity to refuse treatment.[138] It does not follow, though, that an irrational decision is evidence of an irrational person.

[4.71] A person may fully understand the nature of a procedure, but yet have such a fundamental misperception of the reality that surrounds him as to fatally undermine his capacity to give or refuse consent. So, in one American case,[139] a woman required amputation of her feet due to progressive gangrene, but the woman in question refused to accept that such an operation was necessary even when faced with the 'obvious facts that the flesh was dead, black, shrivelled, rotting and stinking'. Her chance of survival following amputation was estimated at 50 per cent while the prospect of death in the short term was close to 95 per cent in the absence of surgery. The woman's refusal of treatment was not valid in the circumstances because she did not or could not apprehend the very basic facts involved in taking the decision, so the court permitted the surgery to take place.

Quick Reference Guide 4.5

Withholding consent

> ❖ Any person who is competent to give consent is also free to withhold consent.
>
> ❖ It is not necessary that a person's reasons for refusing a treatment be rational, so long as the thought processes underlying the refusal are rational.
>
> ❖ A person is at liberty to refuse treatment even where that refusal exposes him to the risk of death or serious harm: the patient 'has a right to be wrong'.
>
> ❖ There are likely to be limitations on the minor's right to refuse medical treatment that would be in that minor's best interests, even where that minor would otherwise be competent to consent to treatment.

---

[138] So in *Re B (Adult: Refusal of Medical Treatment)* [2002] 2 All ER 449, [2002] FCR 1, the court examined the reasons of the woman for wanting her ventilator withdrawn. In *NHS Trust v T (adult patient: refusal of medical treatment) [2004] EWHC 1279 (Fam)* [2005] 1 All ER 387, the court held that the reasons that Ms T gave for refusing blood transfusion ('...my blood is evil...once [clean blood is] given to me, it mixes with my own and also becomes evil...[and] will have increased...the danger of my committing acts of evil') were irrational but also evidence of a disordered mind, so that she lacked the capacity to refuse treatment.

[139] *State of Tennessee v Northern* (1978) 563 SW 2d 197.

Chapter 5

Clinical Records and Prescribing

INTRODUCTION

[5.01] Notes of consultations, together with prescriptions that are given to patients and transmitted subsequently to pharmacists, may constitute the only permanent record of what has taken place during a transaction between clinician and patient. Allegations of wrongdoing or negligence may sometimes stand or fall almost entirely on the representation of events depicted in the written record.

[5.02] A clinical record that contains a detailed account of any examinations, findings and treatment plan leaves fewer opportunities for contradiction or misinterpretation than might a terse few words incorporating personalised, non-standardised and often equivocal abbreviations. Similarly, a prescription that is clear and unambiguous can save all concerned a great deal of trouble. This chapter is concerned not merely with the quality of clinical records but, just as importantly, with the records themselves. Who owns them? Who may have access to them? Do any different rules apply to records held on computer as distinct from paper records? The chapter concludes by providing an overview of the rules on prescribing and the potential consequences for both clinician and pharmacist if a prescription is inadequately written.

THE IMPORTANCE OF THE CLINICAL RECORD

[5.03] Whether one looks at this question from a medical or a legal perspective, the message is simple and intuitive: clear and accurate records are essential to good patient care. Looked at from the healthcare professional's point of view, good notes allow for better continuity of care between clinicians who share the same practice or between those in a multi-disciplinary team that jointly shares responsibility for the care of an individual patient. While this chapter focuses predominantly on the written or computer record of consultations, it should be pointed out that clinical records can take many forms, including:

- patient health records (electronic or paper-based, including those concerning all specialties, and GP medical records);
- accident & emergency, birth, and all other registers;
- theatre registers and minor operations (and other related) registers;
- some administrative records (for example, some personnel records or notes associated with complaint-handling);
- x-ray and imaging reports, output and images;
- photographs, slides, and other images;
- microfiche or microfilm;
- audio and video tapes, cassettes, CD-ROM etc;

- e-mails;
- computerised records;
- scanned records;
- text messages.

[5.04] Good notes stand the test of time, an important consideration when the same set of notes may be handled, referred to and added to by a succession of different people, such as junior doctors consecutively rotating through a consultant's 'team' in a hospital. Clear documentation of what has been done not only facilitates the provision of care but can also minimise the possibility of the repetition of redundant and potentially dangerous tests.[1]

[5.05] From the legal perspective, good clinical records are essential—bear in mind the maxim 'no notes, no defence'. If a patient brings a doctor to court alleging negligence and the doctor has no records, it becomes very difficult for her to defend herself. The greater the deficiency in the records, the more difficult it will be to make out a plausible defence and the more compelling may be the inference that the doctor was in fact negligent. The need to retain records is especially significant if one considers for a moment the pace at which the legal process may move; it can be many years between the occasion that gives rise to the reason for legal action and the legal action itself—see Example 5.1.

Example 5.1

Dr Chekhov works in an exceptionally busy general practice. Amongst her duties is the vaccination of children. In an average week she will vaccinate at least 50 children. In order to maximise throughput she took to recording only the fact of the vaccination and its generic type (for example 'whooping cough') without recording the brand name or identification number of the vaccination or anything about the health of the child.

A child she vaccinated in 1990 began shortly afterwards to experience convulsions. Within two years he was manifesting definite signs of developmental delay. By 1994 there was a firm diagnosis of mental handicap. In 1996, six years after the initial vaccination, the parents initiated legal action against Dr Chekhov, alleging that she failed to check for or to act upon any contra-indications to the vaccination.[2] The parents claim that the child had a fever on the day of the vaccination, which was a contra-indication to the giving of the vaccine and known to increase the risk of serious side-effects. It is also suggested that the

---

1   For example, multiple x-rays of the same area of the body that add nothing to the clinical picture but rather may cumulatively create the risk of radiation damage.

2   We discuss the timeframe within which legal actions for negligence must be brought in Ch 6 'Negligence', para **[6.74]**. However, here it can simply be stated that, pursuant to the Civil Liability Act 1961 as amended, in the case of a child who may have been the victim of negligence the time limit for initiating a legal action (via a Personal Injury Summons, see Ch 9, para **[9.43]**) is two years after the child turns 18. So, a two-year old would have 18 years within which to bring a legal action. Note, however, that although this is the theoretical position the courts may sometime dismiss an action that is brought after a long delay, even if it is brought *within* the time limit laid down by the law: *Toal v Duignan* [1991] ILRM 135. That case concerned a man who was discovered to be infertile at the age of 22, allegedly due to a negligent failure to diagnose an undescended testicle shortly after birth.

child had previously had an allergy to vaccine components and that the doctor failed to ask about allergies. Dr Chekhov disputes this recollection of events.

In a related development, there have been allegations that Unichem, the makers of one particular brand of the vaccine in question, knowingly released a faulty batch of vaccines and they too are facing massive claims for damages, which they have agreed to settle. If the doctor could prove that she had given one of these vaccines, then the company would be liable.

Dr Chekhov's notes cannot confirm that a Unichem vaccine was given and so much time has elapsed that she cannot remember the vaccine used. Similarly, her notes do not record any clinical findings on the child or whether she checked for contra-indications. Again, so much time has passed that she has no recollection of the consultation with which to bolster her inadequate notes.

[5.06] There are two reasons why good notes could help the doctor here. In the first place, thorough notes of the consultation might be able to demonstrate that she had in fact recorded the child as having a normal temperature and that furthermore she had enquired about any allergies and had received a negative response from the parents. In the second place, she might be able to demonstrate that she gave a Unichem vaccine from the defective batch and therefore could plausibly allege that it was the vaccine, rather than any act or omission on her part, that gave rise to the brain damage. Neither avenue is open to her because of the shortcomings of the notes.

[5.07] A clinician's records may be the only link to the past and, what is more, an entry into the clinical record is (or should be) a contemporaneous note of events untainted by any retrospective knowledge that the clinical encounter is now the subject of a legal dispute and so can often be regarded as an honest account of what took place. The permanence of a clinical record also gives it an advantage over human memory and human nature. It is understandable that with the passage of time, and whether or not legal proceedings have issued, either or both of the practitioner and patient may become polarised and perhaps mistaken in their recollection of what took place during their interaction. Extant clinical notes of any encounter that are thorough and unambiguous can be crucial to the determination of what took place. In that way, they may highlight or clarify discrepancies and inconsistencies in the narrative of events advanced by either clinician or patient.

MAKING GOOD NOTES

[5.08] What makes for good records? If a practitioner were to sit down and plan an approach to making good notes, where could she look for guidance? The Irish Medical Council's *Guide to Ethical Conduct and Behaviour* provides a departure point:

'It is in the interest of both doctors and patients that accurate records are always kept. These should be retained for an adequate period (this may be for periods in excess of 21 years)[3] and eventual disposal may be subject to advice from legal and insurance bodies. Patients are entitled to receive a copy of their own medical records, provided it does not put their health (or the health of others) at risk.'[4]

---

[3] The issue of how long medical notes should be maintained for is discussed at para **[5.21]***ff.*

[4] *Guide to Ethical Conduct and Behaviour* (6th edn, Dublin: 2004), para 4.10.

The Medical Council therefore calls for 'accurate' records. Is that enough? An example of the distinction between notes that are merely accurate (the requirement of the Medical Council) and those that are both accurate and comprehensive is set out in Example 5.2:

Example 5.2 Different Note-Taking Standards

Compare these clinical notes for two identical General Practice consultations for two identical complaints, in which precisely the same examination was conducted and precisely the same findings were elicited:

(a) The notes of Dr Keats

20/2

Headache. Flu-like?   Reassure.

(b) The notes of Dr Gogarty

20/2/07

Frontal headache.	Complaining of occasional flu-like symptoms.
On examination:	Temperature normal. Blood pressure 120/80. No photophobia. Pupils equal, reactive to light. Fundoscopy normal. Alert. No vomiting. No rash.
Impression:	Possible viral infection. No evidence of hypertension, meningitis or intracranial lesion. Reassured but to return if symptoms persist.

Ignore for a moment any medical terms in Example 5.2 that are not immediately understandable—the language used is irrelevant to the point being made. Observe instead that strictly speaking both sets of notes are, in the sense of the standard mandated by the Medical Council, accurate. However, they diverge on any reasonable scrutiny of their adequacy, context or comprehensiveness.

Is accuracy enough?

[5.09] The record made by Dr Keats, above, accurately documents the day of the consultation (but not the year) and the likely diagnosis, but leaves out many relevant findings including the rationale for the doctor's decision to merely reassure the patient. Nonetheless, they satisfy the requirement in the Medical Council *Guide* that clinical notes be 'accurate'. It seems self-evident that there is more than mere accuracy to be considered. Clinical record (b) shows how useful it can be to record more than an outline of the practitioner–patient encounter.

[5.10] Suppose that the patient in the above example were to succumb to meningitis three days after the consultation without ever having returned to the doctor who originally examined him. Which set of 'accurate' notes will make the doctor's life easier should it come to defending herself against an allegation that she missed the signs of meningitis? Nothing in the first set of notes suggests that a full examination was carried out (even if it was) or that the findings of that clinical examination were normal (even if they were) or that the patient was invited to return (even if he was). One cannot even be certain of the year in which the consultation took place. It would be difficult to demonstrate, given the death of the patient three days later, that the signs of meningitis were not present at the time of the consultation. 'Accurate' notes are thus far from being the same as adequate notes. The UK General Medical Council turns the thumbnail sketch of the Irish guidelines into a more complete portrait:

'[Doctors should] keep clear, accurate and legible records, reporting the relevant clinical findings, the decisions made, the information given to patients, and any drugs prescribed or other investigation or treatment withholding and withdrawing...[and] make records at the same time as the events you are recording or as soon as possible afterwards'.[5]

[5.11] Both context and detail are critical in the clinical record. If a clinician takes a decision, then there should be enough additional information in the notes to explain and illuminate that decision. Such context makes any subsequent course of events easier to link to, or divorce from, what took place in the clinical setting. The more information a set of notes contains, the less room there is for doubt, if ever the notes are scrutinised. In Ireland, the legal requirement to keep proper records was outlined by the Irish courts in *Toal v Duignan*[6] and one guideline[7] on note-making suggests the following elements as essential to good records:

–   they should facilitate continuity of care;

–   they should be individualised, accurate, up-to-date, factual and unambiguous;

–   they should be legible, signed and dated (and where appropriate, the time of the note should be recorded); the notes should be maintained in chronological order and should, where possible, be consolidated into a single record;

–   they should be contemporaneous;

–   abbreviations should only be drawn from a standardised list approved by the relevant clinical entity; shorthand symbols grading clinical findings should also be standardised

–   errors should be bracketed, struck out with a single line (so that they remain legible) and alterations should be signed and dated;

–   other clinicians referred to in notes should be identified;

–   the nature of advice given to patients should be recorded;

–   where documenting the clinical findings of another person, the fact that the findings are of another person should be stated.

Abbreviations and acronyms in clinical notes

[5.12] Practitioners often work in high-pressure situations where their time might be better spent doing things other than writing. As a result, the medical and paramedical

---

5   General Medical Council, *Good Medical Practice* (London, 2006), para 3(g)–(h). As one author has observed, notes should be written with the writer mindful 'of the possibilities the future holds for that information to be read by many other people than herself.' See Lewis, *Clinical Negligence, a practical guide* (London: 2001), 81.

6   *Toal v Duignan* [1991] ILRM 135. Note also that the Supreme Court has awarded exemplary damages against a doctor who altered notes in order to obscure a failure in care: *Philp v Ryan* [2004] IESC 105, [2004] 4 IR 241.

7   An Bord Altranais, *Recording Clinical Practice—Guidance to Nurses and Midwives* (An Bord Altranais, 2002), s 7.

professions have gradually compiled a lexicon of abbreviations, acronyms[8] and shorthand not immediately accessible to the non-clinician. Abbreviations are not necessarily a problem but they should be used sparingly.

The ideal is that abbreviations, if they are used, should be standardised,[9] conforming to the meaning traditionally given to that symbol[10] or grouping of letters although it is recognised that this standardised understanding of abbreviations is not always possible.[11] If there is the possibility that an abbreviation is ambiguous, then it is preferable that the words be written out in full. In any event the use of a particular abbreviation should always be consistent—the same abbreviation should not be used to mean two different things. Writing a word out in full also has the advantage that one dwells on the word a little longer with the possibility of more time to identify a mistake in what one has written. The clearer notes are, the easier it will be to prove the intention and level of care behind what was written.

Quick Reference Guide 5.1

Good written records

- ❖ Clinical notes are generally the only permanent contemporaneous record of what took place at a consultation. They are not tainted with hindsight and are not subject to any other vagaries of the human memory.

- ❖ Clarity in clinical records is insurance against the passage of time and against misunderstandings on the part of those reading the notes, whether for medical or legal purposes.

- ❖ If a practitioner keeps no notes of a consultation, it will be difficult for her to defend herself against allegations of malpractice, even if those allegations are dubious or unfounded.

- ❖ Clinical records should be both accurate and adequate – they should include not only conclusions reached and decisions taken but the context of any decision or conclusion.

- ❖ If abbreviations are to be used in clinical notes they should be as far as possible standard abbreviations. Whether standard or not, they should be consistent.

---

[8] Sometimes referred to as TLA (three letter abbreviations) or ABA (another bloody acronym). An acronym is a pronounceable word formed from the initial letters of other words. Thus LASER is an acronym whereas HIV is an abbreviation: all acronyms are abbreviations but not vice versa: see Wafula, Krikler and Nicol, 'Acronymophilia: Abbreviations and acronyms are different' BMJ 1994; 309: 1021 (15 October).

[9] For example of an attempt to standardise abbreviations, see Dublin Hospitals Group Risk Management Forum, *Abbreviations Sub-Committee Report* (2002).

[10] Pickup, 'Cause of dosing errors' The Lancet 2003; 362: 252.

[11] One dictionary of medical acronyms and abbreviations lists nine possible meanings for the common abbreviation 'CHD'.

CLINICAL RECORDS – OWNERSHIP AND ACCESS

[5.13] There is no suggestion any longer, in these days of greater patient enlightenment and empowerment, that the doctor is the sole arbiter of what a patient is permitted to see or to know.[12] The days of access to clinical records depending on whether or not doctors—or other clinical practitioners—object to that access are essentially over.[13] The UK National Health Service has long embraced a more patient-centred approach, stating that 'as a matter of principle, patients should be allowed to see what has been written about them'.[14] If we accept that it is a 'matter of principle' that patients should be permitted to see their notes, where does that principle come from, how extensive is it and does an Irish patient have a right of access to his notes?

[5.14] The idea that a patient could have a right of access to his notes was first affirmed by the courts, but more recently legislation has delineated and formalised that right. The question of the right of access is dealt with below. First, however, we need to consider the question of who 'owns' the notes in the first place. If a patient wants access to notes, it can be important for him to know whom he needs to ask.

Who owns the records?

[5.15] We discuss below (see para **[5.26]***ff*) the issue of who may have access to the information contained in clinical records, but it is also important to discuss the question of who owns the records themselves. The issues of ownership and access are conjoined, but still recognisably distinct. A patient may (and generally does) have a right of access to the information contained in a doctor's clinical records, but it does not follow that he has a right to claim the physical notes themselves. As with many legal conundrums, there may be no certain answer to the question of who physically owns clinical notes and the issue often may only be resolved by reference to the particular facts of an individual case. There are four candidate answers of varying plausibility:

1. A clinician

[5.16] If a practitioner is self-employed and in wholly private practice then she will, as a corollary, probably own the materials involved in the day-to-day practice of her profession, including the computers or paper files on which the details of consultations are recorded. In this situation it is the clinician who 'owns' the records, in as much as the paper or disk space on which the information is recorded is hers. Furthermore, the law has tended to recognise that documents prepared by a professional person for a lay client

---

12 The issue of patients' 'right to know' is teased out more thoroughly in the section on 'Informed Consent' in Ch 4 (para **[4.45]***ff*). Contrast the modern approach to access to information with the nineteenth century attitude: 'Your patient has no more right to all the truth than he has to all the medicine in your saddle bags.' Holmes, *Currents and Counter Currents in Medicine* (Boston, 1861).

13 Medical Council, *Guide to Ethical Conduct and Behaviour* (6th edn, 2004), para 4.10: 'Patients are entitled to receive a copy of their own medical records, provided it does not put their health (or the health of others) at risk.'

14 DHSS, *Code on Openness in the NHS* (London, 1995).

are ordinarily to be regarded as the property of the professional.[15] The fact that a doctor uses her property to record information relating to a patient is not sufficient to give that patient a right of ownership over the object on which that information is recorded.[16]

2. An institution

[5.17] In a public hospital or clinic, practitioners generally make notes in charts and on forms provided by the institution. A similar situation would pertain in the case of a clinician in private practice who was an employee of another clinician or partnership of clinicians—it would be the employer who owned the notes. Although the notes are made by the clinician and the information relates to the patient, the documents or computer memory is the institution's and it would therefore 'own' the notes.[17]

3. Both clinician and clinic

[5.18] In Ireland, care of an individual patient can quite easily elide from public to private in nature and back again. Take the example of a patient who has always attended his doctor privately but who, at the age of 70, becomes eligible for a medical card and, while staying with the same doctor, becomes his public patient. The doctor continues to use the same file as she has always done but is now paid for the patient's care by the Health Service Executive. Who owns the notes in this instance, the doctor or the health board?

[5.19] The answer is that the ownership, or proprietary interest to use a legal term, is probably shared between the two. It is unlikely that, once the patient becomes a GMS Medical Card patient, the Heath Service Executive immediately comes to 'own' the chart in which the patient's notes continue to be recorded. But at the same time, it is unlikely that the doctor has quite the same ownership herself from the time that the HSE is in effect contributing towards the costs of the stationery or software being used. It is an anomaly of the two-tiered Irish system and one that is not reducible to a simple answer.

4. The patient

[5.20] Ordinarily the patient will not own his notes but there is nothing to stop him from being given the notes in certain circumstances. A patient who is leaving the country, or changing doctor, may request his notes in order to present them to a new doctor. In such cases it is hard to resist an inference that the patient would own the notes until such time as he chose to present himself to a new practitioner. This is a somewhat implausible

---

[15] See *Breen v Williams* (1996) 70 AJLR 772; *Leicestershire County Council v Michael Faraday & Partners Ltd* [1941] 2 KB 205.

[16] Some legal commentators have queried what would happen if the clinician made her notes on paper belonging to the *patient* (for example, a doctor doing a house-call who, having forgotten the patient's file, borrows paper from the patient to record her findings). The answer appears to be that the notes, having been 'created' by the doctor, would still belong to her.

[17] In the United Kingdom, patients under the National Health System are registered with a particular doctor. However, the notes of that patient remain the property of the local health authority. If the patient dies, leaves the country or is in the process of changing general practitioners, his notes are always returned to the health authority, rather than remaining with the GP.

scenario and indeed it could be argued that, in such circumstances, the patient only has temporary custody of the notes rather than ownership. A patient may also have a right of ownership if he has a contract with his practitioner or clinic that includes a term stating that the practitioner or clinic relinquishes ownership of the notes in favour of the patient. This would also be unusual, but certainly possible. In any event, if notes are to be relinquished to another practitioner or institution, the originator of the notes should either forward a copy and retain the original notes, or vice versa.[18] Handing over the notes does not of course mean forfeiting responsibility for any incidents recorded in the notes.

How long must records be kept for?

[5.21] There is no definite guidance in this area, but this section seeks to offer some clues for the navigations of this uncertain area. The ordinary law, relating to negligence for example, is that a person has a finite length of time in which to bring a legal action. So, in the case of medical negligence causing personal injuries, the person has either two years[19] from the date of the injury or two years from the date on which the person first becomes aware he has suffered an injury through negligence. There can be a considerable gap between an event and the date on which a person discovers that he has suffered an injury as a result of that event, which can in turn greatly delay the commencement of legal proceedings.

[5.22] The issue is furthermore complicated in the case of children and persons who are under a mental disability. The two-year period in the case of a child does not begin to run until he reaches the age of 18 (so a child who suffers an injury at birth has until the day before his 20th birthday to issue proceedings). In the case of a person under a mental disability, the two-year period does not begin to run until the person has recovered (if he ever does) from his mental disability. If he never recovers, then there is in theory no legal time limit within which he must bring his legal action.[20]

[5.23] Although these possibly lengthy, and occasionally indefinite, time limits seem to indicate that doctors should hold on to notes in perpetuity in some cases,[21] there are some mitigating factors. One practical consideration is that where notes are stored

---

[18] Keeping the original notes is generally regarded as the preferable course of action: see Irish College of General Practitioners and the National General Practice Information Technology Group, *An Information Guide to the Data Protection Acts for General Practitioners* (2003):

'[W]here a patient decides to transfer to another doctor, the existing doctor should, in accordance with data protection law and ethical guidelines, facilitate that decision by making available to the patient's new doctor a copy of the patient's health information. The existing doctor should, however, maintain the patient information record accumulated at that time for an adequate period consistent with meeting legal and other professional responsibilities. During that period, the provisions of the Data Protection Acts continue to apply to that information.'

[19] This time period was previously three years, until amended by the Civil Liability and Courts Act 2004, s 7.

[20] Although we note below the effect that delay can have even where a case is technically 'within time'—see fn 13. See also para **[6.77]**.

[21] And this is the opinion of at least one author: see Irvine, 'The Importance of Good Medical Records' (2006) 5 Medical Council Newsletter 1, 5: (contd/)

electronically there is less of a burden involved in storing and preserving them for a prolonged period of time, so long as the storage medium does not become obsolete. There are then three legal considerations. The first is that those cases in which notes should be kept are frequently obvious; there will often have been some manifest component to the case that acts as a 'red flag', whether it be an adverse outcome or a situation where, even if no harm has yet transpired, the doctor herself is nonetheless aware that sub-standard care occurred. This, then, may reduce the number of cases in which ultra-prolonged retention of the notes may be necessary.

[5.24] The second element is again a common sense one. In most cases where negligence has or may have occurred, the time period from which a negligence action may be brought will run from the date of the negligent act or omission, so in the vast majority of cases (although perhaps not including children or those under a mental disability, as we have already noted), the time for bringing an action will expire, at the latest, two years from the last encounter a doctor has with a patient.[22] Even in those cases where the patient is not aware for some time that he has been the victim of negligence (in which case the two years will not start to run until this 'date of discoverability), there is typically a time limit, albeit an indefinite one, within which proceedings must be brought in the interests of fairness.

This notion of fairness is the final consideration: where a long period has elapsed between a negligent act or omission and the commencement of legal proceedings, the courts may nonetheless stop an action from proceeding, even though it is within the applicable time limit, on the basis that too much time has elapsed to allow a fair trial of the matter. This may occur when important witnesses have died and notes have, through no fault of the defendant, been destroyed or lost.[23] But none of these considerations helps in categorically answering the question of how long notes should be retained.

[5.25] The Medical Council observes that it may be necessary to keep notes for as long as 21 years.[24] In the UK (where the time limit for bringing a medical negligence action is

---

[21] (\contd)

'... medical records should be kept indefinitely. A survey by the Medical Defence Union in 2003 revealed that 557 doctors have been involved in negligence claims over the past 15 years where there was a delay of 20 years or more from the date of alleged negligent treatment to the making of the claim.'

[22] In cases where negligence is alleged to have caused death, the two-year time period runs from the date of death or the date on which the dependents of the dead person could first have discovered that there was actionable negligence at the root of the death.

[23] *Toal v Duignan* [1991] ILRM 135. That case concerned a man who was discovered to be infertile at the age of 22, allegedly due to a negligent failure to diagnose an undescended testicle shortly after birth. Although his case was commenced within the technical time limit (ie within three years—as the rule was then; it is now two years—of discovering that the earlier surgery had made him infertile), his action failed because of the time lapse between the alleged failure of the doctors and the patient bringing his action. There have been many criticisms of this decision because the young man could not have discovered his infertility any earlier than the time he brought the action, so that the delay was not his fault.

[24] *Guide to Ethical Conduct and Behaviour* (6th edn, Dublin 2004), para 4.10. This figure of 21 years is presumably computed on the basis of an accident at birth; (contd/)

three years rather than two and the courts have a limited jurisdiction to extend that time),[25] the NHS sets out more specific guidelines for the disposal of certain categories of records—see Table 5.1.

Table 5.1 Disposal of Medical Records—NHS Guidelines

Retention Period	Class of record
– from last chart entry/ date of encounter (unless otherwise stated)	
2 years	– Cause of death counterfoils from death certificates – Serum following needlestick injury or hazardous exposure – Controlled drug prescriptions, records, registers etc
3 years	– Routine occupational health records (unless litigation likely or in being—see below)
6 years	– Hospital acquired infection reports; notifiable diseases books
7 years	– X-ray films
8 years	– *Most* health care records, in whatever form (but *not* those relating to minors or those with mental disorders) – Most notes relating to *deceased persons* (8 yrs from death) – A&E registers – Fertility records, where no live child is born
10 years	– Records of treatment involving *products*, eg family planning records; immunisation/vaccination; joint replacements (including records of batch numbers etc…, where applicable) – Notes of patients who have committed suicide (10 yrs after death) – Notes of deceased patients with *learning disabilities* (10 yrs after death) – GP records of deceased patients (10 yrs after death) – Ambulance records – Frozen section samples

---

[24] (\contd) where an infant is the victim of negligence, the time limit for the commencement of proceedings is until the child is 18, plus two further years (at the time of the last review of the Medical Council *Guide*, the law allowed for a further three years once the child turns 18, hence 21; the figure would now be 20 years). However, as we have noted in the text, 21 years may be an underestimation.

[25] Adapted from Department of Health, *Records Management—NHS Code of Practice* (2006). Note that these are UK guidelines, but they are broadly applicable to the Irish situation. One net effect of this difference is that one year may be substituted from the times set out in the NHS guidelines. Irish courts do not have any discretion to extend the time allowed for the bringing of a legal action, although courts may be asked to determine when a person discovered that he had grounds for a claim: see *Gough v Neary* [2003] IESC 39, [2003] 3 IR 92. In terms of liability for defective products, the law is similar—there is a three-year limitation period running from the date on which the defect occurred or from the date on which the defect could first have been discovered up an absolute maximum of ten years from when the defect occurred (a so-called 'long stop' provision): Liability for Defective Products Act 1991, s 7.

11 years	– Records relating to donor or recipient sera
20 years	– Notes related to the treament of any *mentally disordered* patients still living, including mental health records (where deceased, 8 yrs after death) – Child and family guidance notes
25 years	– Maternity and midwifery records (25 years after last live birth) – Neonatal screening records
30 years	– Clinical psychology notes and counselling records – Notes relating to Creutzfeld-Jacob disease (30 years from date of diagnosis) – Organ donor records (30 years post-transplantation) – Genetic records; records relating to semen or ova – Documents necessary to ensure traceability of all blood products – Homicide/ 'serious untoward incident' reports – Standard operating procedures (current and old)
40 years	– Monitoring records of personnel exposed to radiation or specified substances hazardous to health
50 years	– Human fertilisation records (where there is no evidence of whether or not a child was born; from date of first note)
Until patient is 26 years of age	– All notes relating to treatment of *minors*: includes family planning, vaccination etc
Indefinitely	– Notes relating to pending ongoing litigation until advised by legal advisers (recommended at least 10 years after the legal case is concluded)
Not to be destroyed	– Records of destruction of case notes

Although the guidelines set out in Table 5.1 are UK-based and are hampered therefore by the dissimilarities between both the healthcare and legal systems in Ireland and the UK, it is nonetheless suggested that they provide a reasonable rule of thumb for Irish practitioners when it comes to the question of when to dispose of notes.

Quick Reference Guide 5.2

Owning and retaining records?

❖ In general, clinical records belong to whoever owns the medium on which the records are recorded.

❖ In a private practice setting, the practitioner will generally own records; in an institutional setting, it will generally be the hospital or clinic.

❖ There may be circumstances where ownership of the records is effectively 'shared' between practitioner and institution and rarely circumstances in which the patient may have an ownership interest in the records.

❖ How long a record must be kept for will be a function of:

o The nature of the record

o The nature of the encounter to which – and the person to whom – it relates

o Whether there are any known issues that make it desirable to maintain the notes

---

Patient access to clinical records

[5.26] While the patient may not 'own' the notes, this does not affect his right of access to the notes. Similarly, the fact that a doctor or clinic owns notes does not confer on the owner of the notes the right to deny access when requested by a person with a legitimate interest in those notes. In the context of legal action, clinical notes can and will be requested and disclosed. But there is also a right of access that exists quite aside from access as a corollary of litigation. The courts have come to recognise a right of access to notes, but the predominant right of patient access is now rooted in legislation and in particular data protection and freedom of information legislation. The healthcare systems of other countries[26] and the regulatory authorities in this country[27] have recognised that right of access. We discuss each of these areas below.

Courts and the right of access

[5.27] Although Irish courts have not been asked to consider the issue of rights of access to clinical records, determinations of the matter in other comparable jurisdictions have recognised a right of patient access:

> 'A patient is entitled upon request, to inspect and copy all information in the patient's medical file which the physician considered in administering advice or treatment…The onus is on the physician to justify a denial of access.'[28]

In *McInerney*, the doctor had received reports from five other specialists concerning the plaintiff, but he refused to divulge them to the patient on request, suggesting instead that she contact each of those physicians individually for the information contained in each report. The court found that patients have a legal interest in information concerning them. This interest persists even when the information is conveyed from doctor to doctor, and a doctor who is the recipient of such information assumes an obligation to afford the patient access to that information. Furthermore, rather than the patient having to justify why he should be allowed to see his records, it is the doctor who has to justify any refusal.

[5.28] Other countries have taken a more restrictive approach. English courts[29] conceded that patients have a limited right to access to their medical records, but were unwilling to disturb the right of the doctor to decide whether to accede to a request for information on the basis of the patient's 'best interests', with the patient's 'best interests' to be determined by the doctor rather than the patient. In Australia[30] a court was unhappy to

---

[26] DHSS, *Code on Openness in the NHS* (London, 1995): 'As a matter of principle, patients should be allowed to see what is written about them'. See also the UK Access to Medical Records Act 1988.

[27] *Guide to Ethical Conduct and Behaviour* (6th edn, 2004), para 4.10: 'Patients are entitled to receive a copy of their own medical records, provided it does not put their health (or the health of others) at risk.' This tallies with the position under Data Protection legislation: see para **[5.32]**ff.

[28] *McInerney v McDonald* [1991] 2 Med LR 267.

[29] *R v Mid Glamorgan FHSA, ex parte Martin* [1995] 1 WLR 110.

[30] *Breen v Williams* (1996) 70 AJLR 772.

accept that the patient had any automatic right of access, because that right would automatically clash with the doctor's right to decide on the patient's best interests.[31]

[5.29] An Irish court has never been asked to decide this particular question and the advent of legislation has to a great degree rendered such judicial consideration redundant (although as we will observe below, statutory rights of access to records have not obviated legal disputes about the extent of those rights) and has strengthened the patient's hand when he seeks access to the information in his medical records.

[5.30] From an ethical point of view, if trust is to be a cornerstone of the practitioner–patient relationship, then sharing medical records with the patient may buttress a mutual relationship of trust, confidence and respect. So it is not surprising that—on the whole—the balance of legal opinion on the matter of access to records is that any patient whose records are maintained by a physician should have a right of access to the contents of records without having to resort to legal action. The extent of the right depends on the circumstances. It will certainly include any instructions to the physician to divulge information to a third party.[32] Most issues relating to a patient's rights of access no longer fall to be determined by courts (although courts may be required to intervene where disputes arise), but instead are contained in legislation, to which we now turn.

Statute law and the right of access

[5.31] The two principal laws in Ireland that facilitate the right of individuals to access information, including clinical records, which is held concerning them, are the Data Protection Acts 1988 and 2003 and the Freedom of Information Act 1997.

Data protection legislation

[5.32] Data protection legislation seeks to protect personal information about individuals that is stored on computer or in a structured manual file by institutions or other individuals. Personal information is very widely defined as being any data that can be related to a living individual who can in turn be identified by that data. There are two categories of such data: the first is simple personal data[33] and the second is that which is specifically identified as 'sensitive personal data'. The latter (of more relevance to the medical setting) include:

(a)   the racial or ethnic origin, the political opinions or the religious or philosophical beliefs of the data subject;

(b)   whether the data subject is a member of a trade union;

(c)   the physical or mental health or condition or sexual life of the data subject;

(d)   the commission or alleged commission of any offence by the data subject; or

---

[31]   The court concluded that if there were to be a right of access to medical records, then it would have to come from the Australian Government introducing such a law. In essence, this is what has happened in Ireland with the advent of data protection and freedom of information legislation.

[32]   *C v C* [1946] 1 All ER 562.

[33]   Data relating to a living individual who is or can be identified either from the data or from the data in conjunction with other information that is in, or is likely to come into, the possession of the data controller.

(e)   any proceedings for an offence committed or alleged to have been committed by the data subject, the disposal of such proceedings or the sentence of any court in such proceedings.[34]

It is clear that most doctors will hold information in category (c), above.

[5.33] The fundamental aims of data protection are outlined in the Data Protection Principles,[35] which explain the reasoning and purpose of the laws on personal data and which may be summarised as 8 Data Protection Rules:

1   Obtain and process the information fairly;

2   Keep it only for one or more specified and lawful purposes;

3   Process it only in ways compatible with the purposes for which it was given to you initially;[36]

4   Keep it safe and secure;

5   Keep it accurate and up to date;

6   Ensure that it is adequate, relevant and not excessive;

7   Retain it no longer than is necessary for the specified purpose or purposes;

8   Give a copy of personal data to any individual to whom that data relates, on request.

[5.34] Processing personal data describes almost any use of the data, including collecting and storing information in the first place, altering it, transmitting it to others and deleting it. In general for sensitive personal data to be processed fairly, a number of conditions have to be met.[37] The total number of preconditions that need to be required is extensive and there is a higher onus on the processing of sensitive personal information, such as healthcare information; we set out here some (but not all) of the preconditions, one of which must be met, before healthcare information can be processed:

–   the patient consents;

     the processing is necessary for the discharge of a legal obligation;[38]

–   the processing is necessary in order to protect the vital interests of the data subject;[39]

–   the processing is necessary for the legitimate interests pursued by the data controller or by a third party to whom the data is disclosed;[40]

---

[34] Data Protection Acts 1988 to 2003, s 1(1).

[35] The *Principles* are set out in the Data Protection Acts 1988 to 2003.

[36] In other words, information obtained for one purpose (eg opening a bank account) cannot be used for another purpose (eg 'junk' mail) without consent to the information being used for that purpose.

[37] Data Protection Acts 1988 to 2003, ss 2A and 2B.

[38] Such as the notification of a disease about which a doctor is obliged by law to tell the relevant authorities.

[39] For example a GP who tells a hospital doctor what medications her patient is taking or whose locum requires to see the GP's notes in order to provide clinical care.

[40] For example, research, audit, or financial management by a health institution.

– the information is being processed by a health professional for 'medical purposes' (a very widely defined term).

The questions that a person soliciting personal data (known as a 'data controller') is expected to ask himself in discharging his duties are:[41]

'When people are giving you information,

– do they know what information you will keep about them?

– do they know the purpose for which you keep and use it?

– do they know the people or bodies to whom you disclose or pass it?'

[5.35] Consent to the storage of healthcare personal data can reasonably be implied by a patient's attendance at a clinic or doctor's surgery and the giving of information to the doctor, but it has been argued that as an additional precaution a notice should be displayed in waiting rooms or consulting rooms to formally make patients aware that records compiled during the consultation may be further 'processed' (which term, as we have noted above, includes mere storage of the data) for management, teaching or research processes.[42]

Obligations and rights under data protection legislation

[5.36] The *raison d'être* of the Data Protection Acts 1988 and 2003 is that a person who believes or knows that another person holds information about him in permanent form has the right to (a) know whether information is in fact held and (b) a legal right of access to that information.[43] He also has the right to change or delete elements of that information where it is shown to be inaccurate. The Act creates a Data Protection Commissioner whose job it is to police and enforce the Act and ensure that those in possession of data are discharging their responsibilities.[44]

[5.37] The 'data controller', as the person in charge of the hoarded personal data, has a number of obligations that essentially reflect the Data Protection Rules,[45] while the 'data subject' (the person whose information is being 'processed') has a number of rights when it comes to establishing the existence of stored personal information and assessing that information:[46]

---

[41] http://www.dataprivacy.ie/viewdoc.asp?m=&fn=/documents/responsibilities/3c.htm.

[42] Kennedy & Grubb (eds), *Principles of Medical Law* (Oxford, 1999). However, see Case Study 1/97 of the Data Protection Commissioner in which the Commission highlights that the adequacy of an information notice to inform patients of what will happen to data will depend on the circumstances; in Case Study 1/97, a notice displayed in an Accident and Emergency Department was found to be inadequate for the purpose of informing patients.

[43] A person who holds information about another is called a 'data controller'. A person about whom the information is held is called a 'data subject'.

[44] Data Protection Acts 1988 to 2003, s 8 et seq. See www.dataprivacy.ie (last accessed October 2007).

[45] Data Protection Acts 1988 to 2003, s 2.

[46] Data Protection Acts 1988 to 2003, ss 3–4.

- The data subject can make a request, which must be in writing, about information held in electronic form by the data controller, who has 21 days to reply to the request.
- If the reply confirms that data is held concerning the applicant, the data controller must also disclose, in comprehensible form, the nature of the stored information.[47]
- If the information is wrong in any way, then it must be corrected or deleted, depending on which is the most appropriate in the circumstances.[48]
- The data subject can direct a data controller not to process personal information in a manner that would cause substantial damage or distress.

If a data controller does not comply with the requirements of the legislation, she can be reported to the Data Commissioner or be taken to court by the data subject who is affected by her refusal to comply. The court can order compliance and also compel the data controller to pay damages and the costs of the legal proceedings.

[5.38] Personal information must generally, in accordance with the Data Protection Rules, not be disclosed or used for purposes other than those for which it was given. However, information held about an individual that would otherwise be confidential *may* be disclosed in the interests of preventing crime or protecting the security of the state.[49] It may also be disclosed when required urgently to prevent injury or other damage to the health of a person or serious loss of, or damage to, property, or where requested by a court of law or by the data subject himself.[50]

Restricting the right of access to data

[5.39] There are a number of categories of data that are exempt from disclosure, notwithstanding that they contain personal data. Generic, non-medical, examples include:

- information kept for the purpose of preventing, detecting or investigating offences, apprehending or prosecuting offenders, assessing/collecting any taxes or duties or for anti-fraud functions where disclosure would impede the purpose for which the information is kept;
- where access would be likely to impair the security or the maintenance of good order in a prison or other place of detention;
- where access would be likely to harm the international relations of the State;
- where access is sought to legally sensitive or privileged information;
- where the information is back-up data;

---

[47] If the information communicated to the applicant is of a technical nature that is not likely to be readily understood (medical records might be one example), an explanation should be appended. The data controller may charge a small fee for the release of information. The fee is refundable if information about the data subject turns out to have been inaccurate, incomplete or out of date.

[48] Data Protection Act 1988, s 6.

[49] Data Protection Acts 1988 to 2003, s 8.

[50] These are similar to the general conditions in which practitioner–patient confidentiality may be breached (see Ch 3).

- where granting the request would result in disclosing confidential data about another individual, unless that other individual has consented to the disclosure;[51]

- where an expression of opinion about the data subject (which may normally be accessed) was given in confidence;

- where the information relates to examinations;

- where disclosure would entail disproportionate effort;

- where the person has made previous identical or similar requests and a reasonable period of time has not elapsed since the last request.

Medically relevant grounds for restricting access

[5.40] Research data need not ordinarily be disclosed where that information is (a) kept only for the purpose of statistics or carrying out research; (b) that information is not disclosed to anyone else; and (c) where the results of the statistical work or research are not made available in a form that identifies any of the individuals involved.[52] Similarly, a clinician may pass on anonymised or aggregate data, from which individual patients cannot be identified. Where the communication of research findings would necessarily involve the disclosure of personal data, advance patient consent would be required.

[5.41] Further restrictions can arise as a result of the Data Protection (Access Modification) (Health) Regulations 1989,[53] which provide that health data relating to an individual should not be made available to the individual, in response to an access request, if that would be likely to cause serious harm to the physical or mental health of the data subject. The intention of the Regulations is to:

> 'prohibit the supply of health data to a patient in response to a request for access if that would cause serious harm to his or her physical or mental health. They provide also that such data is to be communicated only by, or after consultation with, an appropriate 'health professional'—normally the patient's own doctor'.[54]

In other words, when access to health data is sought, the opinion of a practitioner may be sought as to whether the information is potentially harmful to a patient's health, in which case the information may be withheld. This does not amount to a blank cheque for the data controller simply to refuse access to all information sought. Instead, she must release any portion of the information sought that is not 'likely to cause serious harm to the physical or mental health of the data subject'. A person who is not a health professional[55] should not disclose health data to an individual without first consulting the individual's own doctor, or some other suitably qualified health professional.

---

[51] Data Protection Acts 1988 to 2003, s 4(4). Although limited disclosure that does not compromise confidentiality may be contemplated.

[52] Data Protection Acts 1988 to 2003, s 5(1)(h). This is similar to the scenario where confidentiality of medical information is not an issue where data is anonymous: *R v Department of Health, ex parte Source Informatics Ltd* [2000] 1 All ER 786 (see para **[3.14]**).

[53] SI 82/1989; similar provisions apply in respect of social work data—the Data Protection (Access Modification) (Social Work) Regulations 1989 (SI 83/1989).

[54] Data Protection (Access Modification) (Health) Regulations 1989, explanatory note.

[55] The data controller may not necessarily herself be a medical professional—she may, for example, be an employee in a government department. (contd/)

Registration with the Commissioner

[5.42] Institutions, companies or individuals (including all healthcare or legal professionals) who store personal data relating to patients or clients must register with the Data Protection Commissioner.[56] Applications to be included on the register must detail the purpose or purposes for which the data are to be kept.[57] The public can access this register through the Office of the Data Protection Commissioner and obtain copies of it. A data controller who should be on the register, but who has not registered, is precluded from keeping personal data. Any breach of the obligation to register may result in a fine.

Freedom of Information Act 1997

[5.43] The Freedom of Information (FoI) Act 1997[58] is distinct from and, in ways, complementary to data protection legislation. It is not merely concerned with the individual's right of access to information relating to the individual in question, but rather it seeks to promote the broader principle of transparency within public bodies. Two key differences from data protection legislation should be made clear:

(a) Data protection legislation is directed at everyone who stores personal data whereas the FoI Act applies only to information that is held by 'public bodies'.

(b) A person can only exercise rights under the data protection legislation in respect of his own personal data, whereas a person seeking information under the FoI Act may seek any information held by that body (subject to the exceptions we discuss below).

The FoI Act applies to any information held in any permanent form, whatever the mode of storage.

---

[55] (\contd) In such a case she would defer the decision to a medical practitioner (the Regulations suggest that the practitioner in question should be the doctor of the person making the application for information).

[56] Data Protection Act 1988, s 16. The Act specifically identifies as obliged to register those who store data relating to 'physical or mental health (other than any such data reasonably kept by them in relation to the physical or mental health of their employees in the ordinary course of personnel administration and not used or disclosed for any other purpose)': Data Protection Acts 1988 to 2003, s 16(1)(c)(iii). Although a new s 16(1) is yet to be commenced, it will not affect the obligation of healthcare practitioners and institutions who store personal data to register with the Data Protection Commissioner. Others who must register include the public sector; financial institutions; insurance companies; those involved in direct marketing, providing credit references and debt-collecting; and anyone keeping personal information about race, political opinions, religion, sexual life or criminal convictions.

[57] Data Protection Act 1988, s 17.

[58] The Act was amended by the Freedom of Information (Amendment) Act 2003. The 2003 Act introduced a number of important amendments to the 1997 Act, notably in relation to s 19 (Government Records); s 20 (Deliberations of Public Bodies); s 24 (Security, Defence and International Relations); and s 47 (Fees), although these amendments largely lie outside the scope of the present text.

What is a 'public body'?

[5.44] Defining what a public body is can be difficult, but the FoI Act provides a lengthy appendix that lists each 'public body' by name (for example, the Government Departments) or by category ('a local authority'); furthermore, other bodies can be declared public bodies for the purposes of the Act. The health boards (now the Health Service Executive) and most of the universities were added after the Act was introduced.[59]

What the Act does

[5.45] The FoI Act 1997 enables, in the words of its preamble:

> 'members of the public to obtain access, to the greatest extent possible consistent with the public interest and the right to privacy, to information in the possession of public bodies and to enable persons to have personal information relating to them in the possession of such bodies corrected...'

[5.46] The three essential rights conferred by the Act are:

- a right to access records held by public bodies;
- a right to have personal information in a record amended where it is incomplete, incorrect or misleading;
- a right to obtain reasons for decisions affecting an individual.

This right of access to records held by a public body,[60] while not limited to personal information controlled by public bodies (although personal information is included in the ambit of the Act), is not absolute. The right to privacy of other individuals who might be affected by the disclosure of information is respected, as is information covered by the Official Secrets Act or otherwise important to the security or stability of the State as

---

[59] An up-to-date list of prescribed public bodies is maintained at http://www.oic.gov.ie/en/ PrescribedPublicBodies/ (last accessed July 2007). A rule of thumb for anticipating whether an organisation is a public body without referring to the Act is to ask whether the body in question is, directly or indirectly, a manifestation or extension of the State. Government departments and local authorities are therefore obviously public bodies, as are bodies set up under the auspices of government departments, such as the Irish Medicines Board. Many bodies specifically established by legislation are also public bodies, such as health boards (established by the Health Act 1970) and those universities established by the Universities Act 1908. Similarly, public hospitals are covered by the FoI Act, while private ones are not. Information they hold will be covered by data protection legislation but not by freedom of information legislation. See Costello, 'When is a decision subject to judicial review? A restatement of the rules' (1998) 33 Irish Jurist 91 for examples of how widely it is possible to interpret the meaning of the word 'public' in the context of law.

[60] Freedom of Information Act 1997, s 6. Public Bodies are also required, under s 15 of the Act, to publish a manual setting out (i) their structure and organisation; (ii) their functions, powers, duties; (iii) services provided for the public and how these may be availed of; (iv) a general description of the rules and guidelines used in implementing its schemes and programmes; (v) classes of records held and the arrangements for enabling the public to access such records; (vi) names and designations of members of the staff of the body responsible for carrying out FoI arrangements; and (vii) rights of review and appeal against the decisions of the body (including rights of review under this Act).

well as other exceptions discussed in the following section. A record does not come within the scope of the FOI Act where it is:

(a)   already publicly available;

(b)   available under another enactment (except the Data Protection Act);

(c)   excluded by the Act (see below).

Making an FoI request

[5.47] Any request is generally made to the head of the public body concerned, in writing and furnishing the information necessary to enable the public body to find the information requested and reply to the application. As with data protection legislation, the applicant must receive a reply to his request for information. The public body may grant or refuse the request for information in full or in part.[61] If the decision is taken to refuse to release the information then the refusal must be based on one of the grounds set out in the Act (and the reason for refusal must be given to the applicant), which can be summarised as follows:

–   that the record does not exist, cannot be found or the request was incorrectly made;[62]

–   that access is not being refused, but deferred;[63]

–   that to disclose the record would prejudice the privacy of another person;[64]

–   that the record requested was created solely to aid government deliberations or the drawing up of legislation;

–   that the record would disclose deliberations of a public body that it would be against the public interest to disclose;[65]

–   that release of the record would affect tests or investigations conducted by the body in question or otherwise adversely affect its functioning;

–   that release of the record would undermine the operation of the Oireachtas, the courts, the prison service, state security or the legal system;

–   that the request is frivolous or vexatious or forms part of a pattern of manifestly unreasonable requests or that the request is voluminous;

–   that a fee or deposit for a previous or current request has not been paid.

The decision regarding access is, nominally at least, taken by the head of the organisation, department or institution that holds the records. In the case of the health board that would be the Chief Executive Officer, but in reality the decision is taken in liaison with the staff involved.

---

[61]   Freedom of Information Act 1997, s 8.

[62]   Freedom of Information Act 1997, s 10.

[63]   For example, until the Government or Oireachtas has finished deliberations concerning the record sought.

[64]   Freedom of Information Act 1997, s 28.

[65]   For example, someone might receive advance notification of planning decisions that might permit him to engage in land speculation.

[5.48] If access is granted, the requester is entitled to have the documents released in a form that he can both understand and access and, as with the data protection legislation, only part of the record may be released where that is the appropriate course of action.[66] If a request is made for personal information in the possession of a public body and that information is inaccurate or incomplete, the applicant has a right to correction or deletion of the erroneous details.[67]

Freedom of information in the clinical setting

[5.49] Clinical records made while a clinician is discharging duties on behalf of a public body (such as a public hospital) can be the subject of a request under the FoI Act 1997. The risk of infringing the confidentiality of medical records relating to an individual other than the person making the request is one of the grounds for refusal of disclosure.[68]

> **Example 5.3**
>
> If A requests information that would involve disclosing otherwise confidential information about B, the request may be refused if there is no reasonable way of excising the information concerning B allowing the release of that portion that does not infringe on B's right to confidentiality. The information may be released if
>
> – person B consents to the release of the information; or
>
> – there is an imminent danger to life or limb that may be averted by the disclosure; or
>
> – there is nothing inherently confidential in the information.

Patients may request their own records under the Act, and will generally be granted access to them. However, in a manner analogous to the operation of the Data Protection (Access Modification) (Health) Regulations 1989,[69] if the release of a medical record might be prejudicial to the physical or mental health of the person making the request, then access may be denied, but in those circumstances the refusal of access must be accompanied by an indication that if the requester so wishes the information will be made available for inspection by a health professional nominated by the requester.[70]

Freedom of information and confidentiality in action

[5.50] If a body takes a decision not to grant access to records, citing one of the grounds for refusal contained in the Act, that is not necessarily the end of the matter. The head of the public body can be asked by the requester or by the Information Commissioner at the behest of the requester to review the decision. The applicant may also appeal the

---

[66] Freedom of Information Act 1997, s 12.

[67] Freedom of Information Act 1997, s 17.

[68] There are some specific exceptions to the rule that confidential information will not be disclosed to third parties under the FoI Act: the Freedom of Information Act 1997 (Section 28(6)) Regulations 1999 (SI 47/1999) provide (at Regulation 3(1): 'a request under section 7 in relation to a record access to which involves the disclosure of personal information…shall, subject to other provisions of the FoI Act, 1997, be granted where…the requester is a parent or guardian of the individual to whom the record concerned relates and that individual [has] not attained full age (within the meaning of the Age of Majority Act, 1985 (No 2 of 1985))…'. See also para **[5.51]**.

[69] See para **[5.41]** above.

[70] Freedom of Information Act 1997, s 26(4).

decision to the Information Commissioner, an office which was created by the FoI Act with responsibility for overseeing the operation of the Act. A decision of the Information Commissioner can be appealed (either by the requester or the public body) to the High Court.[71]

[5.51] In *McK v The Information Commissioner*,[72] a father sought the medical records of his daughter in circumstances where his daughter was a joint guardian of both her father and of another family member with whom she lived. The daughter been admitted to hospital. The father sought information related to his daughter's condition but the joint guardian did not want him to be kept informed and the release of information to the father was refused. He then made an FoI request to the hospital and that was refused, so a review was requested from the Information Commissioner who upheld the decision of the hospital to refuse access on the basis that where there was disagreement between guardians on the release of confidential information relating to a minor, the information would only be released where there was strong evidence that the minor would specifically benefit from that disclosure. Such circumstances were, in the Information Commissioner's opinion, absent. The father appealed the refusal of the Information Commissioner to the High Court, which found in favour of disclosure to the father; the Information Commissioner then appealed that decision to the Supreme Court. The Supreme Court found in favour of the father, acknowledging the particular constitutional position of the family, and stating that '[t]he Commissioner erred in determining that release of the medical information would only be directed where there is tangible evidence that such release would actually serve the best interests of the minor.'[73]

[5.52] In a decision of the Information Commissioner, *ACF and the North Eastern Health Board*,[74] a girl who had spent many of her early years in the care of the heath board sought the records pertaining to her care. The health board refused, arguing that many of the records also contained confidential information about the applicant's family members. The woman appealed to the Information Commissioner, who determined that the confidentiality of individuals who may be affected by another person's request for information must be protected. In addition, it would be more difficult for health boards

---

[71] *ABK and the Eastern Health Board* [1999] IEIC 20 (28 September 1999). The decision of the Information Commissioner was upheld by the High Court in April 2001.

[72] *McK v The Information Commissioner* [2006] IESC 2.

[73] [2006] IESC 2 per Denham J. The Supreme Court also found against the Information Commissioner (by a majority decision) in *Sheedy v Information Commissioner* [2005] IESC 35. See also the High Court decision in *National Maternity Hospital v Information Commissioner* [2007] IEHC 113, arising out of a request by the Parents for Justice group to the National Maternity Hospital for documents held by the hospital in relation to the Dunne (later Madden) Inquiry into post-mortem organ retention. Although the matters were confidential at the time of being prepared (the tribunal of inquiry being ongoing), the tribunal had concluded by the time the matter (the National Maternity Hospital having refused to release the records) came before the Information Commissioner. The Commissioner's decision to direct release of certain of the records was upheld by Quirke J in the High Court.

[74] *ACF and the North Eastern Health Board* [2001] IEIC 4 (4 July 2001).

to liaise with the families of children in care if there was a fear that discussions between health board and family members might subsequently be released. The Commissioner therefore ordered the release of the notes pertaining to all meetings at which the requester was present on the grounds that, given her presence at those meeting, there were minimal confidentiality issues to be considered. The release of all other records was refused.

Quick Reference Guide 5.3

A patient's rights of access to clinical records

❖ A patient's right of access to his records was previously dependent on either the consent of the doctor or a decision of the courts to allow access. In most countries, courts held that patients had at least a limited right to access their notes.
❖ A court will readily find that a person has a right of access to his notes when he needs them for the purposes of exploring or initiating some form of legal action. A patient who authorises the release of his notes for such a purpose should have his wish respected.
❖ More recently, the introduction of legislation has ensured that patients now increasingly have a statutory right of access to healthcare information held about them.
❖ The Data Protection Acts 1988 and 2003 give rights to those whose personal data are held on file by others. The legislation also places obligations on those who hold the data in respect of controlling and processing that information.
❖ The rights of the individual under data protection laws extend to healthcare information and include the individual's right to know whether information is held about him, to know what that information is and to alter or delete that information if appropriate.
❖ Any person or institution holding personal data about an individual is required to register with the Data Protection Commissioner. This requirement extends to those who hold healthcare information.
❖ The Freedom of Information Act 1997 extends to all forms of record and all forms of information (not merely personal data) held by 'public bodies'.
❖ In the cases of both data protection and freedom of information legislation, there are a number of exemptions which can be relied on to decline full (or any) disclosure of information. These include questions of confidentiality or where harm may be done by disclosure.
❖ There are limited situations in which disclosure of personal data to third parties (normally prohibited by the data protection and freedom of information legislation) will be permitted. These include concerns regarding the safety of the individual or other persons. Conversely, certain information may be withheld where to disclose that information would infringe on the confidentiality of third parties.

PRESCRIPTION WRITING

[5.53] A prescription is the other element (together with clinical notes) of the permanent record of the practitioner–patient interaction. It testifies to the therapeutic option chosen by the clinician and, as such, may prove invaluable as legal proof in any dispute that arises subsequently. A prescription is also interesting in that it involves a third party in the transaction between clinician and patient, namely the pharmacist, whose job it is to decipher the prescription and dispense the medication indicated. This section looks at the requirements the law places upon the prescriber and dispenser of medications, both in terms of prescribing rules and of what may happen if a prescription is not properly written.

Why are prescriptions necessary?

[5.54] There are some medications that, while beneficial, need to be used with care, often including in their ingredients a substance that 'because of its toxicity or other potentiality for harmful effect, or the method of its use, or the collateral measures necessary to its use, is not safe for use except under the supervision of a practitioner licensed by law to administer such drug'.[75] Accordingly, relevant regulatory bodies (in Ireland, the Irish Medicines Board) designate certain medicines as being either prescription-only (POM) or available for over-the-counter sale (OTC). In addition there are certain categories of medicines that the Minister for Health can designate as controlled medicines and these are subject to further constraints over and above normal prescription rules (see para **[5.60]**).

Who may write a prescription?

[5.55] Registered medical practitioners, dentists, nurses and midwives have the legal power to write prescriptions for human use. There are slight distinctions between medical and dental prescribing powers,[76] but the similarities outweigh the differences. Prescribing by nurses and midwives is a comparatively recent innovation, first given legislative footing in the Irish Medicines Board (Miscellaneous Provisions) Act 2006 and becoming reality with the Medicinal Products (Prescription and Control of Supply) (Amendment) Regulations 2007 and the Misuse of Drugs (Amendment) Regulations 2007. There are conditions for prescribing of medicinal products by nurses and midwives:

– The nurse/midwife must be employed by a health service provider in a hospital, nursing home, clinic or other health service setting;

– The medicinal product must be one that would be given in the usual course of service provided in the health service setting in which the nurse/midwife is employed;

– The prescription is issued in the usual course of the provision of that health service;

---

[75] Federal Food Drug and Cosmetic Act, 21 USC §353(b)(1).

[76] Dentists, for example, may not generally write repeat prescriptions: see Medicinal Products (Prescription and Control of Supply) Regulations 2003 (SI 540/2003): reg 7(5)(c).

– The An Bord Altranais registration number (also known as the Personal Identification Number (PIN)) must be stated on the prescription written by the Registered Nurse Prescriber.

Furthermore, a registered nurse or midwife who wishes to prescribe must have completed an approved education programme, have the appropriate clinical experience, be registered with An Bord Altranais as a Registered Nurse Prescriber and have the authority from their employing health service provider to prescribe medications within their scope of practice. Nurses and midwives are limited in their power to prescribe controlled drugs (see para **[5.60]**) and a special Schedule (Schedule 8) of the Misuse of Drugs Act 1977 sets out the Schedule 2 and 3 drugs which nurses and midwives are permitted to prescribe and the circumstances in which they may be prescribed.[77]

Any medical, dental or nurse/midwife prescriber who is convicted of an offence under the Misuse of Drugs Act 1977 may have her freedom to prescribe or to work with controlled substances removed or limited in the wake of that conviction.[78]

Prescribing – the legal requirements

[5.56] The Medicinal Products (Prescription and Control of Supply) Regulations 2003 lay down the basic regulations to do with prescribing medicines. They include an exhaustive list of the preparations that must only be dispensed in accordance with a prescription as well as providing for the fact that all 'new' medications must also be prescription-only.[79] They also stipulate that some medicines, which would ordinarily be available only on prescription, may be sold over the counter by virtue of containing a lower dose of the active ingredient or by virtue of the particular form of the active ingredient in the medication. Under the regulations, a prescription must:[80]

– be in ink and be signed by the person issuing it with his usual signature and be dated by him;

– except in the case of a health prescription,[81] specify the address of the person issuing it;

– clearly indicate the name of the person issuing it and state whether he is a registered medical practitioner or a registered dentist; and

---

[77] See generally *The Introduction of Nurse and Midwife Prescribing in Ireland: An Overview* (DOH/HSE, 2007) and *Practice Standards for Nurses and Midwives with Prescriptive Authority* (An Bord Altranais, 2007). Available for download from http://www.nursingboard.ie/en/publications_current.aspx.

[78] Limitations may be imposed by the professional regulatory body after disciplinary proceedings or, where there is an element of urgency, by the Minister: Misuse of Drugs Act 1977, ss 6–10. Prescribing limitations may also be imposed by disciplinary bodies in the case of practitioners whose fitness to practice is impaired by the abuse of controlled substances.

[79] Medicinal Products (Prescription and Control of Supply) Regulations 2003, reg 5.

[80] Medicinal Products (Prescription and Control of Supply) Regulations 2003, reg 7.

[81] A prescription issued under free health care provisions of the Heath Service Executive: see Health Act 1970, ss 59 and 67. Note too that under the Medical Practitioners Act 2007, s 43(8) a doctor's prescription must also include the doctor's Medical Council registration number.

- specify the name and address, and age if under 12, of the person for whose treatment it is issued.

To this should be added as clearly and unambiguously as possible the name (proprietary, generic or both), the preparation, the dose, the frequency and the duration of the medication being prescribed. In general, a prescription that does not indicate otherwise will be dispensed once only. The majority of medications can be written on a 'repeat' prescription where the doctor indicates the she wishes the medication to be dispensed repeatedly for a period of up to six months. Controlled medications may not be repeated; each prescription for a controlled medication may be dispensed only once. It is an offence for a person who is not a practitioner to alter a prescription.[82]

Negligence in prescription writing

[5.57] A prescription should be accurate, appropriate and unambiguous. If a prescription is not clear and, as a result, the wrong medication is dispensed, a doctor may be held to have been negligent. She may not be negligent on her own. The blame may be shared with the pharmacist who fails to spot an error or to clarify any ambiguity that may exist on the prescription.

Case Study 5.1

In one case[83] a GP wrote a prescription for a patient who was suffering from an acute respiratory tract infection. The prescription was for salbutamol, phyllocontin and 'amoxil'[84] 250 milligrammes three times daily for seven days. The pharmacist misread the scrawled prescription and substituted 250mg of daonil, a sugar-lowering medication used by diabetics, instead of the amoxil. The patient was not a diabetic and in any event the dose of daonil dispensed by the pharmacist was several hundred times the recommended dose. The patient suffered a prolonged and catastrophic fall in his blood sugar levels (hypoglycaemia) and irreversible brain damage.

In this case, the pharmacist was held liable for the error in dispensing, but the doctor was also held partially responsible for having written a scarcely intelligible prescription that was readily capable of being misunderstood; liability was apportioned as 25 per cent to the doctor for the manner of the prescription and 75 per cent to the pharmacist for having negligently dispensed the prescription when circumstances (the dose and duration of the medication, together with the other drugs prescribed) should have suggested that daonil was not the drug intended by the prescriber. [85]

[5.58] Another possibility that may transpire with an indecipherable or ambiguous prescription is that the pharmacist may justifiably refuse to dispense the drugs listed for fear of making an error. If the pharmacist's fears were wholly reasonable and harm then resulted to the patient because of the delay in starting the medication, the doctor might

---

[82] Misuse of Drugs Act 1977, s 18.

[83] *Prendergast v Sam & Dee Ltd* [1989] 1 Med LR.

[84] These medications are an inhaler to open the airways, a tablet to improve respiratory function and an antibiotic respectively.

[85] Se also *Dwyer v Roderick* [1983] 80 LS Gaz R 3003, a case in which a doctor prescribed the wrong frequency of the medication. Again liability was split between the two practitioners.

again be liable for having written a prescription that could not be dispensed.[86] The problem of vexing prescriptions may also arise between doctors, as well as between doctors and pharmacists; patients discharged from hospital may have with them a prescription or discharge letter listing medications. The GP, in transcribing a hospital prescription to a GMS prescription or from a discharge note to any prescription, is under a similar duty to the pharmacist who receives a prescription. If she transcribes incorrectly, or transcribes correctly from an initially inaccurate prescription, she may be liable in negligence. Similarly, if she transcribes a medicine that she knows, or ought to know, that her patient should not have been prescribed by the initial prescribing doctor, she may also be liable. Of course, the initial prescribing doctor in the hospital is also under a duty of care to exercise diligence in documenting and prescribing medications.

Emergency prescriptions

[5.59] The 2003 Regulations do allow a pharmacist to dispense medication in an emergency when the doctor is not able to provide a prescription, so long as the doctor undertakes to provide one within 72 hours.[87] The Medical Council *Guide*[88] points out that '[s]hould the need arise to prescribe over the telephone, the doctor should make a record of the call and forward the appropriate prescription to the pharmacist in a reasonable time.'

Controlled drugs

[5.60] The Misuse of Drugs Acts (MDA) 1977[89] created a category of medicine known as *controlled drugs*, including most of the well-known illicit drugs, but also certain therapeutic medications. The 1977 Act fulfils three purposes. In the first place it makes illegal the possession of certain substances and lays down penalties for the possession, trafficking or dealing of those substances. Secondly, it lays down the rules within which certain controlled drugs may be used and classes of person who may possess or supply controlled substances. Finally, the Act allows the Minister with responsibility for the Misuse of Drugs legislation (the Minister for Health) to make wide-ranging regulations to clarify the Act or to amend the list of controlled drugs.[90] Attached to the end of the 1977 Act is a series of appendices, called 'schedules', each of which contains a list of controlled drugs, which tended then to be described in terms of the schedule in which they appear; LSD, for example, might sometimes be called a 'Schedule 1 drug'.

---

[86] *Pharmaceutical Society of Great Britain v Storkwain Ltd* [1985] 3 All ER 4.

[87] Medicinal Products (Prescription and Control of Supply) Regulations 2003, reg 8.

[88] Medical Council, *Guide to Ethical Conduct and Behaviour* (6th edn, Dublin: 2004), para 10.2.

[89] The Act has been updated by the Misuse of Drugs Act 1984 and the Misuse of Drugs Regulations 1988 (SI 328/1988).

[90] For example, the Misuse of Drugs (Amendment) Regulations 1993 moved the hypnotic (sleeping tablet) temazepam from Schedule 4 to Schedule 3 on the basis of evidence that it had become a drug of abuse.

Table 5.2 The controlled drugs schedules

Schedule 1 (sometimes also called CD 1)

Many of the common illicit substances are distinguished not only by their adverse effects but also by the fact that they are held to have no medicinal effects. Such drugs cannot be used except with a special licence. The group includes LSD, cannabis and raw coca leaf (from which cocaine is derived). They may not generally be prescribed.

Schedule 2

Includes most of the opiate analgesics (pain-killers) whose use is characterised by the care required to achieve a balance between their definite clinical benefits and their potential for abuse and addiction. Opiate analgesics are frequently used in severe pain, while cocaine is used as a nasal anaesthetic for certain procedures, so both (and the majority of related compounds, including heroin) are included in Schedule 2.

Schedule 3

Some sedatives, such as midazolam and temazepam, strong pain-killers, barbiturates.

Schedule 4

Most other sedatives belonging to the benzodiazepine group. Other drugs with a reduced content of barbiturates.

Schedule 5

Any of the drugs contained in the previous schedules but which are in a preparation, form or concentration sufficiently different or diluted that the potential for abuse is minimal.

[5.61] The classes of people who may have in their possession controlled drugs (from Schedules 2–5) are largely obvious: doctors, dentists, pharmacists, vets, midwives working in the community[91] and nursing matrons or sisters-in-charge. Special exemptions are also given to those whose job is to test, investigate, inspect or work with controlled substances. Any ship or offshore installation (such as an oil-rig) may maintain a store of controlled drugs under the authority of the person in charge of the vessel or installation, so long as there is not a medical practitioner in the crew. Gardaí and others who come into contact with controlled substances in 'the course of their duty' will also not be guilty of possessing those substances in the criminal sense.

Prescribing controlled drugs

[5.62] The prescribing of drugs from Schedules 1 to 3 is the focus of importantly different restrictions for the purposes of prescribing from those that apply to ordinary prescribing. The reason for the increased stringency is to minimise the possibility that patients or others will alter a prescription[92] and to that end the Misuse of Drugs Regulations add the following extra strictures to the writing of controlled drug (sometimes called MDA) prescriptions:[93]

---

[91] But midwives are only exempted for the possession of pentazocine and pethidine (Misuse of Drugs Regulations 1988, reg 10).

[92] An offence under of the Misuse of Drugs Act 1977, s 18.

[93] Misuse of Drugs Regulations 1988, reg 13.

- All of the information contained on the prescription relating to the dose and amount of the medication must be in the prescriber's own handwriting. A computer or typewritten prescription for a controlled drug is therefore not valid;
- The strength and quantity of the medication must be prescribed in both words and figures. So, if the prescription were for morphine slow-release tablets, the prescription would state (in handwriting)—'morphine slow release tablets 10mg (ten milligrammes); dispense 60 (sixty)';
- It is also not possible for the prescriber to write a 'repeat' prescription for a controlled drug. If a drug is to be dispensed in instalments, then no instalment may be dispensed more than two months after the date on the prescription. In any event, a prescription for a controlled drug may only be dispensed within 14 days of the date on the prescription.

The pharmacist may not dispense the prescription unless she is satisfied that the prescription conforms to the terms above and she recognises or has taken steps to verify the name and signature on the prescription.

[5.63] If a doctor or dentist or pharmacist keeps controlled drugs on her premises, they must be kept in a locked compartment. She must also keep a register of the use of those drugs, which must take the form of a bound book and record the use, purchase, or destruction of any controlled drugs on the premises. The storage arrangements and register may be inspected or requested for inspection by a government inspector.

[5.64] A practitioner who abuses her power to prescribe either by supplying controlled drugs to others or by prescribing them for her own illicit use may be reported to the appropriate disciplinary body. To take the Medical Council as an example, the disciplinary body may impose a range of sanctions; it may suspend the doctor from practice, strike her off the register of practitioners or attach conditions to her continued practice, such as prohibiting her from prescribing controlled drugs. The Minister for Health may also, in extreme circumstances, prohibit a practitioner from prescribing controlled substances as well as notifying her misconduct to the Medical Council or other relevant body.

Chapter 6

Clinical Negligence

INTRODUCTION

[6.01] Negligence is probably the area of clinical practice and the law that most exercises the minds of practitioners. Certainly it is true that litigation against doctors and hospitals in particular is on the increase and that the cost of insurance is rising correspondingly,[1] but the reasons for the increase in medical litigation are not at all clear. Some blame solicitors, others blame the so-called 'compensation culture' and there seems little doubt that the increasing empowerment and enlightenment of patients has gone some way towards ensuring that the traditional deference formerly accorded rightly or wrongly to the medical profession has been eroded. However, the reasons for increasing litigation lie outside the scope of this text.[2]

[6.02] The basic principles of negligence, both for 'general' and 'professional' negligence (the distinction between them is discussed below at para **[6.20]***ff*), are relatively simple. Indeed, negligence has already been discussed in outline in Ch 4 Consent. As was observed then, failure to obtain valid consent[3] to treatment from a patient can be the source of a negligence action.

[6.03] In this chapter we look in more detail at the component parts of negligence, the difference between negligence generally and 'professional' negligence in particular[4] and the categories of acts and omissions that may prove to be the foundation for clinical negligence actions. The chapter concludes by dealing with the ways in which a clinician

---

[1] See 'Ireland discusses how to handle projected increase in medical litigation' (2001) Lancet, 3 March. At the time of this article, the Medical Protection Society stated that the frequency of claims against consultants was projected to increase from 200 to 210 per 1000 consultants (compared with 25 claims per 1000 general practitioners). The Irish Government's bill for state-employed doctors' medical insurance tripled in the 10 years to 2000 while claims against doctors and hospitals in the period 1989–98 rose by 450 per cent. We discuss below the Enterprise Liability Scheme (see para **[6.89]**).

[2] Much personal injuries litigation has been (where there is no dispute about the liability of the defendant) taken out of the adversarial legal process setting by the Personal Injuries Assessment Board (PIAB) Act 2003. However, PIAB does not have any jurisdiction (even if the liability of the defendant is admitted) over personal injury claims 'arising out of the provision of any health service to a person, the carrying out of a medical or surgical procedure in relation to a person or the provision of any medical advice or treatment to a person': PIAB Act 2003, s 3(d).

[3] By way of reminder, valid consent must be (1) voluntary; (2) based on sufficient in formation; and (3) given (or withheld) be a person with the capacity (mental or age) to do so.

[4] This distinction is essentially down to how the expected standard of care is judged: discussed at para **[6.20]***ff.*

can defend an allegation of negligence and by examining how strategies can be put in place to minimise the occurrence and consequences of clinical negligence.

WHAT IS NEGLIGENCE?

[6.04] One definition of negligence is:

> '[T]he omission to do something which a reasonable person, guided upon those considerations which ordinarily regulate the conduct of human affairs, would do or doing something which a prudent and reasonable person would not do.'[5]

The 'neighbour principle'

[6.05] The desire to stop people from negligently doing (or failing to do) something in such a way that they may cause other people harm is of ancient lineage,[6] but it was only in 1932 that the modern law of negligence was formulated. In the now-celebrated case of *Donoghue v Stevenson*,[7] a woman discovered the decomposed remains of a snail in a bottle of ginger ale from which she was about to drink. She brought a case against the manufacturer of the drink for his negligence in having permitted the mollusc to find its way into her drink, seeking compensation for the discomfiture and illness the discovery caused her. Prior to this case, a person could be found negligent towards another only if both parties were bound together by a contract. However, in a celebrated judgment, Lord Atkin laid out the 'neighbour principle', the foundation stone of the modern law of negligence:

> You must take reasonable care to avoid acts or omissions which you can reasonably foresee would be liable to injure your neighbour. Who then, in law, is my neighbour? The answer seems to be persons who are so closely and directly affected by my act that I ought reasonably to have them in contemplation as being so affected when I am directing my mind to the acts or omissions which are called into question.

[6.06] In other words, a 'neighbour' is a person whom you can foresee being affected by your acts or omissions. A person who drives a car at excessive speed can foresee that she may strike a pedestrian; a doctor who operates on a patient can foresee that her patient will be harmed if she conducts herself negligently. Similarly, in *Donoghue v Stevenson,* Lord Atkin determined that a person who manufactures soft drinks can reasonably foresee that a person is going to consume that drink and might therefore be affected by any negligent omission of the manufacturer, such as failing to check for snails. Where a person is my 'neighbour' then I owe that person a 'duty of care' (also sometimes called a 'duty to take care') or, put another way, I am under a duty not to act towards that person in a negligent fashion. So, a driver owes other road-users a duty to take care when driving and a doctor owes her patients a duty of care while treating them. The existence of a duty of care is the very basis of the law of negligence, although other elements must

---

[5]   *Blyth v Birmingham Waterworks Co* (1856) 11 Ex Ch 781 at 784.

[6]   The Code of Hammurabi, one of the world's oldest legal texts, was in probably in existence before 1750 BC. It recognised negligence as a punishable offence, although the punishments were harsher than those imposed today—if an architect negligently constructed a house that collapsed, he and his family could be put to death: see para **[1.16]**.

[7]   [1932] AC 562.

also be present. We turn now to examine these necessary elements common to all negligence claims.

THE ELEMENTS OF NEGLIGENCE

[6.07] In order for a negligence action to succeed, a plaintiff must prove three essential elements on the balance of probabilities:

1. The existence of a duty of care;

2. Breach of duty—ie a failure to reach the required standard of care;

3. Causation—ie that harm or damage is caused to the plaintiff by the breach of duty.

Unless these three elements are present and proved, together with certain other procedural requirements such as the obligation to commence proceedings within a specific timeframe and to move the proceedings along without undue delay (see para **[6.77]***ff* below), then a negligence action cannot succeed. Before looking at each of these elements in detail, we will first consider a thumbnail sketch of their importance.

Example 6.1

Ms Watson is a surgeon. She admitted a patient for removal of a cancerous right kidney. The surgeon discussed the operation with the patient, explaining that the right kidney was to be removed. The patient signed a consent form, agreeing to the removal of the right kidney. However, during the operation, the surgeon removed the wrong kidney and the patient, unable to survive on the diseased kidney alone, died.

[6.08] Looking at Example 6.1 it is easy to discern the presence of the necessary elements of negligence: (a) there is a duty of care owed by surgeon to patient; (b) there was a manifest failure to discharge that duty; and (c) the breach of duty caused the patient's death. Of course, there are many things that might be changed about this example. What if another doctor had recorded the patient as having consented to the removal of the wrong kidney and the operation proceeded without anyone noticing the error? What if the error was noted before the operation started? What if the error had been noticed in time to prevent removal of the wrong kidney, but not before the operation to remove that wrong kidney had commenced (so that the initial damage had to be repaired before the operation on the right side could commence)? To add to this last scenario, what if the patient suffered complications wholly or partly attributable to the extra length of the surgery? In the sections that follow we examine in greater detail each of the three elements of negligence as they arise in and apply to the healthcare setting, as well as aspects of negligence that touch upon the possible variations of Example 6.1 just discussed.[8]

---

[8]   Short answers to each of these questions are as follows: (a) where incorrect consent was taken and the error not noticed, liability is likely to be apportioned between all parties who should have noticed the error, but failed to do so; (contd/)

Quick Reference Guide 6.1

The elements of negligence?

> ❖ Negligence is doing – or failing to do – something in such a way that your act or omission falls below the standard of care you owe to your 'neighbour', causing him harm. Legally speaking, one's neighbour is any person whom one can reasonably foresee as being affected by one's acts or omissions.
>
> ❖ There are three essential elements to proving negligence:
>   1. The existence of a duty of care (or a duty to take care)
>   2. A failure to live up to that duty to take care
>   3. Damage caused to the victim of that failure by the failure

Duty of care

[6.09] Ultimately the question of whether a 'duty of care' exists in any given relationship is allied to the neighbour principle (outlined in para **[6.05]**) and is a question to be decided by the courts: in Irish law a duty of care arises where:

- there is proximity (in the legal sense)[9] between the parties;[10]

- any damage caused by one party to the other is foreseeable;

- there is no strong public policy that would create an exception.[11]

In most areas of social and commercial interaction, a duty of care arises precisely where one would expect it to and clinical practice is no exception. In any therapeutic relationship established between patient and clinician, a duty to take care will invariably be present. A duty of care arises between the clinician and her patient when she

---

[8] (\contd) (b) where the error was noted before the operation started, then there was no harm caused to the patient, so there is no negligence; (c) in the scenario where the mistake was noted after the operation commenced but before the wrong kidney was removed, the negligent doctor will still be liable for the extent to which the operation proceeded; and (d) where the patient dies or suffers other complications attributable to the extra time spent in the operating theatre, the doctor may be held liable to the extent that the extra duration of the surgery may have contributed to the complication. The ingredients of each of these scenarios are discussed in the text. For an example of where liability was apportioned between jointly negligent persons ('joint tortfeasors'), see para **[5.57]**.

[9] In this legal sense, proximity does not necessarily mean closeness in space or time. A manufacturer of a drug that causes birth defects has no proximity in terms of time or geography to a child who may be deformed after his mother takes the drug during pregnancy, but nonetheless there may be legal proximity in that the fact of harm is foreseeable.

[10] We return to the question of proximity below when we look at the duty of care owed by the practitioner to people other than her patient, such as those whom a negligently-treated patient may infect or physically harm (para **[6.10]**).

[11] *Ward v McMaster* [1988] IR 337 (SC), where the court held that there was a strong interest in having a rule against the police being found guilty of negligence when they were investigating crimes. Such a public policy means that the police can divert more energy to the detection of criminal activity and less towards 'defensive policing' to minimise the risk of being sued for negligence.

undertakes to care for the patient, whether on foot of a request for care from the patient himself[12] or following a referral from a colleague.

Duty to persons other than existing patients

[6.10] There are a number of scenarios where a doctor may come into contact with someone who is not ordinarily a patient or where a doctor's negligent acts or omissions may have ramifications for someone who is not a patient. In such cases, does the clinician have a duty to these people who are not, in the ordinary sense of the word, her patients? We consider here the clinician's liability to three categories of person:

– non-patients in need of medical care (including 'Good Samaritan' situations)

– third parties affected by the negligent care given to a patient

– non-patients seen solely for the purposes of medical examinations

(a) Non-patients in need of medical care

[6.11] What happens where a person (who is not ordinarily a patient of the doctor in question) presents for care to a practitioner in circumstances where the practitioner is unable to see the patient, for example where the case does not appear to be an emergency and the doctor's surgery appointment slots are fully booked or where the doctor is going off duty? In general, the principle is that unless a doctor or institution accepts the care of the patient, then no duty of care arises. Conversely, an Australian case has accepted that doctors may owe a duty of care to non-patients where the situation is an emergency, the doctor is in a position to help and the doctor has received a direct request for help.[13] The law on this point in Ireland is not clear. Another situation that may arise in the Irish situation is where a patient is a GMS patient of a general practitioner; in such situations, the doctor is under a contractual obligation (as well as a duty of care) to see her patients. There is nothing in the contract for provision of GMS services to say that such patients must be seen immediately, so the doctor may still exercise clinical judgment as to when that patient should be seen.

[6.12] Similar issues may arise where a doctor stumbles across the scene of an accident. While there is no definite general obligation on a practitioner to provide care to a person

---

[12] *Barnett v Chelsea and Kensington Hospital Management Committee* [1969] 1 QB 428. In this case (which we return to below when discussing causation—see para **[6.58]**) patients presented to the casualty department of the defendant hospital, but a doctor was unable to see them because he himself was sick and he directed the men (who had inadvertently consumed arsenic) to go home and see their own doctors. The doctor was held by the court to have been under a duty to examine the men.

[13] *Lowns v Woods* (1996) Australian Tort Reports 81. A doctor was requested to visit a child who was not his patient, but who was experiencing seizures. He declined to do so. The child suffered brain damage and the doctor was found guilty of negligence. The judgment points out that, although a doctor may feel under a moral obligation to attend someone who is not her patient, this does not necessarily translate into an automatic legal obligation to attend. In this case, Dr Lowns was found to have been negligent because (a) he had no satisfactory excuse for not attending; (b) he knew the child to be nearby; and (c) he had, most importantly, received a direct request to do so. Liability also arose in part because of obligations created by the Australian Medical Practitioners Act 1938.

in a 'good Samaritan' situation or to a person who is not ordinarily her patient, if she does choose to do so, then she will be under a duty of care to treat the patient. Naturally, in such an emergency situation, the skill which the doctor is expected to exercise will be tempered by the nature of the emergency, the setting, the availability or otherwise of back-up care or facilities and so on.[14]

(b) The threat of harm to third parties

[6.13] Sometimes, as a result of a doctor providing treatment to her patient, third parties may be affected. To what extent does the clinician owe these third parties a duty of care? Broadly speaking, the law requires that the identity of the third party who is affected should be foreseeable to the clinician at the time of providing treatment to the patient. In a case where a man underwent a (failed) vasectomy and three years later impregnated a woman with whom he had not been in a relationship at the time of the operation, the court refused the claim of the woman against the doctors, stating that at the time of the operation, the doctors:

> [H]ad no knowledge of her, she was not an existing sexual partner of [the man in question] but was merely, like any other woman in the world, a potential future partner of his, that is to say a member of an indeterminately large class of females who might have sexual relations with [him] during his lifetime.[15]

[6.14] A similar approach applies in those cases where a patient causes physical harm to a third party, for example where he is negligently certified as fit to drive and then injures or kills another road user, or where a psychiatric patient is negligently discharged and then attacks a person. No cases of this nature have arisen in Ireland, but in other countries principles have emerged to suggest that a doctor may be liable to third parties for injuries caused where:

- the injury suffered by the plaintiff was foreseeable;
- there was proximity between clinician and plaintiff;
- the imposition of the duty of care on the clinician is fair in the circumstances.

[6.15] In an English case where a man with a known psychiatric history and propensity for sexual violence against children abducted and killed a four-year old girl, the issue arose as to whether the doctors who had failed to treat the killer were liable for the death of the child. The court held that although the man's actions were foreseeable, the doctors

---

[14] The issue of whether a lower standard of care applies in emergencies is discussed at para **[6.30]**. Many commentators argue that 'professional rescuers' such as the medically qualified should not be exempted from helping in an emergency scenario and that circumstances of a particular situation may mandate that the clinician (as in *Lowns v Wood*, see fn 13) could and should do something to help. See Kennedy & Grubb, *Medical Law* (3rd edn, London 2000), p 298. In Australia, the State of Queensland has a law exempting medical and nursing personnel from liability for negligence when providing emergency care at the scene of an accident or during transport from the accident scene to hospital: Voluntary Aid in Emergency Act 1973 (Qld) s 3.

[15] *Goodwill v British Pregnancy Advisory Service* [1996] 2 All ER 161. Contrast this case (where the person at risk of becoming pregnant could not be foreseen) and so-called 'wrongful conception' cases such as *McFarlane* (discussed at para **[6.38]**), where the identity of the person at risk from pregnancy (the wife of the patient) was obviously foreseeable.

were not liable because the victim was not identifiable to them and so the necessary proximity could not exist.[16] In English law, therefore, if the identity of a potential third-party victim of clinical negligence cannot be foreseen, then the doctor does not owe a duty to that victim; it is not enough that the *risk* is foreseen, it must also be possible to foresee the identity of the third party whom the negligence may foreseeably affect.

[6.16] In the United States, courts have decided that where a doctor has negligently failed to advise HIV-positive patients of their diagnosis, the doctor owes a duty not only to the patient, but may also owe a duty to those whom the patient infects.[17] It is hard to predict what approach the Irish courts would take. It certainly seems reasonable that a practitioner should be responsible for the consequences of her actions when those consequences affect those other than her patient, but it would also be preferable that there is a limit to the size of the group to which the practitioner might be liable. It would seem harsh that if two doctors make the same error, for example, each failing to inform a different HIV-positive patient of his diagnosis, that the extent of each doctor's liability should depend on how promiscuous the patient is and therefore how many people he might infect. The preferable approach in Irish law might be that a doctor who is negligent to one of his patients should also be liable for negligence only to those third parties whom a reasonable person might foreseeably identify as being affected by his negligence.

[6.17] A last category of third party who may be affected by negligence includes those who suffer psychiatric trauma (sometimes called 'nervous shock') as a result of witnessing the distressing consequences of medical negligence or as a result of the manner in which news is relayed to the third party. In general, a duty of care will only attend to such person where a sudden, shocking event[18] witnessed by the plaintiff is especially traumatic,[19] a direct consequence of the negligent medical treatment or its immediate aftermath and directly causes a severe psychiatric reaction. A person may also rarely claim directly for 'nervous shock' where he is the victim of negligently-

---

[16] *Palmer v Tees Health Authority* [1999] Lloyd's Rep Mcd 351 CA. The Court took the view that the most effective way to avert the danger in this case was to warn the person at risk and reasoned that because the child could not have been identified, she could not have been warned. See also *Tarasoff v Regents of the University of California* (1976) 131 Cal Rptr 14 and the discussion of whether there is a 'duty to warn' in Ch 3 'Confidentiality', para **[3.35]**.

[17] *DiMarco v Lynch Homes – Chester County Inc* (1989) 525 Pa 558; *Reisner v Regents of the University of California* (1995) 31 Cal App 4th 1110 In this second case the doctor did not tell the patient she was HIV-positive and was sued by the boyfriend of the patient, who contracted HIV from the patient. The law in the United States generally appears to require that the victim's identity be foreseeable, but note that in *DiMarco* the court suggested that the duty was owed to 'anyone who is physically intimate with the patient' including a person with whom the patient was not involved at the time she was negligently infected with (and advised about) Hepatitis B.

[18] The definition of an event may be elastic: the 14-day decline (leading to death) of a man following a road traffic accident was not regarded as a traumatic 'event' in *Sion v Hampstead Health Authority* (The Times, 10 June 1994, while the delivery and death of an infant over a 48-hour period was regarded as a sufficiently traumatic 'event' in *Tredget v Bexley Health Authority* [1994] 5 Med LR 178. The law in Ireland is that a person's nervous shock must be caused by an event giving rise to actual or apprehended physical injury to the plaintiff or a person other than the plaintiff: *Kelly v Hennessey* [1995] 3 IR 253; *Fletcher v Commissioner of Public Works* [2003] 2 ILRM 94.

communicated information concerning a patient; in one such case, a father attended a hospital to be told his infant son was dead and was given the dead infant to hold until it was realised that a mistake had been made and that the man's son was in fact alive and well.[20]

(c) Medical examinations

[6.18] Where a clinician is employed to conduct an examination for a specific purpose (such as a pre-employment medical or an examination on behalf of an insurance company) of a person who is not ordinarily a patient of the clinician in question, how extensive is the clinician's duty of care to that patient? Historically, all that was asked of the examining clinician in such circumstances was that the examination in question did not cause any harm to the patient and any duty owed by the doctor was to the company employing him and not to the patient.[21] However, there is an increasing body of law[22] to say that the mere fact that a doctor is retained to examine a person on behalf of a third party does not exempt the doctor from owing a duty to that patient. The law in Ireland is not clear on this point.

[6.19] Where the clinician is in the occupational health setting, the position will be slightly different; in that case the clinician owes duties both to the patient/employee to whom the clinician is providing care and to the employer, on whose behalf he is providing that care.[23] While in practical terms the practitioner owes a 'split' duty of care

---

18   (\contd) In *Devlin v National Maternity Hospital* [2007] IESC 50, the Supreme Court found that even where a plaintiff suffers a recognisable psychiatric injury, if there was no 'actual or apprehended physical injury to the plaintiff or a person other than the plaintiff' (*Kelly v Hennessy* [1995] 3 IR 263, per Keane CJ) giving rise to the nervous shock, then the plaintiffs could not recover damages for nervous shock (which allegedly arose in Devlin out of the retention of the organs of a child).

19   *Taylor v Somerset Health Authority* (1993) 16 BMLR. In this case, a widow's visit to a hospital mortuary to see her husband's dead body (where he died following a negligent failure to diagnose heart disease) did not amount to a sufficiently traumatic event. Conversely, following a negligent (because it was unnecessary) mastectomy, a court allowed the husband and son to recover for the 'trauma' caused (in the case of the husband) by seeing his wife naked for the first time after the mastectomy and (in the case of the son) by overhearing the telephone conversation in which the mother was told she had cancer: *Frogatt v Chesterfield and North Derbyshire Royal Hospital NHS Trust* [2002] All ER 218.

20   *Farrell v Avon Health Authority* [2001] Lloyds Rep Med 458.

21   *Kapfunde v Abbey National Plc* (1999) 45 BMLR 176.

22   In *JD v East Berkshire Community Health NHS Trust* [2005] UKHL 23, [2005] 2 AC 373, the House of Lords held that a doctor examining a child on behalf of a health authority in circumstances where there is a suspicion that the child has been abused owed a duty of care to the child but not (and this was a case where the parents had sued the authority having been wrongfully accused of abuse on foot of the relevant examination) to the parents of the child. *Webb v TD* (1997) 95 P 2d 1008 (Montana Superior Court) is American authority for the proposition that a doctor owes a duty to the patient when examining the patient on behalf of an outside agency.

23   This area and its potential conflicts are more thoroughly canvassed in Ch 8 'Health in the Workplace'.

to both parties, it is generally accepted that her duty to the patient predominates in the event of conflict.[24]

The standard of care

[6.20] There is a distinction between the standard of care expected from the 'ordinary' person and that expected from a 'professional' and we begin with an examination of the these two differing standards.

The standard of care of the 'reasonably careful man'

[6.21] In negligence generally (for example, following an accident arising out of a failure to take care when driving), the standard of care, or in other words how careful someone has to be in a situation where he is under a duty of care, is the care 'expected from a reasonably careful man in the circumstances.'[25] A person will be compared to what a reasonable person[26] would have done (or not done) in the circumstances and it is the judge who decides whether or not this standard has been met. The 'reasonable person' test is not without problems. Obviously there are times when the test cannot be applied unstintingly—if someone is blind or missing a limb, he cannot be expected to have precisely the same faculties and powers as the 'ordinary man' and this may have to be taken into account.[27]

Is the ordinary standard of care absolute?

[6.22] The circumstances in which the general standard of care expected might vary include the following:

- the standard expected may be higher if there is a higher probability of an accident in the circumstances[28] or if any accident that occurs is likely to have particularly serious consequences, even if the likelihood of the accident occurring is small;

---

[24] See 'International Code of Ethics for Occupational Health Professionals', *Encyclopaedia of Occupational Health and Safety* (4th edn, 1998), Vol 1, 19.1–19.31.

[25] *McComiskey v McDermott* [1974] IR 75. In *McComiskey*, the plaintiff was being driven in a car by his friend who was a rally driver; the driver was expected in the circumstances to show the care when driving that would be expected of a competent rally driver.

[26] English courts used frequently to refer to what the notional 'man on the Clapham omnibus' would have done in the circumstances.

[27] See McMahon & Binchy, *Law of Torts* (3rd edn, Tottel Publishing, 2000) Ch 7. A blind person will fall below the reasonable person's standard of care if he gets into a car and tries to drive but will probably not do so if he leaves his house unaided and, in attempting to make his way about, occasionally impedes traffic.

[28] Two contrasting clinical examples: in *Plunkett v St Laurence's Hospital* (1952) 86 ILTR 157 (HC), a woman 'hardly able to move' fell off an x-ray couch. This was held to be so unlikely to have occurred that it was found that there was no negligence in failing to have kept a closer eye on her. Conversely, in *Kelly v St Laurence's Hospital* [1989] ILRM 437, an epileptic patient fell from a window when going to a toilet unaccompanied shortly after all of his medications had been discontinued. The likelihood of an accident was greater in this latter case and the hospital was to have breached the expected standard of care.

– a lower standard may be applied if the defendant's conduct fulfils some important social function, such as the saving of a life or if it would be practically impossible in terms of the cost or manpower involved to completely eliminate the risk.

We also discuss below (see para **[6.29]***ff*) whether there are other factors, such as limited resources or inexperience, that might also lower the professional standard of care expected in the clinical setting.

The standard of care of the 'professional'

[6.23] The standard of care expected from the professional is different. It is not a test by comparison with the reasonably careful man, where the judge decides what is 'reasonable care'. Rather, the key words in summarising the approach of the courts to the professional's standard of care are 'qualified deference'. Courts accept that in the rarefied and specialised world of a professional, the profession itself may set its own standards and the courts will generally not interfere with those standards, once the standards appear (to the court) not to be obviously unsatisfactory.

Accordingly, when assessing the standard of care expected of the professional accused of negligence, the comparison made is not with what the courts think the reasonably careful man would have done in the circumstances, but with the practice and standards of that professional's peers. Furthermore, the courts also bear in mind when it comes to the professional that there may be differences in opinion as to what constitutes best practice. This means in effect that a professional may take any one of a number of courses of action without falling below the requisite standard of care, so long as the course of action she takes is supported by some responsible body of opinion within the profession. The professional standard of care has been distilled as follows:

> [The standard of care is] that of the ordinary skilled person exercising and professing to have that special skill, and a doctor...[is] not to be held negligent if he acts in accordance with the practice accepted at that time as proper by a responsible body of medical opinion, notwithstanding that other doctors adopt different practices.[29]

The Dunne test

[6.24] In Irish law, the most important case governing clinical negligence is *Dunne v National Maternity Hospital*,[30] a case arising out of birth injuries suffered by a child born in the defendant hospital. Of greatest relevance to our present discussion, the Supreme Court detailed the test for the standard of care in the medical profession (and by extension comparable clinical professions). The test[31] is reproduced here in full and

---

[29] *Salmond and Heuston on the Law of Torts* (21st edn, London, 1996), 232.

[30] *Dunne v National Maternity Hospital* [1989] IR 91. The test that is set out in the text is from the judgment of Chief Justice Finlay. The classic statement of medical negligence in the United Kingdom is the *Bolam* test (from *Bolam v Friern Hospital Management Committee* [1957] 2 All ER 118: '[A] doctor is not guilty of negligence if he has acted in accordance with a practice accepted as proper by a responsible body of medical men skilled in that particular art.'

[31] *Dunne v National Maternity Hospital* [1989] IR 91 at 109*ff*, per Finlay CJ. Note that a similar restatement of the so-called *Bolam* principles (and in particular the reasoning that there might be circumstances in which the 'professional standard' was obviously flawed) occurred in English law in the case *Bolitho v Hackney Health Authority* [1998] AC 232.

then applied to a clinical example below (see para **[6.18]**) so that we can examine its workings:

1. The true test for establishing negligence in diagnosis or treatment on the part of a medical practitioner is whether he has been proved to be guilty of such failure as no medical practitioner of equal specialist or general status and skill would be guilty of if acting with ordinary care.

2. If the allegation of negligence against a medical practitioner is based on proof that he deviated from a general and approved practice, that will not establish negligence unless it is also proved that the course he did take was one which no medical practitioner of like specialisation and skill would have followed had he been taking the ordinary care required from a person of his qualification.

3. If a medical practitioner charged with negligence defends his conduct by establishing that he followed a practice which was general, and which was approved of by his colleagues of similar specialisation and skill, he cannot escape liability if in reply the plaintiff establishes that such practice has inherent defects which ought to be obvious to any person giving the matter due consideration.

4. An honest difference of opinion between doctors as to which is the better of two ways of treating a patient does not provide any ground for leaving a question to the jury[32] as to whether a person who has followed one course rather than the other has been negligent.

5. It is not for a [judge] to decide which of two alternative courses of treatment is in [her] opinion preferable, but her function is merely to decide whether the course of treatment followed, on the evidence, complied with the careful conduct of a medical practitioner of like specialisation and skill to that professed by the defendant.

The judge also went on to say that: 'General and approved practice [mentioned in parts 2 and 3 of the test] need not be universal but must be approved of and adhered to by a *substantial* number of *reputable* practitioners holding the relevant specialist or general qualification [emphasis added].'

Translating and applying Dunne

[6.25] So, the essential elements of the standard of care expected from the professional medical person are:

– *Comparison with a professional of 'equal specialisation'*

This means that a doctor's acts or omissions will be set against those expected of a comparable doctor—a GP will be compared with the standard of a GP, not a consultant neurologist, even if the problem facing the doctor was a neurological one. In all cases the comparison is with the normal competent

---

[32] At the time, juries were a common feature of clinical negligence actions. There was also a sixth element of the *Dunne* test, which concerned issues arising when medical negligence falls to be considered by a jury. Negligence cases heard by juries are now so rare that this final component is not considered here.

comparable professional. A vascular surgeon will not be compared with the most gifted professor of vascular surgery, but with another ordinary skilled vascular surgeon.[33]

– *Deviation from accepted practice is not negligence*

The deviation has to be one that no other comparable doctor would have taken. So, there is no suggestion that there is only one way of doing everything. So long as the course taken is one that reasonable doctors[34] would adopt (even if not all doctors—or even the majority of them—would have taken that course), then it is not negligent.

– *Blindly following the standard course of action may nonetheless be negligent*

A course of action ordinarily followed by doctors might have inherent and obvious flaws and, if it does, the court may find a practitioner negligent for having followed it. For example, if a hospital's process for monitoring babies during labour has flaws detectable by anyone giving the system any thought, then a gynaecologist could not rely for her defence on the fact that she followed that protocol.

– *An honest difference of opinion between two medical practitioners does not mean that one of them must be guilty of negligence.*

The *Dunne* principles recognise that there may be two ways of doing something or, in other words, that there may be more than one 'general and approved practice'. Any difference of opinion between doctors who adopt different general and approved practices must be both honest and reasonable.

– *A jury or judge is not there to decide whether one course of action is preferable to another*

The question to be decided is simply whether the conduct complained of was negligence, not whether it was less expedient, less convenient or more painful than another approach that might have been taken by the doctor.

[6.26] Essentially, *Dunne* gives limited latitude and qualified deference to professionals in clinical practice. Doctors are allowed to follow an accepted standard within the profession and, perhaps more importantly, to differ from a given accepted practice without the court finding them negligent. A doctor pursuing any course of action must be able to show that her action was consistent with a body (although not necessarily the majority body or even an especially substantial body) of responsible opinion within the profession. However, the deference and latitude are not absolute; the court will refuse to accept the doctor's behaviour, even if she followed general and accepted practice, if that practice itself is obviously flawed.

---

[33] *O'Donovan v Cork Co. Council* [1967] IR 173.

[34] It should be observed that when the court in *Dunne* talks about 'no medical practitioner' following a certain course of action, it means no medical practitioner acting with reasonable care. It would not be enough for a defendant to produce a doctor or two who approved of, or who routinely adopted, the practice of the defendant if it were obvious that approving of the conduct of the defendant was inconsistent with reasonable care.

[6.27] There are reasons why this latitude is afforded to the professions and to the medical profession in particular. Among the most important is that medicine, if it is to advance, needs to be allowed to develop and to explore new avenues of treatment, without a doctor working under the constant fear of being sued every time she pursues an unorthodox, new or not yet wholly proven practice.

[6.28] In Example 6.2, we look at the application of the *Dunne* principles.

Example 6.2

A patient attended for assessment of a blocked carotid artery. The treating consultant vascular surgeon, Dr Jekyll, was aware that some academic papers had recently suggested that patients with a blockage of less than 50 per cent may be better treated without surgery. The patient had a 45 per cent blockage in his artery. The decision was therefore taken to manage the patient conservatively with blood-thinning tablets. Dr Jekyll was the only one of three vascular surgeons in her hospital taking this new approach. A month later, the patient suffered a stroke and died. His wife initiates an action for negligence. She claims that the doctor should instead have performed the operation. Applying the *Dunne* test, was Dr Jekyll negligent?

Here we are concerned not with the existence of the duty of care (although that is obviously present) or whether any negligence caused harm. We instead merely wish to apply the *Dunne* principles in order to ascertain whether the doctor breached the expected standard of care. We examine each element of the *Dunne* principles in the order that they were set out in the case itself (see para **[6.24]**):

1. *Comparison with practitioners of equal specialist skill*

    Dr Jekyll will be compared to the practice of other ordinary skilled vascular surgeons exercising responsible care. Had she been a GP taking the decision to initiate conservative treatment, then she would be compared to the standard of other GPs and so on.

2. *Deviation from accepted practice*

    She has deviated from orthodox treatment but has chosen to follow a new regimen suggested by academic papers. Is her deviation negligent? Only if no other practitioner of equal skill[35] would follow this course. Dr Jekyll's approach is based on academic research. It is therefore likely that there would be little problem in showing that her approach was consistent with a responsible, if novel, body of therapeutic opinion.

---

[35] This requirement set out in *Dunne* appears to suggest that the number of practitioners who would have followed the course of action adopted by a defendant need not be 'substantial' (to use the standard adopted in *Hills v Potter* [1984] 1 WLR 641). In *De Freitas v O'Brien* [1995] 6 Med LR 108,, the defendant succeeded in disproving negligence even where only a tiny minority of neurosurgeons would have followed the course adopted by the defendant. The judgment of White J in *Shuit v Mylotte* [2006] IEHC 89 appears to apply the test that the plaintiff must show that *no* reasonable practitioner would have adopted the course taken by the defendant.

3. *Was the practice she chose to follow inherently flawed?*[36]

   Were it the case that she drew her therapeutic inspiration from a single article and, what is more, an article that was based on obviously poor research or published in a journal known to have a poor reputation for accuracy, then the issue of whether her deviation from accepted practice was justifiable might arise. Let us assume, however, that the alternative treatment was reported in reputable journals (although not yet standard practice in Ireland). The court would then be unlikely to criticise the practice taken by Dr Jekyll as having obvious shortcomings.[37]

4. *Difference of opinion*

   In following this course of action, therefore, Dr Jekyll did differ from her colleagues, but it was an honest and responsible difference of opinion.[38]

5. *The issue to be decided was whether negligence was present*

   The question to be decided is not whether surgery would have been the preferable option. It may well have been (particularly in hindsight), but the issue is whether, taking the facts of the case and the *Dunne* principles into account, the choice of conservative treatment was negligent.

---

[36] In fact, it is a comparative rarity for the court to set aside the evidence of experts in clinical negligence and find that, notwithstanding professional practice, the defendant followed a course of action that was negligent: in *Gottstein v Maguire and Walsh* [2004] IEHC 416, the court held that failing to have someone present in the intensive care unit of the defendant hospital who could replace a dislodged tracheotomy tube (per Johnson J) was 'an inherent defect...which ought to be obvious to any person giving the matter due consideration and having given it due consideration, it is obvious to me.' See also *Roche v Peilow* [1985] IR 232, *Reynolds v North Tyneside Health Authority* (unreported, but cited in Jackson, *Medical Law* (Oxford, 2006), 127) and *Marriott v West Midlands RHA* [1999] Lloyds Rep Med 23. In the latter case, the defendant GP had led expert evidence to say that he had not been negligent in failing to refer a patient back to hospital when he had continuing problems following a head injury: the trial judge refused to accept this professional evidence, describing it as 'not reasonably prudent'. His decision was upheld by the Court of Appeal.

[37] English law, like Irish law, includes the proviso that the court will not automatically accept medical evidence of 'accepted practice' where accepted practice has obvious and inherent problems: *Bolitho v City and Hackney Health Authority* [1997] 4 All ER 771. See Brazier and Miola, 'Bye-Bye *Bolam*: A Medical Litigation Revolution?' (2000) 8 Med Law Rev 85–114; see also Lord Woolf, 'Are the Courts Excessively Deferential to the Medical Profession?' (2001) 9 Med Law Rev 1–16.

[38] The issue of honest disagreement between experts was discussed in *Griffin v Patton* [2004] IESC 46. Where a disagreement is as to which treatment or diagnosis is to be preferred the judge is not entitled to prefer one doctor's opinion over the other; however, where the disagreement is whether the course of action pursued by a defendant is negligent, then the judge may choose the evidence that seems to him the more compelling; per Geoghegan J: 'The fact that one doctor may say in the witness-box that in his opinion, the appellant was not to blame does not in any way oust the normal function of the trial judge on the issues of fact even if the judge takes the view that the doctor giving evidence was giving an honest opinion.' There may nonetheless be circumstances where a judge is unable, having listened to the evidence to decide between the plaintiff and defendant's evidence on negligence: *Quinn v Mid-Western Health Board* [2005] 4 IR 1.

The likelihood on this analysis of events in the light of the *Dunne* principles is that even though the patient died, the surgeon was not negligent.

Are there cases in which the Dunne standard of care would not apply?

[6.29] It is occasionally suggested that there may be circumstances where the standard of care expected from a clinician may be lower that usual. Some authors[39] suggest that circumstances in which one might argue for a lower standard of care include:

– where resources are limited;

– where the situation is an emergency;

– where the doctor is inexperienced (see para **[6.62]** below);

– where the clinician is a practitioner of alternative medicine.

[6.30] In England, courts have been prepared to accept that a lower standard may be permissible where finite resources prevent impeccable care, but nonetheless insist that there is a certain minimum standard that must be met.[40] It is suggested that a similar approach would be taken in Ireland. In the case of emergencies, the English courts have observed:[41] 'An emergency may overburden resources and, if an individual is forced by circumstances to do too many things at once, the fact that he does one of them incorrectly should not lightly be taken as negligence.'

[6.31] As far as cases of alternative practitioners are concerned, where that practitioner is also a medical practitioner, it seems to follow that she will be judged by the *Dunne* standard. However, where she is not a medical practitioner, then the position would seem to be logically that as stated in *Shakoor v Situ*:[42]

> [A] plaintiff may succeed in an action against an alternative practitioner for negligently prescribing a remedy either by calling an expert in the speciality in question to assert and prove that the defendant has failed to exercise the skill and care appropriate to that art [or]... the plaintiff may prove that the prevailing standard of skill and care 'in that art' is deficient in this country having regard to risks which were not and should have been taken into account.

---

[39] See Jackson, *Medical Law* (Oxford, 2006), 133.

[40] *Knight v Home Office* [1990] 3 All ER 237.

[41] *Wilsher v Essex Area Health Authority* [1987] 1 QB 730, [1987] 2 WLR 425, per Mustill LJ at 439. But note that where the setting is one geared towards emergencies (for example, an intensive care unit), such latitude will not apply so readily: *Gottstein v Maguire and Walsh* [2004] IEHC 416.

[42] *Shakoor v Situ* [2001] 1 WLR 410, per Livesey QC. The defendant was a practitioner of Chinese herbal medicine (but not an orthodox doctor) who had prescribed a skin treatment that had a fatal idiosyncratic reaction on the patient. Some reports of this potentially serious outcome had appeared in the medical journals. The court held that, even applying the standard of the orthodox practitioner, the defendant had not been negligent in failing to notice such letters and warnings as had appeared in orthodox medical publications and that even if he had seen those warnings they would not have alerted him to the fact that the preparation was too dangerous to prescribe.

Are all clinicians 'professionals'?

[6.32] In drawing a distinction between 'ordinary' and 'professional' negligence and their differing standards of care, the question then arises whether all healthcare practitioners are professionals for the purposes of negligence—do nurses, radiographers, doctors, dentists and pharmacists and the rest all qualify as professionals? Historically, the courts have occasionally drawn distinctions between different categories within the healthcare sector and in one case, *Kelly v St Laurence's Hospital*, concluded that nurses were not professionals for the purposes of negligence.[43]

[6.33] There appear to be two elements involved in deciding whether a health carer is a 'professional' and will accordingly be judged by the more deferential standard of professional negligence. The first is the possession of a special skill or competence, a skill usually conferred by specialist qualifications. The second is the fact of setting out one's stall as possessing that skill and offering to use it to help people achieve a specific end. A practising doctor or dentist is therefore a 'professional'; she possesses the special skills conferred by a medical or dental degree and—in practising medicine or dentistry—claims to be able to use those skills to effect an improvement in health for those who consult her.

[6.34] Simply claiming to possess a skill is not enough to be termed a professional. A jeweller who pierces ears will not, even though she is performing a surgical procedure (albeit a minor one), be expected to demonstrate the abilities of a surgeon, merely the capabilities the court expects of the average jeweller.[44] Similarly, in one Irish case, a 'bone-setter' claimed to be able to cure TB[45] and the court decided that he was not expected to have the skill of a physician, for he had never said that he was one, but he was expected to discharge the skill he claimed to have, namely that of being able to cure tuberculosis. The patient had died and the defendant was found to have been negligent by the ordinary standard of negligence.

[6.35] Does the decision in *Kelly v St Laurence's Hospital* still apply and does it mean that some paramedical staff are not to be regarded, legally speaking, as professionals? One possibility is that the decision that held that nurses were not professionals was an anomaly, a decision rooted in an old-fashioned mindset or predicated on the non-university-based education that previously characterised nursing training. It seems on balance that a course of study conferring a formal qualification in a particular skill that, first, the public regards as a 'special' skill not possessed by the majority of persons and

---

[43] *Kelly v St Laurence's Hospital* [1989] ILRM 437 (SC).

[44] *Philips v Whiteley (William) Ltd* [1938] 1 All ER 566.

[45] *Brogan v Bennett* [1955] IR 119. Mr Bennett had produced a pamphlet headed 'TB CONQUERED' and charged £100 for a rich person and £20 for the poor. Mr Brogan (who belonged to the latter category) fell for it, as many people still fall for utterly implausible treatments today. He left hospital and attended Mr Bennett who (according to the court's judgment) 'produced a bullet on the end of string and said he was going to x-ray the patient. He then caused the pendulum to oscillate and pronounced the case a fairly bad one. He purported to diagnose the exact percentage of impairment of all the main organs of the patient and claimed that by means of his pendulum he could diagnose the ailments of a person at the other end of the world.'

which, secondly, is used to achieve specific outcomes (such as health gain) would make an individual a 'professional'. Accordingly, on this analysis a physiotherapist or occupational therapist, to take two non-medical examples, both of whom can work independently and take independent decisions on specific treatment plans directed at producing a specific health outcome, could be regarded as 'professionals' for the purposes of negligence. On the other hand, it could be argued that nursing and radiography, which have less therapeutic independence and a role less focused on achieving a certain or specific treatment outcome, may be less likely to be regarded as professions when it comes to the arena of negligence.

HARM AND CAUSATION

[6.36] The final element of proving negligence, along with the existence of a duty of care and a breach of the expected standard of care, is that the breach must cause harm to the victim of the alleged negligence.

Harm or damage

[6.37] Where there is no harm or damage, there can be no compensation for negligence even if in fact a negligent act occurred.[46] Where a patient is prescribed a drug to which he is allergic (in circumstances where the doctor should have known he was allergic to that drug) but the mistake is realised before the patient can take the drug, then no harm has resulted,[47] even though duty of care and a breach of that duty were present. We discuss below (para **[6.40]***ff*) what is meant by 'causing' harm.

Damage can take any number of forms. It may be physical, psychological,[48] psychiatric or financial. So, negligently-performed surgery might result in mood disorders, chronic pain, death, the inability to continue in employment or even all of the foregoing and each can be compensated by the law. However, what is critical is that the damage complained must have been caused by the act of which the patient complains. A patient will also not be harmed if the damage done to him does not leave him, objectively, in a worse state

---

[46] See *O'Connor and Tormey v Lenihan* [2005] IEHC 176 in which the plaintiffs' claim for psychiatric injury arising from the retention of their child's organs by the defendant hospital failed on the ground that it could not be shown that either plaintiff had suffered a recognisable psychiatric injury. Also see *Devlin v National Maternity Hospital* [2007] IESC 50, in which the Supreme Court found that even where a plaintiff did suffer a recognisable psychiatric injury, it followed that because there was no 'actual or apprehended physical injury to the plaintiff or a person other than the plaintiff' (*Kelly v Hennessy* [1995] 3 IR 263, per Keane CJ) giving rise to the nervous shock, the plaintiff's could not recover damages for nervous shock arising out of the retention of the organs of their child.

[47] Although it is possible that the patient's discovery that he 'nearly' took something that might have caused harm could cause a psychiatric reaction that might itself be actionable.

[48] Where a person suffers a psychological outcome that is based on fear that an event may transpire (for example, that as a result of his negligent treatment he may die), the courts will only permit recovery where that fear is a realistic one: *Fletcher v Commissioner of Public Works* [2003] 2 ILRM 94; *Philp v Ryan* [2004] IEHC 77.

than he was in before.[49] Any harm arising as a result of alleged negligence must be foreseeable. The law does not require that clinicians protect or warn against risks that could not have been reasonably foreseen. The Irish courts have cited with apparent approval the following:

'It is axiomatic within the concept of negligence that if a particular danger could not reasonably have been anticipated, the defendant has not acted negligently, because a reasonable man does not take precautions against unforeseeable consequences. This is measured by reference to knowledge at the date of the alleged negligence, not with hindsight.'[50]

'Wrongful conception' claims

[6.38] There are some 'harms' that the law will not compensate as matter of policy, even if they arise from negligence, because the law refuses to recognise the 'harm' as having truly damaged the claimant: one such is a claim for 'wrongful conception', [51] which is the birth of a healthy child as a result of a negligently-performed sterilisation procedure. While the law recognises that a negligently-performed sterilisation operation that results in a woman becoming pregnant, when she would not otherwise have done had the operation been successfully performed, is a legal wrong, it limits the degree to which damages will be recovered. It will allow compensation for the pain and distress of childbirth, but not for the upkeep of the child, unless the child is born with a significant disability. The rule against the recovery of legal damages for the maintenance costs of a normal healthy child was laid down in the case of *McFarlane;*[52] the court held that a

---

49 So, in a case where the plaintiff was left scarred by a cosmetic procedure, the judge had regard to the appearance of her abdomen before the operation, concluding that although she was scarred 'it cannot in my view be said that she has been cosmetically damaged or degraded by the procedure'. The judge awarded reduced damages accordingly: *Taylor Flynn v Sulaiman* [2006] IEHC 160, per Peart J.

50 Jones, *Medical Negligence* (3rd edn, Sweet and Maxwell, 2004); cited in *Geoghegan v Harris* [2000] 3 IR 536.

51 'Wrongful conception' or 'wrongful pregnancy' is distinguished from 'wrongful birth' claims, which imply the birth of a disabled child as a result of inadequate antenatal management and from 'wrongful life' claims, which describe a claim by the neonate that he is suffering because his mother was wrongly advised as to continuation or termination of the pregnancy: Mason, *The Troubled Pregnancy* (Cambridge, 2007), 4. For a general discussion of the issues raised by wrongful conception cases, see generally Mason, op cit and Jackson, *Medical Law* (Oxford, 2006), 658–687. In the present state of Irish law (with its restrictions on abortion and limited availability and regulation of prenatal testing), actions for wrongful birth or life are unlikely. It is interesting to wonder, however, whether an Irish woman who was negligently told (following an antenatal diagnostic test) that her foetus was normal, only to be delivered of a handicapped child would have a legal case on the basis that—had she been told of the abnormality—she would have travelled to Britain for an abortion. If so, to what extent would she be able to claim for damages? See *Lee v Taunton and Somerset NHS Trust* [2001] 1 FLR 419.

52 *McFarlane v Tayside Health Board* [2000] 2 AC 59. The case arose following a failed vasectomy performed on Mr McFarlane. Eighteen months after he was told the procedure had been effective and that he no longer needed to use contraception, his wife conceived and gave birth to a healthy child. (contd/)

woman who became pregnant as the result of negligent medical treatment or advice could recover damages for the pain, suffering and inconvenience of her pregnancy and confinement, but there would be no compensation for the cost of the upbringing of her healthy child.[53] Although in Australia the High Court has held that a doctor may be responsible for the costs of rearing a healthy child born following a negligently-performed sterilisation,[54] when a similar case came to be considered before the Irish courts the High Court followed more closely the English jurisprudence.[55]

[6.39] Where a child is born with a significant disability, courts in England will award the differential between the costs of supporting a normal, healthy child (which are not recoverable) and the costs of upkeep inherent in the raising of a child with significant disability.[56]

Causation

[6.40] When the term 'causation' is used, it refers to whether a particular act or omission caused harm in one of two ways. First is the issue of factual causation—did the act or omission in question factually cause the injury complained? Second is the question of whether, even if the harm was factually caused (or contributed to) by the negligence in question, that harm was not too remote from the incident that allegedly caused it. We examine factual causation (the 'but for' test) and remoteness (sometimes termed 'legal causation') in turn.

[6.41] It is for the plaintiff, as the person alleging negligence, to introduce medical expert evidence that 'tilt[s] the scales decisively in favour of the case on causation contended for by the plaintiff's experts'.[57] Where the plaintiff's evidence does not persuade the trial judge that the alleged act or omission caused the harm complained of, then the judge cannot find in favour of the claimant.

---

52 (\contd) *McFarlane* was upheld by the House of Lords in *Rees v Darlington Memorial Hospital NHS Trust* [2003] UKHL 52, [2003] 4 All ER 987 in the case of a visually impaired woman who, concerned that her blindness would prevent her from being able to care for a child, underwent a negligently-performed sterilisation operation. Furthermore, a majority of the Court (4:3) held that McFarlane applied in the case of *Rees* and the woman was not entitled to compensation for the birth of her healthy child.

53 A claim for loss of earnings due to a 'wrongful pregnancy' was also rejected by the English courts: *Greenfield v Irwin* [2001] 1 WLR 1279.

54 *Cattanach v Melchior* [2003] HCA 38, (2003) 199 ALR 131.

55 *Byrne v Ryan* [2007] IEHC 207. Kelly J considered *Cattanach*, but stated that he 'preferred' the decision in *McFarlane*, without setting out reasons for his preference. Kelly J cited with approval Lord Gill in *McFarlane*: 'I am of the opinion that this case should be decided on the principle that the privilege of being a parent is immeasurable in money terms; that the benefits of parenthood transcend any patrimonial loss, if it may be so regarded, that the parents may incur in consequence of their child's existence; and that therefore the pursuers in a case such as this cannot be said to be in an overall position of loss.'

56 *Parkinson v St James and Seacroft University Hospital NHS Trust* [2001] EWCA Civ 530, [2002] QB 266. Note that 'significant disability' has not been judicially defined.

57 *Quinn v Mid-Western Health Board* [2005] 4 IR 1, per Kearns J at 26 in the Supreme Court. Kearns J cited with apparent approval the trial judge's conclusion: (contd/)

Factual causation (the 'but for' test)

[6.42] The test for whether negligence caused harm as a matter of fact is sometimes termed the 'but for' test,[58] ie whether everything would have been all right 'but for' the negligent act.

Case Study 6.1[59]

Three workmen were turned away from a hospital that they had attended on becoming unwell after drinking tea. The reason they were turned away was that the doctor who should have seen them was himself sick. It transpired that the tea was poisoned with arsenic and one of the men died. His wife sued the hospital, but she lost. Given how long had elapsed between the deceased ingesting arsenic and him presenting to hospital, it was too late for an antidote to be successfully administered; the arsenic would have killed her husband anyway, even if he had been seen and admitted by the doctor. It could not be said therefore that the man would still have been alive but for the actions of the hospital. It was the arsenic and not the doctor's failure to see the patient that caused the death.

[6.43] There are some subtleties involved in the 'but for' test, such as the situation in which two separate but connected acts, one non-clinical and the other clinical, combine to cause the final damage. One example might be the scenario in which a driver hits a pedestrian, putting the pedestrian in hospital with relatively minor injuries, but once in hospital the patient receives negligent treatment that kills him. Detailed consideration of these areas of joint liability lie outside the scope of this book, but it is important to note that they do occur.[60] Another, perhaps more relevant, combination of circumstances is where a variety of medical factors exist which may have caused harm to a patient, such

---

[57]   (\contd)

'I am left, therefore, with two mutually inconsistent bodies of evidence neither of which wholly and satisfactorily resolves the issues in the case. It is not for me…to set myself up as a determining authority in regarding these specialist issues, nor do I attempt to do so. I am unable in this case, however, by the application of common sense and a careful understanding of the logic and likelihood of events, to reach a conclusion that the evidence adduced by the plaintiff establishes her case on the balance of probabilities.'

This does not mean that the mere fact that experts disagree means a trial judge cannot decide between them: see *Griffin v Patton* [2004] IESC 46, per Geoghegan J: 'There is nothing in Dunne to support the view that if two medical experts express an honestly held opinion on the negligence issue to opposite effect, the judge is precluded from making a finding of negligence in relation to the way a particular treatment is carried out.'

[58]   Another formulation of the test for factual causation asks whether the act was 'a material element and a substantial factor' in the damage: see McMahon and Binchy, *Law of Torts* (3rd edn, Tottel Publishing, 2000), para [2.15].

[59]   *Barnett v Chelsea and Kensington Hospital Management Committee* [1969] 1 QB 428. This case also accepted the proposition that not every doctor is under an automatic legal obligation to provide healthcare to everyone who requires it, but rather it depends on the circumstances. In *Barnett*, the fact that a doctor was on duty in the Casualty Department was enough (even though the doctor was himself ill at the time) to create a duty to attend the patients. See also *Lowns v Wood* (1996) Australian Tort Reports 81 and the discussion of duty of care at para **[6.09]***ff*. The 'but for' test was succinctly applied by the High Court in *Cunningham v Governor and Guardians of the Coombe Lying-in Hospital & Ors* [2005] IEHC 354.

[60]   See generally McMahon and Binchy, *Law of Torts* (3rd edn, Tottel Publishing, 2000), Ch 2, para [2.06]*ff*.

that it may be difficult to attribute the harm to any identifiable act or omission and in particular to the negligent act or omission alleged.

Case Study 6.2[61]

A premature baby was suffering from multiple conditions and on two occasions oxygen was given to him in too high a concentration. He was subsequently diagnosed with a condition rendering him almost entirely blind. However, while the excess oxygen (the administration of which was negligent) could have caused this condition, there were four other elements of his treatment (none of which amounted to negligence) that could also have caused the loss of sight. Because it could not be stated with sufficient certainty that the administration of excess oxygen was the cause of the harm, there was no negligence.

Causation and 'loss of a chance'

[6.44] One evolving and sometimes controversial area of factual causation is where the patient is not, as such, directly harmed by the treatment given to him by clinicians; instead the acts or omissions of a defendant cause the patient to lose a chance of recovery that he might otherwise have had.

Example 6.3

A woman attends her GP with a lump in her breast. The doctor examines it and tells her it is nothing serious. Three months later, she re-attends and is again reassured. A further three months later, concerned at the advice she has been given, she attends another doctor who refers her for immediate assessment, which results in a diagnosis of breast cancer. The cancer has spread beyond the breast, with a resultant poorer prospect of recovery.

In Example 6.3, the negligence of the original GP did not cause the woman to develop breast cancer; indeed, even had the GP diagnosed the condition at the first visit, the woman would still have been facing a serious condition requiring extensive and gruelling treatment with a serious prospect of death. To what extent is the GP liable to the woman? The approach taken in UK decisions has been that in order to win such a case, the plaintiff must show that his chance of recovery, prior to the negligence of the defendant, was at least 50 per cent; if he was less than 50 per cent likely to recover prior to the negligence of the defendant, then the plaintiff has no claim, even if his chances of recovery were in fact reduced by the negligence of the defendant.[62] There has been some

---

[61] *Wilsher v Essex Area Health Authority* [1988] 1 AC 1074. A similar conclusion was reached by the Supreme Court in *Quinn v Mid-Western Health Board* [2005] IESC 19, [2005] 4 IR 1 where a claim for birth injuries failed on the basis that the plaintiffs did not prove a specific event (delay in delivery) caused the birth injuries or that early delivery would have averted the birth injuries.

[62] *Hotson v East Berkshire AHA* [1987] 1 AC 750. In *Hotson* the plaintiff had suffered a hip injury that was not properly diagnosed for five days; he went on to develop a severe and permanent hip injury. The medical evidence was that there was only a 25 per cent chance that prompt diagnosis would have led to recovery and so the plaintiff failed in his claim. An example of a successful claim is *Hutchinson v Epsom and St Helier NHS Trust* [2002] EWHC 2363, where a trial judge held that had a patient been warned that continuing drinking would kill him (which warning was not given) he would have stopped drinking completely and his liver condition would not have deteriorated, leading to his death.

mitigation of this harsh position in English law,[63] but it remains the case that where a patient cannot show that his chance of recovery would have been at least 50 per cent but for the negligence of a defendant, his claim will fail.

[6.45] In Ireland the state of the law is not wholly certain, but the position appears to be that a patient may recover for the loss of a chance of recovery. In *Philp v Ryan*, the High Court[64] compensated a man who was told that he had prostatitis (benign inflammation of the prostate gland), when in fact he had prostate cancer. The case turned on whether the doctor had been negligent in failing to communicate certain test results (indicative of prostate cancer) to the plaintiff. In holding that negligence occurred, the trial judge appeared also to consider that the loss of chance of recovery was an injury amenable to monetary compensation but what was not clear is whether the compensation was for the fact that the plaintiff's chances of recovery had been reduced or for the fact that the exacerbation of his condition caused the plaintiff reasonable fear and distress.[65] When the matter came before the Supreme Court,[66] a more robust view was taken:

> I should say that it seems to me to be contrary to instinct and logic that a plaintiff should not be entitled to be compensated for the fact that, due to the negligent diagnosis of his medical condition, he has been deprived of appropriate medical advice and the consequent opportunity to avail of treatment which might improve his condition. I can identify no contrary principle of law or justice...[67]

---

[63] *Gregg v Scott* [2005] UKHL 2, [2005] 2 WLR 268. In this case, a negligent failure to diagnose and refer the plaintiff, had led to a delay in ascertaining that he had lymphoma (a cancer of the immune system), reducing his chances of recovery from 42 per cent to 25 per cent. Applying *Hotson*, the House of Lords held that the plaintiff failed in his claim, but see in particular the contention of Lord Phillips that there might be cases where the loss of a chance was so extreme that a plaintiff who had been less than 50 per cent likely to recover might nonetheless be able to make a successful claim and see also the strong dissenting judgments of Lords Hope and Nicholls. Lord Nicholls stated: 'The law would rightly be open to reproach were it to provide a remedy if what is lost by a professional adviser's negligence is a financial opportunity or chance but refuse a remedy where what is lost by a doctor's negligence is the chance of health or even life itself.'

[64] *Philp v Ryan* [2004] IEHC 77. Loss of a chance was also considered a compensatable injury in *Carroll v Lynch* [2002] IEHC 58.

[65] Per Peart J:
> 'I cannot make a definitive conclusion in relation to whether his life has been shortened, or by how long, simply because the whole question is the subject of debate...but I can conclude on the balance of probabilities, the fear that his life has been shortened is a reasonable fear, and the distress caused to the plaintiff in that regard is reasonable, and for which he is entitled to be compensated.'

[66] *Philp v Ryan* [2004] IESC 105, [2004] 4 IR 241.

[67] Per Fennelly J, at 249 of the reported judgment. The judge continued:
> 'It does not matter that the damage suffered by the plaintiff consists of the loss of an opportunity to avail of treatment. It might, with equal logic, be described as an increased risk of shorter life expectancy. It seems to me as illogical to award damages for a probable future injury as if it were a certainty, as to withhold them where the risk is low on the basis that it will not happen at all.'

The court relied in part on the decision of Ó'Dálaigh CJ in *Dunlop v Kenny* (29 July 1969, unreported). Fennelly J concluded: 'In my view, the plaintiff should receive an award for the loss of the opportunity to be advised correctly and treated accordingly.' Note also that the Supreme Court awarded aggravated damages to the plaintiff on the basis that the defendant had deliberately altered his medical notes in order to cover up his negligence.

[6.46] In the later case of *Quinn*, the Supreme Court was not directly asked to consider whether a 'loss of a chance' had arisen, but the court appeared to indicate a willingness to entertain such arguments,[68] although it also appeared to refer with tacit approval to English law.[69] Other jurisdictions have similarly taken a more patient-friendly view than in the UK of those situations in which negligence reduces a patient's chance of recovery.[70]

Res ipsa loquitur

[6.47] In order to succeed in a negligence action, the plaintiff generally has to prove on the balance of probabilities that the alleged act or omission caused the alleged damage as well as proving that the act itself was negligent. Sometimes, however, the patient will not have to prove that a specific act caused the damage, a scenario called *res ipsa loquitur* or 'the facts speak for themselves'. In medical cases, it may be argued that *res ipsa loquitur* arises where the following circumstances all occur:

- the plaintiff was healthy at the time of a given procedure or treatment;
- the procedure or treatment was of a routine nature, involving no special risks;
- the plaintiff had been entirely in the care and control of the defendant throughout;
- the accident in question is such that in the ordinary circumstances it does not happen if those overseeing the treatment or procedure use ordinary care.[71]

[6.48] Where a claim of *res ipsa loquitur* is made out, the onus is cast upon the defendant to explain the plaintiff's injury and to show that it did not result from any negligence on its part. Alternatively, the defendants may seek to prove that it was not the operation or procedure at issue that caused the damage complained of (see Case Study 6.3).

Case Study 6.3

An eight-year old girl was admitted to a hospital and underwent an emergency operation to remove her appendix, carried out under general anaesthetic. After the operation it appeared initially that the girl was beginning to regain consciousness in the normal manner. However, she experienced a series of seizures, and sank into a coma. The plaintiff was subsequently diagnosed as suffering from irreversible brain damage and never regained consciousness, remaining in a deep coma.[72]

---

[68] *Quinn v Mid-Western Health Board* [2005] IESC 19, [2005] 4 IR 1. Kearns J stated, at 11: 'It is somewhat surprising that the case was presented to the trial judge on an "all-or-nothing" basis. No case was made along the lines that the delay in intervention meant that the plaintiff had "lost a chance" of a better outcome for which she was entitled to be compensated'.

[69] Per Kearns J at 18, referring to *Gregg v Scott* [2005] 2 WLR 268: '[It] is the most recent authority in support of the proposition that actionable claims for "loss of a chance" do not lie. A useful resumé of the relevant policy considerations suggesting why this is the preferred approach appear in the judgment of Baroness Hale of Richmond'.

[70] See *Rufo v Hosking* (2004) NSWCA 391. The court stated (per Santow JA para 26): 'Recovery for loss of a chance can be seen therefore as the corollary of a medical duty of care directed to achieving the best chance of a successful outcome though it call for no more than reasonable care and skill in that endeavor [*sic*]'.

[71] See *Scott v London and St Katherine Docks Co* (1865) 3 H&C 596 at 60, per Erie CJ.

[72] *Lindsay v Mid-Western Health Board* [1993] 2 IR 147.

In a case such as that in Case Study 6.3, the facts may appear to invite the inference that the operation must have caused the damage suffered by the patient, but the plaintiff must still prove that the treatment afforded to him was negligent, and that only the treatment will explain the complications suffered by him. In fact, medical scenarios in which the 'but for' test is set aside in favour of the presumption that there must have been negligence are comparatively rare. This is because the circumstances in which *res ipsa loquitur* will apply in the medical negligence setting require that:

– the plaintiff must prove a negligent act on the part of the defendant;

– the defendant may counter the suggestion of res ipsa loquitur by proving either (a) that it did nothing that could be described as negligent;[73] or (b) that there was another reasonable explanation for the plaintiff's condition aside from negligence.

[6.49] There is also English law to the effect that in some rare cases (in particular, where it is not possible to identify one particular act or one particular party responsible for negligence), where there is evidence of harm being caused arising from negligence, justice may demand that the plaintiff succeed,[74] even if he cannot prove precisely who or what caused his harm. However, this approach appears to have been rejected in Irish law by the Supreme Court.[75]

Legal causation and remoteness

[6.50] As well as factual causation, there is also 'legal' causation, which describes whether a court will attach legal consequences (such as compensation) to the fact that a certain act caused a certain consequence. Even though one thing factually causes another, the law may say that the damage was not 'legally' caused because the harm was too remote from the negligent act or omission. Remoteness may arise in one of two ways.

1. The damage was not foreseeable; or

2. Some new event has occurred that has broken the chain of causation.[76]

The issue of whether or not a particular outcome of medical treatment was foreseeable is rarely in issue: if a surgeon performs an operation upon a person, then any resultant damage is likely to be foreseeable. Examples of where a claim in relation to medical

---

73 In *Doherty v Reynolds and St James's Hospital* [2004] IESC 42 a High Court decision was set aside: the High Court judge had applied *res ipsa loquitur*, but his decision was faulted for failing to give due weight the defendants' evidence as to the steps in place to prevent adverse outcomes of treatment.

74 *Fairchild v Glenhaven Funeral Services* [2002] UKHL 22, [2003] 1 AC 32. In *Fairchild*, the plaintiffs had mesothelioma, which is a form of lung cancer caused only by exposure to asbestos. The plaintiffs could prove that their tumours were caused by exposure to asbestos but could not prove with certainty which of several employers was responsible for the exposure. The court nonetheless allowed the plaintiffs to succeed.

75 *Quinn v Mid-Western Health Board* [2005] IESC 19, [2005] 4 IR 1.

76 For example in *Conole v Redbank Oyster Co* [1976] IR 191, a child was drowned when an unseaworthy boat capsized. The original action was against the boat's owners and manufacturers. The court felt that the manufacturers could not be held to blame. The captain's decision to go to sea, in spite of warnings not to, constituted a whole new act, meaning that liability for negligence lay with the captain, not on the manufacturers. Also called novus octus interveniens.

negligence fails on the ground that the damage caused to the patient was too remote, whether due to lack of foreseeability or due a new intervening event, are rare.[77]

PRACTICAL ASPECTS OF NEGLIGENCE

[6.51] Having considered the theory of negligence and how the law applies those theories, we now turn to consider how the law of negligence applies in the day-to-day setting of clinical practice. We begin by examining the issue of who is the appropriate defendant in a legal action arising out of clinical negligence, before considering how the law of negligence applies to certain clinical scenarios.

Quick Reference Guide 6.2

Exploring the elements of negligence

---

1. Duty of care
- ❖ There is a duty of care when a professional relationship ('proximity') arises between clinician and patient. A breach of duty of care generally only amounts to negligence where the damage caused by the breach is foreseeable.
- ❖ In rare circumstances, a practitioner may owe a duty of care to a person other than her patient.

2. Standard of care
- ❖ The standard of care takes two forms: one for negligence generally and another for professional negligence. Falling below the appropriate standard of care is one of the keystones of negligence.
- ❖ In cases of general negligence, the standard is that expected from the 'reasonable man' in the position of the person against whom negligence is alleged. The judge decides on what is the standard to be expected of the reasonable man.
- ❖ In cases of the professional negligence, the standard is that of the profession itself. A professional accused of negligence will be judged by reference to the conduct espoused by comparable members of the profession. A professional does not have to do what every other comparable professional would do, merely that which is approved of by a reputable body of opinion within the profession.
- ❖ A professional is someone who has special skills (such as clinical skills conferred by education) and who represents herself to the public as capable of practising those skills.

3. Damage and causation
- ❖ The damage cause by negligence can take any form including physical, financial and psychological harm.

4. Cause
- ❖ Simply because something was the *factual* cause of something else does not mean that it was the *legal* cause.

---

[77] But see *R v Croydon Health Authority* (1997) 40 BMLR 40—in this case, a patient underwent a pre-employment chest x-ray on which an abnormality known as primary pulmonary hypertension (PPH) was noted. The patient was not warned that this condition could be exacerbated by pregnancy. She claimed that, had she known of this fact, she would not have become pregnant and claimed, amongst other things, for the costs arising from the birth of her child. The court dismissed that claim on the basis that the birth of a child was too remote an event from the negligence complained of.

Identifying the defendant

[6.52] In many cases, where clinical negligence takes place the identity of the defendant will be clear.

Example 6.4

A patient attends his GP, Dr Urbino. The patient's chart records the fact that the patient is allergic to penicillin, but without consulting the chart or asking the patient whether he is allergic to penicillin, the GP prescribes penicillin. The patient suffers a catastrophic reaction and is left brain-damaged.

In this scenario, the negligence is clear and so is the identity of the person guilty of the negligence: it was clearly the GP. However, matters can sometimes be more complicated.

Example 6.5

A patient attends his GP, Dr Paracelsus. This patient too is allergic to penicillin and has previously had a life-threatening reaction to it. The GP is concerned that his patient has a worsening infection and refers him directly to a local public hospital without initiating any treatment and makes no reference to allergies in the letter which accompanies the patient to the hospital (instead he says 'no relevant medical history'). On arrival in hospital, the patient is seen by a casualty officer who takes a history from the patient, but fails to ask about allergies and marks in the chart, 'No known allergies'. The patient is then seen by a registrar with a view to admission, but by then the patient has deteriorated and cannot give a history of his complaint. The patient is admitted under the care of a consultant, Dr McCormick, but the consultant has not yet seen the patient. The registrar (correctly) wishes to give antibiotics and discusses this with a friend of the patient (who accompanied the patient to hospital) and the friend states, "I could be wrong, but I think he might be allergic to penicillin." The registrar consults the patient's notes and referral letter but sees no mention of allergies and decides to go ahead and give a penicillin-containing antibiotic. The patient suffers a catastrophic reaction.

In this second and more complex example, the guilty party is not as certain. The GP may bear some liability for not having alluded to the patient's allergy in her referral letter; the casualty officer's history-taking was clearly defective and both put the registrar in the invidious position of believing the patient not to have an allergy, but it is the registrar who gave the penicillin and caused the harm. In this setting, three issues may arise:

- the liability of each individual doctor;
- vicarious liability; and
- primary liability of an institution.

[6.53] Some of the need to identify each and every clinician who has been guilty of negligence in order to name them all as defendants (which was previously a feature of many medical negligence claims) has been mitigated by the advent of the Enterprise Liability Scheme (see para **[6.89]** below), which means that the defendant will, in most cases of negligence occurring in the public healthcare system, now be the institution in which the negligence occurred.[78] We concentrate therefore on the issues of vicarious liability and the primary liability of the institution.

---

[78] An example of the difficulties arising with multiple defendants in clinical negligence can be found in *O'Gorman v Jermyn & Ors* [2006] IEHC 398.

Vicarious liability

[6.54] Vicarious liability, an important concept in clinical negligence, describes the fact that in some circumstances the law will hold one party responsible for the negligence of another. Originally vicarious liability was confined to the liability of a master for the acts of his servants, but it now tends to arise most commonly in employer–employee relationships or similar hierarchies.[79] If an employee commits a negligent act during the course of her employment, then the employer may also be held responsible for that negligence even if the employer was not responsible for the negligence.

[6.55] The original test of whether an employer was liable for the acts of its employees was whether the employer exercised control over the activities of the employee. Problems arose with this test when it was applied to clinical situations; hospitals would claim that they had no control over a practitioner's exercise of her clinical skills and courts were for some time prepared to accept this claim.[80] Thus it was the case for many years that if a doctor was negligent, her employers could not be negligent because they did not control her clinical activities. This stricture was gradually relaxed; initially, hospitals could be held responsible if they failed to ensure, at the time of employing them, that staff members were competent, or failed to ensure that hospital equipment was fit for its purpose. However, it remained the case that once a clinician was fit for employment the employer continued to have no responsibility for the actual exercise of her clinical skill.[81]

[6.56] Eventually, a hospital was held accountable for the clinical conduct of one of its radiographers[82] and in the same case the court also stated that a hospital would be responsible for the conduct of its nurses. A hospital was finally held accountable for the misdeeds of a surgeon in the 1950s[83] and the judge stated that:

> [W]hen hospital authorities undertake to treat a patient and themselves select and appoint and employ the professional men and women who are to give the treatment, they are responsible for the negligence of those persons in failing to give proper treatment, no matter whether they are doctors, surgeons, nurses or anyone else.

[6.57] The same principles apply in Ireland;[84] the employer will be responsible for the negligence of clinical employees. Note that it is not only a situation of hospital

---

[79] It may also occur when a firm is held liable for the actions of a partner in that firm. Vicarious liability may go all the way up a chain. So, in theory a hospital may be responsible for the actions of a nurse, the HSE for the hospital and the Minister for Health for the HSE and in theory, all may be sued for their vicarious liability. In *Gottstein v Maguire and Walsh* [2004] IEHC 416, the court held that the second defendant (a consultant surgeon) was vicariously liable for negligent care given to the plaintiff (a patient of the second defendant) in the intensive care unit (ICU), even though the second defendant was not actually caring for the plaintiff in ICU.

[80] *Evans v Liverpool Corporation* [1906] 1 KB 160.

[81] *Hillyer v St Bartholomew's Hospital* [1909] 2 KB 820.

[82] *Gold v Essex County Council* [1942] 2 KB 293.

[83] *Cassidy v Minister of Health* [1951] 1 All ER 574 per Denning LJ.

[84] *Lindsay v Mid-Western Health Board* [1993] 2 IR 147 at 167. In *Byrne v Ryan* [2007] IEHC 207, Kelly J held that a hospital was vicariously liable for the acts of one of its consultant obstetricians in his treatment of a public patient and articulated his reasoning as follows: (contd/)

responsibility for the actions of clinicians. Clinicians who personally employ staff may be vicariously liable for the actions of their staff, for example, a negligent act by a practice nurse or the disclosure of confidential information by a staff member. The two elements of vicarious liability are that:

1. the negligent person must be an employee; *and*

2. the negligence must have occurred in the course of the employee's employment.[85]

The important thing to note about vicarious liability is that it arises where the servant has been negligent and there is a relationship of servant and master present. It is not necessary that the employer be negligent; the relationship is enough. So, in Example 6.5 above, the hospital (and by extension the Health Service Executive) may be held vicariously liable for the shortcomings of the hospital doctors who conspired to mistreat the patient.[86] Historically, the individual doctors (and the consultant, even though he did not see the patient) would also have been sued, but Enterprise Liability (see para **[6.89]**) has led to a somewhat different approach to the naming of defendants.

Who is an 'employee'?

[6.58] This is a vital question. If someone alleges that a hospital is vicariously liable for the conduct of a physiotherapist or person working in the hospital, the institution may be able to avoid vicarious liability if it can prove that the person is not an employee. This is most commonly the case in a private institution.

> **Example 6.6**
>
> A patient is referred by her GP to see a consultant in St Vlad's Private Hospital for a gastroscopy (a camera examination of the inside of the stomach). On arrival, she is seen by a nurse who takes her history, including the fact that she is allergic to penicillin. This sheet is made available to the consultant, who does not consult it properly and after the examination he prescribes penicillin. The patient suffers a reaction.

In this private hospital setting, it is typically the case that the consultant is not employed by the hospital, but rather the arrangement is one whereby a consultant rents rooms and has the use of beds and facilities but is not actually employed by or answerable to[87] the

---

[84] (\contd)

  'The plaintiff was referred not to a particular surgeon but to the Coombe Hospital. She had no say in the choice of who would carry out her sterilisation. It was done by Dr. Murray. He was part of the "organisation" or permanent staff of the hospital [and] the operation was part of a service provided by the hospital to the plaintiff...In my view...the hospital here is liable for any want of care on the part of Dr. Murray.'

[85] See *Health Board v BC* (19 January 1994, unreported) HC. The idea that the negligence must occur during the 'course of employment' is rarely a troublesome one in law. If an employee is doing something that she has been expressly forbidden to do by the employer, this minimises the chance that the employer will be vicariously liable.

[86] It might also be the case that the Health Service Executive would be vicariously liable for any acts or omissions of the GP in circumstances where the patient was a 'medical card' patient of the doctor. Where the patient was a private patient of the doctor, no such vicarious liability could arise.

[87] As we have observed, the test is not whether or not there is a contract of employment, but whether the employer exercises a degree of control over the employee: *Moynihan v Moynihan* [1975] IR 192.

institution in which her consultations take place; she is in what is often called 'private practice'. Is the institution then vicariously liable for the negligence of the surgeon or physician? Or what if the person who commits the negligence is an independent practitioner, working for the hospital without any formal contract of employment?

[6.59] It appears that in the case of a private institution in the current state of Irish law, there is no question of the institution being vicariously liable for the work of private practitioners caring for their private patients.[88] It is possible, although the question has not been dealt with in the Irish courts, that a doctor or surgeon treating private patients in an institution where she is also employed to treat public patients may give rise to a situation where the employer could be vicariously liable for the acts of the doctor or surgeon.[89]

Primary liability of an institution

[6.60] The fact that a private hospital might not be vicariously liable for the negligent treatment meted out by a consultant on its premises does not mean that private (or other) institutions can escape liability by placing it at the door of a particular staff member, for whose actions it is then claimed the hospital bears no liability. An institution (or indeed a semi-state body or government department[90] in certain circumstances) may be held negligent without any recourse to vicarious liability. A hospital that employs incompetent staff or uses outmoded machinery or operates deficient protocols may be primarily liable for negligence, quite aside from any negligence on the part of its staff members.[91]

[6.61] An example of such a situation might be where an institution has defective systems in place, such as a faulty system for reporting the results of blood tests. The staff who act on an incorrect report may not be liable for negligence (although they may be if the report is obviously at variance with the clinical findings), while the hospital could be negligent for having such a system in place assuming that the incorrect report leads to harm to the patient. A potential problem with saying that an institution may itself be liable in negligence is reconciling that potential liability with the fact that a

---

[88] The question was discussed, but not determined, in *Bolton v Blackrock Clinic Ltd* (20 December 1994, unreported) HC, [1994] IEHC 12, per Geoghegan J in the last paragraph of his judgment: 'As the Plaintiff was a private patient of the doctors in a private hospital, the question of vicarious liability *may* not arise. Nor is there any evidence of negligence by the hospital itself or its staff' [author's emphasis].

[89] See the dissenting judgment of Kirby P in *Ellis v Wallsend District Hospital* (1989) 17 NSWLR 553.

[90] Cases against government departments on the basis of failure to take action at the governmental level may well fail by reason of a lack of proximity (see para **[6.09]** above) between government and patient: see *Danns v Department of Health* [1998] PIQR P226.

[91] *Wilsher v Essex AHA* [1986] 3 All ER 801, [1987] 2 WLR 425 (CA), per Glidewell LJ (at 463 WLR): '...there seems to be no reason in principle why, in a suitable case..., a hospital management committee should not be held directly liable in negligence for failing to provide sufficient qualified and competent medical staff.'

hospital may be operating under constrained resources and therefore is unable to provide perfect care in every case.[92]

Lack of experience

[6.62] Is a less experienced practitioner under the same duty as a more experienced one? The court *may* take into account inexperience, but it will expect nonetheless a qualified clinician to be competent and to be as reasonably skilled in her vocation as another inexperienced practitioner. As one judge memorably phrased it (in the context of learner drivers): '[He] may be doing his best, but his incompetent best is not enough.'[93] In general, what is primarily expected of inexperienced doctors is to be aware of what they do not know and, when necessary, to ask for help. In *Wilsher v Essex Health Authority*,[94] it was observed that:

> In my view, the law requires the trainee or learner to be judged by the same standard as his more experienced colleagues. If it did not, inexperience would frequently be urged as a defence to an action for professional negligence. If this test appears unduly harsh in relation to the inexperienced, I should add that, in my view, the inexperienced doctor called upon to exercise a specialist skill will, as part of that skill, seek the advice and help of his superiors when he does or may need it. If he does seek such help, he will often have satisfied the test, even though he may himself have made a mistake.

Does a practitioner have to be right every time?

[6.63] No. There is no onus on the practitioner to be right. If a clinician makes a decision, then all the law asks is that the decision be a reasonable one in the circumstances.[95] The decision must be based on all the available information and the practitioner has a duty to have regard to all available sources of information. As the Supreme Court has stated:[96] 'It is quite clear that a diagnosis which merely proves to be incorrect is not evidence in itself of either want of good faith or want of reasonable care.'

[6.64] In the case of *Collins*,[97] the Supreme Court pointed out that as well as taking the patient's history and description of his symptoms into account, a GP also had to include relevant information from other sources, such as (in the case in question) the patient's wife. In that case, the patient minimised his symptoms while his wife drew attention to

---

[92] In *Bull v Devon AHA* [1993] 4 Med LR 117 (CA), the English Court of Appeal attempted to distinguish between the obligation to provide minimally adequate care and the fact that a hospital should be free to distribute its resources as it saw fit (in *Bull* the hospital was spread across two different sites hampering staff in attending to patients).

[93] *Nettleship v Weston* [1971] 2 QB 691 .

[94] [1987] 2 WLR 425 (CA) per Glidewell LJ at 462.

[95] *Cleary v Cowley* (20 December 2002, unreported) HC. In this case, a senior house officer was held not to have been negligent in diagnosing pneumonia in a patient who had recently been suffering from pneumonia and returned to the hospital coughing up blood. In fact, the patient had a pulmonary embolus and died. It was held that the diagnosis, although not right, was a reasonable and likely one.

[96] *Murphy v Greene* [1990] 2 IR 566, per Finlay CJ at 577.

[97] *Collins v Mid-Western Health Board* [1999] IESC 73, [2000] 2 IR 154 .

the fact that he had a very bad headache and that 'he must be very bad', because he was someone who normally avoided doctors. The doctor had a duty to sift and weigh such information as carefully as he would details gleaned from the patient. In not doing so, he was negligent.

There are certain circumstances in which the practitioner will find it more difficult to be right. One example is where she is attempting diagnosis of a particularly unusual or rare condition; in such a case, the onus is to reach a reasonable (by the standards of an equivalent professional) diagnosis in the circumstances.[98]

Keeping up to date

[6.65] It is clear that any 21st-century practitioner must be practising 21st-century skills. As for how assiduous the clinician must be in staying informed about the latest developments, one judge said the following:

> [I]t would… be putting too high a burden on a medical man [sic] to say that he has to read every article appearing in the current medial press; and it would be wrong to suggest that a medical man is negligent because he does not at once put into operation the suggestions which some contributor or other might make in a medical journal. The time may come in a particular case when a new recommendation may be so well proved and so well known and so well accepted that it should be adopted…[99]

In other words, to miss one reference to a new line of treatment may be unfortunate, but to miss dozens would look like carelessness and the practice of ignoring evolving research will become negligent at some point along the evolution and general professional acceptance of that research (although it may be difficult to identify at what point that transition occurs). There were a number of cases in the early days of HIV infections where doctors escaped liability,[100] but as the state of knowledge changed, so did the onus on doctors to be aware of that change.

Responding when 'on call'

[6.66] Many clinicians will be 'on call' at some time or another in their careers. In most cases, the fact of being on call implies a duty to attend. The specialist doctor on call to casualty will generally have to respond if an emergency within her discipline occurs in the accident and emergency department. A general practitioner will typically be expected to respond to a call from a patient to visit him in his house. But while in certain cases it may be a condition of employment that healthcare personnel respond to a call to

---

[98] *Wolfe v St James's Hospital* (22 November 2000, unreported) HC, [2002] IESC 10.

[99] *Crawford v Board of Governors of Charing Cross Hospital,* (1953) Times, 8 December, per Lord Denning—cited in Mason and Laurie, *Mason and McCall Smith's Law and Medical Ethics* (7th edn, Oxford, 2006), para 9.53.

[100] *Dwan v Farquhar* [1988] Qd R 234: in that case the possibility of HIV transmission through blood transfusion had been first raised in an article published in March 1983; a doctor giving a blood transfusion in May of that same year was held not to have been negligent; see also *H v Royal Alexandra Hospital for Children* [1990] 1 Med LR, (1990) Aust Torts Reps 81-000 (NSWSC), in which the plaintiff failed in his claim for compensation for contracting AIDS from infected blood, because the court held that there was no evidence that it was known at the time of the transfusion that AIDS was transmissible through infected blood.

attend to a patient, there are other circumstances where the clinician has greater latitude. A general practitioner may, on hearing a patient recount his symptoms over the phone, feel that a house call is not indicated. Regardless of the doctor's clinical intuitions, is she under a duty to attend? The answer appears to be in the negative. In one case that concerned a GP's failure to make a house call, the High Court said:[101] 'That is not to say that an obligation can arise in every case where a request is made to a general practitioner to visit the patient at home, to comply with such a request. *That would be wholly unreasonable. Every case must be judged on its circumstances*' [emphasis added].

What is certainly true is that where an institution or individual is represented as being available to provide an out-of-hours service, there should be availability to deal with requests from patients or arrangements should be in place to ensure that alternative coverage is available.

Providing information and obtaining consent

[6.67] This area is dealt with in Ch 4 'Consent'. As we observed in that chapter, where a clinician proceeds without ensuring a patient has given valid consent (that is to say voluntarily, on the basis of the appropriate information and with the requisite capacity), then a negligence action may arise. Where a medical negligence case arises from a deficiency in the consent process and particularly as a result of a failure to warn of a risk, then the biggest hurdle facing a plaintiff is that of causation; the plaintiff must show that 'but for' the failure to warn they would not have undergone treatment. For example, where a patient suffers a side-effect of surgery of which he was not warned and where the failure to warn fell below the standard of care, he must also prove in order to win his case that had the proper warning been given, he would not have undergone the surgery.[102]

Writing references and reports

[6.68] A practitioner who writes a report[103] or a reference[104] about a patient or employee has to be careful that its contents are carefully compiled. In the first place, an inaccurate written description of a patient may be libel. The practitioner may also be guilty of negligent misstatement[105] if what she writes is carelessly wrong and damage is caused, such as making the subject of the reference seem less attractive to potential employees. Another situation in which written negligence may occur is when a doctor is compiling a medical report for a patient, perhaps regarding an insurance policy or a mortgage.

---

[101] *O'Doherty v Whelan* (18 January 1993, unreported) HC.

[102] This is discussed in detail in para **[4.61]***ff*. Note, however, the decision in *Chester v Afshar* [2004] 3 WLR 927, in which the House of Lords appeared to conclude that merely to have deprived the plaintiff of the chance to further consider surgery (including whether she would seek a second opinion or undergo the surgery at the hands of a different surgeon) could be sufficient for the plaintiff to recover damages, even where it was admitted that—had she been given the proper warning—she would have undergone the surgery at some point.

[103] *Hedley Byrne & Co Ltd v Heller & Partners Ltd* [1964] AC 465.

[104] *Spring v Guardian Assurance plc* [1995] 2 AC.

[105] *Hedley Byrne & Co Ltd v Heller & Partners Ltd* [1964] AC 465.

Example 6.7

Dr Svengali is asked to complete a medical report for a patient (A) who is seeking life insurance and who has always been in perfect health. She confuses the patient with another patient (B) who has a similar name but an altogether more chequered medical history. In error, she sends the report of B's ailments to the insurance company, which declines patient A's application for life insurance on the basis of his supposed ill-health. One month later, and before A has had the chance to discover why he was turned down, he dies in a car crash. His widow discovers the error. Had the error not been made her husband would have been insured and she would not now be penniless.

In such a situation, the widow could conceivably be in a position to bring an allegation of negligent misstatement or negligence against the doctor. The test for negligent misstatement is probably the simpler test for general negligence, even if the author of the report is a professional. The court therefore asks itself simply whether the letter or report was reasonable in the circumstances.[106]

Quick Reference Guide 6.3

Aspects of negligence

> ❖ The defendant in a clinical negligence action may be an individual, a combination of individuals or an institution. An institution may be the defendant where:
>
> o it is vicariously liable for the actions of an individual
>
> o the institution itself has been negligent (for example, in the maintenance of equipment)
>
> o there is a scheme in place (such as 'enterprise liability') where the institution voluntarily assumes responsibility for acts of certain individuals
>
> ❖ A clinician 'doing her best' is not enough – she must meet the minimum standard accepted for the profession. Inexperience will not be an excuse: the inexperienced practitioner is in particular expected to know her limits.
>
> ❖ A practitioner does not always have to be right, but has only to reach a reasonable diagnosis or decision in the circumstances of the case.
>
> ❖ Failing to keep up to date may be negligence if the gaps in knowledge are such that no reasonable and comparable professional would have allowed the gaps to accumulate.
>
> ❖ A practitioner is not under an open-ended responsibility to attend on those patients who call upon her. The responsibility varies with the circumstances.
>
> ❖ Failure to obtain valid consent may be negligence. Valid consent must be voluntary and given by someone with the legal capacity – in terms of mental competence and age – to do so. Furthermore the practitioner is under a duty to keep the patient informed of the potential risks of treatment (so-called 'informed' consent).
>
> ❖ A report regarding a patient or a reference regarding an employee may give rise to an allegation of negligence.

---

[106] It may be that the test for professional negligence will apply if the report in question is a wholly clinical one involving the exercise of the practitioner's clinical discretion.

DEFENDING AN ALLEGATION OF NEGLIGENCE[107]

The obvious defence

[6.69] The first avenue open to the practitioner is to argue that a particular act or omission was not negligent at all because any or all of the following circumstances apply:[108]

- no duty of care existed;
- the conduct complained of did not fall below the required standard of care;
- there was no damage;
- if there is damage, it was not caused by the act or omission complained of.

Contributory negligence

[6.70] Sometimes, even if a practitioner is negligent, it may not entirely be her fault. The patient may do something to contribute to his own adverse outcome: this is called contributory negligence. There was a time when, if the victim of negligence contributed at all to his mishap, the wrongdoer was entirely absolved of her responsibility. However, the manner in which the rule is interpreted now is that a person's contributory negligence will simply erode the wrongdoer's responsibility in proportion to how substantial the contributory negligence is;[109] where contributory negligence is present, a court will award damages to a plaintiff but then reduce them according to how they view the plaintiff's contributory negligence. If a plaintiff is 50 per cent responsible for his own misfortune, then his damages may be reduced by up to that amount.

> **Example 6.8**
>
> A patient attends an accident and emergency department with a broken leg. He is seen by a doctor, who diagnoses the fracture correctly but applies a cast negligently to the patient's leg. She advises the patient that for the next few weeks he must avoid putting weight on the leg and to that end she issues him with a pair of crutches. The patient ignores this advice and puts weight on the leg. The badly-applied cast cracks and the leg fracture is worsened, requiring a subsequent operation. The patient sues the doctor for negligence.

The doctor may have been negligent in this case in applying the cast as she did. However, the patient was told not to put any weight on the limb and the doctor could argue that the patient's conduct amounted to contributory negligence. Contributory negligence will not always succeed as a defence. In one case a hospital was found to have inadequately assessed a psychiatric patient, who then jumped from a height

---

[107] A professional negligence action against a practitioner cannot commence unless the plaintiff is in possession of a report from an appropriate expert to state that, in the opinion of the expert, there has been negligence in the treatment of the plaintiff: *Cooke v Cronin* [1999] IESC 54. See Lynch J: 'In all cases of alleged negligence on the part of a qualified professional person in carrying out his professional duties there should be some credible evidence to support the plaintiff's case before such an action is commenced.'

[108] Where a judge reaches the conclusion during a trial that a plaintiff has failed to make out a case of negligence, she may decline to hear further evidence and dismiss the plaintiff's claim: *Orla McCann v Thomas O'Reilly* [2002] IESC 76.

[109] Civil Liability Act 1961, s 34.

injuring himself. The hospital argued that while it was negligent, the patient's conduct amounted to contributory negligence. However, because the patient was not fully in control of her mental faculties at the time, her conduct in jumping out of a window did not constitute contributory negligence.[110] Where a patient's contributory negligence is especially gross, it may exceptionally operate to completely relieve a defendant of liability.[111]

[6.71] Similar to contributory negligence is failure to mitigate damage, which arises when the victim of the alleged negligence fails to take reasonable steps to minimise or to correct any damage caused by the alleged negligence. If a person refuses to do so, for example, by refusing to go for treatment of a condition caused by the alleged negligence,[112] he is failing to mitigate his damage and the court may take this into account when apportioning liability and consequent damages.

The voluntary assumption of risk

[6.72] This occurs when a person is made aware of a risk that something may go wrong but nonetheless agrees to go ahead. In broad terms a person can escape liability for negligence if she can show either:

- that there is a contract that includes a term freeing her from any liability for negligence; or

- that there is some other evidence that shows that the person injured agreed to waive his legal rights.[113]

In theory, this could mean that where a doctor explains to a patient that the procedure the patient is requesting is one that the doctor is not very good at and that may consequently go wrong and the patient nonetheless agrees, the patient is voluntarily assuming the risk of the doctor's negligence, but this is an unlikely prospect in the clinical setting.

[6.73] Practitioners may be affected by voluntarily assuming risk as rescuers in emergency situations. A doctor who works as part of an emergency response team might

---

[110] *Armstrong v Eastern Health Board* (5 October 1990, unreported) HC; conversely, where a patient is in command of his own mental faculties and injures himself when negligently unsupervised, then his actions in injuring himself may amount to contributory negligence: *Reeves v Commissioner of Police of the Metropolis* [2000] 1 AC 360.

[111] *Venner v North East Essex Health Authority* (1987) Times, 21 February. In this case a woman who was admitted for a sterilisation operation was asked whether there was any possibility that she was pregnant. She denied the possibility even though she had had unprotected intercourse and was not using any form of contraceptive. As it transpired she was pregnant at the time of the sterilisation procedure and subsequently gave birth to a healthy child. It was held not to have been negligent of the doctor to have accepted the word of the patient that she could not be pregnant.

[112] In *Bohan v Finn* DPIJ: Trinity and Michaelmas Terms 194, 61 (HC). The plaintiff in this case refused to go into psychiatric hospital for treatment of a psychosomatic complaint arising out of an accident, even though there was more than an 80 per cent chance of recovery. The judge took this refusal into account.

[113] This is the interpretation given by McMahon & Binchy (*Law of Torts*, Tottel Publishing, 2000) to s 34(1)(b) of the Civil Liability Act 1961.

be held to take upon herself any risks inherent in responding to emergency situations, consequently making it difficult for her to sue anyone should negligence result in her injury. Irish law, however, has tended to conclude that a rescuer can have a cause of action against someone whose negligence puts her in danger by creating the situation that leads to the attempted rescue.[114]

The case is brought outside the time limit

[6.74] In the interests of justice, a person cannot sue another person so long after the act complained of that it would no longer be possible for the defendant to defend herself properly, or so long after the act that the time laid down by law for commencing the action has expired. If a physiotherapist made an error of treatment in her early twenties, it would seem unreasonable if the first she hears of legal action is 50 years later, long after she has sold on her practice or destroyed the notes of the initial consultation. Accordingly, there is legislation[115] that sets down the limits within which legal actions must be commenced. In general, no legal action may be commenced after the window of opportunity provided by the Act has passed and in the case of negligence and personal injuries the time limit is two years, which period starts to run from whichever is the later of two occasions:

- the date of the original negligent act or omission; or

- the date when the person becomes aware of the negligent act, the so-called 'date of knowledge'.

[6.75] This second provision, the date of knowledge or date of discoverability,[116] is often important in clinical negligence.

---

[114] *Philips v Durgan* [1991] ILRM 321. In the United States, there is a so-called 'Fire Fighters' Rule' which states that a fire fighter injured in the course of his duty cannot sue the person whose negligence caused the fire, except in special circumstances: *Butler v Union Pacific Railroad Co* (1995) 68 F 2D 378.

[115] Statute of Limitations (Amendment) Act 1991, s 2 (as amended by the Civil Liability and Courts Act 2004). Note that where a plaintiff is a child or under a mental disability, the two-year period will not commence until the child reaches the age of 18 or until the person with the mental disability recovers from that disability.

[116] The relevant statutory provision is:

'(1) For the purposes of any provision of this Act whereby the time within which an action in respect of an injury may be brought depends on a person's date of knowledge (whether he is the person injured or a personal representative or dependant of the person injured) references to that person's date of knowledge are references to the date on which he first had knowledge of the following facts:

(i) that the person alleged to have been injured had been injured,

(ii) that the injury in question was significant,

(iii) that the injury was attributable in whole or in part to the act or omission which is alleged to constitute negligence, nuisance or breach of duty,

(iv) the identity of the defendant, and

(v) if it is alleged that the act or omission was that of a person other than the defendant, the identity of that person and the additional facts supporting the bringing of an action against the defendant;

and knowledge that any acts or omissions did or did not, as a matter of law, involve negligence, nuisance or breach of duty is irrelevant.'

Example 6.9

A surgeon performs an operation on a 20-year-old man to remove a testicle in 1995. During the operation she negligently damages the spermatic cord of the other testicle. In 2000, he marries and attempts to start a family. During investigations conducted to identify the cause of infertility in 2002, it becomes clear that the man is infertile due to damage to the spermatic cord.[117]

If it were the case that the man could only sue the surgeon in the two years after the date of the original injury, he is at an obvious disadvantage, for he could not reasonably have discovered the damage until he first attempted to start a family. So, the law allows people who do not discover that they were victims of a negligent act or omission until many years after the event to commence legal proceedings for that act, so long as they do so within two years of the 'date of knowledge'. The date of knowledge was formerly regarded as the date the patient could have become aware[118] of the existence of the damage caused by the proposed defendant and not the date on which he becomes aware that the damage was caused by a negligent act.[119] However, following the decision of the Supreme Court in *Gough v Neary*,[120] the position now appears to be that the two-year period will only begin to run when a person knows not only that he suffered harm but learns also such additional information (such as the fact that the operation was unnecessary) that:

> would be capable at least upon elaboration of establishing a cause of action even if the plaintiff has no idea that those facts of which he had knowledge do in fact constitute a cause of action … But the adequacy of [the person's] knowledge must be related to the

---

[117] A factual example is *Maitland v Swan and Sligo County Council* [1992] PNLR 368, (6 April 1992, unreported) HC. A surgeon removed a woman's ovary in 1969. In 1971 she learned of the removal. In 1983, she learned that her left ovary was abnormal and that she was infertile. In that case the judge decided that the 'harm' arose when the woman discovered that her remaining ovary was abnormal, not when the original ovary was removed.

[118] The measure of whether a patient could have known of the damage is based on knowledge the patient could be expected to have based on facts known to him or facts that he could have discovered by reference to reasonable expert help. So, our hypothetical infertile patient who knew he was having difficulty conceiving could have known that there was a problem from the time the doctor confirmed that he had problems with his sperm count and before he ever knew there was damage to the spermatic cord.

[119] *Hegarty v O'Loughran* [1990] 1 IR 148. This case concerned damage to the plaintiff's nose allegedly caused by the defendant's treatment. The plaintiff unsuccessfully argued that the time should start to run for the purposes of the Statute of Limitations only when he was aware that negligence caused the harm, not from the (earlier) date when he realised he had suffered harm.

[120] *Gough v Neary* [2003] 3 IR 92. The woman in this case had undergone an emergency caesarean at the hands of an obstetrician in 1992 (and was thus aware of the damage that she had suffered from that time), but did not initiate proceedings until 1998, when certain revelations about excess rates of caesarean sections performed by the defendant became widely publicised. Similarly, in *Fortune v McLoughlin* [2004] IESC 34, [2004] 1 IR 526, the Supreme Court held that the plaintiff (who had suffered brain injuries during delivery of a child in 1993) was not statute-barred in having waited until 2000 to issue proceedings: the court held there must be knowledge that the acts were attributable to acts or omission of the defendant and knowledge that there was a connection between the injury and the matters alleged to have caused the injury

context ... It was only when she discovered that the operation was unnecessary that the period started to run.[121]

[6.76] In *Cunningham v Neary*[122] the plaintiff was in a different position. She had undergone the removal of an ovary by Dr Neary in 1991 and when she became aware of the concerns over Dr Neary's practice in or about December 1998, she had written to the Medical Council expressing her concerns. She consulted a solicitor in 2000 and an expert medical report alleging negligence was in the hands of her solicitor in April 2001. The Supreme Court concluded that by December 1998 at the latest, when she wrote to the Medical Council, the plaintiff had the requisite knowledge and that therefore time (which had not at that point been reduced from three years to two) began to run. As she did not initiate proceedings before December 2001 (even though she had an expert medical report alleging negligence which would have allowed her to do so), her claim failed.

Delay

[6.77] Where the court feels there has been too long a delay in initiating a case, even when the delay was caused only by how long it took the patient to discover the fact of injuries (or is permissible because the plaintiff is still a child or under a mental disability), so that the action is still within the Statute of Limitations, the court may still stop the case from proceeding or continuing.[123] The theory behind this approach is that an excessive lapse of time will make it impossible for the defendants fairly to defend themselves and the interests of justice will be best served by striking out the case. So, even where a patient complies with the timeframes laid down by rule of 'date of discoverability' or is, on the face of the legislation, still entitled to commence his litigation, he may find the courts unwilling to consider his case for reasons entirely beyond his control.

Similarly, where a case has commenced but is pursued too slowly, the court may strike out the claim on the basis that the delay in prosecuting the case is unfair to the defendants.[124]

---

[121] Per Geoghegan J at 126. Note the strong dissenting minority judgment of Hardiman J.

[122] [2004] IESC 43.

[123] *Toal v Duignan* [1991] ILRM 135. In *Kearney v McQuillan* [2006] IEHC 186, the plaintiff issued proceedings within the time allowed by the Statute of Limitations following her discovery in 2002 she may have been the victim of negligent injury (a symphysiotomy), but this discovery was 35 years after the event. Her action was struck out on the basis of delay.

[124] *O'Grady v Southern Health Board and Tralee General Hospital* [2007] IEHC 38. For an example of a case in which lengthy delay did not prejudice a plaintiff's claim, see *Reidy v National Maternity Hospital* [1997] IEHC 143; however, it is increasingly likely that courts will take a strict line on delay in prosecuting claims: see *Gilroy v Flynn* [2004] IESC 98.

Quick Reference Guide 6.4

Negligence: the defences

> ❖ That the act or omission was not negligence, because one of the elements of negligence was absent
>
> ❖ That some negligent act or omission on the part of the patient contributed to the damage that resulted – similar to *contributory negligence* is a *failure to mitigate damage* or the victim acting in such a way as to fail to deal with damage that he knows exists or is likely
>
> ❖ That the victim of the alleged negligence voluntarily accepted the risks of the act or omission and exempted the practitioner from any liability for negligence
>
> ❖ That the victim of the alleged negligence has waited too long to bring his legal action or, having initiated legal action, has delayed in advancing the claim

LIABILITY FOR DEFECTIVE PRODUCTS

[6.78] If someone manufactures a product, then she has a duty of care towards the user of that product. *Donoghue v Stevenson* (see para [6.05]), the defining case in modern negligence, arose from a defective product, namely a drink containing a snail. Historically, a person who sought compensation for damage caused by a defective product had to prove that the manufacturer or producer of the product was negligent by satisfying all the tests for negligence that have been discussed previously. However, this area has evolved greatly in recent years thanks to the Liability for Defective Products Act 1991,[125] which applies the concept of 'strict liability'.

[6.79] Strict liability is a legal rule whereby a court will not concern itself with the question of whether a person fulfils the strict legal tests necessary to be found guilty of the allegation in question. Instead, when it comes to products liability, the court will simply satisfy itself that the product at issue was in fact defective and proceed to automatically hold the manufacturer or producer liable for that defective product. In other words, a company will automatically be considered legally negligent if a product it produces transpires to be defective and—in manifesting its shortcomings—causes death or personal injury to a person or damage to any property (other than the defective product itself). Defective products could include medical equipment, blood products and pharmaceuticals.[126]

---

[125] For a more detailed discussion of this area, see McMahon and Binchy, *The Law of Torts* (3rd edn, Tottel Publishing, 2000), Ch 11. Note that the Liability for Defective Products Act 1991 incorporates a 'long stop' limitation: no legal action may be commenced more than 10 years after the manufacture of the product in question.

[126] Where the problem is with the maintenance of an item, then the person having control of the maintenance and not the manufacturer, will be liable: *Fanning v South Western Area Health Board, Laavei, Eurosurgical Limited and Richard Wolf GMBH* [2005] IEHC 25.

ALTERNATIVE WAYS OF COMBATING NEGLIGENCE

[6.80] Negligence is a huge drain on the resources of institutions faced with enormous bills for compensation and for the insurance of their staff. Similarly, practitioners find themselves faced with ever-spiralling personal indemnity costs. Any action brought by a patient may involve enormous legal costs, often exacerbated by the fact that the losing side will generally also have to pay the costs of the winning side.[127] A further problem is the concern that the increased threat of negligence action results in 'defensive practice' or in other words a tendency to do every conceivable test or to furnish every conceivable treatment so that all bases are covered, although there are those who argue that defensive practice is less common than generally supposed.[128] Others observe that where the State is liable for meeting the costs of medical negligence, the money will in effect place a further drain on already scarce clinical resources.[129] The difficulties of pursuing litigation may also deter deserving persons from doing so and those who might face a large bill for legal costs in the event of an unsuccessful claim may be put off pursuing the claim, notwithstanding that it is a meritorious one.[130] Finally, negligence litigation is an adversarial process, the defence of which is often predicated on silence, denial and unhelpfulness. As one commentator has observed: 'Any effort to prevent injury due to medical care is complicated by the dead weight of a litigation system that induces secrecy and silence.'[131]

[6.81] Doctors and other practitioners are insured against negligence in a number of ways. Some are insured (or indemnified) by their employers and in the public healthcare setting indemnification is increasingly mediated through the Enterprise Liability Scheme (see para **[6.89]**). Other practitioners arrange their own medical indemnity insurance. The insurance premium paid each year means that the insurance company will bear the cost of fighting any negligence action and the cost of any award of damages

---

[127] See fn 1.

[128] See generally Ham, Dingwall, Fenn and Harris, *Medical Negligence: Compensation and Accountability* (King's Fund Institute/Centre for Socio-Legal Studies, 1988). They cite as one example the rise in caesarean sections (CS) performed on women in childbirth. The prevailing opinion, then as now, was that the rise in CS rates was an expression of worries about complications in labour leading to a negligence action. They demonstrated that rates were rising in all countries irrespective of the pattern of medico-legal actions in those countries. See also the discussion in Jones, 'Breach of Duty' in Grubb and Laing (eds) *Principles of Medical Law* (2nd edn, Oxford, 2004), 369. Jones observes that defensive medicine may simply be careful medicine and that doctors remain at all times under a duty of care not to perform unnecessary procedures.

[129] Merry and McCall Smith, *Errors Medicine and the Law* (Cambridge, 2002), 212: 'A medium-sized award [of compensation]…may be crudely translated into ten fewer hip replacements.'

[130] See, for example, Mulcahy, *Disputing Doctors: The socio-legal dynamics of complaints about medical care* (Open University Press, 2003), 64*ff.*

[131] Brennan, 'The Institute of Medicine report on medical errors—could it do harm?' (2000) 342 *New England Journal of Medicine* 1123–5.

made against the clinician.[132] As medical negligence claims in particular have increased in number, the payments expected by insurers have correspondingly increased, especially in the supposed high-risk disciplines.

Table 6.1 Obstetricians' Indemnity Fees by year (€equivalent):[133]

1991	*1992*	*1993*	*1994*	*1995*	*1996*	*1997*	*1998*	*1999*	*2000*
11811	20955	24130	25711	30988	38074	43484	43484	45656	54610

Preventing negligence actions and their consequences

[6.82] Ways of dealing with the problems posed by negligence actions fall into two camps divided along the lines of where they attempt to intervene in the natural history of negligence. There are those measures that try to stop the negligence from occurring in the first place (such as risk management) and those that seek a way to minimise the consequences and costs of negligence actions (such as alternative schemes of compensation).[134]

Healthcare risk management[135]

[6.83] Risk management involves putting into place mechanisms for identifying, prospectively or retrospectively, risks to patients and employees in the healthcare environment. If risk management can identify and eradicate risks, then legal actions arising from those risks may consequently be prevented from occurring in the first place or from recurring. One study has shown that approximately 4 per cent of hospital admissions include at least one adverse event and that in 1 per cent of admissions, the adverse event is due to negligence.[136] Typically then, a risk management system will

---

[132] Note that the indemnification of members by medical indemnity organisations is typically discretionary. It is a term of the cover provided that the indemnifying body may choose not to provide indemnification of a particular clinician in circumstances where is not in the interests of the wider membership of the indemnifying body to do so. The Supreme Court found that there was nothing inherently unlawful about discretionary indemnity in *Barry v Medical Defence Union* [2005] IESC 41. A somewhat more widespread 'discretionary' refusal of cover became a weapon in a dispute between one medical indemnity organisation and the Irish Government following the introduction of the Enterprise Liability and the Clinical Indemnity Scheme: see *Hassett (a minor) v The South Eastern Health Board and Raymond Howard, The Medical Defence Union Limited and MDU Services Limited* [2006] IEHC 105.

[133] From Medical Protection Society, cited in *Medical Indemnity – Proposals for Change*, Department of Health, Dublin 2001. Excluding obstetricians, 'low risk' (as defined in terms of their risk to the insurers) consultants in 2000 were paying €8,000, while 'high-risk' specialists were paying approximately €30,000 *per annum* in indemnity fees.

[134] Note the conclusion of *Learning from Bristol: the report of the public inquiry into children's heart surgery at the Bristol Royal Infirmary 1984–1995* (CM 5207, 2001) which called for the abolition of clinical negligence litigation: see Ch 26, para 28*ff.*

[135] See Cusack, 'Risk Management as a Strategy for Quality' in Leahy and Wiley (eds.) *The Irish Health System in the 21st Century* (OakTree Press, 1998).

[136] Hiatt *et al.*, 'A Study of Medical Injury and Medical Malpractice: An Overview', *NEJM,* 1997, 321:7, 480. Much hinges, of course, on one's definition of an adverse event. However, a similar incidence of adverse events was noted in Department of Health [UK] Expert Group, *An Organisation with a Memory* (DH, 2000); furthermore, the authors of this latter study estimated that up to 70 per cent of adverse events were preventable.

involve a system of reporting mishaps and accidents, including 'near misses'.[137] Such mishaps might include unexpected deaths, complicated in-patient stays (for example, the need for follow-up operations or admission to intensive care) or problems with medication. Once such risks are identified, a mechanism can be put in place to tackle problems that have been isolated.[138]

[6.84] However, healthcare risk management is not merely an expression of common sense but also an articulation of the modern ethical approach to medical errors that has been described in the so-called 'Tavistock Principles', generated by the Tavistock Group[139] in the wake of a US Institute of Medicine paper on creating a safer health system.[140] The most important principles from a clinical perspective include the following:

- Co-operation with each other and with those served by the healthcare system is the priority for those working within the healthcare system.

- All individuals and groups involved in healthcare, whether providing access or services have a continuing responsibility to help improve its quality.

- In developing a culture of safety, clinicians will need to act as role models for their students by applying these principles themselves the next time they encounter a medical error. Practitioners need to 'declare error reduction to be an explicit organisational goal and [devote] a significant proportion of the board and management agenda... to achieving this goal.'[141]

Competence assurance for the clinical professions

[6.85] The medical profession has taken a lead in this attempt to validate, on an ongoing basis, the continuing competence of medical practitioners who have completed their formal training. The Medical Council has undertaken to introduce a process of competence assurance that will assist doctors to continue to update their skills and help those doctors who are shown to have fallen dangerously below the norm. The programmes for keeping practitioners' skills up-to-date include programmes of continuing medical education (CME) and continuing professional development (CPD). At present this scheme is at a pilot stage, although plans for the scheme are long in being.[142] It depends for its operation on the enactment of the Medical Practitioners Act 2007, which gives the Medical Council the statutory authority to implement and regulate the competence assurance process as well as providing it with the necessary teeth to

---

[137] Although 'near miss' is a nonsensical term: to nearly miss something is actually to hit it. The author would always prefer—when flying—to be involved in a near hit than a near miss.

[138] It should be observed that much of this may be easier to achieve in theory than in practice; see Merry and McCall Smith, *Errors Medicine and the Law* (Cambridge, 2001), 2: 'A point which is often misunderstood is that human error, being by definition unintentional, is not easily deterred'.

[139] See 'Shared ethical principles for everybody in health care: a working draft from the Tavistock Group', Smith *et al., BMJ* 1999; 318: 248–251.

[140] Kohn, Corrigan and Donaldson (eds) *To Err is Human. Building a safer health system* (Washington, DC: National Academy Press, 1999).

[141] Reinersten 'Let's talk about error' *BMJ* 2000; 320: 720.

compel participation and to impose necessary guidance or sanction on underperforming practitioners.[143] There are many legal obstacles to be met before competence assurance can be made to operate satisfactorily, including those relating to the confidentiality of proceedings and the sanctions to be imposed on incompetent practitioners, but similar systems operate well in other countries such as Australia and the United States.[144]

No-fault schemes

[6.86] A 'no fault' scheme is one where a person injured by a clinical incident does not have to prove that anyone was at fault for the accident. Furthermore, there are also some schemes in which the patient does not even have to identify the person responsible for the injury. The two best-known schemes are those in Sweden and New Zealand (where compensation is payable for 'personal injury by accident') and both of these schemes do oblige the patient to identify the person responsible for the harm he has suffered.

[6.87] The core elements of the New Zealand scheme have been widely discussed:

- Compensation is payable for 'personal injury by accident', which includes both medical mishaps and medical errors;

- Medical mishaps describe rare severe[145] outcomes from non-negligent medical treatment;

- Medical errors describe medical negligence in the more traditional sense and the patient must show that error caused his injury;

- Compensation is for medical treatment, loss of earnings (up to a defined limit), transport and accommodation costs and death benefits;

- The costs of the scheme come from taxation, premiums charged on medical practitioners and levies on employers.[146]

---

[142] See Medical Council, *Competence Assurance Structures—An Agenda for Implementation* (March 2002). The projected timeframe set out in that document was never met. See also Irish Medical Council Consensus Statement, *Performance in Practice—Maintenance of Professional Standards* (2006). At the time of writing (September 2007), limited pilot schemes of 'Professional Practice Review' (PPR) for general practitioners are in their early stages, involving assessment of the practitioner by patients and colleagues. The other elements of Competence Assurance are Continuing Quality Assurance (in essence, self-directed and small group learning on an ongoing basis) and Performance Assessment (in the case of doctors about whose performance concerns have been expressed or otherwise come to light).

[143] See the discussion of the Medical Practitioners Act 2007 in Ch 2.

[144] For a brief summary of the problems and some suggested solutions, see 'Legislating for Competence Assurance—Cool Water on a Hot Topic?' Mills and Cusack (2000) *Medico-Legal Journal of Ireland* (7)1, 2.

[145] It is rare if less than 1 per cent of people could expect to suffer it following the treatment in question (although not if the patient knew of the risk before treatment started) and severe if the patient is hospitalised or disabled for 14 days or more or if the patient dies. Since 2004, certain common mishaps may now also be compensated.

[146] See, for example, *Making Amends: A consultation paper setting out proposals for reforming the approach to clinical negligence in the NHS* (DH 2003). This report was the basis for the UK NHS Redress Act 2006, the elements of which are set out at s 3(2): (contd/)

The first obvious saving is in legal costs. The person alleging that he is injured has only to prove that he has an injury and that his injury resulted from the allegedly negligent treatment by the institution or practitioner in question. There is therefore less likelihood of having to fight a lengthy legal battle. No-fault can also in theory help to improve standards within the healthcare professions. When incidents are identified, the knowledge of that event can be used by the institution fielding the claim to provide feedback to clinical staff in that and other institutions in order to improve standards and avert further similar incidents.

[6.88] By setting out a standard list of compensation amounts that will be payable to patients in each instance, the introduction of no-fault may also counter the element of lottery involved in court awards of damages. How much a plaintiff receives for an injury in the ordinary clinical negligence action may depend on the performance of his legal team and the particular judge he faces. A no-fault scheme would clarify the injuries for which compensation may be obtained and the extent of that compensation. However, one problem with no-fault compensation is that it has proved to be very expensive. Other 'no fault' schemes that have been proposed include the introduction of no-fault compensation for children born with cerebral palsy.[147]

Enterprise liability

[6.89] Under enterprise liability schemes, responsibility for defending malpractice claims is placed on the institutions that provide care (the enterprises) instead of burdening individual practitioners. In turn, the management of the claim is delegated to the State Claims Agency.[148] The distinguishing feature of enterprise liability is that the aggrieved patient does not need to sue the individual medical practitioner, the hospital and the health board (as is often the case), each represented by separate legal teams who often delay the process (and increase costs) by trying to shift blame or fight the case on different grounds. Instead, a claim under the enterprise liability scheme is handled by a single legal team representing the 'enterprise'—in effect, the Government.

[6.90] Under enterprise liability a health board, hospital or other agency providing healthcare services accepts responsibility for the actions of all staff involved in the provision of clinical services. This means that when a patient who believes that he has

---

[146] (\contd)

'A [redress] scheme must provide for redress ordinarily to comprise—

    (i)   the making of an offer of compensation in satisfaction of any right to bring civil proceedings in respect of the liability concerned,

    (ii) the giving of an explanation,

    (iii) the giving of an apology, and

    (iv) the giving of a report on the action which has been, or will be, taken to prevent similar cases arising...'

[147] This suggested approach is partly based on the fact that there is some medical uncertainty concerning whether there is any human component, negligent or otherwise, in the causation of all cases of cerebral palsy: see 'A template for defining a causal relation between acute interpartum events and cerebral palsy: international consensus statement.' BMJ 1999; 319:1054–9. See also *Purdy v Lenihan* [2003] IESC 7.

[148] Which is a section of the National Treasury Management Agency; see National Treasury Management Agency (Delegation of Functions) Order 2003 (SI 63/2003).

suffered an injury or whose illness has been wrongly diagnosed or treated, wishes to seek compensation for any loss or suffering, he will seek that from the health board or other body involved, rather than having to identify and pursue each individual doctor involved in his care and treatment. The scheme covers all doctors operating in a public hospital, including cases where consultants are caring for private patients in a public hospital.

[6.91] The potential benefits of enterprise liability are intended to be multiple:

- it removes some of the stigma of being sued;
- it removes some of the burden from the plaintiff of having to identify and bring legal proceedings against every doctor who may have been negligent;
- it can be expected to reduce legal and administrative costs by eliminating multiple insurers and requiring only a single legal team to represent the enterprise;[149]
- it ends the situation in which the various defendants expend time and money trying to blame each other (which in turn can be destructive of the relationship between those defendants, who are often co-workers);
- it should create greater incentives and opportunities for health-care institutions to introduce risk management (see para **[6.83]** above) schemes;
- it should speed up the resolution of litigation.

The Enterprise Liability plan includes the creation of a national clinical negligence claims handling agency to manage and coordinate the scheme and to establish a State Indemnity Pool (SIP) as the basis for financing future settlements in respect of clinical negligence claims in the public hospital system. The new body will also oversee the necessary protocol for risk management programmes intended to accompany enterprise liability.

TORT REFORM

[6.92] Negligence is a tort and some countries have introduced reforms to the law of torts in order to make it more different to bring a negligence action. This approach has most commonly been adopted in the United States and has generally taken the form of:

- making it more difficult to sue hospitals or doctors by changing the procedural rules, for example by shortening the limitation period within which the action can be brought, and altering the way in which the law defines the standard of care in matters such as informed consent;
- placing a cap on the damages that can be awarded and the fees that can be paid to lawyers;

---

[149] In the UK, the National Audit Office in *Handling Negligence Claims in England* (NAO, 2001) observed that the length of legal proceedings is such that the average case lasts five and a half years and the legal costs are often greater than the award made to the patient, especially where the compensation awarded to the patient is small.

- compelling potential plaintiffs to go to arbitration;[150]
- reducing payments to take account of any monies received from other sources, such as insurance pay-outs from the patient's own insurance.

California introduced its Medical Injury Compensation Reform Act in 1975, containing many of these new measures. Before the introduction of this legislation, California accounted for almost 30 per cent of all US payments for medical negligence. By 1994 this had fallen to 10 per cent.

---

[150] Arbitration is a system where both parties to a dispute agree to let an independent third party to make a *final and binding* decision on the settlement of the dispute. Typically it is quicker and less expensive than going to court. It is very common in the settlement of disputes between insurance companies and policy-holders.

Chapter 7

The Practitioner and the Family

INTRODUCTION

[7.01] The family is accorded a very special position in Irish society by the Constitution.[1] Although the Constitution does not define what a 'family' is, the courts have on any number of occasions re-iterated the principle that the family exists within a sphere of autonomy into which the law will only rarely intrude. The constitutional rights of the Irish family do not explicitly extend to the non-married family,[2] although a non-married family will attract constitutional protection once the formalities of marriage are completed and the children of a non-married family will be recognised in all respects as equal to those of a married couple.[3] For many years, the Constitution contained a prohibition against divorce[4] and to this day contains a provision that some critics feel enshrines the woman's place as being in the home.[5]

[7.02] Constitutional deference to the family has had a number of consequences. For a long time the most noticeable effect was the bar on divorce, which meant in turn that civil annulment (the ending of a marriage by the courts) took on especial significance as the only way in which a couple could end their marriage while still being permitted to remarry later. Secondly, the constitutional deference towards the family has tended to mean that parents will rarely be displaced as the primary carers or decision-makers for a child.[6]

[7.03] We look in this chapter at the question of marriage or, more particularly, the ending of marriage, and in particular the use of nullity to terminate a marriage. We look also at the issue of domestic violence and how spouses and partners can be protected against it with

---

[1] Article 41.1 of the Constitution states:
   1° The State recognises the Family as the natural primary and fundamental unit group of Society, and as a moral institution possessing inalienable and imprescriptible rights, antecedent and superior to all positive law.
   2° The State, therefore, guarantees to protect the Family in its constitution and authority, as the necessary basis of social order and as indispensable to the welfare of the Nation and State.

[2] *The State (Nicolau) v An Bord Uchtála* [1966] IR 567; *WOR v EH & An Bord Uchtála* (July 1996, unreported) SC.

[3] *KC & AC v An Bord Uchtála* [1985] 5 ILRM 302.

[4] Removed by the referendum on the 15th Amendment to the Constitution, which in turn resulted in the Family Law (Divorce) Act 1996.

[5] Article 41.2 of the Constitution states:
   1° In particular, the State recognises that by her life within the home, woman gives to the State a support without which the common good cannot be achieved.
   2° The State shall, therefore, endeavour to ensure that mothers shall not be obliged by economic necessity to engage in labour to the neglect of their duties in the home.

[6] See the discussion of children and consent to medical treatment in Ch 4 'Consent'.

the help of the courts. Finally we look at issues affecting children and the newborn: child abuse, child protection and Sudden Infant Death Syndrome (SIDS).

MARRIAGE

[7.04] There are three ways of ending a marriage in Ireland: divorce, civil annulment (a declaration by the courts that a marriage is invalid because of some fundamental flaw) and judicial separation. Until the introduction of divorce, annulment was the only legal option for those who wished both to quit a dysfunctional marriage and to have the opportunity of remarrying. While nullity is (since the advent of divorce) no longer the only way of ending a marriage, applications for annulment are nonetheless still initiated from time to time[7] and medical, psychiatric and psychological evidence can each be important in establishing grounds for nullity. Divorce is a more pragmatic legal framework in which medical considerations rarely arise, while there is also the process of judicial separation,[8] which does not end a marriage but rather regulates the agreement of a married couple to live apart, including the dividing of assets and the fixing of maintenance payments. A judicially separated couple remain married and must divorce or seek an annulment before they can legally marry again. Judicial separation is not dealt with further in this text.

Divorce

[7.05] The 15th Amendment to the Constitution allowed for the introduction of legislation to permit divorce[9] and the Family Law (Divorce) Act 1996 now regulates divorce in Ireland. There is no need for either partner to have been at fault for the ending of the marriage—the fact of having lived apart for the requisite aggregate five-year period will suffice. 'Living apart' is an elastic term and has, on occasion in family law cases, been held to include estranged couples who continue to live under the same roof but who have ceased to have anything to do with each other. The main concern of the courts in divorce is to ensure that adequate financial arrangements are put in place to ensure the welfare of the children and of either spouse if he or she was previously

---

[7] See *O'K v O'K* [2005] IEHC 384 (29 July 2005).

[8] Judicial Separation and Family Law Reform Act 1989. Judicial separation is most frequently granted on grounds of adultery, unreasonable behaviour by either party (effectively a breakdown in the relationship) or desertion.

[9] Article 41.3.2°:

> 'Where, and only where. such court established under this Constitution as may be prescribed by law is satisfied that –
> i.   a marriage has failed,
> ii. the failure has continued for a period of, or periods amounting to, at least five years,
> iii. that there is no reasonable possibility of reconciliation between the parties to the marriage, and
> iv. any other condition prescribed by law has been complied with,
>
> the court may in accordance with law grant a dissolution of the marriage provided that the court is satisfied that adequate and proper provision having regard to the circumstances will be made for an dependent spouse and for any child who is dependent on either spouse.'

The referendum was passed by a majority of only 9,114; 50.28 per cent of those who voted supported the referendum, although less than two-thirds of those entitled to vote did so.

financially dependent on the other. There is little in the law of divorce involving clinical practice.

Nullity

[7.06] It had been thought that the introduction of divorce into the Irish statute books would lead to a huge and immediate reduction in the demand for annulment of marriage, but this has not happened to the extent predicted.[10] An application for the annulment of marriage remains the avenue of choice for spouses who seek a totally 'clean break' (there is no provision in Irish law for a clean break divorce); the nature of annulment is that it is a declaration that the marriage is not, and never has been, valid, because of some fundamental failing in the marriage 'contract'. The couple therefore will have no financial commitments to each other.[11]

Understanding nullity

[7.07] The simplest way to understand nullity is to regard marriage as a straightforward contract.[12] In any contract there are certain fundamental conditions that must be met for the contract to be valid and if those conditions remain unfulfilled, the contract can be set aside. So the terms of the contract must be certain and, furthermore, a person entering into the contract must do so voluntarily, must be mentally competent to do so and must not be misled as to the nature of the contract he is entering into. Finally, a contract that binds parties to do something they are not legally permitted to do is also void. All of these requirements apply to the marriage contract and the reason why they can be relevant to the health professional is that medical or psychiatric evidence can be important in determining whether the necessary basis exists for a marriage to be annulled. The ways in which a marriage may be set aside as void are generally divided into four categories, of which the last two, invalid consent and incapacity, are the most important:[13]

- lack of capacity to enter into the marriage contract itself;
- non-observance of the formalities of marriage;
- absence of valid consent due to (a) insanity or lack of mental capacity, (b) being misled as to the nature of the marriage, or (c) duress;
- incapacity to enter into or sustain a normal marital relationship.

---

[10] See 'Changes to law on annulment of marriage sought' (2001) Irish Times, 4 October. This report cites Irish Law Society figures (derived from a report of the Law Society on nullity submitted to the Department of Equality, Justice and Law Reform) that show that applications for nullity continued to rise in spite of the introduction of divorce.

[11] There are a number of practical problems inherent in declaring a marriage never to have existed, but they lie outside the scope of this text.

[12] *Griffith v Griffith* [1944] IR 35.

[13] Technically, nullity takes two forms: in some cases the marriage is declared *void*, meaning automatically that the marriage is at an end and never existed; in other cases a marriage will be declared *voidable*. A declaration that a marriage is voidable does not automatically end the marriage but gives either party to the marriage the right to end it. The distinction need not concern us here and the term 'void' will be used throughout.

The law generally presumes that all marriages are valid until the opposite is proven, just as the law presumes that a person is sane until the contrary is shown.[14] Accordingly, it is up to the person who alleges that a marriage should be annulled (the petitioner) to prove it and the court will require compelling proof.[15]

Lack of formalities

[7.08] The absence of the required formalities has little relevance to clinical practice.[16] Formalities include the specific period of notice that must be given before a couple can marry and a requirement that a couple marry in the place stipulated in the instrument that is used to give notice of an intention to marry.

Lack of capacity and/or proper consent

[7.09] A lack of capacity to enter into the marriage contract can arise in one of four ways:

- one or both partners may be too young to marry;[17]
- one (or both) of the married parties may already be married to another person;
- the partners may be too closely related;
- the partners may be of the same biological sex.[18]

The clinician may be obviously involved in cases where the gender of the spouses is at issue. She may be called upon to certify the nature of an operation, may be involved in a determination of what constitutes 'gender', or may be required to give an opinion regarding to which gender the parties in question belong.

[7.10] Just like consent to a medical or surgical procedure, valid consent to marriage has three ingredients: it must be given by someone with the mental capacity to do so, it must be voluntary and it must be informed. If any of these elements is missing the marriage can be annulled.

Mental capacity and marriage

[7.11] It has been said that 'the contract of marriage is, in its essence, one of simplicity and one which it does not require a high degree of intelligence to comprehend.'[19] So, in one case, the court held that a particular person lacked sufficient mental capacity to

---

[14] See Ch 11 'Law and Mental Health'.

[15] *B (O'R) v B* [1991] 1 IR 289 (SC); *S v K* [1993] 1 Fam LJ 18. The parties to nullity or divorce proceedings are called the petitioner and the respondent.

[16] Note, however, that some nationalities resident in Ireland (including Romanians) who wish to undergo the marriage ceremony of their native country (typically conducted in an embassy or consulate) may sometimes be required to complete certain medical formalities.

[17] A person may marry once he is older that 16 years of age, but the permission of the courts must be obtained for those younger than 18 years: Family Law Act 1995, s 31.

[18] In Ireland, one's biological sex is the sex of one's birth. However, see *Christine Goodwin v United Kingdom* (Application No 28957/95), which said that failing to allow a person to modify identification documentation after a sex change operation was a violation of the right to privacy guaranteed by Article 8 of the European Convention on Human Rights.

[19] See *Shatter's Family Law* (4th edn, Tottel Publishing, 1991), para 5.20. Also 'Mental capacity and Marriage', (1964) 98 ILT&SJ, 159–61.

make a will, yet on the same day had the requisite capacity to get married.[20] If a party to a marriage alleges that the marriage should be set aside because one of the parties was suffering from 'insanity' at the time of the marriage, then the person making the allegation must prove it, which will often involve expert medical or psychiatric opinion that:

> …the respondent [the person named by the petitioner in the nullity proceedings] was suffering from psychiatric disorder *at the time of the marriage* of such a character that it prevented him from giving a full, free and informed consent.[21] [italics added].

It is not enough for the petitioner to prove that the respondent suffered from mental illness before or after the marriage.[22] The defect must have been present at the time of the marriage, although it need not have been manifest at the time of the marriage; note that unlike when it comes to writing a will, it is not the case that a person who suffers from an ongoing mental infirmity can consent to marry during a 'lucid interval' when not afflicted by his illness.[23] Note also that a person intoxicated by drugs or alcohol at the time of his marriage may not be able to give valid consent and it would, depending on the circumstances, be open to a court to annul the marriage.[24]

Informed consent to marriage

[7.12] Historically, it was rare to find a petition for nullity granted on a lack of informed consent; traditionally, a mistake or misrepresentation had to be of a most fundamental nature if it was to be grounds for a decree of nullity. The error would have to concern the very identity of the person whom one was proposing to marry. A mistake or misrepresentation about the nature, character or wealth of a party, or any other matter that did not concern the identity of the parties, was not originally sufficient to allow for annulment.[25]

[7.13] With the passage of time and certainly by the mid-1980s,[26] there was a discernible move away from this hard-line approach and towards pragmatism. An acceptance grew that a mistake as to the character or the nature of a life partner could deal just as fatal a blow to the validity of consent as could a mistake as to identity. So, when a husband concealed from his wife prior to their wedding the fact that he was homosexual, his lack

---

[20] *Park v Park* [1953] 2 All ER 1411.

[21] *ME v AE* [1987] (HC) IR 147 at 151 per O'Hanlon J.

[22] Although a person who had misrepresented his mental health history to his prospective spouse could be said to have misled that person into the contract of marriage, giving rise to grounds for nullity—see para **[7.12]***ff* below.

[23] *Turner v Meyers* (1808) 161 ER 600; see Ch 10 'Law and Mental Health Law,' para **[10.60]** for a review of the question of wills made during lucid periods.

[24] *Legeyt v O'Brien* (1834) Milw Rep 325. In this case, the husband was alleged to have been of unsound mind at the time of the marriage. In fact, he was suffering from *delirium tremens* rather than acute intoxication and accordingly the court found that he was fit to marry.

[25] In *Moss v Moss* [1897] P 263 a woman concealed from her husband the fact that she was pregnant by another man. This was not a ground for nullity.

[26] In particular *N v K* [1985] IR 733.

of candour invalidated her consent and an annulment was granted.[27] There is no need for the mistake or misrepresentation to have been deliberate, simply for it to have occurred may be enough to allow the grant of a decree of nullity.

Duress

[7.14] Consent to marriage must be voluntary; a marriage born out of fear, threats, intimidation or any other form of duress can be annulled. Traditionally some measure of coercion was permissible,[28] but the courts have again moved towards a pragmatic intolerance of involuntary consent. Any pressure that overrides the free will of the person who is 'consenting' to the marriage can be duress, including emotional bullying,[29] pressure due to factors external to the relationship[30] (which might include fear of deportation, for example) or duress from the parents of one or both spouses.[31] Where duress has resulted in psychiatric or psychological features, there may be a role for expert medical evidence in any proceedings.

Inability to enter into or sustain a normal marital relationship

[7.15] This ground for nullity can be divided into two broad areas: (a) physical incapacity; and (b) emotional or psychological incapacity. In both cases, the input of a clinician may be required.

Physical inability ('impotence')

[7.16] This generally refers to inability to consummate the marriage, or whether it is possible for the couple to have sexual intercourse. Either partner's difficulties can be the reason for non-consummation of the marriage and, furthermore, obstacles to consummation may be psychological[32] as well as physical, so that erectile dysfunction or

---

[27] *F v F* [1991] 1 IR 348. Similarly a husband who alleged that his wife, during their chaste courtship, had concealed from him the fact that her torso and limbs were disfigured as a result of childhood burns, was granted a degree of nullity on the grounds that he had been misled as to the physical character of the woman he was marrying.

[28] *Griffith v Griffith* [1944] IR 35. In this case, the moral pressure brought to bear by the parents of a girl who became pregnant outside wedlock was not enough on its own to be considered duress. The mother of a pregnant girl (who falsely accused the petitioner of being the father) threatened the man with commencing criminal proceedings for unlawful carnal knowledge (she was younger than 17 years) if he did not marry her daughter. This threat of legal action amounted to duress and the marriage was annulled. See Haugh J at 52: '...duress must be a question of degree and may begin from a gentle form of pressure to physical violence accompanied by threats of death.'

[29] *B v D* (June 1973, unreported) HC.

[30] *Szechter v Szechter* [1970] 3 All ER 905.

[31] *MK v FMC* [1982] ILRM 277, 2 ILRM 277; *B v O'R* [1991] 1 IR 289.

[32] Historically (as recently as the 1940s) many difficulties that we would now recognise as psychosexual were categorised as "wilful refusal to consummate" rather than impotence. Courts of the time refused decrees of annulment and came close to advocating that husbands in such circumstances should overcome their wives' reluctance by force. Now wilful refusal by either partner to consummate the marriage appears to be grounds for annulment even if it does not constitute impotence once the refusing partner entered into the marriage with the intention of refusing to consummate the marriage: see *S v S* (July 1976, unreported) SC.

vaginismus[33] may equally amount to physical incapacity or impotence. Intercourse must be 'ordinary and complete'[34] and possible without resorting to extraordinary measures, such as the use of extreme force. Ejaculation or pregnancy need not occur and the use of barrier contraception does not prevent consummation from having occurred. The impotence does not have to be uniform, affecting all of that partner's sexual relations—it is sufficient simply for a spouse to be incapable of sexual intercourse with the person to whom he or she is married.[35]

Any impotence must be 'incurable', but this is a term to which the law gives an unusual and woolly definition. Impotence is, legally speaking, incurable when any one of the following criteria is met:

–   when it is in fact medically, surgically or psychologically incurable;

–   when the only cure is an operation with potentially dangerous consequences;

–   when a relatively safe surgical treatment is an option, but the spouse requiring the operation refuses to consent to it;[36]

–   in psychological conditions, where there is a danger, even if the condition is treatable or has actually been treated, of the condition recurring.

Proving non-consummation can be difficult and a court may require convincing evidence before it is prepared to annul a marriage on the grounds of impotence.

Medical inspection

[7.17] Court rules provide that where a petitioner brings a case seeking a decree of nullity on the basis of impotence, the parties must be requested to undergo a medical inspection.[37] Medical inspectors may be appointed by the court or can be agreed between the two parties to the legal case. Where a specialist has already been responsible for the care of the party in question, it will often be she who is requested to prepare a report for the courts. The experts' reports are exchanged between the parties if both sides retain separate experts and, as with all medico-legal reports, the authors can be called to testify and to be cross-examined in court.

[7.18] Any report is intended to help the court, but it is not obligatory for either party to undergo medical inspection (although the parties must be requested to undergo the examination) and the court may nonetheless annul the marriage (in the absence of a medical examination being performed) if it is satisfied that non-consummation is proven.

---

[33]   *EC v KM* [1991] 2 IR 192.

[34]   *D-e v Ag* [1845] 173 ER 1039.

[35]   *R v W* (February 1980, unreported) HC.

[36]   A spouse suffering from impotence cannot—in accordance with the general principle of patient autonomy—be compelled to undergo treatment to correct a cause of impotence if he or she does not wish to consent to it.

[37]   Rules of the Superior Courts, Ord 70, r 32.

Psychological or mental inability

[7.19] The parameters of nullity in pre-divorce Ireland were most fundamentally changed when the courts decided that a person could lack the mental capacity to 'enter into or sustain a proper or normal marital relationship'. Essentially, if evidence suggests that because of 'some inherent quality or characteristic of an individual's nature or personality which could not be said to voluntary or self-induced'[38] a person lacks the capacity to be married, an annulment may be granted.

[7.20] This 'inherent quality' does not have to reach the threshold of being a definite psychiatric or mental illness, although that may be the case.[39] The 'inherent quality' must exist at the time the marriage was entered into, although it need not be that symptoms of the problem were present at the time. Other non-psychiatric grounds for courts finding that a person lacked the necessary quality to enter into or sustain a normal marital relationship include the sexual orientation of one of the spouses, emotional immaturity and incompatibility.

[7.21] Medical evidence may be important in all such cases, especially those argued on psychiatric grounds, because it is necessary to prove that the problem existed, albeit latently, at the time of the marriage. The question is whether the person was suffering from an illness that prevented him from entering into and sustaining a normal marital relationship at the time of the marriage and subsequent recovery from that ailment is not necessarily a bar to a decree of nullity. The court can order the parties to attend for a psychiatric review but, as with investigations and treatment of impotence, the parties are not obliged to attend. The courts have stated that there are times when they will prefer to hear the opinion of experts in the field of psychiatry, rather than that of general practitioners. Where there is a dispute between the evidence offered by both sides, the judge will decide between them on the basis of any reports, testimony and cross-examination.

---

[38]   *UF v JC* [1981] 2 IR 330 at 356 per Finlay CJ.

[39]   In one significant nullity case, the husband suffered from schizophrenia. The court appeared not to be concerned with whether he was 'insane' at the time of the marriage (and therefore unable to enter into the contract of marriage) but instead dwelt on the fact that his illness meant he could not sustain the loving and caring relationship essential to marriage: *RSJ v JSJ* [982] 2 ILRM 263. Similarly, bipolar affective disorder (or manic depression) has been held to be grounds for annulment (*D v C* [1984] 4 ILRM 173), as has personality disorder (*W(C) v C* [1989] IR 696).

Quick Reference Guide 7.1
Clinician involvement annulment

> ❖ A decree of nullity, if granted, has the effect of allowing a marriage to be considered as never having existed. A person who brings a legal case in family law is the petitioner, the other party is the respondent.
>
> ❖ In general annulment will be granted where there is a fundamental flaw in the marriage contract or in one party's ability to enter into the contract or relationship of marriage.
>
> ❖ Specific grounds for annulment can include:
>
>   (i) An inability to enter into the marriage contract because of youth, the spouses being related or of the same sex or because one of the spouses is already married
>
>   (ii) A failure to fulfil the requisite formalities
>
>   (iii) A lack of valid consent due to insufficient mental capacity, a lack of informed consent or duress
>
>   (iv) Inability to enter into or sustain a marital relationship for physical, psychological or psychiatric reasons
>
> ❖ A clinician may be involved in assessing and reporting on the presence or absence of any physical or psychiatric infirmity that is alleged in nullity proceedings. A spouse will be ordered to undergo examination when nullity is alleged on the grounds of 'physical incapacity' (impotence). In cases where psychiatric infirmity is alleged, the concern is generally whether the illness was present at the time of entering into the marriage.

DOMESTIC VIOLENCE

[7.22] Domestic violence is common in Ireland[40] and elsewhere.[41] While there are men who are the subject of violence at the hands of female spouses and while violence can

---

[40] Bradley, Smith, Long, O'Dowd, 'Reported frequency of domestic violence: cross sectional survey of women attending general practice'. BMJ 2002; 324:1–6. This study showed that 40 per cent of women who had ever been in a sexual relationship admitted in a questionnaire to having been a victim of violent behaviour in that relationship. Of that 40 per cent, half had been injured as a result of the violent behaviour they had experienced. The study also demonstrated that doctors in primary care appear only rarely to ask about domestic violence.

[41] Community surveys in the UK have indicated that up to one in four women have experienced domestic violence. Studies in the United States and Australia report that between 5 per cent and 20 per cent of the women attending general practice have experienced domestic violence in the preceding year. See Mooney, *The hidden figure: domestic violence in north London—the findings of a survey conducted on domestic violence in the north London Borough of Islington* (London: London Centre for Criminology, Middlesex University, 1993); Johnson, Sacco, Researching violence against women, Can J Criminol 1995; 37:281–304; Hamberger, Saunders, Hovery, 'Prevalence of domestic violence in community practice and rate of physician inquiry' Fam Med 1992; 24:283–7; Marais, Villiers, 'Domestic violence in patients visiting general practitioners—prevalence, phenomenology, and association with psychopathology' S AfrMed J 1999;89:635–40; Mazza, Dennerstein, Ryan, 'Physical, sexual and emotional violence against women: a general practice-based prevalence study' Med J Aust 1996; 161:14–7; McCauley, Kern, 'The 'battering syndrome': prevalence and clinical characteristic of domestic violence in primary care internal medicine practices' Ann Intern Med 1995; 123:737–46.

occur in same-sex relationships, the archetype is male-on-female violence and the problem appears to be substantial and growing.[42] Legislation exists in the form of the Domestic Violence Act 1996 to help protect spouses (as well as cohabiting partners[43] and former spouses) and children from domestic violence. An order can also be granted to protect parents from violent children over the age of 18 years. There are three types of order:

- barring orders;
- safety orders;
- interim protection or barring orders.

Each may be applied for by a person at risk or by a health service executive (HSE) on behalf of that person. An application for a safety or barring order is made to the District Court or the Circuit Court and a person who breaches an order of this nature can be arrested and prosecuted by the Gardaí. An applicant is a person who requests a barring or safety order; a respondent is the person to whom the order applies. It is important to remember that orders for protection against domestic violence can be made to help married partners, cohabiting partners, children and the parents of adult children when a member of any of those groups is threatened by domestic violence. A woman who is the victim of domestic violence can go directly to the District Court, usually with the assistance of the police and sometimes with supporting clinical evidence from her doctor, to apply for an interim order pending a final court decision.

Safety orders[44]

[7.23] A safety order does not compel a violent partner to leave the family home, but rather directs him to refrain from threatening violence against the applicant or 'putting the applicant in fear'. If the respondent is already living away from the residence of the applicant then he can be directed not to trespass into the vicinity of the place. Curiously, a safety order does not prevent the respondent from returning to the family home and if he does so with the permission of the applicant, he has committed no crime. The theory behind the safety order is that it will restrain less serious threatening behaviour, eg that

---

[42] The number of applications for barring orders rose from just over 2,000 in 1981 to almost 5,000 in 1998: Shannon, *Family Law Loose-Leaf* (Roundhall, 2002), Division F, 5.

[43] A cohabiting partner is defined differently depending on whether a safety order or a barring order is sought. For a safety order a cohabiting partner is a person 'who has lived with the respondent as husband and wife for a period of at least six months in aggregate during the period of twelve months immediately prior to the application' (Domestic Violence Act 1996, s 2(1)(a)(ii)). For a barring order, two conditions apply: first, the applicant must have lived with the respondent 'as husband and wife for a period of six months in aggregate during the period of nine months immediately prior to the application' (s 3(b)). Secondly, the respondent cannot be the subject of a barring order when he has a financial interest in the residence the couple shares that is greater than the applicant's financial interest (s 3(4)). So, if an unmarried couple have been sharing a home for ten years and the man is beating the woman, she cannot seek a barring order if he owns more than 51 per cent of the property even if she is at the risk of serious violence. She can seek a protection order. A similar ownership rule applies to parents seeking a barring order against their children.

[44] Domestic Violence Act 1996, s 2(2).

which falls short of violence, while allowing the couple to continue to live together if they wish to do so, perhaps in an attempt at reconciliation. However, there is nothing to prevent the applicant who has been granted a safety order returning to court to seek a barring order. A person who breaches the terms of a safety order can be arrested and imprisoned.

Barring orders[45]

[7.24] Where the safety or welfare of an applicant or the welfare of an applicant's dependent children requires it, a court can make a barring order. A barring order has two effects: first, the respondent can be directed to leave the place where the applicant lives; secondly, whether the respondent is living with the applicant or not, he can be directed to stay away from the place where the applicant lives until the court directs otherwise. The court can also direct the respondent not to use violent or threatening behaviour towards the applicant or her children and to stay away from the vicinity as well as the home of the applicant. The place the respondent can be directed to stay away from need not be the family home; it can be any location where the applicant is resident.

[7.25] If the applicant and her children were forced by the conduct of the respondent to leave the home they shared, a barring order can have the effect of forcing the respondent to quit the home, allowing the applicant and children to return. The court decides on the duration of a barring order and a person who breaches it may be arrested and imprisoned.

Interim orders

[7.26] Interim orders are a short-term solution, operating to provide immediate protection to an abused partner in the time between when an application for a safety or barring order is first made and when the matter is decided by the courts. An interim protection order[46] (which restrains the respondent from violent or threatening conduct) or an interim barring order (which will have the effect of excluding the respondent from the home) can be sought. Both forms of interim order can be sought on an ex parte basis, without any need for the violent partner to be notified or to be present in court, although in any application for an interim barring order a note must be made of the evidence and be communicated to the absent spouse.[47] An interim barring order will generally only be granted where there is an immediate risk of harm to the applicant or her children if the order is not made and if an interim protection order would not be sufficient.

A Role for the Health Service Executive

[7.27] The Health Service Executive (HSE) can act on behalf of 'aggrieved' individuals and seek safety or barring orders on their behalf.[48] In cases where a woman is the victim

---

[45] Domestic Violence Act 1996, s 3(2).

[46] Domestic Violence Act 1996, s 5.

[47] Domestic Violence Act 1996, s 4. The Act originally provided that an interim barring order could be granted ex parte in exceptional cases where it was in the interests of justice, notwithstanding the fact that the respondent had not been given any notice of the proceedings. However, this provision was ruled unconstitutional in a judgment of the Supreme Court in *Keating v Crowley* [2002] IESC 47 (9 October 2002) and was repealed by the Domestic Violence (Amendment) Act 2002.

[48] Domestic Violence Act 1996, s 6.

of domestic abuse and her doctor advises her to seek the assistance of the court, but she will not through fear, then the doctor may be justified in liaising with HSE social workers. A HSE application can happen when:

- the HSE becomes aware of an incident or a series of incidents that in the opinion of the HSE put a person at risk;
- the HSE has cause to believe that the aggrieved person has been subjected to molestation, violence or threatened violence or has otherwise been put in fear of her safety or welfare;
- threats to the aggrieved person are preventing her from making an application for a barring order or safety order herself; and
- taking into account the wishes of the aggrieved person, an application for a barring order or safety order is the appropriate way to proceed.

Such applications are most likely to be made by HSEs when the person at risk is a dependent child and where the child's safety from physical or sexual abuse can be best assured by barring the abuser from the home. This is an alternative to taking the child into care under the Child Care Act 1991 (see para **[7.42]**). However, there is no reason why the mechanism cannot also be used to protect abused spouses, when those spouses are prevented by fear or threats from taking action to exclude their abuser from the home.

Quick Reference Guide 7.2

Domestic violence

❖ A woman – whether married or not – can take legal action to protect her from anyone who is perpetrating domestic violence against her. The clinician faced with such a woman can advise her to involve the police or social workers in seeking an order from the District Court. This can normally be done at the next available sitting of the court. Parents can also obtain orders against violent adult children in the home.

❖ A barring order compels the violent partner to leave a specified place, such as the family home, and to stay clear of that place and of the person in whose favour the order is made.

❖ A safety order does not compel the violent partner to leave anywhere, merely to desist from threatening or violent behaviour against the applicant for the order.

❖ Interim orders are orders (which can be safety or protection orders) made in the short term to protect the woman until the full facts of the case can be heard. It is an interim order that the victim or person at risk will ordinarily be granted on her first visit to court.

❖ A health board can bring an application for a safety or protection order to court on behalf of a person (partner or child) who cannot – due to fear or threats – bring the application herself.

CHILDREN

[7.28] Certain areas of the relationship between the practitioner and the child have been covered elsewhere in the text, in particular the question of consent.[49] We have mentioned that the child is in an unusual position: the Irish Constitution recognises the rights of the family and the consequent right of parents over the child, but it also recognises the rights of the individual. Irish law is not always clear in its attempts to define where the rights of the child fit into the Constitution. There are decisions that hold that the family is paramount and that the child's individual rights are best served by being subsumed into those of the family (and more particularly the right of the parents to take decisions on behalf of the child). But there are other decisions suggesting that a child's rights should be considered in isolation from the family, with the child regarded first as an individual and only secondly as a member of the constitutional family. It is a complex question that we do not consider in depth here, but it bedevils considerations of a child's right to consent to medical treatment against the wishes of his parents[50] and the question of whether a child at risk should be taken from his family and placed in care.

Children at risk – the principles

[7.29] Recent figures suggest that approximately 5,300 Irish children are in some form of care.[51] The legislation that is predominantly used to take children into care is the Child Care Act 1991,[52] but we have noted already that barring orders and safety orders could also be used to ensure the protection of children at risk.

[7.30] A Government document entitled *Children First: National Guidelines for the Protection and Welfare of Children*[53] was introduced to assist professionals and the relevant bodies in identifying and reporting child abuse and providing services for children and families. The essential principle of legislation governing children at risk is that parents or other legitimate carers such as guardians or step-parents have primary responsibility for the care and protection of their children. When they do not or cannot fulfil this responsibility, then it may be necessary for state services, generally in the guise of the HSE social workers, to intervene. As an aid to assessing when intervention is necessary, the *Children First* Guidelines set out a number of 'principles for best practice in child protection' (see Table 7.1).

---

[49] See Ch 4 'Consent'.

[50] See Mills, '*PKU:* Please Keep Unclear?' (2002) DULJ 23, 180.

[51] It has been suggested that the rise in children in care (doubled since 1989) may in some measure be due to greater awareness and a better response to child protection concerns: see 'Number of children in care doubles since 1989' Irish Times, 18 April 2007. Most children were placed in foster care (60 per cent), followed by foster care with relatives (28 per cent), residential care (8 per cent) or other forms of placement (4 per cent).

[52] Irish law defines children, in terms of abuse or the risk thereof, as unmarried people aged less than 18 years. The Child Care Act 1991 was amended by the Child Care Act 2007, but those amendments are not relevant for the present discussion.

[53] Department of Health and Children (Dublin, 1999). The report (or a summary) may be downloaded from http://www.dohc.ie/publications/children_first.html.

Table 7.1 Principles for Best Practice in Child Protection

i. The welfare of children is of paramount importance.

ii. A proper balance must be struck between protecting children and respecting the rights and needs of parents/carers and families; but where there is conflict, the child's welfare must come first.

iii. Children have a right to be heard and taken seriously. Taking account of their age and level of understanding, they should be consulted and involved in relation to all matters and decisions that affect their lives.

iv. Parents/carers have a right to respect and should be consulted and involved in matters which concern their family.

v. Actions taken to protect a child, including assessment, should not in themselves be abusive or cause the child unnecessary distress. Every action and procedure should consider the overall needs of the child.

vi. Intervention should not deal with the child in isolation; the child must be seen in a family setting.

vii. The criminal dimension of any action cannot be ignored.

viii. Children should only be separated from parents/carers when all alternative means of protecting them have been exhausted. Reunion should always be considered.

ix. Effective prevention, detection and treatment of child abuse require a coordinated multi-disciplinary approach.

x. In practice, effective child protection requires compulsory training and clarity of responsibility for personnel involved in organisations working with children.

xi. Early intervention and support should be available to promote the welfare of children and families, particularly where they are vulnerable or at risk of not receiving adequate care or protection.

Definition, recognition and reporting of child abuse

[7.31] Child abuse has been recognised as a medico-legal phenomenon for more than a century.[54] Diagnosis can be difficult, but there are some indicators that should bring the possibility to mind, the most significant of which is a disclosure or allegation by a child of abuse. Such disclosures should always be taken seriously; one of the most formidable obstacles to the detection of child abuse is a failure to accept that it is a possibility. The abuse of children falls into four broad categories: neglect, emotional abuse, physical abuse and sexual abuse. We examine here the definitions.

Neglect

[7.32] Neglect is best described as harm arising as a result of omissions by—rather than acts of—the parent(s). Whereas physical or sexual abuse may be predicated on a single incident, harm caused by neglect will typically accrue over time. Failing to feed or clean a child or to send him to school can all be examples of neglect and the signs of neglect

---

[54] Tardieu, 'Etude médico-legal sur les sérvices et mauvais traitments exercés sur des enfants.' *Annales d'hygiene publique et de medicine legal*, 1860; 13: 361–398.

can include emotional disturbance, low weight or height for age or obvious indicators such as lack of hygiene or dirty, ill-fitting clothes.

Emotional abuse

[7.33] Emotional abuse arises from the conduct of the relationship between child and parent, with the defining feature commonly a failure on the part of the parent to provide for the child's emotional needs, including the child's desire for affection, approval and consistency. Emotional abuse can come to the surface in a spectrum of ways, ranging from clingy behaviour to total avoidance of the parent in question. Other signs can include inhibited emotional and physical development. The *Children First* document lists some of the following as examples of emotional abuse:

- persistent criticism, hostility or blame-casting, harsh disciplinary regimes;
- conditional parenting (making love and care conditional on certain behaviour);
- emotional unavailability or inconsistency;
- premature imposition of responsibility on a child, unrealistic expectations of a child's capabilities or capacity to understand;
- lack of interest and failure to provide opportunities for emotional and cognitive development.[55]

Physical abuse

[7.34] Physical abuse is also termed non-accidental injury and can demonstrate itself in a number of ways. Some manifestations, eg bruises or burns, are obvious, while others, such as haemorrhages due to shaking, are less so and some, such as Munchausen syndrome by proxy,[56] are insidious and rare in the extreme.

[7.35] There are some factors in the examination or history of a child that may bring to mind non-accidental injury. There may be a lack of correlation between the history related by the parent and the injuries sustained by the child and there may perhaps also be a marked reluctance on the part of the parent or guardian to permit a full examination of the child (for fear that other marks or injuries may be noticed). There can also sometimes be an inexplicable delay in seeking medical help for the child. Socio-economic class is not directly linked to physical abuse of children, but it may be slightly more common in lower socio-economic groups. Common injuries will be external

---

[55] *Putting Children First—Summary Document* (Dublin 1999), 10.

[56] A condition in which parents give false accounts of symptoms in their children and may even fake the signs of their children's illness in order to attract attention to themselves. They seek repeated medical investigations and unwarranted treatment. According to one study, the most commonly reported symptoms are neurological, rashes and bleeding. There is some evidence of collusion by children. It has been suggested that children who have been victims of Munchausen syndrome by proxy will progress to have Munchausen syndrome themselves in adulthood. An early description is contained in Meadow, 'Management of Munchausen syndrome by proxy', *Archives of Diseases of Childhood*, 1985:60(4); 385–93. There are those who suggest that there is tendency to over-estimate its frequency: see Meadows, *Journal of Clinical Forensic Medicine* 1994:1; 121–127. Some attempts have been made to video children in hospital to detect such abuse: Foreman, Farsides, 'Ethical use of covert videoing techniques in detecting Munchausen syndrome by proxy' BMJ 1993; 307:611–3.

(bruising, abrasions, bites and burns), but internal damages such as head injuries, eye damage or fractures are not uncommon. X-ray may show numerous old fractures or periosteum damage or fractures at various stages of healing—other injuries that may demonstrate non-accidental injury are detailed in Table 7.2:

Table 7.2 Possible Indicators of Physical Abuse

Bruising, especially if:

- on a baby less than nine months old (the less mobile a child, the less likely he is to sustain accidental injuries);
- on the cheek or head;
- unusual in shape: consider bites; clusters of disc-shaped bruises may be a sign of tight gripping of the child; there may also be the imprint of something that was used to strike the child (for example, a belt buckle);
- multiple bruises of different ages.

Black eyes

Retinal haemorrhage (which may be due to babies being shaken)[57]

Fractures or other bony damage, especially if:

- in children less than one year old;
- rib fractures, particularly when multiple (so-called 'string of beads' appearance on x-ray);
- other multiple fractures at diffuse locations, whether old or healing;
- epiphyseal displacement;
- perisoteal damage or cortical thickening on x-ray.

Burns and scalds:

- small circular burns may be caused by cigarettes;
- old burn scars may be present;
- burns or scalds in very young (and therefore largely immobile) children may be suggestive of non-accidental injury.
- there may sometimes be extensive scalding of the extremities (typically lower) with a linear demarcation proximally suggestive of immersion in extremely hot liquid.

Bruising or laceration in or around the mouth.[58]

[7.36] In terms of validating an index of suspicion, it may be noted that parents or guardians who physically abuse children may demonstrate some of the following characteristics:

---

[57] Although note the suggestion that retinal haemorrhage with specific characteristics is not in fact pathognomonic of shaking: see Geddes, Plunkett, 'The evidence base for shaken baby syndrome', BMJ 2004; 328:719–720 (27 March).

[58] One common injury, described by Knight in *Legal Aspects of Medical Practice* (5th edn, London: Churchill Livingstone, 1992), is the 'side-swipe' injury—a laceration of the mucosa inside the upper lip around the midline and which may include tearing of the frenum. A similar injury can be caused by forcing a bottle into the child's mouth.

- a male abuser may not be the biological father of the child.

- a female abuser may have had several children in quick succession and may lack coping skills or a support network. Straitened financial circumstances may also contribute.

- younger parents pose a greater risk.

- there may be a history of personality or psychiatric disorder or a criminal record.

- the parent or parents may themselves have been victims of physical or sexual abuse as children.

Sexual abuse

[7.37] Sexual abuse is the involvement of children and adolescents in sexual activities they do not fully comprehend and to which they are unable to give informed consent for the sexual arousal or gratification of another person. The forms which child sexual abuse (CSA) can take are numerous and can include:

- sexual activity, including exposure of the sexual organs, in the presence of a child;

- touching a child or soliciting the touch of a child for sexual gratification or arousal;

- masturbation in the presence of, or with the assistance of, a child;

- sexual penetration (vaginal, anal or oral) of a child by any part of the abuser or using a foreign body;

- consensual sexual activity with a child less than 17 years of age.[59]

Indicators of abuse can include disclosure by the child; failure to thrive; signs of neglect; emotional or behavioural disturbance (particularly sexualised behaviour at a young age); and clear physical signs of abuse, including damage to the ano-genital region. Any symptoms suggestive of sexually transmitted disease in the pre-pubertal child should be considered indicative of CSA until proven otherwise. Where CSA is suspected, specialist care should be involved. The more highly trained the person dealing with a child who has experienced CSA, the less traumatic it will be for the child and any evidence or details from the child may be more accurate. Anatomically correct dolls are often used to encourage children to describe what they have experienced. Physical examination should only be conducted by someone expert in the field and even then diagnoses that are at best controversial and at worst incorrect can occur.

Recognising child abuse

[7.38] There are three generally accepted steps to the recognition of abuse, whether sexual, physical or emotional. The first, and perhaps the most important, is simply to consider the possibility that abuse has occurred when faced with the child who has unexplained injuries, emotional disturbance or behavioural abnormality. The second step is to dwell on whether the possibility may be more than fanciful. Looking through a

---

[59] The legal definitions of crimes such as sexual assault and incest are dealt with in Ch 15 'The Law and Forensics of Sexual Assault'.

child's clinical records or the details of previous accident and emergency department visits may disclose patterns consistent with something more than a tentative diagnosis of child abuse. Knowledge of the broader family history may also be useful in isolating cases of abuse[60] and the clinician should be prepared at an early stage to seek a second opinion, ideally from someone with expertise in the area. The final element is to record information that will be useful in facilitating further investigation if it appears to be warranted. Acting on the suspicion or confirmation of abuse is dealt with below.

Reporting child abuse

[7.39] There is no legal obligation on anyone to report child abuse, whether physical, emotional or sexual in nature. Compulsory reporting of suspicions of child abuse has been mooted,[61] but the suggestion never became law.[62] The approach adopted in Ireland is that while reporting of child abuse remains voluntary, a person who does report abuse is afforded the promise of legal protection so long as she makes her report in good faith. The Protections for Persons Reporting Child Abuse Act 1998[63] shields from legal action any person who in good faith reports suspicions that:

(a)   a child has been, or is being, assaulted, ill-treated, neglected or sexually abused; or

(b)   a child's health, development or welfare has been or is being avoidably impaired or neglected.

[7.40] In other words, there is no obligation on a practitioner to report child abuse, but she will not be answerable to her patient or to the alleged perpetrator if she makes a disclosure to the appropriate authorities, which are defined as a member of the Garda Síochána or a designated officer of the HSE.[64] The patient will not be able to bring a

---

[60]   Southall, Plunkett, 'Covert video recordings of life-threatening child abuse: lessons for child protection.' Pediatrics 1997; 100: 735–760. This study suggested that the abused children were more likely to present with bleeding from the nose or mouth, and more likely to have a family history of sudden and unexpected death or abuse in siblings. In addition, 23 of the abusive parents were diagnosed as having personality disorders.

[61]   The issue was raised in the Law Reform Commission Report, *Report on Child Sexual Abuse* (LRC 32–1990) and the Report of the Kilkenny Incest Investigation Team (Dublin, 1993). The Law Reform Commission recommended the introduction of mandatory reporting of CSA; the Kilkenny Incest Investigation Team called for the introduction of mandatory reporting for all forms of child abuse. The arguments were summarised in Department of Health, *Putting Children First—A Discussion Document on Mandatory Reporting of Child Abuse*, (Dublin, 1996).

[62]   This accords with the position in the United Kingdom where proposals to introduce mandatory reporting were rejected: *Review of Child Care Law: Report to Ministers of an Interdepartmental Working Party* (London: HMSO, 1985). France, Italy, Norway Sweden and Finland are European countries with mandatory reporting in place.

[63]   Protections for Persons Reporting Child Abuse Act 1998, s 3.

[64]   Designated officers are those members of HSE staff who fall into one of the following categories: social workers; childcare workers; public health nurses; hospital consultants; psychiatrists; non-consultant hospital doctors; all other HSEs medical and dental personnel; community welfare officers; speech and language therapists; all HSE nursing personnel; psychologists; radiographers; physiotherapists; occupational therapists; health education officers; substance abuse counsellors and care assistants.

legal action for breach of confidentiality,[65] nor will the alleged perpetrator be able to bring a legal action against the clinician for defamation if the allegation turns out to be unfounded. On the other hand, a person who *deliberately and knowingly* makes a false allegation of child abuse against another may not only be sued for defamation by the person she names but she may also face criminal proceedings under the Protections for Persons Reporting Child Abuse Act 1998.[66] The key therefore is that any allegation of child abuse should be made *in good faith*.

[7.41] Any duty or responsibility to report is therefore moral or ethical, rather than legal. It is arguable that a practitioner who knew of abuse taking place and did not report it, resulting in greater harm to a patient or to others that could have been prevented by the disclosure, could be guilty of professional misconduct and subject to disciplinary action by her professional regulatory body. The *Children First* document lists the following as grounds for concerns that could activate the responsibility to report:

 – a specific indication from the child that she was abused (which should always be taken seriously);

 – a statement from a person who witnessed abuse;

 – illness, injury or behaviour consistent with abuse;

 – a symptom which may not itself prove abuse, but which is supported by corroborative evidence of deliberate harm or negligence;

 – consistent signs of neglect over a period of time.

Children at risk – the practice

[7.42] Dealing with the child at risk, whether it is a risk posed by neglect or by physical, emotional or sexual abuse, is a multidisciplinary matter. The practitioner who suspects or knows that child abuse is taking place should involve those best placed to provide assistance. These will most commonly include HSE social workers and paediatricians. A child at risk may require to be taken into care and thus away from the source of the abuse (or as we have noted already, the abuser may be removed from the environment of the child using a protection order), or may require admission or assessment under the care of an experienced paediatrician.

[7.43] The technicalities of reporting abuse will vary with the environment in which the practitioner finds herself: the general practitioner will need to contact a HSE social worker together with the local paediatric unit, where appropriate. The hospital-based practitioner will contact someone within the hospital. In situations where the picture is uncertain, multi-faceted or evolving, a case conference involving all available staff who have knowledge of the family and child in question may be appropriate; it permits the pooling of information and expertise and can allow a clearer picture to develop.

---

[65] As we have seen elsewhere in the text, a clinician's decision to breach confidentiality can be justified if the intention is to protect her patient, another individual or society as a whole (as it would be, in this case, if the breach of confidentiality protected further abuse) or if compelled to do so by the law. See Ch 3 Practitioner–Patient Relationship and Confidentiality, para **[3.18]***ff.*

[66] Protections for Persons Reporting Child Abuse Act 1998, s 5.

Quick Reference Guide 7.3

The principles and diagnosis of child abuse

> ❖ There are four generally accepted categories of child abuse:
>   o neglect
>   o emotional abuse
>   o physical abuse and
>   o child sexual abuse (CSA)
>
> ❖ Children who are suffering abuse can demonstrate a range of signs, including obvious signs of neglect, poor school attendance, unusual or extreme emotional behaviour, the physical stigmata of abuse and premature sexualised behaviour.
>
> ❖ Physical abuse, or non-accidental injury, can range from the extremely overt to the covert and hard to detect. There are some traits that appear to be more common in parents who perpetrate physical abuse, including not being the child's natural parent, comparative youth, poor financial resources and a lack of coping skills and support networks. Parents who abuse were often themselves victims of abuse in childhood.
>
> ❖ A key to the detection of abuse is being prepared to recognise it as a possibility.
>
> ❖ There is no legal obligation on a person to report suspicions of any form of abuse, but a person who does so will be protected by the Protections for Persons Reporting Child Abuse Act 1998 from any legal consequences once the allegation is made in good faith. There is a strong moral and ethical imperative for health care professionals to report any suspicions of abuse to those who are in a position to help the child.

We have noted that the Irish Constitution gives a special place to the family; this is applicable even in situations where members of the family are suspected of abuse. The family should be kept informed of decisions that are being taken with respect to the child at risk, unless to do so would put the child (or—it is argued—other children within the family) at greater risk.

[7.44] In extreme situations where a child is faced with an extreme risk, the Garda Síochána may be the first port of call. A child should not be left in what appears to the practitioner to be a dangerous situation and both HSE staff (typically social workers) and Gardaí are conferred with powers by the Child Care Act 1991 to allow them to intervene when children are at risk. The Gardaí in particular have the power to seize a child without a court order and take him to a place of safety before handing the child over to the care of the HSE. It is important to stress that the best care of the child at risk will be provided by multidisciplinary teams that combine their skills and knowledge bases.

Care orders

[7.45] When a child is shown or believed to be at risk it may be necessary to remove the child from the scene of the abuse and take him into care. The protocol and categories of care orders are set out in the Child Care Act 1991, but it should be noted that all decisions regarding children's custody are taken in accordance with the so-called welfare principle, which may be expressed as follows:[67]

Where in any proceedings before any court the custody, guardianship or upbringing of an infant...the court in deciding that question, shall regard the welfare of the infant as the first and paramount consideration.

'Welfare' is in turn defined as 'religious and moral, intellectual, physical and social welfare'.[68] What the welfare principle means is that, when considering custody issues, the court will always put at the forefront of its mind the question of what is best for the child, although into the mix of this complex question is also thrown the Constitution and its recognition of the role of the family. Accordingly, the usual starting point is that a child's welfare is best served by being kept with or being returned to the family.

[7.46] It will generally be the HSE that applies to a court for a child care order and the 1991 Act describes the following responsibility of the HSE as well as recognising the complexity of any custody decision:

3. (1) It shall be a function of [the HSE] to promote the welfare of children in its area who are not receiving adequate care and protection.

(2) In the performance of this function, [the HSE] shall—

(a)   take such steps as it considers requisite to identify children who are not receiving adequate care and protection and co-ordinate information from all relevant sources relating to children in its area;

(b)   having regard to the rights and duties of parents, whether under the Constitution or otherwise—

i.   regard the welfare of the child as the first and paramount consideration, and

ii.   in so far as is practicable, give due consideration, having regard to his age and understanding, to the wishes of the child; and

(c)   have regard to the principle that it is generally in the best interests of a child to be brought up in his own family.

Accordingly, while it is the HSE's responsibility to apply for care orders, the courts will only grant an order removing a child from his family when there are compelling circumstances that override the parents' constitutional rights and which mean that the child's welfare is best served outside the family.[69] When a court is deciding, therefore, it must hold the welfare principle paramount but must also have regard to the constitutional rights of the parents and may also as far as practicable give due consideration to the wishes of the child having regard to his age and understanding.[70]

Voluntary care

[7.47] Parents can consent to a child being taken into care and, if this occurs, the child will be kept in care for as long as it appears necessary to the HSE.[71] If the parents withdraw their consent, it may be necessary to apply for a care order from the courts (generally the District Court).

---

67   Guardianship of Infants Act 1964, s 3.
68   Guardianship of Infants Act 1964, s 2, as substituted by the Status of Children Act 1987, s 9.
69   *Re JH, an infant* [1985] IR 375.
70   Child Care Act 1991, s 24.
71   Child Care Act 1991, s 4.

Removal of a child to a place of safety by gardaí without a court order

[7.48] If there is an immediate and serious risk to the health or welfare of a child and no time to wait for the making of any other order (such as an emergency care order), then Gardaí may enter any place without a warrant and remove the child to safety.[72] They may be accompanied by such other persons as may be necessary, such as a doctor or social workers. Once the child is removed, he must be handed over as soon as possible to the HSE, which must then apply for an emergency care order.

Emergency care order[73]

[7.49] When 'there is an immediate and serious risk to the health or welfare of a child' that either necessitates him being taken into HSE care or remaining there,[74] the District Court can make an emergency care order at short notice in response to an application by a HSE. If the child is not already in the care of the HSE, the judge can direct the Gardaí to go and bring the child into the custody of the HSE. The judge may withhold information from the parent concerning the whereabouts of the child if there are extremely strong reasons for doing so[75] and she may also restrict access to the child. The judge may also give consent on the child's behalf to any 'medical or psychiatric examination, treatment or assessment of the child.' Once a child is in care (and assuming that they were not already aware of the proceedings), the child's parents must be notified of the care order as soon as possible.

Interim care order[76]

[7.50] Once any short-term crisis necessitating the Gardaí taking a child to a place of safety or the making of an emergency care order has abated, a child may still need to remain in care pending the court deciding what to do. In that case, a court can make an interim care order allowing the child to remain lawfully in HSE custody until those decisions can be made. For the judge to make an interim care order she has to be happy that an application for a long-term care order has been made or is about to be made and that the circumstances that would justify agreeing to a final decision on a long-term care order exist.

[7.51] Unlike an emergency care order, which can be made without the knowledge of the parents (although they must be told of it as soon as possible afterwards), the parents must be notified in advance of an intention to apply for an interim care order. The judge can also make any other orders she sees fit along with the interim order, including directing medical or other assessments.

---

[72] Child Care Act 1991, s 12.

[73] Child Care Act 1991, s 13.

[74] If he has for example been seized by gardaí and handed over to the HSE or is already a patient in hospital.

[75] *MF v Superintendent of Ballymun Garda Station* [1991] 1 IR 189 (SC). O'Flaherty J said (at 206) that parents of a child in care should be kept informed of their child's whereabouts unless 'very exceptional circumstances can be established to justify a different course.'

[76] Child Care Act 1991, s 17.

Longer-term care order

[7.52] For a care order to be made the judge must be satisfied that:

(a) the child has been or is being assaulted, ill-treated, neglected or sexually abused; or

(b) the child's health, development or welfare has been, or is being, avoidably impaired or neglected; or

(c) the child's health, development or welfare is likely to be avoidably impaired or neglected;

and that the HSE can provide the necessary care.[77] The order can be made for as long as the child remains a child (until the age of 18 or until the person marries, whichever is the sooner) or for any shorter period. Orders shorter than the duration of childhood can be extended. If the child is not already in care the judge can direct the Gardaí to go and get him.

[7.53] The care order has the effect of putting the HSE in the place of the parents and it has the power to decide on all matters affecting the child including medical care and consenting to the issuing of a passport to the child. The 'care' can take the form of foster parents,[78] a residential home, adoption or any 'other suitable arrangements', which can include placement with a suitable relative.

Supervision order[79]

[7.54] Supervision orders are an alternative to care orders where the court is happy that the child can remain within the home but nonetheless some measure of observation is warranted. Any disputes between parents and the HSE about the operation of the supervision order will be officiated by the court if a compromise cannot be reached. Supervision orders have a life span of 12 months but can be extended by the court. The court can punish anyone who obstructs the HSE in its attempts to carry out the supervision order and the HSE may, if carrying out its duties under the supervision order proves impossible, apply for a care order.

---

[77] Child Care Act 1991, s 18.

[78] The rules for foster parents are contained in the Child Care (Placement of Children in Foster Care) Regulations 1995 (SI 260/1995) and the amendments of the Child Care Act 1991 by the Child Care (Amendment) Act 2007 were in large measure concerned with granting increased autonomy to foster parents in relation to the care of a child who has been with the foster parents for more than five years. However, these provisions are not relevant for our present purposes. Note that in 2006 the majority of children in care (60 per cent) were in foster care: see 'Number of children in care doubles since 1989', Irish Times, 18 April 2007.

[79] Child Care Act 1991, s 19.

Quick Reference Guide 7.4

Practical aspects of protecting children

> ❖ Dealing with allegations of abuse is a multidisciplinary matter involving police, social workers and medical and nursing specialists. A case conference may be an important forum in which to pool all available knowledge of a particular child's circumstances.
>
> ❖ In all considerations of child custody, the welfare of the child is of paramount importance. However, the courts also give great weight to the role of the family and the rights of the parents, based on the Irish Constitution's recognition of the family as the fundamental building block of Irish society.
>
> ❖ A child can be taken by the Garda Síochána to a Place of Safety without any form of court order where there is an immediate threat to the child's welfare or safety.
>
> ❖ A parent can consent to a child being taken into voluntary care by the local health board.
>
> ❖ Where there is no consent to a child being taken into care or a child has been taken to a place of safety without a court order, the health board must apply to the courts for a care order. In general, the first order made will be an emergency care order, followed by interim or longer-term care orders as appropriate.
>
> ❖ As an alternative to a care order, a court can put a supervision order in place, allowing the child to remain in the home but also allowing the health board to supervise the ongoing development of the child.
>
> ❖ With the exception of emergency care orders, the family must be kept informed of all stages of the care order process and, unless there are exceptional circumstances, be told of the whereabouts of the child.
>
> ❖ As part of a care order, the court can make any other orders it sees fit for treatment or assessment of the child. Once the health board is awarded a care order for a child, it assumes the role of the child's parent.

Sudden Infant Death Syndrome

[7.55] Sudden Infant Death Syndrome (cot death, SIDS) is the sudden death of an infant, usually younger than one year of age, which remains unexplained after a complete post-mortem investigation, including autopsy,[80] examination of the death scene and review of the case history. SIDS is the single most common cause of death in the post-neonatal period (ie in infants aged one month to one year). In most series, SIDS accounts for 35–

---

[80] Findings at post mortem may include some or all of the following: (i) normal levels of hydration and nutrition; (ii) small amounts of frothy fluid in or about the mouth and nose and occasionally there may be vomitus present; (iii) post mortem lividity, rigor mortis and distortion of the contours of face due to the infant dying while on his stomach or while pressed up against or lying on something in the cot; (iv) unusual positions due to muscle spasms can cause blood pooling and/or pressure marks; (v) internal examination may show pulmonary congestion and oedema and there are intrathoracic petechiae in about 90 per cent of SIDS infants; and (vi) there may also be stomach contents and/or microscopic inflammation in the trachea. The post mortem can be important in disclosing a cause of death other than SIDS, for example, congenital heart disease or, more rarely, pneumonia.

55 per cent of deaths within the post-neonatal period. SIDS comprises approximately 20–25 per cent of deaths in those younger than one year. Despite intensive study and advances in the understanding of associated factors, the specific cause or causes of SIDS remain unknown, although there are racial and familial tendencies (eg it is more common in American blacks, and if one sibling in a family succumbs to SIDS there is a greater risk for remaining siblings) and an association with birth order.[81] The majority of deaths occur between October and March and there is a slightly increased frequency in male children. Children who live in cigarette smoke-filled environments seem to be at greater risk and many victims will have had some form of respiratory tract infection in the weeks leading up to death. There is an association between sleeping in the prone (face down)[82] position and SIDS; there is also an association between lower income and the condition. Death generally occurs when the child is laid down to sleep and there appear to be no sounds or signs of distress. According to the National SIDS Register, over the past two decades the SIDS rate in Ireland has declined gradually from a high of 2.3 cases per 1000 live births in the 1980s (average of 134 per year) to a low of 0.55 per 1000 live births in 2004 (34 deaths).

[7.56] The are a number of medico-legal elements to a diagnosis of SIDS. First, the death must be reported to the coroner, even if the general practitioner or hospital doctor believes that a death was due to SIDS. Similarly, as part of the notification process the Gardaí must attend the scene of death and oversee the formal identification of the baby's body. Investigation is necessary to rule out the small possibility that the death was due to unnatural causes. Both processes, notification of the coroner and involvement of the Gardaí, can be distressing to the family, but they are an inevitable part of the aftermath of SIDS. Because of the coroner notification, there is ordinarily no need for the doctor to complete a Death Notification Form (unless instructed that she may do so by the coroner). Elsewhere in this text we dwell on the importance of recording the details of the scene of a sudden or unexpected death.[83] SIDS provides a rationale for this practice—it was the recording of infant sleeping positions that in part led to the identification of sleeping position as a risk factor in SIDS.[84]

Handling SIDS

[7.57] The sudden death of a child can be devastating for a family and support from those involved in a clinical capacity in the immediate aftermath of the death can help the bereaved parents and siblings to come to terms with what has happened—see Table 7.3.

---

[81] 50 per cent are second born children, 25 per cent first born and the remaining 25 per cent third born or later.

[82] Campaigns to change the sleeping position of infants have been estimated to be responsible for 70 per cent of the observed decline in the frequency of SIDS: see Dwyer, Ponsonby, 'Sudden infant death syndrome: after the "back to sleep" campaign.' BMJ 27 July 1996; 313(7051): 180–1.

[83] See Ch 14 'Forensic Medicine, DNA Testing and Terminology of Injuries', para [14.03].

[84] Bass, Kravath, Glass, 'Death-scene investigation in sudden infant death.' NEJM 1986; 315:100–5. If the practitioner is present at the scene of death, she should observe the location of the infant upon arrival and verify that was the position in which he was found. She should also observe for presence of objects in the original area where the infant was found that could have contributed to death and the temperature of the room or any odours, such as domestic gas.

Table 7.3 Considerations in the wake of SIDS

Clinical elements

– In a hospital, if resuscitation is ongoing ensure the parents are kept informed. If unsuccessful, the news should be broken to the parents in a private environment by someone experienced in doing so.

– If in a position to do so, be prepared to offer a tentative diagnosis of SIDS.

– Obtain a history from the family of events leading up to the death, if possible in the circumstances.

– Explain that the coroner and the Gardaí will necessarily be involved and that a post mortem must be performed, but explain too that this does not mean that blame or suspicion is being cast on the parents. Stress that the death is not the fault of the parents.

– Consider practical advice on the suppression of lactation for breast-feeding mothers or the use of an anxiolytic substance, but remember too that simply making time to listen can be more important than dispensing advice or medication.

– Liaise with some or all of the following as appropriate: the hospital to which the body will be brought; the family doctor; social services; any hospitals that may be sending out appointments to the child (for example the maternity hospital in which he was born).

– Consider whether monitoring will be needed for siblings.

– Follow up with the coroner and pathology departments to ensure that any post-mortem documentation can be processed speedily.

Emotional and psychological elements

– Allow and expect the venting of feelings by the parents; do not feel embarrassed about sharing those feelings or grieving with the parents. Offer to contact anyone the parents wish to have with them.

– When talking about the child, use his name.

– Allow the parents to spend time with their dead child if they wish to do so; make a quiet private room available for them where they can be undisturbed for a time.

– Be conscious of the needs of siblings as well as parents; in the immediate aftermath, simple explanations may suffice, but they will often need to grieve along with the parents.

– People in shock have difficulty retaining information in large chunks. Consider leaving information with parents in the form of a leaflet or the contact number of a local helpline.

– Be aware that the family will need support for months to come as they go through the grieving process.

Chapter 8

Health in the Workplace

INTRODUCTION

[8.01] This chapter opens by looking at the role of the occupational health practitioner and, by extension, at all practitioner-patient interactions in which third parties have an interest, such as medical examinations for insurance policies. We examine how the demands of confidentiality interact with the interest of a third party in the outcome of a consultation or with a request from a third party for information relating to a patient.[1]

[8.02] The second portion of the chapter looks at the legal mechanics of ensuring safety, health and welfare in the workplace – both the approach taken by the and the steps taken by the government to compel employers (and employees) to prioritise safety in the workplace. The areas of occupational health is important to clinicians from a number of perspectives: any clinician may be at any time an employee, employer or occupational health professional and in all three capacities will require an understanding of the principles underpinning the safe workplace.

The chapter finishes with a brief overview of occupational disease, absence from work through illness and medical certification under social welfare legislation.

THE OCCUPATIONAL HEALTH PRACTITIONER

The role

[8.03] Occupational health practitioners work at the interface between employer and employee with the twin aims of safeguarding the health of workers, both individually and collectively, and of promoting safe and healthy working environments. Taking a holistic approach to occupational health, any number of disciplines can be involved: an architect must design a safe and user-friendly premises; a foreman must oversee working practices to ensure they are safe. In this chapter, however, we are most concerned with the particular role of the health professional in the working environment.

[8.04] Any one clinician's involvement in occupational health will fit in somewhere along a spectrum of commitment. At one extreme is the practitioner employed casually by a firm merely to conduct pre-employment medical examinations on behalf of the company. At the intermediate level is the practitioner who provides a part-time commitment to the workplace, while at the other end of this spectrum of commitment, some professionals are employed in a full-time capacity by companies to cater for all aspects of the health of their workforces. It is obvious that those who have different working arrangements with a

---

[1] Note that the issues of liability in negligence to third parties (para **[6.10]**) and disclosure of confidential information to third parties (para **[3.30]**) have been dealt with in greater detail elsewhere.

company, or with any third party, to look after patients will have different responsibilities. The intermittently retained general practitioner has a relationship with the company only in so far as it concerns the individual patient before her, while the part- or full-time occupational health professional will be responsible not just for the individual patients she sees, but will also have a broader duty to the company and workforce as a whole. But whatever the precise relationship, the 'triangular' relationship between practitioner, patient and employer (or any third party)[2] brings with it potential complexity.

The potential conflict

[8.05] The duty a practitioner owes to her patient may be modified by many external factors, some of which are encountered elsewhere in this book: a patient of sound mind and adult years who refuses treatment will, by his refusal, override the clinician's duty to treat; similarly, a doctor may wish to help her patient end his life in accordance with his wishes, only to find that the law against euthanasia and assisted suicide restricts that 'duty'. Another striking example of external factors modifying the doctor's duty to her patient, and a facet of care that is prominent in the setting of occupational health, is confidentiality. A clinician owes a duty of confidentiality to her patient, but in certain circumstances that duty is lifted or modified and in situations where an outside party desires or requires access to information gleaned in a consultation, confidentiality can be especially tested.

[8.06] A practitioner employed by a third party to examine and/or report on a patient has a new ingredient in the already complicated mix of the therapeutic encounter, namely the interests of that third party in the end product. A doctor or nurse providing occupational health services for a company who learns in consultation with her patient of information with ramifications for the patient, for other workers or for the company has a problem. What can she disclose? Does she need the patient's consent? If consent is not forthcoming, can she go ahead anyway?

[8.07] When it comes to any consultation in which a third party has an interest, whether in the employment setting, the certification of illness for State benefits or the completion of insurance questionnaires, the clinician owes duties in two directions. One duty of care extends, as always, to the patient. However, another, sometimes competing, duty is owed to the employer or other third party who:

(a)   is typically paying the clinician for her services and with whom therefore the clinician will have some form of contract; and

(b)   has a vested interest in the outcome of the consultation.

A nurse or doctor working in an occupational health capacity may have signed a contract of employment and must fulfil the terms of that contract, including an implied duty to

---

[2]   Other examples of the clinician being in effect the servant of two masters include responding to requests for information from insurance company (on payment of a fee by that insurance company); working in the social welfare services assessing claims for benefits (or indeed filling in social welfare forms on behalf of patients claiming benefit, for which service the clinician typically receives a fee from the State); employment in the prison or armed services and working for insurance companies.

show loyalty to the company. A clinician who has (or will) receive payment for the completion of an insurance questionnaire or a State benefits form is under a contractual obligation to the third party paying her for her services. These potentially polarising commitments to both patient and third party are significant, particularly where the interests of employer and employee do not converge. The patient may have an illness he wishes to keep from his employer, but the employer may have a strong interest in knowing of that illness in order to protect other employees or to ensure that customers and clients are protected. In other settings, the patient may wish to conceal certain aspects of his medical history from an insurer or to cloak from the State the fact that he is now fit for work.

Resolving the conflict in the occupational health setting

[8.08] We consider in the sections that follow how the clinician operating in the occupational health setting can operate in a manner that discharges duties to her patient (such as the duty of confidentiality) while also facing up to the responsibilities imposed by being employed by a company to deliver occupational health services.

> **Example 8.1**
>
> Mr McMurphy, an employee of Combine Inc., attends Nurse Ratched who is an occupational health nurse in fulltime employment with the same company. He complains of some deafness. He is concerned that he may lose his job, which involves dealing with the public, or be re-deployed elsewhere, which would affect his overtime. His hearing loss is very mild and he asks the nurse not to disclose details of the consultation to the company.

[8.09] The *International Code of Ethics for Occupational Health Professionals* lays down the following basic ethical principles for occupational health practice.

> 'The purpose of occupational health is to serve the health and well-being of the workers individually and collectively. Occupational health practice must be performed according to the highest professional standards and ethical principles. Occupational health professionals must contribute to environmental and community health.
>
> The duties of occupational health professionals include protecting the life and the health of the worker, respecting human dignity and promoting the highest ethical principles in occupational health policies and programmes. Integrity in professional conduct, impartiality and the protection of the confidentiality of health data and of the privacy of workers are part of these duties.
>
> Occupational health professionals are experts who must enjoy full professional independence in the execution of their functions. They must acquire and maintain the competence necessary for their duties and require conditions which allow them to carry out their tasks according to good practice and professional ethics.'[3]

These principles clearly indicate that although a practitioner may take on a duty to a party other than the patient, that duty does not supplant her pre-existing ethical

---

[3] International Commission on Occupational Health, *International Code of Ethics for Occupational Health Professionals*, (3rd updating, 2002) p 4.

principles as a health care practitioner.[4] However, because the practitioner also has a duty to the employer and to the workers collectively, this may sternly test the confidentiality owed to the individual worker. If a worker's lung condition suggests unsafe working practice (such as exposure to dust), the practitioner may owe a duty, not only to the patient but also to the employer who pays her and to the work force, whose care is one of the reasons why the employer is paying her in the first place.

Patient first, then third party

[8.10] The reasons why the patient comes before the employer or any other interested party acting in a similar capacity[5] are essentially threefold.

In the first place, clinicians are retained to carry out clinical duties, which duties necessarily include adherence to the ethical obligations of their professions because if it were not so, she could not be properly said to be discharging her professional duty. In the words of the *International Code of Ethics for Occupational Health Professionals*, occupational health practitioners are 'experts who must enjoy full professional independence in the execution of their functions.' Therefore, the first duty of a health practitioner retained by a company or by a third party is to her patient and this includes ethical aspects of that duty, such as a duty to maintain confidences and the freedom to disclose confidential information only where permitted or mandated by ethical principles or the law.[6] This should be the starting point of the relationship and when it is planned to deviate from this (for example in the case of a pre-employment medical examination, where the entire process is predicated on subsequent disclosure), then the patient must be clearly informed.

[8.11] Secondly, employers owe, as a matter of employment law, a duty of trust and confidence to employees and this would seem to include not tampering with the normal practitioner-patient relationship, unless the patient is aware and has agreed that a particular consultation will be played by different rules, including disclosure of

---

[4]   Westerholm, 'Professional Ethics in Occupational Health–Western European Perspectives', (2007) Industrial Health 45;19–25 – this essay identifies many of the wider ethical challenges posed by changing workforce practices including globalisation of core economic activities; growing dependence on sophisticated technologies; organisational flexibility due to competitive pressures; greater power of management over labour; retrenchment of 'welfare state' societal functions; feminisation and aging of the workforce; expansion of labour in precarious employment; increased ecological changes and marginalisation of sections of the population and workforce.

[5]   It should be observed that the occupational health setting is different from the situation where the clinician is certifying a person as entitled to state benefits or completing a questionnaire for an insurance company. In both of these cases, the clinician does not (except in the most nebulous sense) owe a wider duty equivalent to that owed by the occupational health practitioner to the workforce. Furthermore, where the doctor is completing an insurance questionnaire for a patient, she is ordinarily doing so on the basis of the consent of the patient, typically given in advance as part of the patient's application to the company for insurance, to the disclosure of all relevant medical information by the doctor.

[6]   See the discussion of disclosure of confidential information in Ch 3 'Confidentiality and the Practitioner–Patient Relationship' para **[3.18]***ff*. See also the discussion of the Safety Health and Welfare at Work Act 2005 below at para **[8.37]***ff*.

information to a third party. Trust and confidence between employer and employee are undermined if the employer routinely eavesdrops on therapeutic encounters.

[8.12] Finally, every Irish citizen has a right to privacy, guaranteed by the Irish Constitution and the European Convention on Human Rights.[7] The right to privacy is not absolute and there are situations in which it may be set aside, but it nonetheless provides another strand of logic that says the paramount ethical duty of the clinician towards her patient survives her signing a contract with a third party.

Confidentiality in the occupational health setting

[8.13] The duty owed by the practitioner in the context of third-party interest is therefore first and foremost to the patient and includes the patient's right to expect a veil of confidentiality to be thrown over the consultation. There are (see Ch 3, *Confidentiality and the Practitioner–Patient Relationship*) five broad headings under which confidentiality may be breached. The most important is *when the patient consents* – consent by a patient to the release of confidential information neutralises the doctor's obligation to preserve confidentiality as far as that particular information is concerned. The other exceptions, where a doctor may disclose information *in the absence of consent from a patient*, are:

- when required by law, either by a judge or because of a provision in written law;
- when necessary to protect the patient's own interests, health or welfare (although there is an argument that this does not apply in the occupational health setting – see below);
- when necessary to protect another individual;
- when necessary to protect the welfare of society.[8]

Any breach of confidentiality should be moderated by one further consideration: no more information should be disclosed than is necessary and those details should not be disclosed to any wider a circle of recipients than is required to achieve the aims of the disclosure.[9]

[8.14] It is easy to see how criteria for breaching confidentiality in the absence of consent could be satisfied in the workplace. There is a statutory obligation on employers to report accidents that occur at work. If a doctor working for a company becomes aware of an accident, he would be under a duty, imposed in effect by the law, to appraise the company of the fact that the accident occurred. A worker may come to the attention of the doctor as suffering from an illness that, if he were to continue working, may pose a

---

[7] The right to privacy is discussed in Ch 3, Confidentiality and the Practitioner–Patient Relationship para **[3.04]***ff.* See also Kloss, 'A servant of two masters?', *Occupational Health Review*, March/April 2001, p. 26

[8] The practical applications of these exceptions are dealt with in greater detail in Ch 3, para **[3.18]***ff.*

[9] In *Duncan v Medical Practitioners' Disciplinary Committee* [1986] 1 NZLR 513, doctor was concerned about his patient's heart. The patient was a bus driver and rather than confining his concerns to the relevant authority he also told the patient's prospective passengers. Even if this was a valid ground for breaching confidentiality, the information was not as narrowly disseminated as it should have been.

threat to himself, to other individuals or to society. A machine operative who develops a neurodegenerative condition may be a threat to himself; a soldier with murderous delusions may be a danger to limited (and identifiable) members of his platoon, while a restaurant employee with severe gastroenteritis could pose a risk to wider society. An airline pilot with epilepsy or alcoholism could obviously fulfil all three criteria for disclosure with ease.[10]

[8.15] However, in other cases, there may be no grounds for breaching the confidentiality owed to the patient. A doctor who becomes aware during a consultation with a patient, on an utterly unrelated matter, that bullying is occurring on the factory floor may feel she should communicate that fact to the employer and may safely do without referring to the specific patient and without breaching confidentiality. But what if the matter that is causing concern also relates to the patient's health? In reality, the role of the occupational health professional may often involve a measure of 'qualified confidentiality'.

Example 8.2

Mr McMurphy's (see Example 8.1) deafness was not disclosed to his employer, in keeping with the general principle that an occupational health practitioner's first duty is to her patient. However, he continues to suffer from deafness. Nurse Ratched notices on reading his records that before starting his current job, dealing with the public, McMurphy operated machinery on the factory floor. She recalls that two other patients have consulted her recently regarding hearing loss and examining their records she establishes that they too worked with the same machinery. She wonders if there may be a link and whether the deafness may be noise-related.

McMurphy is still worried that his job may be at risk and refuses to permit disclosure of his health status to the employer. His deafness does not pose a risk to anyone else. What may be done now?

[8.16] One reason why the occupational health professional is in a difficult position when it comes to disclosure of risks she identifies during a consultation lies in the way in which 'knowledge' is defined legally. When it comes to assessing legal liability for a danger that causes damage to a worker, the employer will be deemed to have 'known' of the risk if one of his 'servants' (employees) or 'agents' (people working on behalf of, but not for, the company) knew of the risk. So, if a nurse working for or on behalf of a company knows of a risk, then the company legally 'knows' about the risk and may be held legally accountable for damage caused by that risk. Furthermore, the occupational health professional has an ethical duty to the wider workforce and to the company to make sure that overall health is maximised. There is a strong legal and ethical imperative therefore that the existence of a risk to the health of the workforce should be relayed to the company.

---

[10] On the issue of disclosure of risks posed to third parties, the International Commission on Occupational Health, *International Code of Ethics for Occupational Health Professionals* (3rd updating, 2002) states (at p 8): 'In his advice, the occupational health physician must try to reconcile employment of the worker concerned with the safety or health of others that may be endangered.'

[8.17] This is where a doctrine such as 'qualified confidentiality' may come into the convoluted practitioner-patient-workforce-employer equation. It is not a breach of confidentiality to disclose information about a patient where that disclosure, even though it involves the disclosure of confidential information, will not have the effect of identifying the patient.[11] If a patient will not consent to disclosure of information, it may be enough, where it is feasible to do so – for the clinician to notify the employer of the hazard that was brought to light by the consultation without ever identifying the patient.

A protocol for practitioner-patient encounters in which a third party has an interest

[8.18] If a consultation is explicitly to obtain clinical details for a third party or the practitioner receives a request for information concerning her patient, the patient should ideally be fully informed about what is happening.[12] If he is attending the clinician for examination, the patient must understand why he is there and the likely destination of any information he discloses or relevant data that has been requested from his medical history. He should understand that the consultation is not a routine one, in that relevant details are intended for an outside interest. This is important because the patient, as in all matters relating to confidentiality, is free to withhold his consent. If he refuses to permit disclosure, normal rules of confidentiality apply: the clinician cannot disclose the information without the patient's consent unless one of the exceptions exists – the operation of law or a need to protect the patient, another individual or the welfare of society.

Examinations

[8.19] The patient's consent must be informed not only regarding the fact that information will be disclosed but also the nature and extent of that disclosure. The patient must understand that the clinician is under a duty to be impartial and must release all relevant information requested, whether it is injurious or beneficial to the patient, although it may be possible for the doctor to withhold information selectively on the basis that it is not clinically relevant. The Medical Council formerly offered further guidance on the issue of reporting on patients to third parties and to employers (as a matter of general, rather than occupational health, practice), but that guidance is absent from the most recent edition of the *Guide*.[13] The Irish Faculty of Occupational Health sets out the following principles:

'When performing assessments doctors should ensure that all employees fully and clearly understand:

---

[11] See Ch 3, *Confidentiality and the Practitioner–Patient Relationship*, para **[3.12]**.

[12] See House, *Professional Evaluation – social impact and political consequences* (1993, SAGE publications). House suggests three values that should be in place in situations where the clinician faces multiple loyalties: a) non-coercion, b) non-manipulation and support for democratic values and principles, c) transparency.

[13] *Guide to Ethical Conduct and Behaviour* (5th edn, 1998), para 18.6(4): 'The significance, rather than the precise details, of the medical findings should be conveyed to any third party and then only with the patients' consent'; also para 18.7: 'A doctor when assessing the significance of a particular disability, should interpret the medical findings in terms of the likelihood of the patient continuing to work, if requested to do so. An employer does not have the right to be informed of the clinical details of illness or injury without the consent of the patient.' (Bold type in originals).

- The reason for the examination.
- The form that it will take.
- The nature and scope of advice to be given to the employer.

Individual clinical findings are confidential and information given to the employer should generally be confined to advice on ability and functional limitation. The patient's informed consent should be sought to the disclosure of information where identifiable data is provided for any purpose other than the provision of care or clinical audit, except where disclosure is required by law or the public interest because of risk of death or serious harm. More detailed information should only be disclosed with the consent of the employee. This latter course of action should only be in exceptional circumstances, in individual cases, where more detailed insights on the impact of the condition are necessary and appropriate to enable the employer to come to a decision.'[14]

Forms

[8.20] In some instances, a patient will not attend the clinician in person, for example when information has been required by a third party by way of a questionnaire. In the case of applications for insurance, a form will be sent to the practitioner by the insurer to be completed by her from the patient's records. Written consent should accompany a request and the information should not be disclosed until the clinician is positive that her patient has given his consent. Again, consent should also be informed: it may be prudent to communicate to a patient the information to be disclosed, especially if there is anything in the history that may be contentious, but is necessary for an accurate and complete report. The fact that a person has had a heart attack may be relevant to an application for life insurance; the fact that he was abused as a child and attended counselling in his early twenties may not be relevant, particularly if the patient has no psychiatric morbidity. The question is often one of clinical judgement, although there are strong arguments in favour of disclosing everything that may have relevance for the patient's future health.[15] It is desirable to show the patient the form or questionnaire being completed so that he understands the context of his consent.[16] Patients have a legal right, based on data protection legislation, to see any report that is prepared concerning them.[17]

---

[14] Faculty of Occupational Medicine of the Royal College of Physicians in Ireland, *Guidance on Ethical Practice for Occupational Physicians* (August 2007), pp 2–3.

[15] The risk that may be run by the practitioner who does not disclose everything of relevance is that a withheld fact (such as a long-distant and unrepeated episode of depression) may become vital at a later date (for example where the patient later develops a recurrence of depression). The insurance company may use the non-disclosure by patient and/or doctor as grounds for repudiation of the policy.

[16] *Guide to Ethical Conduct and Behaviour* (6th edn, 2004), para 16.6 (Insurance Reports):

'A doctor who is asked by an insurance company to complete a medical report on a patient must ensure that this is not issued without the informed consent of the patient. Patients should be informed that such reports may be read by non-medical personnel. These reports should be sent to the medical officer acting on behalf of the company.'

[17] See chapter 5, *Clinical Records and Prescribing* para **[5.26]***ff.* In the UK, the Access to Medical Reports Act 1988 and Access to Personal Files and Medical Reports (Northern Ireland) Order 1991 allow patients a statutory right of access in respect of reports written about them for employment or insurance purposes.

Disclosure

[8.21] In any case where the release of confidential material is at issue, any decision, including the reason for the decision, should be documented, whether it is disclosure with the patient's consent, refusal by the patient to permit disclosure or a decision to disclose in spite of refusal. The withholding of consent may have ramifications for the patient, such as foregoing a job offer, losing an existing job or failing to be insured, but that is the patient's choice. Even if a practitioner is an occupational health specialist working full-time for a company, the company has no automatic right to access the patient's records unless the patient consents.[18]

Withdrawing consent to disclosure

[8.22] If a person agrees to undergo an examination by an occupational health practitioner, knowing that the results of that examination are to be disclosed to a third party, and then later withdraws that consent, the clinician will generally be protected from legal action if she discloses that information. The initial consent to disclosure remains valid so long as it was validly given and fully informed. In other words, if a patient knows that a third party has an interest in his consultation with the practitioner and goes ahead with the consultation, then that third party interest is enshrined and will not evaporate simply because the patient has changed his mind.[19] The doctor is not obliged to release the information, she may prefer to respect the patient's withdrawal of consent, and it may be the ethically preferable course of action. However, the legal position appears to be that she will not be liable if she discloses on the basis of the original consent. Obviously, if a patient was not fully informed about the purpose of the consultation or what was to be disclosed, it is likely that the patient could subsequently withdraw consent on becoming aware that the parameters of disclosure were different from what he had been led to believe. The clinician would be bound by a change of mind in those circumstances.

Pre-employment disclosure

[8.23] Sometimes attempts are made to access a prospective employee's full medical history, in the form of his general practitioner's notes, as part of pre-employment screening. While this is not illegal, it is not satisfactory, insofar as the patient may be in effect compelled to consent for fear of losing the job. Seeking such information may be a violation of the constitutional right to privacy unless it could be justified as necessary for the post in question. The UK Faculty of Occupational Medicine argues in its guide to

---

[18] *Dunn v British Coal Corporation* [1993] ICR 591. See also the Faculty of Occupational Medicine of the Royal College of Physicians in Ireland, *Guide to Ethical Practice of Occupational Physicians* (August 2007), p 3: 'Management of personal medical records, and data arising from them, should be in accordance with the current data protection legislation. Personal medical records held by occupational health departments are confidential to the medical and nursing staff. They must be kept in a secure place and neither employers nor their legal advisers have any right of access to confidential clinical information unless they have consent or have obtained legal power through an order of a court of law.'

[19] *Kapadia v Lambeth London Borough Council* (CA) [2000] IRLR 699; *Hammersmith and Fulham London Borough Council v Farnsworth* [2000] IRLR 691.

the ethics of occupational health that pre-employment questionnaires demanding disclosure of the applicant's full general practitioner record should not be entertained.[20]

Disclosure in the employee's interest

[8.24] It is not clear whether an occupational health professional can breach confidentiality where any risk posed is only to the employee himself. It is certainly true that in theory a threat to a patient's own health is grounds for breaching confidentiality, but there are few legal cases that support the contention that the clinician may in practice breach confidentiality in such circumstances.[21]

> **Example 8.3**
>
> Dr. Hibbert, a physician working in the occupational health setting for a nuclear power company, diagnoses Mr Simpson, a company employee, as having a knee injury. The patient's job involves a great deal of climbing ladders, but the injury is not a risk to any other person and the risk posed to the patient is uncertain: it is only a possibility that the requirements of the job will exacerbate the knee problem. The patient refuses the doctor permission to discuss the diagnosis with the employers and says that he will struggle on with anti-inflammatory tablets and a beer- and doughnut-free diet aimed at weight loss.

[8.25] The basis for being reluctant to say that a practitioner may breach confidentiality solely in what she perceives to be a patient's interests is patient autonomy: a person is free to exercise control over himself. The practitioner's ethical code may impels her towards 'doing good' for her patient, a principle that could involve telling the patient to take time off work or, in the last analysis, telling the employer so that he can take steps to save the worker from himself. On the other hand is the patient's autonomy: if the patient does not want information disclosed about him, even though he knows that it would be in his best interests to do so, then who is the clinician to override that refusal in the absence of compelling circumstances? In theory then, if a patient is a risk to himself and to himself alone and refuses his clinician permission to disclose this fact, there is a strong argument to say that the patient's wish should be respected. If the patient discloses a workplace risk that the clinician can disclose without identifying the patient then that risk may be identified, but without identifying the patient.

[8.26] If anything happens to the patient as a result of his refusal to allow his condition to be disclosed so that his situation can be ameliorated, then legal liability is unlikely to attach to the employer: the doctrines of 'voluntary assumption of risk' or of 'contributory negligence' would apply.[22] Accordingly, a patient who knew, but declined to tell his employer, of a problem affecting his health that made it likely that he would be injured at work would have greater difficulty in winning a legal case against the employer.

[8.27] One compromise that may be considered – although it is not always easy, let alone possible – is to ask the patient to agree to allow the clinician to recommend changes to work practices without specifying the reason for the required alterations. This is a

---

[20] Faculty of Occupational Medicine of the Royal College of Physicians, *Guidance on Ethics for Occupational Physicians,* (6th edn, London, 2006).

[21] See the discussion in Ch 3, *Confidentiality and the Practitioner-Patient Relationship*, para **[3.27]**.

[22] See Ch 6 'Clinical Negligence' paras **[6.70]–[6.72]** for more details.

common approach in circumstances where the need for a change is great but the circumstances underpinning the need for change are sensitive, such as psychiatric illness. This approach may help the patient by minimising the chance of worsening any underlying problem and help the employer by preventing the loss of an employee to long term illness or injury. Furthermore, it preserves the confidentiality, albeit in a qualified form, of the patient in question. It seems likely in Irish law that where a patient refuses a doctor or nurse permission to breach confidentiality and the *only* basis for such a breach would be the patient's own interests, then the patient's refusal should probably be respected unless other circumstances exist to override the patient's refusal.

Quick Reference Guide 8.1

Occupational health and confidentiality

- ❖ Any consultation with a patient in which a third party has an interest, or any request for information from a third party concerning a patient, can raise ethical complications.

- ❖ Even if a practitioner is being paid for her services by a third party, her first duty remains to the patient. There are three reasons why the patient comes first: the practitioner's clinical independence and consequent ethical duty, the employer's obligation to be fair to employees and the worker's right to privacy under the Constitution and the European Convention on Human Rights.

- ❖ Confidentiality may only be breached if the patient consents or, assuming the patient does not consent, where (a) the law requires it, (b) there is a threat to the patient, (c) a threat to another individual or (d) a threat to the welfare of society. There is an argument that the patient's own interests may not be grounds for a breach of confidentiality in the occupational health setting.

- ❖ In an occupational health setting (or any other environment where a third party has an interest in information concerning a patient) the patient retains his right to refuse to allow information to be disclosed.

- ❖ The practitioner may consider an approach based on 'qualified confidentiality', where elements of the consultation can be highlighted, such as an identified risk to the other members of the workforce, without naming the patient.

- ❖ A patient who is attending for a consultation, or about whom a request for information is made, will necessitate disclosure of otherwise confidential information to a third party which should be fully apprised of the situation. The practitioner can exercise her clinical judgement: she need only disclose relevant information and even then should use only broad brushstrokes in doing so. The patient should know the extent and nature of any disclosure to which he is being asked to consent.

- ❖ A patient will have the right to see any report written about him, for example by relying on data protection legislation.

- ❖ There is probably no right for a practitioner to override a patient's refusal solely in what she perceives to be the best interests of the patient if the patient withholds consent to disclosure. Compromise may be possible in the sense of requesting changes to the employee's working arrangements without disclosing the reason.

SAFETY, HEALTH AND WELFARE AT WORK

[8.28] There are two mechanisms for ensuring safety, health and welfare at work and for punishing those who fail to maintain satisfactory standards. Firstly, individuals who are injured as a result of accidents at work can seek legal redress for any damage suffered, assuming that the accident is legally the result of the employer's negligence: this is the common law approach.[23] Litigation (or application to the Personal Injuries Assessment Board) is essentially retroactive, in that it punishes employers for lack of care towards the worker who is bringing the legal action. In addition, the Government, through the Safety Health and Welfare at Work Act 1989 (now updated by the Safety Health and Welfare at Work Act 2005 – see para **[8.38]** below) and the creation of the Health and Safety Authority, created legal mechanisms to compel safe workplaces and to punish those employers and employees who fall short of the legal standards. This is the statutory approach to safety at work and is essentially proactive in nature, setting down transparent standards in advance for companies to meet, encouraging companies to meet those standards and, as a last resort, punishing companies that fail to meet them.

Practitioners working in an occupational health setting obviously need to know, at least in outline, the rules laid down by the courts and by legislation, but they are useful too for any practitioner in the workplace, whether employee or employer. The rules on employers' and employees' legal duties extend to almost all work places, irrespective of scale.

Safety, health and welfare at work – the approach of the courts

[8.29] Actions by employees against employers for accidents occurring in the workplace are typically based on an allegation that some act or omission on the part of the employer was negligent and that it caused some damage to the employee. We have seen elsewhere in the text that there are three elements to negligence:[24]

- the existence of a duty of care;
- breach of that duty;
- damage (which must be foreseeable) caused to the person alleging negligence as a result of the breach of the duty of care.

[8.30] Until the beginning of the twentieth century, courts were reluctant to find that employers owed employees any duty of care, but with greater acceptance of workers' rights, so the modern approach evolved: the duty of an employer towards an employee is to take reasonable care for the employee's safety in all circumstances of the case.[25] This duty is not absolute or unlimited: an employer only has to take the steps a reasonable and prudent employer would take in the circumstances. After all, there are some jobs that could not be done if all risk were eliminated, eg, climbing scaffolding will always

---

[23] Historically, the avenue of choice would have been litigation in all cases. However the passage of the Personal Injuries Assessment Board Act 2003 means that where accidents in the workplace occur and there is no argument about the liability of the employer, the matter may be adjudicated by the Personal Injuries Assessment Board.

[24] See Ch 6, 'Clinical Negligence', para **[6.07]***ff.*

[25] *Dalton v Frendo* (15 December 1977, unreported) SC.

involve the risk of a fall, and working with radioactive substances will always involve the risk of exposure. The onus on the employer is to ensure that he takes steps to minimise risks to the employee as far as possible.

[8.31] Any accident or incident that occurs must furthermore and in accordance with the general principles of negligence be foreseeable. In one case, an employee developed folliculitis[26] as a result of exposure to chemicals in the workplace. The evidence showed that there were no other recorded cases of the condition developing in the same circumstances anywhere else in the world: the condition was unforeseeable so there could be no negligence in failing to prevent it. Damage done to the employee need not be physical. A soldier who suffered post-traumatic stress disorder following a tour of duty in the Lebanon during which his employers (the army) had acted in a manner the courts thought negligent was able to win damages.[27]

Sub-dividing employers' liability to employees

[8.32] There are four components of the working environment that can give rise to a legal claim by an employee. The practitioner working in the occupational health setting needs to be conscious of them so that she can work with the employers to minimise any risks of which she becomes aware. The employer must provide employees with the following and a failure to do so can result in a court finding for an employee who brings a case alleging injury caused by the absence of one of them:

- *A safe workplace*: Risks in the workplace cannot be eliminated entirely. One judge stated that 'to make accidents impossible would make work impossible.'[28] Where an employer has taken all reasonable and prudent steps to provide a safe place of work and has complied with any obligations laid down by law, then it is less likely that he will be found negligent.

- *Safe and proper plant and equipment*: Equipment used in the workplace must be used for the purpose it was intended. Misuse of equipment, failure to maintain equipment or a mismatch between the capacity of plant or equipment and the job it is asked to do may all constitute a failure to provide safe plant and equipment.

- *Safe system of work*: This can include a number of elements. Examples can include the duty to ensure that workers use the safety equipment they are supplied with or that they are trained in the safest methods of discharging their duties.

- *Competent and safety conscious staff*: If alleging that an employer's staff were incompetent it must be shown that the employer knew the staff to be negligent or at least had the opportunity to find out about the absence of safe conduct.

Of course these four areas overlap: the lack of competent staff could result in the absence of a safe system of work. Some have argued that all four headings should be

---

[26] An infection or inflammation of the hair follicles.
[27] *McHugh v Minister for Defence* [2001] 1 IR 424.
[28] *Christie v Odeon (Ireland) Ltd* (1957) 91 ILTR 25 at 29 *per* Kingsmill Moore J.

subsumed into the single simple question of the employer owing a broad duty of care to the employees.[29]

<h3 style="text-align:center">Case Study 8.1</h3>

(a) Safe system of work

In one case,[30] a ward attendant was lifting a patient when she suffered a back injury. The injury occurred in 1990. The last time she had been shown lifting techniques had been in the 1970s. In the meantime, the recommended technique for lifting had – perhaps unsurprisingly – changed and the employer had never updated the attendant's training. This was a failure to provide a safe system of work and the employee won her case.

(b) Competent safety conscious staff

In another case,[31] a practice had grown up among the staff in a repair shop of playing practical jokes on each other, during one of which an employee was injured. Because the mischief was short-lived each time and difficult to detect and the employers could therefore not have been aware of it, they were not guilty of failing to provide competent staff. This can be contrasted with another case[32] where an employee had a known track record of playing practical jokes on staff. When his antics resulted in the plaintiff sustaining a broken wrist, the company was found liable for failing to ensure its staff maintained a safe working environment.

Vicarious liability

[8.33] It does not have to be the company itself that causes the accident: 'vicarious' liability can occur, which is the liability of the employer for the acts of one of his employees. So, if one employee is bullying another or the company permits horseplay on the factory floor, the employer may be vicariously liable for injury that results. An employer may also be liable for any faulty equipment that is installed or purchased for use by employees and that subsequently causes harm to an employee.[33] The duty owed to an employee varies with a number of factors, including inexperience,[34] age, training or any disability of the worker as well as any particular dangers involved in the work itself. An employer may also in certain circumstances owe liability to those on his premises who are not employees.[35]

---

[29] *Mulcare v Southern Health Board* [1988] ILRM 689 at 692 *per* Murphy J.

[30] *Firth v South Eastern Health Board* (27 July 1994, unreported) HC.

[31] *Hough v Irish Base Metal Ltd* (8 December 1967, unreported) SC.

[32] *Hudson v Ridge Manufacturing Co* [1957] 2 QB 348.

[33] *Connolly v Dundalk Urban District Council and McMahon & McPhilips* [1990] 2 IR 1 (HC) (affirmed 18 November 1992) SC. The court pointed out that while the employer might be initially liable for damage to the employee, he may subsequently be able to sue the party who sold or installed the machinery or equipment in the first place. Note also the discussion of 'Liability for Defective Products' in Ch 6 'Clinical Negligence' para **[6.78]**.

[34] For example, an apprentice who is being trained will clearly need greater supervision than an experienced employee and accordingly, the duty of care will be higher: *Murphy v Ross* [1920] 2 IR 199; *Campbell v Cox* (15 May 1956, unreported) SC.

[35] Called occupiers liability and covered by the Occupiers Liability Act 1995. The Act requires the owner of any premises to which the public have access to take care that the premises do not present a danger to the public or – if danger cannot be wholly eliminated – to alert the public to the fact that the premises may be dangerous.

Contributory negligence and employee carelessness

[8.34] A worker who takes no regard or too little for his own safety and suffers an accident at work as a result of the negligence of his employers may himself be culpable of contributory negligence,[36] which may partially – or even completely – absolve the employer of any blame.

Case Study 8.2

An experienced fitter took apart a new machine, presuming its construction to be the same as its predecessors. He had no manual because the company had failed to make them available to staff. During the dismantling process, the man heard a noise suggestive of something breaking inside the machine, but continued to take it apart regardless. A portion of the machine came away and damaged the man's hand. The court found the company only 75 per cent liable for failing to provide manuals (and thereby failing to provide a safe system of work) because the employee contributed 25 per cent of the negligence in continuing to work on the machine when he should have known there was something wrong.[37]

Similarly an employee who continues to show disregard for his own safety or that of others may be disciplined or even, as a last resort, dismissed.[38] Under the Safety Health and Welfare at Work Act 2005, an employee who fails to take care of his own safety or that of others[39] may be prosecuted by the Health and Safety Authority. It is also important, however, to observe that while an employee who is at fault for an accident may be denied a legal remedy against her employer, she is still entitled to applicable state disability benefits if she is injured at work because such benefits issue on a 'no fault' basis.[40]

Breach of statutory duty

[8.35] As well as obligations under the law of negligence, employers can also have duties imposed on them by legislation. When an employee sues an employer he can, as well as alleging negligence on the part of the employer, also allege 'breach of statutory duty'. Breach of statutory duty means a failure to live up to the requirements of legislation. This is not the employee accusing the employer of 'breaking the law', but simply a case of asking the court to look at what the legislation says the employer *should* have been doing and to compare it with what in fact the employer was *in fact* doing. The comparison can help the judge to find that the employer has been negligent.[41] We will encounter below a number of regulations that have been introduced to promote health

---

[36] See Ch 6, *Clinical Negligence*, para **[6.48]**.

[37] *Doran v Dublin Plant Hire Ltd* [1990] 1 IR 488.

[38] *Kellegher v Power Supermarkets Ltd* (9 March 1990) EAT. The employee had been engage in horseplay on a fork lift truck.

[39] Safety, Health and Welfare at Work Act 2005, s 13 places safety obligations upon the employee.

[40] Social Welfare (Consolidation) Act 1993, s 48 *et seq.*

[41] *Dunleavy v Glen Abbey* [1992] ILRM 1. One departure in the Safety, Health and Welfare at Work Act 2005 is that the breach of any section of the Act can be used as the basis for a civil claim. Under the 1989 Act, certain duties could not, if breached, be cited as grounds for a civil claim.

and safety in the workplace: any one of them may be cited, if its terms have not been complied with, as evidence that the employer has breached his statutory duty towards the employee. In general, where there has been a breach of statutory duty, a negligence action may be easier to prove.

The employee who is unfit for work

[8.36] An employer, especially where work is hazardous, is under a duty to ensure that his workforce is fit for the duties they are undertaking.[42] This may take the form of a pre-employment medical or may require ongoing health surveillance and an employee who is found unfit for work or who refuses to undergo health surveillance (and has been made aware of the consequences of such a refusal) may be dismissed from her job. There is no absolute duty on an employer to find his employees 'light work' if recommended by a doctor caring for a patient, although it is certainly prudent that they should attempt to do so. If there is no alternative work and if a person is unfit to do the work for which they were initially engaged, then they can be lawfully dismissed assuming all other legal obligations are fulfilled by the employer.

Quick Reference Guide 8.2

Common law approach to safety, health and welfare at work

> ❖ Employers owe their employees a duty to provide a safe workplace, safe and proper equipment and plant, safe systems of work and safe and competent staff. If the employer fails in this duty and an employee suffers physical or psychological damage as a result, she may sue the employer for negligence.
>
> ❖ This duty is not absolute: an employer must take such care for the employee's safety in the circumstances as a reasonable and prudent employer would be expected to take.
>
> ❖ The duty owed to an employee varies with her experience, age, training and any disability. The employee herself may be guilty of contributory negligence if she acts without due regard for her own safety. Contributory negligence on the part of the employee can reduce the liability of the employer. An employee who acts without regard for the safety of others may be dismissed.
>
> ❖ If an employer not only fails in his duty towards the employee but also breaches his statutory duties, he is generally more likely to be found negligent.

Safety, health and welfare at work – the statutory approach

[8.37] The 1983 Barrington Commission Report[43] looked at the question of safety at work and recommended that legislation should be introduced to compel employers and employees to have regard for the need for safety in the workplace and to punish them if they did not do so. The result was the Safety Health and Welfare at Work Act 1989. The Act took the many of legal duties of employer and the employee that had already been recognised by the court and which we have dealt with in the preceding section, such as

---

[42] *Heeney v Dublin Corporation* (16 May 1991, unreported) HC.

[43] Report of the Committee of Enquiry on Safety, Health and Welfare at Work, Government Publications, Dublin, 1983.

the duty to provide safe systems of work, and made them statutory obligations. The process that led to the introduction of the Act was a long one and lies outside the scope of the present chapter, but certain elements can be stated:

– Early legislation for safety in the workplace was the result of attempts to redress the appalling employment conditions that were a by-product of the Industrial Revolution;[44]

– Legislation prior to the 1989 Act was piecemeal and limited in scope and reach (for example, legislation such as the Factories Act 1955 applied only to factories and not to any other workplaces);

– Litigation by employees against employers for failing in their duty to provide safe workplaces was increasing and so were the amounts in damages being awarded by the courts.

– The need was recognised for a statutory and proactive, rather than court-based and retrospective, approach to safety in the workplace.

The Safety Health and Welfare at Work Act was updated in 2005 and it is to this latter statute that we now turn.

Safety, Health and Welfare at Work Act 2005

[8.38] This Act is the law governing safety in the modern workplace. It places legal burdens on both employer and employee as well as regulating and empowering the Health and Safety Authority (HSA), which has the power to enforce the Act and to punish those who transgress. The Act also provides the legal basis for the introduction of specific regulations that put flesh on the bones of the Act itself. The Safety, Health and Welfare at Work Act 2005 can be divided into five broad areas:

– the general duties of employers, employees and other persons such as designers of workplaces and those responsible for the manufacture import and supply of workplace materials and equipment (Pt 2 of the Act);

– principles of protection and prevention in the workplace, including the obligation to identify risks and hazards in the workplace, to produce safety statements and to maintain health surveillance (Pt 3 of the Act);

– the appointment of safety representatives and the holding of safety consultations (Pt 4);

– the establishment and regulation of the Health and Safety Authority (HSA) (Pt 5);

– the HSA's powers of enforcement and its power to regulations and accepted codes of practice (ACoP) for the workplace which constitute legal 'best practice'[45] (Pt 6).

We look now at the four most significant elements of the Act: the general duties it imposes on all involved in the workplace, the Safety Statement, dealing with those who

---

44 For example, an Act for the Preservation of the Health and Morals of Apprentices and Others Employed in Cotton and Other Mills and Cotton and Other Factories 1802. This Act mandated quicklime washings for the factory or mill twice a year, fresh air, suitable accommodation (no more than two to a bed) and working day limited to 12 hours. Only in the mid-nineteenth century did inspectors gain real powers to enforce the laws on safety in the workplace.

infringe safety rules and the health and safety regulations that apply the Act to the specifics of the workplace.

General duties under the Act

[8.39] The Act applies to all workplaces, to all employers and to all employees whether full-time or temporary (defined as those who have entered into a contract of employment with an employer) and it is the duty of every employer to ensure, so far as is reasonably practicable, the safety, health and welfare at work of all his employees.[46] Note that this duty reflects the duty laid down by the courts in that it is not absolute but rather the Act requires the employer to ensure safety only so far as is 'reasonably practicable'.[47] The Act lays out specific areas in which the employer has a duty to take care (so far as is reasonably practicable):[48]

- managing and conducting work activities in such a way as to ensure the safety, health and welfare at work of his or her employees;

- managing and conducting work activities in such a way as to prevent, so far as is reasonably practicable, any improper conduct or behaviour likely to put the safety, health or welfare at work of his or her employees at risk;

- having a place of work that is designed and maintained safely, including access to and exit from the site and the design, provision and maintenance of safe plant and machinery;

- ensuring the safety and the prevention of risk to health at work of his or her employees relating to the use of any dangerous articles or substances or the exposure to noise, vibration or harmful substances;

---

[45] An example of an ACoP is the Health and Safety Authority, *Code of Practice for Employers and Employees on the Prevention and Resolution of Bullying at Work* (Dublin, 2007) – available for download from the website of the Health and Safety Authority: http://publications.hsa.ie/ (last accessed October 2007).

[46] Safety, Health and Welfare at Work Act 2005, ss 8–17. The obligation to safeguard the welfare of employees includes temporary and contract employees.

[47] The Safety, Health and Welfare at Work Act 2005 defines 'reasonably practicable' (s 2(6)): it 'means that an employer has exercised all due care by putting in place the necessary protective and preventive measures, having identified the hazards and assessed the risks to safety and health likely to result in accidents or injury to health at the place of work concerned and where the putting in place of any further measures is grossly disproportionate having regard to the unusual, unforeseeable and exceptional nature of any circumstance or occurrence that may result in an accident at work or injury to health at that place of work.' The words 'reasonably practicable' imply a balancing act between the safety the employer is obliged to provide and the cost, in money and effort, required to achieve that level of safety. Where it would be prohibitively expensive or extremely difficult to put a particular measure in place, the courts seem happy to accept that such a measure is not 'reasonably practicable'. The greater the risk to life and limb of the employee the greater the steps an employer is expected to take: *Daly v Avonmore Creameries Ltd* [1984] IR 131; *Boyle v Marathon Petroleum Ireland Ltd* (1 November 1995, unreported) HC, (12 January 1999) SC.

[48] Safety, Health and Welfare at Work Act 2005, s 8.

- providing safely planned, organised, performed, maintained and revised systems of work;
- providing and maintaining facilities and arrangements for the welfare of his or her employees at work;
- providing the information, instruction, training[49] and supervision to employees necessary to ensure safety, health, and welfare at work of his or her employees;
- identifying hazards and carrying out risk assessments and preparing safety statements and reviewing such hazard assessments and safety statements;
- having regard to the general principles of prevention;[50]
- planning for emergencies;
- reporting accidents and dangerous occurrences where required by law;
- obtaining, where necessary, the services of a competent person (whether under a contract of employment or otherwise) for the purpose of ensuring, the safety, health and welfare at work of his or her employees.

Employers and the self-employed are also required to conduct their business in such a way that it is safe for non-employees so far as is reasonably practicable: a doctor, for example, should make sure her needle disposal system does not present a risk to patients. The employer's duty includes taking care not to present a workplace risk to those visiting the workplace or carrying out work on the premises.

Employees' duties

[8.40] Employees are also under a burden to take reasonable care for their own safety, health and welfare and that of any other person who may be affected by their acts or omissions at work. Employees' duties include co-operating with the employer to ensure safety in the work place and utilising any safety equipment or clothing that is provided. The employee is also under an obligation to report any defect in equipment, machinery, the workplace or the system of work without unreasonable delay. The employee is forbidden by the Act from intentionally or recklessly interfering with any article or system intended to cater for safety, health and welfare in the workplace. [51]

The Act also obliges anyone who makes, designs, imports or supplies any article for use at work to ensure that the article is safe for use, that sufficient information is provided to ensure its safe use and that changes in specification or use must be communicated to

---

[49] Training is a dynamic process. According to the Safety Health and Welfare at Work Act 2005 (s 10(2)–(3)), training shall be adapted to take account of new or changed risks to safety, health and welfare at work and shall, as appropriate, be repeated periodically. Training is obliged to be provided (a) on recruitment; (b) in the event of the transfer of an employee or change of task assigned to an employee; (c) on the introduction of new work equipment, systems of work or changes in existing work equipment or systems of work; and (d) on the introduction of new technology.

[50] The essential principle of prevention is that where possible, any risk should be eliminated; where it cannot be eliminated, it should be controlled; where it cannot be controlled completely, then employees should be provided with such suitable protective clothing and equipment (which should also be maintained by the employer) as is necessary to ensure the safety, health and welfare at work of employees.

those using the article. Similar strictures attach to anyone who is designing or constructing a place of work.[52]

Safety statements

[8.41] Safety statements are a crucial element of the modern workplace and every employer must prepare one for his business.[53] The safety statement has two ingredients: it must be based on an identification of hazards and an assessment of risks[54] in the workplace and it must specify how the employer – in the light of the identification and assessment process – will deal with the identified risks and hazards. The statement must detail how safety is being 'managed and secured' and in particular include:

- resources and arrangements for maximising health safety and welfare of the workforce as well as (new under the 2005 Act) contractors and the public;

- details of the co-operation required from the employees regarding health safety and welfare;

- emergency plans;

- arrangements for employee consultation

- names of the people – or their deputies if the named people are absent – responsible for tasks assigned by the safety statement.

Employees must be consulted as part of the preparation of a safety statement and must be aware of its contents.[55] Employees may appoint a safety representative to liaise with the employer or with any inspector sent into the workplace by the HSA. A person acting as safety representative must be given the necessary training to fulfil the role (together with the requisite leave to obtain that training) and must not be penalised financially or in terms of career prospects for discharging her duties. The safety representative will typically be the conduit for health and safety information going between employees and either the employer or any inspectors representing the HSA. An employer should act on the representations of a safety representative where possible.[56]

---

[51] Safety, Health and Welfare at Work Act 2005, ss 13–14. The 2005 Act also prohibits employees from being under the influence of an intoxicant (which includes drugs or alcohol) to the extent that he or she is in such a state as to endanger his or her own safety, health or welfare at work or that of any other person and provides that an employee may be required by his employer to undergo a 'proportionate' test for an intoxicant, conducted by a registered medical practitioner.

[52] Safety, Health and Welfare at Work Act 2005, s 16. If an article is manufactured outside the State then legal liability under the Act falls on the importer.

[53] Safety, Health and Welfare at Work Act 2005, s 20. See Health and Safety Authority, *Guidelines on Risk Assessments and Safety Statements* (Dublin, 2006)

[54] Risk assessment may include all or any the following: safety audit (usually carried out by external safety experts); safety survey; routine safety inspection; safety tour (typically unscheduled); safety sampling; hazard and operability studies (assessment of the particular risk posed by the engineering elements of machinery) and checklists for processes. Essentially there are two types of measurement of risk: quantitative measurements of risks such as noise and qualitative measurements, such as the assessment of techniques and training for manual lifting.

[55] The 2005 Act includes an express provision that information must be communicated in a language appropriate for the workforce (s 20(3)).

[8.42] A safety statement must be a dynamic document and must change to take account of changing health and safety practices. Those companies that are obliged by law to produce annual reports are obliged to include in their reports an indication of the extent to which the policies set out in a safety statement have been implemented. An inspector from the Health and Safety Authority can ask to see an employer's safety statement, which must be in writing,[57] and if it is deficient she can order it to be remedied within 30 days.

Health surveillance

[8.43] Where appropriate, employers must have health surveillance in place, appropriate to the risks to safety, health and welfare which may be identified by risk assessment.[58] This is particularly the case when employees are working in a hazardous environment or with dangerous substances. The requirement for health surveillance is reiterated in many regulations dealing with the handling of specific substances, such the Biological Agents Regulations 1994 and 1998 (see para **[8.52]** below.

Consequences of breaching the legislation

[8.44] The HSA is given the power, as a last resort, to prosecute those who breach the 2005 Act. However, before that stage is reached the Authority has other powers[59] to coerce employers into co-operating with the law. The HSA appoints inspectors who can visit workplaces and exercise powers of inspection and investigation.[60] If an inspector notes a problem with workplace safety, she can proceed in a number of ways depending on the severity of the breach of an employer's (or employee's – remember that the Act applies to both) liability under the Act. In the last analysis, if attempts at remedial measures fail, the HSA can bring a prosecution against transgressing employers or employees: a court can then fine the company (or its directors) or in certain limited circumstances jail the guilty party.[61]

Improvement direction

[8.45] Used for relatively minor breaches of the law: the inspector indicates areas where improvement is required, to which the employer responds with an improvement plan and a timeframe within which the improvement will be effected.[62]

---

[56] Safety, Health and Welfare at Work Act 2005, s 25.
[57] Safety Health and Welfare at Work Act 2005, s 64(1)(c); the obligation on the employer to amend the safety statement (within 30 days) is set out at s 20(5).
[58] Safety Health and Welfare at Work Act 2005, s 22.
[59] The 2005 Act includes the power of medical inspectors to 'invite' persons to attend for examination or to provide biological samples, but the Act does not appear to compel such persons to attend for medical examination: s 63(1).
[60] Safety, Health and Welfare at Work Act 2005, s 64. The inspectors have wide-ranging powers of entry, as well as authority to demand assistance from employers, access to records, and to take samples from a workplace.
[61] See 'Building firm and director fined for deaths on site', (2001) Irish Times, 22 November. A construction company was fined €250,000 and its director €50,000 for breaches of health and safety law in digging a trench on a construction site. The trench had collapsed killing two men. An employee, the driver of a digger, was also fined, showing the extent of the Act's powers.

Improvement notice

[8.46] Here the Inspector tells the employer what he must do in order to comply with the law, together with the timeframe within which it must do it. The employer must implement the improvements contained in the notice, although he does have the right to take an appeal against the notice to the District Court.[63]

Prohibition notice

[8.47] The inspector may stop the employer from engaging in a particular activity that represents a risk of serious personal injury to employees. Once the notice is issued the employer must cease that activity, even if it means that he cannot carry on any work.[64] This would generally be used where there was a serious and extremely dangerous breach of safety in the workplace. In certain circumstances, the Inspector will go to the High Court to seek a prohibition order, rather than issuing it himself.

Safety, health and welfare at work regulations

[8.48] The Safety, Health and Welfare at Work Act is not an isolated piece of legislation. It serves simply to lay out the broad parameters and principles that underlie safety in the workplace. They are buttressed by a panoply of regulations that govern everything from general interpretation and application of the Act to the specifics of health and safety in certain professions or with regard to certain hazards. It would be impossible in a work of this nature to give detailed attention to every such regulation, but we look below at some that are of most interest to the clinician. Many of these regulations are transpositions into Irish law of equivalent or identical European Directives.[65]

General Application Regulations 2007

[8.49] These regulations are the cornerstone of practical implementation of the 2005 Act. In particular they cover the following elements of safety and lay down the practices that should be adopted by the employer. Sections of general relevance to the healthcare sector are listed below.

- Part 2 – Workplace
    - Workplace safety. equipment and machinery (Chapter 1)
    - Personal protective equipment (Chapter 2)
    - Manual handling of loads (Chapter 3)
    - Display screens (Chapter 4)
- Part 3 - Electricity
- Part 6 – Sensitive Risk groups
    - Protection of pregnant, post natal and breastfeeding employees (Chapter 2)
    - Night work and shift work (Chapter 3)
- Part 7 – First Aid and Safety Signs

---

62 Safety, Health and Welfare at Work Act 2005, s 65.
63 Safety, Health and Welfare at Work Act 2005, s 66.
64 Safety, Health and Welfare at Work Act 2005, s 67. The Act also includes the power to 'name and shame' those upon whom prohibition notices have been served: s 85.
65 See Appendix I for a brief discussion of European law.

The specifics of the General Application Regulations are extensive, but there are some elements that should be highlighted.

First aid[66]

[8.50] First aid arrangements must be specifically included in any safety statement. There should be appropriate facilities and properly trained staff. First aid is defined as the treatment of very minor injuries or alternatively treatment with the aim of preserving life or minimising the consequences of injury until a medically or paramedically qualified individual can arrive. The number of staff to be trained in first aid depends on workplace size and the nature of the work carried on in that workplace: factories and construction sites have a greater requirement for first aid facilities.

Manual handling of loads[67]

[8.51] There are three elements to the health and safety considerations of manual handling of loads at work.

–   The employer must put in place systems wherever possible that avoid manual handling of loads, for example by providing mechanical assistance;
–   Where manual lifting is unavoidable the employer must engage in risk assessment and reduction;
–   The employer is under a duty to provide training and information to employees and to have regard to the particular characteristics of individual employees engaged in manual lifting.

Manual handling is defined relatively broadly: 'any transporting or supporting of a load by one or more employees and includes lifting, putting down, pushing, pulling, carrying or moving a load, which, by reason of its characteristics or of unfavourable ergonomic conditions, involves risk, particularly of back injury, to employees.'[68] In each case the procedures in place should take account of the characteristics of the load in question, the physical effort required in lifting and moving the load, the frequency with which lifting must be done and the environment in which the lifting is done.

Biological Agents Regulations 1994 and 1998[69]

[8.52] These regulations cover workplaces where there is the potential for exposure to biological agents, which include bacteria, viruses, parasites and fungi.

The employer must, as with all regulations of this nature, conduct a full assessment of risks in the workplace and where risks cannot be eliminated, for example in a hospital or research facility, then they must be minimised. All employees must be trained in the necessary procedures to ensure safety and there must be health surveillance available to the employees, should they wish to avail themselves of it (see para **[8.43]** above). There must be training and information available to employees, together with health surveillance. In these and similar regulations,[70] exposure limits are often specified where appropriate.

---

[66] Safety, Health and Welfare at Work (General Application) Regulations 2007, Pt 7, Ch 2.
[67] Safety, Health and Welfare at Work (General Application) Regulations 2007, Pt 2, Ch 4.
[68] Safety, Health and Welfare at Work (General Application) Regulations 2007, reg 68.
[69] Safety, Health and Welfare at Work (Biological Agents) Regulations 1994 (SI 146/1994) and 1998 (SI 248/1998).

Ionising Radiation Order 2000[71]

[8.53] The Radiological Protection Institute of Ireland (RPII) is the equivalent of the HSA when it comes to radiation emissions and was established by the Radiation Protection Act 1991. The powers of the RPII and the regulations governing the use of and exposure to radiation are of particular significance to those working in radiography and radiology. The RPII is concerned with hazards to health associated with ionising radiation and with radioactive contamination in the environment. It also has an advisory function to both the Government and the public and licenses and develops regulations for the use and licensing[72] of any device that is a source of ionising radiation, such as x-ray machines. Today, the number of people holding a licence for ionising radiation devices exceeds 1,250 and includes hospitals, dentists, veterinary surgeons, universities, institutes of technology and industrial users. RPII inspectors have extensive powers under the Radiological Protection Act 1991 to inspect any premises or devices.

[8.54] The key principles for the licensing for use of ionising equipment are:

–   it must be possible to justify the use of the equipment by showing that the benefits it provides to society outweigh the risks posed by radiation ('justification');

–   all exposure to radiation must as low as is reasonably achievable in the circumstances ('optimisation');

–   the sum total of all doses must be kept below the specified limits contained in regulations ('limitation').

[8.55] These principles are enshrined in Irish law by the Ionising Radiation Order 2000. The order provides the framework for the Institute's licensing system and details the general radiation protection requirements and dose limits for all users of ionising radiation.[73] The aim of the regulations is to control exposure to ionising radiation risk and to achieve that aim, not only must the radiation principles of justification, optimisation and limitation be respected, a full risk assessment must also be carried out

---

[70]   Similar regulations are in place for exposure to carcinogens (SI 78/2001) and chemical agents (SI 445/1994).

[71]   The Radiological Protection Act 1991 (Ionising Radiation) Order 2000 (SI 125/2000). See also the European Communities (Medical Ionising Radiation Protection) Regulations 2002 (SI 478/2002), which is concerned with the health protection of individuals against the dangers of ionising radiation in relation to exposures related to medical investigations. These regulation require that a specialist in radiology (or a sufficiently experienced dentist) should be the arbiter of whether a particular dose of ionising radiation should be administered, having regard to the likely risks versus benefits; any registered medical or dental practitioner may request a medical ionizing radiation exposure. See also Medical Council, *Policy Document on the Use of Medical Ionising Radiation* (2005). Available for download from http://www.medicalcouncil.ie/medical_ionising_radiation/default.asp (last accessed October 2007).

[72]   A licence is required for custody, production, processing, handling, holding, storage, use, manufacture, importing into and exporting from the European Union, distribution, transportation, recycling, re-use or other disposal of radioactive substances and nuclear devices and the custody, use or distribution of irradiating apparatus.

[73]   There are also regulations governing the exposure of outside workers to radiation: European Communities (Protection of Outside Workers from Ionising Radiation) Regulations 1994 (SI 144/1994).

as part of the process of minimising exposure. The risk assessment must be submitted with an application for a licence from the RPII. The Act also regulates the provision of health surveillance to those staff working with ionising radiation. Individual dose monitoring must be carried out for all exposed workers by an approved dosimetry service and with regard to record keeping, dose records for Category A (those receiving greatest exposure to ionising radiation) workers must be maintained by an approved dosimetry service for a minimum of 50 years from the date on which the worker ceased to do the work involving exposures. In the case of Category B workers, dose records must be maintained by the licensee for a period of at least five years from the date of measurement.

Quick Reference Guide 8.3

The Safety, Health and Welfare at Work Act and Regulations

> ❖ The Safety, Health and Welfare at Work Act 2005 covers all workplaces and places obligations on both employers and employees to maintain safety, health and welfare at work. The Act empowers the Health and Safety Authority (HSA) to enforce the Act.
>
> ❖ The obligations the Act places on employers are very similar to those that had traditionally been placed on employers by the courts, including the duties to provide a safe place of work, safe systems of work, safe equipment and safe staff.
>
> ❖ The fundamental point of all safety, health and welfare at work legislation is that employers are obliged to identify risks and hazards in the workplace ('risk assessment'). Once risks and hazards are identified, the employer is under an obligation to eliminate them where possible or, where elimination is impossible, to minimise them, for example by the use of training or safety equipment.
>
> ❖ All employers must prepare a Safety Statement for the workplace. A Safety Statement must be based on an identification of hazards and an assessment of risks in the workplace and must specify how the employer – in the light of the identification and assessment process – will deal with the risks and hazards identified.
>
> ❖ Employees should be consulted on safety matters and they have the right to appoint a safety representative who must be consulted on safety matters and whose representations to the employer should be given due weight.
>
> ❖ An employer or employee who breaches the Safety, Health and Welfare Act 2005 may be subject to the attentions of the Health and Safety Authority. They may issue improvement directions, improvement notices and prohibition notices regarding the workplace. In the last analysis they may prosecute employers or employees, who may be fined substantial amounts or sentenced to a term of imprisonment.
>
> ❖ The Safety, Health and Welfare at Work Act is fleshed out by a variety of regulations that apply the principles of the Act to the specifics of general and particular working environments. Important regulations for the healthcare community include the Biological Agents Regulations 1994 and 1998, the Carcinogen Regulations 1994 and the Chemical Agents Regulations 1994.

Safety, health and welfare at work in the health services

[8.56] Specific research has been conducted into health and safety issues in the health services.[74] The report drew attention to the importance of the health care sector as an employer, with over 100,000 people working for it. The *Report of the Health and Safety Authority Advisory Committee on the Health Service* sought to identify and prioritise the principal safety and health problems in the sector and to work out programmes to tackle the problems identified. The most significant areas of concern isolated included the following:

- the need to report and record incidents with potential impact on safety at work;

- the importance of having overarching and well-integrated safety systems in place and in particular valuing the role of the safety representative;

- paying attention to the need to avoid where possible and minimise – where avoidance is not possible – the risks posed by manual handling;

- the need to identify the risks posed by biological (such as needlestick injuries) and chemical hazards;

- the need for good housekeeping in health care facilities to reduce the high frequency of slips, trips and falls;

- improved electrical safety in older premises.

Proposed methods for dealing with shortcomings include the HSA liaising with health service employers, the Department of Health, the health boards and the hospitals to foster a greater regard for safety, health and welfare principles. Specific proposals include encouraging safety committees, multidisciplinary occupational health services and emphasising training and the adoption of 'best practice' protocols.

ILLNESS AND CERTIFICATION OF ABSENCE FROM WORK

[8.57] Employees who have paid the requisite PRSI (pay-related social insurance) are entitled to social welfare benefits when absent from work through illness or through injuries sustained in the workplace.[75] In cases where a person is claiming benefit on the grounds of being unfit for work, it will generally fall to the doctor[76] to certify that a person is – in fact – unfit for work. Benefits are payable once the PRSI requirements are met both to patients who are absent from work through non-specific illnesses and to those whose absence is due specifically to injury or illness sustained at work. The most common forms of benefit paid to those who are unable to work through illness or injury include the following:[77]

---

[74] *Report of the Health and Safety Authority Advisory Committee on the Health Services* (HSA, Dublin, 2001).

[75] Social Welfare (Consolidation) Act 1993, ss 48 *et seq.*

[76] See Medical Practitioners Act 1978 s 59: any certificate required to be signed by a doctor and which is not signed by a doctor will not "be of any validity or effect".

[77] Details on all forms of benefits and specific current entitlements can be found on the website of the Department of Social and Family Affairs: www.welfare.ie.

[8.58] *Illness Benefit* – a payment (formerly known as disability benefit) made to those people who are qualified for the benefit through PRSI contributions and who are unable to work due to illness or injury,. A person who suffers an occupational injury or disease will generally receive a disability payment called *occupational injury benefit* for the first 26 weeks' duration of the injury or illness.

[8.59] *Disablement Benefit* – paid to those who are injured at work or who contract a prescribed occupational disease and whose illness outlasts 26 weeks and whose injury results in the loss of a mental or physical faculty. People with occupational injuries or illness receive other benefits under the Occupational Injuries Scheme, which can include Medical Care[78] and Death Benefit.[79] Disablement benefit can sometimes be paid as a lump sum rather than a periodic weekly or monthly payment.

[8.60] *Disability Allowance* – a weekly allowance paid to people with a disability, typically lasting a year or more, who are aged over 16 years and under the age of 66 years. Payments are dependent on a medical examination and a means test.

Occupational injuries and diseases

[8.61] Occupational diseases are diseases that develop specifically due to the nature of a person's employment. Occupational injuries are injuries sustained at work, including those suffered on the journey to or from work. Benefit is payable to persons who suffer from one of a ranged of occupational diseases prescribed by regulations, acquired while engaged in a job provided for by the regulations and due to the nature of the employment.[80] A variety of conditions fall within the remit of occupational diseases – the adjacent table lists some of the most common and the occupations with which they must be associated for benefit to be payable.

Table 8.1 – Some occupational diseases recognised for social welfare payments and their associated causes

Disease or Injury[81]	*Occupation*
Bursitis or subcutaneous cellulitis of the hand, elbow or knee	Manual labour involving prolonged pressure or friction to the affected part.
Byssinosis	Exposure to cotton or flax in the weaving industry
Nasal carcinoma	Work in wood manufacture or repair; footwear manufacture or repair with leather or fibre board

---

[78] A patient may be entitled to payments to help cover medical expenses incurred as a result of an accident at work or a disease contracted at work if he is not otherwise entitled to free medical care and the expenses are reasonable and necessary.

[79] Death Benefits include Widow's Pension, Dependant Widower's Pension, Orphan's Pension, Dependant Parent's Pension, and Funeral Grant.

[80] For more details, see *A Guide to Occupational Diseases Prescribed Under the Occupational Injuries Benefits Scheme*, Department of Social and Family Affairs, Leaflet SW 33. Available for download at http://www.welfare.ie/publications/sw33.html (last accessed October 2007).

[81] This is not a complete list of all occupational diseases, but represents some of those specified in Department of Social and Family Affairs documentation.

Disease or Injury	*Occupation*
Cramp of hand or forearm	Work involving repetitive movements of fingers, hand or arms
Mesothelioma	Exposure to asbestos through handling, manufacture, or as a result of cleaning, building or maintenance work
Radiation-based illness	Work involving radiation exposure
Hearing loss[82]	Use of or exposure to pneumatic percussive or grinding tools in metallurgy, mining or shipbuilding; exposure to drop-forging or drop-hammering plant; exposure to weaving machinery; exposure to wood-manufacturing or forestry machinery.
Infections, including TB, anthrax, glanders, leptospirosis, brucellosis, streptococcus suis infection, viral hepatitis.	Exposure to the illness in any occupation in which the infection is an occupational hazard (e.g. viral hepatitis is an occupational disease for clinical practice).
Certain forms of poisoning or cancer	Exposure to poisonous or carcinogenic chemicals at work.
Asthma	Exposure to any of the following: animals or insects in research or education; cereal dusts; fumes from 'hardening agents' or resins; isocyanates; platinum salts; proteolytic enzymes; red cedar wood dust.
Dermatitis	Exposure in the course of employment to any chemical or other agent capable of causing dermatitis.

Certification of illness

[8.62] The role of the doctor in certifying absence from work is to examine the patient and, where state benefits are being claimed, complete the requisite forms. The most common forms are:

–   Form MC1, which certifies the initial week of any illness and will suffice on its own to cover any illness or injury lasting fewer than eight days.

–   Form MC2, which certifies either continuing illness (intermediate certificate) or that a patient is fit to return to work after a period of illness (final certificate).

---

[82] Certain conditions attach to the payment of occupational injury benefit for deafness: (i) Hearing loss must amount to at least 50db in each year; (ii) The person must have been in the prescribed occupation for 10 years or more; (iii) Any claim must be made within five years of leaving that employment.

Certificates are issued to doctors from the Department of Social and Family Affairs. A person is unfit to work when he is under the care of the doctor for an ailment and in the opinion of his doctor *either* cannot work because of that illness *or* is advised not to work because of the risk his illness poses to others.[83] Typically the doctor will certify illness by completing the appropriate form with the details of the illness and dates of the period covered by the illness.[84]

[8.63] Payment for certification is arranged by the Department of Social and Family Affairs and not by the patient. The Department rules state that all first certificates of illness or injury should be based on a medical examination to confirm the presence of the ailment in question. Subsequent (intermediate or final) certificates should be predicated on an examination unless the doctor is satisfied on good medical grounds that the illness is continuing. Certificates must generally be:

- completed clearly and legibly;
- written by the certifier in ink (preferably in capital letters) and signed by the certifier in her own handwriting;
- issued by the certifier to the patient and at the time of any examination or as soon as possible afterwards.

Certification is generally weekly, but the Department may permit those suffering from long term illness to submit certificates at longer intervals, such as six months. Where a person is no longer unfit for work, then the doctor can issue a 'final certificate'. Any person claiming disability benefit may be called for assessment by a medical assessor on behalf of the Department and if he is found fit for work, benefit may be discontinued. The patient has the right to take an appeal against the discontinuation of benefit to the Social Welfare Appeals Office.

---

[83] For example, infection in a child care or hospital worker.

[84] On forms MC1 and MC2, there is a box marked 'Code D' which the doctor may tick to denote either that including the precise details of the patient's illness on his form could be detrimental to his physical or mental wellbeing or that disclosure of the illness to a third party could cause distress. In either case, a Medical Officer from the Department will contact the certifying doctor for a confidential report.

Chapter 9

The Practitioner and the Lawyer

INTRODUCTION

[9.01] This chapter looks briefly (and predominantly from the viewpoint of the clinician, rather than the lawyer) at the workings of the legal profession and legal process.[1] We examine in some detail the role of the clinician as witness in both her role as 'witness of fact' and as her role as an expert witness. The final third of this chapter follows the process of clinical litigation from initiation to conclusion, with some comments on the role of the clinician when appearing in court.

THE ROLE OF THE LAWYER

[9.02] For most practitioners the first point of contact with the law will be with a solicitor. Solicitors are traditionally the more public face of the legal profession, acting as a first point of contact for those individuals who have, or believe themselves to have, a problem or grievance of a legal nature. Solicitors carry out all initial correspondence relating to claims, including collating relevant documents and reports necessary to further a claim. In many cases, it may not be necessary to involve a barrister, although it would be unusual in clinical litigation for a barrister not to be utilised.

[9.03] In turn the barrister's role is initially also advisory and is directed at ensuring that all the documentation and information necessary to set out (or 'plead') a person's claim or defence to a claim is obtained. The barrister may also offer initial opinions on the merits or otherwise of a particular case. When a matter becomes contentious, the barrister will draft relevant legal pleadings for the court in order to set out the claim or defence as appropriate. When matters come before the court for oral hearings, it is typically the barrister who will make oral arguments. There are an increasing number of matters in respect of which a person may deal with a barrister directly, without the necessity of going through a solicitor.

[9.04] When a practitioner receives a communication from a solicitor, it will generally be a request for information of some sort. The first obligation on the practitioner is to make sure she understands what is being sought. Lawyers are as guilty as health professionals are of using jargon. It is important to be certain that one understands the legal letter and to seek clarification from the sender if anything is incomprehensible, obscure or equivocal. Most commonly, a solicitor's letter to a practitioner will request information regarding a patient whom the practitioner has treated for injuries in an accident and this form of information, 'the medico-legal report', is dealt with in para **[9.05]***ff.* However, a communication from a solicitor may on occasion be a hostile (or potentially hostile) one, either alleging wrongdoing or seeking information relevant to the investigation of

---

[1]   Further detail on the Irish legal system is provided in Appendix I.

allegations of wrongdoing against the clinician or another third party. In such cases, the matter should be put into the hands of the clinician's insurers or solicitors.

MEDICO-LEGAL REPORTS

[9.05] In theory, any healthcare professional may be called upon to write a professional opinion for use in a legal case. In practice, however, doctors, physiotherapists and occupational therapists write the majority of such reports, predominantly because medico-legal reports are most commonly required for assessing personal injuries together with any relevant opinion on the consequences and treatment of those injuries. It is these three professions that would generally be best positioned to offer such opinions, being the disciplines most likely to be involved in the care of such a patient. Such reports may be written either by practitioners who are charged with the ongoing care of the person in question or by doctors who are simply asked to see the patient for the purposes of assessing disability or recovery.[2]

[9.06] Reports are not only required in relation to injuries; clinicians may also be asked to comment on the standard of care provided in alleged negligence cases. Where negligence is alleged against a doctor, for example, the case against the doctor must be based on the opinion of an appropriate comparable doctor[3] that the treating doctor acted negligently. Conversely, the insurers of the doctor accused of negligence will seek a report from an appropriate doctor to see whether that doctor too believes there was negligence.[4] Such reports are dealt with under the heading of 'Expert Witnesses' (see para **[9.30]***ff* below).

The 'typical' medico-legal report

[9.07] In this section and the sections that follow we look at a hypothetical report concerning personal injuries allegedly caused by negligence, but the same rules and advice discussed here apply generally for any medico-legal opinion on physical or psychiatric injuries that a practitioner is called upon to write.

[9.08] Assume that A was injured when he was knocked down by a car driven by B; legal proceedings for personal injuries are commenced by A, in which A is the plaintiff and B is the defendant. A's doctor receives a letter from the solicitor acting for A,

---

[2]   So, in a personal injuries action arising out of a road traffic accident, a report will probably be sought from all the doctors involved in the patient's routine care. But the patient may also be examined by doctors on behalf of the defendant (whose role is to confirm the extent of injuries and disability) and they too, although not involved in the patient's routine care, will furnish reports.

[3]   See *Cooke v Cronin* [1999] IESC 54 (14 July 1999), in which the Supreme Court approved the decisions of the High Court in *Reidy v The National Maternity Hospital* (31 July 1997, unreported) HC, and *Connolly v James A Casey and Laura Murphy (Trading under the style and title of Casey and Murphy) and Michael Fitzgibbon* [1998] IEHC 90. In the latter case, Kelly J observed:

'I have no difficulty in endorsing the views of Barr J. that the commencement of proceedings alleging professional negligence is irresponsible and an abuse of the process of the Court unless the persons advising such proceedings have reasonable grounds for so doing.'

[4]   For a discussion of what constitutes professional clinical negligence, see Ch 7 Negligence.

requesting a report of the investigation and treatment of the patient's injuries and the doctor's opinion as to the diagnosis and prognosis together with information on any referral to other experts. As outlined above, other medico-legal reports may also be generated by doctors not involved in the patient's actual clinical care, eg the insurers of B may wish to have their own assessment of the plaintiff's injuries and they may therefore ask A to attend a doctor of their choosing. In such a case, the protocol for preparing a report, discussed at paras **[9.13]–[9.29]**, is the same. There are two preliminary questions that might arise: is a clinician obliged to provide a report and to what extent is consent necessary?

Can the request for a report be refused?

[9.09] Looked at in its simplest terms, a request to a doctor to provide information that will help the patient to advance a legal claim against a third party is in effect a request from the patient through his solicitor asking that his own notes be released (together with any relevant medical opinion from his doctor) to help advance his case for compensation. A doctor, like other healthcare professionals, has a duty to care for her patient and it can be argued that furnishing a legal report based on the patient's notes so that a patient can progress a legal action for compensation for a physical or psychiatric injury is an extension of the duty of care. The Irish Medical Council's *Guide to Ethical Conduct and Behaviour* states that:

> Doctors have a responsibility to supply medical reports for solicitors or insurance companies on behalf of patients they have seen or treated professionally or for whom they have been responsible. However such reports should not be given without the patient's permission.
>
> Doctors who perceive a conflict of interest in preparing a report should inform the patient or the patient's legal adviser.[5]

[9.10] The courts have agreed with this approach, reasoning that patients who wish to have their notes released for the purpose of legal action should be able to ask the doctor to release them without having to resort to legal action to compel the release of the notes.[6] Furthermore, under data protection legislation, a patient has a statutory right of access to his records, which can only be refused in exceptional circumstances.[7]

Is consent necessary?

[9.11] Confidentiality is a prerequisite for a properly functioning relationship between healthcare professional and patient.[8] One of the ways in which the general requirement that the clinician must safeguard the patient's confidences may be overridden is where the patient consents to disclosure. Thus it may be possible to infer from a solicitor's letter that the patient has given implied consent to the release of the notes.

[9.12] The situation may not be that simple. It may be that the patient is unaware that a request has issued from the solicitor to the doctor. A patient may be under the impression

---

[5]   *Guide to Ethical Conduct and Practice* (6th edn, 2004) para 8.1.
[6]   *C v C* [1946] 1 All ER 562.
[7]   Data Protection legislation is dealt with in Ch 5 'Clinical Records and Prescribing', see para **[5.32]**ff.
[8]   See Ch 3 'Confidentiality and the Practitioner–Patient Relationship'.

that the solicitor will send him to a third party doctor, rather than relying on information from his own physician. There may be elements in the clinical records that the patient would prefer not to have disclosed, to the extent that the patient would rather discontinue the legal action.[9] It is preferable, as suggested by the Medical Council *Guide* adverted to in the previous paragraph, to elicit express consent from a patient to the disclosure of information to any outside party, even where consent may be inferred from the patient's conduct (such as, in this case, a solicitor's letter). Obtaining consent also allows for a discussion with the patient of any sensitive information that is to be disclosed. Where consent is obtained, it should preferably be recorded in writing.

Contents of a medico-legal report

[9.13] Most legal cases 'settle', which means that the two sides agree on a mutually satisfactory arrangement before the matter reaches court. A court case is expensive and in general the losing side will have to pay all the legal costs of both sides. Therefore, if one side believes that it is going to lose a case, then it may be prudent to minimise losses and to agree a settlement that is not compounded by the addition of lawyers' fees.

[9.14] This is not the universal rule, however. Some cases will go to court and if a doctor writes a medico-legal report for a case she may then be called upon as a witness to testify as to the contents of that report; she should therefore never write anything in a report that she would not be happy to stand over in court. Any report should be factual and neutral; a practitioner is not appearing in court or involved in the litigation in order to take one side or the other.[10] It is up to the patient's legal team, not his doctor, to make the case for the plaintiff or defendant. The role of the medical expert witness is therefore to be objective, fair and truthful; only findings of fact and defensible opinions based on those facts[11] should be included in a medico-legal report and expressed in court. The Medical Council affirms this doctrine of neutrality:

> Reports must be factual and true. They are not to be influenced by the fee or by pressure from anyone to omit some details or to embellish others, and strict accuracy must be observed. They should concentrate on the medical problems referred to and omit extraneous details.[12]

---

[9] The author is aware of at least one case in which a medico-legal report implicitly but inadvertently disclosed the fact that, unknown to the doctor, who reported on the consequences of the accident in all innocence from her clinical records, the patient was involved in an extra-marital liaison!

[10] This principle has an ancient lineage: the sixth-century Code of Justinian drew a distinction between medical and other witnesses, expounding the principle, 'Medici non sunt proprie testes, sed majus est judicium quam testimonius'—a medical expert is most useful when assisting the court, rather than her own side, with testimony (para **[1.20]**).

[11] See Law Society of Ireland, Medico-Legal Recommendations (2003), 5:

> 'Solicitors must be careful to avoid influencing the contents of a doctor's medical report (or what evidence the doctor may give in court if he or she is called to give evidence). The doctor has a duty to provide his or her independent medical opinion on the matters the subject of the report. However where there is a manifest error or misunderstanding on the face of the doctor's report, it is proper for the solicitor to bring this to the attention of the doctor.'

[12] *Guide to Ethical Conduct and Behaviour* (6th edn, 2004), para 8.2. Comparable healthcare professional guidelines do not include formal guidance on this issue and it is suggested that the Medical Council code provides a good 'best practice' indicator.

It should be pointed out that any information withheld from a medico-legal report may subsequently be obtained by other parties to the legal action by a court application to 'discover' the original notes (or copies of them). If this occurs, then divergence between the notes made by the doctor and information contained in any medico-legal report is likely to be apparent.

[9.15] While the practitioner will charge a fee for the report,[13] the payment does not or should not sway her from her duty to report on the clinical facts. Also, while the fee charged by the solicitor to her client may be contingent upon a certain outcome ('no win, no fee'), the practitioner is by no means obliged to operate under the same constraints. Payment of the clinician for a medico-legal report in advance is the norm but any consequent failure by the practitioner to furnish a prompt report is frowned upon by the Medical Council;[14] excessive delay in producing a report or outright failure to provide a report at all, even though a fee has been received from the patient or his solicitor, is unethical conduct.[15]

Quick Reference Guide 9.1

Preliminary issues in medico-legal reports

> ❖ A practitioner may be called upon to write a medico-legal report either regarding a patient whom she has treated or as an independent expert concerning a person she has not treated.
>
> ❖ A request for a medico-legal report in respect of a pre-existing patient cannot ordinarily be refused: a patient has a right to pursue legal action and the clinician will generally not be entitled to stand in the way of the exercise of that right.
>
> ❖ The patient's consent to disclosure of the facts necessary for a medico-legal report should be obtained, preferably in writing. The patient should understand what is to be disclosed.
>
> ❖ A charge may be levied for writing a medico-legal report that may be payable in advance. Once payment is made, it is generally regarded as unethical for the practitioner to withhold the report.
>
> ❖ A medico-legal document produced by an expert is expected to be professional and dispassionate, dwelling only on the facts and avoiding any tendency to be economical with information unhelpful to the patient's cause. A practitioner is under no obligation to change a report at the request of a solicitor if to do so would involve compromising her clinical assessment of the patient.

---

[13] The fee will generally be agreed between the Law Society and the relevant body representing the health professional in question (although such arrangements may be subject to Competition Authority scrutiny). In cases where a patient is in receipt of legal aid, the practitioner will be required to fill in the appropriate form in order to claim payment from the Legal Aid Board.

[14] *Guide to Ethical Conduct and Behaviour* (6th edn, 2004), para 8.4.

[15] *Guide to Ethical Conduct and Behaviour* (6th edn, 2004), para 8.3:

> 'Undue delay in furnishing reports may amount to professional misconduct if such a delay results in the patient being disadvantaged. The report should be supplied within two months of the examination or receipt of a written request, whichever occurred last.'

In some States in the USA, a 'licensed physician' may be charged with a criminal offence if she withholds medical records or overcharges for records necessary to advance a legal claim.

The details of a report

[9.16] The purpose of a medico-legal report is to provide clarity about the past, current and expected future health status of the patient with particular reference to the incident that is the subject of the legal dispute.

[9.17] All the information might be readily available to the doctor if she was the one to treat the patient, but she may also require a further opportunity to examine the patient. This may be necessary to clarify certain matters or to verify that certain problems complained of by the patient have resolved (or are persisting). If a doctor is requested by an insurance company or any other party to a legal action to examine a patient who is not usually the practitioner's own patient, to assess the injuries claimed by the patient, then in addition to assessing the patient she will frequently need to seek the treating doctor's records of previous examinations. This is especially relevant where some time may have elapsed since the original incident. A doctor who has treated a patient and who receives a request from the 'other side's' doctor for a report should provide it.[16] A medico-legal report should contain at a minimum certain information, although not necessarily in the order that is set out below:

(a)   Name, date of birth and occupation of the patient;

(b)   The history of the complaint at issue and brief medical background, where appropriate;

(c)   The findings of any examination;

(d)   The results of any further tests or x-rays;

(e)   Diagnosis;

(f)   The likely medical cause or origin of the diagnosis ;

(g)   Any treatment given;

(h)   The course of the complaint following treatment;

(i)   The future likely course of the complaint including any future needs or treatment.

Fleshing out each of these headings gives a clearer indication of why each is necessary in order to produce a rounded report.

(a) Personal details

[9.18] This information provides clarity and context, establishing the identity and something of the nature of the patient who is under discussion in the report. The age of a patient may go some way towards explaining why his injuries are different from those that might normally be expected from the injury in question. Similarly, a patient's occupation is crucial background information; an innocuous-seeming back injury may present no problems in terms of returning to work for a computer operator but may be an insurmountable obstacle to a professional athlete.

---

[16] There has been a tradition among doctors of minimising the information furnished in such circumstances. Such a practice goes against the notion that the doctor is expected to be fair and unbiased in the medico-legal setting.

(b) History

[9.19] The history of the complaint is one of the most important parts of the whole report. Here it is important to recall the role of the person compiling the report—she is not an advocate for the patient; she is there merely to document the medical facts. The details of the incident that led to the injuries should only be dwelt on insofar as they are medically relevant and should not attribute blame; the doctor will not ordinarily have been a witness to the incident. So a medical report that records that 'A was crossing the road when he was struck by a car' is preferable to a report stating that:

> 'A was crossing when a car—whose driver was looking the other way while talking on his mobile —struck him. The tyres on the car were apparently bald and A smelt alcohol on the breath of the driver when he got out of the car.'

The latter version may be true, but only the fact of the collision is relevant for the doctor's purposes.

[9.20] All relevant information should be included and it may be especially important to secure the patient's consent in this regard. If a person has a pre-existing psychiatric history that has been aggravated by the accident, for example, then that context may need to be documented in the medico-legal report. The patient may need to be informed that the practitioner deems it medically relevant to include such information, so that their consent to the release of that information is valid.

Note also that if a practitioner is preparing second or subsequent reports relating to the same incident, it will be helpful to indicate as much and to refer to any prior reports.

(c) Findings of examination

[9.21] The findings of the examination should be documented as minutely and as clearly as possible in clinical records and medico-legal reports. It may be many months before a request arrives for a medico-legal report of an examination and years before the clinician has to testify. The more accurate and comprehensive records are at the time of an examination, the greater one will appreciate it when it comes to writing or justifying a report.[17]

(d) Results

[9.22] Results of tests or x-rays may add to the picture. If they do not, then reference to them in the report can be cursory or absent.

(e) Diagnosis

[9.23] The diagnosis is the clinician's opinion as to the underlying problem giving rise to the patient's complaints. It may be cross-referenced to any background medical history where that has contributed to the diagnosis.

---

[17] Rather than merely describing a complex scar, drawing its extent as well may be a more vivid stimulant to the memory when it comes to reporting upon it or monitoring its recovery subsequently. The quality of the art matters not one bit—all that is important is that it acts as an aide memoire. Photography is a more accurate but more expensive method of achieving the same end.

(f) Medical cause

[9.24] In all legal cases relating to physical or psychiatric injuries arising from negligence, causation is vital.[18] If the accident in question did not cause the injury in question then the person responsible for the accident cannot be responsible for the injury. This is where the professional skill of the person compiling the report may need to be most carefully applied. It is up to the clinician to express an opinion as to whether the complaint is consistent with the incident alleged. It might not be possible to do so in some cases, either because the doctor lacks the expertise to make a causal nexus (as might be the case with a very rare disease) or because there are other possible causes other than the facts of the legal case being reported upon by the doctor.[19] If a doctor cannot offer an opinion, then that should be stated.

Degree of certainty

[9.25] The required standard of proof is also relevant. In a civil (or non-criminal) case, the person making the allegation has to prove on the balance of probabilities that the incident occurred and that the injuries were a result of the incident. The balance of probabilities merely means whether the various elements of the case were more probably than not related.[20] Accordingly, in most legal cases, a medico-legal report will need at the very least to express an opinion as to whether—on the balance of probabilities—the injuries reported were caused by the incident alleged. So, in a medico-legal report for a civil case it is best to couch one's opinion in terms such as 'reasonable clinical probability' or 'likely' or 'probably', all of which terms mean simply that it is more than 50 per cent likely that the clinical findings are related to any given potential cause.

[9.26] In a criminal case, the standard of proof is more onerous—a person alleging a criminal act (generally the prosecutor is the Director of Public Prosecutions) has to prove the allegations against the accused beyond reasonable doubt. In such cases, medical or other evidence will generally need to be couched in such terms. Doctors will rarely (and other healthcare professionals will almost never) be involved in writing reports for criminal cases unless they are specifically employed in a forensic medical role, but the higher standard of proof necessary is something that may need to be borne in mind.

(g) Treatment

[9.27] Details of medical, surgical and other therapy will go to show how extensive has been the need for care. If referral to other clinicians has occurred this should be indicated so that a report can be sought from that other practitioner if appropriate. If the person writing the initial report has enough details from a professional colleague (for example, in letters from a physiotherapist or hospital specialist) then the nature of that colleague's treatment can be included by reference to the letter.

---

[18] See Ch 6 'Negligence' para **[6.36]***ff*.

[19] An example might be a skin reaction that appears following a hair treatment, but where on the same day the patient was also prescribed medication known to cause skin reactions.

[20] Put more simply, whether the chances were more than 50:50. See *Miller v Minister for Pensions* [1947] 2 All ER 372.

The person compiling the report should not hypothesise on the treatment given by someone else unless she has the necessary information (such as a discharge letter) to give that information.

(h) Present and future course of the injury

[9.28] The overall prognosis gives clarity to the legal proceedings. If a doctor's opinion is that a condition has resolved or stabilised, then the legal action may proceed on the basis that future medical uncertainty has been minimised. However, if the condition has not stabilised or resolved then further reports may be necessary.

The language of a medico-legal report

[9.29] Lawyers and healthcare practitioners can each speak a language that outsiders find difficult to understand, but this esoteric jargon is not always helpful to communication between the professions or between the professions and the public. It is preferable that both camps should use unambiguous English when talking to each other, as free of professional jargon and terminology as possible.

The recipient of a legal letter that is shrouded in complicated legal terms should seek clarification of what is required before acting on an interpretation of its contents that may prove to be incorrect. Similarly, a healthcare practitioner providing a report for a solicitor is doing so in order to make matters clearer, to assist the two sides in dispute and, if necessary, to assist the court of law. Complex medical terms may need translation or elucidation, perhaps in a glossary attached to the report or by putting a layman's translation of each medical word in brackets after the word when it first occurs in the text of the report. References to anatomy may usefully be aided by an indication as to where in the body that particular muscle or tendon or nerve is to be found. A medico-legal report will predominantly be read by people who are not versed in medical or paramedical training and it should always be written with this fact in mind.

EXPERT WITNESSES

[9.30] Witnesses are not usually supposed to give opinions; their archetypal role is to give the facts of what they saw, heard or did. It is then up to the judge or the jury to form an opinion based on the evidence that witnesses give. Experts, however, are an exception to this rule. Judges, lawyers and juries do not know everything and sometimes it is necessary to seek the opinion of someone who is an expert in a particular field. In the case of healthcare or clinical issues in particular, expert opinions are often necessary. We have already discussed expert testimony that takes the form of the medico-legal report, whether that report is prepared by someone who was treating the patient or someone who was simply asked to see the patient for the purposes of assessment. Such doctors can then give an expert opinion on what they saw when they examined the patient, together with an expert opinion on prognosis and causation.[21]

[9.31] We turn now to the other type of expert: experts on facts or situations who may or may not have assessed the patient and who have certainly not treated him in the conventional sense. One example is the doctor who is asked to give an opinion on the care provided to a patient in the context of a medical negligence case or on whether a particular act of alleged negligence caused the harm complained of (eg whether a

---

[21] Such witnesses are sometimes called witnesses of primary fact or 'treating' expert witnesses.

delayed delivery caused a plaintiff's cerebral palsy);[22] another example might be the engineer asked to give an opinion on the state of repair of an item of machinery that was involved in an accident. Such witnesses will typically be professional witnesses who were not involved in any aspect of care of a patient and who do not have any prior connection with either party in the legal dispute but who have the qualifications, experience and reputation to be able to comment with authority on what took place. Their role is to offer an outsider's view of the medical facts. Expert witnesses are required in many cases, not only medical ones. Their role is essentially to discuss and explain issues that are not ordinarily within the knowledge of the judge or of either legal team.

[9.32] As far as principles are concerned, the rules for reports offered by external experts are the same as those for reports prepared on the basis of clinical examinations.[23] They should be truthful, unbiased, objective and fair. Of course, because such witnesses are being retained by one side and because their opinions will not be used if they do not advance the case being brought, expert witnesses may appear to be acting as 'hired guns'. Such a perception is often, but not universally, inaccurate. In many cases there will be scope for an honest difference of opinion and expert witnesses are retained precisely to explore that difference of opinion. We will see when we look below at the recommendations of the Woolf Report, that some jurisdictions have begun to wrestle with the perception of the medico-legal hired gun.[24]

Outline of expert report

[9.33] In order to formulate an opinion, an expert will need to have as many details of the case forwarded to her as possible. In general, when a non-treating expert witness is retained to give an opinion, her report may be accompanied by a curriculum vitae indicating why she is qualified to offer the opinion she has compiled. This summary may include posts held, recent publications and a record of relevant previous cases in which the practitioner in question has acted as an expert witness. While there are no specific rules stipulating precisely what a non-treating expert's report to the Irish courts must contain, some guidelines can be derived from England and Wales, where court rules[25] dictate that an expert's report to the court must do the following:

(1)   give details of the expert's qualifications;

(2)   give details of any literature or other material on which the expert has relied in making the report;

(3)   contain a statement setting out the substance of all facts and instructions given to the expert which are material to the opinions expressed in the report or upon which those opinions are based;

(4)   make clear which of the facts stated in the report are within the expert's own knowledge;

---

22   Such a witness might be termed a 'non-treating' expert witness.

23   An expert retained by one side also has the right to consult, where necessary, with medical advisers to another party in the legal action: *McGrory v ESB* [2003] 3 IR 407.

24   See Friston, 'New rules for expert witnesses—the last shots of the medico-legal hired gun' (1999) BMJ; 318:1365–6.

25   See the section on the Woolf Report at para **[9.34]**.

(5)   say who carried out any examination, measurement, test or experiment which the expert has used for the report, give the qualifications of that person, and say whether or not the test or experiment has been carried out under the expert's supervision;

(6)   where there is a range of opinion on the matters dealt with in the report–

    (a)   summarise the range of opinion; and

    (b)   give reasons for her own opinion.

(7)   contain a summary of the conclusions reached;

(8)   if the expert is not able to give his opinion without qualification, state the qualification; and

(9)   contain a statement that the expert understands his duty to the court, and has complied and will continue to comply with that duty.[26]

Two matters are critically important for the expert witness. The first is that she identifies precisely upon what aspect of the legal case her expert opinion is being sought; and secondly, she must be sure that she does in fact possess the necessary expertise to give an authoritative opinion on the matter in question. A court is entitled to reject, or dilute the importance of, the evidence of a witness whom it feels is not sufficiently expert in the field she is testifying about. It may also be that an expert who purports to give evidence in an area in which she is not, in fact, competent may be open to disciplinary or negligence proceedings where that incompetent evidence leads to an adverse outcome.

The Woolf Report (UK) – a way forward for the Republic of Ireland?

[9.34] The Woolf Report[27] took a panoramic view of the problems facing the administration of the civil justice system in England and Wales. One result of the report was the introduction of a new set of rules that made explicit the role of the expert witness as a helper of the court and not of the side by which she is retained. Lord Woolf explicitly criticised the degree to which expert witnesses had become paid advocates for one side or the other. The report resulted in four main changes to the way in which non-treating expert testimony is to be used in the litigation process in England and Wales:

(i)   Clinical experts are to be appointed jointly, by agreement between both sides or by order of the court. As a result, reports are submitted to the court itself and not to the legal representatives of the parties involved in the legal dispute;

---

[26] Civil Procedure Rules Part 35, Practice Direction 35, para 2.2. In the United States, Federal Court Rules lay out the following contents to be included in a non-treating expert witness's report submitted after 1 December 1993:

    (a)   A complete statement of all opinions reached by the expert, together with the reasons for having reached such opinions;

    (b)   Any relevant data or other information considered by the witness in forming the opinions;

    (c)   Any exhibits to be used as a summary of or in support for the opinions;

    (d)   The qualifications and publications of the expert;

    (e)   A declaration of any financial compensation to be paid for preparation, examination and testimony;

    (f)   A list of other cases in which the expert has testified within previous four years.

[27] *Access to Justice: final report to the Lord Chancellor on the civil justice system in England and Wales* (London: HMSO, 1996), 137; also Woolf 'Medics, Lawyers and the Courts' [1997] 16 CJQ 302. See also Friston, 'New rules for expert witnesses—the last shots of the medico-legal hired gun' BMJ 1999; 318:1365–6.

(ii)   The content of clinical reports given to the courts is now standardised (see the sample contents of non-treating experts report set out at para **[9.33]**), including the requirement that experts set out not only their own personal opinion but also that of 'any other recognised body of opinion'. In other words the report must offer not merely the expert's opinion but also the research that both backs up and even undermines her opinion;

(iii)   Expert evidence will only be required where it is necessary to help resolve the issues before the court and most evidence will be provided in writing. Because the expert is appointed by the court or by agreement, there is less likely to be a requirement for lengthy or combative examination of the witness in court; and

(iv)   The court has greater latitude to limit the amount of money paid to an expert witness.

There are neutral expert clinical witnesses in other countries, such as Germany and Greece, while countries such as the Republic of Ireland continue to permit each party to the case to nominate its own experts.

[9.35] There is one exception built into the Woolf Report which is that, in clinical negligence cases, both sides may use their own experts. The reason for this is because of the very nature of professional negligence.[28] One defence to an allegation of professional negligence is that one's actions were in accordance with a reasonable body of clinical opinion, albeit not the majority school of thought. A single neutral expert may have trouble accurately representing both sides of a potentially complex argument and accordingly in such circumstances the parties to the case may introduce their own witnesses to make the arguments for different bodies of opinion.

Quick Reference Guide 9.2

The non-treating expert witness

❖   A non-treating expert witness is one who was not involved in the care of the patient involved in the legal case, but whose expertise is such that she is in a position to offer an opinion on the facts of the case.

❖   In principle, although an expert witness is normally retained by one side or another in the legal dispute, she is under a duty to be impartial and not to advocate for one result or another. The allegation is often made, however, that some expert witnesses are prepared to act as hired guns.

❖   The ideal non-treating witness's report should give not only the qualifications of the expert to offer an opinion and the opinion itself, but should also include details of any schools of thought inconsistent with the expert's opinion.

❖   In England, the Woolf Report has attempted to reduce the adversarial element of expert testimony by introducing a system where there is only a single, court-appointed expert who reviews all sides of the matter in dispute. The only exception to this new rule is in clinical negligence cases. In cases where an expert is appointed, evidence will as far as possible be in writing.

---

[28]   See Ch 6 'Negligence', and in particular para **[6.23]**.

WHAT HAPPENS TO EXPERT/MEDICO-LEGAL REPORTS AFTER THEY ARE PREPARED?

[9.36] Expert reports in all forms of personal injury cases (which form the vast bulk of cases where expert reports are required) are governed by legislation and court practice rules.[29] The rules only apply in personal injury cases, no matter how those personal injuries were caused, and they apply to the reports or statements of 'accountants, actuaries, architects, dentists, doctors, engineers, occupational therapists, psychologists, psychiatrists, scientists, or any other expert whatsoever'.[30] In addition, the rules only apply to cases taking place in the High Court; there is no obligation to exchange expert reports in the Circuit Court or District Court (although exchange of reports – albeit at a late stage in proceedings – is commonplace in the lower courts).

[9.37] The rules oblige the plaintiff's lawyers to send a list of all experts whom it is intended to call as witnesses in court proceedings. Within seven days, the defendant's legal team must reply with its own proposed list of experts. Within one week of that, both sides must exchange any reports received to date from those experts. Any further reports that arise after that time must be exchanged as soon as possible. Once exchanged, the reports provided by one side to the other can be shown to the recipient's expert who can then assess them and may be able to advise on shortcomings in the expert opinion. If one side feels that the other is not complying with its obligations under the rules, it may bring an application to the court to force the other side to comply with SI 391/1998.[31]

[9.38] The timely exchange of expert reports means that the two sides in a legal dispute can maximise the amount of medical evidence before them in order to reach a prompt decision as to whether or not to proceed with the case, to settle it or to abandon it. This can speed up and lessen the cost of litigation by reducing the number of applications that have to be made to the court in order to force disclosure of reports. Similarly, failure to comply with the rules can result in the report that would have been relied on, if it had been exchanged in accordance with the rules, being rendered inadmissible, or even the whole case being struck out by the judge.

[9.39] One problem with SI 391/1998 is that each side has only to disclose the reports of those witnesses whom it intends to call as witnesses to give testimony in the trial. The potential difficulty with this is obvious. Assume a patient is bringing an action against a radiation oncologist for burns sustained during a procedure. The patient is subsequently referred to ten different doctors by his lawyers, and nine of the physicians say that there

---

[29] Rules of the Superior Courts (No 6) (Disclosure of Reports and Statements) 1998 (SI 391/1998).

[30] Rules of the Superior Courts, Order 39, rule 45(1)(e).

[31] See, for example, *Cheryl Doherty v The North Western Health Board and Brian Davidson* [2005] IEHC 404, Finnegan P. In this case, the defendant sought documents from another party that were referred to in reports disclosed under SI 391/1998. The court held that such documents, not being expert reports or other documents described in the statutory instrument, should not be exchanged, although some of them might be sought by way of legal discovery. Conversely, in *David Payne v Philip Shovlin* [2006] 2 ILRM 1, the Supreme Court held that preliminary reports prepared by experts should be disclosed as well as any final report.

is no evidence that the alleged injuries were caused by the negligence, but rather were possibly caused by something else. Only one doctor asserts that the radiologist's actions were to blame. The lawyers decide to call only this last doctor to give oral evidence; according to SI 391/1998 they are obliged only to declare her report, while the nine unfavourable reports may be ignored. It could be argued that it is up to the defendant radiologist's lawyers to have the plaintiff examined and to obtain any reports that may be favourable to the radiologist's side. But it could also be argued that justice is more satisfactorily served if all legal reports obtained for the purpose of legal action in personal injury cases by both sides were subject to disclosure, rather than permitting each side to cherry-pick favourable medical opinions.

THE COURSE OF LEGAL ACTION

The first steps

[9.40] In talking about 'legal action' here, we focus on civil cases, such as injuries resulting from road traffic accidents or claims of negligence or family disputes. There are important differences between civil and criminal procedure, but it is the former type of case that is far more likely to impact on a clinician's work, life and livelihood.

> **Example 9.1**
> A GP prescribes some antibiotics to a patient. She knew, or would have known had she looked at the chart, that the patient was allergic to penicillin, but nonetheless she prescribed penicillin. The patient suffered a massive allergic reaction and as a complication lost his left leg. The patient believes that the doctor was negligent in prescribing the antibiotics.

What happens once an allegation is made?

[9.41] The patient will go to a solicitor. The solicitor will make some inquiries about the facts and commence assembling the necessary material in order to build the case. Among the first things she must do is notify the doctor of the potential legal case, so the solicitor will write to the doctor, notifying her that it is intended to start legal proceedings for negligence.

[9.42] The doctor will contact her insurers or solicitor and they will handle her legal interests from there. If the insurers are contacted, they will take charge of the case and retain solicitors to defend the case on behalf of the doctor. The doctor's solicitors will contact the patient's solicitors with the simple information that they will be acting for the doctor. Until they hear what the patient's solicitors have to say, they will generally say nothing and admit nothing.[32]

Exchange of pleadings

[9.43] In all cases where personal injuries result and where legal action is taken in respect of those personal injuries, the proceedings are initiated by way of Personal

---

[32] At no stage in proceedings does the clinician's duty of care to the patient abate. It may be that mutual trust between practitioner and patient will have broken down to the extent that the patient may go elsewhere for his medical care. Nonetheless, any clinical issues that arise will still have to be dealt with or forwarded to the patient's new practitioner.

Injuries Summons.[33] The Personal Injuries Summons sets out in a prescribed form who is being sued, the basis on which they are being sued, all particulars of negligence that are alleged and the details of all claims for damages.[34] Legal advice will have indicated the likely monetary value of the case and the proceedings will be initiated in the appropriate court.[35] The most senior court in which a case can be initiated is the High Court. In most civil cases there will be no jury.[36] The appropriate summons is issued through the appropriate court office where it is given the number that will identify the case until it is seen through to its conclusion. A summons is 'served' on the defendant, usually by bringing it or posting it to her home or place of business.

[9.44] The doctor's solicitors may first seek further information (called 'particulars') about the claim before responding. However, they will respond with a defence. The defence must be made within a specified time period (although this is often delayed, especially where matters are complex) and legislation relating to personal injuries actions[37] requires the defendant to admit those matters that cannot plausibly be denied (eg in Example 9.1, the fact that the person was a patient of the doctor in question) while allowing the defendant to deny those matters that the defendant requires the plaintiff to prove, eg that the penicillin caused an allergic reaction and that it was the complications of the reaction that led to the patient's long-term harm. The defence may include allegations against the plaintiff. So, it might be that the doctor in Example 9.1 alleges that she did in fact inquire about penicillin allergy before writing the prescription and that the patient denied having any allergy. If this were proven, it might amount to 'contributory negligence' on the part of the patient, which in turn could reduce the doctor's liability.[38]

---

[33] The Civil Liability and Courts Act 2004 introduced this change in the law. Previously personal injuries litigation proceeded by way of a slow two-step process whereby it could be many years before a defendant knew the details of the allegations against him. In cases where (a) liability is admitted by a defendant and (b) there is no issue of medical negligence, such matters can be dealt with by the Personal Injuries Assessment Board (PIAB), created by the Personal Injuries Assessment Board Act 2003.

[34] Cases that are not for personal injuries will have summonses and pleadings in different forms, but they are not relevant for our present purposes.

[35] The various jurisdictions are as follows: the District Court may award financial damages of up to c.€6,350, the Circuit Court up to c.€38,000 and the High Court all sums above this. If a case changes its value (perhaps because a plaintiff's symptoms worsen or persist), agreement can be reached to allow the court to award damages higher than its usual jurisdiction or the case can be sent on for hearing to a higher court.

[36] The only medical matter in which a jury might sit is an allegation of assault or battery arising out of an allegation that a clinician proceeded without proper consent. Such cases are rare: see Ch 4 Consent, para **[4.12]**.

[37] Civil Liability and Courts Act 2004, s 12.

[38] See Ch 6 'Negligence', para **[6.70]**. Note that the plaintiff is also entitled to raise particulars arising out of the defendant's defence and any counterclaim made by the defendant.

Before the trial

[9.45] Following the exchange of pleadings, other issues may arise. Either side may wish to obtain certain documents from the other side (eg the medical records of the plaintiff after his treatment by the defendant doctor)[39] or may need to get more details of the claim that the other side is making. Sometimes these matters can be dealt with relatively amicably, but in other situations court applications (called 'motions') may be necessary to get one party or other to make certain documents available or to answer certain questions.

[9.46] It might be that after the exchange of pleadings one side or the other realises that it has no arguable case. The doctor's solicitors may, on receipt of an expert medical opinion, realise that the doctor's actions were indefensible; conversely, the patient's legal advisers may discover that some other event (such as the care received in hospital, rather than the doctor's prescription—see Example 9.1) was responsible for the patient's injuries. In the first scenario, a settlement may be agreed, while in the second the case may be discontinued.[40] A settlement of the case can occur at any time, right up to the time of the trial. Sometimes settlements are reached during the trial; a particular witness may give a very different testimony to that expected or new evidence may emerge, resulting in a rapid reappraisal by one side of its chances of success, leading in turn to a decision to settle. The bulk of all legal disputes that get as far as a summons being issued will settle without reaching court.[41]

Appearing in court

[9.47] Evidence in a trial is given under oath, which can involve swearing on the appropriate religious text, or making a solemn non-religious affirmation, that the witness will tell the truth. Lying once under oath is the offence of perjury and can be punished by a jail sentence. In general evidence at a trial is given orally, but it may in certain circumstances also be given by means of a sworn statement, called an affidavit. Oral testimony has an advantage in that it is capable of being tested in court by examination and cross-examination; furthermore, the reaction of the witness to any questioning may be informative for a judge or jury.

---

[39] Parties to a legal action may seek 'discovery' of documents held by the other side (and sometimes by parties who are not involved in the legal proceedings). Where the documents are not handed over and a court application is necessary, then the applicant must show the court that the documents are relevant and necessary for the applicant to fight its corner in the legal dispute. Where the court agrees with the applicant, the documents will generally be 'discovered'.

[40] Although a third scenario might be that the plaintiff belatedly realises that both the GP (in prescribing the penicillin) and a hospital (in the care they provided) were both negligent. In this scenario it may be possible for the hospital to be 'joined' as an additional party to the proceedings subject to the usual rules relating to time limits and delay.

[41] In the *IBEC National Survey of Personal Injury Claims 2000*, a survey was conducted of 2,900 claims for personal injuries showing that less than one in ten of the cases that had been finalised had ever gone to a court hearing. In Byrne & McCutcheon, *The Irish Legal System* (4th edn, Tottel Publishing, 2002) the authors suggest that about 85 per cent of personal injury claims never come to court.

[9.48] In general, the side making the allegation goes first in a trial—in a criminal trial that will be the prosecution; in a civil trial, the plaintiff. The lawyer taking the case (typically a barrister) may make opening submissions to the court and takes the court through the evidence of the witnesses. Each witness is called and invited—through questioning by the lawyer—to relate the facts of the case. In general witnesses who are not expert witnesses are not permitted to express opinions and so their testimony will generally be confined to the facts. The initial process of questioning each witness is called examination-in-chief and after it is concluded the barrister for the other side can question the witness in a process known as cross-examination. The purpose of cross-examination is to point out problems or inconsistencies in the testimony given by the witness and to put to the witnesses matters that have been raised or will be raised later by other witnesses. The process can sometimes be hostile and aggressive, depending on the personalities of the barrister and witness in question. Once the plaintiff has called all its witnesses, it is the turn of the defence and the process of examination-in-chief and cross-examination repeats itself for the defence witnesses.

The judge oversees the running of the court and can give guidance and help to the witness if she feels herself overborne or confused. In most civil cases the judge directs proceedings, resolves disputes arising during the trial and reaches the verdict.

Doctor's evidence

[9.49] When a practitioner is called as a witness in a trial, it will generally be as an expert.[42] Before the trial commences, there may be a pre-hearing consultation with the solicitor or barrister. As an expert, the clinician is entitled and expected to express opinions. These opinions, as we have observed already, must be defensible and based on the facts of the case. She will be examined first by the side calling her as a witness and then cross-examined by the other side. A witness may bring contemporaneous notes (ie notes made at the time of the consultations to which her evidence relates) into the box with her in order to refresh her memory. The advice most frequently given to clinicians appearing in court is hackneyed but nonetheless useful—*dress up, speak up and shut up*. Answers should be honest, objective, accurate, within the witness's sphere of competence and to the point.

An obligation to testify?

[9.50] This question arose in an English case,[43] where a police doctor (not the woman's own doctor) examined a woman on foot of her allegations of sexual assault. The doctor made a written record of her findings, which indicated that the woman showed signs of having been sexually assaulted. When the case was listed for trial, the doctor was notified that she would be required as a witness. Four days into the trial, before she was called as a witness, the doctor went on a pre-arranged holiday and indicated that it would

---

[42] Although this may not always be true. The practitioner may herself be the defendant, as in the example of the doctor who inadvertently prescribed penicillin (Example 9.1). In such a scenario, while other doctors may be called as experts, the doctor herself would predominantly be an ordinary witness and would be confined to testifying about the facts of the consultation and its aftermath.

[43] *Re N* [1999] Lloyds L Rep Med 257, but see fn 44.

be at least a week before she could return. The judge refused to adjourn the trial and the case collapsed without the doctor's testimony.

[9.51] The doctor was found guilty of contempt of court and was fined £3000 sterling. However, the woman who had been sexually assaulted also commenced an action against the doctor, claiming that she had failed in her duty of care by not testifying and was responsible for psychiatric complications experienced by the woman following the collapse of the trial. The court decided that the doctor did not owe the woman any duty of care. In the first place, the police doctor was not the woman's own doctor and was therefore only under a duty of care during the examination not to make the patient any worse. The court drew an analogy with the 'passing doctor' who gives assistance at the scene of a road traffic accident. In such a case the doctor would not be under as heavy a duty to the patient as she would be in the ordinary care of a patient during a non-accidental encounter.[44] The matter would have been different if the doctor had been a doctor chosen by the woman or had been the woman's regular GP. Furthermore, as a matter of policy, courts are reluctant to run the risk that professionals will steer clear of being witnesses for fear of being sued by those affected by their testimony (or in this case, lack of testimony).

[9.52] While the 'passing doctor' is not under a duty to testify, the same could not be said either about the patient's own practitioner or a person who was retained and paid as an expert witness—both would be under a duty to attend. The former would be under a duty to attend as part of the patient's care, the latter as a part of the contract she has agreed with the side for whom she is acting as an expert.[45]

---

44 Clarke LJ did also say it was at least arguable that where a forensic medical examiner carries out an examination and discovers that the person being examined has a serious condition which needs immediate treatment, a duty is owed to the examinee to disclose those facts:*Re N* [1999] Lloyds L Rep Med 257 at 263.

45 Where a witness refuses to attend court, it is possible to ask the court to issue a subpoena on the basis that the witness is necessary. Where a subpoena is issued, the witness is under a legal obligation to attend court.

Chapter 10

Law and Mental Health

Introduction

[10.01] This chapter is concerned with the elements of the human mind and the way in which the law regards those elements, especially when there is any deficiency, aberration or dysfunction of mental processes. We consider firstly the law relating to involuntary detention of the psychiatric patient. The chapter also deals with the way in which 'insanity' operates to influence the legal process, both in terms of 'fitness to plead' and as a defence to criminal charges and we note in particular the differences between 'medical' and 'legal' definitions of insanity. We also consider other 'psychiatric defences' to criminal charges, automatism and diminished responsibility.[1]

Finally we look at the question of making a will. A person who makes a will must be of 'sound mind', but what is a sound mind and what questions should the clinician, who will generally, but not universally, be a doctor, ask when assessing a patient's fitness to make his last testament?

Psychiatric detention – the basis

[10.02] The coming into force of the Mental Health Act 2001 profoundly changed the law insofar as it deals with both the voluntary and involuntary patient in a psychiatric hospital. The treatment of psychiatric patients is different from the treatment of those of sound mind because of three factors:

- the nature of their condition is such that it may affect the individual's capacity to reason;
- they may exercise their capacity to reason in a way that is contrary to their own best interests or to the interests of others (eg they may wish to harm themselves or others or may believe that they are not suffering from any illness);
- there are treatments available that can ameliorate the condition of the unwell psychiatric patient and which may enable them to recommence reasoning in an ordered fashion.

These three factors: (i) the nature and presence of a diseased state causing the patient to lack capacity; (ii) the potentially dangerous effects of that diseased state for the patient and/or others; and (iii) the fact of treatability, combine to justify, in the eyes of medical and legal orthodoxy, compulsory detention and treatment in certain limited circumstances, but 'the question is when social control is justified in a psychiatric crisis.'[2] Compulsory

---

[1] The most detailed review of mental health law is contained in O'Neill, *Mental Health Law* (FirstLaw, 2006). Note that the specific issue of consent and mental capacity has been dealt with in Ch 4 'Consent', see para **[4.32]***ff.*

[2] Bartlett, 'The Test of Compulsion in Mental Health Law: Capacity, Therapeutic Benefit and Dangerousness as Possible Criteria', (2003) 11 Med L Rev 3, 325–352.

treatment is clearly an affront to patient autonomy and must therefore be based on sound clinical judgment and subject to close legal scrutiny. Under previous legislation, the Mental Treatment Act 1945, it could be argued that there was insufficient policing of involuntary psychiatric admissions[3] and the Act had been the subject of legal challenges;[4] newer legislation is aimed at ensuring that the powers of detention afforded to doctors are subject to appropriate checks and balances.

Mental Health Act 2001 – an overview[5]

[10.03] The main elements of the Mental Health Act 2001 are concerned with (a) involuntary detention of persons with mental disorder in approved psychiatric centres and (b) mechanisms for assuring standards of mental healthcare. The Act is divided into six parts, but only three are of real concern in the present chapter. After laying out some introductory information, we will review each of the three most significant parts of the Act in turn: involuntary admission of persons to approved centres (Part 2), independent review of detention (Part 3) and consent to treatment (Part 4).[6]

Mental Health Commission

[10.04] The Act brings into being the Mental Health Commission, which has overarching responsibility for mental health treatment in Ireland and its specific functions include:

- appointing members of the Mental Health Tribunals and the panel of psychiatrists who carry out independent second opinion reviews under s 18 of the Act (see para **[10.19]***ff* below;

- arranging the legal aid scheme for patients whose cases are under review;

---

3 In 2002, prior to the coming into force of the Mental Health Act 2001, there were an estimated 2,500 Irish people involuntarily detained under the 1945 Act. This was approximately 75.3 people per 100,000, one of the highest rates in Europe. In England and Wales at that time, the rate was approximately 49 per 100,000 and in Italy 26 per 100,000. See 'New law to cut psychiatric detentions', Irish Times, 17 April 2002. Tribunal hearings aimed at reducing levels of involuntary admissions commenced from 1 November 2006. At the time of writing it is too soon to assess what effect, if any, the advent of tribunals has had on rates of involuntary admission: see Mental Health Commission, *Annual Report 2006* (Dublin, 2007).

4 *Louis Blehein v Minster for Health and Children* [2004] IEHC 374. The defects of the 1945 legislation had long been recognised by the courts: see *RT v Director of Central Mental Hospital* [1995] 2 IR 65 at 81, per Costello P: '... the State has failed adequately to protect the right to liberty of temporary patients [the 1945 Act term for involuntary patients]'. The death knell for the 1945 Act was sounded by the terms of the settlement reached in the case of *Croke v Ireland* (21 December 2000) ECtHR, which undertook to introduce independent review of compulsory detention. The European case arose out of an earlier decision by the Irish Supreme Court that the absence of an independent review of detention did not violate the plaintiff's constitutional rights: *Croke v Smith* [1998] 1 IR 101.

5 What follows is necessarily an overview: for a thorough review of all aspects of the Act, see O'Neill, *Irish Mental Health Law* (FirstLaw, 2005). See also Kennedy *Annotated Mental Health Acts* (Blackhall Publishing, 2007).

6 Part 1 of the Act is concerned with definitions; Part 5 concerns the registration of approved centres; Part 6 relates to miscellaneous provisions.

–   advising the Minister for Health on matters relating to mental health;

–   drawing up codes of practice for the mental health services;

–   approving psychiatric treatment facilities (referred to as 'approved centres'[7] in the Act); and

–   appointing an Inspector of Mental Health Services for the purpose of assessing and approving centres.[8]

[10.05] The Commission comprises 13 members led by a chairperson. The breakdown of membership is as follows:[9]

–   one barrister or solicitor of at least ten years' standing (ministerial appointee);

–   three medical practitioners, at least two of whom are psychiatrists;

–   two psychiatric nurses;

–   one social worker working in the psychiatric arena;

–   one psychologist;

–   one representative of the general public (ministerial appointee);

–   three representatives of voluntary bodies; and

–   one representative of the chief executive officers of the health boards.

Quick Reference Guide 10.1

Psychiatric disorders and the Mental Health Act 2001

❖   Three factors tend to justify the fact that psychiatric patients, unlike any other patients, may be detained against their will in hospital:
    (i)   the nature and presence of a diseased state
    (ii)   the potentially dangerous effects of that diseased state for the patient and/or others; and
    (iii) the fact of treatability of the condition

❖   The Mental Health Act 2001 is born out of a desire to show greater care when depriving a patient of his liberty. Prior to the introduction of the Act, Ireland had one of the highest *per capita* rates of involuntary admission in Europe.

❖   The 2001 Act replaces the Mental Treatment Act 1945 and came into practical effect with the establishment of the Mental Health Commission in April 2002. The Commission has overarching responsibility for mental health treatment in Ireland.

---

7   The Mental Health Commission will maintain a register of approved centres and the period of registration will be three years. The Commission may attach conditions to the registration of specific centres, including the performance of maintenance or refurbishment, and the specification of minimum staffing numbers and/or maximum resident numbers. See Mental Health Act 2001 (Approved Centres) Regulations 2006 (SI 551/2006).

8   Mental Health Act 2001, ss 50–55.

9   Mental Health Act 2001, s 35. Elected public representatives cannot serve on the Commission and, if serving as members of the Commission, must resign on being elected to public office.

Voluntary admissions

[10.06] The Mental Health Act 2001 has little to say on the subject of voluntary patients.[10] It appears from the Act that insofar as voluntary admission and treatment are concerned, no rules over and above the normal common law rules on consent apply.[11] However, there is one important caveat: where a patient has been admitted voluntarily to an approved institution[12] and wishes to leave, he may be detained for up to 24 hours to be examined (by a consultant psychiatrist other than the one who has been caring for him during his voluntary admission) with a view to establishing whether he fulfils the criteria for involuntary admission.[13] If the patient does fulfil the criteria for involuntary detention, then an admission order may be made.

Involuntary admissions

[10.07] Insofar as involuntary admissions are concerned, the watchwords of the new legislation are 'second opinion' and 'independent review'. Under the Act a patient cannot be involuntarily admitted or, having been admitted, be subject to extension of his involuntary detention or certain treatment protocols without the activation of mechanisms designed to ensure that the rights of the patient are safeguarded. However, patients' rights are balanced against recognition of the need to treat those who are a danger to themselves or to others and who will benefit from treatment but who are incapable of consenting to such treatment.

Criteria for admission

[10.08] For a person to be considered for involuntary admission to an approved institution, he must first of all suffer from a mental disorder, which is defined within the Act[14] as being a mental illness,[15] severe dementia[16] or severe intellectual impairment.[17]

---

[10] Mental Health Act 2001, s 29: 'Nothing in this Act shall be construed as preventing a person from being admitted voluntarily to an approved centre for treatment without any application, recommendation or admission order rendering him or her liable to be detained under this Act, or from remaining in an approved centre after he or she has ceased to be so liable to be detained.'

[11] See, generally, Ch 4 Consent.

[12] The term used in the Mental Health Act 2001 to describe any hospital or other setting that has been approved by the Mental Health Commission.

[13] Mental Health Act 2001, ss 24–25. Under the Mental Treatment Act 1945 the patient could be effectively detained for 72 hours during which period his status as a voluntary patient could be reviewed. One possible criticism of the 24-hour period stipulated by the 2001 Act is that it takes no account of and makes no allowance for weekends or other holiday periods.

[14] Mental Health Act 2001, s 3(2).

[15] 'A state of mind of a person which affects a person's thinking, perception, emotion or judgment and which seriously impairs the mental function of the person to the extent that he or she requires care or medical treatment in his or her own interest or in the interest of other persons'.

[16] 'A deterioration of the brain of a person which significantly impairs the intellectual function of the person, thereby affecting thought, comprehension and memory and which includes severe psychiatric or behavioural symptoms such as physical aggression'.

[17] 'Arrested or incomplete development of the mind of a person which includes significant impairment of intelligence and social functioning and abnormally aggressive or seriously irresponsible conduct on the part of the person'.

Secondly, as a result of the mental disorder, the patient must satisfy one of two criteria:[18]

(a)   Because of the illness, disability or dementia, there is a serious likelihood of the person concerned causing immediate and serious harm to himself or herself or to other persons; *or*

(b)   (i)   because of the severity of the illness, disability or dementia, the judgment of the person concerned is so impaired that failure to admit the person to an approved centre would be likely to lead to a serious deterioration in his or her condition or would prevent the administration of appropriate treatment that could be given only by such admission; *and*

        (ii)   the reception, detention and treatment of the person concerned in an approved centre would be likely to benefit or alleviate the condition of that person to a material extent.[19]

[10.09] In other words, where the basis for admission is harm threatened to the patient or to another person, there is no requirement that the condition be one that will benefit from treatment. Where the reason for admission is that the patient's judgment is impaired (such that he cannot appreciate the need for admission), then it is necessary that admission to the approved centre is likely to benefit or alleviate the patient's condition.

[10.10] Any decision to involuntarily admit must be made in the patient's best interests but also with 'due regard for his dignity and autonomy'.[20] The concept of involuntarily admitting someone while at the same time respecting his autonomy is ostensibly a contradiction in terms, but aims to remind the doctor of her duty to give due weight to any wish the patient might express not to be admitted and to consider the alternatives (such as outpatient treatment) or voluntary admission[21] before a decision is taken to override the patient's preference.

Excluded conditions

[10.11] There are three specific diagnoses excluded from the remit of the Act, the first two of which are characterised by the fact that they do not meet the criterion of being likely to benefit from in-patient treatment, while the third exclusion recognises advances made in the clinical understanding of addiction. So a person cannot be admitted where he is solely:[22]

–   suffering from a personality disorder;

–   'socially deviant';[23] or

–   addicted to drugs or intoxicants.

---

[18] Mental Health Act 2001, s 3(1).

[19] This section and its meaning was considered by Charleton J in *TO'D v Kennedy, HSE & the Mental Health Commission* [2007] IEHC 129.

[20] Mental Health Act 2001, s 4.

[21] Note that when a patient is admitted under s 15 of the Mental Health Act 2001, he must be given a notice that includes the information that he 'may be admitted to the approved centre concerned as a voluntary patient if he or she indicates a wish to be so admitted' (s 16(2)(g)) .

[22] Mental Health Act 2001, s 8(2).

[23] Social deviancy is not defined in the Act.

The Act is therefore somewhat more restrictive than its 1945 counterpart in terms of who may be admitted and specifically precludes addicts from forcible detention in a psychiatric institution as well as certain of those who will not clinically benefit from detention. Any person who fulfils any of the three criteria for exclusion from the Act may still be admitted if he is suffering from a mental disorder within the meaning of the Act as well as one of the excluded conditions.

Process of admission: application and recommendation

[10.12] An application[24] for involuntary admission is made to a medical practitioner by the 'applicant', who may be a spouse [25] or relative of the patient, an 'authorised officer'[26] of the health board or a member of the Garda Síochána.[27] Any other person may also be an applicant, but he must be over 18 and must have no financial interest in the detention of the patient. The applicant must have observed the patient within the 48 hours prior to making the application.

[10.13] The doctor to whom an application for admission is made must examine[28] the patient within 24 hours of the application and decide whether to make a recommendation[29] for admission—if she does so, the recommendation for admission remains valid for seven days.[30] The doctor must inform the person of the purpose of the

---

[24] Mental Health Act 2001, s 9 (or in the case of the Garda Síochána, s 12).

[25] Although 'a spouse of a person who is living separately and apart from the person or in respect of whom an application or order has been made under the Domestic Violence Act 1996' cannot make an application for admission.

[26] 'Authorised officer' is not defined in the Act. Note, however, the Mental Health Act 2001 (Authorised Officer) Regulations 2006 (SI 550/2006) which defines an 'authorised officer' as local health manager, general manager, Grade VIII psychiatric nurse, occupational therapist, psychologist or social worker.

[27] Mental Health Act 2001, s 12 deals with the power of the Garda Síochána to detain a person they believe to be suffering from a mental disorder and to make an application to a registered medical practitioner.

[28] An examination is defined in the Mental Health Act 2001 as 'a personal examination carried out by a registered medical practitioner or a consultant psychiatrist of the process and content of thought, the mood and the behaviour of the person concerned'. Historically, a low standard had been accepted by the courts for a psychiatric examination in primary care: *O'Reilly v Moroney* (16 November 1993, unreported) SC. In that case, the doctor, who was not the patient's usual GP, regarded the patient from a distance and did not physically examine her or put any questions to her. He claimed that he was worried that more detailed examination might exacerbate the situation. The majority of the judges in the Supreme Court felt that he had carried out a sufficient examination, the shortcomings of which were cured in any event by the subsequent examination conducted in hospital. Similar logic was applied in *Murphy v Greene* [1990] 2 IR 566 at 581, per McCarthy J:

> When a medical practitioner is called in to deal with a situation such as existed on the night in question the law does not require a standard of precision such as might be appropriate to other aspects of medical practice.

See also *Liam Dervan v Kay Moran and Jacqueline Cahill* (25 June 2002, unreported) HC.

[29] Mental Health Act 2001, s 10.

[30] Mental Health Act 2001, s 10.

examination unless in his or her view the provision of such information might be prejudicial to the person's mental health, well-being or emotional condition.[31] A doctor cannot make a recommendation if she has a financial interest in the centre to which the patient will be admitted, if she is a relative of the patient or if she is also the person making the application for admission. If a doctor refuses to make a recommendation and the applicant seeks a second opinion, the applicant must tell the subsequent doctor of the prior refusal to make a recommendation.[32]

[10.14] Once a recommendation is made for admission, the onus of getting the patient to hospital falls in the first place on the applicant. If the applicant cannot arrange transport, then the doctor who made the recommendation for admission can arrange transport or contact the institution for which the patient is destined and request staff there to arrange transport, with or without the help of the Gardaí. If requested by the doctor who made the initial application for admission to arrange removal of the patient and there is a serious likelihood of the person concerned causing immediate and serious harm to himself or herself or to other persons, the institution, and the Gardaí where requested in turn by the institution, must comply with that request.[33]

Admission and review of detention

[10.15] Once in hospital, the patient must be seen as soon as possible by a consultant psychiatrist[34] and the patient can be detained for up to 24 hours to facilitate that examination on the authority of a consultant or other registered medical practitioner or nurse. In any event, the patient must be assessed by a consultant psychiatrist within that 24-hour window, who must decide whether or not to complete an admission order.[35] The consultant who examines the patient, if satisfied (a) that the patient is suffering from a mental disorder within the meaning of the Act (ie a mental illness, severe dementia or severe intellectual disability) and (b) that the patient fulfils either of the two criteria for

---

[31] The *White Paper on a New Mental Health Act* (Department of Health, 1995), which formed the foundation of the Mental Health Act 2001, recommended that the nature of psychiatric examinations should remain a question of 'professional discretion' (para 3.19).

[32] Mental Health Act 2001, s 11. It has been held (under the provisions of the 1945 Act) that a professional or personal relationship with the applicant will not suffice to disqualify a doctor from making a recommendation: *Liam Dervan v Kay Moran and Jacqueline Cahill* (25 June 2002) HC.

[33] Mental Health Act 2001, s 13. The Gardaí have the right to enter a dwelling and detain and restrain the patient.

[34] Who must be a consultant psychiatrist in the 'approved centre' in question: *WQ v The Mental Health Commission and others* (2007) Irish Times, 9 July (judgment of O'Neill J, 15 May 2007).

[35] Although note the decision of Charleton J in *TO'D v Kennedy, HSE & the Mental Health Commission* [2007] IEHC 129. In that case, the patient was reviewed just outside the 24-hour window; the judge held that the Mental Health Tribunal had the power to correct that error (under s 18 of the Act) where the error 'does not affect the substance of the [detention] order and does not cause an injustice' (at 23):

> I would specifically hold that the purpose of s 18(1) of the Act is to enable the tribunal to affirm the lawfulness of a detention that has become flawed due to the failure to comply with relevant time limits.

involuntary admission, can then make an admission order.[36] A similar mechanism is involved in the process of extending the detention of a patient who is already involuntarily detained in hospital.[37] The initial admission order remains in force for 21 days.

[10.16] Where a patient is a pre-existing voluntary patient but wishes to leave the approved centre, then where he fulfils the criteria for involuntary admission, he may be detained for up to 24 hours to facilitate examination (by a psychiatrist different from the person who has been caring for him during his voluntary admission).[38] Once admitted he may be transferred at his request, or without request, between institutions assuming those in charge of the two institutions agree to the transfer. This includes transfer to a general hospital for medical or surgical treatment. Any proposed transfer to the Central Mental Hospital must be notified to the Mental Health Commission, which will refer the matter to a tribunal.[39]

[10.17] A patient can be given leave of absence when involuntarily detained and may be discharged at any time if recovery has been effected. Following discharge, any proceedings pending before the mental health tribunal will generally be abandoned unless the patient wishes them to continue.[40]

[10.18] Once a patient is admitted to an approved centre, the differences between the 2001 legislation and its predecessor become most apparent. After an order for admission (or renewal of existing involuntary detention) is made, then a copy of the relevant order goes both to the patient and to the Mental Health Commission. The patient's copy of any order must contain the following information:

- the section of the Act under which he is detained (s 14: admission as an involuntary patient; s 15: renewal of existing involuntary detention);
- that the patient is entitled to legal representation and to communicate with the Inspector of Approved Centres;
- a general description of any proposed treatment;
- that the admission or detention of the patient will be reviewed by a mental health tribunal;

---

[36] Mental Health Act 2001, s 14. The consultant cannot make an admission order if she is a spouse or relative of the patient or if she is also the applicant.

[37] Mental Health Act 2001, s 15. Initial detention is for a maximum of 21 days (s 15(1)) which can be extended for periods of between three months (in the first instance) and 12 months (ss 15(2)–(3)). Under the 1945 Act there was a maximum period of involuntary detention of 24 months (see *JH v Russell and HSE and Mental Health Commission* [2007] IEHC 7). Where a detention order is made (extending a prior admission or detention order), it must be made before the expiration of the previous order. Where a patient's lawful period of detention has lapsed, then a renewal of that detention cannot be made (it is to be presumed that a new admission order is the appropriate course of action): see *AM v Kennedy, HSE & Mental Health Tribunal* [2007] IEHC 136.

[38] Mental Health Act 2001, ss 23–24.

[39] Mental Health Act 2001, ss 20–22.

[40] Mental Health Act 2001, s 28.

– that he can appeal to the Circuit Court against any decision of the tribunal to *renew his detention* (but not against a decision to admit him in the first place unless the patient wishes to argue that he is not suffering from a mental disorder); [41] and

– that he can opt to be a voluntary patient if he prefers.[42]

Quick Reference Guide 10.2

Involuntary admission

> ❖ For the purposes of the Act, adults are those over 18. In most other areas of healthcare, one becomes an adult at the age of 16.
>
> ❖ The Mental Health Act applies only to those who suffer from a 'mental disorder', meaning mental illness, severe dementia or significant intellectual disability. Only those who are suffering from such a condition and who are a danger to themselves or to others or those who would deteriorate if not admitted and who will benefit from treatment but are incapable of consenting to such treatment can be involuntarily admitted.
>
> ❖ The Act excludes those with personality disorders, those who are socially deviant and addicts. The UK has introduced draft legislation to bring those with personality disorders back within the remit of its equivalent to the Irish 2001 Act in view of the potential threat such individuals are thought to pose to society.
>
> ❖ When a patient is a candidate for involuntary admission as a psychiatric patient, an application is made to a doctor, usually by a family member, but it may be a Garda, a health board 'authorised officer' or any other person over the age of 18 years.
>
> ❖ Prior to any admission, a patient must be examined and a recommendation made for admission by a doctor.
>
> ❖ The patient, once in hospital, may be detained for up to 24 hours to facilitate examination by a consultant psychiatrist. A similar detention period applies when a patient's period of hospitalisation is being extended or when a patient who was originally admitted voluntarily wishes to leave the hospital.
>
> ❖ If a patient is admitted or his detention period is extended, he is given a written notification of his detention and of his legal rights. The Mental Health Commission is informed of the admission.

Mental Health Tribunals

[10.19] Once the Mental Health Commission receives its copy of an admission or renewal order it will refer the matter to a mental health tribunal and assign a legal representative to the patient (unless the patient wishes to appoint his own). It will also assign another consultant psychiatrist who will examine the patient, review the patient's

---

41 The details of the appeals process against detention are not dealt with in detail here. In certain circumstances of illegal detention (including psychiatric detention) where the matter is urgent and there is no other immediately available avenue, a person may apply under Article 40 of the Constitution to be released: see *Gooden v Waterford Regional Hospital* [2001] IESC 14.

42 Mental Health Act 2001, s 16.

notes, interview the admitting psychiatrist, and report back to the Commission within 21 days.[43] Each tribunal is a three-person board consisting of a lawyer (a barrister/solicitor of seven years' standing), a consultant psychiatrist[44] and a lay member, which considers the medical and legal propriety of admission or renewal of detention. Put at its simplest, the tribunal assesses whether procedural requirements were wholly or largely complied with during the admission or renewal process and whether the patient is in fact ill.[45] If any procedural shortcomings in the admission of the renewal process are such as to cause an injustice or the tribunal does not believe the patient is ill at the time of the tribunal's assessment, it will overturn the order. Where procedural shortcomings are absent or do not cause an injustice in the case and the patient is in fact ill, then the admission (or renewal) order may be affirmed.[46] In reaching this decision, it will take into account the opinion of the Commission-appointed psychiatrist.

[10.20] The tribunal has 21 days from the making of the initial admission order (or renewal order) to review the decision to admit the patient or to renew his detention. However, the time within which a review must take place may be extended by order of the tribunal at the instigation of either the tribunal or the patient in the first instance (for 14 days), with a further extension (again, 14 days) permitted only at the patient's request and where the tribunal believes the further extension to be in the best interests of the patient.[47] When an extension of the period before tribunal review is decided upon, the existing order remains in force until the deferred review date (unless the patient is deemed fit for release from hospital before that date).

[10.21] The tribunal's decision is communicated to the patient, to the Commission and to the psychiatrist who is caring for the patient. The tribunal can direct the patient or any other person to appear before it. Sittings are held in private and the rules for witnesses and legal representatives are similar to those observed in a court. The tribunal also has a role in overseeing treatment: where any psychosurgery is proposed, the consent of a tribunal must be obtained (together with the consent in writing of the patient —see para **[10.23]**).

---

[43] Mental Health Act 2001, s 17.

[44] Who may be a consultant psychiatrist who has retired not more than seven years previously.

[45] Mental Health Act 2001, s 18.

[46] *MD v Clinical Director of St Brendan's Hospital and Gannon* [2007] IEHC 183. This case confirmed that a renewal order may be made before the expiry of any previous order (although it will not take effect until the expiry of the previous order and even then only if the previous order has been affirmed by a tribunal) and that a simple administrative error (in this case notifying the patient incorrectly of the section under which he was detained) will not invalidate the order and such an order may lawfully be affirmed by the tribunal. Upheld by the Supreme Court: [2007] IESC 37.

[47] Mental Health Act 2001, s 18(4). However, there is no discretion to extend retrospectively the maximum time limit laid down in the Act once it has expired: *AMC v St Luke's Hospital, Clonmel* [2007] IEHC 65. In this case no order had been made extending the time for review and the review did not take place within 21 days.

[10.22] A patient can bring an appeal against his *initial* admission to the Circuit Court only on the basis that he is not suffering from a mental disorder and the case will be heard without identifying the patient. The rationale for anonymity is that if it is found that the patient was not suffering from a mental disorder at the time of his admission, there is no reason why he should be potentially stigmatised by having his legal challenge to his detention publicised. Any renewal of existing detention can be appealed to the Circuit Court on the grounds that either the patient is not ill or that proper procedures were not followed.

Quick Reference Guide 10.3

Mental Health Tribunals

❖ The Mental Health Commission appoints a consultant psychiatrist to review the clinical appropriateness of each admission or proposed renewal of detention. The consultant reports in turn to the Mental Health Tribunal who must then review the legal and medical appropriateness of the detention. Strict time limits are in place for the review process.

❖ The Mental Health Tribunal is a three-member panel: a lawyer, a psychiatrist and a lay member.

❖ The role of the tribunal is to rule whether a patient is continuing to suffer from a psychiatric disorder justifying his detention and whether all procedural safeguards have been followed. The tribunal has the power to correct administrative errors in the admission or renewal process, so long as in doing so, no injustice is created for the patient.

❖ Certain forms of treatment, including electroconvulsive therapy and any course of treatment of longer than three months' duration, are subject to review where the patient cannot or does not consent, either by a second psychiatrist or by the Mental Health Tribunal. Psychosurgery may only be performed with the consent of the patient and the Tribunal.

Treatment of the involuntarily detained patient

[10.23] In keeping with general principles of patient autonomy, consent to any treatment in the psychiatric setting must be obtained voluntarily as far as possible. The consultant psychiatrist must ensure that her patient understands the proposed treatment and that the patient has been given sufficient comprehensible information regarding the treatment before consent can be regarded as valid.[48] Consent is required unless the patient cannot or will not consent because of his condition and the consultant psychiatrist caring for the patient is of the opinion that the treatment is necessary, in which case treatment can be given. However, in certain cases the consultant cannot automatically proceed to treatment without consent, notwithstanding that the patient's refusal may be the expression of his psychiatric illness and therefore not a valid refusal of consent. There are three treatment situations where further authority is required for treatment:

- electroconvulsive therapy (ECT): the consent of the patient or the assenting opinion of a second consultant psychiatrist must be obtained;

---

[48] Essentially 'informed consent'—dealt with in greater detail in Ch 4; Mental Health Act 2001, s 56.

- treatment of more than three months' duration: the consent of the patient or the assenting opinion of a second consultant psychiatrist must be obtained;

- psycho-surgery: the consent of the patient *and* a mental health tribunal must be obtained.

Other issues

Age

[10.24] One somewhat surprising definition is that for the purposes of psychiatric treatment a child is any person under 18 years, other than a person who is or has been married.[49] This contrasts markedly and inexplicably with the approach taken in medical and surgical treatment, which is that one becomes an adult at the age of 16 years.[50] Why this different approach has been taken is not clear. Among other anomalies is the fact that a 17-year-old may be able to consent to voluntary treatment in the community just as any other adult would (see the discussion of the power of 16- and 17-year-olds to consent at para **[4.22]**), but once in an approved institution that person is subject to different statutory rules.[51]

[10.25] For children who require involuntary admission, the Health Service Executive or District Court will need to be consulted when a parent is not available who can, or will, consent to admission.[52] Extensions of detention and treatments such as ECT in the case of minors require the sanction of the court.

Restraints and research

[10.26] The Act specifies[53] that a person shall not place a patient in seclusion or apply mechanical means of bodily restraint to the patient unless such seclusion or restraint is determined, in accordance with the rules made by the Mental Health Commission, to be necessary for the purposes of treatment or to prevent the patient from injuring himself or herself or others, and unless the seclusion or restraint complies with such rules.

A person suffering from a mental disorder who has been admitted to an approved centre under the 2001 Act is not permitted be a participant in a clinical trial.[54]

INSANITY AND THE LEGAL PROCESS[55]

[10.27] The mental health of a person is relevant at two stages in the judicial process. The first is at the initial stage and comprises the fitness of the person to offer a plea in the case; the second comes at the end, when a jury may have the option, in a criminal case, of finding an accused 'not guilty by reason of insanity'. We examine each in turn.

---

[49] Mental Health Act 2001, s 2(1).
[50] Non-Fatal Offences Against the Person Act 1997, s 23.
[51] Mental Health Act 2001, s 25.
[52] Mental Health Act 2001, ss 25 and 26.
[53] Mental Health Act 2001, s 69. See Mental Health Commission, *Code of Practice on the Use of Physical Restraint in Approved Centres* -S33(3)/02/2006 (Nov 2006).
[54] Mental Health Act 2001, s 70.
[55] See O'Neill, *Irish Mental Health Law* (FirstLaw, 2005), Ch 7. The historical position, prior to the Criminal Law (Insanity) Act 2006, is extremely well dealt with.

Fitness to plead/fitness to be tried

[10.28] A person who is mentally impaired—whether his impairment is psychiatric or intellectual in origin—may not be able to stand trial if his state of mind is such that he cannot understand the charges or the evidence against him, cannot instruct or comprehend the advice of a legal team or cannot give evidence. The situation has been summed up as follows:

> 'The issue is not merely that it would be unfair to the defendant to continue with the trial once he has been found unfit to plead, or that it would be unsafe to convict someone who cannot plead... but rather that it is in the nature of a criminal trial that the defendant is capable of playing a rational part in the proceedings.'[56]

The question of 'fitness to plead' is couched in terms of 'sanity' and 'insanity', but as with the McNaghten Rules discussed below (in para **[10.32]**), legal insanity can be a different beast to medical insanity; historically, a person could be found unfit to plead for physical, psychiatric or intellectual reasons.[57] A person may also be technically 'unfit' to plead because of a physical handicap or disability such as deafness. In such a case, the court will arrange translation facilities, such as sign language.[58] The question of fitness to plead is nothing to do with whether or not the accused was insane at the time of the act but whether he is sane at the time of trial. The law on 'fitness to be tried' (as it is now termed) was updated and codified by the Criminal Law (Insanity) Act 2006.[59]

Provisions of Criminal Law (Insanity) Act 2006

[10.29] Under the 2006 legislation, at any stage in criminal proceedings and at the instigation of the prosecution, defence or the court, the issue of the accused's fitness to be tried can be raised.[60] A person will be unfit to be tried where, by reason of a mental disorder, [61] he cannot do one or more of the following:

- – plead to the charge;

---

[56] McAuley, *Insanity, Psychiatry and Criminal Responsibility* (Round Hall Press, 1993) 136.

[57] In *R v Governor of Stafford Prison, ex parte Emery* [1909] 2 KB 81, the accused was deaf, mute and illiterate. He was found unfit to plead due to 'insanity'.

[58] A person may also simply *refuse* to say anything in court: in that case, the court will presume a plea of 'not guilty' and proceed accordingly.

[59] There is some academic discussion about whether the standard required to be fit to stand trial should increase with the seriousness of the offence: see for example, Buchanan 'Competency to Stand Trial and the Seriousness of the Charge' (2006) J Am Acad Psychiatry Law 34:4:458–465. The 2006 Act does not make any specific provision relating to this, but clearly a person's capacity to comprehend evidence (one of the reasons why a person may be unfit to plead) may vary with the complexity of the offence with which he is charged.

[60] Criminal Law (Insanity) Act 2006, s 4. It is not clear whether the issue of fitness to be tried can be raised more than once in trial. This might be necessary where a person is initially found fit to be tried only for his mental condition to markedly deteriorate during the trial; see Conway, 'Fitness to Plead in Light of the Criminal Law (Insanity) Bill 2002', (2003) 13 (4) Irish Criminal Law Journal, 6. It has been suggested that where the mental state of an accused is suspect, the court is under a duty to raise the matter: *Leonard v Garavan* [2003] 4 IR 60.

[61] Under the Criminal Law (Insanity) Act 2006, a mental disorder 'includes mental illness, mental disability, dementia or any disease of the mind but does not include intoxication'. (contd/)

- instruct a legal representative;
- in cases where the choice is open to the accused to be tried by jury, elect for a trial by jury;
- make a proper defence;
- in the case of a trial by jury, challenge a juror to whom he or she might wish to object; or
- understand the evidence.

[10.30] Historically, fitness to be tried was usually decided by a jury in a separate hearing to the trial itself; however, under the 2006 Act the matter now falls to be decided by the court.[62] If the person is found fit to be tried, then the trial proceeds. If the accused is found, on the basis of medical evidence from a consultant psychiatrist, to be suffering from a mental disorder within the meaning of the Mental Health Act 2001, the court may commit the accused to a designated centre or direct that the accused undergo out-patient treatment in a designated centre.[63] The 2006 Act is not clear on how a person is to be treated if he is found unfit to be tried because of a mental disorder within the meaning of the 2006 Act but does not have a mental disorder within the meaning of the 2001 Act. Where detention is ordered, it will continue until the accused is found fit be released by the Mental Health (Criminal Law) Review Board.[64] It appears that the court has no statutory power of committal in such cases, notwithstanding that the accused may be suffering from a 'mental disorder' within the meaning of the Criminal Law (Insanity) Act 2006.[65]

---

[61] (\contd) Note that the definition of a 'mental disorder' under the 2006 Act is different from the definition of the same term in the Mental Health Act 2001 (see para **[10.08]** above). Note too that the definition of a mental disorder does not explicitly include conditions such as personality disorder.

[62] In effect the court charged with deciding whether the accused is unfit to be tried is the court in which the offence would be tried. So, a person charged with a serious offence, such as murder, will be sent forward to the Central Criminal Court (the court in which murders are tried) for determination of the issue of fitness to plead, even if the issue of his fitness is raised on the accused's first appearance before a court (which would be in the District Court). An appeal can be taken against any decision that a person is unfit to be tried (or any decision that a person is— or is not—not guilty by reason of insanity): Criminal Law (Insanity) Act 2006, ss 7 and 8. The details of the appeals process lie outside the scope of this chapter.

[63] Criminal Law (Insanity) Act 2006, s 4 (3) and (5). The court in question has the power to commit a person to detention for up to 14 days in a designated centre and to medical examination in that centre in order to determine whether the accused is suffering from a mental disorder within the meaning of the Mental Health Act 2001. A 'designated centre' refers to the Central Mental Hospital or any other 'hospital or in-patient facility' (providing care to persons with a mental disorder within the meaning of the Mental Health Act 2001) that may be designated by the Minister. It may also include a prison.

[64] Created by the Criminal Law (Insanity) Act 2006, s 12 et seq, the board came into being in late 2006 arising out of a challenge to the detention of a person under the Act who could not appeal to the board for a review of his detention (under s 13(8) of the 2006 Act) because the board had not yet been constituted.

[65] Mills, 'Criminal Law (Insanity) Bill 2002: Putting the sanity back into insanity?' (June 2003) *Bar Review* 8(3), 101.

[10.31] If the clinical director of any designated centre forms the opinion that a patient detained as being unfit to be tried is no longer unfit to be tried then he must notify the court that committed the patient of this fact and the court will deal with the matter as it thinks proper (which may include setting the matter down for a new trial). Where the clinical director is of the opinion that a person detained is still unfit for trial, but no longer warrants in-patient treatment, then the matter is referred to the Mental Health (Criminal Law) Review Board—see para **[10.44]** below.

The defence of insanity

[10.32] The insanity defence was for a long time governed by a loose bundle of rules and guidelines such as the McNaghten Rules,[66] which governed patients suffering from 'insane delusions and insane ignorance',[67] together with further modifications made by the courts to allow for defences predicated on physiological (rather than psychiatric) causes of insanity or manifestations of mental illness less florid than common understandings of the word 'insanity', such as irresistible impulse.[68] As with the law on unfitness to be tried, the law on insanity as a defence to criminal charges was codified by the Criminal Law (Insanity) Act 2006. However, before we examine the provisions of that law, it is helpful first to consider the distinction between medical and legal definitions of the word insanity.

Criminal Law (Insanity) Act 2006: not guilty by reason of insanity

[10.33] According to the Criminal Law (Insanity) Act 2006, in order to mount a defence of 'not guilty by reason of insanity' the jury must accept the evidence of at least one consultant psychiatrist that:

(a) the accused person was suffering at the time [of committing the offence] from a mental disorder, and

---

[66] *Daniel McNaghten* [1843] 4 St Tr (ns) 817. McNaghten had killed the Private Secretary to the British Prime Minister, but claimed he was insane. The judge, when directing the jury, told them they need only be concerned about whether the accused could tell the difference between right and wrong as far as the offence he was charged with was concerned. McNaghten was acquitted. It was felt the law on insanity was unclear and hence the Law Lords (the UK's most senior judges) were asked to set out the ground rules for legal insanity. Their conclusions can be summarised as follows:

   1. Every person is presumed to be sane and to possess a sufficient degree of reason to be responsible for his actions until the contrary is proved.
   2. It is a defence to a criminal prosecution if it is established that, at the time of committing an offence:
      (a) The accused was labouring under a defect of reason resulting from a disease of the mind; *and*
      (b) As a result, he either did not know the nature and quality of his act or if he did know the nature and quality of the act, he did not know the act was wrong.

   The use of the term 'disease of the mind' has been interpreted liberally and has encompassed such diagnoses of 'insanity' as low (and high) blood sugar, epilepsy and sleepwalking.

[67] Charleton, McDermott & Bolger, *Criminal Law* (Tottel Publishing, 1999) 1105.

[68] *Doyle v Wicklow County Council* [1974] IR 55, in particular the judgment of Griffin J. This case made clear that while the McNaghten rules apply in Ireland, they are not necessarily the only determinant of whether a person is legally insane.

(b)   the mental disorder was such that the accused person ought not to be held responsible for the act alleged by reason of the fact that he or she—

    (i)   did not know the nature and quality of the act, or

    (ii)   did not know that what he or she was doing was wrong, or

    (iii)   was unable to refrain from committing the act.[69]

A mental disorder is defined in the Act as including 'mental illness, mental disability, dementia or any disease of the mind but does not include intoxication'.[70] It has been observed already that there is a marked difference between the definition of mental disorder in the Criminal Law (Insanity) Act 2006 and the definition in the Mental Health Act 2001. We return below to the practical consequences of this difference when it comes to dealing with the patient who is not guilty by reason of insanity. First, however, we must consider what the law (rather than medicine) means by mental disorder and in particular by the term 'disease of the mind'.

'Mental disorder' and 'disease of the mind'

[10.34] A person accused of a criminal act can offer the defence of insanity, arguing that he was 'insane' at the time the act was committed. If successful in making this argument (or in other words, if the jury believes him), the accused is found 'not guilty by reason of insanity'—he committed the act, but cannot be considered culpable and is not imprisoned for it. But what does insanity mean in this context? Does it refer only to those conditions that the lay-person or the psychiatrist would deem to be insanity, that is to say of psychiatric origin and causing a frank and florid mental derangement? In fact, the legal definition is rather different.

[10.35] Under the 2006 Act, the accused must now be suffering from a 'mental disorder', which 'include[es] mental illness, mental disability, dementia or any disease of the mind but does not include intoxication'. The definitions of dementia, mental illness and mental disability do not present great problems, but the term 'mental disorder' comprehends the idea of 'disease of the mind' and also appeared in the McNaghten Rules.[71] 'Disease of the mind' is a vexed term when it comes to the defence of insanity, but why?

[10.36] Crucial to any understanding, in the present context, of 'insanity' generally and 'diseases of the mind' in particular, is acceptance of the fact that the law takes a different and more utilitarian view of 'insanity' than that generally adopted in the medical setting. There are two reasons for this. One is that while medicine is prepared to accept the shades of grey inherent in the analysis, diagnosis and treatment of the human mind, such a state of affairs is less tolerable to the law. A criminal case seeks to answer a simple binary question: is the accused guilty or not? There are no 'shades' of guilt or innocence, there is only 'guilty' or 'not guilty'.[72] If the accused argues that he was insane when

---

[69]   Criminal Law (Insanity) Act 2006, s 5(1)(a)–(b).

[70]   Note that the definition of a mental disorder, within the 2006 Act does not explicitly include (or exclude) conditions such as personality disorder unlike the Mental Health Act 2001.

[71]   See fn 66.

[72]   There are some jurisdictions, eg Scotland, that allow for the returning of more ambiguous verdicts, such as 'not proven'.

committing his crime, the law needs a categorical legal test by which it can decide whether the accused was insane or not and therefore whether he can be found guilty or not. The second, and perhaps more important, reason for the divergence in understanding of the term 'disease of the mind' is that the court is not only concerned with obtaining one of two binary answers, but it is also charged with discharging certain public policy considerations, including ensuring that those who are not responsible for their actions are not explicitly punished for them, while also guaranteeing that those who require treatment in order to prevent a recurrence of the criminal act are compelled to receive treatment.[73] So conditions that are non-psychiatric in nature (indeed which are wholly medical) but which disturbed cognitive functioning such that they can be termed a 'disease of the mind', have successfully been used as the basis for an insanity defence. Thus, English decisions have recognised causes for 'legal' insanity as diverse as epilepsy,[74] sleepwalking[75] and hyperglycaemia.[76] The legal test for insanity, therefore, is not whether the person was suffering from a psychiatric condition at the time of the offence, but was suffering from any 'internal' condition, arising in the physiology or biochemistry of the person concerned (without external contributing factors, such as intoxication, a blow to the head or taking medication) such as to cause a derangement of thinking sufficient to constitute a 'disease of the mind'.[77] Because the definition used by the courts is a legal one and not a medical one, some people argue that legal insanity is not a diagnosis at all, but an excuse,[78] allowing those who should be held guilty to escape under the guise of 'insanity'.

[10.37] In all such cases, clinical evidence will have a role to play in determining whether the criteria for legal insanity are present,[79] although the jury is the ultimate

---

[73] See *US v Lyons* 731 F 2d 243 (1984): 'what definition of 'mental disease or defect' is to be implied by courts enforcing the criminal law is, in the final analysis, a question of legal, moral and policy—not of medical—judgement.'

[74] *Sullivan* [1984] AC 196. Epilepsy has also been considered a form of automatism in Irish law (see *Ellis v DPP* [1990] 2 IR 291) and may also—in England—amount to diminished responsibility; which defence epilepsy affords seems to depend on the precise clinical manifestation of the condition in the individual concerned.

[75] *Burgess* [1991] 2 QB 92.

[76] *Hennessy* (1989) Cr App R 10. Hyperglycaemia is an abnormally high blood sugar level, commonly found in untreated or under-treated diabetes. Perhaps perversely at first sight, the courts have also held that *hypo*glycaemia following an insulin injection is not a form of insanity, but a form of automatism. The difference between the two cases appears to be the presence of the 'external' element of an injection in the latter (*Quick* [1973] 3 All ER 347). See the discussion of automatism later in the text.

[77] See Ashworth, *Principles of Criminal Law* (2nd edn, Oxford, 1995) 204–206. See also *R v Sullivan* [1983] 2 All ER 673 (HL): the court in that case defined 'mind' as 'the mental faculties of reason, memory and understanding'.

[78] McAuley, *Insanity, Psychiatry and Criminal Responsibility* (Round Hall Press, 1993).

[79] In England, the Criminal Procedure (Insanity and Unfitness to Plead) Act 1991, s 1(2), demands the evidence of at least two doctors, one of whom must be an experienced psychiatrist.

arbiter of whether a person is 'guilty but insane'. Under the Criminal Law (Insanity) Act 2006, in order for the defence to be pleaded, evidence must be given by at least one consultant psychiatrist and no other classes of doctors are listed as being competent to give evidence relating to the defence.[80] This might lead to the inference that only psychiatric disorders will be contemplated as giving rise to the defence, but that might not be the case. Evidence might be given of a condition such as hyperglycaemia and the psychiatrist may then give evidence of the likely effect of that condition on a person's mental state; in such cases, non-psychiatric conditions causing 'diseases of the mind' might still constitute 'insanity' defences.

Effects of the mental disorder

[10.38] We have discussed the distinction between medical and legal definitions of insanity, but what are the other elements of the act? A person must show that he suffers from a mental disorder and that the effect of that disorder was such that he (i) did not know the nature and quality of the act; or (ii) did not know that what he or she was doing was wrong; or (iii) was unable to refrain from committing the act.

Knowing the nature and quality of the Act

[10.39] Legally speaking, to say that someone 'knew the nature and quality of the act' generally means an ability to comprehend the physical, rather than legal or moral, quality of the act, whether or not the accused could assimilate the consequences. In one case, a patient with bipolar affective disorder who was resident in a psychiatric hospital set fire to a wastepaper basket, which in turn caused a more serious conflagration to erupt. Because he could understand that he was setting fire to a basket, he was held to understand the nature and quality of the act, even if he could not necessarily apprehend the likely result of that act.[81] However, other cases have taken a less restrictive approach to 'understanding' the act and have reasoned that the term could imply a more general consideration of whether the accused truly comprehended what he was doing.[82]

Knowing that what one is doing is wrong

[10.40] Conversely, to say that a person did not know that what he was doing was wrong is a criterion more concerned with the state of moral or legal knowledge of the accused. In England and Canada, the test is predominantly whether the accused knew that the act was legally wrong,[83] while in Australia the courts are more concerned with whether the accused knew his acts to be morally wrong.[84] In Ireland, juries have traditionally been told by the judge before they retire to consider their verdict on insanity that they should consider whether a person claiming to be insane knew the act was morally wrong. However, with the passage into law of the Criminal Law (Insanity) Act 2006, the

---

[80] Criminal Law (Insanity) Act 2006, s 5(1).

[81] *Dickie* [1984] 3 All ER 176.

[82] See *Adamcik* [1977] 3 CCC (2d) 1 (BC CC): a Canadian woman robbed a bank to get money to buy a crucifix she believed was being blasphemously displayed in a shop. Even though she certainly knew she was robbing a bank, she was held not to have understood the nature and quality of her act.

[83] *Windle* [1952] 2 All ER.

[84] *Willgloss* [1979] 2 NSWLR 1.

determination of the verdict of 'not guilty by reason of insanity' falls to the judge and it is not clear what test must or will be applied by the courts.

Inability to refrain from committing the Act

[10.41] The inclusion of this element in the 'insanity defence' under the 2006 Act is recognition of the fact that Irish courts had accepted in a number of cases that a person might be able to plead that he had no control over his acts. As the courts have observed, 'irresistible impulse' is:

> ...a limited form of insanity...that means...an irresistible impulse caused by [a mental disorder]. Merely because an impulse is not resisted does not mean that it is an irresistible impulse. If so, no one could ever be convicted of a crime—they would only have to say, "I found the impulse irresistible". It must be an irresistible impulse not an unresisted impulse to constitute that form of insanity.[85]

Consequence of the 'insanity' verdict

[10.42] The exact consequences depend on the court's findings, aided by medical evidence. We have noted already that the definition of a mental disorder under the Criminal Law (Insanity) Act 2006 is different from that under the Mental Health Act 2001. So a person who is found not guilty by reason of insanity as a result of the mental disorder within the meaning of the 2006 Act faces one of two possible consequences. If the condition in question is not a disorder within the meaning of the 2001 Act, it is not clear that the court has any power to detain the person. However, if the mental disorder that constitutes a defence under the 2006 Act is also a mental disorder under the Mental Health Act 2001, then the court has power over the accused. It can:

– commit that person to a specified designated centre for in-patient care or treatment if the person is suffering from a mental disorder (within the meaning of the 2001 Act); or

– commit that person to a specified designated centre for a period of not more than 14 days[86] and direct that during such period he or she be examined by an approved medical officer in order to ascertain whether the person is suffering from a mental disorder within the meaning of the 2001 Act. If medical opinion is affirmative on that question, the court can direct the committal of the person for in-patient care or treatment.

Instead of prison, therefore, the accused who is found not guilty by reason of insanity goes to a 'designated centre' until such time as he may be deemed fit for release by the Mental Health (Criminal Law) Review Board.[87]

---

[85] *People (DDP) v Courtney* (21 July 1994, unreported) CCA. Not every commentator welcomes the advent of 'irresistible impulse' as a defence in Irish law: see McAuley, *Insanity, Psychiatry and Criminal Responsibility* (Round Hall Press, 1993), 61.

[86] This period of detention can be extended by the court after consultation with a consultant psychiatrist for periods that cannot in total exceed six months: Criminal Law Insanity Act 2006, s 5(3)(b).

[87] Criminal Law (Insanity) Act 2006, s 13. Formerly, an application for release from detention for 'criminal insanity' was made to the Minister for Justice. See *John Gallagher v DPP* [1991] ILRM 339. (contd/)

[10.43] Historically, pleading insanity as a defence was a risky strategy. A person convicted of a crime is sentenced to a pre-determined term imposed by the judge, but a person who is found not guilty by reason of insanity is detained until deemed medically fit for release, an open-ended sentence that may long exceed the term that would have been handed down by the court.[88] It is possible that the creation of the Mental Health (Criminal Law) Review Board may serve to reduce the time served by persons committed to detention under the Criminal Law (Insanity) Act 2006.

Mental Health (Criminal Law) Review Board

[10.44] The review board, created by the Criminal Law (Insanity) Act 2006 is charged with reviewing the detention of those who have been committed to detention arising out of the Act because they were:

(a)   either not guilty by reason of insanity or unfit to be tried; and

(b)   found to be suffering from a mental disorder within the meaning of the Mental Health Act 2001 and therefore committed to detention in a designated centre.

The essential functions of the board are to hold hearings on the detention of persons and to ensure that those persons are legally represented at such hearings.[89] It can request the presence of the patient and any other person (and the production of any relevant document) at its hearings and it is an offence not to comply with a request of the review board or to give false evidence before a hearing. The sittings of the review board are held in private.

[10.45] The review board must review the detention of every patient at intervals of not greater than six months. Certain matters may also be referred to the review board, in particular where the clinical director of a designated centre forms the opinion that a

---

[87]   (\contd) This case concerned a man who was detained following a 'guilty but insane' verdict for the murder of his ex-girlfriend and her mother in Sligo. Following his detention he promptly made application for release, claiming that he had recovered from his mental affliction. The Minister considered the application by appointing a series of advisory committees to inquire into Gallagher's mental state. The first two committees recommended continuing detention and their findings were challenged by Gallagher (*Gallagher v The Director of the Central Mental Hospital* (16 December 1994, unreported) HC, but upheld by the courts. A third committee recommended a phased day release programme and that decision was similarly upheld (*Application of Gallagher (No 2)* [1996] 3 IR 10).

[88]   Critics suggest that detention is, in fact, directed as much at punishment as it is at treatment; see McAuley, *Insanity, Psychiatry and Criminal Responsibility* (Round Hall Press, 1993); German & Singer, 'Punishing the Not Guilty: Hospitalisation of Persons Acquitted by Reason of Insanity' (1976) 29 Rutgers LR 1011. It is sometimes observed that the real significance of the insanity plea lay in the time when the penalty for crimes could include execution; better to endure an open-ended incarceration in a mental institution than be killed, ran the logic. In recent years with the abolition of the death penalty, the significance of the insanity plea has diminished, but the plea is nonetheless still raised on occasion.

[89]   Criminal Law (Insanity) Act 2006, ss 11–13. Procedures to be followed by the board are set out at s 12(6). The board must include (a) a lawyer (of 10 years' experience or more) or judge or former judge as chairman; (b) at least one consultant psychiatrist; and (c) such other members as the Minister chooses to appoint (see Schedule 1 of the 2006 Act).

person detained as being unfit to be tried or not guilty by reason of insanity is no longer in need of in-patient treatment. In all such cases, the review board will consider the matter, calling such evidence as it deems necessary, and can:

> make such order as it thinks proper in relation to the patient, whether for further detention, care or treatment in a designated centre or for his or her discharge whether unconditionally or subject to conditions for out-patient treatment or supervision or both.[90]

A detained patient[91] may also apply to have his case reviewed and the review board must, unless satisfied that such a review is not necessary because of any other recent review undertaken in accordance with the 2006 Act, conduct a review as soon as may be.[92] In such cases, the board can direct (in the case of patients detained as being unfit to be tried) that the person be returned to court to be dealt with as the court thinks proper, or (in the case of any detained patient) it can order discharge, whether unconditionally or subject to conditions, or direct out-patient treatment or supervision or both.

Quick Reference Guide 10.4

Legal insanity and fitness to plead

> ❖ A person may be unfit to plead to a criminal charge. Where that occurs, the person cannot stand trial but may be detained and receive treatment until such time as he no longer requires such treatment. The person may be committed for trial at a later date if he becomes fit to stand trial.
>
> ❖ Where a person is found not guilty by reason of insanity, he is not convicted of the offence, but is instead (and where appropriate) committed to an appropriate centre for treatment.
>
> ❖ The law presumes that everyone is sane. It is up to a person making the claim of insanity to prove that claim. It is the jury who decides whether or not the defence of insanity is accepted.
>
> ❖ Legal insanity only applies when a person has a 'mental disorder' that causes a 'defect of reason'. The defect of reason – the 'insanity' – must relate to the act that the person is accused of. The defect of reason must mean *either* that the accused did not understand the 'nature and quality' of his act or did not understand that his act was wrong or was unable to refrain from committing the act.
>
> ❖ A person who is detained as unfit to be tried or as not guilty by reason of insanity is entitled to have his detention reviewed on a regular basis by the Mental Health (Criminal Law) Review Board.

---

[90] Criminal Law (Insanity) Act 2006, s 13(5), (7) and (8)(b).

[91] Or a person detained under s 202 of the Defence Act 1954; a consideration of the military law applications of the Act lies outside the scope of this chapter.

[92] Criminal Law (Insanity) Act 2006, s 13(8).

Diminished responsibility

[10.46] The defence (or, more accurately, partial defence) of diminished responsibility did not exist in Ireland until the enactment of the Criminal Law (Insanity) Act 2006.[93] The four elements of the defence are as follows:

- the accused must be on trial for murder;

- the court or jury has determined that the accused committed the act alleged;

- the court or jury must find that at the time of committing the offence, the accused was suffering from a mental disorder; and

- that the disorder was not such as to justify finding him or her not guilty by reason of insanity, but was such as to diminish substantially his or her responsibility for the act.

In such a scenario the court or jury can then find the person not guilty of murder but instead guilty of manslaughter on the ground of diminished responsibility.

[10.47] The defence of diminished responsibility could be said to be a catch-all, covering the 'margins' of the legal definition of insanity—those who are not suffering from the more serious mental disorder that is necessary for the 'insanity defence' to be activated, but who are nonetheless not wholly responsible for their actions. Conditions that have established the basis for a defence of diminished responsibility have included personality disorders,[94] depression[95] and epilepsy.[96] The voluntary consumption of alcohol leading to a state of intoxication does not amount to diminished responsibility.

Automatism

[10.48] Distinct from the defences of 'insanity' and diminished responsibility is automatism, which is not dealt with by the Criminal Law (Insanity) Act 2006. A person who is not conscious of his actions is in a state of automatism—the actions of the body are done without any control by the mind.[97] In contrast to the 'insanity' defence which, as we have observed (see para **[10.36]**), is required to be 'internal' in nature, automatism is confined to conduct arising from external factors, eg an insulin injection causing hypoglycaemia.[98]

---

[93] Although it was recommended as long ago as 1978: *Treatment and Care of Persons Suffering from Mental Disorder who Appear before the Court on Criminal Charges*, 3rd Interim Report of the Inter-Departmental Committee on Mentally Ill and Maladjusted Persons (Government Publications).

[94] *Turnball* (1977) 65 Cr App R.

[95] *Ford* [1972] QWN 5.

[96] *Price* [1963] 2 QB 1. Epilepsy—as we have seen—has also been held to fulfil the criteria for insanity and for automatism. Which defence will be raised—whether insanity, automatism or diminished responsibility—on the basis of the accused suffering from epilepsy will probably depend on the precise clinical manifestation of epilepsy in the individual.

[97] *Bratty v Attorney General for Northern Ireland* [1963] AC 386.

[98] *Quick* [1973] QB 910. As we have noted above, the situation where *hyper*glycaemia caused by untreated diabetes is 'insanity' (it is a purely internal factor, although it can be caused by the failure to eat or take insulin, both 'external' factors), while *hypo*glycaemia caused by an insulin injection is 'automatism' is somewhat counter-intuitive.

Traditionally, the ingestion of alcohol was not permitted as grounds for automatism, but that has been thrown into doubt by cases suggesting that, in very rare circumstances, the imbibing of excessive alcohol can lead to a state of automatism.[99] It must be stressed that the circumstances in which the so-called 'drunk's defence' will arise are rare and, in general, where a person deliberately and recklessly brings about the situation in which his automatism arises (for example by drinking to excess), he cannot rely on his intoxication as the basis of a defence. Only if the consequences of his actions are especially unpredictable (such as an extreme physiological and/or emotional reaction to a demonstrably moderate intake of alcohol) might the defence be sustainable.

[10.49] The ups and downs of life, such as the ending of a relationship or dismissal from employment, will not generally ground a defence of automatism, but severe psychological trauma, eg in the context of ongoing domestic violence or post-traumatic stress, may do so. This will generally only be permitted where the person suffering the trauma takes a 'snap' decision to attack or kill a persecutor.[100] Evidence of planning or of acting in a controlled manner prior to the murder will tend to defeat a claim that such a form of automatism was present.[101]

TESTAMENTARY CAPACITY (THE MENTAL CAPACITY TO MAKE A WILL)

[10.50] A will is a very important document[102] and the law takes the giving away (or 'disposing') of property very seriously and will carefully scrutinise transactions that involve personal property changing hands. There are two indispensable precursors to

---

[99] (2002) Irish Times, 17 May, 'Suspended sentence for man who killed baby'; (2002) Irish Times, 6 April, 'REM man beats air rage charges'. In each case, the accused argued that he had experienced a severe and unforeseeable reaction to a mixture of substances (poitín, beer and cider in the former case; sleeping tablets and alcohol in the latter). A similar result occurred in the Canadian case of *Vickberg* (1998) 16 CR (5th) 164, where a combination of psychotropic medication and alcohol induced a state of automatism.

[100] *Falconer* (1989) 46 A Crim R 83.

[101] For example in *The People (DPP) v Courtney* (21 July 1994, unreported) CCA, the accused claimed automatism as a result of his traumatic experiences as a soldier in Lebanon. The fact that he had driven his victim to a secluded spot before killing her tended to suggest that he was not acting in a state of automatism.

[102] The steps involved in 'executing' a will are relatively simple in principle. The will is drawn up, usually by giving instructions to a solicitor although it may be drafted by anyone. The document identifies the property of the person in question and to whom he wishes it to be given. A will must be in writing. It must be signed, although the signature can take the form of almost any written mark. The signing of the will must be witnessed by at least two witnesses, who must also sign. A will may later be altered or revoked. When a will is made, the property left in the will is known as the 'estate' of the deceased. The person responsible for distributing the estate is a 'personal representative', either an 'executor' (appointed in the will) or an administrator (appointed by the court). The personal representative is appointed once the will is 'proved' or 'admitted to probate' in court—generally an administrative step in non-contentious wills, but where there is a dispute as to the will there may be a legal challenge to it. Once the will is admitted to probate, the executors pay all the deceased's outstanding debts, before distributing the rest in accordance with the terms of the will.

making a valid will and even if all other legal formalities are complied with, no will is valid unless:

- the testator (the person making the will; testatrix if she is female) is either over 18 or married;[103] and

- the testator is of sound mind.

It is this second fundamental principle that forms the subject-matter of much that follows: what is a 'sound mind' when it comes to writing a will? When a doctor is asked to certify that a patient has the capacity to make a will, what should she look for?

[10.51] There are two useful starting points. First, it should be noted that the law presumes everyone is sane (and therefore capable of making a will) until the opposite is proven. Secondly, the testator needs only to have sufficient mental capacity at the time he is making the will.[104] Accordingly, it makes no difference if a patient makes a will having only just recovered from a period of mental incapacity, or succumbs to some form of mental incapacity as soon as he has drawn up and signed his will, so long as he possessed a sound mind at the time of making the will. The same principle applies to any later additions (called 'codicils') or alterations or revocations of wills. So a person who makes a valid will, only to develop a condition amounting to an 'unsound mind', will be unable, while of unsound mind, to make any changes to the original will.

[10.52] It is ideally the case that the testator should be of sound mind both at the time of giving instructions about what the will should contain (usually to a solicitor) and when he later signs the will. The law, however, seems happy to separate making a will into two steps: a person who is competent when giving instructions to the person drawing up the document will generally be held to have made a valid will even if some event intervenes that affects his capacity before he can sign it.

Case Study 10.1

In one case,[105] a man had his will drawn up by a friend, but before he could sign it he suffered a stroke that left him unable to speak. The will was read out to him in hospital. After each part, the patient agreed by nodding and then signed the will with an 'X'. The court held that this was a valid will, despite the patient being unable to articulate his wishes prior to signing and despite medical opinion that he was not mentally competent at the time of signing. The crux was that there was evidence from witnesses that the will was wholly in accordance with the deceased's wishes and with the instructions he had given when he did possess the necessary mental capacity.

If a person wishes to challenge a will on the basis that the testator was not of sound mind at the time of making the will, then the onus of proving lack of capacity is generally on

---

[103] Succession Act 1965, s 77.

[104] *Re JR* [1993] ILRM 657.

[105] *Re Glynn* [1990] 2 IR 326. See also the rule in *Parker v Felgate* (1888) 8 PD 171. A similar rule has been applied in the case of a person drawing up his own will and deteriorating and dying before he could sign it: *In the Estate of Wallace: Solicitor of the Duchy of Cornwall v Batten* [1952] TLR 925.

the person making that allegation.[106] A doctor who is asked to assess a patient's competence to make a will should bear in mind that the will may later be challenged and should therefore carefully document any decision taken and the basis upon which the decision was taken

What constitutes a 'sound mind'?

[10.53] A sound mind is similar to the concept of 'capacity' encountered in the context of consent to medical treatment[107] and is a highly individualised matter. There is no fixed diagnosis or exhaustive list of symptoms to which the clinician can refer in order to decide categorically on the soundness of mind of a patient; rather there are degrees of judgment and common sense involved. Testamentary capacity disappears somewhere along a spectrum between obvious capacity and manifest incapacity but where precisely the transition occurs is uncertain. In the politically incorrect but evocative language of the time, one judge summarised the problem:

> There is no difficulty in the case of a raving madman, or a drivelling idiot, in saying that he is not a person capable of disposing of property; but between such an extreme case and that of a man of perfectly vigorous understanding, there is every shade of intellect, every degree of mental incapacity. There is no possibility of mistaking midnight for noon, but at what precise moment twilight becomes darkness is hard to determine.[108]

[10.54] In general the mental standard for disposing of one's worldly goods in a will is a relatively high one; in one case, a person was held to have the necessary mental capacity to consent to getting married, but not—on the very same day—to make a will.[109] Judges have tied themselves into knots attempting to define the phrase 'sound mind', with the word 'mind' causing especial problems; one judge sub-divided mental functioning into the distinct elements of 'mind, memory, understanding, thought, judgement and reflection'[110] in a misguided attempt to bring some clarity to affairs. Courts have recognised that the mind need only be defective in one respect for it to be unsound, but they have also concluded that the defect in question must go the very root of the person's ability to make a reasoned decision how to dispose of his property. So, the presence of any mental impairment is only relevant if it has a bearing on the will.[111] Ultimately, the approach taken by the courts is similar to the 'capacity' approach mentioned in the chapter on consent to medical treatment[112]—there is no automatic presumption that a person is automatically unfit to make a will merely because he suffers from mental illness or organic deterioration of the brain. Instead, each individual must be considered

---

[106] *Blackhall v Blackhall* (28 June 1996, unreported) HC. On the other hand, if a person is known to have suffered from an illness affecting mental capacity and a suggestion is made that the will was made during a 'lucid interval' (see below), then the person claiming the existence of a lucid interval will have to prove the truth of that claim.

[107] See Ch 4.

[108] *Boyse v Rossborough* 6 HLC 1 at 45, per Cranworth LJ.

[109] *Re Park* [1954] P 112 at 136.

[110] *In the Estate of Bellis, Polson v Parrott* 45 TLR 452.

[111] *Banks v Goodfellow* [1870] QB 549 at 559 per Cockburn CJ.

[112] See Ch 4 'Consent'.

separately and courts have tended to look at the precise details of the individual's mental capacity, rather than the general category into which the testator fits. Essentially, the testator must be '...able to appreciate his position; he must be able to appreciate his property, to form a judgement with respect to the parties whom he chooses to benefit by it after his death...'[113]

[10.55] Mere perversity in the testator is not enough; sociopathic or personality disorders that cause the testator to behave in a perverse manner, for example by precluding his family from the will, do not necessarily amount to unsoundness of mind.[114] Considerations of mental capacity are concerned therefore not with the nature of the decisions themselves (although in some cases, decisions made by a testator might be indicative of failing cognitive powers, eg proposing to leave one's worldly goods to a long-deceased family member) but with the thought processes that underpin the decision; a finding of a lack of capacity will generally only arise in the presence of some form of organic or psychiatric disease. The doctor therefore has to decide not only whether a person is suffering from a disease that might cause an unsound mind, but also whether that condition is such as to impair the person's capacity to make a will. The essential questions are:

- Does the patient understand the general nature and effect of a will?[115]
- Does the patient know the extent of the assets to be distributed in the will?[116]

---

[113] *Sefton v Hopwood* 1 Fos & F 578.

[114] Part IX of the Succession Act 1965 (s 117) affords the family of the deceased protection from being cut out of wills, whether motivated by malice or by unsound mind. The spouse of the deceased has a claim on the property of the deceased, while children of the deceased have a right to be provided for by the courts out of the deceased's property in circumstances where the deceased has failed in his 'moral duty' to do so in the will. In the case of *Bird v Luckie* (1850) 8 Hare 301, the court observed that there is no requirement that the person behaves 'in such a manner as to deserve approbation from the prudent, the wise or the good'.

[115] The important elements to be understood are set out in *Assessment of Mental Capacity— Guidance for Doctors and Lawyers* (2nd edn, London: BMA, 2004), 66: in terms of the nature of the will the patient should understand that (i) he will die; (ii) the will will come into effect on the patient's death and not before; and (iii) he can change or revoke the will at any time, providing he has the capacity to do so. In terms of the effect of making a will, the person should understand (and where necessary, make choices relating to): (i) appointing an executor; (ii) whether gifts are outright or conditional; (iii) that property disposed of or money spent during his remaining lifetime might have an effect on what is left in the will; (iv) that a beneficiary might die before him; (v) that the new will displaces any previous will. The Law Reform Commission *Consultation Paper on Law and the Elderly* (LRC CP 23–2003) stated (at para 2.37) that '[g]uidelines on the assessment of testamentary capacity should be drawn up by the Law Society and the Medical Council for the assistance of both solicitors and medical practitioners. This has not occurred.

[116] The test of whether a patient knows the extent of his assets may not be so strictly applied in cases where the estate is exceptionally large and where it would be an extreme feat of memory to recall its exact details: *In the Estate of Agnes Blackhall, dec'd* (28 June 1996, unreported) HC, (1 April 1998, unreported) SC.

- Is the patient able to bring to mind the people (be they family members or others) who should be considered as beneficiaries of the will?

A court, in keeping with the presumption of sanity, will generally presume a testator to have been competent to make the will unless that presumption is contradicted by 'firm medical evidence by a doctor in a position to assess the testator's mental capacity'.[117]

Psychiatric conditions and the unsound mind

[10.56] Psychiatric conditions are therefore not automatically a bar to making a will. The sole issue arising with a patient's psychiatric condition is whether it affects the making of a will. If it does, then the will cannot be valid. In certain circumstances, where only one portion of a will is affected by a psychiatric condition which operates to undermine the testator's capacity, then that portion may be struck out where it is possible to do so, with the remainder left intact.[118]

[10.57] Alcoholism is not automatically a bar to a valid will, but acute intoxication or acute alcohol withdrawal at the time of drawing up the will or instructing a solicitor would probably render the will void. Similarly, brain damage caused by chronic alcohol abuse, such as Korsakoff's syndrome, could bring with it a lack of capacity.

Cognitive impairment and the unsound mind

[10.58] There are many facets to cognitive function and impairment of any one element will not necessarily destroy testamentary capacity, so long as it does not affect the ability to understand the issues involved in making a will. Simple failures of memory, occasioned either by the great size of the property to be dealt with[119] or by a minor slip in recall will not void a will.

[10.59] Cognitive impairment can generally be assessed either by the clinician's knowledge of the patient or preferably more formally by using an objective test, such as the Mini-Mental State Examination.[120] Such tests record the cognitive state of the patient as a numerical result based on the answers to a series of questions relating to the orientation of the patient in place, time and person, his memory, and his ability to comprehend and carry out instructions. If a general practitioner conducts such a test and the result is borderline, then repeating the test or referral to a specialist in psychology or medicine or psychiatry of the elderly, may be the appropriate course to take.

---

[117] *Re Corboy* [1969] IR 148 at 167 per Budd J.

[118] In *Bohrmann* [1938] 1 All ER 271, an English man suffered from a delusion that the local council was persecuting him and for that reason made a codicil (addition) to his will that substituted US charities for the English charities originally specified. Because the man's delusions led him to this conclusion, the codicil was struck out and the rest of the will was valid. Even though he suffered from schizophrenic delusions, the delusions did not affect the rest of his will, save for that single portion.

[119] *Estate of Agnes Blackhall, dec'd* (28 June 1996, unreported) HC, (1 April 1998, unreported) SC.

[120] There are many such tests. One such is contained in Folstein, J Psychiatric Research *(1975)* 12:189–198. The lower the score, the more likely the patient is to be demented.

Lucid intervals and the unsound mind

[10.60] Many conditions, psychiatric as well as physical, follow a pattern of remissions and relapses where the condition improves for a time, followed by a return to the status quo. Alzheimer's disease is an example of an organic condition that can evidence such fluctuations in mental capacity, while many psychiatric conditions have a similar course. A will made during a so-called 'lucid interval' will be valid, but it is necessary when a patient is known to suffer from a disorder likely to have had a bearing on testamentary capacity, to prove that the lucid interval was in fact present on the occasion when the will was made.[121] In other words, the normal pattern of presumption is reversed and a doctor called upon to certify a patient during a 'lucid interval' should record the absence of those symptoms that would otherwise render the will invalid. A patient who normally suffers from delusions should be thoroughly questioned to ensure the absence of any delusions relating to the will or to establish the presence of insight into his condition (when a patient has insight into the facts of his condition, the courts can take that insight as evidence of a sufficient recovery).[122] A patient suffering from cognitive impairment will require a test of cognitive function to verify that his comprehension and reasoning faculties are, on the occasion in question, sufficient for him to instruct a solicitor and to sign a will.

The doctor's role summarised

[10.61] When a doctor is called to see a patient with a view to assessing his capacity to make a will, then she must bear in mind three critical areas of enquiry:[123]

   i.   defining the diagnosis;

   ii. quantifying any resultant disability;

   iii. interpreting how the disability affects the making of a will.

It may often be wise to assess a patient on more than one occasion if in doubt, or to consider referral to a colleague more experienced in the assessment of capacity. The patient should understand the reason for the examination so that consent to it is validly obtained.

[10.62] Background information may also need to be brought to bear on the examination. In this respect, the patient's own doctor can often be the best person to conduct an examination; she is likely, not only to know the patient, but also to have an appreciation of the patient's broader social and financial circumstances, both of which are potentially important factors in assessing whether the patient appreciates what is involved in making his will. Where a doctor is not the patient's own clinician, she should consider informing herself about such matters (perhaps from more than one source to avoid being misled), as well as familiarising herself with the clinical history, before

---

[121] *Cartwright v Cartwright* (1793) 1 Phillim 100. When the testator was known to suffer from a condition that affected his capacity, it is up to the person who claims that a will was made during a period of recovery to prove that allegation.

[122] *Re Dyce Sombre* 1 M'N&G 116, per Cottenham LJ.

[123] See also *Assessment of Mental Capacity—Guidance for Doctors and* Lawyers (2nd edn, London: BMA, 2004).

assessing the patient. Where information comes from a person with an interest in the outcome of the assessment, it may need to be treated with caution.[124]

[10.63] Attempts should also be made to maximise the patient's testamentary capacity so that he is not seen in circumstances unrepresentative of his general mental state. Steps that can be taken include the following:

– treat underlying conditions that may impair soundness of mind, such as infections and depression;

– recognise that a patient's mental powers may fluctuate and that any impairment may be temporary—delaying or repeating an assessment may be appropriate;

– consider that apparent deficiencies in mental functioning may in fact be deficiencies in the power of communication, such as dysphasia[125] after a stroke, and attempt to overcome those hurdles;

– conduct the assessment, where possible in circumstances and surroundings where the patient feels most comfortable—consider whether the presence of a third party might help or hinder matters.

In circumstances where the doctor is happy that a patient is fit to make a will, she may be required to confirm the fact not only in her medical notes, but generally also by acting as a witness to the will. Whatever opinion the doctor reaches, then she should record her opinion in her medical notes together with the reasons for reaching that conclusion.[126]

[10.64] If a will is later challenged, then the doctor may have a role in testifying as to the patient's testamentary capacity. This may take the form of a sworn statement (an affidavit) concerning the clinical facts or it may involve a court appearance as a witness. In any situation when reporting her deceased patient's testamentary capacity, the doctor owes a duty of impartiality in reporting clinical facts. She should also as far as possible respect confidentiality, respect for which, according to the Medical Council's *Guide to Ethical Conduct and Behaviour*, is a professional obligation extending beyond the grave.[127]

---

[124] A doctor may wish to disqualify herself from conducting such an assessment where she knows she is likely to be a beneficiary in the will of the patient being assessed.

[125] The loss or impairment of the power of speech.

[126] *Duffy v Duffy* (10 August 1994, unreported) HC; *Kenward v Adams* [1975] CLY 3591; *Re Simpson* (1977) 121 SJ 224. The importance of medical evidence in such cases is sometimes referred to as the 'golden rule': see *Assessment of Mental Capacity—Guidance for Doctors and Lawyers* (2nd edn, London: BMA, 2004); the book also contains (at appendix G) a helpful template letter of instruction for solicitors to send to a GP requesting an assessment of a patient's mental capacity prior to making a will.

[127] *Guide to Ethical Conduct and Behaviour* (6th edn, Dublin, 2007), para 19.1. See Ch 3 'The Practitioner–Patient Relationship and Confidentiality', for a discussion of whether confidentiality does in fact the death of a patient.

Table 10.1 A Suggested Checklist for the Medical Certification
of Testamentary Capacity

–   Not every condition that affects the mind will necessarily mean that a patient cannot make a will, nor will every irrational decision regarding a will indicate an unsound mind or lack of capacity.

–   The key is that any deficit must go to the heart of the ability to make a will; define the diagnosis, quantify resultant disability and interpret how the disability could affect the making of the will.

–   Ask whether the patient suffers from any psychiatric condition, organic brain disease or any other cognitive impairment unrelated to a specific psychiatric or organic disease.

–   If the patient does suffer from a psychiatric or cognitive impairment, does it result in a situation where the patient is unable to appreciate any or all of the following:

–   the general nature and effect of a will (or of a change to a will)?

–   the approximate extent of the assets covered by the will?

–   the people (family or others) who should be named as likely beneficiaries of the will?

–   Both elements— an unsound mind and the operation of that defect on testamentary capacity —must be present for the person to lack testamentary capacity. It may be wise to examine a borderline patient on more than one occasion or to enlist outside help in cases of uncertainty.

–   All the necessary clinical and non-clinical information should be in place to allow the doctor, especially if she is not familiar with the patient, to assess the patient and his circumstances.

–   Take steps to maximise the potential of the person being assessed. Such steps may include: treating underlying conditions; deferring or repeating the examination; overcoming communication difficulties and conducting the examination in the most comforting, familiar and secure (for the patient) environment possible.

Chapter 11

The Extremes of Life I: The Beginning

INTRODUCTION

[11.01] This chapter and the one that follows are about those who are at either extreme of being: in this chapter we look at issues that arise in relation to existence before, during and immediately after time spent in the womb. In the next chapter, we consider those issues that arise at the end of life. The two particular areas of focus in this chapter are abortion and assisted human reproduction, both of which (as will be seen) exist in something of a vacuum in Ireland insofar as legislation is concerned. We also examine the law on infanticide, which was belatedly brought up to date by the Criminal Law (Insanity) Act 2006.

ABORTION IN IRELAND

[11.02] In the sections that follow we look, in chronological fashion, at the processes that led to the modern Irish position on abortion, before examining the current Irish position.

The evolution of current Irish law on abortion

[11.03] Abortion in Ireland is covered by legislation that pre-dates the foundation of the State: the Offences Against the Person Act 1861. The Act sets out the following crimes relating to abortion and the maximum sentences (in brackets) that may be imposed on those found guilty of such crimes:[1]

- performing or procuring an abortion (life imprisonment);

- providing the equipment or 'poison or other noxious thing' used to perform an abortion (five years);

- concealing the death of a child, whether it died before, during or after birth (two years).

[11.04] In England the legal position under the Offences Against the Person Act 1861, before laws were enacted to permit abortion on specified grounds,[2] evolved to reach a position whereby a doctor could justify performing an abortion, notwithstanding the ban imposed by the Act, if the termination of pregnancy was being performed in order to protect the physical and mental well-being of the pregnant woman in question.[3] In other

---

[1] Offences Against the Person Act 1861, ss 58–60.

[2] Abortion Act 1967.

[3] *R v Bourne* [1939] 1 QB 687, per Naghten J:

> If the doctor is of the opinion on reasonable grounds and with adequate knowledge, that the probable consequence of the continuance of the pregnancy will be to make the woman a physical or mental wreck, the jury are quite entitled to take the view that the doctor who, under those circumstances and in that honest belief, operates, is operating for the purpose of preserving the life of the mother. (contd/)

words, abortion remained illegal, but a doctor would have a defence if she could show that the abortion was necessary to safeguard the life or health (whether physical or mental) of the mother. As we will observe below, the effect of the *X* case[4] judgment in Ireland is somewhat similar in nature.

1983 Referendum

[11.05] There was no tendency towards, or enthusiasm for, altering the law on abortion in Ireland along the lines elucidated in the English case of *R v Bourne*.[5] Indeed, the Eighth Amendment to the Constitution, passed in 1983, was thought to have copper-fastened the prohibition against abortion. By placing a constitutional guarantee on the life of the unborn, it was anticipated that only by a further countermanding constitutional amendment could that guarantee ever be threatened in any way.[6] The net result of the 1983 referendum was to insert the following into the Irish Constitution:

> The State acknowledges the right to life of the unborn and, with due regard to the equal right to life of the mother, guarantees in its laws to respect, and, as far as practicable, by its laws to defend and vindicate that right.[7]

[11.06] However, there was a problem: no law was ever introduced to explain precisely what this constitutional amendment meant and, in particular, to clarify exactly what was implied by 'the equal right to life of the mother'. The Supreme Court further determined in 1988 that the provision of information to women who proposed travelling to Britain for an abortion was illegal.[8] Thus, it was widely presumed that the net effect of the Eighth Amendment was to make abortion definitively illegal in Ireland. When it fell to the Supreme Court to consider the prohibition on abortion in Ireland in 1992, their response was both eagerly awaited and surprising.[9]

The X case

[11.07] In 1992 the Supreme Court was asked to rule upon the predicament of a 14-year-old girl who was pregnant as a result of rape and who wished to travel to the United Kingdom for an abortion, but who was prevented from doing so by the authorities once her plight became known to them. The High Court had upheld the position of the authorities and issued an injunction against the minor travelling to Britain for a

---

3   (\contd)
    In the *Bourne* case, the girl was the 14-year-old victim of an assault and rape by a number of soldiers. For an excellent discussion of this case, see Brookes and Roth, '*Rex v Bourne* and the medicalization of abortion' in Clark and Crawford (eds), *Legal Medicine in History* (Cambridge University Press, 1994).

4   *Attorney General v X* [1992] IR 1.

5   Conversely, the law on abortion in Great Britain was codified by the Abortion Act 1967: see para **[11.19]** below.

6   If the ban on abortion was only dependent on the Offences Against the Person Act 1861, the Act could have been repealed and replaced by a decision of the Oireachtas, perhaps by an Act permitting abortion. Only the Irish people, by referendum, may change the Constitution.

7   Article 40.3.3°.

8   *Attorney General (SPUC) v Open Door Counselling Ltd* [1988] IR 593.

9   *Attorney General v X* [1992] IR 1.

termination, on the basis that to do so would be to fail to vindicate the rights of the unborn. Expert evidence had been presented that the girl would be a suicide risk if not permitted to terminate the pregnancy. The Supreme Court placed great reliance on the fact that the Constitution recognised 'the equal right to the life of the mother'. The court reasoned that this particular clause clearly envisaged that abortion would sometimes be permissible, for example including the scenario of 'double effect'.[10] Accordingly, the court was prepared to find that where the right to life of the mother was threatened, as it was in the *X* case by the risk of suicide, then the mother's right to life could permit her to have an abortion and that such an abortion would not violate the provisions of the Offences Against the Person Act 1861. The conclusion of the court, in deciding that the girl should be permitted to travel for an abortion was as follows:

> ...[T]he proper test to be applied is that if it is established as a matter of probability, that there is a real and substantial risk to the life, as distinct from the health, of the mother, which can only be avoided by the termination of her pregnancy, such termination is permissible, having regard to the true interpretation of Article 40, s 3, sub-s 3° of the Constitution.[11]

In other words, the constitutional amendment of 1983, far from providing a bulwark against abortion, instead afforded a springboard for the Irish courts to hold that abortion is legal in certain circumstances. Those circumstances must pose a 'real and substantial risk' to the life, and not merely the health,[12] of the mother and could include a risk to life in the form of threatened suicide. Furthermore, the court's decision meant that an Irish citizen was free to travel outside the jurisdiction for the purpose of procuring a termination of her pregnancy.[13]

1992 Referendum

[11.08] Following the *X* case, further constitutional amendments, crafted in the light of the judgment of the Supreme Court in the *X* case, were put forward for approval or rejection by the Irish people. While the electorate rejected a provision that would allow for termination of pregnancy in limited circumstances including a real and substantial

---

[10] See para **[12.24]**. Also see fn 40 below.

[11] [1992] 1 IR 1 at 53 per Finlay CJ. As with many legal cases involving personal rights, it can be argued that there is a degree of balancing involved between the different rights, and it could be argued too that at the core of the *X* case judgment is pragmatism. If the right to life of the child were to be defended to its uttermost limit in the circumstances of the case, one possible outcome could be the suicide of the mother, with the resultant loss of both of the lives that the Constitution was attempting to protect. Similarly, if the threat was a physical one, refusal to countenance saving the mother's life could result in the loss of both lives. Note however the countervailing argument that undergoing abortion increases the possibility of mental ill-health in the mother and that, as a matter of medical fact, medical scenarios in which the doctor must choose between the life of the mother and the life of the foetus are extremely rare.

[12] This contrasts to the approach of the English courts (pre-Abortion Act 1967): in *R v Bourne* [1939] 1 QB 687 the threat of the woman becoming a 'physical or mental wreck' was sufficient to provide a defence to a doctor accused of performing an abortion.

[13] See para **[11.13]** below.

risk to the life of the mother but *excluding* the threat of suicide,[14] two new constitutional provisions relating to abortion were accepted:[15]

– Nothing in Article 40.3.3° would limit the freedom to travel between Ireland and any other state;[16]

– Nothing in Article 40.3.3° would limit the freedom to make available information relating to services lawfully available in another state.

The Supreme Court's consideration in the *X* case of Article 40.3.3°, an article which had been thought to foreclose any possibility of abortion in Ireland, thus had far-reaching consequences. While the Constitution and the Offences Against the Person Act 1861 still nominally banned abortion, the ban was effectively limited by the terms of the Supreme Court's decision.

2002 Referendum

[11.09] A succession of governments declined to introduce legislation that would crystallise the law on abortion in Ireland. After a protracted period of consultation,[17] the Government proposed a further constitutional amendment in 2002. The proposed amendment took the novel step of inserting a change in the Constitution that would make the protection of the 'life of the unborn in the womb' dependent not on a provision in the Constitution itself but on the Protection of Human Life in Pregnancy Act 2002, which Act would be brought into law only if the amendment were passed. The key provisions of the proposed legislation were as follows:[18]

– No person would be permitted to carry out or effect an abortion in the State;

– Abortion was defined as 'the intentional destruction by any means of unborn human life after implantation in the womb of a woman';

– Abortion did not include the carrying out of a medical procedure by a medical practitioner in the course of which or as a result of which unborn human life is ended, where the procedure is, in the reasonable opinion of the practitioner, necessary to prevent a real and substantial risk of loss of the woman's life other than by self-destruction.

---

[14] The rejected amendment read:

'It shall be unlawful to terminate the life of an unborn unless such termination is necessary to save the life, as distinct from the health, of the mother where there is an illness or disorder of the mother giving rise to a real and substantial risk to her life, not being a risk of self-destruction.'

Two-thirds of those who voted in the 1992 referendum rejected this particular amendment, while just over two-thirds of voters accepted the amendments permitting travel and information relating to abortion.

[15] The Thirteenth and Fourteenth Amendments to the Constitution, formally enacted in December 1992.

[16] One issue that arises is whether the abortion for which a woman wishes to travel is one that falls within the terms of the *X* case judgment, namely whether there is a 'real and substantial risk to the life of the mother': see para **[11.13]** below.

[17] All-Party Oireachtas Committee on the Constitution, *5th Progress Report—Abortion* (Government Publications, 2000).

[18] Twenty-fifth Amendment of the Constitution (Protection of Human Life in Pregnancy) Bill 2001, Second Schedule.

[11.10] If passed, the 2002 amendment would therefore have modified the *X* case position in a similar way to the amendment rejected in 1992. Abortion would be unlawful.[19] It would not, however, be an offence for a medical practitioner to perform a termination with the aim of averting a real and substantial risk to the life of the mother, but such a risk could not include the threat of suicide. The amendment to the Constitution was narrowly defeated, so the Protection of Human Life in Pregnancy Act 2002 was not introduced and the law remained unchanged. We look below (para **[11.12]**) at how this leaves the law on abortion in Ireland.

The Medical Council's position

[11.11] In mid-2001 and as part of the penumbra of the referendum to amend the Constitution, the Irish Medical Council set about changing the expression of its stance on abortion contained its *Guide to Ethical Conduct and Behaviour*. After a certain amount of disputation, a compromise was achieved, which reads:[20]

THE CHILD IN UTERO

The Council recognises that termination of pregnancy can occur when there is a real and substantial risk to the life of the mother and subscribes to the views expressed in Pt 2 of the written submission of the Institute of Obstetricians and Gynaecologists to the All-Party Oireachtas Committee on the Constitution...[21]

As can be seen from the text of the submission of the Institute,[22] it does not say much, although it does state at para 2 that '[t]here is a fundamental difference between abortion carried out with the intention of taking the life of the baby, for example for social reasons, and the unavoidable death of the baby resulting from essential treatment to protect the life of the mother'. But the Institute's submission does not define 'essential

---

[19] Note that abortion was defined as the destruction of life after implantation in the womb and not after fertilisation: see para **[11.15]** below.

[20] *Guide to Ethical Conduct and Behaviour* (6th edn, Dublin, 2004) para 24.6.

[21] *Fifth Progress Report—Abortion* (Government Publications, 2000) A407. The written submission of the Institute of Obstetricians and Gynaecologists to the All-Party Oireachtas Committee on the Constitution was as follows:

The Institute of Obstetricians and Gynaecologists is the professional body representing the speciality of Obstetrics and Gynaecology in Ireland. The Executive Council of the Institute has examined the Green Paper on Abortion and the members have been consulted. We welcome the Green Paper, which provides a comprehensive, up to date and objective analysis of the issues arising in the care of the pregnant woman. Our expertise is in the medical area and our comments are confined to these aspects.

In current obstetrical practice rare complications can arise where therapeutic intervention is required at a stage in pregnancy when there will be little or no prospect for the survival of the baby, due to extreme immaturity. In these exceptional situations failure to intervene may result in the death of both mother and baby. We consider that there is a fundamental difference between abortion carried out with the intention of taking the life of the baby, for example for social reasons, and the unavoidable death of the baby resulting from essential treatment to protect the life of the mother.

We recognise our responsibility to provide aftercare for women who decide to leave the State for termination of pregnancy. We recommend that full support and follow up services be made available for all women whose pregnancies have been terminated, whatever the circumstances.

[22] See fn 21 above.

treatment' and is careful to say in Pt 1 of its submission that its opinion is a 'medical' one, suggesting that the Institute is avoiding, rather than necessarily rejecting, consideration of the psychiatric imperative for termination. Nothing in the *Guide* or in the Institute's submission suggests that the latter's submission is an exhaustive opinion and for the Medical Council to say that it *subscribes* to the views in the submission is very far indeed from saying that it is *bound* by that submission.

✱ Current position

[11.12] A doctor in Ireland could, according to the Supreme Court, perform an abortion where there was a real and substantial risk to the life of the mother, including the risk of suicide and, in addition, the Constitution now enshrines a freedom to travel for an abortion and a right to provide information to women regarding the availability of abortion in other countries.

Freedom to travel

[11.13] The distinction had been drawn by the courts between a 'right' to travel and an altogether more limited 'freedom' to travel. In the case of *A and B v Eastern Health Board*,[23] it appeared to be implied by the court that the freedom to travel was limited only to those cases where the abortion for which the woman was travelling was one that, if performed in Ireland, would be lawful here. In the 2007 case of *D v Health Service Executive and Attorney General*, the High Court took a less restrictive view. In the earlier case, the girl in question had been a teenage rape victim who was, on the available medical evidence, suicidal, thus fulfilling the *X* case criteria. In the later case, the woman was 17 and carrying an anencephalic foetus, but she was not suicidal and there was no specific risk to her health. The abortion for which she wished to travel to Britain was one that was lawful in Britain (see para **[11.19]** below), but not lawful in Ireland. Furthermore, the 17-year-old would ordinarily have been competent for the purposes of consenting to medical treatment, but was restricted in the instant case by the fact that she was the subject of a care order. The court gave her permission to travel.[24]

Providing information

[11.14] After the passage of the constitutional amendment allowing for information about abortion to be furnished, the Government introduced legislation to govern the provision of that information.[25] As far as clinicians are concerned, the Act makes it unlawful to advocate or promote abortion when providing information, although

---

[23] *A and B v Eastern Health Board* [1998] 1 IR 464 per Geoghegan J at 483:

> But the fact that there may be different views as to the importance of the constitutional right to travel does not in my view affect the issue of whether the District Court under the Child Care Act 1991, can actually exercise a jurisdiction authorising travel for a particular purpose, namely, for an abortion in circumstances where the proposed abortion would not be allowed under Irish law. I think that the court would be prevented from doing so by the terms of the right to life of the unborn expressed in the Constitution and as the Supreme Court have held, unaffected by "the travel amendment".

[24] See 'Court rules "Miss D"can travel to UK for abortion' (2007) Irish Times, 10 May. Note that at the time of writing (October 2007) no written judgment is available.

[25] Regulation of Information (Services Outside the State for Termination of Pregnancies) Act 1995.

'advocacy' and 'promotion' are not defined in the Act. If information regarding services for the termination of pregnancy is given, it must be given in the context of 'truthful and objective' information about all options open to the pregnant woman and the information must relate to services that are legal in the state to which the information refers.[26] Information on abortion cannot be provided by a person who has (or whose employer has) a financial interest in the provision of abortion services outside the State, which may include receiving financial benefits, such as donations or commissions, from a body that provides services for the termination of pregnancies.[27]

Somewhat counter-intuitively, even though:

(a)   a practitioner may legally give information to a patient relating to a termination of pregnancy outside the State;

(b)   the woman may travel outside the State for that termination of pregnancy; and

(c)   most commentators[28] feel that a necessary consequence of the decision in the *X* case is that abortion is in certain circumstances legal in Ireland,

the 1995 Act insists that the practitioner may not assist in the making of an appointment for her patient. She may however furnish the patient with relevant 'medical, surgical, clinical, social or other like records or notes relating to [the patient]'.[29]

When does pregnancy begin?

[11.15] There are many dimensions to any discussion of when human life begins, but we are concerned here only with the legal position and its effect on clinical practice. It is the teaching of many churches and the belief of many individuals that life begins at the moment of conception, but the legal position appears to be different. This legal distinction is important insofar as a legal definition of pregnancy (and thus human life)[30] beginning with fertilisation could have an impact on methods of contraception such as post-coital contraception (the 'morning after pill') and intrauterine contraceptive devices (the IUCD or 'coil') that operate as post-fertilisation contraceptives. If the law identifies fertilisation as the starting point of pregnancy, then the operation of such contraceptives could, legally speaking, be regarded as abortion. The approach that appears to be favoured by Irish lawmakers is that life begins at implantation and a number of sources

---

[26]   Regulation of Information (Services Outside the State for Termination of Pregnancies) Act 1995, s 5. Note that a 'woman' is defined in the Act as a 'female person': there is therefore no apparent lower age limit on the provision of information to minors. The Act in effect means that abortion can only be discussed in the context of exploring the other available options open to the pregnant woman, namely keeping the child and giving the child up for adoption.

[27]   Regulation of Information (Services Outside the State for Termination of Pregnancies) Act 1995, ss 6 and 7.

[28]   See *Shatter's Family Law* (4th edn, Tottel, 1999) para 1.103.

[29]   Regulation of Information (Services Outside the State for Termination of Pregnancies) Act 1995, s 8.

[30]   A discussion of whether the human life that begins in early pregnancy is morally equivalent with that of a born person also lies outside the scope of the present text.

support this contention. One semantic reason was identified by the report on abortion produced by the All-Party Committee on the Constitution:[31]

> The Family Planning Act 1979 specifically prohibits the importation, sale and distribution of abortifacients. In as much as the morning after pill [and by logical extension, the IUCD] is available and prescribed the legal presumption must be that it is not regarded as an abortifacient.

[11.16] Similarly, when the Protection of Human Life in Pregnancy Bill was drafted with the intention of being enacted were the 2002 amendment passed, the Bill defined abortion as 'the intentional destruction by any means of unborn human life *after implantation in the womb* of a woman.'[32] Looking abroad for guidance brings home a similar message. Modern English legislation[33] and case law[34] uniformly supports the idea that implantation rather than fertilisation is the legal point at which pregnancy (and therefore legally relevant human life) starts. The judgment of the High Court in *MR v TR*[35] dealing with the 'right to life' of un-implanted frozen embryos, also seems to lend itself to the view that in the present state of the law constitutional protection for the unborn is only afforded once implantation in the womb of a fertilised embryo has taken place.

Abortion and homicide

[11.17] In many jurisdictions, as far as the law is concerned, abortion (even where it is the deliberate termination of *in utero* life) is regarded as an act legally distinct from murder or manslaughter. Murder is the killing of another person where there is an intent to kill or to cause serious injury to the person killed.[36] Manslaughter is the killing of another where there is no specific intention to kill or cause serious injury, or where the killing is the result of provocation leading to a loss of self-control, or where the accused used force he believed to be necessary in the circumstances (perhaps in self-defence). For a homicide (either murder or manslaughter) to be committed, the prevailing opinion in countries such as England is that the person killed must, at the time of the alleged

---

[31] All-Party Oireachtas Committee on the Constitution, *5th Progress Report—Abortion* (Government Publications, 2000) 102 (material in square brackets added).

[32] Second Schedule to the Protection of Human Life in Pregnancy Bill 2002 (italics added).

[33] Human Fertilisation and Embryology Act 1990, s 2(3). See also the New Zealand Crimes Act 1961 (amended 1977), s 182A.

[34] For example *R v Dingra*, unreported (1991) Daily Telegraph, 25 January. Note, however, that while some recognition is given to the foetus under English law, it does not possess a separate legal existence capable of recognition and protection by the courts equivalent to that of a born person: *Re F (in utero)* [1988] 2 All ER. As in Ireland, it appears to be the case that – legally speaking – emergency contraception is not regarded as an abortifacient: *R (on the application of Smeaton) v Secretary of State for Health* [2002] 2 FLR 146.

[35] *MR v TR, Anthony Walsh, David Walsh and the Sims Clinic* [2006] IEHC 221 and 359. The earlier of two judgments delivered in this case (at [2006] IEHC 221; [2006] 3 IR 449) also confirmed the necessity for the consent of both parties to the creation of the embryo before frozen embryos could be implanted in the woman.

[36] Criminal Justice Act 1964, s 4.

killing, have been both alive and capable of sustaining independent life; in short, he must have been born. One judge summed up the issue as follows:

> A baby is fully and completely born when it is completely delivered from the body of its mother and it has a separate and independent existence in the sense that it does not derive its power of living from its mother. It is not material that the child still be attached to the mother by the umbilical cord.[37]

In English law, if injuries are inflicted on a pregnant woman that also affect the foetus and the baby is subsequently born alive, but dies as a result of the injuries, then the attacker can be convicted of the child's manslaughter.[38]

Quick Reference Guide 11.1

Abortion and the law in Ireland: the current position?

> ❖ Legally speaking, the approach taken by legislators and the courts is that human life in pregnancy begins at implantation.
>
> ❖ A necessary and obvious consequence of the decision in the X case is that abortion would, in those circumstances where there is a real and substantial risk to the health of the mother including the risk of suicide, be legal in Ireland.
>
> ❖ A practitioner may legally give information to a patient relating to a termination of pregnancy outside the State. She may not, however, make an appointment for her patient.
>
> ❖ A woman has the freedom to travel outside the State for a termination of a pregnancy so long as the termination of which she wishes to avail herself is one that is legally available in the country to which she is travelling.
>
> ❖ It is the case in Irish law that an assault giving rise to the death of *in utero* life might give rise to a charge of murder.

[**11.18**] The situation may be more complicated in Ireland: the Irish Constitution contains a guarantee to respect the life of the unborn, while having regard to the equal right to life of the mother.[39] In theory then, if

(a)   the rights to life of the mother and unborn are equal; and

(b)   to kill the mother would be murder,

---

[37]   *R v Hutty* [1953] VLR 338, per Barry J.

[38]   *Attorney General's Reference (No 3 of 1994)* [1997] 3 All ER 936. This 'born alive' principle was also applied in the US case of *US v Spencer* 839 F 2d 1341 (9th Cir 1988). America has also passed the Unborn Victims of Violence Act of 2004 (18 USC 1841), criminalising the killing of a foetus during certain violent crimes against the person. Thirty-four individual states of the USA also have similar legislation.

[39]   Article 40.3.3° (inserted by the Eighth Amendment to the Constitution). Note also the decision of the Court of Human Rights in *Vo v France* (53924/00) (2005) 40 EHRR 12 in which the court decided (by 14 to 3) that the foetus did not have a right to life within the meaning of Article 2 of the European Convention of Human Rights. The applicant had alleged a violation of Convention on the ground that the conduct of a doctor who was responsible for the death of her child in utero was not classified as unintentional homicide.

then to kill the unborn child could reasonably be regarded[40] under the Constitution as murder or manslaughter. On the other hand, it could be argued that, in terms of legislation, abortion is clearly regarded as different from murder; it was, for example, dealt with in its own provisions of the Offences Against the Person Act 1861, separate from those dealing with murder and manslaughter.[41] Similarly, the fact that there are circumstances in which termination of the unborn may be legally performed in Ireland also appears to put the act of termination in a legal category that is distinct from the deliberate killing by a medical practitioner of a 'born' person, which is not countenanced in any way by Irish law.

The law on abortion in Great Britain

[11.19] On the basis that the majority of women in Ireland who opt for termination of pregnancy set out for England,[42] it is sensible to briefly set out the law in Britain[43] when it comes to abortion. As we have noted, information on abortion can only be provided and women may only travel for terminations when those terminations are legal in the destination country, so knowledge of what constitutes a legal abortion in Britain may be relevant for the clinician. As in Ireland, the British law nominally prohibits abortion but legislation, in the form of the Abortion Act 1967, also creates an exception. A termination of pregnancy will not be an offence:

> when a pregnancy is terminated by a registered medical practitioner, if two registered medical practitioners are of the opinion, formed in good faith:
>
> (a)   That the pregnancy has not exceeded its 24th week and that the continuance of the pregnancy would involve risk, greater than if the pregnancy were terminated, of

---

40   This appears to be the view in Charleton, McDermott & Bolger, *Criminal Law* (Tottel Publishing, 2000) para 7.54. Another (ethical rather than legal) distinction that is sometimes drawn between different acts causing the death of a foetus or embryo is the doctrine of 'double effect' which applies where a particular (morally unsatisfactory) outcome is foreseen but unintended and is necessary to achieve a morally defensible aim. So, emergency surgery to save the life of a pregnant woman where, without the surgery, both mother and foetus will die and where the surgery necessarily involves the death of the foetus, would be morally defensible (to a person opposed to abortion) under the doctrine. There are many criticisms of this approach: see Glover, *Causing Death and Saving Lives* (Penguin, 1990) Ch 6.

41   Although the Offences Against the Person Act 1861 no longer governs the law on homicide in Ireland, the fact that, under the Act, murder and manslaughter were regarded as separate and distinct from abortion seems nonetheless a relevant observation.

42   Figures issued by the British Department of Health in June 2007 showed that the number of women who gave Irish addresses at British abortion clinics fell to 5,042 in 2006 from 5,585 in 2005: see 'Groups welcome falling abortion figures' (2007) Irish Times, 20 June (see also *Women and Crisis Pregnancy* (Dublin: Government Publications, 1998)). The figure may be higher: it is believed that many women give false addresses. It has also been suggested that more women are travelling to countries other than Britain.

43   The law is governed by the Abortion Act 1967, amended by the Human Fertilisation and Embryology Act 1990; the Act does not extend to Northern Ireland. For more on the law on abortion in the UK, see Kennedy & Grubb, *Medical Law* (3rd edn, Tottel Publishing, 2000) Ch 11.

injury to the physical or mental health of the pregnant woman or any existing children of her family; or

(b)   That the termination is necessary to prevent grave permanent injury to the physical or mental health of the pregnant woman; or

(c)   That the continuance of the pregnancy would involve risk to the life of the pregnant woman greater than if the pregnancy were terminated; or

(d)   That there is a substantial risk that if the child were born it would suffer from such physical or mental abnormalities as to be seriously handicapped.[44]

It should be noted that there is only a time limit of 24 weeks[45] for the termination of pregnancy where there is a risk of physical or mental injury to the pregnant woman. No time limit applies to any of the other grounds. In any event, there is no necessity under English law that the risk must be one to the life of the mother as is the case in Ireland; a threat posed to her health or even to the health or welfare of any children she already has will suffice. The UK Act allows doctors to opt out of a termination if they are conscientiously opposed to the procedure and the procedure is not immediately necessary to save the life of the mother,[46] but the doctor is still obliged to refer her patient to someone who will provide the service.[47] The right to opt out only applies to those who actively participate in the termination and not to those who are ancillary to the process or procedure.[48] Note too that a father has no right under English law (or indeed

---

[44]   Abortion Act 1967, s 1. There is no definition of what constitutes a 'serious handicap' sufficient to allow a termination (up to term) on these grounds: see Wicks, Wyldes and Kilby, 'Late Termination of Pregnancy for Fetal Abnormality: Medical and Legal Perspectives' (2004) Med L Rev 12(3) 285–305. The British Medical Association and the UK Royal College of Obstetrics and Gynaecology have called for the revision of the Abortion Act 1967 so that, in the first trimester women are not required to meet medical criteria for abortions and the requirement for two doctors to confirm that the abortion meets the legal criteria is removed. The issue of reducing the upper time limit beyond which an abortion may not be procured (except in the case of 'severe handicap', the definition of which has also been criticised) has been discussed in the UK: see British Medical Association, 'Abortion time limits: a briefing paper from the BMA' (London, 2005), 34–35.

[45]   See Kennedy & Grubb, *Medical Law* (3rd edn, OUP, 2000) 1422 for a discussion of the question of the date from which the 24 weeks should begin to run. In the interests of legal certainty, the conventional medical practice of dating the start of pregnancy from the first day of the last menstrual period should probably be followed: see Francis and Johnston, *Medical Treatment Decisions and the Law* (Tottel Publishing, 2001) 78.

[46]   Abortion Act 1967, s 4(2).

[47]   Analogous provisions exist in the Medical Council *Guide to Ethical Conduct and Behaviour* (6th edn, Dublin, 2004) para 2.6: Conscientious Objection:

> If a doctor has a conscientious objection to a course of action this should be explained and the names of other doctors made available to the patient.

[48]   So a secretary could not refuse to type referral letters and claim conscientious objection: *Janaway v Salford AHA* [1989] AC 537.

under the law of most countries) to intervene in a woman's decision to consent to an abortion.[49]

INFANTICIDE

[11.20] We mentioned in para **[11.17]** that for a killing to be homicide, the victim must have been born. There is one further qualification that is of interest here. A mother who kills her child in the first year after its birth and who does so as a result of mental imbalance caused by that birth, may be found guilty of infanticide rather than homicide. The necessary elements are that (i) the killing must be committed by the mother of the child; (ii) it must occur at some time in the child's first year of life; (iii) the woman must cause the death by some 'wilful act or omission';[50] and (iv) the mind of the killer must be disturbed at the time of the killing. If the killing does not fulfil each of these criteria, the killing is likely to be murder or manslaughter. Either the prosecuting authorities can bring an accusation of infanticide instead of murder against the mother or the accused herself can raise the question of infanticide at her trial and it is then open to the jury to find her guilty of that rather than homicide if they choose to do so. Infanticide, if it attracts a custodial sentence at all, is often punished comparatively lightly.

[11.21] Infanticide is a crime that may only be committed by a mother; fathers cannot commit it—a gender-specific element that has come in for criticism. It has also been argued that the leniency afforded to mothers who kill infants of less than one year is disproportionate to the gravity of the crime and the risk faced by infants.[51] The necessary mental imbalance required for a verdict of infanticide was also for a long time not entirely clear.[52] The Royal College of Psychiatrists, when submitting evidence to a UK commission considering infanticide, called for the recognition of social and psychological as well as psychiatric factors as mental triggers for infanticide, including 'overwhelming stress' from the social environment or from the addition of a new member to a household already struggling with poverty. They also advocated a failure of bonding between mother and child due to illness or disability as a possible cause. The commission, however, was reluctant to accept these contentions.[53]

[11.22] In Ireland the law on infanticide was amended by the Criminal Law (Insanity) Act 2006 and the law on infanticide is now as follows:

---

[49] *Paton v Trustees of British Pregnancy Advisory Service* [1979] QB 276; *Paton v United Kingdom* (1980) 3 EHRR 408. In the USA the Supreme Court has said that a woman is not under any obligation to consult her husband, let alone seek his consent to termination: *Planned Parenthood of SE Pennsylvania v Casey* (1992) 112 S Ct 2791.

[50] For example, smothering the child would be an 'act'; failing to feed it would be an 'omission'.

[51] Maier-Katkin & Ogle, 'A Rationale for Infanticide Laws' [1993] Crim LR 903. For more detail on the principles underpinning infanticide, see Oberman, 'Mothers Who Kill' 34 Am Crim LR 1 (1997).

[52] The Infanticide Act 1949 spoke (s 1(3)(a)) of the balance of the mind being disturbed 'by reason of the effect of lactation'—lactation has for many years not been regarded as a cause of such a disturbance.

[53] Criminal Law Revision Committee, 14th Report (1980), paras 100–114; Draft Criminal Code (Law Com No 177) clause 64.

A woman shall be guilty of…infanticide if—

(a) by any wilful act or omission she causes the death of her child, being a child under the age of twelve months, and

(b) the circumstances are such that, but for this section, the act or omission would have amounted to murder, and

(c) at the time of the act or omission the balance of her mind was disturbed by reason of her not having fully recovered from the effect of giving birth to the child or by reason of a mental disorder[54] consequent upon the birth of the child

and may for that offence be tried and punished as for manslaughter and, on conviction may be dealt with…as if she had been found guilty of manslaughter on the grounds of diminished responsibility.[55]

Assisted human reproduction

[11.23] Assisted human reproduction (AHR) is predominantly a response to infertility[56] and a detailed discussion of the various types of AHR methods lies outside the scope of the present text. Broadly speaking, AHR refers principally to reproductive procedures that involve the handling of gametes[57] and embryos, namely assisted insemination (AI) and in vitro fertilisation (IVF).[58] Four relevant facts relating to IVF should be noted:

- Mature human ova do not do well in frozen storage.[59] It is for this reason that eggs are fertilised and stored as early embryos;

- Obtaining eggs from a woman is an invasive and difficult procedure. The woman is typically given medication to encourage a 'hyper-ovulatory' state and

---

[54] A mental disorder within the meaning of the Criminal Law (Insanity) Act 2006; the Act defines a 'mental disorder' as 'mental illness, mental disability, dementia or any disease of the mind but does not include intoxication'. Obviously, where the mental disorder affecting the mother is sufficiently serious, she may in fact be in a position to plead that she is not guilty by reason of insanity. See Ch 10 'Law and Mental Health', para **[10.32]**.

[55] Infanticide Act 1949, s 1(3) as amended by the Criminal Law (Insanity) Act 2006, s 22. Diminished responsibility is dealt with in Ch 10 'Law and Mental Health', para **[10.46]**.

[56] One in six couples is subfertile and many will seek intervention in the form of assisted reproduction: see Cahill and Wardle, 'Management of Infertility' BMJ 2002; 325:28–32. Infertility or subfertility are generally recognised when a couple does not conceive after two years of regular unprotected intercourse.

[57] That is to say, sperm and eggs.

[58] The essential difference between them is that AI involves the handling of male gametes only with fertilisation taking place within the female body (*in vivo*), while IVF involves the handling of both male and female gametes and fertilisation takes place outside the body (*in vitro*). The first successful IVF birth was Louise Brown in 1978; human donor insemination dates back to at least the nineteenth century.

[59] However, there have been great advances in harvesting immature eggs (oocytes) which can be stored frozen and then matured in vitro. Initial evidence suggests that the fertilisation rate of such eggs is low, but successful fertilisations have resulted. Such advances may circumvent some of the issues arising from the disposal of frozen embryos and may also in turn undermine the 'surplus embryo' argument in favour of embryo research.

a large number of eggs (eight on average, but it may be as many as 40) are then harvested for use;

- Because of the problems with storing eggs, already noted, all of the eggs are fertilised prior to storage;

- Good practice is not to implant too many fertilised embryos into a woman at one time in order to achieve a balance between maximising a successful outcome and minimising the risks of a high-number multiple pregnancy. Usually two (or exceptionally three) fertilised embryos are transferred into the womb.

A corollary of this is that extra frozen embryos are often left in storage after the completion of IVF. These frozen embryos can be a boon where a cycle of IVF treatment has failed (the success rate is only one in four, even in young healthy women) and a couple wish to go through it again or where the couple wishes to have further children. However, where they do not wish to use those embryos, then the issue arises of what can or should be done with those embryos assuming that there are no willing recipients for them and that they are reaching the end of the indeterminate but finite period during which they can be stored without degrading.

The Irish situation

[11.24] There is no legislation in Ireland governing assisted human reproduction, although there has been some case law.[60] The main discussion on the issue in Ireland was contained in the *Report of the Commission on Assisted Human Reproduction*.[61] It made a wide range of recommendations and certain of its 'headline' recommendations are set out below:

Main recommendations of the Commission on assisted human reproduction

Regulatory issues

[11.25]

- A regulatory body should be established by an Act of the Oireachtas to regulate AHR services in Ireland;

- Appropriate guidelines should be put in place by the regulatory body to govern the freezing and storage of gametes and the use of frozen gametes and the regulatory body should, in accordance with statutory guidelines, have power to address cases where gametes are abandoned, where the commissioning couple cannot agree on a course of action, where couples separate or where one or both partner(s) dies or becomes incapacitated;

- Centres that collect and store gametes and that generate and store embryos should be regulated and licensed by the regulatory body.

---

[60] *MR v TR* [2006] IEHC 221 and 359, [2006] 3 IR 449.

[61] Department of Health and Children (Dublin, 2005). Available for download at http://www.dohc.ie/publications/cahr.html (last accessed October 2007). Note that the headings within which the main recommendations are grouped in the text represent the author's own loose classification of the recommendations.

Clinical practice and storage issues

[11.26]

- Superovulation should be allowed (although service providers should facilitate users who wish to avoid any treatment that might result in the production of 'surplus' embryos;

- Appropriate guidelines should be put in place by the regulatory body to govern the number of embryos to be transferred in any one treatment cycle and when to transfer embryos;

- It should be obligatory for all recognised providers of AHR services in Ireland to obtain written informed consent for all the services they provide. Each stage of the AHR process should be covered by comprehensive consent procedures;

- Where there is objective evidence of a risk of harm to any child that may be conceived through AHR, there should be a presumption against treatment.

Donation and surrogacy issues

[11.27]

- Donation of sperm, ova and embryos should be permitted and should be subject to regulation by the regulatory body subject to appropriate guidelines governing the selection of donors: to screen for genetic disorders and infectious disease; to set age limits for donors; and to set an appropriate limit on the number of children to be born by the use of sperm or ova from a single donor;

- Any child born through use of donated gametes or embryos should, on maturity, be able to identify the donor(s) involved in his/her conception; donors should not be able to access the identity of children born through use of their gametes or embryos but should, if they wish, be told if a child is born through use of their gametes;

- Donors should not be paid nor should recipients be charged for donations per se. This does not preclude payment of reasonable expenses and payment for AHR services;

- In donor programmes, the intent of all parties involved—that the donor will not have any legal relationship with the child and that the woman who gives birth to the child will be the child's mother—should be used as the basis for the assignment of legal parentage; the partner, if any, of a sperm recipient should be given a legal commitment to be recognised as the child's parent; the gestational mother of an egg recipient should be recognised as the legal mother of the child; and her partner, if any, should be recognised as the child's second legal parent;

- Payments for donations or surrogacy should be on an expenses-only basis.

Pre-implantation and research issues

[11.28]

- Human reproductive cloning and the generation and use of interspecies human embryos should be prohibited;

301

– Preconception sex selection should be permitted only for the reliable prevention of serious sex-linked genetic disorders but not for social reasons;

– Research on gametes should be permitted provided it is governed by strict conditions set out by the regulatory body and subject to informed consent from donors.

Miscellaneous issues

[11.29]

– Counselling from suitably qualified professionals should be provided before, during and after AHR treatment and to all donors of sperm, eggs and embryos;

– Services should be available without discrimination on the grounds of gender, marital status or sexual orientation subject to consideration of the best interests of any children that may be born.

The voice of dissent

[11.30] One interesting feature of the Commission's report is that a small but significant number of the recommendations were not unanimous. Several recommendations, especially those activating differing views of the moral and legal status of the embryo, were the subject of dissenting opinions.[62] The non-unanimous recommendations included the following:

– The options (to be regulated by the regulatory authority) available for excess frozen embryo would include voluntary donation of excess healthy embryos to other recipients, voluntary donation for research or allowing them to perish;

– The embryo formed by IVF should not attract legal protection until placed in the human body, at which stage it should attract the same level of protection as the embryo formed in vivo;

– Surrogacy should be permitted and should be subject to regulation by the regulatory body and the child born through surrogacy should be presumed to be that of the commissioning couple;

– Embryo research, including embryonic stem cell research, for specific purposes only and under stringently controlled conditions, should be permitted on surplus embryos that are donated specifically for research. This should be permitted up to 14 days following fertilisation…The generation of embryos through IVF specifically for research purposes should be prohibited;

– Regenerative medicine[63] should be permitted under regulation;

– Pre-implantation genetic diagnosis (PGD) should be allowed, under regulation, to reduce the risk of serious genetic disorders.

---

[62] See 'Expressions of Dissent', *Report of the Commission on Assisted Human Reproduction* (2005), 80–85.

[63] The report defines 'regenerative medicine' as follows:

Regenerative medicine (also known as therapeutic cloning) involves the creation of a cloned embryo using non-diseased donor cells from a patient with a degenerative disease or disorder. The objective is to use the cloned embryo to generate a stem cell line (immortalising those cells) that, in turn, can be used to generate a particular tissue for treatment of the disease in question.

Case law on AHR in Ireland

[11.31] In the case of *MR v TR*,[64] the High Court held that consent was an essential precursor to every step of the assisted reproduction process and that consent given by the genetic father to the formation of a frozen embryo was not tantamount to consenting to that embryo being implanted. So where (as in this case) the couple were now estranged, the woman could not rely on his consent to the creation of the embryos to have them implanted; the estranged husband would be required to give further consent to implantation. The court furthermore held that for the purposes of the Irish Constitution, unimplanted embryos could not be regarded as the unborn and thus did not have the protection of Article 40 of the Constitution.

Legislative response

[11.32] At the present time there is no indication of forthcoming legislation to put the regulation of assisted human reproduction in Ireland onto a firm statutory footing. However, we turn now to examine some relevant issues in assisted human reproduction and consider how they have been dealt with in the neighbouring jurisdiction.

Issues in Assisted Human Reproduction (AHR)

Regulating AHR—the UK model

[11.33] The UK Human Fertilisation and Embryology Act 1990[65] governs the whole area of assisted reproduction and embryo research. The legislation established the Human Fertilisation and Embryology Authority (HFEA),[66] which has responsibility for:

- regulating and inspecting standards to ensure that all UK treatment clinics offering in vitro fertilisation (IVF) or donor insemination (DI), or storing eggs, sperm[67] or embryos, conform to high medical and professional standards and are inspected regularly;
- licensing and monitoring human embryo research.[68]

A licence, which may be granted by the HFEA, is necessary to carry out any of the activities covered by the legislation. The activities authorised by the licence can only be

---

[64] *MR v TR* [2006] IEHC 221 and 359, [2006] 3 IR 449.

[65] The Act is further supplemented by statutory instruments: the Data Protection (Miscellaneous Subject Access Exemptions) Order (SI 419/2000) and the Human Fertilisation and Embryology (Special Exemptions) Regulations 1991 (SI 1588/1991).

[66] The Authority itself is a 21-member panel appointed by the Secretary of State for Health. A majority of the Authority must be drawn from disciplines other than medicine or human embryo research. Website: www.hfea.gov.uk (last accessed October 2007). New regulatory legislation is contemplated in the form of the Draft Tissues and Embryos Bill, which is intended to revise the law on assisted reproduction and embryology, and to establish the Regulatory Authority for Tissue and Embryos (RATE).

[67] Including ovarian and testicular tissue from children who are undergoing treatment, such as radiotherapy, that will have the effect of rendering then infertile.

[68] The IVF-related research that has been licensed includes pre-implantation genetic diagnosis (PGD) for medical reasons (therefore excluding its use for purely social or cultural sex selection). See HFEA, *HFEA/Advisory Committee of Genetic Testing Consultation Document—Pre-Implantation Genetic Diagnosis* (London, 1999). (contd/)

carried on in premises to which the licence relates and under the supervision of the 'person responsible'.[69] The HFEA is required by law to publish a Code of Practice.[70] Any decision to licence a treatment service must take account of the welfare of any child who may be born as a result of treatment.[71]

Who should have treatment?

[11.34] Under UK law, IVF or AI treatment will not be given to any woman unless to do so would be consistent with the welfare of any child she may give birth to (including the need of that child for a father) and the welfare of any other children who may be affected by the birth of a sibling.[72] It is also acceptable to limit the maximum age of a woman to whom state-funded IVF treatment may be given. The English courts have held that, in view of the limited budgets available for IVF and the fact that effectiveness of IVF diminishes with age, it is permissible to set a maximum of age for women who will be given IVF treatment.[73] The Irish Commission on Assisted Reproduction has recommended that there be no discrimination on the basis of gender, marital status or sexual orientation, but did not make any explicit comment on age limits.

[11.35] Age limits also apply to the donation of eggs and sperm: 55 years for male donors; 35 years for female donors and a lower limit of 18 years for both sexes.[74] Donations can also be stored and screened for certain diseases, such as HIV and cystic fibrosis. There are limits too on the number of live births any one donor's donated

---

[68] (\contd) Both PGD and pre-natal diagnosis (for example, amniocentesis) involve ethical and legal complications. A prenatal diagnosis of a severe genetic abnormality may lead the couple to seek an abortion. Pre-implantation diagnosis raises the problems of disposal of fertilised, but not implanted, embryos affected by the genetic condition. PGD is available currently in the UK only to those couples with a family history of severe genetic disorder (see para 26 of the *Consultation Document*).

[69] Human Fertilisation and Embryology Act 1990, s 12(a). The 'person responsible' may be a human person, a body corporate, a partnership or unincorporated association (s 46).

[70] HFEA, *Code of Practice* (7th edn, January 2007).

[71] Human Fertilisation and Embryology Act 1990, s 13(5).

[72] Human Fertilisation and Embryology Act 1990. Note that s 13(5) says that the welfare of any child born as a result of treatment includes 'the need of that child for a father', which appears to militate against IVF or AI for single or lesbian mothers. Note too that there is evidence to suggest that donor insemination children brought up by single mothers may 'do better' than those brought up by married couples: see Murray and Golombok, 'Solo mothers and their donor insemination infants: follow-up at age 2 years', 20 Human Reproduction (2005) 1655–1660. The repeal of s 13(5) has been recommended: House of Commons Science and Technology Committee, *Human Reproductive Technologies and the Law—Fifth Report* (HMSO, 2005) para 101 et seq.

[73] *R v Sheffield Health Authority, ex parte Seale* (1994) 24 BMLR 1. The woman in this case was over 35 years and the rules stipulated that in view of the greater failure rate of IVF in older women, the cut-off age for treatment should be 35. English courts have also upheld a rule limiting the number of embryos that may be implanted during any single cycle of IVF: *R v Human Fertilisation and Embryology Authority, ex parte Assisted Reproduction & Gynaecology Centre and* H [2002] EWCA Civ 20 (31 January 2002).

[74] Jackson, *Medical Law* (Oxford, 2006) 831.

gametes will ordinarily be used for. A maximum of two eggs or embryos may be tranferred during a single cycle of infertility treatment in women aged under 40 years, with no exceptions, and no more than three in women over this age. This limitation aims to reduce the risk of multiple births in women undergoing infertility treatment, while maximising women's chances of having a healthy baby.

Use and storage of sperm (or eggs) taken without consent

[11.36] In the UK, the sperm of a deceased husband cannot be used by his surviving spouse for the purposes of donor insemination without him having given his consent when alive and it may be withdrawn once given. In all cases, consent is an indispensable precursor to the use of eggs or sperm for IVF. In one case,[75] a woman's husband had passed into a coma due to meningitis. Sperm was obtained by electro-ejaculation and, following her husband's death, the woman sought to undergo donor insemination using her dead husband's sperm. The HFEA, which oversees all donor insemination treatment in the UK, refused, in the absence of the husband's consent to the storage and use of the sperm, which was required by the law,[76] to give its permission to treatment or its consent to the export of the sperm for treatment abroad. The court confirmed that in all cases consent must be obtained for the harvesting and use of sperm or eggs and where there is no consent, there can be no legal storage or use. Where consent to the use of sperm has been given, but then withdrawn, the later withdrawal of consent will be binding unless it can be shown that there was something defective (for example that it was involuntary) about the withdrawal of consent.[77] The same consent requirement is true for the implantation of embryos.[78]

The right to information of those born as a result of fertility treatment

[11.37] In the UK a person over the age of 18 years who applies to the HFEA has the right to find out whether he was born as the result of fertility treatment. This can include the necessary information to ensure that the applicant is not about to marry someone to

---

[75] *R v Human Fertilisation and Embryology Authority, ex parte Blood* [1997] 2 All ER 687, [1997] 2 WLR 806. It has been argued in this case that, quite aside from questions of the use of sperm, taking the sperm from the comatose husband in the first place was illegal, as it was done without consent and in the absence of a necessity. It has been suggested that sperm could rarely be removed in an unconscious person's 'best interests': see McClean, *Review of the Common Law Provisions Relating to the Removal of Gametes and the Consent Provisions in the Human Fertilisation and Embryology Act 1999* (Department of Health, London, 1998). The law has been amended to allow a man whose sperm is used after his death to be recognised as the father of any resultant children (provided he gave his written consent to being recognised as their father while still alive): Human Fertilisation and Embryology (Deceased Fathers) Act 2003.

[76] Human Fertilisation and Embryology Act 1990, s 4(1).

[77] *Centre for Reproductive Medicine v U* [2002] EWCA Civ 565.

[78] See also *Evans v Amicus Healthcare Ltd* [2004] EWCA Civ 727 (25 June 2004); *Evans v The United Kingdom* (Application No 6339/05), Fourth Section (7/3/06) Grand Chamber of the ECHR (10 April 2007). This case concerned a woman who had entered into IVF with her partner in anticipation of treatment for ovarian cancer that would render her permanently sterile. He gave his consent to the creation of embryos, but by the time they came to be used the couple had separated and he refused to give consent to the embryos being implanted. Ms Evans failed in both the domestic courts and the European Court of Human Rights.

whom he is related. Many countries, including Sweden,[79] and the state of Victoria in Australia,[80] have laws providing that children will have the right on attaining adulthood to know the identity of the donor. From April 2005 the law changed in the UK to permit children born as a result of donated sperm to learn the identity of the donor once they reach the age of 18.[81] The first cohort of children in the UK able to avail of this new legal right will turn 18 in 2023. The Irish Commission on Assisted Reproduction has recommended that children should, on reaching maturity, be able to learn the identity of any donor whose donation resulted in their birth.

Who are the parents of a child born through assisted reproduction?

[11.38] The Human Fertilisation and Embryology Act deals with the issue thus:

Maternity:[82]   The woman who is carrying or has carried a child as a result of the placing in her of an embryo or of sperm and eggs … is to be regarded as the mother of the child.

Paternity:[83]   If a woman is married at the time of undergoing assisted reproduction therapy and the sperm with which she is inseminated is not her husband's, then assuming her spouse consented to her undergoing treatment, he will be legally regarded as the father of the child. If unmarried, then her male partner will be regarded as the child's father, if the couple went through treatment 'together'.[84] Where the woman has no male partner or where, if she is married, her husband does not consent to the treatment, then the child will have no father.

Where the sperm that is used is not the sperm that was consented to by the male partner (ie where the wrong sperm was used) then the male partner will not be recognised as the father because the consent that was given was not to the sperm that was, in fact, used.[85]

---

79   Insemination Act 1984. Research into the Swedish law has suggested that lifting anonymity does not result in a fall in donors: Daniels, 'The Views of Semen Donors Regarding the Swedish Insemination Act 1984' (1998) 3 Med Law Int 117. Cited in Kennedy & Grubb, *Medical Law* (3rd edn, Butterworths, 2000) 1325–1332.

80   Infertility Treatment Act 1995.

81   The Human Fertilisation and Embryology Authority (Disclosure of Donor Information) Regulations 2004. Concerns about the effect of the lifting of anonymity appear to have been misplaced; the number of men registering as donors in the UK rose by 6 per cent in the year following the removal of donor anonymity: http://www.hfea.gov.uk/en/1523.html (last accessed October 2007). The amending regulations arose in part because of a judicial finding that failing to provide information to the offspring of donors might amount to a breach of Article 8 of the European Convention on Human Rights: see *R (on the application of Rose) v Secretary of State for Health* [2002] EWHC 1593 (Admin), [2002] 3 FCR 731.

82   Human Fertilisation and Embryology Act 1990, s 27.

83   Human Fertilisation and Embryology Act 1990, s 28.

84   The man himself does not have to undergo any treatment: it is enough that the treatment service was requested by the man and woman together; see *U v W (Attorney General intervening)* [1998] 2 FLR 282.

85   *Leeds Teaching Hospital NHS Trust v A* [2003] EWHC 259, [2003] 1 FLR 1091. In this case a couple (both white) went for IVF treatment but the woman gave birth to mixed-race babies. It transpired that the wrong sperm, that of a black man, had been used. Although Mr A could not legally claim automatic paternity under s 28(2) of the Human Fertilisation and Embryology Act 1990, the court observed that the defect could be corrected by adoption orders.

[11.39] Recommendations along broadly the same lines as those used in the Human Fertilisation and Embryology Act 1990 have been made by the Irish Commission on Assisted Human Reproduction: where donation or surrogacy take place, the fact that the parties intend that the recipient be the parent of the child will be in large measure determinative of matters. Similarly, the partner of any recipient will be recognised as the child's other parent. Issues that have arisen in Ireland in the absence of legislation include the issue of the parental rights of a donor of sperm to a lesbian couple.[86]

Sex Selection and Pre-Implantation Genetic Diagnosis (PGD)

[11.40] Sex selection describes the process whereby embryos of one particular sex are chosen for implantation. PGD is where the embryos are screened[87] for the presence of particular disease states with a view to not implanting embryos that have a particular disease state. The two may go hand in hand in circumstances where a sex-linked disease (ie a disease that affects children of only one sex, such as haemophilia) is the condition that is being screened out. Another method of sex selection is 'sperm sorting', which is the separation of sperm carrying X chromosomes from those carrying Y chromosomes prior to fertilisation in order to determine the sex of the offspring. Both are permissible under UK law, once the reasons for doing so are wholly medical rather than social in nature. The treatment centre proposing to carry out PGD must have specific permission from the HFEA for the condition that is to be screened. There is much debate about the acceptability of screening for defects in embryos. Among the issues that are raised and which were recognised by the Irish Commission on Assisted Human Reproduction are:

(a)   Can it ever be acceptable?[88]

(b)   How severe does a condition have to be before it can be screened out?[89]

(c)   What about conditions that will not affect the child, but will arise in later life?[90]

(d)   What if a couple (eg a deaf couple) wish to ensure that their child shares a disability with its parents?[91]

[11.41] The issue of PGD has also arisen in the context of 'saviour siblings': embryos selected for a particular tissue type that will make them a good donor match for an existing child who could potentially be saved from a life-threatening condition with a

---

[86]   *McD v L* [2007] IESC 28; see also 'Sperm donor seeks joint custody of boy' (2007) Irish Times, 20 July. The Supreme Court granted a temporary injunction (by a majority decision) restraining the lesbian couple from taking the child to live permanently in another country without consent of the sperm donor. See also the Australian case *Re Patrick* (2002) 28 Fam LR 579.

[87]   The screening is facilitated by the removal of one or two cells when the embryo is at an early stage of development, which does not compromise the viability of the embryo.

[88]   See King, 'Preimplantation genetic diagnosis and the "new" eugenics', (1999) Journal of Medical Ethics 25;176–81.

[89]   Holm, 'Ethical Issues in Preimplantation Diagnosis' in Harris and Solm (eds), *The Future of Human Reproduction* (Oxford, 1998).

[90]   Robertson, 'Extending preimplantation genetic diagnosis: the ethical debate' (2003) 18 Human Reproduction, 465–71.

[91]   Savulescu, 'Deaf lesbians, "designer disability" and the future of medicine' (2002) BMJ 325; 771–773.

transfusion from the new 'selected' sibling. The English House of Lords determined that the UK HFEA could legally licence treatment clinics to provide tissue-typing services in the context of a child with a condition who could potentially be treated with tissue from a new sibling with the correct tissue type.[92] The Irish Commission on Assisted Human Reproduction has recommended (with expressions of dissent) that both sex selection and (with expressions of dissent) PGD be permitted for medical reasons.

Human rights and AHR

[11.42] It is frequently argued in AHR legal cases[93] that the human rights of persons seeking to avail themselves of AHR are being breached in circumstances where a person is denied access to fertility treatment or denied the right to use fertilised embryos already created. Broadly speaking, the human rights most commonly invoked are the right under Article 8 of the European Convention on Human Rights to respect for privacy and family life; the right under Article 12 to found a family; and the right under Article 14 not to be discriminated against.

[11.43] When tested in the courts, a reasonably consistent jurisprudence emerges. In respect of the 'right to a family', the courts will not grant that right in circumstances where to grant a person's application to have a child would, in effect, make another person a parent against his or her will; in other words, there is a flipside to the rights to respect for privacy and family life or to found a family, which is the right *not* to do those things.[94] Similarly, the mere fact that the right to found a family is delayed (eg by incarceration in prison)[95] is not enough to found a successful claim; the right can only be relied on where founding a family is prevented, not simply postponed.

Embryo research

This area is dealt with in Ch 17 'Research, Stem Cells, Embryos and Genetics'.

---

[92] *Quintavalle (Comment on Reproductive Ethics) v Human Fertilisation and Embryology Authority* [2005] UKHL 28. HFEA guidelines originally stipulated that the sibling to be treated must have a genetic condition, but this criterion was set aside in a review of HFEA guidelines in 2004. Tissue-typing is only available as an option of last resort, when all other potential donor sources have been researched. The issue of bringing a child into the world to act as a donor 'at lifelong risk of exploitation' is discussed in Wold, Kahn and Wagner, 'Using Preimplantation Genetic Diagnosis to Create a Stem Cell Donor: Issues, Guidelines and Limits' (2003) 31 Journal of Law, Medicine and Ethics 327; 327–39; also Sheldon and Wilkinson, 'Hashmi and Whitaker: An Unjustifiable and Misguided Distinction' (2004) 12 Med L Rev 2, 137–163.

[93] *Evans v Amicus Healthcare Ltd* [2004] EWCA Civ 727 (25 June 2004); *Evans v The United Kingdom* (Application No 6339/05), Fourth Section (7/3/06) Grand Chamber of the ECHR (10 April 2007).

[94] *Evans v Amicus Healthcare Ltd* [2004] EWCA Civ 727 (25 June 2004); *Evans v The United Kingdom* (Application No 6339/05), Fourth Section (7/3/06) Grand Chamber of the ECHR (10 April 2007).

[95] *R v Secretary for State for the Home Department, ex parte Mellor* [2001] EWCA Civ 472, [2001] 3 WLR 533.

SURROGACY

[11.44] Surrogacy arises where a woman acts as the carrier of a child on behalf of another couple; the nature of the surrogacy may vary from being inseminated with sperm (such that the surrogate is the genetic mother of the offspring) or being implanted with an embryo (so that there is no genetic relationship between surrogate and offspring).[96] It is difficult to police surrogacy by insemination, because there need be no third party clinician or institution involved, but surrogacy by implantation of an embryo necessitates medical intervention. The issues that arise with surrogacy are issues relating to parenthood and, often as a corollary, custody, although disputes arising out of surrogacy arrangements are rare.[97]

[11.45] It is not clear what the legal position is in Ireland when it comes to surrogacy.[98] The conclusion of the Irish Commission on assisted reproduction was (with one member of the Commission dissenting) that surrogacy should be permitted subject to regulation. The majority of the Commission also considered that the child born through surrogacy should be presumed to be the child of the commissioning couple. Furthermore, women who decide to participate as surrogate mothers should be entitled to receive reimbursement of expenses directly related to such participation. Finally, the child born through surrogacy, on reaching maturity, should be entitled to access the identity of the surrogate mother and, where relevant, the genetic parents.

The law in the United Kingdom

[11.46] UK law is that while it is not illegal to enter into a surrogacy agreement, the agreement will not be enforceable.[99] In other words, a couple cannot sue the surrogate if she does not hand over the baby and, by extension, nor can the surrogate sue the commissioning couple for failing to hand over any money due to her or for failing to take the baby from her. Nor can a person enter into a surrogacy arrangement for profit,[100] although it has been observed that payments which appear to be for sums greater than expenses (which may lawfully be paid to the surrogate) have been authorised by the UK courts.[101]

[11.47] Under English law the surrogate who undergoes the pregnancy and birth is the child's mother.[102] The competing legal approach (and the one recommended by the Irish

---

[96] Sometimes known as 'partial' and 'full' surrogacy respectively.

[97] Estimated at 4–5 per cent of cases in the UK: see Brazier, *Surrogacy: Review for Health Ministers of Current Arrangements for Payments and Regulation* (London: HMSO, 1998) para 6.22.

[98] For an excellent and thorough discussion of the history and comparative law of surrogacy, see Madden, *Medicine Ethics and the Law* (Tottel Publishing, 2002) Ch 7. See also section 7.4 of the *Report of the Irish Commission on Human Reproduction*.

[99] Surrogacy Arrangements Act 1985, s 1(b).

[100] Surrogacy Arrangements Act 1985, s 2.

[101] Jackson, *Medical Law* (Oxford, 2006) 876.

[102] Human Fertilisation and Embryology Act 1990, s 27(2): The woman who is carrying or has carried a child as a result of the placing in her of an embryo or of sperm and eggs … is to be regarded as the mother of the child.

Commission on Assisted Human Reproduction) is that the intention of the parties should determine parenthood—if the surrogate intends that the child is to be given to the commissioning couple and the surrogate was impregnated on behalf of the commissioning couple with the intention of them taking the child, then those intentions will determine parenthood and the commissioning couple will be regarded as the parents. So, the fact that the parties intended that the commissioning couple would raise the child means that the couple is obliged to do so (even if, for example, the child is born with a disability). Under the English approach, the commissioning couple can walk away, leaving the surrogate as the mother of a child she may never have wished to raise. The issue of who is the father of a surrogate child, especially where the child is conceived using the sperm of someone other than a commissioning male, has proved extremely complex in English law and we do not dwell on the complexities here.[103]

---

[103] See Jackson, *Medical Law* (Oxford, 2006) 879–881.

Chapter 12

The Extremes of Life II: The End

INTRODUCTION

[12.01] This chapter examines the legal issues that arise towards the end of life. We look at issues relating to death itself, such as whether there is a 'right to die' in Irish law; the distinction between killing and 'letting die'; 'do not resuscitate' orders and the law on euthanasia and assisted suicide. However, we also consider planning for the end of life and look at the law on advance statements and other legal methods that may (or may not) be used to map out the final episodes of a person's life story.

DEATH AND DYING

[12.02] There is no formal definition in Irish law of what constitutes death. In many countries, including the UK, the point of death is taken to be when brain death occurs and the Irish Medical Council envisages brain death as being the principal diagnostic criterion of death in the context of harvesting organs for transplantation.[1]

Treatment of the dying patient

[12.03] There is certainly no legal question that, as a matter of clinical necessity or inevitability, doctors may take steps to desist from futile treatment.[2] There is therefore no legal or moral stigma attached to calling a halt to a prolonged but fruitless resuscitation attempt on a patient who has suffered a cardiac arrest. Similarly, there can be no problem with turning off the life-support machine of a patient who has suffered brain stem death, although as we will observe below (see para **[12.11]**), consultation with the family of the patient before discontinuing life-preserving treatment is the legally preferable course of action. The Medical Council *Guide* says of care for the dying patient:

---

[1] Medical Council, *Guide to Ethical Conduct and Behaviour* (6th edn, 2004) para 21.1: 'Brain death should be diagnosed, using currently accepted criteria, by at least two appropriately qualified clinicians, who are also independent of the transplant team.'

[2] Where a doctor has formed a reasonable and responsible clinical judgment that treatment is not required and where that treatment would be against the 'best interests' of the patient (see para **[12.11]** below), the law will generally not compel her to provide it: *Re J (a minor) (wardship: medical treatment)* [1992] 4 All ER 614 (CA); see also *Wyatt v Hospital Hospital* [2005] EWCA Civ 1181. In *An NHS Trust v MB* [2006] EWHC 507 (Fam), the English High Court drew a distinction between withdrawing and withholding treatment. In the case of a child who was dependent on a ventilator, had no hope of recovery and was likely to deteriorate, the court refused to allow the withdrawal of ventilation, but directed that in the event of deterioration of the child's condition the following interventions could be withheld: (i) Cardio pulmonary resuscitation, or bag ventilation beyond 20 minutes, or the siting of an intravenous line or interosseous needle (CPR); (ii) ECG monitoring as an indicator for, or adjunct of, CPR; (iii) The administration of intravenous antibiotics; (iv) Blood sampling.

Where death is imminent, it is the responsibility of the doctor to take care that the sick person dies with dignity, in comfort, and with as little suffering as possible. In these circumstances a doctor is not obliged to initiate or maintain a treatment which is futile or disproportionately burdensome. Deliberately causing the death of a patient is professional misconduct.[3]

[12.04] However, there are many greyer areas and in particular those relating to patients who are not clinically dead or to patients for whom death is not imminent, but who have no hope of recovery and who in neither case can communicate their wishes. There is also the issue of the patient who expresses the wish to be allowed to die. Lastly, there are those who request help in securing a peaceful death on their own terms, through the active intervention of euthanasia or assisted suicide. Each of these scenarios is discussed below.

Treatment of the patient with no hope of recovery

[12.05] What about the patient who, although death is not imminent, has no realistic hope of recovery? Here there are two distinct answers, depending on the ability of the patient to communicate and reason.

Competent patients

[12.06] Where a person can communicate his wishes, is competent to do so (in terms of mental function and age) and does so voluntarily and on the basis of the requisite information, then the normal rules of consent (discussed in Ch 4 'Consent') apply. Such a person may refuse treatment that he regards as unwelcome and can do so 'notwithstanding that the reasons for making the choice are rational, irrational, unknown or even non-existent.'[4] The Irish courts have recognised that there is, in effect 'a right to choose to die':

The consent which is given by an adult of full capacity is a matter of choice. It is not necessarily a decision based on medical considerations. Thus, medical treatment may be refused for other than medical reasons or reasons most citizens would not regard as rational, but the person of full age and capacity may make the decision for their own reasons.[5]

This right, as we will observe when we consider the *Ward of Court* case below (para **[12.08]**ff) does not extend to a right to enrol others in assisting one to die and it is not certain whether it amounts to a right to refuse what is called 'basic care'.[6] Of course, it is

---

[3] Medical Council, *Guide to Ethical Conduct and Behaviour* (6th edn, 2004) para 23.1

[4] [1992] 4 All ER 649, per Lord Donaldson. See Ch 4 'Consent' para **[4.65]**.

[5] *In Re A Ward of Court (withholding medical treatment) No 2* [1996] 2 IR 79 at 156 per Denham J. The right to withhold consent to medical treatment, as articulated in the *Ward of Court* case, was approved by the Supreme Court in North Western Health Board v W (H) ([2001] IESC 70; [2001] 3 IR 622). See also the English case of Re B (Adult: Refusal of Medical Treatment) [2002] 2 All ER 449; [2002] FCR 1, in which a competent ventilator-dependant patient secured a legal right to direct doctors to turn off her ventilator.

[6] The English Law Commission report *Mental Incapacity* (Report No. 231, para 5.34) found that an advance refusal of treatment should not be permitted to include a refusal of basic care, defined in the report as 'care to maintain bodily cleanliness and to alleviate severe pain as well as the provision of direct oral nutrition and hydration.'

not necessary that a patient be dying or facing a condition from which he will not recover; the right to refuse treatment encompasses the trivial as well as the life-threatening. The refusal of treatment by a competent adult is dealt with at greater length in Ch 4, Consent (see para **[4.65]**).

Incompetent patients

[12.07] Where a patient cannot communicate with carers, due perhaps to advanced dementia or a persistent vegetative state, the problem of deciding between treatment and non-treatment in the face of a life-threatening condition is more fraught. In that setting, how can one know the patient's wishes and, if one does not know the patient's wishes, how is the decision to be taken on whether or not to continue with (or to initiate) treatment that, while it may be of some benefit to the patient (eg by treating an infection), can never effect a recovery or an appreciable remission in the patient's condition? In short, is there any right for the incompetent patient to die or, perhaps more accurately, to be allowed to die? If so, how extensive is that right and how is it to be activated?

A right to die

[12.08] There is no room in a book of this nature for a consideration of all relevant aspects of the right to life: questions of the moral value of life and the lengths that should be pursued in order to preserve it also lie outside the scope of this text. Instead, we focus simply on the legal position in Ireland, both what the law permits and what it forbids. Broadly stated, while Irish law mandates respect for life, it does not mandate the preservation of life at all costs: 'To care for the dying, to love and cherish them, and to free them from suffering rather than simply to postpone death, is to have fundamental respect for the sanctity of life and its end.[7] How, though, is the decision to 'free a person from suffering' to be taken where a patient cannot consent (or withhold consent) to dying?

Ward of court case — 'best interests'

[12.09] A woman underwent a minor operation in 1972 at the age of 22 years and during the operation suffered a series of cardiac arrests resulting in profound brain damage. She became a patient in a long-stay hospital facility and in 1974 was made a ward of court.[8] The woman was in what was described as a near-persistent vegetative state ('near-PVS')[9]. She was almost entirely unresponsive, totally unable to care for herself and was

---

[7] In Re A Ward of Court (withholding medical treatment) No. 2 [1996] 2 IR 79 at 156 per Denham J.

[8] See Ch 4 'Consent' para **[4.41]**. Note the proposition in the Law Reform Commission, *Report on Vulnerable Adults and the Law* (83–2006), that the ward of court system be abolished and replaced with a guardianship system instead.

[9] PVS has been described as a 'twilight zone of suspended animation where death commences while life, in some form continues' (*Rasmussen v Fleming* (1987) 154 Ariz 207 at 21). It is an irreversible condition of 'unawareness of self and environment'. The diagnosis is not frustrated by the presence of movements that are 'non-purposeful and explicable as a reflex response', but according to some guidelines nystagmus, a 'menace response' to threats and the tracking of objects with the eye *do* militate against the diagnosis: (contd/)

fed artificially until 1992 by a nasogastric[10] tube and thereafter by a gastrostomy[11] tube. Part of the reason for replacement of the former with the latter was the woman's apparent resistance to the insertion of the nasogastric tube. Without such feeding and without the intervention of medical care during times of clinical crisis (such as when she suffered infections), she would have died. The mother of the ward (who was also the committee of the ward)[12] applied to the courts for permission to withdraw further life-sustaining treatment, including artificial feeding.[13] Evidence before the court suggested that if feeding were discontinued the woman would die without distress in the space of approximately two weeks. The court laid down guidance for the refusal of life-sustaining treatment by the competent person that we have already commented upon (see para **[12.06]** above), but in this section of the text we are more concerned with the reasoning of the court when it comes to withholding or withdrawing treatment from the incompetent patient.

[12.10] Upholding the decision of the High Court, the Supreme Court determined that in the case of a patient suffering from PVS, treatment could be withdrawn and laid down the following markers:

– Treatment decisions on behalf of the incompetent patient should, in the first instance be taken by the family of the patient, in the light of available medical opinion;

– Feeding of the woman by means of a nasogastric tube and subsequently by a gastrostomy tube was inherently artificial and also a form of treatment;[14]

---

[9] (\contd) see 'The Permanent Vegetative State, a review by a working group convened by the Royal College of Physicians', Journal of the Royal College of Physicians (March/April 1996) 30(2). At least one subsequent English case (*NHS Trust A v H* [2001] FLR) found deficiencies in the College of Physicians definition and preferred the definition contained in Andrews, 'International working party on the management of the vegetative state: summary report' Brain Injury 1996, 10(11) 797–806; this latter report found that tracking and vague localisation to touch or sound can be consistent with PVS. PVS is regarded by some as a burden on the family (who are unable to mourn), on carers and on the State (which must spend its limited resources on the care of long term patients who have no prospect of recovery).

[10] A very narrow tube inserted through the nose and down into the stomach, through which food can be introduced.

[11] A tube that travels through an opening made in the abdominal wall and therefore directly into the stomach.

[12] The person appointed by the Court to take non-contentious decisions on behalf of the ward: see Ch 4 'Consent' para **[4.41]**.

[13] The institution in which the woman was resident had already agreed that it would not use antibiotics in the event of any further infections.

[14] Although the Supreme Court found that artificial hydration and nutrition comprise treatment that can be withheld or withdrawn in a patient's best interests (and English courts have reached the same conclusion), the Medical Council does not share this view (Medical Council *Guide to Ethical Conduct and Behaviour* (6th edn, 2004) para 22.1: 'Access to nutrition and hydration remain (*sic*) one of the basic needs of human beings, and all reasonable and practical efforts should be made to maintain both.' What characterises 'reasonable and practical efforts' is not stated and this is perhaps deliberate, in order to allow for the exercise of clinical judgement as each individual situation demands.

- Taking decisions of such magnitude involves a balancing of all of the issues involved, but the paramount concern will be the 'best interests'[15] of the patient. The views of the family were important, but could not be the sole decider of the case;

- The court should, if involved in making such a decision, approach the matter from the standpoint of a 'prudent, good and loving parent' in deciding what course should be adopted.

[12.11] In other words, it could be (and in this case, was) in a person's best interests to be allowed to die. The decision is predominantly a medical one, taken in consultation with family members and where a court is involved (as it may be in the case of a dispute), it will decide from the standpoint of a 'prudent, good and loving parent'. The right to life, concluded the Supreme Court, includes the right to die peacefully and naturally and not to have life 'artificially maintained by the provision of nourishment by abnormally artificial means which have no curative effect and which are intended merely to prolong life.'[16]

[12.12] The Medical Council approximately reflects this position:

> For the seriously ill patient who is unable to communicate or understand, it is desirable that the doctor discusses management with the next of kin or the legal guardians prior to the doctor reaching a decision particularly about the use or non-use of treatments which will not contribute to recovery from the primary illness. In the event of a dispute between the doctor and relatives, a second opinion should be sought from a suitably qualified and independent medical practitioner.[17]

In these cases of 'proxy consent', where someone other than the patient authorises treatment decisions in respect of a mentally incompetent patient, what does this term 'best interests' mean and are there other means for deciding on treatment withdrawal in the case of incompetent persons?

Best interests test

[12.13] The court in *Re A Ward of Court* favoured the definition of 'best interests' adopted by the UK House of Lords in the case of a young man left in a PVS in the aftermath of the Hillsborough football stadium disaster:[18]

> 'It is crucial for the understanding of this question that the question itself should be correctly formulated. The question is not whether the doctor should take a course which will kill his patient, or even take a course which has the effect of accelerating his death. The question is whether the doctor should or should not continue to provide his patient with medical treatment or care which, if continued, will prolong his patient's life... The question is not whether it is in the best interests of the patient that he should die. The

---

[15] See the discussion of 'best interests' when it comes to *giving* treatment to incompetent patients in Ch 4 'Consent' para **[4.37]**.

[16] *In Re A Ward of Court (withholding medical treatment) No 2* [1996] 2 IR 79 at 156 per Hamilton CJ.

[17] Medical Council, *Guide to Ethical Conduct and Behaviour* (6th edn, 2004) para 22.1.

[18] *Airedale NHS Trust v Bland* [1993] AC 789 at 868 per Lord Goff. English law has subsequently put the best interests test on a statutory footing: Mental Capacity Act 2005.

question is whether it is in the best interests of the patient that his life should be prolonged by the continuance of this form of medical treatment or care.'

Courts have further refined this 'best interests' test for withdrawing treatment from the incompetent patient by stating, as in Ireland, that the wishes of the family should be taken into account. Additional ingredients of the best interests tests include stipulations, as in Irish law, that where a court is charged with making a decision, then the decision should be taken from the standpoint of a 'prudent good and loving parent'. In England the courts have expressly reasoned that previously expressed wishes of the incompetent patient, even if not of sufficient force to determine the matter,[19] should also be factored into any decision.[20]

A competing view – substituted judgment

[12.14] The best interests test can be contrasted with the so-called 'substituted judgment', which is the preferred approach to treatment (and treatment withdrawal) decisions concerning the incompetent patient in the US. It has been described as follows:

> The proxy, or court, does not attempt to decide what is in the 'best interests' of the patient, but rather what decision would be made by the individual if he were competent. The court 'dons the mental mantle of the incompetent and substitutes itself as nearly as possible for the individual in the decision making process'[21]...It has been raised in cases involving incompetent persons to help establish whether, for example, to consent to the withdrawal of life support systems or to certain usual or controversial types of medical treatment, such as shock therapy or psycho-surgery.

---

[19] For example an advance directive (see para **[12.31]***ff*). See also *Re T (Adult: Refusal of Treatment)* [1992] 3 WLR 782 per Lord Donaldson at 787:

> Consultation with the next of kin has a further advantage in that it may reveal information as to the personal circumstances of the patient and as to the choice which the patient might have made, had she been competent to take it...they are factors to be taken into account by [the practitioner] in forming a clinical judgment as to what is in the best interests of the patient.

[20] Note also that the Supreme Court did not criticise the High Court for also having taken into account evidence of what the incompetent ward herself would have wanted: *In Re a Ward of Court* [1996] 2 IR 79 at 115 per Hamilton CJ:

> The learned trial judge [ie, in the High Court] further stated:

>> Whilst the best interests of the ward is the acid test, I think that I can take into account what would be her own wishes if she could be granted a momentary lucid and articulate period in which to express them and if, despite what I have already said, I can form a view on the matter. I think that it is highly probable, and I find the evidence of the family on this aspect of the case to be clear and convincing, that the ward would choose to refuse the continuance of the present regime to which she is subjected... and would instead choose the withdrawal of such abnormal, artificial feeding resulting in an immediate reduction of bodily functions and their attendant indignities and a peaceful death in accordance with nature within two weeks or so.

> This finding by the learned trial judge that the ward would... choose the withdrawal of such abnormal, artificial feeding resulting in an immediate reduction of bodily functions and their attendant indignities and a peaceful death in accordance with nature within two weeks or so was based on evidence from the family which he found to be clear and convincing.

[21] *Superintendent of Belchertown State School v Saikewicz* 370 NE 2d 417 (1977).

It is a controversial concept, not least because of the inherent difficulties of attempting to assess what an incompetent patient would have decided were he competent, whether that assessment should be subjective or objective and, if objective how can it really differ from the 'best interests' test.[22]

[12.15] The substituted judgment test is 'less overtly paternalistic than the best interests test, since it attempts to extend the principle of self-determination to patients who are in fact incapable of making their own decisions'.[23] But the difficulties of substituting one person's judgment for that of another, no longer competent, person are obvious.[24] The other issue is whether there is as much practical difference between the best interests test and the substituted judgement test in circumstances where the former frequently may, as we have already observed, involve an inquiry (via the next of kin) into the values and circumstances of the incompetent patient.

Limits on the right to die

[12.16] The *Ward of Court* case, although it permits the death of patients to occur in certain circumstances, is not a manifesto for euthanasia, nor does it create an untrammelled right to die. To be sure, the case upheld the doctrine of the patient's autonomy[25] and the right to consent to or withhold consent to treatment as he sees fit. Furthermore, the court took a stance that artificial life-sustaining treatment (including the withdrawal of artificial hydration and feeding) could be lawfully withheld when it is a patient's best interests to do so.[26] However, the decision on withdrawing treatment applied only to patients who meet four criteria:

---

[22] Dworkin, 'Law and medical experimentation' (1987) 13 Monash University Law Rev 189, 200.

[23] Jackson, *Medical Law* (Oxford, 2006) 205.

[24] See Elliott, 'Patients doubtfully capable or incapable of consent' in Kuhse and Singer (eds), *A Companion to Bioethics* (Blackwell, 1998) 452–62. An example of the use of the substituted judgment test is found in Re *Lucille Boyd (1979) 403 A 2d 744 (DC Cir)*—in this case the woman had prior and strongly-expressed religious views that stood in opposition to her proposed treatment:

> If the court decides that Mrs Boyd would reject psychotropic drugs on religious grounds if presently competent and fully aware of her situation, it must refuse to authorise such treatment unless the government can demonstrate that a particular "compelling state interest" would justify overriding Mrs Boyd's putative choice.

[25] As well as recognising how autonomy could be infringed by invasive feeding of the unresponsive patient: see the judgement of Denham J.

[26] The right of doctors to withdraw treatment from patients at the end of life was challenged in the English case of *R (on the application of Leslie Burke) v General Medical Council* [2005] 3 WLR 1132, [2006] QB 273. Although the High Court ([2005] QB 424) initially affirmed the wish of Mr Burke (who suffered from a progressive neurological condition) that artificial nutrition and hydration would not be withdrawn from him during the last stages of his illness, the Court of Appeal reversed that decision and stated that clinical judgment would be the determining factor in treatment withdrawal (at 296 and 301, per Lord Philips):

> The proposition that the patient has a paramount right to refuse treatment is amply demonstrated by the authorities... The corollary does not, however, follow, at least as a general proposition. Autonomy and the right of self-determination do not entitle the patient to insist on receiving a particular medical treatment regardless of the nature of the treatment. In so far as a doctor has a legal obligation to provide treatment this cannot be founded simply upon the fact that the patient demands it. (contd/)

(a)   they are in effect insensate;

(b)   they have no prospect of recovery;[27]

(c)   they are being kept alive by 'artificial' means, and

(d)   it would be in their 'best interests' to be allowed to die.

[12.17] The Chief Justice was explicit:

> [The issues in the case] are not about euthanasia and are not about putting down the old and the infirm, the mentally defective or the physically infirm but are about the question whether, under our law and Constitution, artificial feeding and antibiotic drugs may be withheld from the [woman in the *Ward of Court* case].[28]

There is therefore no legal authority in Ireland for euthanasia (in the sense of the deliberate shortening of a person's life by a physician) or assisted suicide. Therefore, while it may be possible to omit the continuation of artificial life-sustaining treatment. it is not permissible to take an explicit step with the intention of shortening a patient's life and this is true even if the patient asks for such steps to be taken[29] and '[e]ven in the case of the most horrendous disability, any course of action or treatment aimed at terminating

---

[26]   (contd/)

> The source of the duty lies elsewhere...So far as ANH (artificial nutrition and hydration) is concerned, there is no need to look far for the duty to provide this. Once a patient is accepted into a hospital, the medical staff come under a positive duty at common law to care for the patient and where ANH is necessary to keep the patient alive, the duty of care will normally require the doctors to supply ANH. This duty will not, however, override the competent patient's wish not to receive ANH...

> We have indicated that, where a competent patient indicates his or her wish to be kept alive by the provision of ANH any doctor who deliberately brings that patient's life to an end by discontinuing the supply of ANH will not merely be in breach of duty but guilty of murder. Where life depends upon the continued provision of ANH there can be no question of the supply of ANH not being clinically indicated unless a clinical decision has been taken that the life in question should come to an end. That is not a decision that can lawfully be taken in the case of a competent patient who expresses the wish to remain alive.

[27]   The question of whether the diagnosis of PVS is always made with sufficient certainty to validly underpin decisions to withdraw life-sustaining treatment in a patient's 'best interests' has also been raised: see Andrews, 'Misdiagnosis of the vegetative state: retrospective study in a rehabilitation unit'. BMJ (1996) 313: 13–16. According to this paper, 42 per cent of patients in one unit had been incorrectly diagnosed (one 'PVS' patient was dictating letters to his wife!). A diagnosis of PVS should be made and confirmed by at least two specialists, as well as being kept under regular review, before the diagnosis can be satisfactorily accepted: Giacino, 'The minimally conscious state: Definition and diagnostic criteria.' (2002) 58 Neurology 349–353. See also fn 9.

[28]   *In Re a Ward of Court (withholding medical treatment) No 2* [1996] 2 IR 79 at 100 per Hamilton CJ: see also, at 120, 'the Court can never sanction steps to terminate life.'

[29]   The point was articulated as follows in *Airedale NHS Trust v Bland* [1993] AC 789 at 865, per Lord Goff: '[To] act is to cross the Rubicon which runs between on the one hand the care of the living patient and on the other hand euthanasia.' Of course, there is no reason why it could not or should not be argued that *withdrawing* treatment such as artificial feeding is indeed an act. See the discussion of 'killing and letting die' at para **[12.19]***ff* of the text.

life or accelerating death is unlawful.'[30]A practitioner, whatever her clinical discipline, who administers medication to a patient for the purpose of ending his life would be guilty of murder or manslaughter.

[12.18] A category distinction is in effect made between, on the one hand, withholding or withdrawing treatment that is of no benefit and which will 'allow nature to take its course' or giving treatment that may have the unavoidable consequence of hastening a patient demise (see 'double effect' below—para **[12.24]**) and, on the other hand, taking steps explicitly and deliberately aimed at causing death, even if the motives for doing so are compassionate. The English courts have been asked to consider a request from a woman (in the end stages of motor neurone disease) for a declaration that her husband would not be prosecuted if he aided her in committing suicide: the House of Lords[31] and the European Court of Human Rights[32] both rejected her application. Of particular significance was the Court of Human Rights' declaration that the right to life recognised by the European Convention of Human Rights did not bring with it a right to have that life ended and nor did refusal of a right to assisted suicide amount to 'degrading' treatment of the woman.[33] It is anticipated that an Irish court would take the same approach. Conversely, the right of a competent patient to direct that treatment, even if life-sustaining, be withdrawn appears to be beyond doubt.[34]

Killing and letting die: a distinction without a difference?

[12.19] There are tensions created by the distinction between what the law allows and what it forbids: tensions that represent an intersection between law, morality and clinical pragmatism. The distinction often delineated between acts and omissions is in particular a tenuous one—is it truly an 'omission' rather than an 'act' to switch off a life-support machine or to stop feeding a patient? Many writers have explored some of the complex

---

[30] *In Re A Ward of Court (withholding medical treatment) No 2* [1996] 2 IR 79 at 120, per Hamilton CJ.

[31] *R v Director of Public Prosecutions and Secretary of State for the Home Department, ex parte Mrs Dianne Pretty* [2002] 1 AC 800.

[32] *Pretty v The United Kingdom* (2002) 35 EHRR 1. See the appendix for a brief account of the role of the European Court of Human Rights.

[33] The right to life is guaranteed by Article 2 of the European Convention on Human Rights; degrading treatment is prohibited by Article 3 of the European Convention on Human Rights. See Freeman, 'Denying Death its Dominion: Thoughts on the Dianne Pretty Case' (2002) 10 Med L Rev 3, 245–270, at 270:

> The courts came to the only conclusion open to them. But the time has come for a rethink...On suicide the law is unclear, on its relationship to other end of life decisions it is confused. The ban on assisted suicide is ineffective (a regulated system would stifle more abuse), morally obtuse (it discriminates against the disabled and privileges the incompetent over the competent) and, though controversial, out of line with popular opinion. (Had Mr Pretty assisted his wife's suicide, would he have been prosecuted? Would a jury have convicted? Would he have been imprisoned?). We can regulate very much better than we currently do.

[34] *Re B (Adult: Refusal of Medical Treatment)* [2002] 2 All ER 449; [2002] FCR 1. In this case a competent, ventilator-dependent woman wished to have her ventilator turned off by doctors, allowing her to die. See the further discussion of this case in Ch 4 'Consent' para **[4.65]**.

issues involved in the fraught relationship between patient autonomy and the presence or absence of a 'right to die'.[35]

[12.20] There are critics who point out that there is no material difference between 'letting someone die' and killing them. Those who endorse the decisions of the courts in cases such as *Re Ward of Court* point to the fact that it is the underlying disease that is responsible for the death of the patient and not the withdrawal of treatment; the withdrawal of treatment merely permits natural death to occur.[36] However, there are those who hold contrary views; either any attempt to draw a distinction along these lines is meaningless[37] or where we do draw such a distinction we should be careful about where and how we do it. One criticism made of the *Ward of Court* case is that the Supreme Court confused the value of the woman's life with the quality of her life and decided on the basis of the latter.[38] Where the distinction is blurred between killing and 'letting die' and especially where an argument can be made that there is little difference between them, one of two conclusions may flow. One is that it is inherently wrong to withdraw treatment and just as bad as killing that person. The other, perhaps more controversial, position is that in circumstances where treatment is to be withheld or withdrawn in the knowledge and intention that the patient will die, would it not be morally equivalent to kill the patient?[39]

[12.21] The distinction between permissible and impermissible clinical involvement in death appears to be, in part, how justifiable the clinical outcome is: where the choice is between death and what can scarcely be called life, then withdrawal of treatment is acceptable (as is death by double effect—see para **[12.24]**). However, where the choice is a stark one between life and death, the law argues that the clinician should always, in her action, choose life. But this distinction operates without considering autonomy: if the incompetent patient's life can be ended without his consent but in his best interests, where does that leave the patient who is competent but terminally ill and expresses a wish to end his life? He can opt to refuse all treatment, feeding and hydration and can starve to death and the law cannot intervene in any way, so long as the patient is of sound mind.[40] He can hoard some of his medication and administer it to himself. He can wait until he is terminally ill and further treatment may be withdrawn. But he cannot

---

[35] Doyal and Doyal, 'Why active euthanasia and physician assisted suicide should be legalised' BMJ 2001; 323 1079–1080; British Medical Association *Withholding and withdrawing life-prolonging medical treatment: guidance for decision making* (BMA Books, London, 2001), 1–14.

[36] See McGee, 'Finding a way through the ethical and legal maze: withdrawal of medical treatment and euthanasia' (2005) 13 Med L Rev, 357–385.

[37] See Kuhse and Singer, 'Killing and letting die' in Harris (ed) *Bioethics* (Oxford, 2001) 42–61 .

[38] Keown, *Euthanasia, Ethics and Public Policy* (Cambridge, 2002) Ch 19.

[39] Kuhse and Singer, 'Killing and letting die', *op cit*.

[40] Courts have directed the forced feeding of a mentally disturbed individual who has refused food with the intention of causing his own death: *R v Dr Collins and Ashworth Hospital Authority, ex parte Brady* [2000] Lloyd's Rep Med 359. However, they will not intervene in the case of a patient of sound mind who is refusing food and English courts have also opted for stating that refusing food and drink is not suicide (because food and drink in the hospital setting can be regarded as medication): *Secretary of State for the Home Department v Robb* [1995] 1 FLR 412.

request that he be helped to end his life or that his life be ended sooner than it would otherwise end.

[12.22] A contrary argument is that all life is worthwhile and that the clinical professions should not be terminating anyone's life, whether by assisted euthanasia or by withdrawing artificial feeding. Considerations of whether to withdraw treatment should be rooted solely in futility, in the burdensomeness of treatment and be confined to medical treatments only (and not, for example, nutrition and hydration, however administered) and furthermore should be independent of whether the patient's life is 'worth living' or whether the decision is in the patient's 'best interests'. Furthermore, opponents of life-ending acts or omissions argue that withdrawing treatment for severely incompetent patients must never be done with the intent of causing death even if death is a foreseeable consequence. It can only be done to relieve suffering.[41]

[12.23] The arguments can, and do, go on forever[42] and it would impossible to rehearse them all here. Much of the logic for drawing the line at 'omissions' is a fear of the slippery slope (see para **[12.28]**), that permitting the active ending of life in certain circumstances at the request of a patient opens the floodgates. The position taken by the law against permitting medical euthanasia or assisted suicide is an example of the balancing of different forms of rights. The right of autonomy in the case of euthanasia is abridged in the interests of protecting the old, the infirm and the vulnerable who may, the law fears, be unwitting victims of a decision to countenance legalisation of —or turning a blind eye to—life-shortening interventions.

Double effect

[12.24] One widely-recognised exception to the proscription against acting to shorten a patient's life is the principle of 'double effect'. A patient, for example a terminally ill patient with cancer, may be in such extreme and debilitating pain that high doses of morphine are necessary to relieve his symptoms. It may be the case that the required dose hastens the patient's death[43] as well as relieving the symptoms. Such a 'double effect' scenario is not regarded as legally or ethically blameworthy; the primary aim of the clinician in giving the morphine is to relieve pain and suffering, not to cause death (even if she is aware, from clinical experience, that death may result).[44] Indeed, if the legal position were not so, doctors might be inhibited from relieving their patients'

---

[41] See generally, Keown, *Euthanasia, Ethics and Public Policy* (Cambridge, 2002) Chs 19–21.

[42] See for example Finnis, 'A philosophical case against euthanasia' and Harris, 'The philosophical case against the philosophical case against euthanasia', both in Keown (ed) *Euthanasia Examined* (Cambridge University Press, 1995) 23–35; also Weir, 'The Morality of Physician-Assisted Suicide'. (1992) 20 Law, Medicine & Health Care 116; Blake, 'Physician-Assisted Suicide: A Criminal Offence or a Patient's Right?' (1997) 5 Med L Rev 294.

[43] Although this stark scenario is less likely to occur with modern pain-relieving opiate-analogue medication that gives equivalent pain relief to morphine without some of the potentially lethal side-effects such as respiratory depression.

[44] In *R v Cox* (1992) 12 BMLR 38, an English doctor administered to a patient who was in chronic pain—at her request—a fatal dose of potassium chloride, which was not an analgesic medication in any conventional sense. The patient (who was not terminally ill, merely suffering from severe and chronic pain) died and the doctor was convicted of attempted murder (because evidence was obliterated by the cremation or the patient, he could not be accused of murder). See Gillon et al, 'When doctors might kill their patients' BMJ 1999; 318:1431–3 (editorial).

symptoms for fear of being guilty of homicide. The key is that the doctor stops when she has given enough medication to relieve the relevant symptoms; she must not continue beyond that point or her intention may be doubted.[45] Similar scenarios arise with the patient who is manifestly dying; there will not be an obligation on the clinical team, having duly weighed the medical issues, to prolong life through enforced feeding or futile treatment through tubes or drips or by forlorn attempts at resuscitation.

Euthanasia and assisted suicide[46]

[12.25] In Ireland both voluntary euthanasia and assisted suicide are prohibited by the law.[47] The former describes the situation in which a person A kills person B at the request of person B, in circumstances where B wishes and intends his life to be ended and is mentally competent to take the decision that his life be ended. The latter term describes where person A affords to person B the means necessary for person B to end his life and where person B then uses those means in order to end his life. Both are sometimes casually regarded as an inseparable entity, but that is not so—the two are obviously different and in the USA, for example, the state of Oregon has legalised assisted suicide while keeping voluntary euthanasia outside the law.[48] We look here at the experience of a jurisdiction which has legalised euthanasia and assisted suicide.

Voluntary euthanasia and assisted suicide—the Dutch experience[49]

[12.26] One of the very few countries[50] to have formally enshrined assisted dying in legislation is Holland with the passage of the Termination of Life on Request and

---

[45] Note that there is much criticism of the moral and logical coherence of the principle of double effect; see Gillon, *Philosophical Medical Ethics* (Wiley, 2003) Ch 21. The doctrine of double effect is also invoked to distinguish (morally wrong) abortions from those cases in which the death of a foetus is a foreseen but unintended consequence of trying to save the mother (eg life-saving surgery to the womb or chemotherapy to treat cancer).

[46] See Stoffell, 'Voluntary euthanasia, suicide and physician-assisted suicide' in Kuhse and Singer (eds), *A Companion to Bioethics* (Blackwell, 1998) 272–279.

[47] Criminal Law (Suicide) Act 1993, s 2(2).

[48] State of Oregon Death With Dignity Act 1997.

[49] The US state of Oregon in 1997 enacted the Death with Dignity Act, legalising physician-assisted suicide (patients receive, upon written request, the medications—typically barbiturates—necessary to end their lives), but not euthanasia. See Chin *et al,* 'Legalized Physician Assisted-Suicide in Oregon—The First Year's Experience' NEJM 1999:340; 577. The text of the Act is available at http://www.oregon.gov/DHS/ph/pas/ors.shtml (last accessed October 2007). According to the 9th Annual Report (2007) on Oregon's Death with Dignity Act, 65 prescriptions for lethal medications under the provisions of the Death With Dignity Act (DWDA) were written during 2006: of these, 35 patients took the prescribed medications, 19 died of their underlying disease without taking the prescribed medication, and 11 were still alive at the end of 2006. In addition, 11 patients died during 2006 after taking medication prescribed under the Act prior to 2006, resulting in a total of 46 DWDA deaths during 2006. In 2001, the total was 21.

[50] Belgium also has a euthanasia law: see Adams and Nys, 'Comparative Reflections on the Belgian Euthanasia Act 2002' (2003) 11 Med L Rev 3, 353–376. France is, at the time of writing, mulling proposals to legalise euthanasia: see Lewis, 'The evolution of assisted dying in France: a third way?' (2006) 14 Med L Rev 1, 44–72.

Assisted Suicide (Review Procedures) Act.[51] The historical process that led to the current state of affairs lies largely outside the scope of this text,[52] but the present position is this: in Holland, euthanasia and assisted suicide are both formally illegal, although they have both long been categorised differently from, and have attracted far lighter punishment than, murder or manslaughter. However, the legislation creates an exception to the illegality: where a doctor is involved in an act of euthanasia or assisted suicide, she will not be prosecuted if she adheres to the requirements of the law. The Dutch Criminal Code in relation to euthanasia reads as follows:

> Any person who terminates another person's life at that other person's express and earnest request shall be liable to a term of imprisonment or a… fine.

> The [above] act… shall not be an offence if it is committed by a physician who fulfils the due care criteria set out in section 2 of the Termination of Life on Request and Assisted Suicide (Review Procedures) Act, and if the physician notifies the municipal pathologist of this act…[53]

This exception only applies to doctors, so that in all other circumstances euthanasia and assisted suicide remain illegal. The patient in question must be suffering unbearably, hopelessly and without any prospect of improvement.[54] A doctor is not obliged to perform euthanasia but, where she has a conscientious objection, she must refer the patient to another practitioner who would in principle be prepared to consider the request. The Dutch Criminal Code requires the doctor to show she has fulfilled the 'due care' criteria laid down in the Termination of Life on Request and Assisted Suicide (Review Procedures) Act.[55] The physician must demonstrate six things to show 'due care' has been taken:

---

[51] See De Haan, 'The New Dutch Law on Euthanasia' (2002) 11 Med. L Rev 3, 57. Australian law had a brief flirtation with euthanasia: the Northern Territory Government enacted the Rights of the Terminally Ill Act 1995 (NT), only for it to be subsequently and retrospectively invalidated by a decision of the Australian Federal Government which removed individual states' powers to introduce euthanasia laws (Euthanasia Laws Act 1995).

[52] See Griffiths, Bood and Weyers, *Euthanasia and Law in the Netherlands* (Amsterdam University Press, 1998) Chs 2–4. In 1984, a Dutch court accepted in the *Schoonheim* case (N.J. 1985, 106) that euthanasia could be legal in certain circumstances. The general practitioner had in that case performed euthanasia on a 95-year-old woman who had requested it. The rules for reporting deaths were also subsequently changed to allow doctors to voluntarily report to the prosecuting authorities, via Regional Review Committees, details of acts of euthanasia performed. The authorities would then generally not prosecute, assuming that the facts indicated that the doctor had complied with rules set down by the government and by the courts in the *Schoonheim* case. These informal rules were then reiterated in the Termination of Life on Request and Assisted Suicide (Review Procedures) Act.

[53] Section 293 (1) & (2). There are identical provisions for assisted suicide (s 294(1) & (2)).

[54] The majority of cases of euthanasia are for patients with cancer. In 2000, there were 2123 reported cases of euthanasia of which 1893 (89 per cent) involved patients with cancer: Dutch Regional Review Committees Report 2000, cited in De Haan, 'The New Dutch Law on Euthanasia'. (2002) Med. L. Rev 57.

[55] Section 2(1). The Dutch law also recognises the validity of advanced directives, or 'living wills', that request euthanasia (see para **[12.32]***ff* below).

- She was satisfied that the patient made a voluntary and well-considered request for euthanasia;
- She was satisfied that the patient was suffering unbearably and hopelessly and that there was no alternative treatment available;
- The patient was informed about his position and prospects for improvement;
- The doctor's decision about the hopelessness of the patient's position had been reached together with the patient;
- An independent doctor was consulted (and examined the patient);
- The patient's life was terminated with due medical care and attention.

[12.27] The precise meaning of each of these criteria remains to be fully explored, but it has been established that euthanasia can occur before the patient enters the terminal phase of an illness and that a patient's suffering may be psychological or psychiatric rather than physical. It is not necessary that the request is made to the physician in writing, but it must be voluntary and must be made by someone who is able to reason in an ordered fashion. Minors between the age of 12 and 15 years may request euthanasia and it may be carried out with their parents' consent; those of 16 years and over may take the decision alone, but their parents should be consulted.[56]

A slippery slope?[57]

[12.28] It is interesting—although in the longer term perhaps not significant—to note that in the two years to 2002, the number of deaths due to 'mercy killing' reported in Holland fell and that this fall appears to have been sustained.[58] Whether this indicates that so-called 'slippery slope' arguments against voluntary euthanasia or assisted suicide need to be treated with scepticism[59] is not clear; the apparent decline may be due to under-reporting of deaths or may be due to advances in training in palliative care.[60]

---

[56] Termination of Life on Request and Assisted Suicide (Review Procedures) Act, s 2(3) & (4).

[57] A 'slippery slope' in the bioethical sense of the word describes a process that commences by having (at least arguably) morally laudable intention but which has the capacity to be turned to immoral ends. For a discussion of some aspects of the 'slippery slope' debate, see Macklin, 'Which way down the slippery slope?—Nazi Medical Killing and Euthanasia today' in Harris (ed.) *Bioethics* (Oxford, 1999) 109–130.

[58] The number of Dutch euthanasia cases in 2005 fell to 2,325 from 3,500 in 2001. Assisted suicides dropped to 100 from 300. Reporting of cases of euthanasia and assisted suicide by doctors is thought to be in the order of 80 per cent: see 'Euthanasia Cases Fall in Netherlands' (2007) The Guardian, 11 May.

[59] Criticism, and a defence, of the Dutch system are contained in the following two articles: Jochemsen and Keown, 'Voluntary Euthanasia Under Control? Further Empirical Evidence from the Netherlands' *Journal of Medical Ethics* 1999; 25:16; Van Delden, 'Slippery Slopes in Flat Countries—A Response' *Journal of Medical Ethics* 1999; 25:22. A more up-to-date assessment discussion of whether there is a 'slippery slope' in the context of modern medical killing is contained in Smith, 'Evidence for the Practical Slippery Slope in the Debate of Physician-Assisted Suicide and Euthanasia' (2005) Med L Rev 13(1), 17–44.

[60] Many of those involved in palliative care argue that improvements in palliative symptom relief can help to militate against the suffering that leads to euthanasia or assisted suicide requests: see Jeffrey, 'Active euthanasia—time for a decision' (1994) British Journal of General Practice 44, 136–8.

'Do not resuscitate' orders

[12.29] A feature of hospital care is the annotation of a patient's chart with a 'DNR' (Do Not Resuscitate) order, indicating that a patient is not for attempted resuscitation in the event of cardiac or respiratory arrest. Often such decisions are non-contentious and perfectly justifiable, yet one must be conscious that entering a DNR instruction in a patient's chart is not a step that should be taken lightly and one that should arguably be rooted in respect for autonomy. A frail and unwell patient may nonetheless be immaculately capable of taking his own decision on resuscitation and may well benefit from resuscitation. Alternatively, family members may wish to be consulted on any such decision, although it is the patient, if competent, who should be the final arbiter of all decisions concerning his healthcare. There are many considerations that influence a decision whether or not to resuscitate, including the fact that CPR (cardiopulmonary resuscitation) is only effective in approximately one in five cases and the fact that a patient may be extremely ill,[61] but paramount among the considerations should be consent and autonomy.

Quick Reference Guide 12.1

The 'right' to die and euthanasia

> ❖ No legal blame attaches to deaths that result from a decision to allow a dying patient to die peacefully and without further intervention or to abandon futile attempts at treatment or resuscitation. Similarly, 'double effect' deaths that occur as a natural corollary of symptom relief are not unlawful.
>
> ❖ There is a right to choose to die. A patient of adult years and sound mind may choose to refuse lifesaving or life-prolonging treatment even if the inevitable conclusion is the patient's death. The reasons for refusing treatment do not have to be rational.
>
> ❖ In certain circumstances – which include patients who are in a PVS (persistent vegetative state) or a near-PVS – it may be legally permissible to withdraw artificial life-prolonging treatment, which the law holds to include artificial feeding methods. This might be termed a 'right to be allowed to die', based on the premise that the right to a peaceful and dignified death – when there is no prospect of recovery – is a part of the right to life.
>
> ❖ The decision to withhold treatment in cases where there is no prospect of recovery should be taken in the patient's 'best interests', judged from the standpoint of a 'prudent, good and loving parent'. The Medical Council does not agree with the Supreme Court that nutrition and hydration are artificial treatments, preferring to see them as basic needs.
>
> ❖ The *Pretty* case suggests that while the right to life may include the right to a peaceful and dignified death due to the withdrawal of treatment, it does not include a right to have one's life ended by euthanasia or assisted suicide.
>
> ❖ The law in Ireland and England draws a distinction between acts that are intended to end or shorten life and selective non-treatment that may have the effect of permitting a patient to die. The distinction – which is arguably a tenuous one – is aimed at erecting a bulwark against euthanasia.
>
> ❖ Holland and Belgium are the only European nations that permit at present euthanasia and that have formally legislated for its provision.

---

[61] Vos, Koster, 'In-hospital cardiopulmonary resuscitation: pre-arrest morbidity and outcome.' (1999) Arch Intern Med 159: 845–850.

[12.30] Lack of transparency can characterise the DNR order; decisions may be made by the clinical team without proper discussion with the patient or his family.[62] It is true that a patient or family member may, when told of the diagnosis and prognosis and the likelihood of emerging from CPR alive or with the same quality of life, opt to decline resuscitation,[63] but that probability does not justify failing to consult with a fully-informed patient about proposed treatment or non-treatment.[64] English courts have decided that DNR orders are legal although they should be based on appropriate guidelines and it is similarly likely that responsibly-made DNR orders would be upheld in Ireland. In *Re R (adult: medical treatment)*, the only case in these islands to formally consider 'not for resuscitation' orders,[65] the court was strongly persuaded by the joint British Medical Association/Royal College of Nursing statement on DNR orders[66] (see Table 12.1) and in the absence of an Irish equivalent, they are a useful indicator of how DNR decisions should be made.[67]

---

[62] Age Concern England. *Turning your back on us—older people and the NHS* (Age Concern, London, 2000).

[63] Many patients and family members recognise that conversations about death are an important part of their care and it is doctors and nurses rather than patients who find such conversations difficult. See Krumholz, 'Resuscitation preferences among patients with severe congestive heart failure: results from the SUPPORT project' Circulation 1998; 98: 648–655.

[64] Some studies suggest that only one-third of patients subject to DNR orders in the USA are involved in making DNR orders (see Levin, 'Life-sustaining treatment decisions for nursing home residents: who discusses, who decides and what is decided?' J Am Geriatr Soc 1999; 47: 82–87). Even if involved, many patients appear to have a poor grasp of the decision they have taken (see Sayers, 'An analysis of CPR decision-making by elderly patients' J Med Ethics 1997; 23: 207–212). DNR orders are more common for older people and, in the US, for black people, alcoholics, non-English speakers, and people with HIV. It has been suggested that doctors have stereotypes of who is worth saving and who is not (see Thompson, 'Do patients' ethnic and social factors influence the use of do-not-resuscitate orders?' Ethnicity Dis 1999; 9: 132–139.)

[65] And also that decisions on DNR may be taken for incompetent patients in certain circumstances by doctors even against the wishes of the guardians of the incompetent patient: *Re R (adult: medical treatment)* (1996) 31 BMLR 127 (Fam Div).

[66] *Decisions Relating to Cardiopulmonary Resuscitation—A Joint Statement from the British Medical Association, the Resuscitation Council (UK) and the Royal College of Nursing* (London, 2001).

[67] The US state of New York has legislation regulating DNR orders (Article 29-B, Consolidated Laws of the State of New York). Its essential ingredients are (i) all patients should be resuscitated unless an individual patient consents to the making of a DNR order; (ii) before giving consent to an order that he is not for resuscitation, the patient must be informed of the particulars of his condition, including diagnosis and prognosis and the risks and benefits associated with resuscitation in his case, together with the consequences of refusing resuscitation; (iii) consent must be given in writing or orally before two witnesses; (iv) consent can be given by all adults of sound mind, by parents on behalf of children or by a family member or 'designated decision-makers' (for example under an Advance Statement); (v) the consent can be revoked at any time by telling any staff member in the institution; (vi) an order may be made without consent only in the rare circumstances where a discussion with the patient intended to explore the issue would cause the patient 'injury', but a second opinion must be obtained before taking such a step; (vi) the order must be kept under weekly review in a hospital and two-monthly review in a nursing home.

Table 12.1 A Framework for DNR Decision-Making

Effective, sensitive communication is essential, and advance discussion with the patient or family should be encouraged, but not forced. The information imparted in such discussions should be realistic and outline both the limitations[68] and potential benefits of treatment.

Decisions must be based on the individual patient's circumstances, not for wholesale categories of patient, and should be reviewed regularly.

Competent patients should be involved in discussions about attempting CPR unless they indicate that they do not want to be. Where patients lack competence to participate, people close to them can be helpful in reflecting their views. Patient autonomy is always an important consideration and there may be a role for the advance directive, or 'living will' (see para **[12.32]** below).

Written information on policies should be available for patients and families.

In emergency situations, where no advance decision has been made or is known, CPR should generally be attempted unless:

(a)   The patient has refused CPR; or

(b)   The patient is clinically in the terminal phase of illness; or

(c)   The burden of the treatment outweighs the benefit.

Medical staff should not be compelled to provide treatment where such treatment is clearly inappropriate.

PLANNING FOR THE END OF LIFE

[12.31] What of those who have made a decision on their future treatment (or more pertinently for our present purposes, non-treatment) and wish to have that decision respected at a time when they are no longer capable of expressing that decision? Or alternatively, what of those who wish to repose decision-making responsibility in the hands of another person? We have already looked at the question of wards of court,[69] but wards are those who have *already* lost the power to make their own decisions and hence the courts appoint a 'committee' to take non-contentious decisions on behalf of the ward, while the courts reserve the right to take more contentious decisions. There is really only one mechanism open to the person who is presently competent to make decisions but who knows or fears that he will one day lose that competence and that is the advance statement about medical treatment. We also discuss power of attorney, but predominantly to highlight its limitations when it comes to medical treatment.

---

[68]   Burdens of resuscitation could include the risk of brain damage (if resuscitation is protracted or slow to be implemented) or physical damage as a direct result of the CPR process, such as fractures or internal organ rupture.

[69]   See Chapter 4 'Consent' para **[4.41]**. See also O'Neill, *Wards of Court in Ireland* (FirstLaw, 2004).

Advance statements about medical treatment

[12.32] Advance statements (or living wills or advance directives) are instructions, typically in writing, about how a patient wishes to be treated in the event of certain circumstances arising in the future and if, at the time of those circumstances arising, the patient is unable to consent (or withhold consent) himself. Not all advance statements are legally binding, as we will see below, but they may furnish a potentially vital piece in the jigsaw of ensuring treatment of the incompetent patient that is consistent with the patient's wishes and values. An advance statement, in effect, allows a patient to participate in decisions about his care after he has lost the power to express his opinion contemporaneously. Advance statements can operate in many scenarios, including temporary loss of capacity due to psychiatric illness,[70] but here we are concerned predominantly with advance statements activated near the end of life or with implications for the end of life. There are a variety of forms that such a statement can take, including any one or a combination of the following:[71]

-   a general statement of a person's aspirations and preferences that does not expressly request a certain form of treatment or non-treatment;

-   a statement of beliefs, often in the form of answers to a set of questions about the individual's wishes for the present and desires for the future;

-   a statement that names another person who should be consulted in the event of incapacity arising (this overlaps with the 'power of attorney'—see para **[12.38]**);

-   a clear instruction refusing some or all medical interventions—sometimes called an 'advance directive' (because it 'directs' a specific course of action) rather than an advance statement;

-   a statement that specifies a condition or clinical state which, should it arise, is the limit beyond which no further life-sustaining treatment should be administered.

[12.33] Anticipatory decisions or expressions can be roughly divided into wishes, statements and directives. There is no law governing advance statements in Ireland and the courts have not considered the matter explicitly, but one can draw upon the experience of other countries and reason that, under certain circumstances, an advance statement that refuses certain treatment or refuses treatment in a certain set of circumstances will be binding on clinical staff. English courts have agreed that, if contemporaneous refusal of treatment by a competent patient is binding, then '[t]he same principle applies where the patient's refusal to give his consent has been expressed at an earlier date, before he became unconscious or otherwise incapable of communicating it.'[72]

---

[70] Although a psychiatric patient would not be permitted to refuse in advance treatment authorised under the Mental Health Act, he may do so regarding other medical or surgical treatment.

[71] See British Medical Association, *Advance Statements About Medical Treatment* (BMA Books, 1995). The first law providing for the legalisation of the 'living will' was the Natural Death Act 1976 in California.

[72] *Airedale NHS Trust v Bland* [1993] AC 789 at 866 per Lord Goff. See also *Re C (adult: refusal of medical treatment)* [1994] 1 All ER 819.

[12.34] The author is of the opinion that an advance statement, properly made and containing no directives that were themselves unlawful, would be acceptable to Irish law; it appears to be the only logical corollary of the decision in the *Ward* case, with its categorical exaltation of personal autonomy.[73] The only advance refusal of care that will never be binding, because refusal will affect others beside the patient, including staff, family members and other patients, is refusal of basic care, such as hygiene measures and the relief of pain or distress.[74] Medical Council guidelines, as we have observed, indicate that basic care also includes hydration and nutrition.[75]

[12.35] An advance statement can be a formal written statement, although it can sometimes be recorded serially through the narrative of a patient's clinical notes, and may even be made orally, although a written record is preferable; an oral statement will not constitute a binding advance directive unless it is made repeatedly and consistently. The existence of an oral advance wish regarding treatment should be recorded in writing by the practitioner and its accuracy should be attested by a witness. Advance statements should be regularly reviewed. A person who has become reconciled to his illness, or whose views have changed over the passage of time, may not realise that he needs to alter a directive and a clinician's opinion that the patient's mind remains unchanged may be wide of the mark: 'the healthy do not choose in the same way as the sick'.[76]

If refusal of treatment, recorded in the form of an advance directive, is to be binding, then it must have been a voluntary[77] and informed decision, made at a time when the patient had the mental capacity to refuse treatment and the refusal must envisage the scenario currently facing the patient. As was observed in Ch 4, the general legal

---

[73] *In Re A Ward of Court* (withholding medical treatment) No. 2 [1996] 2 IR 79. The Supreme Court explicitly endorsed the decision in *Airedale NHS Trust* (see fn 73 above). The Law Reform Commission in its report *Vulnerable Adults and the Law* (LRC 83–2006) did not deal with the issue of advance statements on the basis that the Irish Bioethics Council was due to publish a report on the subject. The Irish Council for Bioethics (ICB), in its report *Is it Time for Advance Directives?* (2007) stated (at p 6):

> It has been suggested [by the LRC] that it should be possible for an individual to make a legally binding advance directive, provided that the decisions within that directive are themselves legal. However, in its final report…the LRC concentrated on "the limited context of certain healthcare decisions which might be conferred using an enduring power of attorney", as opposed to dealing with the issue of advance directives directly.

Of course, the reason why the LRC did not deal with it was because it thought the ICB would do so: in the end the ICB does not offer an opinion on the lawfulness of advance statements in Ireland although it does acknowledge the force of autonomy and the right of the competent adult to refuse treatment.

[74] The English Law Commission, in their report in *Mental Incapacity* (Report No 231, para 5.34) found that a refusal of treatment should not be permitted to include a refusal of basic care, defined in the report as 'care to maintain bodily cleanliness and to alleviate severe pain as well as the provision of direct oral nutrition and hydration.'

[75] See fn 14.

[76] Report of the House of Lords Select Committee on Medical Ethics (HMSO, 1994) 41.

[77] *Re T (adult:refusal of medical treatment)* [1992] 4 All ER, [1993] Fam 95. Situations where a decision may be less than ideally voluntary may include the immediate aftermath of a devastating prognosis or straight after admission to hospital.

approach is that the more serious a decision, the greater the mental capacity that is required to underpin that decision.[78] A decision to refuse treatment, with death as the almost inevitable result, requires greater mental capacity than a refusal of treatment where the consequences are negligible. Any refusal can be for irrational reasons or for reasons that most people would strongly disagree with, but that is not the point. Autonomy exercised by a patient with the mental capacity to do so is generally binding and there is no reason in theory that an advance directive should be any different, once the scenario envisaged in the directive has eventuated.

Mental capacity and the advance statement

[12.36] Mental capacity therefore arises at two junctions on the journey between conceiving of an advance statement and death: first, when the patient makes his statement; and, secondly, when it is sought to rely upon that statement. In the former instance, the patient must possess mental capacity, while in the latter he must lack it, such that the statement is the only possible way of ascertaining his views. While the law will presume a patient possesses the capacity to make a decision until the contrary is proven, there are matters that need to be considered with the patient who wishes to draft an advance statement refusing treatment:

– Does the patient have a broad understanding of what treatment is at issue and the circumstances in which it may be used, together with a comprehension of the benefits, risks and alternatives to that treatment?

– Does the patient have sufficient powers of memory to be able to retain the information long enough for the decision to be properly informed.

– Does the patient understand the consequences of refusing treatment?

– Is the patient making a free choice?

– Has capacity been maximised through the removal or amelioration of any factors that would tend to undermine it, such as infection, certain medications or a strange environment?[79]

[12.37] Where the clinical team is aware of the existence of an advance statement by a patient, they should consult that statement before proceeding to treatment. If the advance decision indicates a wish or a broad statement of values, then the clinical team may wish to be bound by that statement or may factor it in to the care given to the patient but they are not obliged to do so. If the statement nominates a person who should be consulted about treatment decisions, then that person should be consulted, although his opinion is not necessarily binding. However, a statement containing an express refusal of treatment in certain circumstances or an express refusal of certain treatment should be considered as binding when it fulfils the following criteria:

– it is clear and unambiguous;

– it was made originally by a person who had the mental capacity to do so;

– it envisages the circumstances that have presently arisen;

---

[78] See para **[4.34]**; see also *Re T* [1992] 4 All ER, [1993] Fam 95, per Lord Donaldson.

[79] British Medical Association, *Advance Statements About Medical Treatment* (BMA Books, 1995).

– it is a voluntary statement;

– the patient is not capable of giving a contemporaneous consent or refusal.

It should be noted that there are many critics of advance directives: criticisms include the fact that doctors are slow to act on them so that directives have little practical effect; that the statements themselves are frequently not of sufficient clarity to be reliably acted upon;[80] and the fact that an advance statement made when a person is well may not, in fact, reflect how the person feels once they lose competence.[81]

Enduring power of attorney

[12.38] We mentioned in the previous section that one form the advance statement may take is naming a designated decision-maker. In Ireland, this form of statement may have legal force when a patient has given 'power of attorney' to the person named in the statement, allowing that person to take legally binding decisions on his behalf. However, although the Powers of Attorney Act 1996 allows a person (the 'donor') to appoint another person (the 'attorney') to take 'personal care decisions' on his behalf in the event that the donor loses capacity,[82] the Act does not seem to envisage that those personal care decisions specifically include healthcare decisions. The Law Reform Commission has recommended that an enduring power of attorney should be capable of permitting an attorney to make certain healthcare decisions on behalf of the donor where the donor lacks capacity to make the decision.[83]

---

[80] Fagerlin and Schneider, 'Enough: The Failure of the Living Will' (2004) Hastings Center Report 34(2): 30–42

[81] Buchanan, 'Advance directives and the personal identity problem' in Harris (ed) *Bioethics* (Oxford, 2001) 131–156; Maclean 'Advance Directives, Future Selves and Decision Making' (2006) Med L Rev. The clash, in terms of personal identity, is between those who believe that the autonomy of the person making the directive (at the time of making the directive) is paramount, so that the directive must be relied upon even if the person appears to be happy in their present state (eg a person with advanced dementia, but otherwise mobile, happy and pain-free) and those who feel that the present condition of the person, and not merely his prior autonomous wishes, have a role to play in whether an advance statement should be relied upon. The former position is adopted by academics such as Ronald Dworkin and the latter by academics including Rebecca Dresser; see Dworkin, 'Life Past Reason' in Kuhse and Singer (eds) *Bioethics—An Anthology* (2nd edn, Blackwell, 2006) 357–364 and Dresser 'Dworkin on Dementia: Elegant Theory, Questionable Policy, 365–373.

[82] Under the Powers of Attorney Act 1996, the power of the attorney is only activated when the donor loses competence; prior to that point, he remains in control of his own affairs.

[83] Law Reform Commission, *Vulnerable Adults and the Law* (LRC 83–2006) para 4.32. The Commission also recommended that certain major healthcare decisions such as non-therapeutic sterilisation, the withdrawal of artificial life-sustaining treatment and organ donation should be specifically reserved for the High Court (para 6.72). The draft legislation prepared with the report also advocates a system of personal guardians (to be overseen by a new Office of the Public Guardian) to operate as a more flexible proxy decision-maker in circumstances where a person may possess the capacity to take certain decisions, but lack it in respect of others. Where an enduring power of attorney is activated and registered, any powers of an assisting decision-maker which conflict with those of an attorney will cease to have effect unless the Guardianship Board (which will have actual responsibility for the appointment of personal guardians) determines otherwise.

[12.39] There is a specific form for creating an Enduring Power of Attorney and if the form is not used, then the power cannot be exercised. The powers that can be transferred include responsibility for any one or more of the following:

- all or part of the donor's property, business or financial affairs;
- personal care decisions affecting the donor;
- making appropriate gifts or donations on behalf of the donor;
- any other specified things.

Any power given to an attorney can be subject to any specified conditions or restrictions. The attorney has a duty to ascertain as far as possible past and present wishes of the patient and factors that will inform his decisions. If possible, the attorney should involve the donor in decisions,[84] or family and any other person named by the donor or involved in his care. All decisions must be taken in the donor's best interests. An attorney must be over 18 years of age and have no vested financial interest in the donor (eg being the owner of a nursing home in which the donor is resident).

Clinician's role in enduring power of attorney

[12.40] Clinicians may be involved at a number of stages in the process. A doctor may be required to assess the patient at the time of making the power of attorney to ensure that he has the necessary mental capacity to give away the power of attorney. A patient who lacks mental capacity cannot make a power of attorney document (and similarly, it is only when a person has lost mental capacity that the power of attorney is activated). According to the English Law Commission, a person lacks mental capacity:

> [i]f at the material time
>
> (a) He is unable by reason of mental disability to make a decision for himself on the matter in question, or
>
> (b) He is unable to communicate his decision on that matter because he is unconscious or for any other reason.'[85]

[12.41] An English discussion document on the topic recommended that 'continuing power of attorney' (as it was called in the document) should extend to treatment decisions.[86] This power was proposed to be limited to situations where the donor was known, or was believed by the attorney, to lack capacity to refuse or consent to treatment. No attorney should be allowed to consent to the refusal of basic care or to consent to treatment where a patient had refused treatment by means of advance directive refusing that treatment. The attorney, it was recommended, should not be allowed to withhold consent to life-sustaining treatment unless expressly authorised to do so.[87] This would appear to be the logical approach for Irish law to take.

---

84 Powers of Attorney Act 1996, s 6(7)(b): this provision in the Act seems to disagree with the principle that the donor must have lost mental capacity before the power is activated.

85 English Law Commission Report, *Mental Capacity* (No. 231, 1995). Mental capacity is dealt with at greater length in Ch 4 'Consent', para **[4.32]***ff.*

86 English Law Commission Report (No 231, 1995) on *Mental Capacity,* para 7.7 *et seq.*

87 Many of these recommendations have been espoused in the English Mental Capacity Act 2005.

Chapter 13

Coroners and the Aftermath of Death

INTRODUCTION

[13.01] Death is one circumstance that regrettably, yet inevitably, must be dealt with by almost all health professionals at some time in their careers. In many cases, the cause of a person's death will be clear and the aftermath for family and professionals left behind is, from a legal perspective, uncomplicated. In such cases, a doctor will be in a position to sign a death notification form that will allow the family of the deceased or the institution in which the death occurred to register the death.

[13.02] It is nonetheless one of the more unpleasant and inconvenient facets of mortality that people will sometimes die suddenly and in suspicious or untoward circumstances. Where there is uncertainty about the circumstances of death, or in other situations circumscribed by the law, certain investigations may be necessary and these inquiries are most commonly the remit of the coroner.

[13.03] This chapter looks at some of the principal consequences for clinicians of patients' deaths. We look at the history and the modern role of the coroner, who is the individual principally responsible for the investigation of the circumstances that surround certain categories of death. As we will see, the coroner is not responsible for the attribution of blame for that death; investigations into the blame attaching to death are the responsibility of the police and final decisions on individual culpability are generally made by a court of law. Instead, the coroner is concerned only with the factual and relatively immediate causes and scenario of the death. This chapter also considers the question of the certification of the uncomplicated death.

[13.04] Quite aside from the question of the death itself, other consequences can arise from a patient's demise, such as a previously expressed desire for cremation. We also examine the issue of post mortems and consent to organ retention.

DEATH CERTIFICATES AND THE REGISTRATION OF DEATH

[13.05] A doctor involved in the care of a patient who has passed away will frequently be asked to complete and sign what is often called a 'death certificate', but is more correctly termed Part 1 of a 'Death Notification Form'.[1] This document is necessary for two

---

[1] The 'Death Notification Form' was introduced by the Civil Registration Act 2004 and replaced the Medical Certificate of Cause of Death. The obligation to complete and sign Pt 1 of the form and to return it to a family member is contained in s 42 of the Act. Where there is no family member, the form should be returned to an authorised officer of the hospital (if the death occurred in hospital) or to an undertaker or other qualified informant.

reasons. First, the family require it in order that they may register the death, which in turn will furnish them with acceptable proof of death for any administrative tasks in which they may need to engage to regularise the affairs of the dead person, such as redeeming insurance policies. Secondly, it is compulsory in Irish law to register every death with the Registrar of Births and Deaths[2] and the cause of death stated on the medical certificate is entered verbatim onto the register of deaths by the registrar. This register is then used for epidemiological and statistical analysis, a reason why certificates regarding cause of death should be completed as carefully and accurately as possible by the doctor.[3]

[13.06] Part 1 of the Death Notification Form is a statement of the 'disease which was directly responsible for the death'[4] together with any pre-existing conditions that gave rise to the condition directly responsible for death. Only a doctor may certify the cause of death and even then the doctor certifying the cause of death must be one who has been personally in attendance upon the deceased during his last illness. As we will see below, one situation in which the coroner's role is activated is where no doctor has seen the deceased during the month preceding death. In such circumstances, the coroner may satisfy herself that no further investigation is necessary, and permit the Death Notification Form to be signed.

Completing the Death Notification Form

[13.07] Any term used in defining or describing the medical cause of death should be as precise and accurate as possible. For example, the anatomical and clinical precision of 'acute infero-lateral myocardial infarct' would be far preferable to the vagueness of 'heart disease' and a certification of 'post-operative death' should be accompanied by the details of the operation and the condition for which the operation was being performed. A wholly schematic example of a correctly completed Death Notification Form is set out below at Figure 13.1.

---

[2] The Births and Deaths Registration Act (Ireland) 1880, amended by the Vital Statistics and Births, Deaths and Marriages Registration Act 1952, the Births, Deaths and Marriages Registration Act 1972 and the Stillbirths Act 1994. Registrars operate under the auspices of the Health Service Executive and each county will generally have one registrar.

[3] We have already observed (see Ch 1 'Introduction and History', para **[1.05]**) that the information contained on death certificates is often inaccurate: see James and Bull, 'Information on death certificates: a cause for concern?' J of Clin Path 1996;49(3):213–6; Doyle, Harrison and O'Malley, 'A study of selected death certificates from three Dublin teaching hospitals' J Pub Health Med 1990;12(2):118–23. See also Gawande, *Complications* (Profile Books, 2002) 191 et seq.

[4] From 'Notes and Suggestions Regarding Certification of Causes of Deaths', which accompanied each book of Medical Certificates of the Cause of Death.

Figure 13.1 Schematic Example of Completed Pt 1 of Death Notification Form

I	I	Approximate interval between onset and death
Disease or condition directly leading to death[5]	(a) Acute renal failure *due to or as a consequence of*	5 days
Antecedent causes[6]	(b) AIDS-associated renal disease *due to or as a consequence of* (c) HIV/AIDS	9 months 5 years
II	II	
Other significant conditions[7]	Hypertension *Mycobacterium avium* complex infection	8 months 2 months

Registration of death

[13.08] If a death occurs in hospital, the hospital will typically register the death with the Registrar of Births, Deaths and Marriages. Deaths that occur at home or at a nursing home must be registered with the local registrar by a 'qualified informant' attending the registrar's office. A qualified informant is defined as:

– a relative of the deceased[8] who has knowledge of the required particulars in relation to the death and who is not incapable of complying with these procedures by reason of ill-health;

– a person present at the death;

– any other person who has knowledge of the required particulars;

– if the death occurred in a building used as a dwelling or a part of a building so used, any person who was in the building or part at the time of the death;

– if the death occurred in a hospital or other institution or in a building or a part of a building occupied by any other organisation or enterprise, the chief officer

---

5 This does not mean the mode of dying ... it means the disease, injury or complications which caused death.

6 Morbid conditions, if any, giving rise to the above cause, stating the underlying condition last.

7 Contributing to the death but not related to the disease or condition causing it.

8 Civil Registration Act, s 37(1)(a). Such a person is under a duty to register the death within three months. Persons other than relatives are obliged to (i) within three months of the death, give the Death Notification Form to a relative of the deceased who is capable of registering the death; or (ii) register the death as soon as possible if no relative of the deceased exists or can be found; or (iii) register the death as soon as possible if more than three months have elapsed since the death and the date the death notification form was received by them.

of the institution, organisation or enterprise (by whatever name called) or a person authorised by the chief officer to perform his or her functions;

– a person who found the body of the person concerned or who took charge of that body or who procured the disposal of that body; or

– any other person who has knowledge of the death.

The informant who goes to register the death must bring to the registrar the completed Death Notification Form, which is then used to complete the death registration form.

[13.09] Deaths referred to the coroner[9] are registered when the registrar receives a certificate of the post-mortem examination or inquest from the coroner. The coroner is involved in circumstances where there is a suggestion of uncertainty, suddenness, wrongdoing or violence (or any combination of the four) attaching to the death or where—as already adverted to—the deceased has not been seen in the month leading up to his passing away. Only when a death is properly registered does a Death Certificate issue.

Quick Reference Guide 13.1

'Death certificates'

❖ Death certificates are more properly called Death Notification Forms, Part 1.

❖ All deaths must be registered by law and the death certificate enables that to be done. Only if the death is registered can proof be issued from the Registrar of Birth to allow the family to deal with the aftermath of the death.

❖ The information provided on Death Notification Forms is also used for statistical and demographic purposes. Information provided on the certificate should therefore be as accurate as possible for this reason.

❖ The notification of the death, together with the presentation of the Medical Certificate of the Cause of Death must be done by a 'qualified informant'.

THE CORONER

[13.10] The role of the coroner probably represents the most highly engineered interface between law and medicine in the British Isles.[10] A coroner must be legally qualified or medically qualified or both[11] for she makes legal determinations based on medical facts

---

[9] Civil Registration Act 2004, s 41 provides for death not being registered until the matter has been referred to the coroner. Where the result of a coroner's investigation includes a finding that the cause of death is different from that originally recorded on the Death Notification Form, the coroner can communicate that fact to the appropriate registrar and the register will be amended accordingly (s 41(3)). Note that under the Coroners Bill 2007, the coroner may issue a 'fact of death' certificate, prior to the determination of the cause of death (s 34).

[10] A more exhaustive account of the coroner's history, role and powers is contained in Farrell, *Coroners: Practice and Procedure* (Round Hall, 2000), Ch 1.

[11] See Department of Justice, Law Reform and Equality, *Review of the Coroner Service—Report of the Working Group* (Dublin, 2000): one recommendation made is that specialist coroner training programmes should be introduced to formalise instruction in both medical and legal matters, focusing predominantly on the discipline in which the particular coroner is not already qualified.

of the cause of death and her decisions are generally legally binding (although coroners' decisions may be appealed to the courts). The dovetailing of the two disciplines could scarcely be more neatly arranged; the role of the coroner has been described as coordinating the medical and legal aspects of investigation into sudden or unsatisfactorily explained deaths. A summation of the coroner's role was contained in one review of the Irish coroner service:[12]

> The coroner performs a public service by making inquiries into sudden and unexplained deaths, independently of the medical profession, the Gardaí, the State or any parties who might have an interest in the outcome of death investigation... In other words, society is demanding that no death be left uninvestigated unless there is a clear and certifiable reason for that death.

The evolution of the modern office of coroner has been a slow process unfurling over centuries. The coroner initially acted as little more than a fundraiser-in-chief for the Crown until many of the office's powers gradually eroded or were whittled away, leaving only the duties we now recognise as lying within the province of the coroner.

Basic principles of the coroner's role

[13.11] The modern coroner presides over a system for investigating and certifying deaths in situations where there is some question, doubt or lack of clarity concerning the death. In many cases there is little need for the coroner to do anything other than satisfy herself that no further investigation or formal inquest is required, but where necessary she does have broader powers to conduct an investigation or to constitute an inquest. The investigation may be relatively informal, but at the other extreme a coroner's inquest, should one be called, is in effect a court investigating the circumstances of death, but without apportioning blame for the death. A coroner, like a judge in a conventional court, can swear in witnesses and hear testimony that helps to clarify or indicate the cause of death. The objective of an inquest, and the overarching role of the coroner, is to establish the answers to four basic questions pertinent to the death being scrutinised: *Who* is the deceased? *How* did the deceased meet his end? *When* did the deceased die? *Where* did death occur?[13] However, the one thing that a coroner may not do is attribute blame for any death which is investigated.

---

[12] Department of Justice, Law Reform and Equality, *Review of the Coroner Service—Report of the Working Group* (Dublin, 2000) 25.

[13] Department of Justice, Law Reform and Equality, *Review of the Coroner Service—Report of the Working Group* (Dublin, 2000) preamble:

> It is critical to focus on the fact that the coroner service is a service for the living. It serves and reassures society as a whole by public investigation of sudden or unexplained death. It informs and supports the bereaved by establishing the cause of death—a service often critical to the process of mourning and adaptation especially where the circumstances of death may have been unusual or tragic.

Not all commentators take such a rosy view of the coroner's role in these islands: see Pounder, 'The coroner service—A relic in need of reform' BMJ 1999; 318:1502–3:

> Every coroner's investigation is an enforceable intrusion by the state into what would otherwise be a private family matter—the death of a loved one. Striking the correct balance between the reasonable needs of the state to investigate and the rights of the next of kin to privacy and religious ritual is not easy, and present evidence suggests that it is not done well....

While that may be the principal role of the modern coroner, the office has nonetheless an ancient lineage that needs some exposition in order to put its current functions in context.

History of the coroner's office

[13.12] The role of the coroner, although much about it has changed with the passage of time, is encrusted with history. Its precise roots are shrouded in antiquity; some legal historians argue that the office dates back to the time of the Roman Empire, but while that contention is possible there is little evidence to support it with any certainty. Most commentators tend to accept that the history of the coroner's office in Ireland can most accurately be traced back to 12th-century Norman-controlled England.[14]

Origins

[13.13] In 1194, Richard I of England (the Lionheart) instituted the office that is undoubtedly the linear predecessor to the modern-day coroner. Money was the main motivating factor: Richard had been captured in Austria and imprisoned near the Danube while making his way back from the Third Crusade, and was held ransom for a sum that all but bankrupted the Crown treasury. Richard's plenipotentiary in England[15] decided therefore to institute a new office with responsibility for securing more revenue for the Crown. This new office would also simultaneously—and, from a political point of view, conveniently—undermine the corrupt and rapacious Sheriff system, which was both the object of popular loathing and a drain on the public coffer due to embezzlement by the Sheriffs. In the 1194 document, an edict called the 'Articles of Eyre' declared that 'in every country of the King's Realm shall be elected three knights and one clerk to keep the pleas of the crown'.[16]

[13.14] The edict was originally in Latin and from the Latin word *corona*, meaning crown, came the word coroner (via the word 'crowner', which was current for several centuries). The first mention of coroners in Ireland is in 1264 and, according to some sources, the coroner may first have followed his Norman creators across the Irish Sea as early as 1212.[17] It should be pointed out that for many years the coroner's powers in Ireland only spread as widely as English rule was recognised. In many areas the Norman law espoused by the coroner existed side by side with ancient Irish Brehon law.

Duties of the ancient coroner

[13.15] 'Keeping the pleas' meant recording details of legal disputes that arose in the coroner's district and which required to be heard either in local courts or before the more

---

[14] Mention of the office of coroner does feature enigmatically and tantalisingly in some documents from as early as the eighth to tenth centuries, but these documents offer no context to confirm whether it is a still-earlier predecessor of the modern post.

[15] Richard never learned English and spent as little time in England as possible.

[16] Article 20. An 'eyre' was a travelling court that stopped in each township to hear major cases that had accumulated since the last visit of the court. Minor cases would be heard in the Sheriffs' Courts.

[17] Otway-Ruthven, *A History of Mediaeval Ireland* (London, 1968) Ch 5 (cited in Farrell *Coroners: Practice and Procedure* (Dublin, 2000)). Dr Farrell plumps for a date in 1215 as being the origin of the office of coroner in Ireland.

senior judges who would visit each district periodically to hear cases. As it could be many years between each judicial visit, careful compiling and tending of records was vital, lest cases that should be heard might be forgotten.[18] Coroners were in theory prohibited from hearing the cases themselves, but many did so until the practice was formally countermanded by the Magna Carta in 1215.

[13.16] The coroner investigated and recorded any offence that might subsequently give rise to a fine (and hence revenue for the crown), safeguarding the results of the investigation until the case could be heard. Offences the coroner investigated included the principal role that survives to this day, namely sudden deaths (especially murders), but also robberies, rapes and assaults. The coroner also had responsibility for determining the ownership of any buried treasure (treasure trove) and other somewhat more unusual duties.[19]

[13.17] Norman laws concerning death in mediaeval England and Ireland were especially complex and any breach of the duties placed on the individual who discovered a dead body or on the district in which the death occurred could be punished by heavy fines. Hence sudden death, suspicious or not, represented a potentially lucrative source of income for the state coffers. Any deviation on the part of citizens from the Byzantine rules laid down by the law in cases of possible murder would be noted down by the coroner and might subsequently be punished. Coroners were initially obliged to be Knights of the Realm and had to satisfy a certain minimum property threshold, the theory being in part that the wealthier a coroner was, the smaller would be the temptation to skim off illicit commissions or to take bribes. Coroners were elected, but only by a limited electorate: typically only the local landed gentry.

[13.18] It was during the late 13th century that the coroner's inquest began to be formalised, although it long remained a more unwieldy affair than modern hearings; the membership of juries could run into three figures, while jurors could also be called as

---

[18] One writer records a gap of 44 years between visits of the court, so coroners had to be patient as well as meticulous.

[19] One of the more curious and long-lasting of the coroner's historical powers was *deodand*—an ancient legal tradition where the object responsible for a person's death was believed to be cleansed by its forfeiture to the Church or to the Crown. The fatal object (examples include a sword, an animal, a mill wheel, even a tree) could therefore be confiscated by the coroner for the Treasury or its estimated monetary equivalent given to the victim's family as partial compensation. In one of those occasional oversights that pepper legal history, deodand survived into the nineteenth century, when legal applications for deodand-based recompense were made by the families of individuals killed in locomotive accidents. A case in 1839 involved a man and a horse killed by a locomotive at a crossing; a jury at the inquest in that case awarded the family £1400, the full value of the locomotive engine. Deodand was abolished in 1846, presumably to the enormous relief of the fledgling railway industry. A coroner also took charge of felons who chose to 'abjure the realm': certain classes of criminal could, after making a full confession and forfeiting their possessions, safely quit the kingdom in accordance with a formal and tortuous set of rules. Failure to adhere to the rules or to leave the country in time made the abjurer fair game, his head 'forfeit to any man who can lift a sword'. See also fn 23.

witnesses. The inquest was traditionally held at the site of the death or crime and the coroner was required to conduct an examination of the corpse or victim and record the clinical findings associated with the murder, rape or assault. Not until 1836 was a coroner permitted to hire an outside medical expert to conduct a post mortem.[20]

[13.19] The coroner would also be present at any trials by ordeal in order to record the results.[21] The coroner's role at the ordeal was in essence to assess whether the alleged wrongdoer undergoing the ordeal should subsequently (and often posthumously) be required to forfeit his goods to the Crown. One additional duty of the early Irish coroner was the 'presentment of Irishry'. Unless it could be proved otherwise, any murder victim was presumed to be Norman and a consequent fine[22] was levied on the Irish population of the locality in which the body was found. To avoid the fine, the natives had to prove— by way of a 'presentment' typically made by the relatives of the dead man —that the victim was Irish.

[13.20] Few of the coroner's historical roles[23] survive into the present. The longest lasting is obviously the coroner's role in the investigation of death, while the coroner's responsibility for dealing with treasure trove (the determination of the value and ownership of precious gold and silver artefacts) persisted into the 1990s.[24]

---

[20] One commentator points out that a medical expert would not often have been necessary: given the available implements, mediaeval murders were rarely subtle affairs. In England, the coroner was obliged to view the body of the deceased until 1980. In 1767, a surgeon was appointed to assist the coroners of Dublin (see Farrell, fn 10 above, 19). In Ireland, s 27(1) of the Coroners Act 1962 places an obligation upon the coroner to view the body prior to an inquest unless a Garda gives evidence that she has viewed the body of the deceased. Section 32 of the Coroners Bill 2007 does not require the coroner to view the body: the coroner may direct a member of the Garda Síochána or such other person as may be thought appropriate to view the body and give evidence as to identity.

[21] Trials by ordeal were a primitive method for ascertaining guilt or innocence, most strongly associated in the popular consciousness with the detection of witchcraft, but also the investigation of murders and other serious offences. Ordeals could include being bound and thrown into deep water; floating meant guilt, sinking (and therefore sometimes drowning) signified innocence. Other ordeals included bringing the alleged perpetrator before the body of the victim— if the victim's wounds began to bleed again, then guilt was determined.

[22] Called the *murdrum*.

[23] Easily the most esoteric of the coroner's mediaeval duties was the obligation to investigate certain catches made by fishermen, namely sturgeon and whale, all of which belonged to the Crown, and failure to yield up the catch or its monetary equivalent to the royal coffers would result in a fine.

[24] Coroners Act 1962, s 49: this section originally regulated the coroner's powers in this respect, but the National Monuments (Amendment) Act 1994 transferred all duties to do with precious artefacts found in the Republic to the Director of the National Museum in Dublin, an apportionment of responsibility more in keeping with the purpose of contemporary treasure trove. There is no mention of treasure trove in the Coroners Bill 2007.

Quick Reference Guide 13.2

History of the coroner

> ❖ The coroner's office is of late 12th century origin in England and dates back to the early 13th century in Ireland.
>
> ❖ In essence the role of the coroner was as a fundraiser for the crown. He fulfilled this role by investigating and recording the details of matters that would have to be determined later by the courts (called 'keeping the pleas'). The courts would hear the cases and the fines they imposed would be directed to the state coffers.
>
> ❖ The main areas of concern for the coroner were those involving violent crimes, but the job also involved determining the ownership of buried treasure ('treasure trove') as well as certain other matters including *deodand,* the presentment of Irishry and abjuration of the realm.
>
> ❖ The coroner's inquest was initially an unruly affair, taking place at the scene of the crime and featuring an enormous jury.
>
> ❖ The evolution of more orthodox – to modern eyes – forms of taxation led to the diminution of the coroner's fund-raising role and left the office with its current predominant focus on sudden and unexplained deaths.

The modern coroner

[13.21] Over the years, many of the powers of the coroner were stripped away. Taxation gradually became a more rational process and thus revenue to the Crown increasingly came through more uniform and orthodox channels. By 1500, the Eyre—the wandering court for which the coroner had to 'keep the pleas'—was long gone, Acts of Parliament had been passed to limit or eliminate many of the powers of the coroner and Justices of the Peace assumed a more important role. The coroner became predominantly concerned with investigations of death.[25]

Law in flux

[13.22] The law that regulates the modern office of coroner in Ireland is contained in the Coroners Act 1962 and the legislation has in turn been fleshed out by decisions of the Irish courts. The 1962 Act took the various statutes that had previously formed an ill-fitting patchwork cloak of guidance for the coroner and consolidated them, updating and replacing laws that dated back as far as the thirteenth-century reign of Edward I.

[13.23] Preparation of the ground for reform of the coroner service has been underway for some time. In 2000 the Department of Justice, Equality and Law Reform published its *Review of the Coroner Service*, compiled by a working group appointed by the Department.[26] The working group made more than 100 recommendations for reform of

---

[25] The vast plethora of legislation that punctuated the transition from mediaeval to modern coroners is dealt with in Farrell, *Coroners: Practice and Procedure* (Dublin, 2000) Ch 1.

[26] Department of Justice, Equality and law Reform, Dublin, 2000. Available for download from http://www.justice.ie/en/JELR/ReviewCoronerService.pdf/Files/ReviewCoronerService.pdf (last accessed October 2007). See also Pounder, 'The coroner service—A relic in need of reform' BMJ 1999; 318:1502–3. The need for reform in the UK was also highlighted in The Shipman Inquiry Third Report, *Death Certification and the Investigation of Deaths by Coroners* (Cm 5854)(July 2003).

the coroner service, including the establishment of a Coroners Rules Committee, which prepared Coroners Rules, published in 2003.[27] Certain changes relating to the calling of medical witnesses, the serving of summonses and the failure of witnesses to attend were ushered in by the Coroners (Amendment) Act 2005. However, thorough reform is promised by the Coroners Bill 2007. It is proposed in the text that follows to deal with the legislation that remains in force (Coroners Act 1962), but also to highlight where appropriate both in the text and in footnotes the important and material changes that will be made should the Coroners Bill 2007 become law. Note, however, that there has been criticism of the 2007 Bill (including from coroners), so the final form of any legislation, if enacted, may be different from that which is described in this chapter.

Who can be a coroner?

[13.24] The Coroners Acts (Ireland) of 1829 and 1846 stipulated that the only requirement to be a coroner was that the prospective coroner should satisfy a certain property threshold. The 1881 Act of the same name adopted a more inclusive approach, necessitating only that a coroner be a surgeon, physician, solicitor, justice of the peace or barrister. The 1962 Act required that any coroner should have at least five years' experience as a registered medical practitioner, a barrister or a solicitor.[28] The Coroners Bill 2007 maintains the same requirement.[29]

[13.25] Each coroner has a deputy (termed an 'assistant' in the Coroners Bill 2007) who acts for the coroner if the principal is away or ill. Coroners have frequently been part-time holders of their office; however, the Coroners Bill 2007 provides that coroners appointed after the legislation comes into force will not be permitted to hold any other paid employment,[30] although assistant coroners may hold office on a part-time basis.[31]

Organisation of the coroner service

[13.26] The coroner service is administered on a geographical basis, divided largely along county or borough lines; coroners are no longer elected but, under the 1962 Act, are appointed[32] and paid[33] by the relevant local authority. There are 48 coroner districts in total in the Republic of Ireland, each of which is served by a coroner and her deputy.[34]

---

[27] *Report of the Rules Committee* (Department of Justice, 2003). Available for download at http://www.justice.ie/en/JELR/coronersfulljob.pdf/Files/coronersfulljob.pdf (last accessed October 2007).

[28] Coroners Act, 1962, s 14(1). As of 2000, about half of the coroners working in the Republic of Ireland were medical practitioners while half were legally qualified. One or two had a foot in both camps—see *Review of the Coroner Service—Report of the Working Group*, above.

[29] Coroners Bill 2007, s 19(2).

[30] Coroners Bill 2007, s 19(7).

[31] Coroners Bill 2007, s 18(4). Unlike under the 1962 Act, where the coroner appoints her deputy (and may also cancel the appointment of any deputy, so long she has appointed a replacement), assistant coroners will be appointed under the 2007 Bill by the Government.

[32] In general the coroner must live within the district for which she is responsible unless she has obtained permission of the Minister for Justice, Equality and Law Reform to do otherwise: Coroners Act 1962, s 8(2).

[33] Coroners Act, 1962 s 9(1).

[34] Coroners Act, 1962 s 12.

Many of the larger counties are divided into several districts, while smaller or sparsely populated counties may be served by a single coroner. Each of the cities of Dublin, Cork, Waterford and Limerick has its own coroner.[35]

[13.27] Under the 1962 Act, coroners have responsibility for investigating sudden, suspicious or unnatural deaths that occur in their geographical area of responsibility. It is the place of death that is generally determinative of which coroner will investigate a death, although an investigation may be moved to the jurisdiction of another coroner by agreement. This might occur when two people who were injured following the same accident were moved to different hospitals under the jurisdiction of two different coroners and subsequently died in those hospitals. Even though the deaths might have occurred in two separate coroner districts, the investigations or inquests into the deaths—after all, the result of a single accident—may be heard by the coroner for only one of the districts, perhaps the one where the accident took place.[36]

Proposed changes in the Coroners Bill 2007

[13.28] Under the Coroners Bill 2007, new national offices of Chief Coroner and Deputy Chief Coroner are created and will be appointed by the Government. The Government, rather than local authorities, will also take over the role of appointing coroners and assistant coroners. The role of the Chief Coroner is to:[37]

- provide leadership and direction in all coronial matters;
- ensure the efficient and effective management of coronial matters;
- determine the allocation of coroners, assistant coroners and coroner's officers to regions, subject to the right of the Minister for Justice to set the number of coroner regions in the country;
- determine expeditiously appeals or applications to him or her under the Act;
- liaise with other statutory bodies charged with the investigation of accidents, incidents or diseases which have or may have caused or resulted in a reportable death;
- ensure that proper and effective communication is made with the public regarding the role and activities of the Coroner Service;
- ensure that all necessary training and development is provided to coroners; and
- provide advice to the Minister on coronial matters.

---

[35] The boundaries between adjoining areas over which any combination of coroners has jurisdiction may be redrawn under the 1962 Act by the Minister for Justice, Equality and Law Reform, assuming all the relevant districts affected are under the control of the same local authority (Coroners Act 1962, s 6(3)). In certain circumstances, coroners' districts may be amalgamated (Coroners Act 1962, ss 6(4) and 7); this might occur with depopulation or if the service in an area were to be taken over by a full-time, rather than part-time, coroner.

[36] Coroners Act 1962, ss 17–21; see also Coroners Bill 2007, ss 28–29. Where a person dies in a region other than the region in which they were ordinarily resident prior to death, it is the region of residence in which any investigation will take place: Coroners Bill 2007, s 28(2).

[37] Coroners Bill 2007, s 14. The precise role of the Deputy Chief Coroner is set by the Chief Coroner, but duties include discharging the functions of the Chief Coroner when circumstances require.

Under the 2007 Bill, the broad principle that coroners investigate certain categories of deaths in the districts for which they have responsibility will continue to hold true, but the categories of death that must be investigated are broadened (see para **[13.32]**). The Bill states explicitly that 'the Coroner Service shall operate on a regional basis' and the Minister for Justice will determine the number of regions.[38] Each region will have no fewer than two coroners and no fewer than one assistant coroner. The 2007 Bill also creates another new role, known as the Coroner's Officer (who may be a member of the Garda Síochána) to assist the coroner in the discharge of his functions.[39]

Duties of the coroner

[13.29] The coroner makes inquiries into sudden and unexplained deaths acting independently of outside influences, but how many such deaths are there? According to figures from 2000, approximately 32,000 deaths occur each year in the Republic of Ireland, of which 7250 (22 per cent)[40] are reported to a coroner. Under the 1962 Act, there are certain categories of death which *must* be reported to the coroner in charge of the area in which the death took place:[41]

- where there is reason to believe that the deceased person died, either directly or indirectly, as a result of violence or misadventure or by unfair means;

- where there is reason to believe that the deceased person died, either directly or indirectly, as the result of negligence or misconduct or malpractice on the part of others;

- where there is reason to believe that the deceased person died, either directly or indirectly, from any cause other than natural disease.

---

[38] Coroners Bill 2007, s 12. The determination of the number of regions is to be made with regard to s 12(3): (a) the size of the population in the proposed region and its distribution; (b) the mortality rate; (c) the configuration of cities, towns and hospitals; (d) the likely availability and distribution of support services; and (e) the opinion of the Chief Coroner. In certain circumstances, deaths of persons ordinarily resident in Ireland that occur outside the State may be investigated. The circumstances require the sanction of the Chief Coroner and include where the death—although occurring abroad—arose from circumstances within the State; where the deceased was abroad in the service of the State; where the death was the result of (a) murder, manslaughter or infanticide, (b) drunk or dangerous driving or (c) assisted suicide: Coroners Bill 2007, s 31. Any body repatriated into, or removed from, the State must be notified to the coroner for the region in which the body is to be disposed of: Coroners Bill 2007, ss 39–40.

[39] Coroners Bill 2007, s 21. Coroners' officers have, if directed by the coroner, powers of entry search and seizure; the coroner has similar powers but it seems most likely that these powers would ordinarily be exercised by coroners' officers: Coroners Bill 2007, s 37. Entry into a dwelling place can only be with the consent of the owner or with a warrant from the District Court.

[40] *Review of the Coroner Service–Report of the Working Group*, above. This figure is appreciably lower than in the United Kingdom, where 190,000 (approx 33 per cent) of all deaths in England and Wales were reported to the coroner in 1996. In 1970 that number was 130,000, or 20 per cent. See Tarling, *Coroner Service Survey* (London: Home Office Research and Statistics Directorate, 1998).

[41] Coroners Act 1962, s 18(4).

Furthermore, even if a death is thought to be a result of natural causes, it must nonetheless be reported to the coroner if the deceased was not seen by a medical practitioner within one month before his death. There are also certain categories of person laid down in the Coroners Act 1962 who are obliged by law to notify the coroner if they become aware of a death that occurs in any of the circumstances outlined above. These categories are very broad:

> Every medical practitioner, registrar of deaths or funeral undertaker and every occupier of a house or mobile dwelling and every person in charge of any institution or premises, in which a deceased person was residing at the time of his death who has reason to believe that the deceased person died [in any of the circumstances outlined above]...[42]

[13.30] However, the obligation on any of these persons to inform the coroner is purged once the person, instead of informing the coroner of the death, notifies a Garda of the rank of sergeant or higher.[43] The obligation to notify the appropriate coroner for the region in which the body was found or in which the death occurred then passes to the Garda.

Proposed changes in the Coroners Bill 2007

[13.31] Under the Coroners Bill 2007, the categories of reportable death are greatly expanded and may be categorised as follows:[44]

Mechanism/circumstances of death

– Where death was (a) violent or unnatural, (b) due to unknown causes, (c) accidental, (d) suspicious, (e) suicide, suspected suicide or suspected assisted suicide;

– Where the deceased was not seen by a registered medical practitioner within the 28 days preceding death;

– Death due to possible negligence, misconduct or malpractice;

---

[42] Coroners Act 1962, s 18(4). Under the Coroners Bill 2007 (s 26(4)) it is sufficient to notify any member of An Garda Síochána–there is no minimum rank specified. Under the 2007 Bill, the categories of person obliged to report a death are also broadened: (a) any registered medical practitioner or registered nurse having had responsibility for, or involvement in the care of, the deceased person in the period immediately before his or her death or having been present at his or her death; (b) the funeral director responsible for the disposal of the body of the deceased person; (c) an occupier of a house or other dwelling, including a mobile dwelling, in which the deceased person was residing at the time of his or her death; (d) the person in charge of any public or private institution or premises... in which the deceased person was residing or receiving treatment or care at the time of his or her death; (e) a person having care of the deceased person immediately prior to his or her death, the person in charge of the aircraft or vessel, which the deceased person was on at the time of his or her death...: Coroners Bill 2007, s 25(3). In cases where death occurs on a vehicle, plane or vessel in transit the obligation is to report the death as soon as possible after disembarkation.

[43] Coroners Act 1962, s.18(5).

[44] Coroners Bill 2007, s 25 and Third Schedule (note that this is the author's view of how reportable deaths may be categorised and not how they are set out in the legislation). This list may be further amplified by the Minister following consultation with the Chief Coroner and with the approval of the Oireachtas (s 25(2)).

– Death due to want of care, exposure or neglect;

– Death that may specifically be due to (a) accident at work, occupational disease or industrial poisoning; (b) alcohol, drugs or other substance; (c) Transmissible Spongiform Encephalopathy (eg, Creutzfeldt-Jakob Disease; (d) Methicillin-Sensitive Staphylococcus Aureus (MRSA).

Location/context of death

– A death occurring within 24 hours of admission to a hospital or other health institution;

– Any death which may have occurred during an operation, or before recovery from the effects of anaesthetic, or from a diagnostic or therapeutic procedure regardless of the length of time between the procedure and death (including any non-conventional medicine or procedure);

– Any death of a child in care;

– Any death that occurs in

    o   an institution … where the person was being detained involuntarily;

    o   Garda/military/prison custody (including where the person was in custody immediately before death, but not necessarily at the time of death);

    o   a remand centre or a children detention school within the meaning of the Children Act 2001;

    o   any public or private institution for the care of elderly or infirm persons.

Mother/Child circumstances

– Any maternal death that occurs during or following pregnancy (up to a period of six weeks post-partum) or that might be reasonably related to pregnancy;

– Infant deaths, including Sudden Infant Death Syndrome and non-accidental injury;

– Unnatural stillbirths and intra-uterine deaths.

Other

– Where a body is to be removed from or repatriated to the State;

– Where human remains are discovered and/or where a body is unidentified;

– Where a member of the family of the deceased cannot be traced;

– Where a satisfactory certificate of the cause of death is not procurable from a registered medical practitioner.

Coroner's response to a reported death

[13.32] The coroner is required to investigate all deaths reported to her that fall within her region of responsibility,[45] but is not required to hold an inquest in every case. If the coroner is satisfied in the circumstances that there was nothing untoward about the

---

[45] Coroners Bill 2007, s 28. There is no obligation to investigate deaths that have occurred more than 70 years ago, although such deaths may be reported to the Chief Coroner, who may direct that an investigation should take place: Coroners Bill 2007, s 30.

death, then she may direct the doctor to issue a death certificate without further investigation and certainly without requiring an inquest.[46] Under the 2007 Bill, the coroner can arrange for the body to be identified by a Garda or coroner's officer and can, where it is necessary, take possession of the body for the purposes of any investigation.[47]

Example 13.1

A patient who had not been seen in the month prior to his death but who was known to have a long history of heart disease and complained to his General Practitioner over the telephone of chest pain and weakness. He died before the doctor could attend. As the patient had not been attended by his doctor in the 28 days prior to death, the GP was required to notify her local coroner's office.

The history and circumstances reported to the coroner in Example 13.1 could lead her to the conclusion that a heart attack was to blame and she may be happy in those circumstances to direct the attending physician to issue a Death Notification Form. In other circumstances, the cause of death may be less clear and the coroner may direct that further investigation, often a post-mortem[48] examination, be held to establish the cause of death.

Example 13.2

Take the example above of the cardiac patient but alter the scenario insofar as there was no witness to the final symptoms of the deceased. Let us say instead that he died in his sleep and was found dead by a relative the next day. Again, he was not seen by his doctor in the previous month.

Post-mortem examinations

[13.33] The inference in Example 13.2 might be that heart disease was to blame because of the long-standing history of heart disease, but the coroner may prefer to confirm that particular hypothesis in this scenario by ordering that a post-mortem examination be conducted. The coroner does not conduct the post-mortem herself, but instead relies on facilities and personnel provided by local hospitals;[49] the body will therefore be moved to a local hospital so that the examination can be conducted. The post mortem is performed by a single doctor (typically a pathologist) but *cannot* be carried out by:

- a doctor who is not a pathologist *and* who was involved in the care of a patient in the final month of that patient's life; or

---

[46] A coroner may discontinue any investigation if (a) following a post-mortem examination the cause of death is established and a medical certificate of the cause of death is procurable and a certificate has been given to the appropriate registrar by the coroner; (b) he or she has no reasonable cause to suspect that the death occurred in a manner, place or circumstance where an inquest would be necessary; or (c) he or she considers that it is no longer necessary to continue the investigation: Coroners Bill 2007, s 42(1).

[47] Coroners Bill 2007, s 33.

[48] A post mortem may—at the discretion of the coroner—involve only an external examination of the body to rule out signs of violent death: *Hanley v Cusack* [1999] IEHC 6.

[49] This reliance on facilities that are often already overburdened and over which the coroner has no prior call can lead to long delays in obtaining the results of post mortems. The ability to direct a post mortem is set out at Coroners Bill 2007, ss 74 and 75.

– a doctor, whether a pathologist or not, whose care of the deceased may, in the opinion of the coroner, be called into question at the inquest.[50]

[13.34] The reason for this is obvious: either of the above conducting the post mortem would raise the uncomfortable spectre of bias or of conflict of interest. If a doctor cares for a patient who dies suddenly, perhaps after an operation or within moments of a visit by her GP, it would be wholly inappropriate for that surgeon or that GP respectively to perform the post mortem.

[13.35] If the post mortem demonstrates death due to natural causes, the coroner can then issue a Coroner's Certificate, which is her equivalent of the Death Notification Form and which indicates that she is satisfied that a death certificate should issue for the deceased. The Coroner's Certificate is communicated to the Registrar of Births and Death for the district in order that the death can be formally registered.

[13.36] In cases where the cause of death is strongly suggestive of an unlawful killing, the post mortem will generally be conducted by a State Pathologist at the request of the coroner, subject to the approval—which is never withheld—of the Minister for Justice, Equality and Law Reform. In circumstances where a suspicion of violent or unnatural death comes to light *after* the burial of the deceased and that suspicion is communicated to the coroner by a senior Garda, the coroner for the area may request the Minister to order that the body be exhumed and—if the body is exhumed—the coroner's powers are precisely as if the body had never been interred in the first place.[51]

Proposed changes in the Coroners Bill 2007

[13.37] Under the 2007 Bill, once a coroner is conducting an investigation into the death of a person, she can issue a Fact of Death Certificate which allows (once the coroner has no further use for the body) next-of-kin to dispose of the body and which allows the family to make any claims from social welfare or other statutory body. As the circumstances of death have yet to be investigated, the Fact of Death certificate can only confirm that death has occurred and can make no reference to the cause of death.[52] The

---

[50] Similarly, a coroner (or deputy coroner) may not act as coroner in a case where she (as a doctor) treated the patient within a month of his death or (as a solicitor) drafted the will of the deceased. Nor may a coroner who is a solicitor or barrister act in any legal case arising out of any matter that may have come before her while acting as coroner or deputy coroner. Under the Coroners Bill 2007, s 76(6), the only limitation on doctors who may perform a 'post mortem or special examination' is that it may not be 'a registered medical practitioner who had attended the deceased within 28 days of the person's death'.

[51] Coroners Act 1962, s 47. Under the Coroners Bill 2007, s 44(3), there is no obligation on a coroner to exhume a body in circumstances where the need for an inquest (whether compulsory or optional) comes to light after a body has been buried and where 'the coroner determines that no good purpose will be effected by exhuming the body for the purposes of an inquest.' The coroner can direct an exhumation under the 2007 Bill pursuant to s 78 where (i) there are grounds for believing that a person's death was a reportable one; (ii) exhumation is or reasonably may be necessary for the performance of the coroner's (or another coroner's) duties; (iii) a post mortem or special examination is necessary; (iv) the burial or cremation took place before an ongoing investigation was completed; or (v) a new inquest is to be held. The coroner may also direct an exhumation where requested by certain categories of persons.

[52] Coroners Bill 2007, s 34.

coroner is also obliged to keep the family (and such other persons that the coroner deems appropriate) informed of the nature and progress of any investigation.

'Special examinations' and post mortems under the 2007 Bill

[13.38] Similarly under the proposed new legislation, a coroner can direct post-mortem and special examinations be carried out as part of the death investigation.[53] The coroner will be obliged to direct a post mortem when requested in writing (with reasons) to do so by a senior Garda or army officer, by a person authorised by legislation to investigate certain accidents, diseases or incidents or by the Garda Ombudsman Commission. A post mortem is also obligatory when, in the opinion of the coroner, the death occurs:

- in a violent or unnatural manner;

- from unknown causes;

- in or immediately after being in Garda Síochána, military or prison custody;

- in custody in a remand centre or a children detention school, each within the meaning of the Children Act 2001, or immediately after being in such custody;

- in an institution administered by or on behalf of the State, including a hospital or other institution for the care and treatment of mentally ill or intellectually disabled persons, where the deceased was being detained involuntarily, or immediately after being so detained;

- of a child in care;

- in circumstances which, under provisions in that behalf contained in any other enactment, require that a post mortem or other special examination should be held;

- in an unexplained manner;[54] or

- as a result of an industrial accident or disease.

Where a coroner requests a post-mortem examination or special examination of a body, the person conducting the examination is authorised to remove from the body and preserve, for such period as the coroner shall direct, any body parts or material which relate to the circumstances, including the cause, of death of the deceased person.[55] The Bill also permits the coroner to direct that relevant medical notes be made available to the person conducting the post-mortem or special examination.

---

[53] Coroners Bill 2007, s 74. A 'special examination' means an 'examination by way of analysis, test or otherwise of material be it tissue, organs, biological fluids or other parts or contents of the body obtained from the body of the deceased person in the course of a post-mortem examination, or of any other substance or thing relevant to such post-mortem examination.'

[54] It is not at all clear to the author what the distinction is between deaths that occur 'from unknown causes' and those that occur 'in an unexplained manner'. Where a post mortem is directed, the coroner is under an obligation to keep a member of the family of the deceased informed.

[55] Coroners Bill 2007, s 76(1). Where practicable, the coroner must inform a family member or longstanding friend of the deceased of the need to retain body parts and the body parts may be returned to the family or friend.

Quick Reference Guide 13.3

The role of the coroner outlined

❖ Substantial changes to the manner in which the coroner discharges her duties have been proposed by the Coroners Bill 2007.

❖ The principal power of the modern coroner is the investigation of sudden or unexplained deaths, through the use of informal investigations, post mortems or inquests.

❖ To be a coroner, one must be a lawyer or a registered medical practitioner of at least five years' standing. A coroner has responsibility for a particular geographical district and may discharge her duties in a full- or part-time capacity.

❖ The coroner investigates sudden, suspicious or unnatural deaths occurring in her area of responsibility.

❖ Certain deaths must be reported to the coroner including those involving potential foul play, malpractice or unnatural causes. Any death of a person who has not been seen in the month preceding death must be reported to the coroner.

❖ There are certain categories of person, including medical practitioners and any one in charge of an institution or premises where such a death occurs, obliged by law, if they know of such a death to notify the coroner.

❖ In essence, the coroner has four questions to pose and to answer:

o *Who* died?

o *When* did he die?

o *Where* did he die?

o *How* did he die?

❖ In answering these questions, the coroner is forbidden by law from apportioning any blame for the death.

❖ The coroner has discretion over whether to investigate certain deaths and, in such cases, informal inquiries may be sufficient to satisfy the coroner of the cause of death. If not, she may proceed to order a post mortem or to hold an inquest.

❖ Once the coroner is satisfied as to the identity of the deceased and time, place and cause of death, she may either direct the medical practitioner to issue a Death Notification Form or issue a Coroner's Certificate, either of which will allow the death to be registered.

INQUESTS

[13.39] If a post mortem does not disclose a natural cause of death, then the coroner *may* at her discretion proceed to hold an inquest to try to establish the cause of death[56] and there are other circumstances (discussed below—see para **[13.43]**) where the coroner must hold an inquest. However, first we will examine the nature and purpose of an inquest. In a traditional court case there are battle lines drawn between one side and another; one side has made an allegation that it is trying to prove, while the other side is

---

[56] Cusack, 'The Coroner's Court' (1995) Medico-Legal Journal of Ireland 1, 82.

attempting to put the opposite case. In a criminal case, for example, the State is trying to prove that the accused committed a crime, while the accused is trying to establish his innocence or, at the very least, raise a reasonable doubt as to his guilt.

[13.40] There is no such conflict at an inquest: the coroner is simply inquiring as to the facts of death and is expressly forbidden by legislation from attributing any blame for the death.[57] An inquest may involve a jury (see para **[13.50]** below) being called upon to consider and reach a verdict. It may involve witnesses being called and testimony being heard, but it cannot, as we have observed already, involve a finding of guilt against any party. Unlike a civil or criminal court case, where the various parties involved can call witnesses, at an inquest only the coroner herself may call witnesses. The legal framework of the coroner's inquest is usually described as 'inquisitorial',[58] rather than the 'adversarial' system of the criminal and civil courts. The coroner is the questioner seeking to determine the four cardinal facts already referred to:

- who died?
- when did he die?
- where did he die?
- how did he die?[59]

In addition to answering these questions, the coroner (or the jury) will return a verdict on the death,[60] without attributing blame for the death. The principle of the coroner's inquest was described in this way by the UK Committee on Death Certification and Coroners in 1971 (Broderick Report), cited in the Irish *Review of the Coroner Service*:

> [T]he function of an inquest should be simply to seek out and record as many of the facts concerning the death as the public interest requires, without deducing from the facts any determination of blame.[61]

---

[57] Coroners Act 1962, s 30; see also Coroners Bill 2007, s 46(5)(b) and s 54(3).

[58] Coroners Bill 2007, s 27(1): 'An investigation by a coroner into the death of a person shall be inquisitorial in nature.'

[59] This is formalised in the Coroners Bill 2007, s 46: 'The purpose of an inquest shall be to establish— (i) the identity of the deceased, (ii) when and where the death took place, (iii) in so far as practicable, the circumstances in which the death took place including the medical cause of death, and make findings in respect of these matters...'

[60] Under the Coroners Bill 2007, s 46 there is an obligation to return a verdict. Available verdicts are discussed below at para **[13.54]**.

[61] See also *R v South London Coroner, ex parte Thompson* (1982) SJ 625, per Lord Lane:

> [A]n inquest is a fact finding exercise and not a method of apportioning guilt. The procedure and rules of evidence which are suitable for one are not suitable for the other. In an inquest, it should not be forgotten that there are no parties, there is no indictment, there is no prosecution, there is no defence, there is no trial, simply an attempt to establish the facts. It is an inquisitorial process, quite unlike a trial...

[62] In *Morris v Dublin City Coroner* [2000] 3 IR 592 (HC), 603 (SC); [2000] IESC 24 (SC) the court agreed that police under a verifiable death threat from a paramilitary organisation could give evidence screened from the public gallery, but not from the coroner, jury, legal representatives or press. (contd/)

An inquest is held in public.[62] The usual venue is a courtroom in the coroner's geographical area of responsibility, but this is not uniformly so. The body is not generally produced at an inquest and the jury, if there is one, does not have to view the body.[63]

Reasons for deciding to hold an inquest

[13.41] There are circumstances in which a coroner is obliged to hold an inquest and we discuss those in the next section. However, where there is no such compulsion on the coroner, then she has discretion on whether to hold an inquest. That discretion to hold an inquest is typically exercised in circumstances that have been identified by the courts:[64]

- to determine the medical cause of death;
- to allay rumours or suspicions;
- to draw attention to the existence of circumstances which, if not remedied, might lead to further deaths;[65]
- to advance medical knowledge;

---

[62] (\contd) The presence of the press as reliable reporters of what takes place at the inquest is sufficient to give it the required quality of being held in public. The Report of the Coroners Rules Committee (2003), above, recommends (Rule 6.10) witness anonymity where (a) there is a threat to the personal security of a Garda or to a member of the Defence Forces or their families, (b) there is a threat to the personal security of any witness, or their family, (c) there is a threat to national security. This rule is not reflected in the Coroners Bill 2007, although the name and address of a witness may be withheld at an inquest in certain circumstances (s 61). There is provision in the Coroners Bill 2007, s 49(2)–(3) for excluding persons from all or some of an inquest in limited circumstances. Any such exclusion may be appealed to the Chief Coroner.

[63] The Coroners (Ireland) Act 1846 permitted the coroner to order that the body be brought to the nearest convenient tavern until the inquest could be heard. Nowadays the body will have been brought to a mortuary for post-mortem investigations and will usually have been buried by the time an inquest takes place.

[64] *Farrell (Dublin City Coroner) v Attorney General* [1998] 1 IR 203. These recommendations were in turn based on the United Kingdom Committee on Death Certification and Coroners (Broderick Report, 1971). In the Coroners Bill 2007, s 44 the coroner has discretion to hold an inquest (a) if a medical certificate of the cause of death of a person is not procurable and the coroner, having investigated the circumstances of the death of that person … is unable to ascertain the cause of death, the coroner may, if he or she considers it appropriate so to do, hold an inquest in relation to the death or (b) if he or she has reason to believe that any death notified to her has occurred in such circumstances that an inquest is appropriate, even if the body has been destroyed or is irrecoverable.

[65] So, for example, in a situation where lack of institutional care was responsible, the coroner may hear evidence as regards that lack of care (but without explicitly laying blame for that death at any individual door); see *Northern Area Health Board v Geraghty (Coroner for County Dublin)* [2001] 3 IR 321. See *R v HM Coroner for Inner London North (ex parte Touche)* [2001] EWCA CIV 383, where the court held that a coroner's decision not to hold an inquest where there were obvious questions of lack of care was irrational and directed that one be held.

[66] In other words there may be legal consequences for the family of the deceased, depending on the cause of death that is established. (contd/)

–   to preserve the legal interests of the deceased person's family, heirs or other interested parties.[66]

Obligatory inquests

[13.42] While the coroner has the discretion to hold an inquest in most cases, there are other circumstances where she is obliged to do so. According to the Coroners Act 1962:

> [W]here a coroner is informed that the body of a deceased person is lying within his district, it shall be the duty of the coroner to hold an inquest in relation to the death of that person if he is of the opinion that the death may have occurred in a violent or unnatural manner or suddenly and from unknown causes or in a place or in circumstances which [because of any provision laid down in other laws] require that an inquest should be held.[67]

There are also obligations on the coroner to hold inquests that are created by legislation other than the Coroners Act 1962: the Defence Act 1954[68] requires that an inquest must be held in the case of any person dying while serving a sentence in a military prison or detention barrack.

Changes proposed by the Coroners Bill 2007

[13.43] Under the Coroners Bill 2007, an inquest must be held where a death occurs:

–   in a violent or unnatural manner;

–   from unknown causes;

–   in or immediately after being in Garda Síochána, military or prison custody;

–   in custody in a remand centre or a children detention school, within the meaning of the Children Act 2001, or immediately after being in such custody;

–   in an institution administered by or on behalf of the State, including a hospital or other institution for the care and treatment of mentally ill or intellectually disabled persons, where the deceased person was being detained involuntarily, or immediately after being so detained;

–   of a child in care; or

–   in circumstances which, under provisions in that behalf contained in any other enactment, require that an inquest should be held.[69]

Inquests directed by the Attorney General

[13.44] An inquest may also be ordered by the Attorney General[70] in any situation where the Attorney General thinks that such an inquest is required in the public interest or in

---

[66]   (\contd) If a coroner's inquest holds that a person was the victim of an accident rather than having killed himself, such a decision may have ramifications for insurance policies, reputation and so on.

[67]   Coroners Act 1962, s 17 .

[68]   Defence Act 1954, s 238.

[69]   Coroners Bill 2007, s 43. In countries such as Scotland, reforms introduced have included fewer mandatory inquests, limiting them only to deaths in custody and accidents at work: see Pounder, 'Law and forensic medicine in Scotland' Am J Forensic Med Pathol 1993;14:340–9.

[70]   Coroners Act 1962, s 24. See also Coroners Bill 2007, s 45, which gives the Attorney General the same powers, save that they must be exercised in consultation with the Chief Coroner.

the interests of justice, even in circumstances where the body is irrecoverably lost or destroyed. If such an order is made, *any* coroner, even one who does not have jurisdiction over the area where the death occurred, may be directed to conduct the inquest, irrespective of any previous inquests or inquiries. The Attorney General's power to do so has been confirmed by the Irish Supreme Court[71] but only if the power is not exercised unreasonably or irrationally.

Conduct of the inquest

[13.45] Evidence can be given in written[72] or oral form. During the inquest, the coroner can call witnesses if she chooses and those witnesses may be examined under oath. Although the coroner may receive submissions from interested parties about which witnesses should be called, the final decision rests with the coroner. Under the 1962 Act, refusal to attend or, having attended, refusing to take an oath or to answer questions is contempt of court and the High Court is empowered to deal with the matter; contempt may be punished by a fine, a prison term, or both. The coroner herself cannot take action for contempt of court; her powers are only those laid out in the Coroners Act 1962.[73]

Witnesses

[13.46] A witness who testifies before a coroner's inquest is treated as if he were a witness before the High Court and is entitled to all of the safeguards and protection that would be afforded to him if he were testifying before that court. These might include the right not to testify about certain material that is legally privileged.[74] There are no other express limits to the power to call witnesses.[75] In general, anyone who wishes to testify may indicate his desire to give evidence before the inquest and will be heard so long as the coroner believes that the evidence is relevant to the inquiry being conducted. So, a person who has a series of grievances that he wishes to air and which have no bearing on the matter under investigation may be prevented from taking the stand or be permitted to do so only if their testimony confines itself to relevant matters.

---

[71] *Farrell (Dublin City Coroner) v Attorney General* [1998] 1 IR 203. In England, the courts have forced a coroner to hold an inquest when the coroner initially declined to do so on grounds that the court felt were irrational: *R v HM Coroners Court of St Pancras* [2001] Lloyds Law Reports Medical 67.

[72] Coroners Bill 2007, s 51: the coroner appears to have extensive powers under this section to receive written rather than oral evidence.

[73] Coroners Bill 2007, ss 63–65: the coroner can summon any witness to appear and direct the witness to take an oath, answer questions and produce any document, substance or other item.

[74] Legal privilege, in brief, refers to protection from legal action for statements made during the discharge of duties that are privileged, such as lawyer–client discussions, what a priest hears in confession, a judge's ruling or a speech made in Parliament. For a more detailed discussion, see McGrath, *Evidence* (Round Hall, 2004).

[75] See Coroners Act 1962, s 26(2): this section limited the coroner to being able to call a maximum of only two registered medical practitioners to give evidence: *Eastern Health Board v Farrell* [2000] 1 ILRM 446 (HC); [2001] 4 IR 627 (SC) and in particular the judgment of Hardiman J in the Supreme Court. This limitation on medical witnesses was repealed by the Coroners (Amendment) Act 2005, s 1(a).

Privilege

[13.47] During the inquest, the coroner herself also has judicial 'privilege', meaning that she is immune from legal action for anything she says or does provided always that she is acting within her powers.[76] In *Desmond v Riordan (Coroner for City of Cork)*[77] a pop concert promoter sought to sue a coroner for defamation based on unflattering observations the latter had made during an inquest into the death of a teenager who had drowned while swimming the River Lee in an attempt to gain access to a concert. The court reasoned that:

> [A] coroner enjoys absolute privilege in respect *of anything that he says while he is performing his duties as a Coroner* in the holding of an inquest in accordance with … the Coroners Act 1962 … Once, however, he strays outside of the functions which he is required to perform under the Act which are defined …as being to ascertain the identify of the person in respect of whose death the inquest is being held and how, when and where the death occurred and *once he knows that he is no longer performing one of these functions* he ceases to enjoy this privilege [italics added].

[13.48] In other words, a coroner—like a judge—is free from the inhibiting threat of being sued as long as she acts at all times within the powers that are given to her by legislation. One corollary of the fact that the inquest is a fact-finding exercise rather than a trial is that the coroner will not be obliged to adhere as strictly to the rules of the courts, such as notifying every single party to the inquest of every evidential matter that may be brought up.[78]

Legal aid

[13.49] Historically there was no provision for legal aid to families of deceased who were unable to afford legal presentation,[79] but the Coroners Bill 2007 does propose a limited legal aid scheme for the family (or where there is no family, a friend of long standing) at an inquest where the coroner certifies that:

---

[76] Intra vires, to use the legal term; the legal term for operating outside one's legal powers is ultra vires.

[77] *Desmond v Riordan (Coroner for City of Cork)* [2002] 1 ILRM 502.

[78] *Northern Area Health Board v Geraghty (Coroner for County Dublin)* [2001] 3 IR 321, per Kelly J:

> The necessity to disclose material prior to a hearing and the extent of such disclosure will very much depend on the nature of such a hearing … I would be slow to hold that an inquisitorial procedure whose verdict cannot impose civil or criminal liability of any sort on any person requires the full panoply of natural justice requirements of disclosure in advance of the hearing to be applied to it as would be the case, for example, in a criminal trial.

Interested parties may be able to establish sufficient grounds why certain documents should be released by the coroner: see *Ramseyer v Mahon (Acting Coroner for the County of Offaly)* [2004] IEHC 70. The decision of the coroner in this case to refuse to release unsworn depositions was upheld by the High Court, but then overturned by the Supreme Court: *Ramseyer v Mahon (Acting Coroner for the County of Offaly)* [2005] IESC 82. The Coroners Bill 2007, s 50 allows for the Coroner Service to adapt rules and procedures for the taking and recording of evidence and receiving submissions.

[79] See *Magee v Farrell* [2005] IEHC 388.

a. The deceased was in custody at or immediately before death or the death occurred in a healthcare institution where the deceased was involuntarily detained or the death was of a child in care or the death gives rise to complex issues of major public importance,

AND

b. There is significant public interest in the legal aid being afforded in all the circumstances, including whether the person could participate without legal aid, the nature and seriousness of the allegations likely to be raised and whether other investigations are likely.[80]

Juries

[13.50] Under the Coroners Act 1962, a jury may consist of anything from six to 12 people (but the Coroners Bill 2007 permits a jury of between five and seven members)[81] and they are generally sworn in before the inquest commences, although the 2007 Bill envisages a scenario where it becomes clear during an inquest that a jury is required and allows for a jury to be sworn in at that stage. The jury's duty is to reach a verdict and if it cannot do so, then under the 1962 Act (and under the 2007 Bill) the coroner can discharge the jury and hear the case afresh with a new jury. Once a majority of the jury is agreed on a particular verdict, the coroner will accept that verdict.

The coroner has a certain degree of discretion about whether to empanel a jury depending on the circumstances of the case[82] but again her discretion is circumscribed— some inquests *must* take place before a jury if the coroner believes that:

– the death was the result of murder, manslaughter or infanticide;

– the death occurred in circumstances where an Act other than the Coroners Act 1962 states that an inquest must be held; [83]

– the death occurred in circumstances where—under provisions contained in any Act other than the Coroners Act 1962—a Minister, government department or inspector working on behalf of a Minister or government department must be notified of the death;[84]

– the death was the result of using a vehicle in a public place;

– the death occurred in circumstances that would, were they to continue or to recur, constitute a danger to the health and safety of the public or a section of the public.

---

[80] Coroners Bill 2007, s 86(1)–(4).

[81] Coroners Bill 2007, s 69(1). Where a juror is discharged or dies during an inquest, the inquest may continue unless lost jurors mean that the jury comprises fewer than five members, in which case a new inquest must be held: s 72(3).

[82] Coroners Act 1962, s 40.

[83] For example the General Prisons (Ireland) Act 1877, s 56 mandates the holding of an inquest 'on the body of every prisoner who may die within the Prison.' Similarly, s 238 of the Defence Act 1954 covers deaths in military custody and explicitly mandates both that an inquest be held and that a jury be empanelled.

[84] This would commonly occur under the Health, Safety and Welfare at Work Acts, which require that any accident at work must be notified to an inspector of the Health and Safety Authority.

Proposed changes in the Coroners Bill 2007

[13.51] Under the Coroners Bill 2007, the grounds for empanelling a jury are augmented and clarified. According to the Bill, a jury must be sworn if, before or during the inquest, the coroner becomes of the opinion that the death:[85]

- may have been murder, infanticide or manslaughter;

- may have occurred in Garda, military or prison custody, or immediately after being in such custody;

- may have resulted from an act or omission of a member of the Garda Síochána, a member of the Defence Forces or a prison officer in the purported execution of his or her duty;

- may have occurred in custody in a remand centre or a children detention school, within the meaning of the Children Act 2001, or immediately after being in such custody;

- may have occurred in an institution, administered by or on behalf of the State, including a hospital or other institution, for the care and treatment of mentally ill or intellectually disabled persons, where the deceased was being detained involuntarily, immediately after being so detained;

- was of a child in care; or

- occurred in a place or in circumstances which, under provisions in that behalf contained in any other enactment, require that an inquest should be held with a jury.

An inquest may also be held with a jury if the coroner considers that the death gives rise to issues of major public importance or where the death of the deceased occurred in circumstances the continuance or possible recurrence of which would be prejudicial to the health or safety of the public or any section of the public.

The conclusion of the inquest

[13.52] In many cases the evidence illuminating the facts surrounding death is simple and clear-cut. Witnesses and post-mortem reports will combine to provide an unambiguous description of the circumstances of the death. However, in some more contentious cases there may be some dispute as to the facts or the interpretation given to the facts by certain witnesses. Those involved at an inquest are entitled to have legal representation at the inquest to ensure that the coroner follows due procedure in complex situations and remains within her powers and also to verify that the rights of participants in the inquest are not abridged in any way. The coroner will permit—if permission is sought—examination of witnesses by an interested party or by the legal representative of an interested party but will not permit that interested party to call its own witnesses: only the coroner may call witnesses at an inquest. Interested parties to an inquest can include

---

[85] Coroners Bill 2007, s 66(2)–(3). Any decision not to hold an inquest with a jury may be appealed to the Chief Coroner. There does not appear to be a power to appeal against a decision of the coroner to swear in a jury. The most obvious change in the 2007 Bill is the end to the obligatory jury inquest in all cases of road traffic accidents.

the following, but the list is not necessarily exhaustive, as the final category in the list below suggests:

- the family or next-of-kin of the deceased;

- representatives of an institution where the deceased was residing at the time of death;

- those factually responsible for the death in some way, such as the driver of a motor vehicle involved in an accident that claimed the life of the deceased;

- representatives of insurance companies;

- where death results from an accident at work: trade union representatives; the employer of the deceased; Health and Safety Authority inspectors;

- others who are considered interested parties at the coroner's discretion.

The coroner must record in writing the names and addresses of any witnesses and keep a record of documentation arising at each inquest, namely the details of depositions (written submissions) to inquests, witnesses, post-mortem results and verdicts returned at inquests.[86] The 1962 Act does not oblige the coroner to prepare a written judgment or report. The coroner is also ordinarily obliged to circulate all statements (such as witness statements) and documents furnished to the inquest among the interested parties at the inquest, but there may be circumstances in which such statements can be withheld by the coroner.[87]

Proposed changes in the Coroners Bill 2007

[13.53] Under the 2007 Bill the coroner is obliged to prepare and publish a written report at the conclusion of the inquest detailing:

- the findings made and the verdict returned;

- a brief description of any evidence received by the inquest;

- any facts established by the inquest in relation to matters the subject of the inquest;

- any recommendations made by the inquest; and

- such other matters as the coroner should think appropriate.

Before publishing such a report, a copy should go to the Chief Coroner and to any person interested in or likely to be affected by the report. Certain information, including that which might prejudice the security or safety of the state may be withheld from a coroner's report.

---

[86] Coroners Act 1962, s 29. See also Coroners Bill 2007, s 52.

[87] See *Anne Morris and John Morris v Brian Farrell* [2004] IEHC 127. In this case the coroner refused to release documents relating to a Garda investigation to the family of the deceased, even though the State and the Garda Síochána had waived its right of confidentiality over the documents. The court held that the coroner could not rely on the confidentiality of the documents in the circumstances, but was entitled to withhold them unless the family could prove that they were prejudiced by the withholding of the documents. See also *R v H M Coroner, ex parte Peach* [1980] QB 211.

Verdicts

[13.54] Once all the evidence is heard from witnesses or from reports submitted to the inquest, the coroner or the jury, if a jury has been empanelled, will endeavour to reach a verdict, which may include one of a range of verdicts. The Report of the Coroners Rules Committee (2003) stated that the following verdicts are available at an inquest:

- accidental death;
- death by misadventure;[88]
- medical misadventure;
- suicide/self-inflicted death/deceased took his own life;[89]
- unlawful killing;[90]
- want of attention at birth;[91]
- stillbirth;
- occupational disease;
- industrial accident;
- in accordance with the findings of a criminal court;
- death by natural causes;
- open verdict.[92]

Notwithstanding the above list, a verdict can be relatively expansive and narrative in nature.[93] A coroner's verdict may subsequently be challenged by any party with a

---

[88] Misadventure can be described as the unintended outcome of an intended action. So, medical misadventure is where there is an unintended action in a medical context or where complications arising from a medical procedure cause death: *Report of the Coroners Rules Committee* (2003), 36.

[89] *Report of the Coroners Rules Committee* (2003): declaring a verdict of suicide the coroner/jury must be sure that (a) the deceased took his or her own life, (b) the deceased was intent on taking his or her life, (c) there is proof beyond reasonable doubt that the injuries sustained were self-inflicted and (d) the deceased had such intention.

[90] *Report of the Coroners Rules Committee* (2003): returning a verdict of unlawful killing the coroner/jury must confirm that (a) there are no criminal proceedings, (b) unlawful killing is proved beyond reasonable doubt, (c) the investigation by the Gardaí has ended and (d) no person is, expressly or by implication, named for the killing.

[91] *Report of the Coroners Rules Committee* (2003): in returning such a verdict the coroner/jury must confirm that (a) the child was abandoned, (b) the child's mother was never found, (c) no other person is under criminally identifiable suspicion of the death and (d) proof of the above three items is secured beyond reasonable doubt.

[92] *Report of the Coroners Rules Committee* (2003): an open verdict should be returned if there is insufficient evidence to record any other specified verdict.

[93] *Farrell (Dublin City Coroner) v Attorney General* [1998] 1 IR 203. In that case, the jury's verdict was in effect natural causes, but was recorded in full as 'acute cardiac failure and pulmonary oedema and that was due to an episode of hypertension possibly due to an anaphylactic reaction to penicillin combined with severe coronary arterial disease and hypertensive cardiac disease'.

legitimate interest in bringing the challenge (called a locus standi) by means of an application to the High Court for judicial review.

[13.55] On retirement, resignation or dismissal, the coroner must return all documentation to the county registrar. All the documentation generated by the coroner is public and the 1962 Act stipulates that a copy of any documentation must be given to anyone who requests it.

Recommendations

[13.56] As well as reaching a verdict with or without a jury, the coroner may also issue any general recommendations that she may think necessary to minimise the recurrence of similar avoidable tragedies.[94] Examples of such recommendations include a verdict returned by the Dublin City Coroner's Court that called for a dangerous junction, which had been the scene of several previous accidents, to be remedied.[95] These recommendations have no legal force in that the coroner cannot compel action to achieve the ends stipulated in her recommendation, but they do satisfy the coroner's role as a servant of the public interest.

Changes proposed in the Coroners Bill 2007

[13.57] The 2007 Bill provides that where an inquest has addressed a recommendation to a Minister of the Government, a local authority or a statutory body, a response to the recommendation must be given to the coroner concerned in writing no later than six months from the date of receipt of the recommendation and shall indicate the measures, if any, taken or proposed to be taken on foot of the recommendation.[96]

Postponing an inquest in the interests of justice

[13.58] In a situation where criminal charges are being considered or pursued against any individual in respect of a death that is being investigated by the coroner, a senior Garda (or, in the 2007 Bill, an army officer or an authorised officer of a statutory body charged with investigating certain accidents, incidents or diseases) may request the coroner to adjourn the inquest until such time as the criminal matters or other relevant investigations are concluded. The coroner is obliged to accede to that request.[97] The

---

[94] Coroners Act 1962, s 31.

[95] 'Cyclist was crushed by Truck' (2002) Irish Times, 24 January. See also a call from a Galway coroner for a national policy to ensure safer building sites after the death of a schoolboy night watchman on one site: 'Coroner calls for inspection of building sites' (2000) Irish Times, 29 January.

[96] Coroners Bill 2007, s 54(1).

[97] Coroners Act 1962, s 25. See also the case of *Costello v Bofin* (21 November 1980, unreported) SC, which confirmed that the coroner is obliged to adjourn the inquest at the request of the gardaí, but may only do so for a specified period. Similar provisions are set out in the Coroners Bill 2007, s 57. There is also provision in the Bill (s 58) for an adjournment where a tribunal or commission of investigation has been established by the Oireachtas and where that tribunal or commission will investigate the same subject-matter to be covered by the inquest. An inquest adjourned under ss 57 or 58 of the 2007 Bill need not be resumed unless the coroner considers there are sufficient reasons for doing so. If resumed, the matter should be treated as if it were a new inquest.

reason for this is to ensure that the coroner's inquest would not compromise the criminal proceedings by appearing to prejudge the matter (which could in turn prejudice public opinion, making a fair trial impossible). Of course if the criminal process results in the conviction of an individual for an offence such as murder or criminal negligence, it might then be redundant to bring the inquest to its conclusion (a verdict of unlawful killing would after all add little to the overall picture) and the coroner may decide not to reconvene the inquest. Conversely, if the criminal proceedings fail to materialise or to secure a conviction, it may be that the coroner will wish to resume the inquest in order to reach a verdict in the interest of the grieving family and in the wider public interest.

Quick Reference Guide 13.4

The inquest

❖ An inquest may become necessary when further investigations are necessary to determine the answers to the four key questions for the coroner: Who? When? Where? How?

❖ In general an inquest will occur either when mandated by law or when informal or post-mortem investigations have failed to answer questions concerning the death.

❖ The coroner has discretion to call an inquest in many cases, but when (a) she is of the opinion that the death may have been sudden, violent or unnatural or (b) a provision in any other law demands an inquest, then one must be held.

❖ When the coroner is deciding whether or not to hold an inquest, there are five principal grounds on which she will generally decide to do so:

    (i)   To determine the medical cause of death;

    (ii) To allay rumours or suspicions;

    (iii) To draw attention to the existence of circumstances which, if not remedied, might lead to further deaths;

    (iv) To advance medical knowledge;

    (v) To preserve the legal interests of the deceased person's family, heirs or other interested parties.

❖ At an inquest there is no adversarial competition between two sides, simply an attempt to determine the facts leading to the death. The coroner decides what witnesses are to be called. A witness who refuses to attend or testify may be reported to the High Court for contempt of court.

❖ An inquest is generally heard in public; there may be a jury, but there are certain circumstances in which there must be a jury, including road traffic accidents (although this requirement will be removed by the Coroners Bill 2007). The inquest can hear from any interested party.

❖ Persons involved in an inquest may have legal representation, but they cannot call witnesses.

❖ A coroner is exempt from legal action against her for anything she says or does while acting in her role as coroner.

❖ At the end of the inquest, the jury – if there is one – will make findings or return a verdict and the coroner may make recommendations. The verdict or the recommendations must not apportion blame and the investigation must only concern itself with the proximal medical cause of death.

The conclusion of the coroner's role

[13.59] Once the coroner is satisfied that the cause of death has been established without the need for further enquiries, she may direct the doctor caring for the patient to sign the death certificate. However, in more complicated cases, where a post mortem or inquest is conducted, the coroner then assumes responsibility for issuing a coroner's certificate to the registrar of births and deaths containing all the necessary details to allow the death to be registered and which—as already outlined—takes the place of the medical certificate of cause of death. If a death certificate had already been issued but the cause of death upon it has subsequently been adjudged incorrect, an amending certificate may be issued, detailing the new cause of death as amended.[98] The coroner does not need to retain the body of the deceased until the utter end of any investigation and if she feels no purpose would be served by retaining the body, it may be released for burial or cremation even before an inquest has taken place.[99]

Limits of the coroner's powers

[13.60] In reaching a conclusion to each case, the coroner must satisfy herself that one question paramount among the four posed has been answered: how the person died. When it comes to this question of 'how?' there has in recent years been some degree of disagreement about how far the coroner's enquiries should be permitted to go in order to obtain an answer. Section 30 of the Coroners Act 1962—as we have already seen—is one of the most important provisions of the legislation, limiting the degree to which the coroner can raise questions of criminal and civil liability in examining the cause of death. In addition, s 31 prohibits the 'censure or exoneration' of any person. How to reconcile these limits with the ambition of the coroner to get as close as possible to the source of the cause of death? What in any event is meant by the 'cause' of death? Some coroners have questioned whether ss 30 and 31 of the Act confine them solely to examining only the immediate medical cause of death or whether they have a wider-ranging remit.

Case Study 13.1

The case of *Eastern Health Board v Farrell (Dublin City Coroner)*[100] reflected some of these issues and provided the answer that, for the time being, constitutes the limits to a coroner's inquisitorial powers. The Dublin City Coroner was conducting an inquest into the death from aspiration pneumonia of a young man who had suffered from mental retardation since infancy. However, it was suggested at the inquest that his brain damage was itself a possible consequence of the administration of the pertussis (whooping cough) vaccine in infancy. The coroner wished to call witnesses to examine this claim, while the Eastern Health Board argued that for him to do so would lie outside his powers under the Coroners Act and would in any event be counter-productive.

---

[98] Coroners Act 1962, s 51.

[99] Coroners Act 1962, s 51. The decision to release the body for cremation rather than burial will often have to be a more considered one. Cremation will after all destroy any evidence and later exhumation will not be an option.

[100] *Eastern Health Board v Farrell (Dublin City Coroner)* [2000] 1 ILRM 446 (HC), [2001] 4 IR 627 (SC).

The Supreme Court determined that the vaccination as a 'cause' of death was too indirect to be legitimately investigated by the coroner, upholding an earlier High Court ruling that the role of the coroner is to investigate the 'proximal medical cause' of death.[101] The decisions in both the High Court[102] and the Supreme Court [103] did however afford the coroner some latitude in determining the cause of death.

Blame and the coroner

[13.61] It can be seen that verdicts such as 'unlawful killing' or 'medical misadventure' may mean that the coroner can walk a fine line when it comes to the rule that her inquests should neither make a finding of guilt nor attribute blame to any person. The avoidance of blame can be a far-reaching doctrine. In the case of *The State (McKeown) v Dr Thomas Scully*,[104] the inquest returned a verdict that included a finding of suicide. At the time suicide was illegal,[105] meaning that according to the verdict, the deceased was guilty of the criminal offence of having killed himself. Because a coroner is forbidden from considering questions of criminal liability or attributing blame, the High Court quashed the verdict reached at the inquest and furthermore the court also stated that there was insufficient evidence in any event to have reached a finding of suicide in the first instance.

---

[101] In the Supreme Court, the ruling of Hardiman J differed from the other judges in that it was predicated on the fact that Dr Farrell had already heard evidence from two medical witnesses. Introducing a third witness to expound on the alleged link between the pertussis vaccine and mental retardation would have violated the Coroners Act 1962, s 26(2), which imposed a ceiling of two medical witnesses. This limitation on medical witnesses was repealed by the Coroners (Amendment) Act 2005, s 1(a).

[102] Per Geoghegan J in the High Court:

> I think it would be unwise to set down any hard and fast rules but in each case, the Coroner should be investigating what is the real and actual cause of the death. This death it appears to me, was caused by pneumonia. Any conceivable link with the three-in-one injection [of which the whooping cough vaccine was a part] is too nebulous and indirect to make it appropriate for an investigation by the Coroner.

[103] The Chief Justice in the Supreme Court pointed to the absurdity of giving the coroner no leeway at all:

> It cannot have been the intention of the Oireachtas that, in the case of a road accident, for example, the verdict should be simply confined to a finding in accordance with the pathologist's report and that the coroner or jury would be precluded from finding that the deceased had met his death while travelling in a motor car which collided with another vehicle.

See also *Northern Area Health Board v Geraghty (Coroner for County Dublin)* [2001] 3 IR 321. In that case, the court held it was acceptable for a coroner to hear evidence about the nursing care provided in the hospital where the deceased last resided in order to establish whether that may have been an element in the death.

[104] *The State (McKeown) v Dr Thomas Scully* [1984] ILRM 133.

[105] It remained so until the Criminal Law (Suicide) Act 1993. Similar considerations and conclusions arose in the case of *Greene v McLoughlin (Coroner for Galway West)* (26 January 1995, unreported) SC.

Changes proposed in the Coroners Bill 2007

[13.62] Under the proposed new legislation, the role of the coroner's inquest in determining the cause of death is to establish 'the circumstances in which the death took place including the medical cause of death.'[106]

THE RETENTION OF BODY TISSUES AFTER DEATH

[13.63] In 1999 it became clear that Irish hospitals, and in particular paediatric hospitals, had engaged in the retention of body parts and other tissues, without having obtained consent to that retention. The revelation mirrored similar disclosures in the United Kingdom. The one legal case brought by parents seeking damages for the trauma caused by the retention of their child's organs was not successful.[107]

The Dunne Inquiry/Madden Report

[13.64] Although there is much debate about the moral seriousness of organ retention, the Government commissioned an investigation into the practice of post mortems in Ireland.[108] Although no legislation has yet been introduced as a result of the recommendations (save for draft legislation, already discussed, to reform the coroner service), a number of recommendations were made:

-   a need for legislation dealing with tissue removal and retention;[109]

-   a system of authorisation (rather than consent) as a necessary precursor to any organ removal or retention of body organs or tissues accompanied with all information necessary (if desired by the parents/guardians) concerning the reasons for, nature of and potential benefits of the post-mortem examination;

---

[106] Coroners Bill 2007, s 46(1)(a)(iii).

[107] *Angela O'Connor and Jason Tormey v Michael Lenihan* [2005] IEHC 176 and reported in (2005) Medico-Legal Journal of Ireland 11, 2. See also *AB v Leeds Teaching Hospital NHS Trust* [2004] EWHC 644: in this latter case, it was held that doctors could owe a duty of care to a mother after the death of her baby; therefore the practice of not warning parents that a post-mortem examination might involve the removal and retention of an organ could not be justified in all cases. Where the claimants had no right of burial and possession of organs lawfully removed at post mortem and retained, there was no action for wrongful interference with the body of the child. One of the three claimants succeeded in a claim for psychiatric damage; the claims of the other two plaintiffs failed.

[108] Department of Health and Children, *Report of Dr Deirdre Madden on Post Mortem Practice and Procedures* (2006). The investigation had originally been conducted by Anne Dunne SC, but was delivered to the commissioning department unready to be published. Dr Madden completed the report. Available for download: http://www.dohc.ie/publications/madden.html (last accessed October 2007). Note that the recommendations of the Madden Report discussed in the text are necessarily a summary of the wide-ranging conclusion of the Report.

[109] Although the terms of reference concerned the retention of the organs of children, the report stated (at recommendation 1.9): 'it is clear that human tissue legislation is urgently required to deal with issues relating to removal, storage and uses of human biological material from the living and the deceased.' A later Working Group on Post Mortem Practice was asked to consider the question of organ retention in adults and children (see para **[13.67]**).

– any organ removal and/or retention must be necessary for the purposes of diagnosis and parents should be advised of any reasons for removal or retention, the duration of retention and options regarding return and/or disposal of the organs;

– no supply of any organs to a third party without the knowledge and authorisation of the parents;

– standardised forms and information booklets;

– reform of the coroner service;

– reform of hospital post-mortem policy;

– public information and education about post-mortem examination and the need for organ removal and/or retention;

– training of doctors and nurses in practical, procedural and ethical issues;

– the authorisation of organ retention for research purposes.

'Authorisation' for organ retention

[13.65] The reliance on 'authorisation' rather than consent to the removal and retention of organs is derived from an equivalent Scottish report[110] and reasoning behind it is articulated as follows:

> The Report takes the view that the use of the word 'authorisation' rather than 'consent' clarifies the scope of the decision-making powers of parents in these circumstances. It also meets the concerns of those parents who do not wish to receive information about post-mortem examination and/or organ retention, but who nonetheless do not object to these procedures being carried out. 'Consent' requires the provision and comprehension of information, whereas 'authorisation' does not impose this requirement. Parents may thus authorise procedures without having information forced upon them.[111]

Working group on post-mortem practice

[13.66] Arising from the Madden Report, a working group was established with terms of reference to consider the application of the recommendations in the Madden Report on Post-Mortem Practice and Procedure, to babies who died before or during birth, minors and adults.[112] The working group reiterated the call for legislation so 'no post-mortem examination will be carried out on the body of a deceased person, and that no organ or tissue will be retained from a post-mortem examination for any purpose without knowledge and appropriate authorisation.' Among the features of such proposed legislation would be the possibility of a person authorising his own post mortem before he dies. Alternatively, he could nominate a specific person to take that decision. However, absent advance authorisation or a specific nominee, it would be open to clinical staff to seek authorisation from family members according to a strict

---

[110] *Independent Review Group on Retention of Organs at Post-Mortem, Final Report* (HMSO, 2001).

[111] *Report of Dr Deirdre Madden on Post Mortem Practice and Procedures* (2006), 117.

[112] Department of Health and Children, *Report of the Working Group on Post Mortem Practice* (Dublin, 2006).

hierarchy;[113] the decision of the 'highest ranking' person would determine the matter and where there was disagreement between two family members of the same rank, then the post mortem would not be carried out. Interestingly, the working group also called for the authorisation by under-16s of their own post mortems, or those of any children they might have, to be regarded as valid.[114]

[13.67] It also stressed the need for greater information for the public, including standardised information sheets and authorisation forms. In cases of early miscarriage, the working group drew a distinction between identifiable foetal remains and non-identifiable foetal remains and recommended that authorisation was only required for examination of the former. The working group's request that 'legislation should clearly set out the circumstances in which a post-mortem examination of a foetus or stillborn child may be carried out in both coroner's and non-coroner's cases' has been met in part by the Coroners Bill 2007 (see para **[13.31]**).

UK law

[13.68] In England[115] the Human Tissue Act 2004 regulates the storage and use of all human organs and tissue from the living,[116] and the removal, storage and use of tissue and organs from the deceased, for specified health-related purposes and public display. The main features of the Act (which would likely be a template for any equivalent legislation in this jurisdiction) include:

- Consent (not authorisation) is the fundamental principle underpinning the lawful retention and use of body parts, organs and tissue;

- It lists the purposes for which consent is required;[117]

---

[113] The levels of hierarchy are as follows: (i) spouse/partner; (ii) parent/child; (iii) brother/sister; (iv) grandparent/grandchild; (v) stepfather/stepmother; (vi) half-brother/half-sister; (vii) step-brother/step-sister; (viii) child of brother/sister; (ix) long-standing friend.

[114] See the discussion of the rights of the minor to consent to medical treatment in Ch 3 'Consent' para **[3.24]***ff.*

[115] And in Scotland, the Human Tissue (Scotland) Act 2006, which deals with three areas: (i) tissue donation primarily for the purpose of transplantation, but also for research, education or training and audit; (ii) tissue removal, retention and use following a post-mortem examination; and (iii) for the purposes of the Anatomy Act 1984 as amended for Scotland by the 2006 Act. It utilises the principle of authorisation rather than consent as the basis for lawful use of tissues.

[116] The Human Tissue Act 2004 does not deal with the removal of tissue from living persons, which is dealt with in accordance with existing principles of consent—see generally Ch 3 Consent.

[117] Which include the following: anatomical examination; determining the cause of death (except where ordered by a coroner); establishing after a person's death the efficacy of any drug or other treatment; obtaining medical information about a person that might be relevant to someone else, such as genetic information; public display; research; transplantation; (the following apply only to tissues taken from a dead person) clinical audit; relevant education or training; performance assessment; public health monitoring. No consent is required for tissues already held in storage prior to the coming into force of the Act in 2006.

- It establishes a Human Tissue Authority to ensure compliance. The Authority will issue good practice guidelines in statutory codes of practice and will also licence and inspect post-mortem activities.

Cremation

[13.69] Formal rules applying to cremation in Ireland were introduced in 1989.[118] Cremation must be authorised by the medical referee attached to the crematorium, based on certificates completed and furnished by the doctor who attended the deceased. The rules on cremation are obviously somewhat tighter than they might be in the case of burial. Cremation by its very nature reduces the body to a form which makes later investigation of an alternative cause of death—such as foul play—practically impossible;[119] accordingly, it is necessary to be absolutely certain that there is no irregularity in the background to an application for cremation. The medical referee, before authorising a cremation, must be satisfied that:

(a)   the attending doctor, who must have been registered for at least three years, has completed and signed a certificate in the prescribed form (form 'C'—see Appendix III) stating the cause of death; or

(b)   if the attending doctor is not available or has not been registered for the requisite three years, form 'C' has been completed and signed by another doctor registered for at least three years, and that the second doctor has viewed the body and made such inquiries as she deems necessary to satisfy herself as to the cause of death before signing the certificate; or

(c)   the death has been reported to the coroner and the medical referee is in receipt of a completed certificate in the prescribed form (form 'D'—see Appendix III) from that coroner.

A doctor who is related to the deceased or who has a financial interest in the affairs of the deceased (such as being named in the will) cannot sign the cremation form.[120] In the case of a death reported to the coroner where the coroner is satisfied as to the cause of death, a coroner's certificate circumvents the need for a form signed by doctors and the cremation may go ahead. The coroner may—as has already been mentioned—release

---

[118] The Dublin Cemeteries Committee Rules 1989. Professor Knight, in his book *Legal Aspects of Medical Practice,* relates the story of eccentric Welsh GP, William Price, who attempted to cremate his infant son (named Jesus Christ Price) after the child's death in 1884. At the time cremation was illegal and Dr Price was tried. He conducted his own defence and was acquitted. The British Government felt obliged thereafter to legislate for cremation and introduced the 1902 Cremation Act. Dr Price was an extraordinary figure: he became fascinated by the pagan rites of the ancient druids, carried out his own rituals around a supposedly ancient stone on a hill above Pontypridd, dressed frequently in a fantastic costume of green and blue and capped by an animal skin.

[119] This was an issue in the case of Dr Harold Shipman and the subsequent inquiry recommended a strengthening of the procedural steps prior to cremation: see The Shipman Inquiry Third Report, *Death Certification and the Investigation of Deaths by Coroners* (Cm 5854)(July 2003).

[120] Rule 19.8.

the body for burial or cremation when she is satisfied that no purpose would be served by retaining the body further.

[13.70] The appropriate form must usually reach the crematorium before mid-afternoon of the day before cremation is scheduled to take place. This ensures that there is ample time for the medical referee to instigate any necessary investigations or clarifications prior to authorising or refusing the cremation. If the forms are not correctly filled or the medical referee is not happy with the information supplied, she can attempt to get further information from the signatories of the form or from anyone else having knowledge of the death. If the medical referee is still not satisfied she may perform an examination of the body, extending—with consent of the next of kin—to 'internal dissection' if necessary to rule out any reason why the body should not be cremated. It follows that the medical referee has the discretion to refuse to authorise cremation.[121] A Garda, not below the rank of Superintendent, may put a stay on cremation where further examination of the body is or may be necessary.[122]

[13.71] One aspect of the examination after death of a body intended for cremation is to ensure that there are no prostheses left *in situ*. Of particular concern are cardiac pacemakers or any radioactive devices, neither of which responds especially well to the high temperatures of the crematorium. In particular, mercury batteries in a pacemaker may explode.

---

[121] Forms also exist for the separate cremation of the body parts of a deceased. Typically these will have been organs retained during post-mortem examination and released subsequent to the interment or cremation of the rest of the body. The institution that held the body organs certifies that there is no reason why the organs or body parts should be further examined and that they are suitable for cremation. Such a form may be (although there is no explicit legal requirement) completed by a medical practitioner, but may also be completed by another representative of the hospital or other institution.

[122] Rule 19.9.

Chapter 14

Forensic Medicine, DNA Testing and Terminology of Injuries

INTRODUCTION

[14.01] This chapter (together with Ch 15, which is concerned with rape and sexual assault) contains an outline of those elements of legal medicine that are often called 'forensic medicine'. It is in this realm of forensic medicine that the practitioner may become a part of the criminal justice system (and occasionally the civil system in matters such as paternity: see para **[14.32]**), using clinical skills to identify clues that could rule out or confirm foul play. This chapter and the one that follows are by no means exhaustive of the subject they describe; they serve predominantly to outline the elements that should be in the mind of the practitioner, who will typically be a doctor or a forensic science specialist, when faced with the dead or injured individual.

[14.02] For most clinical practitioners, involvement with the dead or injured body will rarely go beyond the administrative or the clinical, but there are times when circumstances conspire to demand at least something of the detective from the clinician. This may be because of her job (such as a pathologist) or because of geographical isolation in rural practice that means that the local doctor may be the only person at the scene of a death for some hours after a body has been discovered. It is true also that the need for some measure of forensic skill may arise in the more commonplace scenario of the consulting room, where any clinical professional may be required to compile a medico-legal report detailing the clinical findings (physical or psychological) arising from examination of the victim (or even the perpetrator) of injuries. Clarity and certainty in descriptions and conclusions can be vital to the usefulness of any report and its defensibility in the face of later scrutiny. Knowing the terminology of injuries, together with the degree to which any injuries identified are consistent with events alleged by a patient, can be the foundation upon which plausible and sustainable conclusions are built.

THE DOCTOR AND THE DEAD BODY

[14.03] Post-mortem 'clerical' issues, such as referral to the coroner and death certification have been dealt with in Ch 13. To summarise, in cases where death is sudden, overtly suspicious, occurs in certain institutional or contextual settings, or where the deceased has not been seen in the month preceding his death, the coroner will need to be informed.[1] It may also, depending on circumstances, be necessary to notify the police. It will then be a matter for the police or the coroner to notify the Chief State Pathologist should the situation require it. In this chapter, however, we are more concerned with the

---

[1] See Ch 13 'The Coroner and the Aftermath of Death' para **[13.29]**ff.

dead body itself, including the signs that may lead a clinician to suspect foul play and to identify such features as the cause or time of death.

External examination of the body

[14.04] Where there is any suspicion as to the cause of death or any possibility that further examination of the body in situ will be required, then the body and the setting in which it has been discovered should be disturbed as little as possible. It is important, however, not to neglect to confirm that death *has* actually occurred. Clearly, palpation of an accessible pulse should take place to ensure that death has in fact occurred, but there may be cases (such as the discovery of a decomposing body) in which not even this step will be necessary. While confirming the fact of death may involve compromising potential evidence, it may also (if the person is not in fact dead) permit the opportunity of downgrading the scene to one of death to one of an assault or overdose, as the case may be, and also allows for the possibility of getting the person to hospital in time to avert death.

[14.05] However, even though disturbance of the body should be kept to an absolute minimum, external examination of the body at a remove can nonetheless speak volumes as to possible causes of death. The skin may be a cherry-pink colour after carbon monoxide poisoning[2] and acute septicaemia or asphyxiation may leave the body with obvious petechial marks[3] on the skin. Obvious injuries may be evident and their appearance and location should be recorded. Common external indicators of the cause of death include:

- petechial haemorrhages around the eyes and ears or on the face in cases of strangulation or asphyxiation;

- bruises on the face: the face bruises easily and may demonstrate signs of injury, notably around the neck and under the chin (especially in cases of manual strangulation);

- if there is bleeding, its source should be established: is it from an obvious wound, or from the mouth ears of some other orifice? Bear in mind that hair may conceal serious head wounds;

- if touching the body to establish the absence of life, is it cold and/or stiff? Within the first 36 hours after death, one (far from accurate) rule of thumb is that the greater the frigidity and rigidity of the body, the longer it has been since death. We discuss the difficulties of establishing time of death in para **[14.08]***ff.*

Detailed investigation of the dead body in cases of foul play or suspicious deaths will typically fall to the Chief State Pathologist (or a deputy) or in cases where the coroner is

---

[2]   Carbon monoxide (CO) poisoning may occur accidentally (commonly due to malfunctioning heating systems in poorly ventilated spaces where incompletely combusted oxygen in the form of CO is allowed to accumulate) or deliberately (as in suicide with car exhaust fumes). See also para **[14.56]** below.

[3]   Petechiae or petechial marks are small areas of bleeding visible just beneath the surface of the skin.

involved, a local pathologist. Nonetheless, it is useful for the physician to be aware of certain clues that may be present on or around the body.

The scene of death

[14.06] Many clues can be gleaned from the death scene that will prove useful where death has been overtly violent or is otherwise sudden and unexpected. The position of the body should be noted but, as already outlined, the body and the surrounding scene should not be disturbed unless absolutely necessary or unless the attending clinician is experienced at death scene investigations.

[14.07] One should note the presence, location and nature of any substances, instruments or other objects that might be linked to the death. If a person is found dead in bed and on a bedside cabinet are several empty bottles of tranquilisers or anti-depressants, this may indicate to the doctor that an overdose may have caused (or at least contributed to) death. Torn or unusually arranged clothing or missing undergarments may indicate a physical or sexual assault.[4] The nearby presence of a firearm or a bloodstained implement, when coupled with wounds to the body, may also be an important indicator of cause of death.

Time of death

[14.08] It is always difficult, and sometimes impossible, to be certain of the time of death and the longer the period that elapses after death, the more difficult that task becomes. All methods for measuring the time of death have inherent shortcomings and the best that can ever be offered by the clinician is a 'window' of time within which death is most likely to have occurred. A doctor who ties herself to too specific a time of death without good reason may be offering a hostage to fortune—if her estimation of the time of death is shown to be inaccurate, that may in turn cast a pall of doubt over any other findings she may make.

Immediately after death: body temperature

[14.09] In the first day or so after death the core temperature of the body falls gradually to the temperature of the surrounding environment. For the first few hours after death occurs, the temperature of the corpse typically remains static (the 'plateau' phase) and then begins to fall over a period of about 24 hours to the ambient surrounding temperature. Then as decomposition begins (although the time at which decomposition starts is very variable indeed: see para **[14.14]**) the temperature of the cadaver may actually rise a little.

[14.10] Taking a measurement of the core temperature therefore, either rectally, which is the method of choice, or from the axilla (assuming that the arm can be brought against the body to close off the thermometer from the surrounding air), the external auditory

---

4   Although as Professor Knight observes in *Legal Aspects of Medical Practice* (5th edn, 1992), missing or disarranged undergarments may merely indicate that the death occurred suddenly while the deceased was dressing or defecating.

meatus or deep in the pharynx or nasal passages, can give a *very approximate* indication of time lapse since death.[5]

Limitations in short-term estimations of the time since death

[14.11] Temperature curve estimates of the time since death are obviously susceptible to any number of interfering factors: the person who dies of hypothermia will obviously have a very different temperature drop after death compared to a person who dies of a fever. Indeed, in the case of hypothermic death, two potentially confounding factors exist: first, that the starting temperature at the time of death is by definition low; and, secondly, that if the prevailing environment continues to be cold, the fall of the core temperature to that of the ambient environment may be accelerated. Conversely, in the case of a person dying with a fever, analogous factors apply in reverse: the starting temperature is higher than expected. There are many other factors that can stymie attempts to estimate the time of death from body temperature:

- the initial plateau phase: even for two identical bodies in identical settings, the duration of the initial steady temperature may be very variable;

- the ambient temperature: weather conditions may accelerate or retard the fall in body temperature;

- clothes worn by the deceased;

- the amount of fat on the body will alter the rate of core body temperature change.

In warm weather, climatic conditions may markedly accelerate the process of decomposition, as well as altering the cooling curve.

Overcoming the limitations

[14.12] An experienced forensic scientist may be able to adjust for any number of variables, but it remains the case that relying on temperature alone in the immediate aftermath of death will never afford more than an approximate time of death. Among the methods used to try to compensate for the many variables are tools such as the Henssge nomogram,[6] which attempts to factor in confounding elements to give a more accurate estimate of time of death. However, even this mechanism has errors that are measured in

---

[5] Wherever the temperature is taken, the measuring device (ideally a long thermocouple probe to assay deep rectal temperature) should be left in situ for some time to stabilise. Serial measurements of the change in temperature over time are preferable to a single measurement. Taking rectal temperature may be contra-indicated when there is any suspicion of rectal trauma, such as may occur in a sexual assault. If the temperature must, for whatever reason, be taken in the axilla (arm pit) or deep in the pharynx, then 3 or 4°c should be added to the recorded temperature in an attempt to more accurately reflect the core temperature.

[6] Different Henssge nomograms are used when the environmental temperature is above or below 23.0°C. The nomogram method may be used in conjunction with other methods, such as electrical stimulation of muscle or pupillary response to drugs (see text) to reduce error margins. See Henssge, 'Death time estimation in case work I. The rectal temperature time of death nomogram.' Forensic Science International 38 (1988), 209–236.

several hours. Other methods that can be used as adjuncts to body temperature nomograms[7] include:

– electrical muscle stimulation: the response of muscles (in particular the small muscles around the eye but also larger muscles) to electrical stimulations can persist for up to 20 hours after death, dwindling as the post-mortem interval lengthens;

– pupillary response to drugs: the excitability of the iris following sub-conjunctival injection of certain drugs can be an indicator of time since death. The degree of excitability diminishes with the lapsing of time since death;

– vitreous humour potassium levels: there is a linear relationship between time since death (for up to five days) and the rise in potassium concentration in the vitreous humour of the eye. However, this is not an especially reliable method;[8]

– rigor mortis: see below.

Rigor mortis

[14.13] The stiffness of the body in the first day or two after death is often thought of as furnishing important clues as to the time when death occurred, but as with body temperature, the presence or absence of stiffness may confound as much as it enlightens. Rigor mortis occurs after death when the body's oxygen-starved muscle cells produce high levels of lactic acid due to the breakdown of glycogen, which in turn causes the actin and myosin proteins in muscles to fuse and form a gel. It is this fusion which causes stiffness and rigor persists until the process of decomposition begins to take hold. Rigor mortis can commence at almost any time after death[9] and one rule of thumb is that 'rigor mortis commences in six hours, taking six hours to become fully established, remains for 12 hours and then passes off over the next 12.'[10] It should be noted though that this rule of thumb can only be applied with great caution. Another approximate guide to the time of death occurring in temperate countries (such as Ireland) can be derived from a combination of body temperature and rigor mortis (see Table 14.1), but it must always be borne in mind that the determination of time of death is rarely, if ever, a precise science.

---

[7] There are also other models that attempt to cater for changes or irregularities in the ambient temperature of the setting in which the body is cooling (for example, where a person is killed in one place and then—after a few hours—moved to another, colder setting): see Mall and Eisenmenger, 'Estimation of time since death by heat-flow Finite-Element model part II: application to non-standard cooling conditions and preliminary results in practical casework' (2005) Leg Med (7)2; 69–80.

[8] Other less-than-reliable methods include assessment of gastric contents in circumstances where the time and nature of the last meal of the deceased are known.

[9] There is some (possibly apocryphal) evidence to suggest that rarely the onset of rigor mortis may be instantaneous.

[10] Knight, *Legal Aspects of Medical Practice* (5th edn, Churchill Livingstone, 1992), 145.

**Table 14.1 Temperature and stiffness as approximate
indicators of time since death**

Body Temperature	Body Stiffness	Estimated time since death
Warm	Not stiff	Dead fewer than 3 hours
Warm	Stiff	Dead between 3 and 8 hours
Cold	Stiff	Dead between 8 and 36 hours
Cold	Not stiff	Dead more than 36 hours

The medium term after death

[14.14] In a temperate setting, decomposition commences approximately two to three days after death but yet again the ambient surroundings have a significant part to play. A body in a very cold environment may not decompose at all until the weather warms up, while a body in a warm and humid environment may move into the decomposition phase very quickly (in a matter of a few hours). The process of decomposition begins in the area of the gut, which is rich in bacteria that rapidly multiply unchecked, so that the abdomen is the first to discolour; gas production, a by-product of bacterial activity, leads to the rupture of the intestines and to the spread of the bacteria. With time the putrefaction spreads, distorting the face and body cavities. The skin breaks down after approximately one to two weeks. Decomposition and dispersal of the body may also be affected by the action of scavenging animals. Decomposition may also be retarded by immersion in water (although the presence of sewage may increase the rate) and burial in the ground (which also retards colonisation by insects such as blowflies—see para [14.16]). In certain conditions, decomposition will not occur in the conventional manner and instead adipocere[11] formation (damp conditions) or mummification (dry conditions) will take place.

[14.15] Decomposition is yet again an unreliable indicator of time since death. It is true that different organs do start decomposing at different times after death, so the degree of progression of decomposition may have some value in estimating time of death. However, the reality is that the information provided by such decomposition is variable and often equivocal and will again only offer the opportunity to fashion an approximate window (see Table 14.2) of time within which the death is most likely to have occurred.

---

[11] A chemical change of all or (more typically) part of the body's fat, converting it to a grey-ish waxy soapy compound, called adipocere, that may persist for many years and that can retain the shape of the original fatty tissues, so that the body and even facial appearance or wounds (such as bullet holes) remain recognisable.

Table 14 .2 Approximate stages of decomposition in a temperate setting

Stage	Description
Initial Decay	The cadaver appears fresh externally but is decomposing internally (starting in the gut) due to the activities of bacteria, protozoa and nematodes before death
Putrefaction	The cadaver swells due to gas production, accompanied by odour of decaying flesh
Black Putrefaction	Flesh of creamy consistency with increasing black discoloration. Body begins to collapse as gases escape. Odour of decay very strong
Butyric Fermentation	Cadaver drying out. Some flesh generally still remains initially. 'Cheesy' odour develops.
Dry Decay	Cadaver almost dry; rate of decay slows

Forensic entomology

[14.16] One forensic discipline that can assist in working out an approximate time of death in the medium to long term after death is 'forensic entomology', which is the application of the study of insects and other arthropods to legal issues. The most relevant insects for the purposes of this discussion are the carrion feeders (typically blowflies) that are attracted by the decomposing flesh of the body. The females lay their eggs or deposit larvae on the body, especially at the natural orifices and in any wounds. Many of these insects go through dependable and predictable life-cycle phases (although the rate is subject always to climatic conditions). The forensic entomologist can look at insect pupae or larvae obtained from a body and, by identifying the species[12] and gauging where that specimen is in its lifecycle, offer an insight into the time since death. Of course, this technique is to some extent hamstrung by the imprecision inherent in pinpointing when decomposition began, thus attracting insects to the cadaver in the first place.

[14.17] Different types of insects may yield different information, by virtue of their preference for different body parts. Beetles that scavenge bone, for example, have to wait until bone is exposed. Predatory beetles or parasites that feed on maggots (the larval stage of most blowfly species) have to wait until other insects have arrived and deposited their eggs. Some insects specialise in colonising very decayed bodies and their larvae would not be expected until three to six months after death. Where a forensic entomologist is involved in a scene-of-death investigation, his or her role will generally include the following:

- – recording the scene;
- – collecting climate data from the scene;

---

12 Different species are attracted to bodies at different stages in the decomposition process. Also the fact that a species found on a body is not one that would ordinarily be found at the locus where the body was discovered might indicate that the body had been moved after being colonised by the insect in question.

- collection of specimens from the body and surrounding area before removal of the remains;

- collection of specimens from directly under and in close proximity to the remains once the body has been removed.

The longer term after death

[14.18] Once decomposition of the soft tissues is complete, any dogmatically precise assertion of the time of death becomes extremely difficult. A body left in the open air will decompose to a skeleton in approximately one year, depending on both weather conditions and the activity of scavengers and insects. At this late stage in the process, scrutiny of the remaining bony tissues and teeth (although hard tendon tags may also persist) will be all that is open to the investigating clinician. The primary role of the expert in such cases will be distinguishing old remains (which may have some forensic and criminal relevance)[13] from ancient remains, which will be more properly the province of the archaeologist.

Forensic dentistry (or odontology)

[14.19] Where only hard tissues remain following complete decomposition, then teeth, which have great resistance to processes such as putrefaction or fire, may be the most useful body parts remaining. The precise arrangement of teeth and fillings is practically unique to each individual and if dental records can be found for comparison, they can be as useful as fingerprints. Although the dental perspective will not be of use in specifically identifying the time since death, it may fulfil the equally, if not more, important task of identifying the deceased[14] by comparison of the dentition of the cadaver with dental records of those who are candidates for a match with the deceased. Even if only a few teeth are available and too few for certain identification, a forensic odontologist may be able to offer an age estimation of the dead person, as well as other clues, such as smoking habits, overall oral hygiene and other features that may match ante-mortem records. Where the subject has no teeth, information can nonetheless be obtained from the study of dentures or by x-raying the mouth and skull. Other possible roles for the forensic odontologist include:[15]

- age estimations of both living and deceased persons including neo-natal remains;

- analysis of bite marks found on victims of attack;[16]

---

[13] See the Coroners Bill 2007, s 30: there is no obligation on the coroner to investigate deaths that have occurred more than 70 years ago, although such deaths may be reported to the Chief Coroner, who may direct that an investigation should take place.

[14] Indeed, once the deceased is identified it may be circumstantially easier to work towards a time of death. Hitler's right-hand man, Martin Borman, and one of the Führer's doctors, Ludwig Stumpfegger, escaped from the Reich Chancellery building in May 1945 and were never seen again. Their bodies were unearthed during building work in Berlin in 1972 and were identified with certainty from their WWII-era dental records. It is presumed that, faced with capture by the Russians, they killed themselves.

[15] See www.bafo.org.uk, the website of the British Association of Forensic Odontologists (last accessed October 2007).

[16] Although this can be an imprecise science: Pretty, 'The barriers to achieving an evidence base for bitemark analysis' (2006) Forensic Science International 159S, S110–S120.

- identification of bite marks in other substances such as wood, leather and foodstuffs (and analysis of weapon marks using the principles of bite mark analysis);
- presentation of bite and weapon mark evidence in court as an expert witness;
- assistance in building up a picture of lifestyle and diet at an archaeological site.

Identifying dead bodies

[14.20] Deaths frequently occur of those whom it is difficult to identify. A body may be unrecognisable due to the time since death, the nature of the incident (a conflagration being one example) or simply because there is no immediate evidence as to who the deceased is such as the location of the body at or near a residence or place of business, missing person registers or documentation found on or near the body. In the absence of such indicators, factors useful for building up a picture of the identity of an unknown deceased include the following:

- bodily dimensions (height, weight);
- coloration (hair, skin, eyes);
- sex;
- age (x-rays of epiphyses can be useful in those younger than their 20s; dentition may also be especially helpful as a determinant of age in the young);
- deformities, such as missing limbs or digits;
- scars or other marks, such as tattoos or piercings;
- dentition (see 'forensic odontology' at para **[14.18]** above);
- DNA profiling (see para **[14.21]** below).

Quick Reference Guide 14.1

The dead body

> ❖   Many clues about the cause of death may be gleaned from the scene of death. However, it is important to bear in mind that where a death is obviously due to foul play, too much untrained tampering at the scene of death may result in evidence being destroyed.
>
> ❖   A cursory external examination can point to obvious clinical signs of a cause of death as well as affording the opportunity to confirm death.
>
> ❖   Nearly all methods of estimating the time since death are unreliable: the best that can usually be obtained is an approximate time window during which death is most likely to have occurred.
>
> ❖   In the immediate aftermath of death (first 36 hours), the temperature and stiffness of the corpse may afford some guidelines.
>
> ❖   With the passage of time, the presence of decomposition and the stage it has reached may also be an aid to estimating when death occurred; once decomposition is complete, methods for determining time since death are scanty, but they may include the use of forensic dentistry or forensic entomology.
>
> ❖   Other aids to identifying the deceased include bodily dimensions; coloration; sex; age (estimated by x-ray or dentition); deformities; scars, tattoos or body piercing; DNA profiling.

DNA identification

[14.21] DNA technology has revolutionised the ability to identify people using their 'genetic fingerprint'. It is of particular importance in the criminal justice setting, where the possibility of identifying a perpetrator has been hugely augmented not only by the advent of DNA technology but by its further refinement which now permits identification on the basis of the smallest of residues left at a crime scene.[17]

Although DNA is often referred to as a genetic code, in fact there is much of DNA that does not appear to carry genetic information. Only about 10 per cent of the entire length of a DNA molecule is used for genetic coding; the rest is silent. The English scientist Alec Jeffreys observed that these redundant segments of DNA[18] were hugely variable between individuals, but were completely consistent for any given individual and were inherited reliably from parents. It is this 'hypervariable' material that forms the basis for DNA testing.

[14.22] DNA is not only recovered from the scene of criminal activity. It may also be garnered from criminal suspects[19] or from others who wish to (or who are compelled to) provide samples for the purposes of civil legal issues, such as the settlement of paternity disputes. The simplest method of obtaining material for genetic analysis is a mouth swab which will readily provide cells from the buccal mucosa or a hair root; however, other sources include traces of blood, semen and saliva, which may be left at the scene of a crime. For the purposes of identification of dead bodies, DNA can also be obtained from bone, although post-mortem samples are inferior to living samples; in deceased persons where decomposition is not advanced, muscle, spleen and (where decomposition is advancing) bone marrow are good sources.[20] Trace DNA may even sometimes be obtained from items touched by an individual, such as the inside of gloves. In the case of

---

[17] 1ng of template DNA (equivalent to 10 nucleated cells) is sufficient for the generation of a DNA profile using polymerase chain reaction (PCR): see Bär, 'DNA profiling: evaluation of the evidentiary value' (2003) Legal Medicine 5, S41–S44. Even if DNA cannot identify a particular person (because no match is currently available), analysis may suggest certain characteristics of a suspect, such as ethnic origin: see Wetton, Tsang and Khan, 'Inferring the population of origin of DNA evidence within the UK by allele-specific hybridization of Y-SNPs' (2005) Forensic Science International 152, 45–53.

[18] These redundant segments are also known as 'stutters', 'minisatellites' or 'hypervariable regions'.

[19] See below: para **[14.16]**. Testing of DNA samples in state criminal investigations is carried out by the State Forensic Science Laboratory. The Forensic Science Laboratory works in four areas: (i) biology, dealing with biological samples mainly involved in offences against the person; (ii) chemistry, dealing with physical and chemical examinations and involved mainly in offences against property; (iii) drugs, analysing materials thought to contravene the Misuse of Drugs Acts; and (iv) DNA—DNA analyses and comparisons are frequently carried out on samples from the other three sections.

[20] Saukko and Knight, *Knight's Forensic Pathology* (3rd edn, 2004), 106. Obviously, where the deceased person has been the victim of an assault, further samples capable of identifying the assailant will need to be taken from locations such as the rectum, vagina or fingernails as appropriate in the circumstances. See the following chapter for more details of the examination of the sexual assault victim.

assault or sexual assault, material that accumulated during attempts to fight off an attacker may be obtained from under the victim's fingernails and may permit identification of the assailant. Also, after a sexual assault, semen may be deposited on or in a victim. In crimes where there has been more than one perpetrator or where there has been contamination of the crime scene, there may be more than one DNA fingerprint at the scene. The sample sources to be matched do not have to be identical—one does not, for example, have to match blood with blood. The DNA in every cell is identical, so the DNA contained in the bulb of tissue at a hair root taken from a suspect can be compared satisfactorily with a sample of semen thought to have come from the same person.

[14.23] As DNA tests have become more sensitive, they have increasingly permitted the analysis of samples retained during now-dormant criminal investigations that were commenced before the advent and refinement of DNA profiling and which remained unsolved until DNA linked the crime to a particular suspect. Similarly, the increased finesse of DNA profiling techniques has allowed smaller and smaller samples to yield significant results.

Obtaining and analysing a DNA sample

[14.24] Although there is a wide range of techniques that may be employed, most share the common features set out below:

1. Where there is only a small amount of DNA available, it may need to be amplified. PCR (polymerase chain reaction)[21] mimics DNA's self-replicating properties to make up to millions of reliably identical copies of the original DNA sample in only a few hours. Where there is sufficient genetic material for testing, this step may not be required.

2. The sample is then digested by 'restriction endonuclease enzymes', each of which recognises a particular known DNA sequence called a restriction site and cuts the DNA there. The result is many fragments of varying sizes.

3. The samples are separated by gel electrophoresis: the digested DNA is placed in a well at the end of a lane in a gel (a gelatine-like material solidified in a thick slab).[22] Mild electric current applied to the gel slowly separates the various fragments by length, because shorter fragments migrate further in response to the current than longer, heavier fragments.

4. The resulting fragments (or 'bands') are transferred to a sheet of nylon by a process known as southern blotting and the DNA is denatured ('unzipped') by heating, separating the double helix of the DNA into single strands.

---

[21] One common PCR-based method is Short Tandem Repeats (STR).

[22] Digested DNA from the suspect or from the person being compared (for example, the putative father in the case of the investigation of paternity) may often be placed in another well on the same gel. Control specimens of DNA fragments of known size, and—where appropriate—DNA specimens obtained from a victim may also be run on the same gel to compare with and rule out any contamination by the victim's own DNA.

5. A probe is applied. The probe is a single strand of DNA tagged with a radioactive compound[23] that binds to or 'hybridises' its complementary sequences when it is applied to the samples of denatured DNA.

6. Excess hybridisation solution is washed off, and the nylon membrane is placed between sheets of photographic film. Over time, the radioactive probe material exposes the film where the biological probe has hybridised with the DNA fragments. The result is an autoradiograph, or an autorad—essentially a photograph of bands that represent specific DNA fragments.

The process can be repeated with different probes that bind to different sequences of DNA. Three to five different probes are typically used, testing for matches in different parts of the DNA, although the number depends in part on the amount of testable DNA recovered from the crime sample. The ideal result will be a set of autorads, each of which shows the results of comparisons between a different part of the sample obtained (eg from the crime scene) and the sample it is being checked against (eg from a suspect).

[14.25] If, on visual inspection, the DNA band patterns for the suspect and the evidence sample appear to be aligned on the autorads, this impression is verified by a computerised measurement. If the two bands fall within a specified length, a match is declared for that probe or allele. For forensic purposes, a match means that the patterns are consistent with the conclusion that the two DNA samples came from the same source. Taken together, the collective results of the probes form the 'DNA profile'.

Samples for forensic analysis—Irish law

[14.26] The Criminal Justice (Forensic Evidence) Act 1990 allows for the taking of forensic samples from a suspect for the purpose of forensic analysis where that person is either in custody under suspicion of having committed a serious criminal offence[24] or is detained in prison and suspected of a serious offence unconnected with the reason for his detention. The samples that may be taken are:

- samples of (i) blood, (ii) pubic hair, (iii) urine, (iv) saliva, (v) hair other than pubic hair, (vi) a nail, (vii) any material found under a nail;

- a swab from any part of the body other than a body orifice or a genital region;

- a swab from a body orifice or a genital region;

- a dental impression;

- a footprint or similar impression of any part of the person's body other than a part of his hand or mouth.

---

[23] Often radioactive phosphorus-32. Different laboratories may use different probes and where different probes are used, test results are not readily comparable. Another type of DNA analysis uses a multi-locus probe, which hybridises with multiple locations simultaneously, yielding a more complex DNA pattern.

[24] See s 2(1) of the Criminal Justice (Forensic Evidence) Act (as amended): s 4 of the Criminal Justice Act 1984 (suspected of an offence where, on conviction, the sentence would be a minimum of five years); s 30 of the Offences Against the State Act; s 2 of the Criminal Justice (Drug Trafficking) Act 1996; or s 50 of the Criminal Justice Act 2007.

[14.27] Authorisation for the sample to be taken must come from a senior member of An Garda Síochána and the investigating member must have reasonable grounds to suspect the involvement of the person in the crime alleged and believe that the sample requested will tend to prove or disprove the involvement of the person in question. The suspect must also be told:

(a)   the nature of the offence in which it is suspected that that person has been involved;

(b)   that an authorisation for the taking of the sample has been given by a senior member of An Garda Síochána…and of the grounds on which it has been given; and

(c)   that the results of any tests on the sample may be given in evidence in any proceedings.

In respect of certain samples,[25] the consent of the suspect is required[26] for the purposes of lawfully obtaining a sample; however, the Act permits a judge or jury to draw the appropriate inferences (namely, that the suspect may have something to hide) if the suspect refuses unreasonably to provide a sample.[27]

The future of forensic sampling in Ireland

[14.28] Note also the publication in February 2007 of an outline Criminal Justice (Forensic Sampling and Evidence) Bill 2007[28] which, if passed into law, will repeal the Criminal Justice (Forensic Evidence) Act 1990. The main features of the 2007 Bill are:

–   the establishment of a DNA database comprising electronic storage of profiles derived from samples taken or recovered from crime scenes, suspects, convicts and volunteers; mass screening[29] samples; samples from or relating to missing persons and an elimination index;[30]

–   the DNA database will be divided into two 'divisions', the investigation division and the identification division;

–   samples may be taken from persons detained under the same provisions of the law as currently apply to the Criminal Justice (Forensic Evidence) Act 1990;

---

[25]   Section 2(4)(b) of the Criminal Justice (Forensic Evidence) Act 1990 (as amended by s 14 of the Criminal Justice Act 2006). The samples in respect of which consent is required are blood, urine, pubic hair, swabs taken from anywhere other than the mouth and dental impressions.

[26]   Where the suspect is under 14, the consent of parents/guardians is required; between the ages of 14 and 17 the consent of both parents/guardians *and* the suspect is required—see also para **[4.25]**.

[27]   Criminal Justice (Forensic Evidence) Act 1990, s 3. This section does not apply to minors or in circumstances where consent was refused by someone other than the suspect himself (eg his parents).

[28]   Based on the Law Reform Commission *Report on the Establishment of a DNA Database* (LRC 78–2005, November 2005).

[29]   This refers to the taking of samples from a defined group of people as part of the investigation of a particular arrestable offence.

[30]   This refers to samples from persons who may be in a position (by virtue of their official roles) to inadvertently contaminate a sample or an investigation scene.

- the samples that may generally be taken without consent under the outline Bill are mouth swabs and hair samples only, unless the samples are required for evidential purposes, when consent is required only for blood, pubic hair and urine samples;

- increased powers to take samples from persons in prison, including those who have been placed on the sex offenders register in accordance with the Sex Offenders Act 2001;

- specific limits placed on the duration of storage.

It is not clear the degree to which the Bill will be altered before becoming law; nor is there a clear timetable for its enactment.

DNA as evidence and the 'chain of evidence'

[14.29] DNA evidence may be used before a court. It may be useful in settling custody disputes between 'parents' by establishing that one of them is or is not the father of the child in question. It can also provide crucial evidence of the involvement of an accused person on trial in circumstances where there is no other identification evidence. Courts have accepted that DNA evidence is acceptable in criminal cases to prove the identity of a perpetrator[31] and laid down the rules by which the jury should attempt to judge the worth and weight of that evidence.

[14.30] The main obstacles to the use of DNA evidence are to do with statistical errors in weighing the probative value of the evidence and ensuring that a jury is accurately informed about the likelihood of a sample having come from a particular person.[32] Ordinarily, where there is a match between the DNA of a suspect and samples found at a crime scene, the possibility that the sample came from another person can be measured in tens of millions; however, there are confounding factors that can undermine such seeming statistical certainty:

- how common the DNA segments are in a particular population;

- how common they are within any segment of that particular population (eg within an ethnic group);

- the existence of siblings who have not been properly excluded as suspects.

It is important to remember that what is being compared in DNA profiling is not an entire genome, but rather segments. While the possibility that there may be a match between the segments tested and equivalent segments in a random person who is not a suspect is always low, it does remain at least a statistical possibility and is one that must be confronted by prosecutors, judges and juries when weighing up DNA evidence.

[14.31] As with any form of evidence, it is important that a court can be sure that the evidence will not have been contaminated in any way; this is the so-called chain of

---

[31] *Dennis John Adams (No 2)* (CA) (Crim Div) 16 October 1997.

[32] Henderson, 'The use of DNA statistics in criminal trials' (2002) Forensic Science International 128 183–186; Bär, 'DNA profiling: evaluation of the evidentiary value' (2003) Legal Medicine 5S41–S44; Fung, Hu and Chung, 'On statistical analysis of forensic DNA: theory, methods and computer programs' (2006) Forensic Science International 162, 17–23.

evidence—a sample that could be used in evidence must be carefully shepherded through the testing process. This is typically achieved by the completion of a series of forms that make clear the origin of the evidence as well as documenting who has possession of the evidence at any given time and what has been done to the evidence (and by whom).

DNA, blood and paternity testing

[14.32] DNA can also be used to establish the paternity of a child,[33] and it is increasingly the method of choice for doing so. It has the advantage over blood testing (see the following section) that it can actually identify a person as the father of a child, rather than acting merely as an exclusionary test. A DNA profile is created for both parents and the child. The bands are compared first between child and mother. Once the bands that match between mother and child have been accounted for, the remainder must come from the father. If there is no match between those remaining bands and the father's profile, then he is not the father. On the other hand, if there is a match, the chances are greater than 99.5 per cent that he is the father.

Blood testing

[14.33] Blood group genes are passed on from parent to offspring and all possibilities are combinations derived from the letters A, B and O (each of which represents a 'blood group antigen'). Each parent has a blood group determined by two of the letters (including the possibility of a homozygous pair, AA or BB) and each parent donates one of those antigens to the child. Therefore, a blood group antigen cannot be present in the child unless it is also present in at least one parent and, furthermore, if one parent possesses a homozygous allelic pair[34] (AA or BB) then that gene must be present in all of his or her progeny. The various ramifications are worked out in Table 14.3 for convenience.

---

[33] In Ireland a parent can seek a 'declaration of parentage' under the Status of Children Act 1987. This might be done where maintenance payments are being sought (or avoided). The Act only explicitly provides for the use of blood samples, but the courts have held that DNA profiling may be used: see *JPD v MG* [1991] 1 IR 47.

[34] Each of the human body's cells contains 23 paired chromosomes, one of each pair inherited from each parent, and these chromosomes store the body's genetic information. Each little parcel of code is called an allele. If the corresponding alleles on each chromosome (the allelic pairs) are identical, they are called homozygous (allelic) pairs. When humans reproduce, each parent provides one of each pair of chromosomes and the other parent provides the other. Hence a parent who has the blood group called AB (where A is on one chromosome and B on the other) will donate *either* an 'A' genetic code or a 'B' genetic code to the child. A parent who has an AA code *must* donate an A, and so on.

Table 14.3 Blood Group Combinations

1st Parent	2nd Parent	Potential Offspring	Impossible Offspring
O	O	O	A, B, AB
O	A (AA, AO)	O, AO	B, AB
O	B (BB, BO)	O, BO	A, AB
A (AA, AO)	A (AA, AO)	O, AA, AO	B, AB
1st Parent	*2nd Parent*	*Potential Offspring*	*Impossible Offspring*
A (AA, AO)	B (BB, BO)	O, AA, AO, BB, BO, AB	No grouping impossible
B (BB, BO)	B (BB, BO)	O, BB, BO	A, AB
O	AB	AO, BO	O, AB
A (AA, AO)	AB	AA, AO, BO, AB	O
B (BB, BO)	AB	BB, BO, AO, AB	O
AB	AB	AA, BB, AB	O

There are a number of other blood tests that can be done in addition to blood grouping to assess the likelihood of paternity[35] so that the total chance of correctly excluding a father wrongly accused of paternity from the possibility of being the father using such systems is 93 per cent. A person's blood group remains constant throughout life except for transient disturbances that may occur after blood transfusion. It is important to bear in mind that no one should undergo a blood test for paternity within three months after a blood transfusion.

---

[35] Other red cell antigen systems that can be typed include the following factors: Rhesus, Duffy, Kidd, Kell, and Luthran. The serum protein systems that can be typed include haptoglobins, while red cell enzymes systems that can be typed include erythrocyte acid phosphatase, glutamate pyruvate transaminase and phosphoglucomutase.

Quick Reference Guide 14.2

DNA and blood grouping

❖   Thanks to the polymerase chain reaction step in DNA sampling, it has become possible to extract meaningful amounts of DNA for analysis from the smallest samples.

❖   DNA can be assayed easily from a blood sample, a swab of the inside of the mouth, or a sample of hair, skin or sperm. Legislation has increased the power of investigating authorities to take samples for DNA testing from criminal suspects.

❖   With a good sample and reliable testing it is possible to obtain a DNA match between a test sample and a suspect (or other donor) sample that is so accurate that it practically excludes the possibility of anyone else in the world being a match for the sample.

❖   DNA sample matches are admissible evidence in court and can be used to help secure a criminal conviction. Like all other evidence, DNA must be handled with care and transferred scrupulously from person to person during the investigation of a crime in such a way as to rule out the possibility that the evidence has been tampered with.

❖   DNA is analysed by a method known as Restriction Fragment Length Polymorphism (RFLP). The steps involved may, depending on the method employed, include collection of the sample, digestion of the sample by enzymes, electrophoresis, Southern blotting and comparison by way of autorads between the sample and the suspect (or other donor) sample.

❖   DNA or blood testing can both be used for paternity testing. Blood sampling is cheaper and there is a greater than 90% chance of reaching a correct conclusion. Blood testing is sufficiently accurate for it to be accepted as evidence by the courts in civil cases. DNA testing is more accurate, but also more expensive.

DESCRIBING INJURIES

[14.34] The need to document injuries may arise in any number of scenarios. It may form part of the routine admission of a patient to hospital following an accident or assault or it may arise as a necessary part of the compilation of a medico-legal report. Whatever the circumstances, it is important to be aware of the words and terms that are properly used to describe certain injuries.[36] If healthcare professionals adhere to correct terminology and demonstrate internal consistency in the use of such terms in their note-taking, then life becomes easier both for the clinician consulting her own notes, possibly after the passage of some considerable time, and for any third parties who have to read those notes. Accurate descriptions of injuries at the time of the original examination will help in compiling any report, which may not be required for months or even years after the event. This is especially true if, as may happen in the hospital setting, the clinician with responsibility for compiling a report and therefore with responsibility for deciphering the initial consultations may not be the same person who dealt with the patient who is the subject-matter of the report. The usefulness of drawings (or where

---

[36]   Milroy and Rutty, 'If a wound is "neatly incised" it is not a laceration' (1997) BMJ; 315:1312.

possible, photographs) as an unambiguous *aide memoire* or guide cannot be overstated when it comes to trying to describe injuries at a later date.[37]

[14.35] As with all medical interventions, consent to disclosure of information will be necessary unless there are forces operating to make disclosure obligatory or desirable even in the absence of consent.[38] Consent should be obtained from the patient, at the time of examination, to the later disclosure of that information or perhaps more appropriately consent can be sought at the time when disclosure is required or being contemplated.

Injuries common in assaults or accidents

[14.36] While all of the injuries below are dealt with as if they were separate entities, it is a truism that they often co-exist in a single patient; a person in a road traffic accident who strikes his head on a windscreen or on the ground could expect to suffer lacerations, abrasions and contusions. However, each class of injury has different characteristics and it is important to be aware and confident of the distinctions between each, so that the presence of injuries can be accurately catalogued, whether present in isolation or as part of a spectrum of physical trauma.

Abrasions

[14.37] Abrasions are essentially scrapes or scratches; they are superficial wounds to the skin's surface that do not penetrate to the full thickness of the skin, although they may nonetheless be deep enough to bleed. They generally occur when the skin rubs against a rough surface. The skin or the rough surface (or both) may be in motion at the time of contact, so a person who is flung headlong along a road surface may sustain abrasions, as may a person who is dealt a glancing blow from an object such as a weapon. Abrasions may sometimes contain foreign bodies[39] although ordinarily they are too superficial to do so. Abrasions may also on occasion record a relatively faithful impression of the object that caused them (for example the weave of a particular rope). Abrasions can also become more livid after death.

[14.38] Careful examination of abrasions can disclose the direction of the contact that caused the injuries; small skin tags will generally be found at the end of the abrasion where the abrading surface parted contact with the skin.

Contusions/bruises

[14.39] Contusions are essentially bruises, which in turn are the accumulation beneath the skin's surface of blood released from small (or sometimes larger) blood vessels following a blow. Bruises are variable in size, nature and duration, depending on where the bruising occurs. The extent of a bruise can be variable in size, nature and duration, also depending on where the bruising occurs. Although the extent of a given bruise caused by any particular injury can be unpredictable, intra-dermal bruises (occurring

---

[37] See Ch 9 'The Practitioner and the Lawyer', for a more detailed description of medico-legal reports.

[38] See para **[3.15]** for a discussion of the circumstances in which consent may not be necessary for the disclosure of confidential information.

[39] So, after a road traffic accident, abrasions may contain tiny fragments of glass.

just below the level of the epidermis) can occasionally reflect the nature and dimensions of the object that caused the physical insult. The soles of boots, for example, may sometimes leave such accurate marks that it is possible to identify with some certainty the pattern on the sole.

[14.40] Whether a bruise occurs depends on how much room there is for blood to collect beneath the skin. The more lax the overlying skin and the less dense the tissue beneath the skin, the more likely bruising is to occur. Similarly, where skin is stretched taut over bony prominences, such as the cheek or the jaw, bruising is more common (as are lacerations—see para **[14.42]**). The very young, the very old and those with bleeding disorders (or on 'blood thinning' medication such as warfarin) bruise most easily. Even firm gripping of a child's arm may result in contusions, typically a series of discrete disc-shaped bruises corresponding to each fingertip. Clusters of bruises may be indicative of repeated blows. Some implements, such as belt buckles or rod-like instruments, may leave characteristic marks. On children, any such marks should at least raise the possibility of child abuse. A bite, if it does not break the skin, may leave two sets of 'mirrored' semi-circular bruises (the services of a forensic odontologist—see para **[14.19]** above—may help in the documentation and identification of such marks).

[14.41] As bruises age, they change colour, which can be a useful, although not especially accurate, adjunct to verifying when an alleged incident took place. The rate of colour change of bruises is highly variable, but the colour progression is generally the same: new bruises are purplish in colour, changing to become brownish and then altering to green-yellow, before resolving over a week or two. Superficial bruises may disappear much more quickly than this. The colour changes are due to the breakdown of the blood products in the bruise.

Lacerations

[14.42] A laceration is not, in the conventional sense of the word, a cut. Rather, it is a wound penetrating the full depth of the skin, but which is caused by a blunt or relatively blunt object, rather than by a sharp edge. A blow to an area of skin that is taut over a bony surface (such as the scalp) is particularly likely to result in a laceration. Such a wound may resemble an incision, but what will distinguish a laceration from an incision on close examination is the presence of the signs of crushing around the margins of the laceration wound. On the scalp, for example, hairs will often be forced into a laceration wound by the impact. In other areas of the body, foreign bodies may be forced into the wound, which by contrast is an unusual event with an incision. Lacerations also tend (although this is not universal) to bleed less than incisions, because the blunt trauma to the blood vessels encourages coagulation of blood.

[14.43] The fact that a laceration may contain a foreign body should be borne in mind. Such wounds should not generally be closed up without being explored. Any discovered foreign body should, where possible, be retained, labelled and stored, especially where legal action is a possibility.

Incisions

[14.44] Incisions are penetrating wounds caused by sharp objects and they fall into two categories: the 'stab' wound (which is deeper than it is long) and the 'slash' wound (which is longer than it is deep). As with abrasions, slash wounds should have their direction and dimensions recorded, using drawings if possible. The sharper the weapon, the smoother the edges of the incision will be. In many cases, the deeper end of a slash wound is where the cutting edge first went into the body, but this is not always true. A stab wound may not reveal much unless it is explored at a post-mortem examination, but the two extremities of the (usually elliptical) entrance wound may indicate whether the weapon had two sharp edges (in which case, there will usually be a neat cut at both edges of the wound), one sharp edge (the skin will often be split rather than cut at the extremity of the wound where the blunt edge when into the skin), or two blunt edges (skin split at both extremities).

[14.45] Foreign bodies, although not often a feature of incisions, should still be borne in mind; there may be a part of the weapon (such as a piece of glass) contained in the wound that may be invaluable at a later date in linking the injury to a particular implement.

Fractures

[14.46] The clinically-trained reader will not need an account of fractures at this point, but it may be useful to point out certain characteristic features that may occur in the forensic or medico-legal setting. The driver of a car who braces himself against an impending impact by firmly clutching the steering wheel or forcing his feet down on the pedals will often suffer fractures of the wrist, forearm or lower limb. A person who fends off an attacker may also sustain factures in his attempts at self-defence. The non-clinically trained reader should be made aware that, in terms of bones, a 'fracture' is synonymous with a 'break'.

Underlying damage

[14.47] Even if examination suggests minimal damage to the external surface of the body, it is always worth considering the possibility of moderate, or even severe, underlying harm. Even a small penetrating injury or blunt trauma to the abdomen or flanks can cause kidney, liver or spleen damage and these possibilities should always be considered. A person who has received a kick or other blow to the loins should, as well as undergoing a physical examination, be asked to provide a urine sample to exclude damage to the kidneys.

Head injuries

[14.48] Without going in to the physics that underpin this anatomical irregularity, the practitioner should always be aware when it comes to head injuries that there are critical differences in the location of skull fractures depending on whether or not the head was moving at the time of the impact. If the stationary head is struck by a moving object, then any fracture (and underlying brain damage) is likely to be at the site of the impact. Conversely, if the moving head strikes a stationary object, then injury to the skull or the brain tissue may occur at the point diametrically opposite the contact *as well as* at the point of contact. This is known as a *contre-coup* injury and should be considered in patients suspected of having sustained a head injury.

Discussion of the various types of brain haemorrhage that may accompany a head injury lies outside the scope of this text.

Burns

[14.49] In clinical practice, only the hospital doctor or nurse is likely to encounter extensive burns or scalds,[40] but the question of classification of burns may nonetheless be relevant for any practitioner who is compiling a medical report following an assault or accident. The extent of burns may usually be approximately gauged by the so-called 'rule of nines':[41] each whole arm and the head equates to roughly 9 per cent of the body surface, while each leg and each of the front and back of the torso constitutes 18 per cent.[42] Any description of burns should ideally indicate the area affected, the extent of the burn, the shape of the burn and the severity ('degree') of the burn. There are three degrees of burn:

First Degree	Superficial redness (erythema) and blistering
Second Degree	Full thickness of skin affected, exposing underlying tissue. Typically painless, because of extensive damage to the nerves which would ordinarily carry pain sensation.
Third Degree	Severe damage to underlying tissue, exposing bone and muscle. A person who has suffered third degree burns will often have severe muscle contractures and skin-tearing due to the shrinkage of tissues exposed to high heat.

A burn can occur at quite low temperatures if exposure to the heat source lasts long enough; so sitting by a fire or even prolonged exposure to a hot water bottle or electric blanket may sometimes cause burns, especially in the elderly. Burns are occasionally a feature of severe child abuse.[43] There may be evidence of small circular burns, caused by cigarettes, or of scalding a limb with a horizontal margin around the proximal end, a sign of the limb having been lowered into very hot water.

Electricity burns

[14.50] Burns can also be caused by electricity and come in two forms. The burns caused by firm contact with the electrical source will often result in a blister-type lesion surrounded by a paler area of skin. Lighter contact with an electrical source may leave a small pit, but it can be very hard to find the mark. Extremely high electrical currents can cause very severe burns.

Firearm/bullet wounds

[14.51] The various types of wound caused by bullets may not be of immediate concern to the doctor or nurse who is attempting to resuscitate a gun shot victim but, at the same

---

[40] The distinction is rarely clinically significant, but scalds classically refer to burns caused by liquids.

[41] In younger children the proportions are somewhat different: the head equates to more than 9 per cent and each leg to less than 18 per cent.

[42] The remaining approx 1 per cent is accounted for by the genital area, the palms of the hands and the soles of the feet.

[43] See Ch 7, para **[7.34]***ff.*

time, the nature of a wound can provide an indication of the sort of weapon used. Noting and recording the type of wound may be of importance both as a permanent record should the original wound be obliterated by surgical intervention and as an indicator of what is to be expected internally should the patient require an operation. The main differences in the type of wound caused by a bullet generally depend on the velocity of the bullet as it enters the body:

Low Velocity	The damage essentially results from the bullet slowing down, transferring its kinetic energy to the surrounding tissues by way of friction and heat damage. A bullet that does not slow down (for example, passing through the body without encountering bone or a major organ) is less likely to cause serious damage.[44]
High Velocity	The slowing of the projectile is still relevant, but there are other factors too. A very high velocity projectile may be accompanied by a shock wave, causing compression and severe damage to surrounding tissues. High velocity bullets can cause cavitation wounds that are greater than the size of the bullet would seem to suggest.

A gunshot wound should result in an entry wound and an exit wound unless the bullet has struck a bony object or was of sufficiently low velocity to come to rest in the body.[45] With high velocity bullets the exit wound may be several times larger than the entry wound. Other clues to distinguish entry from exit wounds include the fact that an entry wound will typically have inverted edges and the exit wound everted edges, although this guideline is subject to a number of modifying factors.

Shotgun injuries

[14.52] Shotguns are among the most common legally-held firearms and it is therefore a weapon that is used in suicides with some frequency. However, because of their regular use on farms and for hunting, accidents are also common. A shotgun discharges lead pellets from cartridges[46] consisting of a plastic or cardboard cylinder with a brass plate at one end and a 'wad' at the other to hold the pellets in the cylinder. The plate contains a primer which, when struck by the hammer of the shotgun, explodes to propel the shot (and the wad) from the barrel of the gun. As the shot moves away from the end of the barrel, it begins to spread out. A small amount of the explosive propellant will also escape from the barrel and travel a very short distance from the muzzle.

[14.53] Calculating the distance between the weapon and the victim of the shooting at the time of firing may enlighten the investigation of a shotgun death. A 'contact' wound may suggest a suicide or that someone was able to approach the victim very closely

---

44 Although this is not always true, a bullet may pass quickly through the body, but still sever a major artery, for example.

45 This is not uncommon in shotgun injuries.

46 Different types of cartridges can contain pellets of different sizes.

before discharging the weapon. The distance the victim was from the weapon as it discharged may be demonstrated by some or all of a variety of defining characteristics:[47]

Contact Discharge	There may be contusions (bruising) caused by the pressure of the barrel against the body. The entry wound may be almost circular, approximating to the size of the barrel (or barrels) of the shotgun, but if the weapon is discharged over bone (the skull or sternum, for example) the pressure of gases between skin and bone may result in a larger, more ragged wound. There may be burn or other marks caused by escaping flame, soot and gas (from the exploding propellant in the primer) especially with older weapons or cartridges. Any hairs or clothing fibres may be obviously singed. The wad from the cartridge will be in the wound.
Close Firing (cm)	There may be singeing around the edges of the wound and soot staining or 'tattooing' caused by escaping, unburned, propellant. The wound will be circular if the gun was discharged straight at the wound, but elliptical if discharged at an angle. The wound will usually contain the wad from the cartridge.
Discharge Within 2m	Once the cartridge was discharged more than (approximately) 30cm away, soot deposition is uncommon, but tattooing with unburned propellant may still occur. The margins of the wound will be more irregular as the pellets begin to spread out. The wad will generally (but less frequently than in the case of closer discharge) be found in the wound.
Discharge Beyond 2m	No soot, no tattooing, and wad less likely to be in the wound as the distance increases. The neatly circumscribed single wound is increasingly likely to be replaced by a series of different wounds inflicted by individual pellets as the distance increases.

In any event, with shotguns exit wounds are rare if the area of the body the pellets are passing through is dense.[48] If they do occur, then exit wounds may often be multiple, either because of the dispersal of the shot or because of shattering and fragmentation of bone. There will be no signs of discharge, such as burning or tattooing, on an exit wound. If there is a particular weapon known or suspected to have been involved in the death, it can be test-fired and the spread pattern of shot from that weapon can be

---

[47] The following descriptions assume that the wounds in question are inflicted directly onto skin unless otherwise stated. Overlying clothing can make a big difference, eg 'tattooing' is less likely if clothing intervenes between cartridge and skin, and clothing should always be retained to assist in analysis.

[48] Shotgun wounds to the mouth are common in suicides. In such instances, exit wounds are typical and substantial.

compared with some forensic accuracy to that on the body and used to estimate the distance at which it was fired.

Other bullet injuries

[14.54] Most other long-barrelled guns, as well as most handguns, are 'rifled', meaning that the internal aspect of the barrel is grooved in such a way as to impart a spin to the departing bullet.[49] This means the bullet travels faster, further and straighter. As with shotgun injuries, there are telltale elements associated with the distance from which the gun is fired (but the injuries are more likely to be consistent with those cause by high-velocity projectiles):

Contact Discharge	Over soft tissue, the wound will typically be round with abrasions reflecting the calibre (diameter) of the barrel. Smoke and tattooing may mark the skin, but they are less likely than with shotgun wounds. More damage to the skin is likely if the gun is fired with the muzzle over bone; in such cases, the entry wound will often be star-shaped (stellate) rather than round and the edges of the wound may be everted rather than inverted.
Discharge Within 1m	The entrance wound will generally be inverted. There are often two 'rings' around the margin of the wound. Closer to the wound will be grease-soiling (the *grease collar*) caused by the bullet effectively wiping itself clean as it passes through the skin.[50] The outer ring will comprise abrasions or contusions (the *contusion collar*) caused by the bullet forcing itself through the skin, traumatising the skin in the process. There may be damage to the skin caused by the heat and debris from the discharge of the gun.
Discharge Beyond 1m	There will rarely be any signs of detonation (tattooing or burns). The entry wound will be similar regardless of any further increase in distance. Unlike the shotgun, there is no pattern of spreading pellets to help to assay the distance. All that can be confirmed is that the weapon was fired from far enough away that it is unlikely to have been a self-inflicted wound

Exit wounds of rifled bullets are often, but not universally, larger than entry wounds and again the presence of fragmented and expelled bone may result in multiple exit wounds.

---

[49] The rifling of the barrel also leaves a reproducible mark on the bullet. This means that if a suspect weapon is recovered, it can be test-fired and the marks it leaves on a bullet compared with the impressions left on the bullet retrieved from a shooting victim. Because of the history of paramilitary activity on this island, there have long been strict controls on the private ownership of handguns and rifles (long barrelled sporting/military weapons). However, such weapons are commonly used by criminals.

[50] This may be absent if the bullet passes through clothing

The higher the velocity of the weapon, the larger the exit wound is likely to be. There will be no signs of discharge, such as burning or tattooing, on an exit wound.

Gunshot suicides

[14.55] Evidence of a gun discharged against the skin is generally, but by no means absolutely, indicative of suicide. The trajectory of the bullet can help to corroborate this theory. Common sites for the fatal injury include the head, the chest and, rarely, the abdomen.[51] Handguns are often used to inflict injuries to the head, in particular the temple, mouth or underside of the chin. Atypical wound locations may suggest murder rather than suicide. About one in five suicides will be discovered still clutching the weapon. High velocity bullets may be associated with 'splash-back' of blood onto the hand or hands holding or steadying the weapon.

Strangulation/asphyxia

[14.56] In many cases, the fact of strangulation or asphyxia may be obvious; hanging is a common method of suicide,[52] but in other circumstances the identification of asphyxia may be more difficult. It may occur at three levels: there may be no oxygen available in the atmosphere (where poisonous gases have accumulated, for example); there may be a mechanical obstruction (internal or external) to oxygen reaching the lungs;[53] or there may be a problem with the lungs or heart preventing the harnessing of available oxygen. Only the second of these, mechanical obstruction, will generally result in obvious signs of what took place, although some forms of gas poisoning (such as carbon monoxide) may result in a recognisable discoloration of the skin.

[14.57] The supposed 'cardinal' signs of mechanical asphyxiation are cyanosis,[54] congestion and petechial haemorrhage.[55] All of these signs occur because the mechanical obstruction of breathing causes two effects: first, pressure increases markedly within the veins that return blood to the heart; and, secondly, veins become unable to return sufficient blood to the heart. These signs are most commonly seen on the face, where the pressure change and the accumulation of oxygen-poor blood are

---

[51] For handgun and shotgun suicides the approximate distribution of wounds is: 80 per cent head, 15 per cent chest and less than 5 per cent abdomen. Other long-barrel-rifled weapons are associated with fewer head injuries and a greater preference for the chest and abdomen.

[52] In judicial executions by hanging, the aim is not to asphyxiate but to break or dislocate the neck of the victim (at the level of the first cervical vertebra) causing near-instantaneous death: the length of the rope and the drop through the trapdoor are calculated accordingly, bearing in mind the weight of the person to be killed. In suicide and ad hoc hanging in lawless situations, death by asphyxiation is more likely; death may also occur suddenly due to pressure of the rope on the carotid arteries, leading to cardiac arrest. See *Lachman's Case Studies in Anatomy* (4th edn, OUP, 1997) Ch 9, 'The Anatomy of Hanging'.

[53] There are a huge number of potential causes for this: manual strangulation, hanging, choking or plastic bags (children's accidents, suicide and sexual thrill-seeking are all causes of plastic bag asphyxiation). Pressure to the chest is a common cause of asphyxia in the crushing of panicked or compressed crowds. Asphyxia due to compression of the chest is sometimes referred to as 'traumatic' asphyxia.

[54] A blue-ish tinge to the skin caused by lack of oxygen.

[55] Small bruise-like areas of bleeding under the skin.

most severe. Petechiae are also common on the lung and its lining, the pleura. Even in the absence of external pressure (eg choking on food), cyanosis and petechial haemorrhages may occur, although congestion is less likely.

[14.58] The signs are not universal: they are often scanty or absent in the very old or very young. Sometimes, too, initial asphyxiation can lead to abrupt death due to a reflex cardiac arrest.[56] Such sudden deaths may eschew the build-up of pressure and fall-off in oxygen concentration that lead to the signs of strangulation and asphyxia.

[14.59] Where strangulation is suspected, there are other signs that may help in diagnosis. As well as cyanosis, congestion and petechiae, there may be bleeding from the nose and mouth (and sometimes the ear) and indicia of strangulation, such as disc-shaped bruises consistent with an assailant's fingers or rope marks may be present on the neck. At post mortem, the hyoid bone and/or the thyroid cartilage may be broken.

---

[56] This occurs due to stimulation of the vagal nerve, which reacts by slowing the heart to a standstill (called a vagal response). Indeed, very rarely sudden death can occur in otherwise healthy individuals as the result of a vagal response to a playful blow or touch to the neck.

Quick Reference Guide 14.3

Describing injuries and wounds

❖   Accurate recording of the name and extent of any injury at the time of any examination can greatly aid recall should it come to having to report or testify on clinical findings.

❖   Drawings and photographs can be included in clinical notes as more accurate documents of the injuries recorded.

❖   Abrasions are scratches or scrapes: superficial wounds to the skin that do not penetrate the full thickness of the skin, although they may be deep enough to bleed. They generally occur when the skin is rubbed against a rough surface.

❖   Contusions are essentially bruises, Their colour change (purple-brown-green/yellow) as they resolve may give some indication of the time frame within which the bruises were incurred.

❖   Lacerations are wounds penetrating the full depth of the skin, but caused by a blunt or relatively blunt object rather than by anything sharp. Lacerations frequently bleed less that incisions and the edges of the wound frequently show crushing.

❖   Incisions may be stab wounds (deeper than they are long) or slash wounds (longer than they are deep).

❖   Underlying damage should always be considered in conjunction with the external evidence of injury. Head injuries may sometimes be accompanied by damage to area of the skull and brain diametrically opposed to the site of impact: *contre-coup* injuries.

❖   Burns are extremely common injuries and can have a number of causes. A burn caused by a liquid is sometimes termed a scald. Burns in infants may sometimes be an indicator of non-accidental injury. Burns caused by electricity can be very variable in nature, but may be extensive when caused by high-current shocks.

❖   The key element of bullet wounds is that the characteristics of the wound change most significantly in proportion to three factors:

    o   the speed of the bullet

    o   the distance of the victim from the muzzle when the gun was discharged

    o   whether a wound is an entry or exit wound

❖   The 'cardinal' signs of mechanical asphyxiation are cyanosis, congestion and petechial haemorrhage.

Chapter 15

The Law and Forensics of Sexual Assault

INTRODUCTION

[15.01] There are two aspects to this chapter. First is a discussion of what constitutes rape and sexual assault in Ireland and secondly, we look at the clinical approach to the diagnosis, investigation and recording of the evidence of sexual assault.

[15.02] In the Republic, heterosexual acts, not including intercourse, are permitted between consenting partners aged 15 years or older; the legal right to consent to heterosexual or homosexual intercourse is conferred on the occasion of a person's 17th birthday, although there is active debate over proposals to lower the age of consent to 16. Any sexual conduct not prohibited by law is permissible between consenting partners, on condition that it does not cause physical harm[1] or otherwise offend public decency. The frequency of rape and sexual assault cannot be stated with certainty. One study (in the United Kingdom) has suggested that in a single year as many as one in 200 women were raped and one in 100 had been the victim of some form of sexual victimisation, including rape. One in 20 women surveyed admitted to having been raped since the age of 16. Current partners or acquaintances were the most common perpetrators.[2] Quite aside from these statistics, the reasons why the law intervenes in the conduct of individuals' sexual practices were summarised by the Wolfenden Committee:[3]

> [T]o preserve public order and decency, to protect the citizen from what is offensive and injurious and to provide sufficient safeguards against exploitation and corruption of others, particularly those who are especially vulnerable because they are young, weak in body or mind, inexperienced or in a state of special physical, official or economic dependence.

The question of child abuse—aside from the issues of the detection of the clinical signs of sexual assault—is covered in Ch 7 'The Practitioner and the Family'.

---

[1] See *Brown* [1994] 1 AC 212. See Charleton, McDermott and Bolger, *Criminal Law* (Tottel Publishing, 1999): the authors argue that sexual conduct that gives rise to mental damage may also be illegal. The charge that would be brought against those involved in such acts, whether causing mental or physical damage, would be one of assault.

[2] UK Home Office, *Rape and Sexual Assault of Women: Findings from the British Crime Survey* (HMSO, 2002). These figures may underestimate the prevalence of rape and sexual victimisation: the British Crime Survey did not cover institutions, the homeless or women under the age of 16, thus excluding some 'high risk' women; furthermore, interviews were not always conducted in private, possibly inhibiting disclosure. Others put the figure for the percentage of women who have been raped between 14 per cent and 25 per cent: see Goodman *et al*, 'Male violence against women: current researches and future directions' (1993) Am Psychologist 46; 1054–58.

[3] The Wolfenden Committee on Homosexual Offences and Prostitution (Cmnd 247) 1957. Also see Card, 'Sexual Relations with Minors' 1975 Crim L Rev 371.

THE CATEGORIES OF SEXUAL CRIME

Incest

[15.03] Incest was criminalised in Ireland in 1908 and the law was updated in 1995.[4] The law only covers actual sexual intercourse that occurs between those members of a family who are within the 'forbidden degrees of relationship'. If there is no intercourse, then even if the act involves those within the relationships covered by incest legislation the crime that has been committed is one of sexual assault. If a person over the age of 17 years consents to incestuous intercourse, that will not afford a defence to the perpetrator. In a case where both participants are 17 years or older, both will be guilty of an offence, although the person who perpetrates the sexual act (typically the male, and envisaged as such in the 1908 Act) will be guilty of the more serious offence. A man guilty of incest may be sentenced for up to a maximum of life in prison,[5] while a woman similarly convicted of engaging in incestuous intercourse may receive a sentence of up to seven years in jail.

[15.04] The relationships prohibited cover 'any male person who has carnal knowledge of a female person, who is to his knowledge his grand-daughter, daughter, sister or mother'.[6] Incest cannot occur between a father and his stepchildren or adopted children, an anomaly when one considers the frequency with which sexual abuse is perpetrated by a stepfather on his stepchildren.[7] This shortcoming in the legislation has come in for criticism from a number of quarters,[8] as has the fact that incest cannot legally occur in the absence of sexual intercourse.

Child sexual abuse

[15.05] This area is dealt with in greater detail under the broad heading of 'Child Abuse' in Ch 7 'The Practitioner and the Family' (para **[7.37]***ff*). For the purposes of brief elucidation here, let it be said that a person under 17 years cannot legally consent to sexual intercourse and a person under 15 years cannot legally consent to any sexual act. The penalties for defilement of a child younger than 15 are greater than those for defilement of a minor who is under 17. The abuser cannot claim that his (and it is

---

4   Punishment of Incest Act 1908 and the Criminal Law (Incest Proceedings) Act 1995. This latter Act essentially allows for incest trials to be conducted in private (although the press may be present) and for the accused to be afforded anonymity: the anonymity is for the benefit of both the victim (to minimise the trauma of the trial) and the accused (who, were it not for the 1995 Act, may be acquitted only to find that his name and alleged offences have been trumpeted in the media with potentially harmful consequences). The details of the case may be published or broadcast, but not the identity of the accused and the victim or any details that would tend to identify them. A breach of an anonymity order is punishable by a jail sentence of up to three years or fine up to €12,700 (s 4).

5   'Life' imprisonment normally means a sentence of seven to ten years.

6   Punishment of Incest Act 1908, s 1(1). Contrary to popular belief, first cousins are not covered by incest legislation.

7   A point made in Law Reform Commission, *Child Sexual Abuse* (LRC 32–1990), see Appendix 1.

8   English Criminal Law Revision Committee, 15th Report, 1984 (Cmnd), paras 8.25–8.35.

typically a male abuser) victim consented, although he can plead the defence that he honestly believed the child to have attained the age of 15 or 17 years (as appropriate).[9]

[15.06] It is also important to note that the clinician is not under an *obligation* to disclose information about child sexual abuse received from the victim if she feels it would be detrimental to the therapeutic relationship. However, she may do so without fear of legal action by her patient or the alleged perpetrator.[10]

Rape

[15.07] Rape is different from many other crimes in terms of what must be proved if the guilty person is to be convicted. In general, if the prosecution wishes to prove that a person committed a crime, they have to prove two things: first, that the accused did the crime he is accused of and, secondly (and just as importantly), that he intended to do the crime he committed.[11] This second element is the so-called 'mental element' or mens rea of the offence. In rape cases, however, there is a second 'mental element' added to the mix: the need to prove that the victim did not consent to the act in question. In other words, rape—unlike most other crimes—is not merely concerned with the mindset of the perpetrator but also that of the victim.

[15.08] Rape happens when a man penetrates, or continues sexual intercourse with, a woman who is not consenting to sexual intercourse (or has withdrawn her consent to intercourse) and where the man, knowing that she is not consenting or that she may not be consenting, continues with the sexual act. It is up to the jury to decide whether they accept a contention of the accused that he 'believed' the woman was consenting to sex. A jury can reach a conclusion that the man believed the woman was consenting by reference to what the 'ordinary person' would have believed in the circumstances. If a jury believes that there were 'reasonable grounds' for a man to believe that the woman was consenting, then it is entitled to find him not guilty.

Consent and rape

[15.09] A woman may withdraw her consent to sexual intercourse at any time during the act: consent to penetration is not tantamount to consent to continuation or completion of the sexual act. Nor does silence amount to consent. The law is that 'failure or omission by [a] person to offer resistance to the act does not of itself constitute consent to the act.'[12] Evidence capable of indicating that consent was not given, even if refusal was not formally or explicitly expressed, includes:

> ... evidence of threats issued by the defendant. It may be evidence that the complainant [victim] was by reason of drink or drugs incapable of giving consent or incapable of being aware of what was occurring. It may be evidence that by reason of age or lack of understanding due to mental handicap the complainant did not give consent. The jury may accept that the complainant was asleep when sexual intercourse occurred or that she was tricked into giving her consent in the belief that the defendant was her husband or partner.

---

[9]   Criminal Law (Sexual Offences) Act 2006.
[10] Protections for Persons Reporting Child Abuse Act 1998. See para **[7.39]**.
[11] Or that he was reckless regarding whether his conduct would result in the criminal act.
[12] Criminal Law (Rape)(Amendment) Act 1990, s 9.

We do not for a moment suggest that these examples exhaust the possible factual situations which may arise.[13]

Historically, a crucial element of rape was that not only did the prosecution have to prove penetration but also that ejaculation had happened. However, the law now is that once there is penetration of the vagina by the penis then rape has occurred.[14] Until 1990 Irish law did not recognise that it was possible for rape to occur within marriage, although it did state that a husband could not use any more than 'gentle violence' to coerce his wife into sexual congress.[15] This obvious gap in the law was corrected by the Criminal Law (Rape)(Amendment) Act 1990.[16]

[15.10] The Law Reform Commission suggested the following definition of consent to sexual intercourse:[17]

1. 'Consent' means a consent freely and voluntarily given and...a consent is not freely and voluntarily given if it is obtained by force, threat, intimidation, deception or fraudulent[18] means.

2. A failure to offer physical resistance to a sexual assault does not of itself constitute consent to a sexual assault.

Alleging rape

[15.11] Historically, there appears to have been a belief that women routinely made false allegations of rape. A celebrated judge of the eighteenth century described rape as 'an accusation easily to be made and hard to be proved and harder to be defended by the party accused though never so innocent.'[19] Because of the intimate circumstances in which a rape or sexual assault can occur and the consequent lack of witnesses to confirm or deny the allegation, there was a traditional reluctance on the part of the courts to accept a rape victim's word at face value in order to avoid 'successful' false

---

[13] *Malone* [1998] 2 Cr App R 447. Other examples of where consent is not truly given are where a woman consents through fear (*Olugboja* [1982] QB 320) or where the person initiating the sexual encounter is in a position of authority over the woman in question and she acquiesces in recognition of that authority (eg a teacher and a student: *O'Connor* (1998) 123 CCC (3d) 487).

[14] See Criminal Law (Rape) Act 1981, s 1(2): '... intercourse is deemed complete on proof of penetration only.' It has been decided in Irish law that 'if the male organ is proved to have entered the opening of the vagina this amounts to penetration even if there is no emission [of semen].' This means that if rape is alleged by a virgin whose hymen is intact after the assault, the fact that the hymen is intact does not automatically preclude penetration having occurred. See *The People (AG) v Dermody* [1956] IR 307.

[15] *McN v McN* [1936] IR 177.

[16] Criminal Law (Rape) Act 1990, s 4. The Act also abolished the legal supposition that any male under the age of 14 was incapable of rape.

[17] Law Reform Commission, *Rape and Allied Offences* (LRC 24–1988), 9.

[18] See *Williams* [1923] 1 KB 340 where a man told the woman that sexual intercourse was a medical procedure that would improve her singing voice and for that reason alone she consented. The fraud implicit in what the man said was so profound that it rendered the woman's consent meaningless and therefore a rape was committed.

[19] M Hale, Historica *Placitorum Coronae*, Vol 1 (London: Nott and Gosling, 1734) 635–636.

allegations.[20] This reluctance was at one time so marked that the jury was formally warned that it was dangerous to convict a man of the rape of a woman in the absence of any corroborating evidence.[21] The modern evidential rule is that it is up to the judge to decide whether she thinks it appropriate in the circumstances of the case to warn the jury of the dangers of convicting the accused of rape solely on the uncorroborated evidence of the alleged victim.[22] This has replaced the obligation to warn in *all* cases, a requirement suggestive of an institutional belief that women could not be trusted when they made allegations of rape. The need for the judge to consider whether a warning about corroboration is needed applies to allegations of both rape and sexual assault.

[15.12] The fact that a woman tells someone she has been raped is not corroboration as such, but it may be important evidence that tends to show the consistency of a victim's allegation of rape or sexual assault. For example, if a woman describes a rape in some detail to her doctor (or to a family member or friend) soon after it happened, and her account tallies closely with the later statement made to Gardaí, this may be suggestive that the allegation is true. This issue of 'previous consistent statements' is dealt with in more detail at para **[15.38]**.

Sexual assault

[15.13] Sexual assault occurs when a person intentionally assaults another person and the attack has an element of indecency to it. It is up to the jury to decide whether an assault is a sexual assault or not, although in general the sexual element of the assault may be all too clear. Unlike rape, which is by definition perpetrated by a man upon a woman, sexual assault is gender-neutral and people of either sex may be convicted of it. There is also an offence entitled 'aggravated sexual assault' which is 'a sexual assault that involves serious violence or the threat of serious violence or is such as to cause injury, humiliation or degradation of a grave nature to the person assaulted.'[23]

---

[20] Estimates of false allegations are unreliable but some Canadian research suggests that the figures may be as high as one in 20. Other authors have suggested a one in 50 chance of a false allegation (see Charleton, McDermott and Bolger, *Criminal Law* (Tottel Publishing, 1999), para 8.150).

[21] 'Corroborating evidence' is evidence that tends to support the allegation being made. DNA testing of sperm emitted during the commission of the alleged crime may corroborate the woman's story that the accused was the person who had sexual intercourse with her. Similarly, marks of injuries on the woman's body may be inconsistent with the assailant's story that the victim consented and may instead be corroborating evidence for an allegation of rape or assault.

[22] Criminal Law (Rape)(Amendment) Act 1990, s. 7. The fact that the warning is now optional does not mean that it may always be omitted. There may still be cases in which it is desirable for the judge to warn of the dangers of convicting on the uncorroborated evidence of the alleged victim: *The People (DPP) v Reid* [1993] 2 IR 186. However, the circumstances in which a warning need be given are only where there is a strong doubt concerning the veracity of the victim's evidence and where a judge does not give a warning in other situations, that is unlikely to be grounds for an appeal: *People (DPP) v JEM* (1 February 2000, unreported) CCA.

[23] Criminal Law (Rape) Amendment) Act 1990, s 3(1).

The Criminal Law (Rape) Amendment) Act 1990 addressed the fact that certain acts, analogous to rape, were not properly covered by the criminal law. There was no mechanism, to take two examples, for appropriately prosecuting homosexual rape or acts of forced oral sex. Accordingly, the Act provided for a new offence, sometimes referred to as 'section 4 rape', so-called because it was introduced in that section of the 1990 Act:

[S]exual assault that includes

(a)   penetration (however slight) of the anus or mouth by the penis, or

(b)   penetration (however slight) of the vagina by any object held or manipulated by another person.[24]

Bestiality

[15.14] Vaginal or anal intercourse with any animal remains a crime under the Offences against the Person Act 1861.[25]

Homosexuality

[15.15] Homosexuality is no longer a crime, but it would still be possible for someone to be prosecuted for a homosexual act. The reason for this is that it was not until 1993 that the law changed to permit homosexual acts between consenting males[26] over the age of 17 years. Given that homosexuality only became legal from when the Act came into force in 1993, a person could still technically be convicted of a homosexual encounter that occurred before 1993.

[15.16] In 1990 the Irish Law Reform Commission proposed that the same legal regime should exist for consensual homosexual activity as for heterosexual.[27] Nothing happened until 1993, which is strange when one considers that laws such as the Prohibition of Incitement to Hatred Act 1989 made it illegal to discriminate against people because of their sexual orientation;[28] in other words, it was illegal to discriminate against homosexuals, even though the state itself was arguably discriminating against homosexuals by making certain physical expressions of their sexual orientation illegal. Intercourse between consenting males is legal if both partners are over 17 years and neither partner is mentally impaired. The same applies to anal intercourse between a man and a consenting woman.

---

24   Criminal Law (Rape) Amendment) Act 1990, s 4(1).
25   Offences Against the Person Act, s 61.
26   Criminal Law (Sexual Offences) Act 1993. Lesbianism was never outlawed in Britain or Ireland. The reason for this is often apocryphally stated to be that Queen Victoria refused to believe that lesbianism could exist and argued therefore against any need to ban it.
27   *Report on Child Sexual Abuse* (LRC 32–1990)(September 1990).
28   Prohibition of Incitement to Hatred Act 1989, s 1(1).

Quick Reference Guide 15.1

The essentials of the sexual crimes

❖ By law, sexual acts (not including intercourse) are permitted between consenting partners over the age of 15 years. Sexual intercourse is legal from the age of 17 years.

❖ The basis of laws against sexual crimes includes the need to preserve public order and decency and to safeguard the weak, young or inexperienced individual against exploitation or corruption.

❖ Incest is sexual intercourse between a man and his daughter, grand-daughter, sister or mother. If there is no sexual intercourse or the relationship is not one of those listed, it cannot be incest. Consent is not a defence to incest.

❖ A person younger than 17 years cannot consent to sexual intercourse and a person less than 15 cannot consent to any sexual act.

❖ Rape is sexual intercourse with a woman without her consent or the continuation of sexual intercourse after she has withdrawn her consent. Whether a woman consented to intercourse is judged by whether the 'reasonable person' in the circumstances would have believed her to be consenting. Silence or acquiescence does not necessarily amount to consent.

❖ Sexual assault covers most other sexual crimes, including the area of 'aggravated' sexual assault – sexual assault with violence or the threat of violence – and 'section 4 rape'.

❖ Bestiality is vaginal or anal intercourse with an animal and is a criminal offence.

❖ Homosexual acts carried out before the decriminalisation of homosexuality in 1993 could still – in theory at least, but not in practice – be regarded as criminal acts.

SEXUAL CRIMES AND THE PRACTITIONER[29]

Allegations against the practitioner

[15.17] A practitioner may on occasion be exposed to the possibility of allegations of sexual assault arising following an examination or procedure. Two scenarios in particular call for the practitioner to be attuned to the sensitivities of the clinical situation. One is where a patient is under an anaesthetic and the other is where the doctor is conducting an intimate examination of a patient.

Anaesthesia

[15.18] The patient who is succumbing to, or emerging from, the effects of anaesthesia may be susceptible to vivid sensations that may include imagining an encounter of a sexual nature. Of course, it may also be the case that a sedated patient could be the victim of a sexual assault while disabled by anaesthesia. In any event, the presence of another member of staff who can corroborate what took place while the patient was

---

[29] In this section and the sections that follow, the convention used elsewhere in the text of describing the practitioner as 'she' and the patient as 'he' is abandoned for obvious reasons and pronouns are used in the manner necessary to make sense of the text.

under anaesthesia will militate against any unfounded allegations being made by the patient.[30]

Intimate examination

[15.19] The second scenario, when a doctor is conducting an intimate examination on a patient, is far more common and there are some practitioners who argue in favour of the presence of (or at least the offer of) a chaperone in all such cases.[31] The reality and diversity of clinical practice is such that in many instances it will not be feasible to provide a chaperone. A doctor in a hospital may have little problem finding a nurse to act as a chaperone during the examination, but it may be more difficult for the general practitioner in a practice that lacks a nurse or where the nurse is engaged in her own clinical duties. It is also true that not all patients wish to have a chaperone present during examination, while some actively prefer to undergo examination without a chaperone. The gender of the patient, taken together with the nature of the examination and gender of the clinician or of the available chaperone seem to underpin whether a patient will express a preference regarding a chaperone. Research suggests that most women want to be offered a chaperone and that furthermore they feel uncomfortable asking for one if it is not offered. More women prefer having a third party present when the examining clinician is male; fewer if she is female. In general, patients are happy simply to have one of their family members present as chaperone. Men, particularly teenagers, may find the presence of a female nurse as observer during genital examination unwelcome. However, a substantial proportion of patients in primary care, the arena in which chaperones may be hardest to come by, are unconcerned as to whether a chaperone is present or not, a fact that may be indicative of the easier familiarity and closer therapeutic relationship often characteristic of primary care.[32]

A legal need for chaperones?

[15.20] The offer of a chaperone should probably always be made, together with an explanation that if a chaperone is not available at that time, the patient may need to

---

[30] There was for a long time a practice of permitting medical students to perform 'practice' internal examinations on women while they were anaesthetised. It is hoped that this practice has disappeared with practitioners' increasing awareness of the need for consent in such situations. Of course, with the patient's consent, it is possible to perform such examinations.

[31] Bignell, 'Chaperones for genital examination' BMJ 1999; 319:137; Conway and Harvey 'Use and offering of chaperones by general practitioners: postal questionnaire survey in Norfolk' BMJ 2005;330: 235-236; Rosenthal *et al.* 'Chaperones for intimate examinations: cross-sectional survey of attitudes and practices of general practitioners' BMJ 2005; 330: 234–235.

[32] See the following: Penn and Bourgnet, 'Patients' attitudes regarding chaperones during physician examinations' J Fam Pract 1992; 35: 639–643; Webb and Opdahl, 'Breast and pelvic examinations: easing women's discomfort' Can Fam Physician 1996; 42: 54–58; Phillips, 'Teenagers' preferences regarding the presence of family members, peers and chaperones during examination of genitalia' Pediatrics 1981; 68: 665–669; Ng, 'The practice of rectal examination' Postgrad Med J 1991; 67: 904–906; Jones, 'Patients' attitudes to chaperones' J RCGP 1985; 35: 192–193; Cohen, McLean and Barton, 'Use of chaperones in general practice: Chaperones protect both parties' BMJ 2005; 330: 846–847.

return when a chaperone is available or with a family member who can act as a chaperone.

[15.21] It is certainly true that doctors in particular have been accused of unprofessional conduct and sexual assault after non-chaperoned examinations. In one study, 8 per cent of women reported experiences where they felt a doctor had conducted a gynaecological examination in a 'less than professional manner'.[33] It is often suggested that by way of medico-legal prophylaxis, a third party should always be present during genital examination[34] but this can be difficult to arrange in every setting and, what is more, if the patient does not want a chaperone to be present, should that reluctance be overridden by the clinician in the interests of medico-legal protection? In addition, some clinical set-ups will not lend themselves to the presence of a chaperone unless the patient brings one to the consultation. There is no legal obligation on a practitioner to have a chaperone present for examinations or when a patient is anaesthetised. However, it would be desirable and preferable firstly to make one available if the structure and manpower of the healthcare facility in question permits it and, secondly, not to object if a patient wishes to be accompanied by a chaperone of his or her own choosing.[35]

---

[33] Webb and Opdahl, 'Breast and pelvic examinations: easing women's discomfort' Can Fam Physician 1996; 42:54–58. 'Unprofessional' behaviour in this study included overexposure of the woman's body, unusual positioning of the woman for examination and inappropriate comments, gestures or facial expressions.

[34] Bignell, 'Chaperones for genital examination' BMJ 1999; 319:137.

[35] In December 2001, the UK General Medical Council published guidelines on intimate examination (which it defines as examination of the breasts, genitalia or rectum). The full text is at http://www.gmc-uk.org/guidance/current/library/intimate_examinations.asp (last accessed July 2007). Its recommendations (in addition to those outlined in the text above) include the following:
  - Explain to the patient why an examination is necessary and give the patient an opportunity to ask questions.
  - Explain what the examination will involve, in a way the patient can understand, so that the patient has a clear idea of what to expect, including any potential pain or discomfort.
  - Obtain the patient's permission before the examination and be prepared to discontinue the examination if the patient asks you to. Record the fact of the patient's permission.
  - Keep discussion relevant and avoid unnecessary personal comments.
  - Offer a chaperone or invite the patient (in advance if possible) to have a relative or friend present...If for justifiable practical reasons you cannot offer a chaperone, you should explain that to the patient and, if possible, offer to delay the examination to a later date. You should record the discussion and its outcome.
  - Give the patient privacy to undress and dress and use drapes to maintain the patient's dignity. Do not assist the patient in removing clothing unless you have clarified with them that your assistance is required.

Quick Reference Guide 15.2

Chaperones and intimate examinations

❖ Patients who are under anaesthesia or recovery from anaesthesia may sometimes experience vivid dream-like memories of an encounter of a sexual nature. It is better and, at any rate, best clinical practice to be accompanied by at least one person who can act as a witness to what occurred while a patient was under anaesthesia.

❖ Some patients prefer to have a chaperone present when undergoing intimate examinations and there are those clinicians who argue that chaperones should be present for all such assessments.

❖ Patient preferences and manpower issues both need to be taken into account when considering whether a chaperoned examination is to be the norm for any given health care setting.

❖ There is no formal legal obligation to provide a chaperone.

The examination of the rape or sexual assault victim

[15.22] A person who alleges that she has been the victim of a sexual assault presents particular problems for the practitioner (typically the doctor, but it may also be the accident and emergency nurse and, later in the process. it may be a psychologist) who must deal with the patient. Any clinical findings may be used in evidence in subsequent legal action and a further complicating factor is that the examining clinician may not be experienced in noting or understanding the clinical findings. Evidence relating to a rape or sexual assault may be subtle, hard to obtain and easy to contaminate or destroy.

[15.23] As we have noted already, corroboration may be important in any allegation of sexual crimes and particularly in cases of rape. The evidence gleaned from a meticulous examination may ultimately prove crucial in confirming the victim's story or in exonerating an innocent accused. A patient undergoing examination after a sexual assault may not have decided whether or not to pursue criminal charges, but the doctor should nonetheless proceed as if criminal proceedings are inevitable and adhere to the highest standards of history-taking and evidence-gathering.

[15.24] A forensic examination should take place as soon as possible after the incident and prior to the victim bathing or showering. Ideally, the examination should be conducted by a doctor skilled in careful and thorough assessment in the wake of an alleged sexual assault. There is a strong argument that the doctor should be of the sex preferred by the victim in the circumstances, in order to minimise any trauma involved in an examination that by its very nature will be intimate. At the same time, a determination to provide a female rape victim with a female doctor should also be tempered by the realisation that an inexperienced doctor may not be able to obtain evidence or put the patient at her ease as well as an experienced examiner, of whatever sex, may do.

Consent to forensic examination

[15.25] The victim who is being examined or her guardian if he or she is a young minor[36] should be asked to consent in writing to the examination taking place. The

---

[36] But note the discussion of consent by minors in Ch 4 (para **[4.24]***ff*).

doctor should have the correct tools for the job of properly examining a patient after a sexual assault. This is sometimes referred to as a 'rape kit'. The examination should take place in an environment of appropriate privacy and where the facilities are available to maximise the quality of the examination (adequate lighting and an examination couch are two of the minimum requirements). If the victim is still upset or nervous at the prospect of the examination, the presence of a family member or a chaperone may help the patient through the process. There are a number of considerations that arise when seeking consent to examination of the victim of sexual assault:[37]

> *Temporary loss of capacity due to intoxication:* in such circumstances the forensic assessment should normally be deferred until the patient's capacity to consent has returned. The duration of the deferral will depend on the type, time, amount and quantity of the substances that have been consumed. It may be necessary to assess the patient repeatedly within a given period to determine if the patient's capacity has returned.

> *Serious injury:* the family of the patient should be informed and, assuming the patient is unconscious, as much of the examination as is possible should be done. The patient should be informed as soon as possible of what was done. The circumstances that necessitated carrying out the examination without express consent should be documented.

> *Mental disorder:* the individual patient's capacity to consent to (or refuse) the forensic examination should be gauged. If it is not possible for the patient to consent, then the decision should be taken with the patient's family or carers. Similarly, the circumstances of proceeding to examine the patient without consent should be documented.

> *Children:* as the author has argued elsewhere in this text,[38] a mature minor's consent to medical treatment, including forensic examination, is arguably valid in Irish law. If parents withhold consent in the instance of a young minor (perhaps because a parent is responsible for perpetrating or enabling the assault) it may be necessary to consider making the child the subject of a care order.[39]

The examination

[15.26] In essence, the examining clinician's medico-legal duties following a sexual assault are threefold:

(a) Performing a careful medical assessment to provide corroborative evidence in a claim of sexual assault. Evidence is sought that may demonstrate (as appropriate):

    – that a sexual assault has taken place within the period of time claimed

    – that the victim did not consent

    – the identity of the assailant

    – the site or sites on the body where the assault took place

(b) Keeping detailed and exact records made at the time of the examination

---

[37] Summarised from Education and Research Committee of the Association of Police Surgeons, *Consent in Relation to Complaints of Sexual Assaults* (May 2001).

[38] See Ch 4 'Consent' para **[4.24]***ff.*

[39] See Ch 7 'The Practitioner and the Family' para **[7.45]**.

(c)   Providing a subsequent expert opinion on the significance of any findings in relation to allegations of sexual assault to the police and possibly later to the court.

There is also the doctor's medical duty to care for the patient by treating any injuries and arranging for appropriate follow-up care.

History

[15.27] The doctor needs to get the patient to relate the history of what occurred. The details of the assault can help to inform the examination that follows. As well as the history of the assault, the general medical history of the victim should be canvassed. A victim of a sexual assault may be composed after the assault (a 'dissociative' state), but may also be in such an understandable state of emotional derangement as to make it impossible to establish a coherent history. In such cases it may be beneficial to return to the details of the assault and the victim's medical history again at the end of the consultation.

A truncated sexual history may be clinically important.[40] If a person has had unprotected intercourse with another partner in the same general time period as that in which the sexual assault occurred, this may have ramifications for the identification of any semen that is obtained as a result of the examination. Semen may be recoverable from the vagina or anus, depending on the assault, up to 72 hours after the alleged assault.

Gleaning evidence

[15.28] The time of the examination and how much time has elapsed since the alleged assault should be recorded. Any information or samples obtained during an examination following sexual assault should be treated with reverence for their potential use as evidence. Drawings or photographs can be enormously useful in helping to capture the precise location, extent and shape of injuries. All specimens obtained should be labelled and the labels should detail:

- the nature of the specimen;
- the anatomical source of the specimen;
- the person from whom and by whom the specimen was obtained;
- the time and date obtained.

Procedure and potential findings

[15.29] The general demeanour of the victim should be noted, including damage to clothing and mental state. Potential evidence will ultimately be forwarded to the Forensic Science Laboratory. Clothing worn during the attack should be retained for forensic examination.[41] There may be fibres or bodily fluids belonging to the assailant on the victim's clothes. The victim will need to undress, traumatic as this may be, in

---

[40] Although this part of the history may not be admissible in the courtroom as evidence. The prior sexual history of the victim (whether with the accused or another) cannot be used in evidence merely to cast doubts on the victim's character, but it may be used where it may tend to suggest that the victim consented or that the accused may have been mistaken about whether she consented (see Criminal Law (Rape) Act 1981, s 3).

[41] A family member should be asked to bring in a change of clothing.

order to facilitate the examination. The Forensic Science Laboratory *Sexual Offences Examination Form* should be used where available.[42]

Approximately 70 per cent of adult victims of a rape or serious sexual assault will have some external signs of injury. Children are less likely to show signs of physical injury following sexual assault, either because they are less likely to be aware of what is happening to them or because their struggles are more easily subdued. External examination should be as minute as possible and the following signs in particular should be sought:

- Obvious injuries such as abrasions and contusions, especially those consistent with the victim having been struck or tightly gripped. Teeth marks or petechiae caused by suction by the mouth[43] on the skin may also be present;

- Dirt, mud or grass stains, all of which may be consistent with a struggle on open ground or with clothing having been removed during the attack;

- Semen may be deposited almost anywhere on the body, although common external sites are the torso, thighs or face. The area surrounding the vagina or rectum may also show signs of seminal deposition.[44]

[15.30] Samples of semen can be obtained either by absorption onto swabs, by being snipped off with any hairs to which it is attached or by being carefully washed with sterile saline into a sample container. Hairs on the body that appear not to belong to the victim should also be retained, as they may belong to the assailant. Physical examination should also include the fingernails of the victim under which hair or skin of the assailant may have accumulated as the victim attempted to fight him off.

[15.31] Ano-genital examination should take notice of any obvious physical injuries; following penetration, such injuries are likely to include contusions, abrasions and lacerations. Severe vaginal injuries are rare, but signs of less severe injury are found in about one-third of rape victims. If there is any bleeding from the vagina it is important to exclude menstruation as the cause of that bleeding. The extent of the injuries to the vagina or the anus depends on:

- the degree of force used;
- the type and size of any implement, if used;
- the size, lubrication and elasticity of the orifice;
- the age of the patient.

[15.32] The pubic or anal hair should be combed to isolate any of the assailant's pubic hairs that may have been shed in that area. A sample of the victim's pubic hair should also be taken. Vaginal swabs (or where appropriate, anal swabs) should be performed.

---

[42] The form should also be available in paediatric units. See 'Care of the Adolescent Sexual Assault Victim—A Policy Statement' Paediatrics (2001) 107; 6:1476–1479.

[43] So-called (and in these circumstances misnamed) 'love bites'. See para **[14.19]** for a discussion of the potential role of the forensic dentist/odontologist with respect to bite marks on assault victims.

[44] As an aid to locating semen, it should be noted that it may sometimes fluoresce under Wood's Light.

The hymen of a female victim may have been ruptured in the assault. In the pre-pubertal victim, the hymen is thin and inelastic and may be obviously and painfully torn.[45] Attempted masturbation or oro-genital contact with a pre-pubertal girl is unlikely to cause damage to the hymen. In the older victim the hymen may be absent for reasons other than penetration.

A blood sample or some other source of DNA should also be taken from the victim. This can be compared with any DNA results that show up in forensic analysis, helping to exclude any samples that merely identify the victim.

Other considerations

Psychological

[15.33] The examining doctor should bear in mind the state of mind of the victim and there are three simple statements that should form a part of the examiner's repertoire during the course of the examination and in the longer-term aftermath following a sexual assault or rape. They may all bear repeating on more than one occasion:

- – 'You are safe now';
- – 'I am sorry this happened to you' or another similar expression of empathy and of your belief in the worth of the patient;
- – 'This [the attack] is not your fault'.

Sympathetic and empathic care can help to reduce the impact of the physical and psychological trauma of the assault, to support existing and emerging coping skills and to set the tone for resumption of normal functioning. Any attack victim should be allowed to tell their story and the listener should acknowledge their trauma and try to recognise that a crime has been committed. Victims often feel guilty for not struggling. Reinforce the fact that this may have helped them survive the assault.

[15.34] Psychologically, it is impossible to gauge just how traumatic a sexual assault will be on the victim. The impact of the abuse is related to the age of the victim, the extent and duration of the assault, the number of perpetrators, the use of violence during the attack, the relationship if any between victim and assailant and the response of others to any disclosure of any abuse[46] or assault. There are classically short- and long-term consequences of an assault. The short-term or 'acute-phase' response will arise over the initial weeks and may include:

- – fear, shock, disbelief, denial;
- – somatic complaints (the expression of psychological disorders through the medium of physical symptoms);
- – acute anxiety, nightmares, insomnia and lack of concentration;
- – obsessive washing;
- – mood swings, fear, guilt, anger, desire for revenge.

---

[45] Examination of children in cases of suspected child sexual abuse may disclose a notched or scarred hymen as an indicator of previous assault.

[46] Finkelhorn and Browne, 'The traumatic impact of child sexual abuse: a conceptualisation' Am J Orthopsychiatry 1985; 55: 530-541

[15.35] In the longer term (which may extend over very many years), different problems may predominate. Measurable long-term psychiatric consequences are present in 25 per cent of victims of sexual abuse, compared with an incidence of 6 per cent of the same symptoms in the non-abused population).[47] Sometimes a victim may cope very well until circumstances—such as the trial (or release) of the assailant—conspire to cause a setback. A quarter of women continue to experience serious negative effects a year after the event.[48] Features of long-term adjustment include the following:

- a person may elect to undergo major lifestyle changes, such as moving to a different area or changing jobs;
- phobic behaviour may emerge, triggered by general or specific stimuli;
- somatic symptoms/ chronic pain;
- recurrent nightmares;
- sexuality issues;
- substance abuse or other destructive behaviour.

Medical

[15.36] Any person who has been a victim of sexual assault may be at risk of sexually transmitted diseases and a woman may be at risk of pregnancy. The history taken from a rape victim should include attention to menstrual dates, any pre-existing pregnancy and any contraception that is being used. A series of follow-up visits should be arranged to allow testing for the presence of sexually transmitted infections, although only with the consent of the patient.[49]

Table 15.1 Suggested Timetable for Testing for Infection

At 2–3 weeks	Test for Gonococcus, Chlamydia, Trichomoniasis, and do cervical cytology. Do pregnancy test, where appropriate
At 6 weeks	Syphilis serology and test for hepatitis B/ C
At 3 months	HIV test[50] and repeat hepatitis B/ C

Active Hepatitis B immunisation should also be offered, where appropriate, with the first dose of vaccine given within seven days of the attack. Also, where appropriate and

---

[47] Mullen et al. 'Childhood sexual abuse and mental health in adult life' Brit J Psychiatry 1993;163: 721-732. Watkins and Bentovim, 'The sexual abuse of male children and adolescents: a review of current research.' J Child Psychol Psychiat 1992; 33:197–248.

[48] Rothbaum, 'A prospective examination of post traumatic stress disorder in rape victims' J of Traumatic Stress 1992; 5:455–475.

[49] Because patients may fail to attend for follow-up, it is sometimes suggested that all serious sexual assault should be given a prophylactic antibiotic at the time of the original examination to minimise the possibility of subsequent development of bacterial STDs. The antibiotic chosen will depend on regional bacterial resistance and prevalence patterns.

[50] HIV testing should be accompanied by appropriate counselling, the details of which lie outside the scope of this book.

with any necessary consent, emergency post-coital contraception[51] may be prescribed, although this will not extinguish the need to do a subsequent pregnancy test. The probability of conception from a single, random, unprotected intercourse is estimated to be between 2 per cent and 4 per cent, while the likelihood of conception from a single, unprotected, mid-cycle intercourse is at least 10 per cent and may be as high as 30 per cent[52] if the attack was on the estimated day of ovulation.

Legal

[15.37] We observed above that the fact of the complaint to the doctor about the rape or sexual assault might be important from the point of view of evidence should the matter ever come to trial. Quite aside from the evidence gathered by a doctor who conducts an assessment or examination on a victim of sexual assault, there is also the fact of the victim telling someone about the attack.

[15.38] In general, the fact that someone tells someone else about a crime that was perpetrated against her is not admissible in evidence. However, an exception is made to this so-called 'rule against previous consistent statements' in the case of sexual assaults. A complaint by a victim about a sexual attack, including but not limited to rape, made to any person soon after the attack,[53] voluntarily and at the first reasonable opportunity, can show the consistency of the victim's allegation when compared to any statement made later to the police. This consistency may in turn lend credence to arguments that the allegation of the assault was not fabricated and that consent was absent. The complaint must be made at the first opportunity and must be made without any more than light prompting.[54]

[15.39] Thus, a doctor may be in a position of having to furnish two forms of evidence. There is first the evidence gleaned from examination, which should be minutely detailed and will generally be presented with the doctor acting in the role of treating expert witness.[55] Then there is also the fact that the doctor might have been the audience for the earliest possible complaint of the assault and she may therefore be asked to testify to this fact as well, but this time as a normal witness. It is a further reason why notes of consultations relating to rape and sexual assault should be carefully recorded. In an accident and emergency department environment, a nurse or a casualty officer may be the witness to the earliest complaint, while a more experienced doctor in forensic examination may be the expert witness as to the findings of examination.

---

[51] In countries such as New Zealand, it is a legal requirement to offer protection against pregnancy after rape, or to refer the victim to another doctor who will do so: Contraception, Sterilisation and Abortion Act 1977. There is no equivalent legislation in Ireland.

[52] Barret and Marshall, Population Studies 1969:23:455–61.

[53] How soon after the attack is not clear. It appears to vary with the precise circumstances of the case.

[54] See Ní Raiftearaigh, 'The Doctrine of Fresh Complaint in Sexual Cases' 1994 ILT 160.

[55] See Ch 9, para **[9.30]**.

Quick Reference Guide 15.3

Examination and follow-up of the sexual assault victim

- ❖ The examination and history taken from a sexual assault victim has strong legal as well as medical significance. It is always best if someone trained in such an examination is available to conduct it.

- ❖ The sooner a forensic examination can be conducted after the assault, the easier it may be to glean relevant findings/evidence.

- ❖ The examination should be conducted only with the consent of the patient and should take place in an environment and a manner that does not exacerbate the traumatic experiences of the victim.

- ❖ The purpose of the examination is both medico-legal and medical – to obtain evidence and to diagnose any problems that may need treatment or follow-up. A sexual history is important as it may help to explain the finding of semen inconsistent with sexual assault by the alleged assailant. A history of the attack may be difficult to obtain from a distressed patient in the aftermath of an assault. It may be necessary to return to the history of the assault on more than one occasion.

- ❖ All evidence collected during examination should be carefully gathered, stored, sealed and labelled.

- ❖ External examination is important as signs of injury, staining of clothing or skin and the presence of semen deposited on the body may all be important evidence.

- ❖ Anal or genital examination may indicate the fact of assault as well as the violence, nature and extent of the assault.

- ❖ Examination and follow-up should pay careful attention to the psyche of the victim. Affirmation of the fact that the victim is not to blame for the attack is important. Psychological reactions to sexual assault can be manifold, grave and long lasting.

- ❖ Medical considerations include testing, with the patient's consent, for pregnancy and the presence of sexually transmitted disease. Emergency contraception ('the morning after pill') should be offered together with any appropriate active immunisations.

- ❖ All records of the history and examination, together with the fact of the complaint itself, may ultimately be admissible as evidence in a future criminal trial.

Disclosure of past sexual abuse or assault

[15.40] The disclosure of past sexual abuse, either in childhood or in earlier adulthood, may sometimes be made to a practitioner, particularly to a doctor or nurse and often in the context of a related consultation, such as a discussion relating to a psychiatric problem. In general, such disclosures will only be made when the patient feels he or she is in a safe, sensitive and confidential environment. The news may be delivered spontaneously or it may be mentioned in response to careful questioning by the doctor, eg 'I am going to ask you a question you may not have been asked before and you don't have to answer it if you don't want to. Has anyone ever made you have sex that you didn't want and didn't agree to?'

[15.41] There is no need to press for full details of the abuse or attempt to deal with all the issues raised in a single consultation, but the clinician who attempts to elicit the details of past sexual assault should bear in mind that a patient who discloses a history of sexual assault will need not only the care of the doctor, but of a trained counsellor too.

Managing the disclosure

[15.42] It is important to provide an empathic, non-judgmental and affirmative response to allow the patient to answer as fully as she feels comfortable with—the patient's first need is to be heard. A simple statement about the widespread incidence of sexual abuse may help the patient feel less isolated. Check whether the patient is safe now and if other family members or others potentially affected by the abuser are safe. Offer an examination to check physical injuries, scars or medical conditions related to the abuse. Normal findings may address and assuage the patient's unspoken concerns. When performing a physical examination, request permission for even minor procedures—be gentle, take time, and give encouragement. Involve the patient, ensure the patient understands that consent to the examination is not final and can be withdrawn at any stage in the procedure.

[15.43] For most patients a routine enquiry about past abuse does not precipitate a crisis, but it might. Advise the patient that many people find it helpful to talk things over with a trained sexual abuse counsellor and refer if this is their wish. The clinician should know her limits—if she has not had in-depth training in counselling or other 'talking therapies', such as psychotherapy, she should not usually attempt to be a sexual abuse counsellor for her patient, unless the patient declines a referral to another professional. Some patients require increased attention and medical care for a while following disclosure because of the emergence of delayed symptoms. Patients previously employed and coping may need time off work after disclosure and in the early stages of recovery. Problems that may preface, accompany or follow a declaration of previous sexual abuse include:

- alcohol problems;
- eating disorders;
- anxiety or sleep disturbances;
- depression or general stress;
- problems with current relationship or with previous relationships.

[15.44] Ask the patient how the abuse has affected or still is affecting his life and what he wants to do about this. The patient's decision concerning what action he wishes to take should be respected *as far as possible*. On some occasions it may be appropriate to talk to the patient about making a complaint to the police and if a patient declines to do so, there may be a question of the doctor being obliged to breach confidentiality in the interests of protecting other potential victims of an identifiable abuser who continues to be a risk to others. The breach of confidentiality may be kept to a minimum by identifying the potential abuser without identifying the source of the information. One of the generally accepted exceptions to the general requirement of maintaining confidentiality is when there is an identifiable risk to a specific person or where there is a risk to the welfare of society.[56] It is beyond argument that an ongoing risk of sexual

---

[56] Ch 3 'Confidentiality and the Practitioner-Patient Relationship' para **[3.21]**.

abuse of children or adults would in all but the most unlikely circumstances merit such a breach of confidence.

Reporting child abuse—historical or otherwise

[15.45] The specific question of child abuse is dealt with in the context of Ch 8 The Practitioner and the Family, but it is worth pointing out at this juncture that the Protections for Persons Reporting Child Abuse Act 1998[57] protects any person from legal action who reports—in good faith—her suspicions that:

(a)   a child has been or is being assaulted, ill-treated, neglected or sexually abused; or

(b)   a child's health, development or welfare has been or is being avoidably impaired or neglected.

[15.46] In other words, while there is no obligation on a practitioner to report child abuse, nor will be she be answerable to her patient or the perpetrator if she makes such a disclosure to the appropriate authorities. Conversely, a person who deliberately and knowingly makes a false allegation of child abuse against another may not only face legal action by the person she names but may also face criminal proceedings under the Act.[58] The key therefore is that any allegation of child abuse should be made in good faith. Note, however, that many HSE and other institutions do have a policy of reporting disclosure of abuse.

---

[57] Protections for Persons Reporting Child Abuse Act 1998, s 3.
[58] Protections for Persons Reporting Child Abuse Act 1998, s 5.

Chapter 16

The Practitioner and the Driver

INTRODUCTION

[16.01] Health care professionals interact with drivers in a number of ways and this chapter looks at some of the most important. Many of the situations in which the interaction occurs may seem to be purely administrative but as we will see, there are complications that can arise in areas as seemingly simple as the certification of fitness to drive and as complex as dealing with the possibly intoxicated driver. In situations concerning the drunk driver in particular, there are legal rules at play of which the clinician needs to be aware so that she can be sure that she is discharging her legal responsibilities while, at the same time, protecting the rights of any patient under her care.

This chapter deals with certification of fitness to drive and the challenges created by those patients who are no longer fit to drive. Also important is the question of driving under the influence of drugs and alcohol and this chapter looks at the law regarding driving while intoxicated and the potential role of the doctor or other clinician in a number of scenarios that can occur with the drunken driver.

PRACTITIONERS AND THE DRIVING LICENCE

[16.02] The general rules for the medical standards that apply to drivers are set out in legal form in the Road Traffic (Licensing of Drivers) Regulations 1999 (hereafter the 1999 Regulations).[1] However, they are also laid out in a putatively more user-friendly format in a Department of the Environment booklet intended for medical and paramedical professionals (see para **[16.05]**ff below).[2]

Categories of licence

[16.03] There are 14 specific categories of motorised vehicle for which a licence may be obtained, ranging from mopeds to substantial heavy goods vehicles, but as far as the doctor is concerned there are only two broad classifications of licence for the purpose of medical certification: Group 1 consists of all motorcycles, cars and tractors (with or without trailers), while Group 2 in effect comprises all vans, trucks and buses.

[16.04] The essential difference between the groups, as far as the practitioner is concerned, is the nature of the examinations that must be carried out and certified before a prospective driver can be declared fit to sit behind the wheel of the relevant vehicle. Group 2 vehicles are heavier, they have lower braking capacity and are generally regarded as higher-risk.

---

[1]   SI 352/1999; amended by the Road Traffic (Licensing of Drivers) (Amendment) Regulations 2004, which are discussed below: para **[16.17]**.

[2]   Department of the Environment and Local Government, Medical Aspects of Driver Licensing— A Guide for Registered Medical Practitioners (1999).

Accordingly, the standard of physical and mental fitness required on the part of the driver is higher and it is the doctor who has the responsibility of assessing that this standard is met. So, a person applying for a Group 1 licence is obliged to undergo an eyesight test, which may be conducted by an optician or a registered medical practitioner. Group 1 applicants are not, however, ordinarily obliged to undergo a medical examination: a medical assessment of a Group 1 licence applicant is required only where the applicant:

- is over 70 years of age;[3] or
- suffers from any of the disabilities listed as requiring a medical report (these conditions are set out at para **[16.12]** below);
- has a history of alcoholism or epilepsy;
- takes, on a regular basis, drugs or medicaments which would be likely to cause the driving of a vehicle by him or her in a public place to be a source of danger to the public.

On the other hand, every person seeking a Group 2 licence must undergo a full medical examination conducted and recorded by a registered medical practitioner[4] and the medical examination 'shall take due account of the additional risks and dangers involved in the driving of such vehicles'.[5]

Table 16.1—The Classes of Driver Licence (figures in brackets denote the minimum age for holding the licence)

Group 1 Licences

M	Mopeds (age 16)
A1, A	Smaller motorcycles (age 16); motorcycles over 125cc (age 18)
W	Work vehicles and tractors with or without trailers (age 16)

Group 2 Licences

C, C1, EC, EC1	Vehicles with a capacity of not more than 8 people with (C1) or without (C) an upper limit of 3,500kg (age 18)
D, D1, ED1, ED	Vehicles with a capacity greater than 8 people and with (D1) or without (D) a maximum capacity of 16 people (age 21)

---

[3] There is some evidence to suggest that this singling out of over 70s is not rooted in fact. In the UK, only 6 per 1000 male drivers in the 65–74 age group were involved in crashes, compared with 21 per 1000 in the 25–34 age group. However, fatality rates are disproportionately higher in older drivers (in the US in 1997 fatality rates in over 65s were 12.7 per 100,000, compared with 10.3 per 100,000 25–64 year olds). See OECD, *Ageing and Transport: Mobility Needs and Safety Issues* (Paris, 2001) Ch 3. Of course, one reason why over-70s appear to be safer drivers is because of the mandatory medical examination, which weeds out those who should not be driving.

[4] The result of the examination is recorded on Form D 501. Eyesight is certified on Form D 502.

[5] Road Traffic (Licensing of Drivers) Regulations 1999, Sch 6.

Certification of fitness to drive

[16.05] The purpose of medical certification of drivers 'is to keep the more seriously affected drivers off the roads or to restrict their driving within the limitations [imposed by] their disability.'[6] A patient who has received a completed form regarding their eyesight (or medical condition) from their doctor concerning fitness to drive has one month to file that form with their application. If they fail to do so, the findings on the form lapse and the applicant must submit himself for a further examination.

Eyesight examination

[16.06] The first port of call for an applicant for a driver's licence falling into the classification of Group 1 may be an optician rather than a medical practitioner. A person who does not fulfil the criteria for a compulsory medical examination (or who does not declare that he suffers from any condition which would necessitate a medical examination) need only undergo an eye test, which may be conducted by an optician.[7] It may be that an optician will identify a problem during ophthalmic examination suggestive of an underlying illness that may be incompatible with driving, such as diabetes, in which case it would be expected that she would decline to sign the form, directing the applicant to seek a medical opinion.

As far as determination of capacity to drive is concerned, there are four elements to assessment of eyesight set out in the 1999 Regulation: visual acuity, field of vision, night vision and the presence of any progressive eye disease.

Group 1 applicants

[16.07] A person applying for a Group 1 licence and who has vision in both eyes must have (with corrective lenses if necessary) a visual acuity of not less than 0.5, using both eyes together.[8] He must also have a horizontal field of vision of not less than 150 degrees. A person with one eye is permitted to drive but he must have a visual acuity of not less than 0.6[9] and an unrestricted field of vision in that eye. Furthermore, the monocular vision must have existed for long enough for adaptation to the new state of affairs to occur.[10] There is no limitation on the permitted strength of corrective lenses.

Group 2 applicants

[16.08] A person making an application for a Group 2 licence must have (again with corrective lenses where necessary) a minimal visual acuity of 0.8[11] in the better eye and 0.5 in the worse eye. There are conditions attached to the use of corrective lenses by Group 2 applicants that are not imposed on applicants for Group 1 licences. If corrective lenses are used in the case of the former, then either the unrestricted acuity in each eye must read 0.5 or else the minimum acuity must be achieved either:

---

[6]   Department of the Environment and Local Government, *Medical Aspects of Driver Licensing* (1999) 2.

[7]   Road Traffic (Licensing of Drivers) Regulations 1999, reg 42(6).

[8]   This equates to 6/12 using a metric Snellen Chart.

[9]   Equating to 6/10 using a metric Snellen Chart.

[10]   Usually adaptation to monocular vision takes a matter of months rather than weeks or years.

[11]   6/7.5 using a metric Snellen chart.

– by correction by means of glasses with a power not exceeding plus or minus 8 dioptres; *or*

– by means of contact lenses.

Anyone with monocular vision or who suffers from diplopia (double vision) cannot be certified as fit to drive vehicles that fall into the Group 2 category. Any deteriorating vision in applicants over the age of 40 must be investigated before that person is certified as fit to drive; this would appear to be one circumstance that would warrant referral by an optician to a registered medical practitioner.

A gap in the rules?

[16.09] There is no obligation under Irish regulations requiring a test for colour blindness or a declaration by an applicant that he suffers from colour blindness. This is at odds with the policy in certain other countries, such as Australia and the United States. In the United Kingdom, however (whose fitness to drive criteria we discuss extensively below), colour blindness is not considered to inhibit driving and does not form part of assessment. Colour blindness, which is typically genetically inherited, occurs in as many as 8 per cent of men and in about 0.2 per cent of women and the majority of those affected will have difficulty with red, green or both colours—important colours when it comes to driving.

[16.10] Drivers with a severely impaired red colour perception defect (protans) have, according to some studies, a reduced visual distance for other vehicles' rear lights and for red traffic signals and consequently they have an increased nose-to-tail collision rate when driving. It is arguable that irrespective of current guidelines doctors should screen for colour blindness as part of the eyesight test for a driving licence. It is at least arguable that male applicants in particular might undergo testing for severe red perception difficulty and should be under a legal obligation to declare whether they suffer from such a condition.

Medical examination

[16.11] When a medical examination is conducted by a doctor on an applicant for a driving licence, the doctor has a number of options upon the completion of the assessment. The applicant can be certified as:

(a)   unfit to drive;

(b)   fit to drive with no requirement for review;

(c)   fit to drive, but with review of fitness to drive in one, three or ten years' time.

The first category is self-explanatory and covers those drivers who simply should not be on the road. Similarly, the second category needs little illumination, save to point out that there are some limitations on the freedom of the doctor to certify that a patient does not need further review (which is where the third category, in part at least, comes into play). Persons over the age 70 can be certified as fit to drive for maximum period of three years at a time only. Similarly, in the case of certain medical conditions, such as insulin-dependent diabetes (in the case of an applicant for a Group 2 licence only), a doctor may only certify fitness to drive for a period of one year at a time. Lastly, any person applying for any Group 2 licence can only be certified as fit to drive for a maximum of ten years at a time. The last category of driver to whom time-limited certification might apply is the driver who does not currently fall into the class of mandatory time-limited certification but who is suffering from a medical condition that, although it does not currently affect capacity to drive, is likely to do so in the future, making re-assessment medically desirable.

The obligatory medical examination

[16.12] We have noted already those who must undergo mandatory medical examinations: (i) all applicants for Group 2 licences; (ii) all Group 1 applicants who are over 70 years of age; (iii) all Group 1 applicants who are suffering from 'diseases or disabilities where a report is required';[12] (iv) those with a history of epilepsy or alcoholism; and (v) those who regularly take medication or drugs that may dangerously impair performance on the road. The 'diseases or disabilities where a report is required' are as follows:

- alcoholism;
- any physical disablement which is likely to affect ability to drive safely;
- any illness which requires the regular use of psychotropic substances;
- any illness or disease which requires the regular use of medications likely to affect ability to drive safely;
- cardiovascular diseases;
- diplopia, defective binocular vision or loss of visual field;
- serious hearing deficiency;
- diabetes;
- epilepsy;
- encephalitis, multiple sclerosis, myasthenia gravis or hereditary diseases of the nervous system associated with progressive muscular atrophy and congenital-myotonic disorders;
- diseases of the peripheral nervous system;
- trauma of the central or peripheral nervous system;
- cerebrovascular diseases;
- lesion with damage to spinal cord and resultant paraplegia;
- mental disturbance due to disease or trauma of, or operation upon, the central nervous system;
- severe mental retardation;
- psychosis, psychoneurosis or personality disorders;
- serious diseases of the blood;
- any disease of the genito-urinary system (including renal disorder) which is likely to affect ability to drive safely.

One problem is that the doctor who is unfamiliar with a patient's history will need to take a full medical history and conduct a full examination in order to ascertain the presence or absence of any of the exhaustive, and not always clearly defined, list of

---

[12] Road Traffic (Licensing of Drivers) Regulations 1999, Sch 4.

illnesses that would preclude or limit certification of fitness to drive. Some are conditions of which the patient may well be unaware. The lack of definition of terms such as 'serious' diseases of the blood is also unhelpful: what conditions are serious and what are not? The 1999 Regulations are silent on whether it is up to the doctor to simply rely on the patient's declaration of whether or not he suffers from any of the conditions or whether the doctor is, in fact, required to exclude the presence of all of the above conditions. In practice, the onus appears to be on the applicant to declare his fitness to drive and in situations where the doctor has no reason to believe the patient is unfit to drive and where an examination is not otherwise mandatory, she may confine herself to administering an eye test.

Conducting a medical examination

[16.13] Once an examination is required, the 1999 Regulations and *Medical Aspects of Driver Licensing* state that the examination should take account of the applicant's 'general health insofar as it affects the ability to drive'. Furthermore, as we have already noted above, where the applicant is seeking a Group 2 licence, the medical practitioner must take due account of the additional risks and dangers involved in the driving of such vehicles. The health parameters that fall to be considered in a fitness to drive assessment under the 1999 Regulations are very general indeed and include an assessment of both physical and mental health.[13] The fundamental test that the examining doctor is expected to apply when considering the health status of an applicant for any category of licence is whether any defect would render the applicant a danger to other road-users.

[16.14] However, the Irish Regulations fail to offer specific guidelines or a definitive list of conditions that would make the applicant a danger to other road users. In this respect Irish guidelines fare very poorly when compared to the fitness to drive guidance provided by the UK Driver and Vehicle Licensing Authority (DVLA), whose regulations act as an invaluable resource[14] for patching the many gaps left in the Irish Regulations. In the sections that follow, consideration of the Irish medical guidelines will draw upon the UK Regulations where they add clarity to the Irish situation. It should be remembered, however, that the UK guidelines are not Irish ones and that where there is divergence, the Irish guidelines will always apply. However, the UK guidelines are relied on in places in this chapter, precisely because of the frequent weakness of Irish guidance.

---

[13] The requirements for examination are set out in the 1999 Regulations, Pt 2, reg 1(1) and in Medical Aspects of Driver Licensing (see above): the medical examination shall take account of the following aspects of the applicant's physical and mental condition: conditions of (i) the cardiovascular system; (ii) the haemopoietic system; (iii) the endocrine system; (iv) the respiratory system; (v) the gastro-intestinal system; (v) the genito-urinary system; (vi) the nervous system; (vii) the mental system; and (viii) general physique and physical disabilities; and (ix) ear conditions.

[14] DVLA Drivers Medical Group, At a Glance: Guide to the Current Medical Standards of Fitness to Drive (2007): see http://www.dvla.gov.uk/medical/ataglance.aspx (last accessed October 2007).

Hearing

[16.15] Although 'serious hearing deficiency' is listed in the 1999 Regulations as one of the conditions necessitating a medial examination, there is, in fact, no real requirement to examine the hearing of Group 1 applicants, even though the medical examination is in theory necessary because of the hearing loss. This is because there is nothing in the regulations entitling the doctor to find that an applicant for a Group 1 licence is unfit to drive by reason of deafness.

[16.16] Conversely, for Group 2 licences only[15] there is an express statement that 'fitness to drive shall not be certified if the applicant's hearing is so deficient that it interferes with the proper discharge of his duties.' However, there is no elaboration in the regulations as to what constitutes either sufficiently good hearing or the 'proper discharge' of a driver's responsibilities. Accordingly, the decision is apparently dependent on the subjective judgment call of the individual physician, who may not be at all conversant with the nuances of the applicant's job. In the United Kingdom, the DVLA Medical Regulations state the following regarding profound deafness in Group 2 applicants:

> Of paramount importance is the proven ability to be able to communicate in the event of an emergency by speech or by using a device e.g. a MINICOM. If unable to do so the licence is likely to be refused or revoked.[16]

In other words, the DVLA perceives the primary difficulty as not being one of the ability to hear but the ability to warn and be warned in an emergency. This approach goes some way towards helping to identify what may be meant by the Irish Regulations' reference to an applicant's 'discharge of his duties' and also seems to imply that in the ordinary course of events, deafness is unlikely to be a bar to a Group 2 licence applicant. In the UK, as in Ireland, deafness (even profound deafness) is not a bar to holding a Group 1 licence.

Heart disease

[16.17] The 1999 Regulations state the following in terms of heart conditions relevant for the purposes of driving:

> Any disease capable of exposing an applicant for a first licence or a driver applying for a renewal of a licence to a sudden failure of the cardiovascular system such that there is a sudden impairment of the cerebral functions constitutes a danger to road safety.

That covers myriad illnesses and the guidelines do not parse or expand upon this broad statement. The conditions (together with the consequences of the relevant diagnosis) expressly referred to in the 1999 Regulations[17] and the *Medical Aspects of Driver Licensing* are:

---

15 Road Traffic (Licensing of Drivers) Regulations 1999, Sch 6, Pt 2, reg 3.
16 DVLA Drivers Medical Group, Ch 8.
17 Road Traffic (Licensing of Drivers) Regulations 1999, Sch 6, Pt 2, reg 4(3).

- serious arrhythmia resulting in loss of consciousness:[18] shall not be certified as fit to drive;[19]
- pacemakers: may drive but should be regularly reviewed;
- abnormal blood pressure: may not be fit to drive depending on other findings on medical examination;
- angina during rest or emotion: shall not be certified as fit to drive;
- myocardial infarction: may be certified as being fit to drive subject to regular medical review.

All considerations of cardiovascular health have to be weighed more carefully when it comes to drivers applying for Group 2 licences, taking due account of the additional risks and dangers involved in the driving of such vehicles.

Specific heart disorders

[16.18] The UK DVLA lists a larger number of specific conditions and how they should be approached with regard to each of the two groups of applicant.[20] Common cardiac conditions dealt with in the UK guidelines, together with the limitations they impose upon the driver, include the following:

---

[18] It is not clear whether this refers to an ongoing risk of loss of consciousness or a historic loss of consciousness; it seems logical that it refers to the former and that once the risk of loss of consciousness is minimised by treatment, then the applicant is fit to drive again. However, note the DVLA guidelines on arrythmia at Table 16.2.

[19] Persons with 'ventricular tachyarrhythmias treated by an implantable cardioverter-defibrillator (ICD)' who are in New York Heart Functional Class III shall not be certified as fit to drive. Those in Class I or II can be certified as fit to drive if certified by a consultant cardiologist. The New York Heart Association Classification is a gradation of the severity of symptoms in patients with congestive heart failure that operates approximately as follows:

I   Symptoms develop at extreme levels of exertion (Workloads >7 METs);
II   Symptoms develop at moderate levels of exertion (Workloads 4–7 METs);
III Symptoms develop at mild levels of exertion (Workloads <4 METs);
IV   Symptoms of CHF are present at rest.

One method of measuring units of work is the MET. One MET is the utilisation of 3.5ml oxygen/kg/min and is the typical amount of oxygen used at rest.

[20] DVLA Drivers Medical Group, above, Ch 2. A Left Ventricular Ejection Fraction of < 0.4 is considered an automatic bar to Group 2 Entitlement. Table 16.2 is a summary of guidelines relating to common conditions and conditions imprecisely referred to in the Irish guidelines. The 'exercise/functional testing' referred to for Group 2 drivers is 'exercise evaluation...performed on a bicycle or treadmill. Drivers should be able to complete 3 stages of the Bruce protocol or equivalent safely without anti-anginal medication for 48 hours and should remain free from signs of cardiovascular dysfunction during exercise or the recovery period. In the presence of established coronary heart disease exercise evaluation shall be required at regular intervals not to exceed 3 years.'

Table 16.2—Common Heart Conditions and Driving Restriction (from UK DVLA Guidelines)

Condition	Group 1	Group 2
Angina	Driving must cease when symptoms occur at rest or at the wheel. Driving may recommence when satisfactory symptoms control is achieved	Licence refused or revoked with continuing symptoms (treated and/or untreated) Re-licensed if: (1) symptom-free for at least 6 weeks (2) the exercise/functional test requirements can be met (3) there is no other disqualifying condition.
Angioplasty/ CABG/Acute coronary syndromes (including myocardial infarction)	May return to driving from 1 (angioplasty) to 4 weeks (MI/CABG) after the procedure or event	Disqualified for at least 6 weeks after angioplasty and 3 months after CABG or acute coronary event after the procedure or event and (1) must meet exercise/ functional test requirements (2) must be no other disqualifying condition.
Hypertension	No problem if medication tolerated	Disqualified if resting blood pressure over 180mmHg (systolic) or 100 mm Hg (diastolic) until successfully treated without side effects that impair driving.
Arrythmia	Driving must cease if the arrhythmia has caused or is likely to cause incapacity. Driving may be permitted when underlying cause has been identified and controlled for at least 4/52.	Disqualifies from driving if the arrhythmia has caused or is likely to cause incapacity. Driving may be permitted when: – the arrhythmia is controlled for at least 3 months – the LV ejection fraction is satisfactory (fn 21) – no other disqualifying condition

Condition	Group 1	Group 2
Implantable Cardioverter Defibrillator (ICD)	Patients with ICDs implanted for sustained ventricular arrhythmias should not drive for a minimum period of from 6 months to 2 years if the arrythmia caused incapacity, depending on the precise circumstances of the condition. 1 month off the roads if no incapacity with arrythmia and otherwise stable from a cardiovascular point of view.	Permanently bars

Diabetes and other endocrine disorders

[16.19] Diabetes, whether controlled by insulin injections or tablets, is not an automatic stumbling block to obtaining a Group 1 licence, once the applicant remains under medical supervision.[21] A candidate for a Group 2 licence with non-insulin-dependent diabetes may be certified as fit to drive, but insulin-dependent diabetes is a bar to certification for a Group 2 licence unless there are exceptional circumstances,[22] as certified by a consultant endocrinologist with an interest in diabetes and, even in such exceptional circumstances, the applicant or driver is subject to annual medical review. Drivers or applicants with endocrine disorders other than diabetes cannot drive where the condition means that they would be a danger to other road-users.

Neurological problems, including epilepsy

[16.20] According to DVLA guidelines, epilepsy is the most common cause of loss of consciousness at the wheel. The regulations in Ireland on epilepsy were amended in 2004 to bring them more closely into line with the practice in other jurisdictions.[23] While under the new amended Regulations, applicants for Group 2 licences are still

---

[21] Road Traffic (Licensing of Drivers) Regulations 1999, Sch 6, Pt 2, reg 5(1). The DVLA adds the rider that the Group 1 driver must recognise warning symptoms of hypoglycaemia and meet the required visual standards. He can only be certified as fit to drive for 1–3 years. In the UK any insulin-dependent diabetic who did already have his licence by 1991 may not hold a Group 2 for a Heavy Goods Vehicle or a Public Carriage Vehicle.

[22] It is not clear whether these circumstances are confined to medical circumstances or whether they might include psychological or socio-economic factors.

[23] Road Traffic (Licensing of Drivers) (Amendment) Regulations 2004 (SI 705/2004). Previously in the case of persons with epilepsy, fitness to drive could only be certified for a limited period in relation to Group 1 license applicants where the applicant has not suffered any epileptic attack during the 12-month period preceding the date of medical examination. Under the old dispensation, all episodes of epileptic activity (including auras or seizure warnings in which consciousness is retained) counted as seizures.

permanently barred from holding a driving licence once they have been diagnosed with epilepsy, a Group 1 applicant may be certified for a limited period in relation to vehicles of category A1, A, B, EB, M or W, where he:

(i) has not suffered any epileptic attack during the 12-month period preceding the date of medical examination; or

(ii) has only had nocturnal seizures over a period of two years preceding the date of medical examination, and certification of this fact is by a consultant neurologist;

(iii) has only had a single provoked seizure and such seizure was prior to the six-month period preceding the date of medical examination, and certification is by a consultant neurologist; or

(iv) has only had simple partial seizures where awareness is fully maintained at all times, and certification of this fact is by a consultant neurologist.

In the UK, applicants for Group 2 licenses are not excluded in perpetuity solely because they have suffered from epilepsy at some time in the past. Instead, a person who has been fit-free for ten years or more without medication may subsequently apply for a Group 2 licence. This seems a sensible approach, but the law in Ireland remains that anyone who has ever suffered seizures must be refused a Group 2 licence on medical grounds. In the UK, patients are also forbidden from driving while anti-epileptic medication is being withdrawn.

Other neurological conditions

[16.21] Patients who have any form of paralysis or other cerebrovascular disease may be certified as fit to drive if surrounding circumstances so permit, including the possibility that they may need a vehicle that has been modified to suit their condition. Any such certification must be time-limited in order to allow for regular review. Applicants for Group 2 licences are barred if they have suffered from a cerebrovascular disease or lesion with resultant damage to the spinal cord and paraplegia. Other neurological conditions, aside from epilepsy, enumerated by the Irish regulations are:

(a) encephalitis, multiple sclerosis, myasthenia gravis, hereditary diseases of the nervous system associated with progressive muscular atrophy and congenital myotonic disorders;

(b) diseases of the peripheral nervous system; or

(c) trauma of the peripheral nervous system.

In each case of neurological disease, the question of fitness to drive should be judged on the merits of the individual case and fitness to drive should, where certified, be only for a limited period in order to facilitate regular review of progress or deterioration.

[16.22] There is no explicit provision that Group 2 applicants should be refused if they suffer from conditions (a)–(c) above. It is likely that, by analogy with the general policy regarding type-2 licence diseases, greater scrutiny and reluctance to certify should be brought to bear upon applicants for licences to drive larger vehicles. This would tally with the DVLA philosophy that neurological conditions other than epilepsy are not a bar to Group 2 licenses once there is no evidence of deterioration. After a stroke or transient ischaemic attack (TIA), the UK DVLA guidelines state that Group 1 licence-holders are not permitted to drive for at least a month after the event and Group 2 licence-holders or applicants may not drive for 12 months after a stroke or TIA.

Mental disorders

[16.23] Applicants for a Group 2 licence who suffer from mental illness are not explicitly precluded from holding licences but the regulations repeat the mantra that any medical examination concerned with mental disorders 'shall take due account of the additional risks and dangers involved in the driving of such vehicles.' There is no psychiatric condition that is automatically a bar to driving. The categories of mental disorder of concern to the certifying doctor are set out by the regulations:[24]

(a)   severe mental disturbance, whether congenital or due to disease, trauma or neurosurgical operation on the central nervous system;

(b)   severe mental retardation;

(c)   psychosis, which in particular has caused general paralysis; or

(d)   severe behavioural problems due to dementia; psychoneurosis; or personality defects or disorders leading to seriously impaired judgement, behaviour or adaptability.

In all of the above cases, certification may be for only a limited period when deemed necessary in order to permit regular review. In the United Kingdom, severe anxiety or depression, a psychotic episode and dementia are all bars to driving until the condition is investigated and treated. UK drivers with stable anxiety and depression and whose medication does not interfere with their performance behind the wheel may continue to hold both Group 1 and Group 2 licences.

Alcohol

[16.24] An applicant who has in the past suffered from alcoholism[25] should be considered for limited certification only, so that his continuing sobriety can be kept under review. Active alcoholism is an obvious reason for the refusal of certification.

Drugs – illicit and prescribed

[16.25] The regulations stipulate that anyone who is 'dependent upon psychotropic substances or, if...not dependent upon such substances, regularly abuses them' shall not be certified to drive. However, it appears that a person who is *prescribed* such medications may be certified as fit to drive, so long as the medication does not hamper his ability to drive. There is some confusion here: what about a patient who is both prescribed 'psychotropic' medication and also dependent upon those medications? For example, a doctor may be prescribing a course of sedatives or heroin substitute intended to wean a patient off an addiction. If that patient is 'dependent' upon prescribed medication, but otherwise unaffected by the medication in terms of fitness to drive, may he be certified as fit to drive? What—in any event—does 'psychotropic' mean? The term is not defined in the 1999 Regulations; does it include anti-depressant tablets, short-acting sleeping tablets or depot injections of anti-psychotic medication or does it indeed

---

24   Road Traffic (Licensing of Drivers) Regulations 1999, Sch 6, Pt 2, reg 6.

25   Alcoholism is not defined in Medical Aspects of Driver Licensing or in the 1999 Regulations.

include non-pharmacological compounds such as caffeine? The answers to these questions are not contained in the guidelines.

[16.26] According to the UK DVLA medical guidelines, 'the prescribed use of [benzodiazepines] at therapeutic doses, without evidence of impairment, does not amount to misuse/dependency for licensing purposes.' It seems logical that the real test under the Irish legislation is not an abuse/dependency/prescription distinction, but rather an assessment of whether an applicant is, as a matter of fact or of probability, impaired by any compounds (medicinal or illicit) he is taking. The question of driving under the influence of alcohol and drugs is reviewed in the second half of this chapter.

Other health considerations

[16.27] The regulations on certification of fitness to drive further require the physician to take into account diseases of the blood, renal disorders, organ transplants and 'any disorder not mentioned... which gives rise to, or is likely to result in, functional incapacity affecting safety at the wheel.'[26]

DISCUSSION – ETHICAL AND LEGAL ASPECTS OF DRIVER LICENSING

[16.28] When it comes to driver licensing, much appears to hinge on the doctor's clinical judgment and common sense. There will be many situations in which the doctor may be tentative and uncertain about the wisdom of allowing a particular patient out on the roads, eg the patient known to have failing eyesight who nonetheless satisfies the legal limit on the day of examination. Such a patient may be fit to drive now, but is unlikely to be fit to drive in one year's time (the shortest period for which an applicant may be certified as fit to drive). In all such borderline cases it will be important for the doctor to document the decision taken and the reason she took that decision.

Ethical aspects

[16.29] Confidentiality is an important consideration in the context of certification of fitness to drive. When a person applies for a licence, it is up to that person to declare any illness that may preclude him from driving or that may limit the life span of his licence. Most patients will do so, but what about the patient who suffers from epilepsy and withholds that information from the licensing authority and from the doctor or optician who conducts the eyesight test? The fact that an optician's report is all that may be required from an applicant who chooses not to declare an illness or submit himself to medical examination, demonstrates the degree to which the whole edifice of driver certification is erected on the foundational principle of full disclosure by the patient.

> **Example 16.1**
>
> A person with poorly-controlled epilepsy is seeking a Group 1 licence. He arranges for his eyesight test to be conducted by an optician who is unaware that the applicant suffers from epilepsy and that he has had recent seizure activity. Subsequently, the patient's GP spies her patient, whom she knows to be epileptic, behind the wheel of his car. What should she do?

---

[26] Road Traffic (Licensing of Drivers) Regulations 1999, Sch 6, Pt 2, reg 12.

Medical confidentiality is important, but as we have seen,[27] the requirement to maintain confidentiality is modified in certain circumstances and among those is the exception created by a situation where it is necessary to betray confidentiality in order to protect the welfare of society. So disclosure to protect society from the release of a dangerous prisoner would be valid grounds for disclosure[28] and so would disclosure to take a potentially lethal driver off the roads.[29] The Irish Medical Council *Guide to Ethical Conduct and Behaviour* does not deal specifically with the issue of driving, but the UK General Medical Council suggests the following protocol:[30]

> Where patients have conditions [that do or may in the future affect the patient's ability to drive] you should:
>
> a. Make sure that patients understand that the condition may impair their ability to drive. If a patient is incapable of understanding this advice, for example because of dementia, you should inform the DVLA immediately.
>
> b. Explain to patients that they have a legal duty to inform the DVLA about the condition.
>
> If patients refuse to accept the diagnosis or the effect of the condition on their ability to drive, you can suggest that the patients seek a second opinion, and make appropriate arrangements for the patients to do so. You should advise patients not to drive until the second opinion has been obtained.
>
> If patients continue to drive when they may not be fit to do so, you should make every reasonable effort to persuade them to stop. This may include telling their next of kin, if they agree you may do so. If you do not manage to persuade patients to stop driving, or you are given or find evidence that a patient is continuing to drive contrary to advice, you should disclose relevant medical information immediately, in confidence, to the medical adviser at the DVLA.
>
> Before giving information to the DVLA you should try to inform the patient of your decision to do so. Once the DVLA has been informed, you should also write to the patient, to confirm that a disclosure has been made.

[16.30] Note that, unlike in the UK DVLA, there is no medical department within the Irish licensing authorities whom the doctor may contact with queries or as a first port of call where she has concerns about a patient's fitness to drive. The importance of telling only the relevant authorities was stressed in *Duncan v Medical Practitioners' Disciplinary Committee* where a doctor warned not only the relevant authorities of the fact that a particular driver suffered from a heart condition that made it unsafe for him to drive, but also a number of his patients and, eventually, even the media. The New Zealand High Court, in affirming a decision to erase the doctor's name for the register

---

27 See Ch 3 and in particular para **[3.21]***ff*.

28 *W v Egdell* [1990] 1 All ER 835.

29 This point was accepted by the court in *Duncan v Medical Practitioners' Disciplinary Committee* [1986] 1 NZLR 513—the problem in that case (discussed in the text) was the nature of the disclosure more than the fact of disclosure.

30 http://www.gmc-uk.org/guidance/current/library/confidentiality_faq.asp#q17.

said that 'a doctor who has decided to communicate [confidential information] should discriminate and ensure the recipient is a responsible authority'. [31]

Legal consequences

[16.31] Any disclosure by a clinician of the risk posed by a driver would be immune from legal action once the breach of confidentiality was grounded upon an appreciable risk and notified only to relevant authorities. It has, however, been suggested that a doctor or other health professional who negligently failed to establish a patient's fitness to drive could be liable for negligence to the victims of any injury caused by the patient on the roads as a result of the patient's lack of fitness to drive. As the law stands, it is uncertain that any attempt to sue the clinician would succeed. In the United States, attempts to sue the doctor have been rejected[32] and it is likely (but not certain) that such a case against an Irish clinician by those injured as a result of shortcomings in the certification of an applicant's fitness to drive would also fail. The only circumstances in which a case might succeed would be when it is possible to foresee not only the possibility of damage to a third party but also the identity of the third party who is at risk.[33]

DRIVING, ALCOHOL AND DRUGS

[16.32] Drinking and driving has been illegal in Ireland since 1961, when the first Road Traffic Act was passed, although the original Act has been amended on a number of occasions since then. It is these later amendments, particularly the Road Traffic Acts of 1994 and 1995, that are of most relevance to health practitioners, especially doctors. The Road Traffic Act 1994 is the statute predominantly responsible for the modern form of drink-driving legislation in Ireland. The most recent amendment of drink-driving legislation, allowing for mandatory alcohol testing checkpoints (or random testing), was contained in the Road Traffic Act 2006.

Alcohol limits for drivers

[16.33] The Road Traffic Act set down the maximum permissible levels of alcohol in the three types of sample that may be provided by a driver suspected of being intoxicated: blood, alcohol and breath. Blood samples are generally taken by doctors. Urine and breath samples will generally be provided by the suspect to a member of Garda Síochána. The basic law on drunk driving is as follows:[34]

---

[31] *Duncan v Medical Practitioners' Disciplinary Committee* [1986] 1 NZLR 513. See the discussion of prudent disclosure of confidential information at para **[3.30]**.

[32] *Crosby v Sultz* 592 A 2d 1337 (Pa, 1991).

[33] See *Palmer v Tees Health Authority* [1999] Lloyd's Law Reports Medical, 351. See *Reisner v Regents of the University of California* (1995) 31 Cal App 4th 1110. This area is discussed further in Ch 6 'Negligence' (see para **[6.10]**). Also of relevance is the idea of 'duty to warn', discussed in Ch 3 Confidentiality and the Practitioner-Patient Relationship (see para **[3.35]**).

[34] Road Traffic Act 1961, s 49, as amended by the 1994 Act.

- A person shall not drive or attempt to drive a mechanically propelled vehicle in a public place while he is under the influence of an intoxicant to such an extent as to be incapable of having proper control of the vehicle.[35]
- A person shall not drive or attempt to drive a mechanically propelled vehicle in a public place while there is present in his body a quantity of alcohol such that, within 3 hours after so driving or attempting to drive:
  - the concentration of alcohol in his blood will exceed a concentration of 80mg of alcohol per 100ml of blood.
  - the concentration of alcohol in his urine will exceed a concentration of 107mg of alcohol per 100ml of urine.
  - the concentration of alcohol in his breath will exceed a concentration of 35μg of alcohol per 100ml of breath.[36]

[16.34] The Road Traffic Acts 1961–2006 also include regulations permitting the relevant Minister to make orders changing the permissible limits of alcohol in breath, urine or breath. There is increasing pressure from Europe to vary Irish limits downwards; the amount of alcohol permitted in the systems of drivers in Ireland is the joint highest in Europe.

Quick Reference Guide 16.1

Confidentiality, ethics and the unfit driver

❖ In general, the onus appears to be on the driver to declare the presence of illness that may render him unfit to drive.
❖ If a doctor is aware that a patient is suffering from an illness that renders him unfit to drive but nonetheless continues to drive, that knowledge may place her in a difficult position.
❖ A clinician may breach confidentiality when it is in the interests of the welfare of society, in the interests of an identifiable individual at risk or when it is in the interests of the patient himself. Keeping an unsafe driver off the road may fulfil any of those categories.
❖ The first step should be to obtain the patient's agreement to ceasing to drive or to the release of the information that renders him unfit to drive. In the absence of such consent, the doctor would be justified in disclosing the information in her possession to the relevant authorities.
❖ If disclosure is made, it should be to the smallest number of recipients consistent with achieving the aim of the breach of confidentiality.
❖ A practitioner is unlikely, as the law stands, to be successfully sued by a person injured by a driver who was wrongly certified by the practitioner as fit to drive.

---

[35] Road Traffic Act 1961, s 49(1), as amended. An 'intoxicant' mentioned in s 49(1) includes alcohol, drugs or any combination of drugs or any combination of drugs and alcohol: Road Traffic Act 1961, s 50, as amended by the Road Traffic Act 1994. There is also an offence under s 50 of being drunk while in control of a vehicle, even though the person may not actually have been driving the vehicle at the time.

[36] Road Traffic Act 1961, s 49(2)–(4).

Drink driving alcohol levels

[16.35] Only Ireland, the United Kingdom, Luxembourg and Italy permit a legal limit of 80mg of alcohol per 100ml of blood. In all other European Union Member States, the upper limit is 50mg per 100ml and in Sweden (the only exception) the level is lower still at 20mg per 100ml. In 2001, the European Commission adopted a recommendation[37] that blood alcohol limits be harmonised at a maximum of 50mg alcohol per 100ml of blood for drivers generally, with a maximum permitted level of 20mg alcohol per 100ml of blood for:

- commercial drivers;
- motorcyclists; and
- inexperienced drivers.

This position has been reiterated in the EU White Paper *European Transport Policy for 2010: time to decide*.[38]

Dealing with drunk drivers

[16.36] Members of the Garda Síochána have extensive powers to stop, detain and investigate those whom they suspect of driving under the influence of alcohol. Where a driver has, in the opinion of a member of the Garda Síochána:

- consumed intoxicating liquor;
- is or has (with his vehicle) been involved in a collision; or
- is committing or has committed an offence under the Road Traffic Acts 1961 to 2006,[39]

then a member of the Garda Síochána may require that person to provide a specimen of breath for analysis at or near the place where he has been detained and may hold the person at that place for up to an hour to allow a breathalyser machine to be brought to the scene. Refusing to provide a specimen is an offence. A person may be arrested on suspicion of being intoxicated or he may be requested to accompany a Garda, although not formally under arrest, to a station to provide a blood or urine specimen. If a person refuses to accompany the Garda, he may then be placed under arrest. Under 2006

---

[37] A recommendation is not binding on Member States, although often indicative of the direction that future legislation will take

[38] COM (2001) 370. See in particular Pt 3. The report points to the anomaly of a driver crossing the Channel from England to France with a legal amount of alcohol in his blood on one side of the border, becoming illegal when he crosses into France. See also OECD, *Safety on Roads— What's the Vision?* (Paris, 2002), 63–68. This report also documents the steady decline in the rate of drink driving noted by most countries surveyed during the 1980s and early 1990s. However, rates of improvement have declined or halted in most nations. It also observes that alcohol consumption by pedestrians is a contributing factor in many accidents. Among the mechanisms reported by the OECD as successful in reducing rates of drunk driving is the use of random breath testing. United States figures included in the report suggest that the raising of the legal drinking age to 21 also contributes to a reduced rate of drunk driving accidents.

[39] Road Traffic Act 1994, s 12, as amended by the Road Traffic Act 2003, s 2.

legislation,[40] the Garda Síochána may also establish checkpoints for the purpose of carrying out random mandatory alcohol testing ('random breath testing'). It is an offence to refuse to provide such a sample if requested.

Quick Reference Guide 16.2

Drink-driving limits

Blood	80 milligrammes (mg) alcohol per 100 millilitres (ml) blood
Urine	107 mg alcohol per 100 ml urine
Breath	35 microgrammes (µg or mcg) alcohol per 100 ml exhaled breath

[16.37] There are certain circumstances, once a person has been detained under suspicion of driving when intoxicated, where the process of investigating intoxication may intersect with the role of the health professionals. Moving through the drink-driving 'process', one can identify those points at which that process may intersect with the duties of clinicians.

[16.38] Once a person is brought to a Garda station, then the doctor may be involved. A person may be brought to a Garda station on foot of a failed preliminary breath test, or where he has been arrested because, in the opinion of a member of the Garda Síochána, he has been under the influence of an intoxicant and was driving or attempting to drive. A person brought to a Garda station under these circumstances is required to:

– permit two specimens of breath to be taken for determining alcohol concentration in the breath; and/or

– permit a designated doctor to take a blood sample; or

– provide for the designated doctor a specimen of urine.

This obligation to provide a sample extends to any person who is admitted to or attends at a hospital as a result of alleged drink-driving.[41] A person who is in hospital or who is otherwise not under arrest, but who rather has voluntarily accompanied a Garda to a police station may be required to undergo a blood or urine test conducted by a designated doctor. A doctor will be called to the station in order to take the sample. The doctor can express the opinion that on medical grounds the taking of a particular sample would be inadvisable, and another form of sample should be taken. Accordingly, if a doctor felt that a blood sample should not be taken, then a urine or breath test would be taken instead. If the person refuses to provide any specimen at all, then that is an offence. It should be noted that 'designated doctor' means designated by the Garda Síochána and not by the patient. Each Garda station will typically have a doctor or a roster of doctors

---

[40] Road Traffic Act 2006, s 4. Random breath testing is not, therefore, completely random as it can only take place at a checkpoint established for the purposes of conduction mandatory alcohol testing. Away from such checkpoints, the normal rules apply: the Garda must form the opinion that the driver (i) has consumed intoxicating liquor; or (ii) is or has (with his vehicle) been involved in a collision; or (iii) is committing or has committed an offence under the Road Traffic Acts 1961 to 2006, before a preliminary breath sample can be requested.

[41] Road Traffic Act 1994, s 15; see below.

upon whom they can call for the purposes of attending to take samples. A fee is payable for attendance by the doctor in a range that depends on the day of the week and/or time of day of the attendance at the Garda station or hospital.[42]

[16.39] There are strict requirements in place regarding the handling of specimens obtained from a suspected drunken driver. These stipulations are to ensure that their integrity as potential evidence in a criminal case will not be challenged. A drink-driving suspect who was able to challenge the probity of the evidence against him could expect to have any prosecution against him overturned for fear that the unsound evidence would result in an unsafe conviction.

Breath samples[43]

[16.40] Two breath samples are obtained[44] from the suspected drunken driver and, where there is any discrepancy in the results obtained from the two samples, the lower of the two results is the one taken into account for the purposes of evidence. This approach ensures that any measuring error inherent in the process is weighted in favour of the accused. In fact, for the purposes of any prosecution that results from a sample in excess of the legal limit, not only is the lower figure used, but an additional 17.5 per cent is subtracted from the lower reading to allow for any variability in the analysis and the apparatus used, in order to ensure that a person is not convicted on the basis of mere statistical error. In essence, the accused is given the benefit of any doubt. If the two results tally exactly then either may be used. A statement of any reading that exceeds the legal limit is produced in duplicate and given to the suspect, who must sign both readings and return one to the Garda. These readings may then be used in evidence.

Blood and urine samples

[16.41] Of more concern to doctors is the procedure regarding urine and blood samples taken from suspected drunk drivers under the Act.[45] Any specimen obtained must be divided into two parts and sealed 'forthwith'. The person who furnished the sample is offered, in writing, the opportunity of retaining one of the two sealed containers holding a portion of the relevant sample. The doctor must also complete a form to accompany the sample which must be forwarded to the Medical Bureau of Road Safety 'as soon as practicable' after the detained person has had his opportunity to retain a portion of the

---

[42] Additional samples taken from other people in custody during a single visit to the Garda station or hospital are reimbursable at a lower rate. An additional fee is also payable if a station or hospital visit lasts longer than one hour.

[43] The machine used is an 'intoxilyser'. The Medical Bureau of Road Safety (see para **[16.45]**) evaluated different types of instruments from June 1999 to September 1999 (see Reynolds and Kearns, 'Introduction of Evidential Breath Testing in Ireland' (2001) Medico-Legal Journal of Ireland 7, 9) and the intoxilyser machine was adopted for use in Ireland. It operates by measuring infra-red wavelengths and, entertainingly enough, the infrared measurements of the intoxilyser are dependent upon the operation of the physics equation known as Beers Law.

[44] Gardaí are the individuals responsible for obtaining breath samples and the procedure they must follow is laid down in the Road Traffic Act 1994, s 17.

[45] Road Traffic Act 1994, s 18.

sample. If the detained person has declined to retain the portion of the specimen that was offered to him, then both are forwarded to the Bureau. The same process applies to both urine and blood samples. What happens to the sample once it reaches the Medical Bureau of Road Safety is dealt with below.

Samples in hospital

[16.42] One power accorded to the Gardaí by the Road Traffic Act 1994[46] is to request that a sample for alcohol analysis be provided by a person in hospital and to achieve that end they are also given the power to enter a hospital without warrant for the purposes of securing that sample. Similarly, a designated doctor has the right to enter the hospital in order to take a sample. Clinicians should be aware that if they are acting as the designated doctor, they have this power. Similarly, practitioners caring for a hospitalised patient who has been involved in a road traffic accident should be aware that the police and the designated doctor have the legal power to require that a specimen of blood or urine be taken for the purposes of analysis of alcohol concentration or the presence of any other intoxicant.

Consequences of failing a drink-driving test

[16.43] Automatic disqualification from driving applies to all drink-driving convictions but the minimum period varies depending on the alcohol levels in individual cases. As observed above, there are certain situations where a person's refusal to adopt a certain course is itself an offence, eg refusing to provide a sample, without a 'special and substantial reason' for such refusal[47] or refusing to sign the print-out of the results of an analysis of a breath sample. Disqualification orders are made by a court and the duration of the driving bans for different levels of intoxication (and for repeat offences) was amended by the Road Traffic Act 2006.[48] Mandatory disqualification also applies in the case of a person who refuses to supply a sample for the purposes of analysis and in the case of a person who is intoxicated to such a degree as to be 'incapable of having proper control of the vehicle'.[49] Details of the minimum disqualification periods if convicted of a particular offence are as set out in Table 16.3:

---

[46] Road Traffic Act 1994, s 15.

[47] Road Traffic Act 1994, s 23.

[48] Road Traffic Act 2006, s 6(1)(b), amending s 26(4)(b) of the Road Traffic Act 1961. The 2006 Act also includes an option of a fixed fine (€300) and disqualification (six months) for drink-driving offenders who have a blood alcohol content between 80mg and 100mg per 100ml of blood (or equivalent breath and urine levels). If the driver accepts the penalty and disqualification, then no court proceedings will issue. If they do not accept the penalty and the matter goes to court, the disqualification on conviction is one year: see Road Traffic Act 2006, s 5. At the time of writing (October 2007), s 5 had not come into force.

[49] Road Traffic Act 1961, s 49(1) as amended by the Road Traffic Act 2006, s 6(1)(a).

Table 16.3—Minimum Disqualification Periods

Offence		Minimum Period	
		1st Offence	*2nd or Subsequent Offence*
1. Alcohol level/100mls			
Blood	81 mg–100 mg		
Urine	107mg–135mg	1 year	2 years
Breath	36µg–44µg		
Blood	101 mg–150 mg		
Breath	135mg–200mg	2 years	4 years
urine	45µg–66µg		
Blood	>150 mg		
Urine	>200mg	3 years	6 years
Breath	>66µg		
2. Refusal offences		4 years	6 years
3. 'Drunk and incapable'		4 years	6 years

[16.44] People who have been disqualified for the first time and for a period of more than two years are allowed to apply to the court to have their disqualification removed and their driving licence restored. At least half of the period of disqualification must have elapsed before an application can be made. In addition to disqualification, a court can impose a jail sentence or fine on anyone who is convicted of drunk-driving: under the 2006 Act, a person convicted of drunk-driving or of having an alcohol level above the legal limit may also be liable to a fine of up to €5000 or to imprisonment for a term not exceeding six months or to both. Any decision of a lower court (in general driving offences are heard in the District Court) may be appealed to a higher court by either the accused or by the Director of Public Prosecutions. The latter may transpire if the DPP (the prosecuting authority) feels that the punishment handed down is too lenient. A person disqualified from driving may also be ordered to re-sit his driving test.

The Medical Bureau of Road Safety

[16.45] The Medical Bureau of Road Safety (MBRS) was established in 1968 under Pt V of the Road Traffic Act 1968 and the duties of the MBRS were set out most recently in the Road Traffic Act 1994.[50] Its primary role is to take receipt of samples of urine or blood provided by those suspected of driving under the influence of intoxicants and test them for the presence of intoxicants. The Bureau issues certificates in respect of the results of these analyses, which may then be used as evidence in the prosecution of individuals whose samples demonstrate the presence of an intoxicant.

---

[50] Road Traffic Act 1994, s 19(1).

[16.46] The process of taking and splitting samples from a suspected drunk driver has already been described (see para **[16.42]**). Any relevant samples are forwarded to the MBRS and as soon as practicable after it has received a specimen forwarded to it, the MBRS analyses the specimen and determines the concentration of alcohol or (as may be appropriate) the presence of a drug or drugs in the specimen.[51] The MBRS then certifies (on a special form for the purpose) the results of testing and returns the results of the analysis to the Garda station from which the specimen originally emanated as soon as is practicable. A copy of the certificate is also forwarded to the person who provided the specimen for testing. The certificate issued by the MBRS must contain the following particulars:

- name and address of the person from whom the specimen was taken, or who provided the specimen;
- the nature of specimen (whether blood or urine);
- the date and time when the specimen was taken or provided;
- the name and address of the Garda station or hospital at which specimen was taken or provided;
- the Garda station from which the specimen analysed was forwarded (in the case of those specimens taken or provided in a hospital);
- the result of the analysis;
- the signature of person who carried out the analysis.[52]

[16.47] The Bureau is overseen by a five-member board, headed by a director, and appointed by the Minister for Transport.[53] Other roles of the MBRS include the provision of equipment for the taking of blood and urine specimens, research on drinking and drugs in relation to driving, including methods of determining the amount of alcohol or drugs in a person's body. Figures released in the MBRS Annual Reports also serve to offer a snapshot of the way in which the Bureau operates.

---

[51] Testing is conducted using gas chromatography.
[52] Road Traffic Act 1994, s 19; SI 351/1994, reg 4 and Second Schedule.
[53] The MBRS was transferred from the responsibility of the Minister for Environment and Local Government in 2002.

Quick Reference Guide 16.3

Driving, alcohol and drugs

❖ Driving, or attempting to drive, while under the influence of alcohol or intoxicants is a criminal offence, punishable by time in jail, a fine, disqualification or any combination of the three. The punishment varies with the gravity of the offence

❖ Alcohol concentration can be measured in breath, blood or urine samples. The maximum permitted concentration is different (but equivalent) for each of the three forms of sample. 'Random' breath testing is now permitted by law.

❖ A doctor will be involved in the drunk-driving detection process when a urine or blood sample is required from a patient. The 'designated doctor' will usually obtain the sample at a Garda Station, but she has the right to enter a hospital and take a sample from a patient there. A 'designated doctor' can indicate that any particular sample should not be taken for medical reasons, in which case an alternative form of sample will be sought.

❖ In order not to inhibit their value as evidence there are safeguards attaching to the manner in which any sample should be taken and handled. In particular, blood and urine samples are divided into two portions and sealed, with one being offered to the suspected drunk driver. The sealed sample that is retained by the doctor is forwarded to the Medical Bureau for Road Safety (MBRS) for analysis.

❖ The MBRS sends the results of its analysis back to the Garda Station where the sample originated. The certificate accompanying the results must contain certain information to ensure that its evidential value is secure.

❖ There is a realistic probability that in the near future European pressure will lead to a reduction in the Irish maximum blood alcohol level for driving from 80mg per 100ml (the joint highest in Europe) to 50mg per 100ml.

Chapter 17

Research, Embryonic Stem Cells and Genetics

INTRODUCTION

[17.01] This chapter examines a number of areas affiliated to the overarching concept of advances in medical science. We look first at legal aspects of clinical research, before turning to Irish (and other) legislation on embryonic stem cell and genetic research and treatment.

CLINICAL RESEARCH

[17.02] The bulk of the law on clinical trials in Ireland is provided by the European Communities (Clinical Trials on Medicinal Products for Human Use) Regulations 2004.[1] The 2004 Regulations define a 'clinical trial' as

> [A]ny investigation in human subjects, other than a non-interventional trial,[2] intended–
>
> (a) to discover or verify the clinical, pharmacological or other pharmacodynamic effects of one or more investigational medicinal products, or
>
> (b) to identify any adverse reactions to one or more such investigational medicinal products, or
>
> (c) to study absorption, distribution, metabolism and excretion of one or more such investigational medicinal products, or
>
> (d) to discover, verify, identify or study any combination of the matters referred to at subparagraphs (a), (b), and (c),
>
> with the object of ascertaining the safety or efficacy of such products, or both.

---

[1] SI 190/2004.

[2] The Directive of 2004 does not apply to 'non-interventional trials', which are defined as 'a study of one or more medicinal products which have a marketing authorisation, where the following conditions are met: (a) the products are prescribed in the usual manner in accordance with the terms of that authorisation; (b) the assignment of any patient involved in the study to a particular therapeutic strategy is not decided in advance by a clinical trial protocol but falls within current practice; (c) the decision to prescribe a particular medicinal product is clearly separated from the decision to include the patient in the study, (d) no diagnostic or monitoring procedures are applied to the patients included in the study, other than those which are ordinarily applied in the course of the particular therapeutic strategy in question, and (e) epidemiological methods are to be used for the analysis of the data arising from the study.' Non-interventional trials are therefore not subject to any legislative control.

[17.03] The 2004 Regulations further define a 'medicinal product'[3] as:

(a) Any substance or combination of substances presented as having properties for treating or preventing disease in human beings; or

(b) Any substance or combination of substances which may be used in or administered to human beings either with a view to restoring, correcting or modifying physiological functions by exerting a pharmacological, immunological or metabolic action, or to making a medical diagnosis.

Insofar as the 2004 Directive applies to any given trial, it supplants the provisions of the earlier legislation, namely the Control of Clinical Trials Acts 1987 and 1990. However, where a proposed trial does not come within the remit of the 2004 Directive, but does come under the aegis of the 1987 and 1990 Acts, those acts will continue to apply.[4] We focus here, however, on the Directive of 2004.

CLINICAL TRIALS ON MEDICINAL PRODUCTS FOR HUMAN USE REGULATIONS 2004

[17.04] Under the Regulations, the Irish Medicines Board is designated as the competent authority for administering the Regulations and granting permissions to clinical trials. The most significant elements of the Regulations are:

– ethics committees;

– the clinical trials authorisation process;

– good practice in clinical trials;

– pharmacovigilance;

– manufacture, importation and labelling of investigational medicinal products.

We focus here on the issues of ethics committees, the authorisation process and good practice (including pharmacovigilance). In essence, to get permission for a clinical trial in Ireland, three conditions must be satisfied:

1. The Minister of Health (the 'Ethics Committees Supervisory Body') must give permission;[5]

2. The Irish Medicines Board must grant an authorisation;

---

3   Citing the definition of 'medicinal product' in Directive 2001/83/EC on the Community Code Relating to Medicinal Products for Human Use.

4   The long title of the Act of 1987 makes clear that the overlap between the two is considerable and that therefore it will almost always be the 2004 Directive that has force: 'An Act to provide for control over the administration of one of more substances or preparations to persons for the purpose of ascertaining the effects (including kinetic effects) of the administration of such substances or preparations on those persons where such administration may have a pharmacological or harmful effect [and] to provide for ethics committees in relation to the foregoing.' The 1987 and 1990 Acts are most likely to apply to trials on non-medicinal products, as the definition of the conduct of a clinical study in the Acts is not confined to active substances but covers trials using 'substances or preparations...where such administration *may* have a pharmacological or harmful effect' [italics added]

5   Clinical Trials on Medicinal Products for Human Use Regulations 2004, reg 6.

3.   Any sponsor of the trial (or the person authorised to act on his behalf) must established in the EU.

Ethics committees

[17.05] Ethics Committees are under the supervision of the Minister for Health, who may either recognise committees appointed by institutions or appoint her own committees with either national responsibility or responsibility for particular classes of clinical trial.[6] Where the Minister recognises an ethics committee, she must indicate to them their terms of reference and in particular the geographical area and classes of clinical trials over which they have power. An ethics committee may have its recognitions revoked by the Minister in certain circumstances.[7]

[17.06] Ethics committees, when appointed, must consist of both expert members and lay members,[8] with a maximum size of 21 members, of whom at least one third must be lay members and at least half of those lay members must be persons who are not and never have been health care professionals. The duration of a person's appointment to an ethics committee is not fixed and will be defined by the terms of her appointment. The appointing authority will also appoint a chairperson, a vice-chair (and an alternate vice-chair). Each committee may set out its own procedural and standing rules, subject to approval by the Minister, although the Regulations set out that no committee may give ethics committee approval to a trial unless, at a minimum, the chairperson and six other members are present at the meeting.[9] Each ethics committee has limited powers to appoint sub-committees and deputies and to co-opt up to two extra members. The committee must also prepare an annual report.

Application for Ethics Committee Approval[10]

[17.07] No trial may commence without ethics committee approval. Application must be made by the chief investigator of the trial and may be made to only one ethics

---

[6]   Clinical Trials on Medicinal Products for Human Use Regulations 2004, regs 6–7. Prior to approving any ethics committee created by an institution (an 'appointing authority'), an application must be made to the Minister (the 'Supervisory Body'), who must be satisfied that the proposed arrangements for the membership and operation of the committee would enable the committee to adequately perform the functions of an ethics committee and to comply with the provisions of Sch 2 of the Regulations.

[7]   Clinical Trials on Medicinal Products for Human Use Regulations 2004, regs 6–7.

[8]   Clinical Trials on Medicinal Products for Human Use Regulations 2004, sch 2, reg 1: An 'expert member' is 'a health care professional or who has professional qualifications or experience relating to the conduct of, or use of statistics in, clinical research, unless the said qualifications or experience relate only to the ethics of clinical research or medical treatment'; a lay member is 'a member of an ethics committee who is not an expert member and who is not and never has been a registered medical practitioner or registered dentist and who does not in the course of his or her employment or business provide medical, dental or nursing care or participate in the promotion or conduct of clinical research'.

[9]   Including at least one expert member and at least one person who is (a) not and never has been a healthcare professional and (b) not a chairperson, member, director, officer or employee of a health service body.

[10] Clinical Trials on Medicinal Products for Human Use Regulations 2004, regs 12–13.

committee[11] and should be made to a committee that is (a) recognised in relation to the particular class of clinical trial into which the proposed clinical trial falls and (b) has geographical authority for

- the whole State; or

- that part of the State in which the chief investigator is professionally based; or

- a particular institution or group of institutions in which the chief investigator is professionally based.

The application must be made in writing and accompanied by the necessary particulars and documents required by applicable European rules.[12] The ethics committee has a specified period of time in which to reply to any application,[13] although that time does not continue to run where the committee notifies the applicant that further information is required.

Consulting experts

[17.08] It is open to the ethics committee to consult a specialist committee where the application relates to a clinical trial of:

(a) medicinal products for gene therapy or somatic cell therapy, including xenogenic cell therapy; or

(b) medicinal products containing genetically modified organisms.

There is also a requirement for the ethics committee to consult relevant experts in cases where:

- any subject participating in a clinical trial is to be a minor and the committee does not have a member with professional expertise in paediatrics;[14] or

- where any subject participating in a clinical trial is to be an adult incapable by reason of physical or mental incapacity of giving informed consent to participation in the trial and the committee does not have a member with

---

[11] Even if the trial will be conducted at a number of centres, each of which may be an institution with its own ethics committee.

[12] The full panoply of documentation required to support a clinical trials application is not considered here.

[13] Usually 60 days, but in the case of a clinical trial involving a medicinal product for gene therapy or somatic cell therapy or a medicinal product containing a genetically modified organism then (i) where a specialist committee is consulted, 180 days, or (ii) where there is no such consultation, 90 days. Where the clinical trial involves a medicinal product for xenogenic cell therapy, there are no specified time limits. Where a trial protocol is amended by a sponsor, the ethics committee has 35 days to consider any substantial amendment to that protocol and respond to it – Clinical Trials on Medicinal Products for Human Use Regulations 2004, reg 21(6).

[14] Before giving its opinion, the committee 'shall...obtain advice on the clinical, ethical and psychosocial problems in the field of paediatrics which may arise in relation to that trial.' Clinical Trials on Medicinal Products for Human Use Regulations 2004, reg 13(7).

professional expertise in the treatment of (a) the disease to which the trial relates, and (b) the patient population suffering that disease.[15]

Ethics Committee Opinions

[17.09] In giving its opinion the ethics committee is required to consider the following matters:

- the relevance of the clinical trial and its design;
- whether the required evaluation of the anticipated benefits and risks (see para **[17.14]** below) is satisfactory and whether the conclusions are justified;
- the clinical trial protocol;
- the suitability of the investigator and supporting staff and the investigator's brochure
- the quality and adequacy of the facilities for the trial;
- the adequacy and completeness of the written information to be given and the procedure to be followed for the purpose of obtaining informed consent to participation in the trial;
- if the subjects are to include persons who because they are minors are incapable of giving informed consent or who are adults but who are incapable by reason of physical or mental incapacity of giving informed consent, whether the research is justified having regard to the conditions and principles laid down in Sch 1 (see para **[17.16]***ff* below);
- the arrangements for the recruitment of subjects;
- the provision made for indemnity or compensation in the event of injury or death attributable to the clinical trial, including any insurance or indemnity to cover the liability of the investigator and sponsor;
- the amounts and, where appropriate, the arrangements for rewarding or compensating investigators and trial subjects, including the terms of any agreement between the sponsor and the owner or occupier of the trial site which are relevant to those arrangements.

Application for authorisation to conduct a clinical trial

[17.10] Applications to conduct a trial are made once ethics committee approval has been received and are made to the Irish Medicines Board. The full details of the application process are not considered here, but in outline the process involves an application in writing to the Board containing all relevant details of the proposed trial. The precise details of the application process vary depending on whether the application relates to a trial of general medicinal products,[16] of medicinal products for gene therapy

---

[15] Before giving its opinion, the committee 'shall...obtain advice on the clinical, ethical and pyschosocial problems, in the field of that disease and the patient population concerned, which may arise in relation to that trial.' Clinical Trials on Medicinal Products for Human Use Regulations 2004, reg 13(8).

[16] Clinical Trials on Medicinal Products for Human Use Regulations 2004, reg 15.

(and similar technologies)[17] or medicinal products with 'special characteristics'.[18] Where an application is made, the Board can approve or reject the proposal (although, in the case of trials of general medical products only, the Board can approve the request subject to conditions). There is also a protocol for the sponsor of the trial to submit an amended request in circumstances where authorisation has not been granted or has been granted subject to conditions.

[17.11] In the case of applications relating to gene therapy and similar technologies, the Board is obliged to refuse authorisation if the use of gene therapy products in that trial would result in modifications to any subject's germ line genetic identity. The Board may also consult the Advisory Committee for Human Medicines or any such other body or committee as the Board may consider appropriate, prior to deciding to authorise any trial.

Provisions also exist for the modification of any protocol by the Board or by a sponsor, together with procedures for the acceptance or rejection of those modifications.[19]

Conduct of clinical trials

[17.12] Under the Regulations, it is obligatory that no trial be conducted or sponsored otherwise than 'in accordance with the conditions and principles of good clinical practice.'[20] Where a trial is a commercial clinical trial with the sponsorship of the pharmaceutical industry or in other circumstances where the investigator-sponsor has a commercial or financial interest in the outcome, then investigational medicinal products used in the trial, and any devices used for the administration of such products must be made available to the study participants free of charge.[21]

[17.13] In terms of what constitutes good clinical practice, the regulations set out that the trial must be carried out in accordance with the terms of the authorisation given[22] and that there must be urgent safety measures in place.[23] Where the Board has concerns about the safety of any trial or about whether the terms of the authorisation given by the Board are being observed it has the power to suspend or terminate a trial.[24] Records of

---

[17] Clinical Trials on Medicinal Products for Human Use Regulations 2004, reg 16. The classes of trial covered by this regulation are those involving '(a) medicinal products for gene therapy and somatic cell therapy, including xenogenic cell therapy and (b) medicinal products containing genetically modified organisms.'

[18] Clinical Trials on Medicinal Products for Human Use Regulations 2004, reg 17. 'Special characteristics' means (a) medicinal products which are not the subject of a product authorisation in force in pursuance of the Medicinal Products (Licensing and Sale) Regulations 1988 and referred to in Pt A of the Annex to Regulation 2309/93/EEC or (b) a biological product of human or animal origin, containing biological components of human or animal origin or a product the manufacturing of which requires such components.

[19] Clinical Trials on Medicinal Products for Human Use Regulations 2004, regs 19–22.

[20] Ibid, reg 24.

[21] Ibid, reg 24(3).

[22] Ibid, reg 25.

[23] Ibid, reg 26.

[24] Ibid, reg 27.

any adverse events must be notified to the sponsor and be collated and retained by the investigator; the Board has the power to request copies of those records at any time.[25] Where serious adverse events occur, they must, where they are fatal or life-threatening, be recorded and reported as soon as possible to the Board, to the equivalent competent authorities in all other EEA states and to the relevant ethics committee, as soon as possible and, in any event, within seven days of the serious reaction occurring. Other, non life-threatening, events need only be reported to the same authorities within 15 days (although they, too, should be reported as soon as possible). Trial sponsors are also obliged to report on a regular basis to the board in respect of all serious adverse affects occurring in the 'reporting year' as a result of the use of the relevant product in trial both within and outside the State.

General principles

[17.14] The principles of good practice applicable to all clinical trial are also set out in Sch 1 of the Regulations.[26] The overall conditions and principles that apply to all clinical trials are:

Conditions

1. The foreseeable risks and inconveniences have been weighed against the anticipated benefit for each subject of the clinical trial and other present and future patients;

2. The anticipated therapeutic and public health benefits justify the risks;

3. The medical care given to, and the medical decisions made on behalf of, subjects shall be the responsibility of an appropriately qualified registered medical practitioner or, where appropriate, of an appropriately qualified registered dentist;

4. Provision has been made for insurance or indemnity to cover the liability of the investigator and sponsor which may arise in relation to the clinical trial.

Principles

5. The rights of each subject to physical and mental integrity, to privacy and to the protection of the data concerning him or her in accordance with the Data Protection Acts 1988 and 2003, are safeguarded.

Consent

[17.15] Consent to a clinical trial will only be valid where:

1. the subject has had an interview with the investigator, or another member of the investigating team, in which he or she has been given the opportunity to understand the nature, objectives, risks and inconveniences of the trial and the conditions under which it is to be conducted;

2. the subject has been informed of his or her right to withdraw from the trial at any time;

---

[25] Ibid, reg 29.
[26] Clinical Trials on Medicinal Products for Human Use Regulations 2004, Sch 1, Pt 2.

3. the subject has given his or her informed consent[27] to taking part in the trial;

4. the subject may, without being subject to any resulting detriment, withdraw from the clinical trial at any time by revoking his or her informed consent;

5. the subject has been provided with a contact point where he or she may obtain further information about the trial.[28]

What is not explicit in the Regulations is the degree of disclosure required from investigators. It is presumed that full disclosure of all possible risks is required.[29] It is unlikely that there is any role for a medically paternalistic approach such as 'therapeutic privilege'[30] when it comes to obtaining consent for clinical trials.

Consent and minors

[17.16] Where a minor is to take part in a clinical trial, there are a number of extra strictures around consent.[31] Every person with parental authority[32] must give informed consent to the minor's participation in the trial and must be provided with a contact point where he or she may obtain further information about the trial. Furthermore the person with parental authority must be informed of the right to withdraw the minor from the trial at any time, without detriment to the minor.

[17.17] There are a number of extra safeguards: the consent of the person with parental authority must represent the minor's presumed will and be given in consultation with the registered medical practitioner who has been treating the minor. Interestingly, the minor himself must receive information according to his or her capacity of understanding,

---

27 Informed consent is defined in the Regulations as follows: 'a person gives informed consent if his or her decision to take part, or that a subject is to take part, in a clinical trial:

    (a) is given freely after that person is informed of the nature, significance, implications and risks of the trial; and

    (b)(i) in the case of a subject giving consent himself or herself—

        (I) is evidenced in writing, dated and signed, or otherwise marked, by that subject so as to indicate his or her consent, or

        (II) if the subject is unable to sign or to mark a document so as to indicate his or her consent, is given clearly to the investigator or another member of the investigating team, in the presence of two witnesses present at the same time and recorded in writing;

    (ii) in the case of another person giving consent, is evidenced in writing, dated and signed, or otherwise marked by that person so as to indicate his or her consent.

28 Clinical Trials on Medicinal Products for Human Use Regulations 2004, Sch 1, Pt 3.

29 Courts have decided the same thing: see the Canadian case of *Halushka v University of Saskatchewan* (1965) 53 DLR (2d) 436.

30 The withholding of information from a patient in what is perceived by the doctor as the patient's own interests: see ch 4, 'Consent' para **[4.53]**.

31 Clinical Trials on Medicinal Products for Human Use Regulations 2004, Sch 1, Pt 4. 'Minor' is defined in the Regulations as a person under 16 years of age.

32 The Regulations are unclear as to whether the consent of one person with parental authority will suffice or whether the consent of every person with parental authority over the minor in question is required.

from staff with experience with minors, regarding the trial, its risks and its benefits[33] and the explicit wish of a minor who is capable of forming an opinion and assessing information given to him to refuse participation in, or to be withdrawn from, the clinical trial at any time must be considered by the investigator. No incentives or financial inducements can be given to the minor or to a person with parental responsibility for that minor, except provision for compensation in the event of injury or loss. Furthermore, the clinical trial must relate directly to a clinical condition from which the minor suffers or is of such a nature that it can only be carried out on minors and some direct benefit for the group of patients involved in the clinical trial is to be obtained from that trial. The clinical trial must be

- necessary to validate data obtained in other clinical trials involving persons able to give informed consent or by other research methods.
- impossible to conduct properly without using minors.
- designed to minimise pain, discomfort, fear and any other foreseeable risk in relation to the disease and the minor's stage of development.

Lastly, the risk threshold and the degree of distress have to be specially defined and constantly monitored and the interests of the patient always prevail over those of science and society.

Consent and mentally incapacitated adults

[17.18] Similar conditions and principles to those used for minors apply to the consent of mentally incapacitated adults to participation in clinical trials. The principal difference is that the role of parent is occupied in the case of an incapacitated adult by his legal representative. Other differences are that in the case of an incapacitated adult:

- there must be grounds for expecting that administering the medicinal product to be tested in the trial will produce a benefit to the subject outweighing the risks or produce no risk at all, and
- the clinical trial relates directly to a life-threatening or debilitating clinical condition from which the subject suffers.

Otherwise the conditions and principles are the same as those applicable to a minor.

HUMAN CELLS AND TISSUES

[17.19] We have observed elsewhere (see Ch 11) the recommendations of the Commission on Assisted Human Reproduction relating to the regulation of embryo creation and storage. Issues relating to the storage of tissue such as embryos, but also including substances such as stem cells and other human material are dealt with in the European Communities (Quality and Safety of Human Tissues and Cells) Regulations 2006.[34] These Regulations lay down standards of quality and safety for human tissues and cells intended for human applications, in order to ensure a high level of protection of

---

[33] See the discussion of the rights of minors to consent to medical treatment in Ch 4, 'Consent' para **[4.24]***ff.*

[34] SI 158/2006. These Regulations give effect to Directive 2004/23/EC of the European Parliament and of the Council of 31 March, 2004 (contd/)

human health. They apply to the donation, procurement, testing, processing, preservation, storage and distribution of human tissue and cells intended for human applications and of manufactured products derived from human tissue and cells intended for human applications.

Role of the IMB

[17.20] The Irish Medicines Board (IMB) has been designated as the competent authority for the purposes of these new directives.[35] As a result the IMB is obliged to authorise all sites carrying out any prescribed activities in accordance with the regulations and organise inspections and appropriate control measures to ensure that the requirements of the directives are complied with.

Tissue establishments

[17.21] The Regulations create 'tissue establishments', which are defined as 'a tissue bank or a unit of a hospital or another body where activities of donation, procurement,[36] testing, processing, preservation, storage or distribution of human tissues and cells are undertaken.' These Tissue Establishments are required to:

- comply with the requirements laid down in European Communities (Quality and Safety of Human Tissues and Cells) Regulations 2006 and other relevant Regulations;

- apply to the IMB for authorisation pursuant to Regulation 6 of the 2006 Regulations;

- undergo inspections by the IMB in order to obtain authorisation and regular inspections thereafter;

- notify the IMB of any substantial changes they intend to make in the prescribed activities they undertake;

---

[34] (\contd) setting standards of quality and safety for the donation, procurement, testing, processing, preservation, storage and distribution of human tissues and cells and Commission Directive 2006/17/EC of 8 February, 2006 implementing Directive 2004/23/EC of the European Parliament and of the Council as regards certain technical requirements for the donation, procurement and testing of human tissues and cells. See also Commission Directive 2006/86/EC, setting out the traceability requirements, notification of serious adverse reactions and events and certain technical requirements for the coding, processing, preservation, storage and distribution of human tissues and cells.

[35] See IMB, *Guidance on the regulatory requirements for the procurement, in the Republic of Ireland, of human tissues and cells intended for human application* (Dublin, 2007); available for download from http://www.imb.ie/publication.asp?todo=showpublication&id=390 (last accessed October 2007).

[36] 'Procurement' is defined as 'a process by which tissue or cells are made available'; a 'procurement organisation' is a health care establishment or a unit of a hospital or another body that undertakes the procurement of human tissues and cells and that may not be authorised as a tissue establishment. Activities specifically listed by the Irish Medicines Boards as coming within the rubric of the term 'procurement' in the legislation include the collection of umbilical cord stem cells or the collection of skin cells for cosmetic uses.

- keep a record of their activities, including the types and quantities of tissues and/or cells procured, tested, preserved, processed, stored and distributed or otherwise disposed of, and on the origin and destination of the tissues and cells intended for human applications;[37]

- submit an annual report on these activities to the IMB;

- notify the IMB of, and provide the IMB with a report analysing the cause and ensuing outcome of—

  (a) any serious adverse events and reactions, which may influence the quality and safety of tissues and cells, and

  (b) any serious adverse reactions observed during or after clinical applications, which may be linked to the quality and safety of tissue and cells.

Regulation of procurement of human tissue and cells

[17.22] Regulation of the procurement of human tissues and cells depends on where the tissue processing establishment is located. Where a tissue procurement site is supplying a tissue establishment in the Republic of Ireland, the act of procurement will be regulated through the inspection and authorisation of the Irish tissue establishment which processes the tissue or cells. The procurement site does not need to be independently authorised but will be listed as a 'site of procurement' on the tissue establishment's authorisation and will be inspected as part of the inspection of that tissue establishment. Where a tissue procurement site is supplying a tissue establishment outside the Republic of Ireland, that procurement site will be required to apply directly to the IMB for authorisation.

[17.23] In order for the procurement of human tissues and cells to be authorised by the IMB:

- staff carrying out the procurement of human tissues and cells must be fully and appropriately trained.[38]

- the tissue establishment or procurement organisation must have written agreements with the staff or clinical teams responsible for donor selection,[39] specifying the procedures to be followed to assure compliance with the selection criteria for donors.

- the tissue establishment or procurement organisation must have written agreements with the staff or clinical teams responsible for tissue/cell procurement,[40] specifying the type(s) of tissues and/or cells and/or samples for testing, to be procured and the protocols to be followed.

---

[37] A 'human application' is 'the use of tissues or cells on or in a recipient and extracorporal applications'.

[38] Persons who have successfully completed a training programme specified by a clinical team specialising in the tissues and cells to be procured or a tissue establishment authorised for procurement.

[39] Unless they are employed by the same organisation or establishment.

[40] Unless they are employed by the same organisation or establishment.

> – there must be standard operating procedures (SOPs) for the verification of:
>
> > o donor identity; [41]
> >
> > o the details of donor or donor family consent or authorisation;
> >
> > o the assessment of the selection criteria for donors;
> >
> > o the assessment of the laboratory tests required for donors;
> >
> > o procedures for procurement.[42]
>
> – procurement must take place in appropriate facilities, following procedures that minimise bacterial or other contamination of procured tissues and cells.[43]
>
> – procurement of tissues and cells from living donors shall take place in an environment that ensures their health, safety and privacy.
>
> – where appropriate, the staff and equipment necessary for body reconstruction of deceased donors shall be provided and such reconstruction must be completed effectively.

EMBRYONIC STEM CELLS AND CLONING

[17.24] Stem cells are cells which have the potential to become any required body cell (pluripotential cells) if stimulated appropriately and they are potentially a rich source of cells that may be utilised for the treatment of certain medical conditions. There are three widely recognised categories of stem cell:[44]

> – embryonic stem cells, which are found in early human embryos which can be created by IVF, by cloning techniques or from already existing cell lines;
>
> – embryonic germ cells, which are found in the primitive reproductive organs of the developing foetus and can be obtained from cadaveric foetal tissue;

---

[41] A unique identifying code shall be allocated to the donor and the donated tissues and cells, during the procurement or at the tissue establishment ensuring proper identification of the donor and traceability of all donated material. The coded data shall be entered onto a register provided for the purpose. Donor documentation shall be maintained in accordance with point 1.4 of Annex IV of Directive 2006/17/EC.

[42] There must also be SOPs for packaging, labelling and transportation of the tissues and cells to the point of arrival at the tissue establishment or, in case of direct distribution of tissues and cells, to the clinical team responsible for their application or in the case of tissue/ cell samples, to the laboratory for testing.

[43] Furthermore, procurement materials and equipment shall be managed in accordance with the standards and specifications (laid down in 2006/17/EC, Annex IV section 1.3) and with due regard to relevant national and international Regulations, standards and guidelines covering the sterilisation of medicines, medical devices and surgical instruments. Also, sterile, single-use instruments and collection devices shall be used for tissue and cell procurement unless the use of sterilised reusable instruments is justified.

[44] Stem cells are cells that can divide to produce either cells like themselves (self-renewal), or cells of one or several specific differentiated types. Stem cells are not yet fully differentiated and therefore can reconstitute one or several types of tissues. Those that have the potential to form many different types of tissue are 'pluripotent' cells. There remains some dispute about the precise taxonomy of stem cells.

—   adult stem cells, which can be obtained from adult tissues, such as the bone marrow, brain, intestine and blood cells.

[17.25] It is embryonic stem cells that have the greatest capacity to be encouraged to develop into other forms of cells and therefore have the greatest potential in the area of treatment. The creation of embryos through cloning is the mechanism that is currently thought to offer the best opportunity for deriving embryonic stem cells. Although this text is not concerned with the scientific minutiae of stem cell research, it is appropriate to point out that there are two types of cloning:[45]

—   *Therapeutic cloning*

A human embryo is created by somatic cell nuclear transfer (SCNT)[46] in order to obtain embryonic stem cells for research or therapeutic purposes. If the somatic cell is supplied by a patient, any embryonic stem cells isolated from the cloned embryo could be used to make cells and tissue that would be compatible with the patient's immune system because they have the same genetic material. In this way, therapeutic cloning could allow 'customised' embryonic stem cells to be generated thus avoiding, for example, problems of rejection.[47]

—   *Reproductive cloning*

An embryo created by (SCNT) is implanted into a womb in the hope of producing a viable foetus and bringing it to term. The clone would be a near identical genetic copy of the adult whose somatic cell nucleus was used for cloning.

[17.26] The distinction between reproductive and therapeutic cloning is an important one and the world's governments have taken a firm stance against reproductive cloning insofar as it has the potential to produce cloned humans.[48] In the UK, such cloning as is

---

[45]   An excellent guide to the basic of stem cells was published by the Irish Council for Bioethics, *Stem Cell Information Leaflet*, (2007). The definitions of therapeutic and reproductive cloning are taken from that publication.

[46]   SCNT is the 'scientific name' for cloning: 'the nucleus (where the genetic material is carried) of a somatic cell (any cell of the body except for sperm and egg cells) is injected, or transplanted, into an egg that has had its nucleus removed. The resulting embryo is a near identical match to the individual or animal that the original somatic cell was taken from. SCNT has been used by scientists to clone animals for a number of years, the most famous example being Dolly the sheep. Recently, scientists have used cloning to fuse human somatic cells with animal eggs. The resulting embryos are known as human-animal hybrids. Cloning requires a large supply of human eggs, and their production and isolation involves physical risks for the women donors. It is hoped that by creating hybrid embryos, scientists could avoid using eggs from women to produce embryos for stem cell research' – Irish Council for Bioethics, *Stem Cell Information Leaflet*, (2007), p 3.

[47]   It is also sometime argued that therapeutic cloning can also enable scientists ultimately to learn about the mechanisms of reprogramming adult cells to behave like embryonic stem cells again. If this line of research were successful, adult cells reprogramming would make it unnecessary to resort to using embryos to derive stem cells.

[48]   Human reproductive cloning is banned in the United Kingdom: the terms of the Human Reproductive Cloning Act 2001 mean that nobody in the UK is allowed to use cell nuclear replacement, or any other technique, to create a child. (contd/)

permitted is regulated by the Human Fertilisation and Embryology Authority (HFEA),[49] which has the power to license[50] defined centres to carry out defined activities.[51] Ireland has not expressly banned cloning, whether therapeutic or reproductive. Research on adult stem cells is legal in Ireland and is currently being conducted in a number of locations. In some cases, this research has been publicly funded. The legal situation regarding embryonic stem cell research in Ireland is less well defined and only research using embryonic stem cells from animals is currently carried out in Ireland.[52] Ireland does not have specific legislation dealing with stem cell research or research on embryos produced, but not used, during IVF treatment.[53] The Medical Council states that 'the creation of new forms of life for experimental purposes or the deliberate and intentional destruction of in-vitro human life already formed is professional misconduct'[54] and further that 'any fertilised ovum must be used for normal implantation and must not be deliberately destroyed.'[55]

[17.27] The question of whether embryonic cells can be produced solely for the purposes of research is the area of cloning that most exercises the minds of the lawyer and the ethicist at the present stage of the cloning debate. The ethical debate involves resolving the fact on the one hand that pre-pregnancy life will be created (and ultimately destroyed) for the purposes of research and on the other hand that the resulting research could have huge benefits for humankind. The question of the creation of the embryo is in particular coloured by the questions over whether the embryo constitutes a 'life': if it does, then what are its rights and – if it has any rights – how can they be reconciled with

---

[48] (\contd) There are some who argue that reproductive cloning could be carefully regulated rather than prohibited: see Harris, '"Goodbye Dolly?" – The Ethics of Human Cloning' (1997) 23 *J of Med Ethics* 353. For a thorough analysis of the potential 'harms' of human cloning (and whether in fact they constitute reasons to ban cloning), see Robertson, 'Liberty, Identity and Human Cloning' (1998) 76 Texas LR 1371, cited at length in Kennedy & Grubb, *Medical Law* (4th edn, Butterworths, London, 2000) pp 1251–1265. A more sceptical view can be found in Holm, 'The Ethical Case against Stem Cell Research' (2003) 12 *Cambridge Quarterly of Healthcare Ethics* 372–83.

[49] See the discussion of the HFEA in Ch 11 *The Extremes of Life I: The Beginning*, para **[11.33]***ff.*

[50] The power of the HFEA to regulate cloning was challenged (and upheld) in *Regina (on the application of Quintavalle) v Secretary of State for Health* [2003] UKHL 13, [2003] 2 All ER 113.

[51] In 2007, the HFEA approved in principle the carrying out of 'hybrid' cloning, which is the insertion of a human nucleus into the cytoplasm of an animal cell from which the animal nucleus has been removed: see http://www.hfea.gov.uk/en/1581.html (last accessed October 2007).

[52] Irish Council for Bioethics, *Stem Cell Information Leaflet*, (2007), p 5.

[53] See the discussion in Ch 11 *The Extremes of Life I: The Beginning*, para **[11.23]***ff.*

[54] Medical Council, *Guide to Ethical Conduct and Behaviour* (6th edn, 2004), para 24.1.

[55] Medical Council, *Guide to Ethical Conduct and Behaviour* (6th edn, 2004), para 24.5. Note that these proscriptions apply only to doctors and do not apply to non-medically qualified scientific personnel. It is also not clear the extent to which this ethical guidance is consistent with the decision of the High Court in *MR v TR, Anthony Walsh, David Walsh and the Sims Clinic* [2006] IEHC 359, which held that frozen, unimplanted embryos were not 'unborn' within the meaning of Art 40.3.3° of the Irish Constitution.

the way in which the embryo is used? At the other extreme is the opinion that an embryo is no more than a clump of cells. In general, those considering the matter from a legislative viewpoint have tended to adopt an 'intermediate position that a human embryo has a special status as a potential human being, but is not of the same status as a living child or adult.'[56] Respect for the special status (the 'rights') of the embryo is weighted against the benefit to be obtained from violating any right to life the embryo possesses.

The potential ingredients of stem cell legislation[57]

[17.28] This intermediate position is being adopted by many countries and is further modified by a determination to avoid creating embryos purely for research purposes and to completely restrict the use of embryos for reproductive cloning. Elements that statutory approaches to cloning technologies cloning tend to share include:[58]

  - an absolute ban on the cloning of humans for reproductive purposes;[59]

  - a time limit from fertilisation beyond which the embryos cannot be used for research; [60]

  - an insistence that there must be strong scientific merit in, and no alternative to, any decision to permit the use of embryonic stem cells for the purpose of research. Decisions must be made on a case-by-case basis by an approved statutory body (in the UK, the HFEA) to whom those requiring a licence for research must apply;

---

[56] 'Ethical, Legal and Social Issues in Human Stem Cell Research, Reproductive and Therapeutic Cloning – A Report from the Bioethics Advisory Committee, Singapore (2002) 24.

[57] For a discussion of many of the issues arising see Holm, 'Going to the Roots of the Stem Cell Controversy' (2002) 16 *Bioethics* 493–507.

[58] See the Opinion of the European Group on Ethics in Science and New Technologies to the European Commission, No 15, 14 November 2000, *Ethical Aspects of Human Stem Cell Research and Use*. This opinion in particular cautions against rushing headlong into the use of embryonic stem cells for research that, regardless of its promise, remains largely speculative: see para 2.7.

[59] For example the UK Human Reproductive Cloning Act 2001; see also the EU Charter of Fundamental Rights (2000): Art 3, Ch 1 prohibits the reproductive cloning of human beings. See also the Council of Europe Protocol on the Prohibition of Cloning Human Beings, which came into force in March 2001. The 'protocol' is added to the Convention on Human Rights and Biomedicine and bans 'any intervention seeking to create a human being genetically identical to another human being, whether living or dead'. The Protocol leaves it to countries' domestic law to define the scope of the term 'human being'. The protocol has not been ratified by Ireland.

[60] In the UK, the time limit is 14 days:Human Fertilisation and Embryology Act 1990, s 13. The 14-day timeline is derived from the work of the Warnock Committee in the UK (discussed in Warnock, 'Experimentation on human embryos and fetuses' in Kuhse and Singer, *A Companion to Bioethics* (Blackwell, 1998), 390–6) which reasoned that the primitive streak (the precursor and first indication of the developing spinal cord) was 'one reference point in the development of the human individual'.

–   expressly limiting the categories of purpose for which it is lawful to license embryos; [61]

–   embryonic stem cells should only be used where adult and embryonic germ cells are not satisfactory. The first ports of call for embryonic stem cells, if required, should be:

o   existing stem cell lines held in laboratories,

o   surplus embryos originally created for purposes of medically assisted reproduction but not used for that purpose.

It is thought preferable by many authorities to use such embryos for research rather than simply destroying them.

–   only if such routes are not productive will the use of embryos created through therapeutic cloning for research purposes be considered;[62]

–   commercial trade in embryonic material is typically prohibited, as is the creation of cloned embryonic material for the purposes of producing human life;[63]

–   fully informed consent to the provision and use of material for the purpose of stem cell cloning a research must be obtained.

GENETICS AND THE USE OF GENETIC MATERIAL

[17.29] The use of genetic material in medical research is increasingly commonplace and the possibility looms ever larger that human and other genetic material may yet have

---

[61]   See Human Fertilisation and Embryology Act 1990, Sch 2(3): 'A licence…cannot authorise any activity unless it appears to the Authority to be necessary or desirable for the purpose of—

(a)   promoting advances in the treatment of infertility,

(b)   increasing knowledge about the causes of congenital disease,

(c)   increasing knowledge about the causes of miscarriages,

(d)   developing more effective techniques of contraception, or

(e)   developing methods for detecting the presence of gene or chromosome abnormalities in embryos before implantation, or for such other purposes as may be specified in regulations.'

The Act also states that no licence can be granted unless the use of the embryos is necessary for the research. The Human Fertilisation and Embryology (Research Purposes) Regulations 2003 added further permitted purposes: (a) increasing knowledge about the development of embryos, (b) increasing knowledge about serious disease, (c) enabling any such knowledge to be applied in developing treatments for serious disease.

[62]   See House of Lords Stem Cell Research Committee, *Stem Cell Report* (2002), para 4.28. This report highlights that situations in which embryos might be created for the purpose of research might be where the act of fertilisation itself is what is under study, for example examining the fertilisation of eggs that have been frozen or refining techniques such as intra-cytoplasmic sperm injection.

[63]   Directive 98/44/EC on the legal protection of biotechnological inventions stipulates that 'processes for cloning human beings' and 'uses of human embryos for industrial or commercial purposes… shall be considered unpatentable'.

an enormous role to play in the future of medical diagnosis and treatment. The issues that gene research and therapy raise are ones that legal and ethical opinion has begun to face only in recent years.[64] In some ways, the principles of DNA-related law and ethics are uncomplicated: issues of consent and information and patient autonomy remain, or should remain, at the forefront of all considerations and the rules for consent in the fields of genetics or assisted reproduction are broadly no different from the rules in other areas of clinical practice. Problems most starkly arise in the practice rather than the principles of DNA research work.

[17.30] There are two facets to DNA research. In the first place there is the harvesting of genetic material for specific directed research, such as studies of the genetic basis for cardiovascular disease. But secondly and perhaps more importantly there is the question of storage and later research on that genetic material in circumstances where that later use does not tally with the initial immediate purpose for which it was given. Later research, with new techniques and researchers armed with new knowledge, may disclose information about genetic disorders or predispositions afflicting the original donor: should the donor be told? The genetic material may subsequently turn out to have commercial value in treatment or further research: should the original donor come in for a cut of any profits? We look at these two questions below.[65]

The process of harvesting, storing and using genetic material will be done in one of several ways:

–   'unlinked': where there is no longer any identifying link between the donor and the sample

–   'coded': where the genetic material is anonymised and no longer directly linked to the original donor but the donor may nonetheless be identified through the code system

–   'linked', where the original donor continues to be linked or identified directly with the sample

Consent issues

[17.31] Issues of consent in the field of genetics are, as we have noted, especially complex when a patient donates his genetic material not merely for an immediate research purpose, but also for later and often unspecified research use. If consent is given now, but the material may later be used for purposes not yet invented or thought of, then how are those future circumstances to be catered for? The UK Genetics Commission has observed that:

---

[64]   Note the provision in the Clinical Trials on Medicinal Products for Human Use Regulations 2004, reg 16, whereby the Irish Medicines Board is obliged to refuse authorisation to any application for a trial utilising gene therapy if the use of gene therapy products in that trial would result in modifications to any subject's germ line genetic identity.

[65]   Many of the issues raised by genetics in clinical practice have been identified and summarised by the Health Research Board: Sheikh A., *Genetic Research and Human Biological Samples – The Legal and Ethical Considerations* (Health Research Board, 2002). Available for download from the Health Research Board website at www.hrb.ie/storage/researchfunding/fundingpolicies/geneticresearch.pdf (last accessed, October 2007).

'Genetic research is subject to the same standards as any other branch of medical research in that informed consent is required from the donor at the time a sample is obtained.'[66]

The Nuffield Council on Bioethics recognises that genetic material that is analysed for the presence of diseases may disclose the presence either of the particular disease being researched or of other conditions. The question then is whether information gleaned from the sample should be relayed back to the original donor.

'To provide an individual with information from a research study about gene mutations which they might or might not carry and which, at the time samples and information were collected, could not have been foreseen, could be to give them information they would choose not to have, and/or information for which they or other members of the family are not prepared or cannot understand in terms of its implications.'[67]

[17.32] The Working Party of the Nuffield Council therefore makes the following recommendations on donor consent to the taking of genetic material:[68]

– As a general rule, those who consent to take part in research should be told that individual information derived from analysis of their DNA will not be given to them. This is especially true where any information on genetic predisposition suggests a weak susceptibility to illness.[69]

– In any research study that could yield genetic information which is clinically relevant to a research participant and/or their relatives, consent to that research should make it clear whether or not such information will be made available. If it is to be made available, then before consenting to the research an individual should receive genetic counselling. They should also give written consent to make clear whether they wish a designated medical adviser to receive any relevant information or whether they would prefer to receive such information themselves.

[17.33] In view of the potentially complex uses of genetic material after initial donation, the US National Bioethics Advisory Committee has identified that consent forms may need to consider offering the donor all or any of the following options:

(a) refusing use of their biological materials in research,

(b) permitting only unidentified or unlinked use of their biological materials in research,

(c) permitting coded or identified use of their biological materials for one particular study only, with no further contact permitted to ask for permission to do further studies,

---

[66] UK Human Genetics Commission. *Whose Hands on your Genes? – A discussion document on the storage, protection and use of personal genetic information* (2001) 23.

[67] Nuffield Council on Bioethics, *Report on Mental Disorders and Genetics: The Ethical Context* (1998), para 7.23. Available for download: www.nuffieldbioethics.org/go/screen/ourwork/mentaldisorders/introduction (last accessed October 2007).

[68] Ibid, para 7.24*ff.*

[69] And presumably it is less true where the genetic information provides extremely strong evidence of a very serious condition that would benefit from the earliest possible intervention.

(d)   permitting coded or identified use of their biological materials for one particular study only, with further contact permitted to ask for permission to do further studies,

(e)   permitting coded or identified use of their biological materials for any study relating to the condition for which the sample was originally collected, with further contact allowed to seek permission for other types of studies, or

(f)   an open-ended consent permitting use of their biological materials in any form for any kind of future study.[70]

Essentially then, there are two limbs to patient consent for the use of genetic information. First is consent to the use of the research for which the sample has be taken and second is consent to the storage and future use of the genetic material.[71] If a person consents only to the first, then the material should subsequently be destroyed and only if specific consent has been given to storage and future use can that be done. Patients should also have the opportunity to change their minds where necessary.[72] If consent is absent, then the material cannot be used.

Financial considerations

[17.34] One difficult area of genetic research is the fact that it is possible to patent (and therefore effectively to own) genetic material that has been subject to research and development.[73] Patients and researchers need to be clear of the limits and consequences of ownership of genetic material. The Medical Research Council made the point in a report on genetic research:

> 'Research participants may be particularly sensitive to the idea of a company or an individual making a profit out of the tissue that they have freely donated. It is important that research participants are made aware of the potential benefits of allowing commercial access, and that the role of any one individual's sample in the generation of future profits is likely to be minimal as well as impossible to quantify. Given the possible sensitivities, it

---

[70] National Bioethics Advisory Commission (NBAC). *Research Involving Human Biological Materials: Ethical Issues and Policy Guidance* (1999), Recommendation 9.

[71] The fact that consent is required for use of a sample beyond the original purpose for which it was taken was identified in *Moore v Regents of the University of California* (1990) 793 P 2d 479 (Cal Sup Ct). Here a doctor took samples from a patient with a hairy cell leukaemia and entered into an arrangement (without the express consent of the patient) with a pharmaceutical company to clone and patent those cells. This was a breach of the doctor's duty to obtain consent.

[72] British Medical Association, *Consent Tool Kit* (BMA Books, 2001), 9: 'Consent should be considered as a process, not an event, and it is important that there is continuing discussion to reflect the evolving nature of treatment.'

[73] See the EU Directive on the Legal Protection of Biotechnological Inventions. To comply with the Directive, a person from whose body the material used for an invention is taken must have had an opportunity of expressing free and informed consent (Recital 26). The directive became law in Ireland with the European Communities (Legal Protection of Biotechnological Inventions) Regulations 2000 (SI 247/2000). See also: Sheikh, A. 'Owning' Life: New Frontiers in Patent Law, Genetics and Biotechnology' (1999) 5 *Medico-Legal Journal of Ireland* 1: 23 and Nuffield Council on Bioethics, *The Ethics of Patenting DNA* (London, 2002).

is essential that research participants are made aware that their sample or products derived from it may be used by the commercial sector, and that they will not be entitled to a share of any profits that might ensue.'[74]

The reality then is that a patient involved in genetic research should be made aware that legally they will have no right to any share in profits that may emerge, but nonetheless, their consent to the use of their genetic material in the commercial environment should be sought.

---

[74] Medical Research Council, *Human tissue and biological samples for use in research Operational and Ethical Guidelines* (2001). Para 4.2: available for download from http://www.mrc.ac.uk/Utilities/Documentrecord/index.htm?d=MRC002420 (last accessed October 2007).

Appendix I

An Introduction to the Irish Legal System

INTRODUCTION

[A.01] The Irish legal system is a blend, in part at least, of everything from the mediaeval to the ultra-modern. Some laws remain in force that were originally enacted in the sixteenth and seventeenth centuries (including fundamental rules relating to the buying and selling of property) while, in more modern times, the complexities of social structures, technology, commerce and international relations are such that new laws and other legal rules, particularly those derived from Ireland's membership of the EU, are enacted on an almost daily basis. The law of Ireland is susceptible to any number of influences that shape its form and overall direction. Irish law is most fundamentally underpinned by our written Constitution, but law also arises from enactments of the Oireachtas, from the decisions of Irish courts and, perhaps most significantly of all in recent years, from Europe. The different types of law can be confusing, even to lawyers, but some generalisations can be made and this appendix attempts to distil some of those generalisations for the non-legal reader. It does not attempt to be an exhaustive guide to Irish law, but simply to give a flavour of its overall structure and influences.[1]

LEGAL SYSTEMS

[A.02] Ireland operates under a common law system, which is a legal heritage that comes with our colonial past and one shared with countries such as Australia, Canada and the United States. There are other countries that follow what is often called a civil law or codified system. We look at the two systems below.

The common law system

[A.03] Common Law does not exist in a single book. Rather it is a broad descriptive term with two generally accepted meanings, one broad and one more constrained but both of which combine to give us the legal systems that we operate under.

[A.04] The narrower definition of the term 'common law' refers to the way in which the gradual accumulation of the experience of the courts over the years, documented in the recorded decisions handed down by the courts, has established binding legal rules. Long before there was the amount of legislation that there is today, most areas of legal uncertainty were policed by the courts. With each decision, a little more certainty was created and that decision became a precedent for later decisions. This system of common law precedent continues today: if a case comes before a court, the court can look back to any earlier decisions concerning similar facts and circumstances and it will be guided by

---

[1] For a more exhaustive review, see generally Byrne and McCutcheon, *The Irish Legal System* (5th edn, Tottel Publishing, 2001).

those decisions if it is appropriate to be so guided. These common law rules represent the way in which the courts have viewed society's disputes over the years and their attempts to solve them have become a source of legal certainty. In general, if the decision has previously been made by a higher court, then a lower court must follow the earlier decision, or precedent, of the higher court. Contradictions or qualifications of earlier decisions will normally only be made by a court of equal or higher standing to the court that created the earlier precedent.[2] Courts will typically only depart from earlier precedent if a decision they are considering is different in an important way from the previous decision or if to follow the previous decision would be unreasonable or unjust.[3] So, if a District Court is faced with a case very similar to one which the Supreme Court (see para **[A.23]** below for a discussion of the hierarchy of the courts) has previously decided, it would be a brave District Justice indeed who ploughed the lonely furrow of disagreeing with the Supreme Court's precedent unless there were exceptional circumstances that justified her doing so. Conversely, the Supreme Court will be free to revise or 'distinguish' (the term used where there are particular aspects of two or more superficially similar cases that permit them to be treated differently) any domestic court's earlier decision.

[A.05] The second and broader definition of the term 'common law' refers to the way in which this judge-made, precedent-based law exists alongside written legislation and, together with that statue law, forms an overarching system of legal rule. The decisions of courts continue to form a set of legal rules, but only when the decision involves an area of the law not covered by legislation or involves an area of legislation that is unclear and requires clarification by the courts.

Example A.1

There is very little legislation on negligence in Ireland. Accordingly, it has fallen to the courts to decide the common law rules on what constitutes negligence.[4] However, if the government were to introduce a law that defined clinical negligence and set out rules for compensation, then that new law would replace the latitude of the courts. Nonetheless, the courts would retain a role in interpreting the legislation. Examples of the role of the courts being circumscribed by law include the Statute of Limitations, which sets strict time limits within which a legal action may be brought, although leaving to the courts certain issues of interpretation, such as the 'date of discoverability' of an injury.[5]

In practical terms a common law system means that the courts and the elected lawmakers operate in tandem to set out and administer law: the Oireachtas makes law and the courts interpret that law in the light of the facts of cases before it and in the light

---

[2] Although there are exceptions: in *Geoghegan v Harris* [2000] 3 IR 536, the High Court significantly re-assessed the decisions of the Supreme Court in *Walsh v Family Planning Services* [1992] 1 IR 496 and *Bolton v Blackrock Clinic* (20 December 1994, unreported) SC – see para **[4.56]**.

[3] See para **[6.05]**: the case of *Donoghue v Stevenson* [1932] AC 562 revolutionised the law of negligence because one of the judges was prepared to depart from the precedents that said that negligence could not exist where there was not a contract.

[4] Discussed generally in ch 6.

[5] See Ch 6 'Clinical Negligence', para **[6.75]***ff.*

of any ambiguities created by the legislation. Where there is no applicable government-made law or where statutes require interpretation, the courts apply the 'common law' body of decisions made by previous courts. The common law system has been described by one English judge as 'common sense under a wig'.

[A.06] There is one especially useful consequence of the fact that common law systems exist in different countries, which is that common law countries tend to share broadly similar cultural and social norms expressed through similar written laws and analogous traditions of legal decision-making. As a result, the courts of common law jurisdictions tend to interpret those written laws and earlier decisions in a manner with which a court in Ireland can identify and that, using principles and logic, can be applied to the Irish setting. Many enlightened decisions in various areas of law have been made first in one jurisdiction before spreading – sometimes unchanged, sometimes modified – to some or all other common law countries.[6] If an issue is being tried before an Irish court and no Irish law (government- or judge-made) has ever considered the matter, the court may therefore look to similar decisions made in other common law jurisdictions (such as England or Australia) and be informed, persuaded or guided by such decisions, although of course an Irish court is never bound by the decisions of courts outside the jurisdiction, however august they may be. For readers of this book, one practical consequence of this approach is that frequent references are made throughout the text to cases decided in other countries. These cases are not always indicative of the law in Ireland but they often point to the way that such cases might be decided in Ireland or to an alternative point of view that an Irish court might, or should, consider when approaching or re-visiting a particular issue.

Quick Reference Guide A.1

The common law system

> ❖ Common law legal systems involve a combination of two elements:
>
> > o The first is the 'common law' itself – the body of decisions made by courts and forming precedents on which later courts can base their decisions when faced with similar facts and circumstances.
> >
> > o The second element is the existence of a legislature that can introduce statute laws alongside the common law courts. In areas of human life where there are no statute laws, the courts continue to base their decisions on the common law, but where there are statute laws, the courts' role changes to one of application and interpretation of those laws.
>
> ❖ Most countries that were hosts to English influence during their history have common law systems, including the USA, Canada and Australia.
>
> ❖ Decisions made in the courts of other common law countries can sometimes be helpful to courts in Ireland when they are considering matters that have not previously come before Irish courts.

---

[6]   Examples include the 'patient centred' approach to information disclosure in consent: see Ch 4 'Consent', para **[4.48]***ff.*

The civil law system

[A.07] A contrasting system used in many of our European neighbours is the civil law system (which should not be confused with the more restrictive term 'civil law' that is sometimes used in Ireland to refer to private legal disputes – see para **[A.20]** below). At the risk of gross over-simplification, a Civil Law system can be taken to describe writing a legal code of rules so compendious that it hopes to deal with every eventuality that may arise in the field of human intercourse. Judges then apply this formal, and hopefully exhaustive, set of rules to any dispute that comes before them. In essence then, unlike common law, which takes its inspiration from written legislation or the decisions of the courts or both together, civil law has only one principal source, namely the written code. Previous decisions made by similar courts in similar circumstances are sometimes used in the civil law systems of nations such as France and Germany, but to a far smaller degree than in the common law world.

THE MECHANISMS OF LAW

[A.08] The law of any land, whether a common law country such as Ireland or a civil law nation such as the Netherlands, has a number of engines creating law. In Ireland there are a number of sources of law creation and application. A fundamental source is the Constitution, the set of rules with which all other laws and all legal conduct must conform, although its significance is in some measure limited by the consequences of Ireland's European obligations (see **[A.35]***ff*). The Constitution is the basic charter of the State and any rule or law that conflicts with it is not valid. Within the constraints of the Constitution, the courts and the legislature then operate side by side to make or interpret law as appropriate. Above the national level, European commitments mean that rules can be made for Ireland by the EU or judgments handed down by the European Court of Justice or the European Court of Human Rights that have the force of law throughout Ireland. Irish lawmakers and Irish courts are subservient to and bound by the decisions made by the courts and lawmakers of the European Union. We will look at each of these driving forces in turn.

Quick Reference Guide A.2

The Constitution

❖ The Constitution is a blueprint for the operation of the Irish State. The present Constitution dates from 1937.

❖ Any law or conduct that is incompatible with the Constitution will be struck down by the courts. The President can refer any new Bill (the precursor to an Act of the Oireachtas) to the Supreme Court so that the court can gauge its constitutionality.

❖ The Constitution guarantees a number of rights to citizens. Some are explicitly expressed in the Constitution, while others have been implied by the courts – the 'unenumerated' rights.

❖ The Constitution separates powers and gives them to different bodies: only judges may decide the law, only the legislature may make the law and only the government may run the country.

❖ The Constitution can be changed by referendum and any law or act can be challenged regarding its constitutionality by means of judicial review.

The Constitution

[A.09] In a manner of speaking, the Constitution is a blueprint for the running of the Irish State and a working knowledge of the Constitution goes a long way towards outlining how Ireland operates in the legal sense. The Constitution is the supreme benchmark for Irish law, so that if a law or activity is unconstitutional, it is not valid. Only the two highest courts in the land – the High Court and Supreme Court – can take decisions regarding the Constitution, including deciding whether a particular activity or law is unconstitutional or determining the meaning of a particular section of the Constitution. No person or is immune from the provisions of the Constitution and that includes the courts and the State itself.

[A.10] The first Irish Constitution was born when the State became independent in 1922, but in 1937 a newer Constitution of Ireland, Bunreacht na hÉireann, was introduced and it continues in force to this day. The Constitution lays down the manner in which the country is to be run, delineating and delimiting the structures and role of Government, the manner in which elections are to be carried out, as well as the roles of judges and the President. There are certain aspects of the Constitution that directly relate to the application of law to clinical practice, such as the competing rights of the mother and the unborn child. The Constitution both explicitly and tacitly circumscribes the rights of the individual citizen and by extension, therefore, it also limits the degree to which any individual or institution may impinge upon another's rights.

[A.11] Any law that is enacted by the Oireachtas must be compatible with the Constitution. Before the President signs an Act of the Oireachtas (which is a necessary precursor to it becoming law), she has the option to refer it to the Supreme Court, which can assess its constitutionality. Thus, the Regulation of Information (Services Outside the State for Termination of Pregnancies) Bill 1995[7] was referred to and found to be constitutional by the Supreme Court, while other legislation, such as The Matrimonial Home Bill 1993, was found to be repugnant to the Constitution because it violated the right to private property contained in the Constitution. If only one part of a law is unconstitutional, then, in certain circumstances, that unconstitutional part may alone be removed or set aside and the rest of the law permitted, so long as the severance of the offending portion does not make a nonsense of the law.

Express rights

[A.12] As we have mentioned, the Constitution guarantees to the citizen a number of rights, some expressly, some tacitly. The right to liberty is one example of an expressly guaranteed right; the Constitution adverts to the fact that 'No citizen shall be deprived of his personal liberty save in accordance with the law.'[8] This in turn automatically trammels the right, to take a clinical example, of a doctor to compulsorily detain an individual who has a psychiatric disorder unless she has followed a protocol laid down by law, in this case the Mental Health Act 2001.[9]

---

[7] See Ch 11, 'The Extremes of Life I: the beginning', para **[11.14]**.

[8] Art 40.4.1°. Other express rights include, among many, the right to a fair trial (Art 38.1), the right to own property (Art 43) and the right to express one's opinion subject to public order and morality (Art 40.6).

[9] The legal safeguards in place for the involuntary detention of those with psychiatric conditions are dealt with in Ch 10, 'Law and Mental Health'.

Implied or 'unenumerated' rights

[A.13] Furthermore, the courts over the years have recognised other rights that although not explicit in the Constitution can be inferred from the guarantee contained therein that the State will 'respect and, as far as practicable, by its laws defend and vindicate the personal rights of the citizen.'[10] Using this guarantee, the courts have 'found' rights in the Constitution that are not expressly listed in it: these are often known as the unenumerated rights. Unenumerated rights of the citizen that the courts have recognised and which have repercussions for clinical practice include:

- the right to bodily integrity;[11]
- the right to privacy;[12]
- the rights of the child;[13]
- the right to travel out of the State; and[14]
- the idea that the right to life includes a correlative right to die.[15]

None of these constitutional rights is absolute: they exist, to use the words of the Constitution itself, 'as far as is practicable' and where necessary one right may need to be limited in order to protect another more important right.

Separation of powers

[A.14] Another aspect of the Constitution that is of relevance to the practitioner in the disciplinary setting is the 'separation of powers' doctrine, which means that powers are distributed to the various organs of State and only those organs given a power under the Constitution may exercise that power. Accordingly, only the government (meaning the Cabinet) should run the country, only the legislature (meaning the Oireachtas) should make laws and only the courts should administer justice. One consequence of this is that only a judge may determine those legal matters that have far-reaching consequences for the citizen, such as the deprivation of a practitioner of her livelihood due to a punitive sanction imposed by a body such as the Medical Council. This is the fundamental reason why a decision of the Medical Council (or any similar disciplinary body with such powers) to suspend or strike off a medical practitioner for serious professional misconduct must be ratified by the High Court before it can take effect. The Medical Council (and other similar bodies), therefore, may hear a fitness to practise case and

---

10 Art 40.3.1°.
11 *Ryan v Attorney General* [1965] IR 294; decisions such as this provide the basis for the right to refuse treatment articulated in *Re a Ward of Court (withholding medical treatment) (No 2)* [1996] 2 IR 79. See Ch 4, 'Consent'.
12 *Kennedy v Ireland* [1987] IR 587; decisions such as this underpin the constitutional facet of the right to medical confidentiality. See Ch 3, 'Confidentiality and the Practitioner-Patient Relationship'.
13 *G v An Bord Uchtála* [1980] IR 32 and *PW v AW* (21 April 1980, unreported) HC for contrasting views of the rights of the child within a family. See also chapter 4 (in particular para **[4.24]***ff*) and Ch 7, The Practitioner and the Family.
14 *The State (M) v Attorney General* [1979] IR 73. See also Ch 11, 'The Extremes of Life I: the beginning'.
15 *Re A Ward of Court (withholding medical treatment) (No 2)* [1996] 2 IR 79.

make a recommendation, but only a judge may rule on the validity of any decision they make that affects the individual doctor's career.[16]

Changing and challenging the Constitution

[A.15] The Constitution is not a testament written in stone. It can be amended and has been on a great number of occasions. Some amendments have been necessitated by membership of European institutions, while other amendments were motivated by the attempt to secure peace in Northern Ireland. Of particular relevance to medical practice is the 14th Amendment, which in 1982 inserted Article 40.3.3° ostensibly to enshrine the right to life of the unborn child.[17] No authority but the people of Ireland can amend the Constitution. The Government is expressly prohibited by the terms of the Constitution itself from amending the Constitution without a popular vote: amendments to the Constitution are approved or rejected by referenda in which all Irish citizens over the age of 18 are entitled to vote.[18] An individual or institution may also approach the High Court and ask it to decide whether a particular decision or purported act is unconstitutional. This process is usually called judicial review and will often concern the decision of a public body, which includes the Medical Council, a Government Department and most of the Universities[19] (although not the Royal College of Surgeons in Ireland).[20]

The legislature

[A.16] The legislature is the Oireachtas, the collective term for the Dáil and the Seanad combined. It is the Oireachtas that generates the majority of legislation that has the force of law in Ireland. Legislation, or statute law, is essentially written law produced by a law-making body. Article 15 of the Constitution lays down the rule that only the Oireachtas may make laws, which are therefore usually called Acts of the Oireachtas or primary legislation. Laws that were enacted by the British Parliament for Ireland prior to independence in 1922 remain in force as long as they have not been expressly repealed or supplanted by a more modern law. Legislation also includes rules made by Ministers as a result of previous Acts of the Oireachtas. An Act will often bestow a power on a

---

[16] *Re Solicitors Act 1954* [1960] IR 239. In this case the Law Society, the solicitors' equivalent of the Medical Council, struck off two solicitors guilty of misconduct. The two solicitors argued successfully that this was the exercise of a far-reaching judicial power by a non-judicial body. Accordingly, when the Medical Practitioners Act 1978 was passed, it included the stipulation that all decisions of erasure and suspension affecting doctors had to be ratified by the High Court. In *M v Medical Council and Attorney General* [1984] IR 485, this approach was held to be legally sufficient. This approach is present in all statutes relating to clinical disciplinary procedures (except the Opticians Act 1956). See Ch 2.

[17] See Ch 11, The Extremes of Life I: the beginning, para **[11.05]***ff*.

[18] Arts 46 and 47.

[19] In *Flanagan v University College Dublin* [1988] IR 724, a student was accused by the college of plagiarism She sought judicial review of the college's actions, asking the court among other things to answer the question of whether her constitutional right to fair procedure had been infringed. The court held that it had been and overturned the decision of the college.

[20] RCSI has been traditionally regarded by the courts as a private body: *Rajah v Royal College of Surgeons in Ireland* [1994] 1 IR 384.

relevant Minister to take further decisions that are in keeping with the original act. The Misuse of Drugs Act 1977 gives the Minister for Health the power to amend the lists of various controlled drugs, a power that has been exercised on a number of occasions.[21] Secondary legislation, as it is sometimes called, is also used as the mechanism by which many European Union rules come to be included in Irish laws. These secondary rules are generally in the form of Statutory Instruments (SIs).

Passing legislation

[A.17] Legislation essentially tries to reduce rules of conduct to a fixed and written formula, and typically those rules are stated as precisely as possible. A statute comes into being through a stepwise process involving both houses of the Oireachtas and the President. A Bill is drawn up, containing the legislation that it is intended to enact. In theory, any Senator or TD can introduce such a Bill, but in practice, for the bulk of new legislation, it tends to be the Minister for the Department that oversees the area for which the legislation is being introduced. A Bill generally goes through five stages (see Table A.1), although there are exceptions.

Table A.1 – The stages by which a Bill becomes an Act

- First Stage: permission is sought from the House to circulate the Bill, drafted in outline form.

- Second Stage: a debate on the generality of the Bill in which its principal provisions are outlined. At this stage the Bill may be voted down but if it is not, matters progress towards the Bill becoming an Act of the Oireachtas.

- Third Stage: also called the Committee Stage. Once a Bill has reached this stage, it can no longer be voted down in its entirety and the debate turns to the individual sections of the Bill. The debate is often conducted, not by the whole house, but by a Special Committee, consisting of members of both the Dáil and Seanad in proportion to their parties' strength in the Oireachtas.

- Fourth Stage: the report on progress made in the Committee Stage, when amendments recommended by the Committee may be inserted into the legislation.

- Fifth Stage: essentially a formality and results in the final form of the Bill.

[A.18] One the Bill is passed by a vote of both Houses,[22] it is signed by the President, at which point it becomes an Act of the Oireachtas. The fact of the President having signed the Bill is published in *Iris Oifigiúil* (the Official Gazette of the Government). Before signing the bill, the President may, as already mentioned, use one of the few powers she is given under the Constitution[23] and send a Bill for scrutiny by the Supreme Court in order that they can assess whether the new Bill is constitutional. The fact of an Act being passed (and signed into law by the President) does not mean that the new statute automatically becomes law: many Acts of the Oireachtas contain a provision to the effect that the law (or sections of it) will come into force only on a day appointed by the

---

[21] The Misuse of Drugs (Amendment) Regulations 1993, for example, moved the sleeping tablet temazepam from schedule 4 to schedule 3 on foot of evidence that it had become a drug of abuse.

[22] Although there are circumstances in which legislation may be rushed through.

[23] Art 26.

Minister. So, the Mental Health Act 2001 was passed in 2001, but came into force in a stepwise fashion and was only fully 'commenced' in 2006.[24] A published Act will have a short title by which it will tend to be colloquially known, such as 'The Misuse of Drugs Act 1977' but it also has a long title.[25] The long title will tend to set out the broad parameters of the act and draw attention to any other Acts that the new Act is repealing or amending.

The courts

[A.19] The courts oversee the administration of Irish justice and arbitrate nearly all legal disputes in the State, especially those involving civil or criminal matters and the interpretation of legislation or the Constitution. Indeed, according to the Constitution, the courts are the only body empowered to make judicial determinations between parties that have legal differences, although in certain circumstances other 'quasi-judicial' bodies, such as the Employment Appeals Tribunal, may do so. Broadly speaking, there are two categories of legal case: criminal and civil. In general, this book is predominately concerned with civil legal cases, but it is important to understand the difference between the civil and criminal legal systems.

Criminal and civil law

[A.20] The phrase 'civil law' has a meaning in Ireland different from that imported by an exhaustive code of written law such as characterises the legal systems of countries like France or Germany (see para [A.07] above). In Ireland, the phrase is more usually used as an antithesis to 'criminal law', although the division between the two is not always a clear one. Criminal law is largely concerned with the rules laid down by society for the good of society as a whole. If these rules are broken, then society, represented in Ireland by the Director of Public Prosecutions, initiates criminal proceedings against the person accused of breaking the law. Murder, theft and drunk-driving would all constitute examples of criminal offences. Civil law is largely concerned with private disputes, whether between individuals or between companies or between companies and individuals. Claims for accidents in the workplace, legal action against a practitioner for negligence and divorce proceedings are all examples of civil legal actions. The key distinction between criminal and civil legal proceedings, and indeed the principal reason for the difference between them, lies in the consequences. A civil claim is usually for damages or for an injunction or some similar order.[26] A successful criminal prosecution, on the other hand, will often result in a fine (paid to the State) or, more pertinently, a term of imprisonment.

---

[24] The Mental Health Commission was established in 2002 (Mental Health Act, 2001 (Sections 1 to 5, 7, 31 to 55) (Commencement) Order, 2002 (SI 90/2002), a large part of the remainder of the Act followed on foot of the Mental Health Act 2001 (Commencement) Order 2006 (SI 411/2006).

[25] Which, in the case of the Misuse of Drugs Act, ran to a total of 98 words.

[26] A declaration that an offending party should cease what he is doing (for example, that he should stop extending his house onto my property or claiming to use my name to endorse a product).

Burden of proof

[A.21] Because the consequence of a criminal conviction can potentially be more serious than a finding of guilt in a civil matter, the 'burden of proof', that is the degree to which the person making the allegation has to prove that allegation, is far greater in a criminal case. In a criminal case, the charge, eg that X murdered Y, must be proved 'beyond all reasonable doubt'. In a civil case, the argument, eg that X was negligent in her medical treatment of Y, must be made out merely 'on the balance of probabilities'. The phrase 'beyond reasonable doubt' is one that many judges have had difficulty defining, but can be said to mean that the jury[27] must have no substantial worries that its decision to convict an accused person is the wrong one. On the other hand, the 'balance of probabilities' merely means 'more likely than not'. If it were the case that criminal cases were decided only on the balance of probabilities, the legal system would run the risk of jailing many innocent people and so, even at the risk of seeing some guilty people (that is to say those whose guilt cannot be proved beyond reasonable doubt) go free, the higher standard is imposed in all criminal cases.

[A.22] The fact that the fine or term of imprisonment is 'given' to the State rather than to the person affected by the criminal act is another distinction between criminal and civil matters. If a person wins damages in a civil case, then that person will generally receive the damages.

Example A.2

A good example of the way the different burdens of proof, and indeed the different consequences of civil and criminal law, operate was provided by the protracted saga of O.J. Simpson's prosecution for the murder of his ex-wife, Nicole Brown Simpson and her friend, Ron Goldman, in the 1990s. In a criminal court, he was acquitted of murder; the jury found that he had not been proved guilty beyond all reasonable doubt. However, the families of the victims brought a private civil case against Simpson. Again (under the US system) there was a jury but in this case, because it was a civil case, they had only to consider whether the case was proven on the balance of probabilities. Simpson was found guilty at the second hearing of 'willingly and wrongfully' causing the two deaths. Again, because it was a civil case, he could not be jailed, but was instead ordered to pay $33m to the families of the victims.

It is also worth observing that a single event can have both criminal and civil consequences. The two elements, criminal and civil, will be the subject of separate trials and each will be governed by the rules applicable to each. This might mean, for example, that arising out of the same crash, a person might face actions for both negligence (prosecuted by the victim of any injuries and decided on the balance of probabilities) and drunk-driving (prosecuted by the State and decided beyond reasonable doubt).

---

[27] Another difference between civil and criminal cases is that there is generally a jury in all but the most minor (or 'summary') criminal cases, whereas civil matters are ordinarily decided by a judge, sitting without a jury.

The hierarchy of the courts

[A.23] Irish courts are hierarchical in nature. Aside from the obvious differences in authority that accompany ascension through the hierarchy, there are some practical differences. One key difference is the power – or jurisdiction – of each court in question. On the criminal side, the cases any court can hear are limited by the jurisdiction of the court: the District Court may generally (there are some exceptions) hear only minor, or summary, cases, while there are other more serious cases that must be heard in the Central[28] or Special[29] Criminal Courts.

Table A.2 – The hierarchy of the Irish courts (highest first)

Civil	Criminal
Supreme Court	Supreme Court
High Court	Court of Criminal Appeal
Circuit Court	Central Criminal Court (or Special Criminal Court for certain offences)
District Court	Circuit Court
	District Court

Civil courts

[A.24] On the civil side, each court has an upper limit to its 'monetary jurisdiction', which means that there is a limit to either the amount of damages (see below) the court may award at the end of a case or the maximum value of any goods or contract that can form the subject matter of the case the court is hearing. In essence, the higher the court, the greater is its monetary jurisdiction.

Table A.3 – Monetary jurisdiction of the civil courts

District Court	max €6,348.69
The Circuit Court	max €38,092.14
High Court	min €38,092.14 with no upper limit

Accordingly, if a person sustained comparatively minor (but not trivial) cuts and bruises following a trip and fall in a supermarket and chose to pursue legal action, the Circuit Court might be the most likely port of call. If, on the other hand, catastrophic injuries resulted from a road traffic accident, then the High Court would almost certainly be the forum. There is no upper limit to the amount of damages that the High Court can award. A similar hierarchy exists for disputes over property and the court in which any dispute is heard depends on the rateable value of the land in question.

[A.25] The Supreme Court does not feature in the table concerned with monetary jurisdiction and that is because it exists solely to resolve issues that remain unresolved by the lower courts and to hear appeals from decisions of the High Court. Generally, each court can hear appeals from the court or courts below it. If a case involves the

---

[28] Such as rape or murder.
[29] Terrorism and organised crime cases are generally heard in the Special Criminal Court.

Constitution, it may only be heard in the High Court or the Supreme Court. Note that any decision of the High Court or of the Supreme Court on almost any matter relating to European law may be appealed to the European Court of Justice and any decision of the European Court of Justice is binding on the Irish Courts. Cases concerning human rights may also be brought on appeal to the European Court of Human Rights, the decisions of which must be borne in mind and applied by Irish courts where relevant.[30]

Quick Reference Guide A.3

Damages

❖ Damages awarded by a court as compensation at the end of a legal case can be 'special' or 'general'.
❖ Special damages are generally for concrete and measurable expenses such as loss of income.
❖ General damages cover for pain and suffering.
❖ Rarely aggravated or exemplary damages may be awarded in circumstances where the court seeks to punish especially egregious behaviour by a party to legal action.

Damages – 'special' and 'general'

[A.26] 'Damages' is the term used to describe the money that is paid out in compensation for any harm done by a wrongdoer once it is shown that the wrongdoer was legally responsible for that harm. The damages may be paid by the wrongdoer personally, but will frequently be paid out by an insurer. The extent of damages depends on the effect of a wrongful act on a particular person. So, a knee injury that might not be especially injurious to a sedentary office worker might be catastrophic to a successful professional footballer's career and it would be expected that the damages awarded in the latter case would be more significant.

[A.27] The underlying principle of damages is that the compensation attempts to leave the plaintiff no worse off than if the wrong had not been committed in the first place,[31] but this is not a universally simple process. In some cases, compensation may be easy: if X destroys Y's unoccupied car, then the damage can be rectified by X replacing Y's car. However, if a negligently performed operation leaves a patient with lifelong, irremediable pain, how might that pain be adequately compensated in circumstances where it cannot be cured? Accordingly damages are multifaceted and apportioned to compensate for different forms of loss. There are 'special' damages and 'general' damages. Special damages compensate for concrete losses that can be quantified precisely, such as loss of earnings (past, present and future) and medical expenses (which may include the costs of medical care into the future). General damages are more flexible and include compensation for pain and suffering, for 'loss of amenities' (eg the

---

[30] European Convention on Human Rights Act 2003.
[31] Also called *restitutio in integram.*

loss of the use of an eye or a limb) and for reduction in life expectancy. Payments tend to be made on a once-off lump sum basis, but may sometimes be payable in instalments.[32]

Criminal courts

[A.28] On the criminal side, the hierarchy of the courts is somewhat different and so is the manner by which it is determined what court will hear a particular case. A criminal case almost always has an initial hearing in the District Court where the case (if it is a minor one) is allocated a hearing date before the District Court (where there is no jury) or sent forward for hearing to whichever more senior court is appropriate for the crime in question. A person who is accused of a criminal offence may be entitled to bail, allowing him or her to remain free until the trial takes place, but the courts have considerable powers to refuse bail when it is possible that a person might commit further crimes while on bail. An appeal against a criminal verdict from the District Court is taken to the Circuit Court, while an appeal from the decision of any other court may be taken to the Court of Criminal Appeal and may, rarely, proceed to the Supreme Court.

Coroners' courts and other tribunals

[A.29] Separate from the Criminal and Civil Courts, there is a system of Coroners' courts. The Coroner's Court has an important role to play in exploring the causes of certain types of death and has many powers similar to a conventional court.[33] There are some other bodies that have powers similar to the courts (quasi-judicial bodies), including the Fitness to Practise Committee of the Medical Council, which has certain powers similar to those of the High Court. As a logical corollary of the powers of the Coroner's Court and disciplinary bodies such as the Medical Council, any person appearing before them is entitled to legal representation and to expect that proper and fair legal procedure is followed.[34]

The legal profession

[A.30] Some commentators in the arena of legal medicine liken the division between barrister and solicitor to that between general practitioner and specialist among physicians. It is a useful metaphor, but should not be taken too far. In the first instance, general practitioners and consultants belong to the same profession, that of medicine, and are bound by the same regulatory body, the Medical Council. Secondly, at any stage in a doctor's training she may elide from one speciality into another with far greater ease than a barrister may become a solicitor or vice versa. Conversely, in the legal profession, there are two different, if superficially similar, professions with separate regulatory bodies and a measure of inter-professional rivalry and while those differences can be both underestimated and overstated by turns, they are nonetheless important.

---

[32] Courts may also sometimes award 'aggravated' or 'exemplary' damage in order to express disapproval of or deter especially egregious conduct, such as deliberately altering clinical records: see Supreme Court decision in *Philp v Ryan* [2004] IESC 105, [2004] 4 IR 241.

[33] See Ch 13, 'Coroners and the Aftermath of Death'.

[34] Fair procedure before disciplinary bodies is discussed in Ch 2, 'Healthcare Professions and Regulation', para **[2.58]***ff*.

Solicitors

[A.31] Solicitors are often a person's first contact with the law. If a member of the public has a legal query, the first person they must generally approach is a solicitor, although there is an increasing amount of 'direct professional access' to barristers. Some areas of law are to all intents and purposes the sole province of a solicitor, such as the uncomplicated sale of a house (conveyancing) or the drawing up of wills. A solicitor may represent her clients in court, although this is a more common occurrence in more minor offences tried before lower courts. The profession is regulated by the Law Society of Ireland, which also oversees legal training for student solicitors and exists as a statutory body, similar to the Medical Council and its analogues.[35] After completing a degree or diploma in law, students sit a series of exams, which if successfully negotiated, permit them entry into the professional training course for solicitors at Blackhall Place in Dublin. During their training, aspirant solicitors must also serve an apprenticeship to an established solicitor. Like barristers, solicitors may be in general practice or specialise in certain areas, such as company law; they also have, unlike barristers, a limited entitlement to advertise their services.

Barristers

[A.32] The barrister's professional environment is sometimes collectively known as the Bar. All Barristers are required to be members of the Law Library in the Four Courts in Dublin and have a degree or diploma in Law coupled with one year's full-time study at the Honourable Society of King's Inns in Dublin. After completing the King's Inns degree of Barrister-at-Law, the would-be barrister must also serve an apprentice year (called 'devilling') to a more experienced 'master' after which he or she is free to set up in independent practice. The Bar is not a statutory profession, although it is self-regulated under the aegis of a body called the Bar Council, which is elected by and from the members of the Law Library. A barrister's work generally comes from being 'briefed' by a solicitor to act for a client. Not all such instructions will result in a court appearance: the barrister's role is frequently solely to advise in writing on a legal point or even to caution against proceeding to court action at all. There are two tiers of barristers, junior and senior counsel, the latter also known as the 'inner bar' or 'silks' and denoted by the letters SC after their names. For junior counsel, much of her work may involve drafting pleadings and other paperwork or conducting more routine administrative court proceedings. The Senior Counsel is perhaps the individual more likely to do high-profile courtroom work, especially in more complex cases.

Judges

[A.33] Judges are chosen from the ranks of solicitors and barristers (although some may come from academia, they will have previously have qualified as a solicitor or barrister). According to the Constitution, the President appoints judges to the Bench, but elsewhere in the Constitution it is also stated that the President will act 'only on the advice of the Government' (meaning, in this case, the Cabinet). The Judicial Appointments Advisory Board, comprising a mixture of legal and lay individuals, was established in 1995 with the task of preparing lists of candidates for the Bench and bringing transparency to the

---

[35] The Solicitors Acts 1954–1994.

appointment of judges. Any solicitor or barrister who has been in practice for up to ten years may be appointed a Judge of the District or Circuit Court. In turn, increasing seniority as a judge, coupled with the requisite experience as a solicitor or barrister, qualifies a judge for appointment to the High and Supreme Courts, although rarely judges are appointed directly to the higher courts. Judges serve in office until they are anything between 65 and 72, the age depending on the date of their appointment and the court in which they serve – Supreme and High Court judges retire at 72. A judge may only be removed from office, according to the Constitution, 'for stated misbehaviour or incapacity'[36] in which case, a resolution calling for that judge's removal must be passed by both the Dáil and Seanad.

[A.34] A judge's job is often described as 'finding' the law. If the application of a particular written piece of legislation is at issue, the judge will interpret the legislation. If the matter concerns a legal dispute, he or she will, in accordance with the principles of common law already outlined, be guided by relevant statute law, decisions taken by previous courts in similar circumstances, by the arguments of barristers and by the evidence of witnesses. If a jury is involved in a case, the judge's job is to make sure that the trial is conducted fairly and to use her experience and knowledge of the law to guide the jury before it retires to reach its verdict.

EUROPEAN LAW

[A.35] Since Ireland's accession to the European Economic Community in January 1973, the influence of Europe on Irish law has been immense. The reality is that European Union membership necessitates and imposes a legal order that has its source outside the State, an imposition that is manifestly necessary when one considers the aims of the EU: fostering closer political and economic relationships, while also creating an open economic environment by assuring as far as possible the free movement of goods, workers, capital and services. In terms of legal institutions, four principal organs constitute the EU: the Commission, the Council of Ministers, the European Parliament and the Court of Justice.

The European Commission

[A.36] The Commission has hitherto comprised nominees from each of the Member States, but as the European Union enlarges, smaller nations will hold Commissionerships only on a rotating basis. Each Commissioner has a specific policy area of responsibility, operating under the direction of the President of the Commission. The Commission as a whole works to produce a legislative programme for the EU. Traditionally the Commission's power was huge and it was in effect the paramount law-making body in the EU, but more recent treaties (including the Treaty of Amsterdam) have reined in its powers somewhat, compelling it to co-operate and collaborate more with the Parliament and the Council of Ministers. The Commission is sometimes referred to as the 'guardian of the Treaty'. If a member state steps out of line with respect to its Treaty obligations, it is the Commission that will normally institute normative legal proceedings against the errant State.

---

[36] Art 35.

The Council of Ministers

[A.37] The Council represents the governments of the Member States. At meetings of the Council, a Minister who has responsibility for the policy area under discussion at the meeting and who is authorised to take decisions on behalf of her Government attends on behalf of each Member State. There are different Councils dealing with each area of Community policy: a Council of Health Ministers oversees health discussions, Finance Ministers (ECOFIN) discuss fiscal affairs and so forth. The Council of Ministers takes decisions on the basis of a complex voting system that reflects the population and influence of each Member State.

The European Parliament

[A.38] The Parliament is directly elected by the people of Europe and each country has a number of MEPs (Members of the European Parliament) approximately relative to its population, although this arrangement is somewhat skewed in favour of the smaller nations. Within the parliament, members tend to ally themselves first along national party lines and then along international lines of broadly shared political philosophy. The Parliament has seen an incremental growth in its power in the last generation or so, to the extent where it may now successfully object to proposed legislation without fear of simply being overruled by a vote of the Council or Commission.

The European Court of Justice

[A.39] The European Court of Justice (ECJ) hears all cases that concern alleged violations of the various European treaties. If a person or another body, such as the European Commission, alleges that a country is violating its obligations under the treaty, then he may bring an action at first in the courts of that country or in the ECJ. Any decision made by the ECJ is binding on all Member States and on the courts in the Member States.

The effect of EU membership

[A.40] EU membership is important to Ireland's laws for a number of reasons, of which the most significant is that it creates a whole new legal order and limits Irish sovereignty in as much as Irish courts and law-makers are bound by the provisions of European law and by the decisions of the European Court of Justice. Furthermore, Ireland cannot enact laws or engage in conduct contrary to the provisions of the European treaties without risking legal retribution from the European Commission or an adverse finding against the State in the ECJ. We have noted above that the Irish Constitution states that only the Oireachtas may exercise law-making powers,[37] so how is European Union membership compatible with that statement? The short answer is that in order to contemplate membership of the EEC, there needed to be a referendum in 1972 on a Constitutional amendment to bring the demands of the Irish Constitution and the prospective demands of EEC membership into harmony. The section of the Constitution that was originally amended and which has been amended repeatedly to take account of the ever-expanding reach and nature of the European project is Article 29. The Irish courts have conceded

---

[37] Art 15.

that, in signing up to the European treaties, Ireland was 'signing up to a moving train' and, as part of the journey, it has proved necessary to go to the country repeatedly to seek approval of European treaties.

EU law-making

[A.41] Laws from Europe have a number of forms. Obviously, the various treaties themselves are binding and must be obeyed by signatories to the treaties, but in order to further the aims of the treaties, the institutions of the EU have a number of legislative weapons in their armoury: regulations, directives and decisions.

Table A.4 – How the EU makes laws

Regulation:	A regulation is a rule made by the EU that is applicable to all Member States without any further ado. It becomes binding as soon as it is introduced, without any need for the Government of that Member State to introduce any new legislation.
Directive:	A directive is a rule made by the EU that is applicable to all Member States, but which leaves to the Government of the Member States the question of precisely how that directive is implemented, so long as it is done within a certain time-frame. Usually, this will necessitate the introduction of new legislation and/or the amendment of existing legislation to achieve the end sought by the Commission or Council. Failure to enact the directive will result in the Commission taking legal action against the recalcitrant Member State.
Decision:	A decision is normally directed at one particular Member State or one particular dispute. It is binding on those concerned in the dispute. For example, in 1993 the Irish Government sought to provide Aer Lingus with a cash injection. This could only be done after Commission approval was sought in the form of a Decision.

European decisions have 'direct effect' on Irish law. What this means is that once a law is made in Europe, it becomes, as a matter of course, the law of Ireland, even if the State has not taken the necessary steps to formally incorporate it into Irish law. While there may be various administrative requirements necessary to formally integrate the EU rules into Irish law, it is nonetheless the case that an Irish citizen may rely on the new directive or regulation as directly applicable from the moment of its adoption by the EU.

[A.42] There are few areas of Irish life upon which European law has not impinged. One clear example is the workplace: as an essentially economic entity, the EU is intimately concerned with satisfactorily regulating the means, methods and conduits of economic productivity. Similarly, rules on safety in the workplace, rules of labour law, the international recognition of qualifications and the free flow of information are all examples of EU legislative concerns. Conversely and comparatively speaking, some areas of domestic Irish law, relating primarily to property or family, are only barely touched upon by European Law, but as legislation and policy of an increasingly social nature emanates from the European Union and its law-making bodies, this is a situation that seems likely to change.

Human rights law

[A.43] Ireland is a signatory to the European Convention on Human Rights and Fundamental Freedoms and is therefore obliged, especially since the passage of the European Convention on Human Rights Act 2003, to have regard to the rulings and decisions of the European Court of Human Rights.

THREE IMPORTANT SUBSETS OF LAW

[A.44] In the course of legal education, students are taught law, not as a generic mass of principles, statutes and rulings but according to certain divisions, most of which are logical, some of which are more time-honoured and traditional. Three main areas of law encountered in this book are worth examining in a little more detail here. All are civil, rather than criminal, areas of law and are generally decided according to common law principle or, in other words, by reference to how courts have decided similar cases in the past.[38]

Tort

[A.45] Tort is an area of law that recognises the general rights of individuals (or indeed of companies) and helps the individual or company protect those rights as far as possible with appropriate remedies such as damages. If a person is injured by a careless driver or by medical negligence, then he may can bring a case against that person under the tort (which essentially comes from a French word for 'wrong') of negligence against the person who injured him. Important torts include negligence,[39] defamation (libel and slander), trespass (including trespass to the person or battery) and liability for defective products.

Contract

[A.46] The concept of the law of contract is almost self-explanatory and is concerned with the making an enforceability of contracts between parties. In the clinical setting it may be relevant in the context of private healthcare, where alongside the ordinary duty to take care there may also be a contractual aspect to treatment[40] and contract law is also applicable to the employment relationship. There are three elements to a valid contract:

- an offer;
- an acceptance;
- consideration.

'Consideration' is the legal term for something that is transferred from one party to another in order to cement the contract: in general that means money, such as a payment

---

[38] Although there are some exceptions: the Liability for Defective Products Act 1991 may have a relevant input into any case arising from negligently manufactured or maintained equipment, for example.

[39] See Ch 6, 'Clinical Negligence' and Ch 4, 'Consent'.

[40] See Ch 3, 'Confidentiality and the Practitioner-Patient Relationship', para **[3.55]** for a discussion of the role of contract law in the practitioner-patient relationship.

of some kind, but it can take other forms.[41] If a nurse is offered a job and she accepts that job and the employer agrees to pay the nurse for taking the job, there is a valid contract of employment.[42]

[A.47] A contract can be written or oral and can be open-ended or for a fixed period. The employment contracts of most junior doctors, for example, are for a fixed length of time, at the end of which period the contract expires and the employment ends. A contract will generally contain terms or conditions that attach to a contract and which must be satisfied if the contract is to be valid. A term may also be implied into a contract: for example, there is an implied term in every contract that any salary agreed in the contract will be paid. Some contractual terms can outlive the contract: some employment contracts contain terms to the effect that after the employee leaves her job, she will not set up in competition within a certain area close to the location of her current employer for a certain length of time. Such 'restrictive covenants' are valid only so long as the restriction they place on the employee is not too great.

Equity

[A.48] Equity is a body of law concerned with ensuring fairness in the outcome of the legal process. It exists alongside the law of tort and has much in common with contract law: for example, equity will often operate to force a person to honour a contract that he is attempting to avoid. Where the law does not formally protect a person's rights and a serious injustice would result from not protecting those rights, equity will typically step into the breach. The key element is fairness, equity tries to promote fairness and prevent unfairness in human legal relations. Common equitable approaches to the law include:

- injunctions, which prevent a person from doing or continuing to do something;
- specific performance, which involves forcing a person to do something he signed a contract to do, but which obligation he is now trying to avoid;
- estoppel, which prevents someone from trying to get out of a promise or undertaking made to another person in circumstances where it would be unfair to allow him to escape the promise; and
- undue influence, which may allow a person to escape from a contract or promise made because he came under 'undue (or excessive) influence' to enter into the contract or promise.

---

[41] Such as a promise not to pursue a certain course of action in exchange for the contract being agreed.

[42] Note that the Medical Council (*Guide to Ethical Conduct and Behaviour* (6th edn, 2004), para 4.9) lays down rules for doctors who have accepted posts of employment:

'A doctor, having formally accepted any post, including a locum post, must not then withdraw without due cause unless the employer will have time to make other arrangements to ensure that patient care is not compromised'.

Appendix II

Glossary of Legal Terms and Abbreviations

IMPORTANT ABBREVIATIONS USED IN THE TEXT

This list does not include every abbreviation in this book, but focuses on those that recur most frequently and which are likely to be a source of confusion for the reader not versed in their meaning but also a potential source of further information for those interested in reading outside the confines of this book.

AC	Appeal Cases (England & Wales)
AJLR	Australian Journal of Law Reports
All ER / AER	All England Reports
BMJ	British Medical Journal
BMLR	British Medical Legal Reports (England & Wales)
CCA	Court of Criminal Appeal (Ireland)
CJ	Chief Justice
Cr App R	Criminal Appeal Reports (England & Wales)
DLR	Dominion Law Reports (Canada)
DULJ	Dublin University Law Journal
EWCA	England and Wales Civil Appeals
EHRR	European Human Rights Reports
ELR	Employment Law Reports
FAM LJ	Family Law Journal
HC	High Court
HL	House of Lords (United Kingdom)
HMSO	Her (or His) Majesty's Stationery Office
IESC / HC / IC	Irish Electronic Supreme Court / High Court / Information Commissioner Reports
ILRM	Irish Law Report Monthly
ILT(R)	Irish Law Times (Reports)
IR	Irish Reports
J	Judge/Justice *or* (depending on context) Journal
JAMA	Journal of the American Medical Association

KB	Kings Bench (England & Wales)
LJ	Lord Justice
LRC	Law Reform Commission
LS Gaz R	Law Society Gazette Reports (England & Wales)
Med LR	Medical Law Reports (England & Wales)
MLJI	Medico-Legal Journal of Ireland
NEJM	New England Journal of Medicine
NSWLR	New South Wales Law Reports (Australia)
NZLR	New Zealand Law Reports
per	In the words of… (in the context of a quotation from a particular judge)
QB	Queens Bench (England & Wales)
RPC	Reports of Patent Cases (England & Wales)
SI	Statutory Instrument
SC	Supreme Court
unreported	When a judgment is recorded as 'unreported' it means that it has not been included in any one of the books of legal reports, such as the Irish Reports. Unreported judgments will generally be available from behind the issue desk in the law section of academic libraries. With the advent of online resources, it is becoming less common for a legal case to remain unreported.
WLR	Weekly Law Reports (England & Wales)

Appendix III

Cremation Certificates

CREMATION CERTIFICATE

This form is issued by   Glasnevin Crematorium Limited Finglas Road, Glasnevin, Dublin 11. Tel: 01 - 8305211   **FORM C**
                  Web Site. www.glasnevin-cemetery.ie   email: cemetery@indigo.ie

These Certificates should be in the hands of the Medical Referee.
NOT LATER THAN 3.00PM ON THE DAY PRIOR TO THE CREMATION.

PURSUANT TO THE BYE LAWS MADE BY GLASNEVIN CREMATORIUM LIMITED

The Doctor signing this form must be fully registered on the Medical Register of Ireland for at least three years. Completion of this form is mandatory. All the questions must be answered to complete the Certificate for the purposes of Cremation.

The doctor Completing the Certificate must see the **body before and after death.**

The medical Certificate is Strictly Confidential.

PLEASE PRINT IN BLACK PEN ONLY

I Hereby certify that the answers given below are true and accurate to the best of my knowledge and belief.

Name ....   (Signature) ....
                                        Date: ....
(please insert name here in block capitals).   (Address) ....

Telephone No.   ....

Registered Qualification ....
Month .... Year ....
of Full Registration on The Medical Register of Ireland

MUST BE AT LEAST 3 YEARS QUALIFIED

MEDICAL CERTIFICATE
FORM C

I am informed that application is about to be made for the cremation of the remains of:-
(Name of Deceased) ....
(Address) ....
(Occupation or Description) .... (Age) ....

HAVING SEEN AND IDENTIFIED THE *BODY BEFORE AND AFTER DEATH.*

I give the following answers to the questions set out below:-

1. (a) Were you the regular attending doctor of the Deceased   )   (a) ....

     (b) If so, for how long?   )   (b) ....

2. (a) Did you attend the Deceased during his or her last illness   )   (a) ....

     (b) If so, for how long?   )   (b) ....

3. When did you last see the Deceased alive?   )   Date ....

     (say how many days or hours before death)   )   Days or Hours ....

4. (a) How soon after death did you see the body?   and   )   (a) ....

     (b) What examination did you make?   )   (b) ....

5. On what date and at what hour did he or she die?   )   Date .... Hour ....

6. (a) What was the place where the Deceased died?) (a) ....

     Give address and

     (b) Say whether Deceased's own residence, lodging, hotel,

     hospital, nursing home etc.) (b) ....

---

7. (a) Are you a relative of the Deceased;) (a) ....

     (b) If so, state relationship) (b) ....

---

8. Have you, so far as you are aware, any pecuniary interest

    in the death of the Deceased.) ....

---

9. Cause of death and duration of last illness: **NO ABBREVIATIONS**

I.	I.	Approximate interval between onset and death
Disease or condition directly leading to death	(a) .... due to (or as a consequence of)	
Antecedent causes. Morbid conditions, if any, giving rise to the above cause, stating the underlying condition last	(b) .... due to (or as a consequence of) (c)	
II. Other significant conditions contributing to the death but not related to the disease or condition causing it.	**II.**	

NOTE: **IF DEATH IS NOT DUE TO NATURAL CAUSES, CORONERS CERTIFICATE IS REQUIRED FORM D.**

---

10. (a) State how far the answer to the last question

     is the result of your own observation.) (a) ....

     (b) If not your own observation, what was the

     source of your information?) (b) ....

---

11. (a) Have you or any other doctor made a Post Mortem

     examination of the body.) (a) ....

     (b) If "YES" state by whom the examination was made.) (b) ....

---

12. By whom was the Deceased nursed during his or her

    last illness.) ....

    (Give names and say whether professional nurse,

    relative etc. If the illness was a long one this

    question should be answered with reference to

    the period of four weeks before the death).) ....

CORONER'S CERTIFICATE FOR CREMATION

.

CORONER'S CERTIFICATE FOR CREMATION

I Certify that:-

I am satisfied that there are no circumstances likely to call for a further examination of the body.

PARTICULARS OF DECEASED PERSON

Full Names ....

Sex ....

Age ....

Date of Death ....

Place of Death ....

(Please insert name here in block capitals) ....

Signature ....

Coroner for the   of

Date ....

(1.)	Has the Deceased been fitted with	
	(a) A Cardiac Pacemaker	) (1.) (a) Yes/No ....
	(b) A radio-active or other implant	) (b) Yes/No ....
	(c) Other Prosthesis	) (c) Yes/No ....

(2.)	If the answer to (a) (b) or (c) above is in the	
	affirmative has this been removed?	) (2.) Yes/No ....

NOTE: CREMATION MAY BE REFUSED IF ANY PROSTHESIS IS NOT REMOVED.

NOTE: This Certificate is issued for the purposes of cremation only and must be delivered to the Medical Referee appointed by Glasnevin Crematorium Limited. The Cremation cannot be proceeded with unless this Certificate is so delivered.

13. Who were the persons present (if any) at the moment
of death.   ) ....

14. In view of your knowledge of the Deceased's
habits and constitution, do you feel any doubt whatever
as to the character of the disease or the cause of death
stated in 9. above?   ) ....

15. Have you any reason to suspect that the Deceased person died either directly or indirectly as a
result of:

   (a) Violence or misadventure   (a) Yes/No
   (b) Unfair means   (b) Yes/No ....
   (c) Negligence or misconduct   (c) Yes/No ....
   (d) Malpractice on the part of others   (d) Yes/No ....
   (e) Any cause other than natural illness   (e) Yes/No ....
   or disease for which he/she had been seen   ....
   and treated by a registered medical
   practitioner within one month before his/her death;

16. Do you know or have you any reason to suspect that the
death occurred under or within 24 hours of an anaesthetic   )

17. (a) Have you any reason to suspect that the death of the
Deceased should properly be reported to the Coroner?   )   (a)
   (b) If YES state why   )   (b)..

18. Have you any reason whatever to suppose a further
examination of the body to be desirable?   )

19. (a) Did you sign the Medical Certificate of the Cause of Death?)   (a)
   (b) If not who has?   )   (b)...

20. (1.) Has the Deceased been fitted with
   (a) A Cardiac Pacemaker   ) (1.)   (a) Yes/No
   (b) A radio-active or other implant   )   (b) Yes/No.....................................
   (c) Other Prosthesis   )   (c) Yes/No ....

   (2.) If the answer to (a) (b) or (c) above is in the
affirmative has this been removed?   ) (2.)   Yes/No

NOTE: CREMATION MAY BE REFUSED IF ANY PROSTHESIS IS NOT REMOVED.

N.B.   HAVE YOU SIGNED THIS FORM
N.B.   THE DOCTOR SIGNING THIS FORM MUST BE FULLY REGISTERED ON THE IRISH MEDICAL
        REGISTER FOR AT LEAST THREE YEARS.
NOTE: THIS CERTIFICATE MUST BE HANDED TO OR SENT TO THE MEDICAL REFEREE IN A SEALED
        ENVELOPE TO ARRIVE NOT LATER THAN 3PM ON THE DAY PRIOR TO CREMATION.

Index

All references are to paragraph numbers